THE OXFORD H

MW01076855

PHILOSOPHY
AND LITERATURE

THE OXFORD HANDBOOK OF

PHILOSOPHY AND LITERATURE

Edited by
RICHARD ELDRIDGE

OXFORD
UNIVERSITY PRESS

OXFORD
UNIVERSITY PRESS

Oxford University Press is a department of the University of Oxford.
It furthers the University's objective of excellence in research, scholarship,
and education by publishing worldwide.

Oxford   New York
Auckland   Cape Town   Dar es Salaam   Hong Kong   Karachi
Kuala Lumpur   Madrid   Melbourne   Mexico City   Nairobi
New Delhi   Shanghai   Taipei   Toronto

With offices in
Argentina   Austria   Brazil   Chile   Czech Republic   France   Greece
Guatemala   Hungary   Italy   Japan   Poland   Portugal   Singapore
South Korea   Switzerland   Thailand   Turkey   Ukraine   Vietnam

Oxford is a registered trade mark of Oxford University Press
in the UK and certain other countries.

Published in the United States of America by
Oxford University Press
198 Madison Avenue, New York, NY 10016

Library of Congress Cataloging-in-Publication Data
The Oxford handbook of philosophy and literature / edited by
Richard Eldridge.
p.   cm.
Includes bibliographical references and Index.
ISBN 978-0-19-518263-7 (hardcover); 978-0-19-996549-6 (paperback)
1. Literature—Philosophy.   I. Eldridge, Richard Thomas, 1953–
II. Title: Handbook of philosophy and literature.
PN45.O84 2009
801—dc22   2008041062

Printed in the United States of America
on acid-free paper

PART II. PERIODS AND MODES

10. Realism 223
    Bernard Harrison

11. Romanticism 247
    Nikolas Kompridis

12. Idealism 271
    Toril Moi

13. Modernism 298
    Philip Weinstein

14. Postcolonialism 322
    Simona Bertacco

PART III. DEVICES AND POWERS

15. Imagination 349
    Kirk Pillow

16. Plot 369
    Alan Singer

17. Character 393
    Stanley Bates

18. Style 420
    Charles Altieri

19. Emotion, Memory, and Trauma 442
    Glenn W. Most

PART IV. CONTEXTS AND USES

20. Literature and Knowledge 467
    John Gibson

Contents

Contributors ix

Introduction—Philosophy and Literature as Forms of Attention 3
Richard Eldridge

Part I. Genres

1. Epic 19
   Gregory Nagy

2. Lyric 45
   Susan Stewart

3. Tragedy 71
   J. M. Bernstein

4. Comedy 95
   Timothy Gould

5. Pastoral 117
   Mark Payne

6. Satire 139
   R. Bracht Branham

7. The Novel 162
   Anthony J. Cascardi

8. Autobiography and Biography 180
   Stephen Mulhall

9. Experimental Writing 199
   R. M. Berry

21. Literature and Morality 486
     Ted Cohen

22. Literature and Politics 496
     Fred Rush

     Index 517

Contributors

CHARLES ALTIERI teaches in the English Department at University of California, Berkeley. His most recent books are *The Particulars of Rapture* and *The Art of Twentieth Century American Poetry*. He is working toward a book on the poetry of Wallace Stevens.

STANLEY BATES teaches philosophy at Middlebury College. He has written on ethics, aesthetics, film, Kant, Thoreau, Wittgenstein, and Cavell, He is the coeditor of *Walter Cerf: A Personal Odyssey*, to which he contributed an introductory essay.

J. M. BERNSTEIN is University Distinguished Professor of Philosophy at the New School for Social Research. Among his books are *The Fate of Art, Adorno: Disenchantment and Ethics*, and *Against Voluptuous Bodies: Late Modernism and the Meaning of Painting*. He edited and introduced *Classic and Romantic German Aesthetics*. He is currently working on a book provisionally titled *Torture and Dignity*.

R. M. BERRY is coeditor of *Fiction's Present: Situating Contemporary Narrative Innovation* and author, most recently, of the novel *Frank* and story collection *Dictionary of Modern Anguish*. His critical writings have appeared in *Soundings, Symploke, Philosophy and Literature, Narrative*, and various anthologies. He is currently professor and chair of English at Florida State University.

SIMONA BERTACCO is assistant professor of English literature at the University of Milan. Her research focuses on issues in postcolonialism, women's and gender studies, and translation studies. Her publications include *Out of Place: The Writings of Robert Kroetsch, Postcolonial to Multicultural: An Anthology of Texts from the English-Speaking World*, and *Sul Corpo: Culture/Politiche/Estetiche (On the Body: Cultures/Politics/Aesthetics)*, coedited with Nicoletta Vallorani.

R. BRACHT BRANHAM teaches classics, comparative literature, and philosophy at Emory University. He is coeditor (with M. O. Goulet-Cazé) of *The Cynics: The Cynic Movement in Antiquity and Its Legacy* and editor of *Bakhtin and the Classics* and *The Bakhtin Circle and Ancient Narrative*.

ANTHONY J. CASCARDI is director of the Townsend Center for the Humanities and Ancker Professor in the departments of Comparative Literature, Rhetoric, and Spanish at the University of California, Berkeley. He is the author of numerous essays and books, including *The Subject of Modernity* and *Consequences of Enlightenment*, and is editor of *Literature and the Question of Philosophy*. He serves on numerous boards and as the general academic editor of the Penn State series of books in Literature and Philosophy.

TED COHEN is professor of philosophy at the University of Chicago. He is a past president of the American Society for Aesthetics and of the Central Division of the American Philosophical Association. He is the author of *Jokes: Philosophical Thoughts on Joking Matters* and *Thinking of Others: The Talent for Metaphor.*

RICHARD ELDRIDGE is Charles and Harriett Cox McDowell Professor of Philosophy at Swarthmore College. He is the author of *On Moral Personhood: Philosophy, Literature, Criticism, Self-Understanding; Leading a Human Life: Wittgenstein, Intentionality, and Romanticism; The Persistence of Romanticism; An Introduction to the Philosophy of Art*; and, most recently, *Literature, Life, and Modernity*; and he is the editor of *Beyond Representation* and *Stanley Cavell.*

JOHN GIBSON is associate professor of philosophy at the University of Louisville. He is the author of *Fiction and the Weave of Life* (Oxford UP, 2007) and coeditor of *A Sense of the World: Essays on Fiction, Narrative and Knowledge* and *The Literary Wittgenstein*. He is currently working on a new book titled *Poetry, Metaphor, and Nonsense: An Essay on Meaning.*

TIMOTHY GOULD is professor of philosophy at the Metropolitan State College of Denver. He has written articles on Kant's aesthetics, Emerson, Thoreau, Nietzsche, Romanticism, and Wittgenstein and is the author of *Hearing Things: Voice and Method in the Writing of Stanley Cavell*. He is completing a book manuscript titled *The Names of Action*, with chapters on Austin, Wittgenstein, Cavell, Emerson, Marx, and Nietzsche. He has also been writing a series of essays on narrative in comedy, history, movies, autobiography, and trauma, tentatively titled *Saving the Story.*

BERNARD HARRISON currently holds an Emeritus Chair in Philosophy at the University of Utah. At the University of Sussex, where he taught from 1963 to 1992, he profited from the presence of a stellar group of colleagues in literary studies, including A. D. Nuttall, Stephen Medcalf, and Gabriel Josipovici. His interests include the interfaces between literature, moral philosophy, and the philosophy of language. His books include *Fielding's Tom Jones: The Novelist as Moral Philosopher, Inconvenient Fictions: Literature and the Limits of Theory*, and (with Patricia Hanna) *Word and World: Practice and the Foundations of Language.*

NIKOLAS KOMPRIDIS is currently a visiting professor in the Department of Political Science and the Centre for Ethics at the University of Toronto. He is the author of *Critique and Disclosure: Critical Theory between Past and Future* and numerous articles on topics in political philosophy, aesthetics, and critical theory as well as the editor of *Philosophical Romanticism*. He is now working on three forthcoming books, *The Freedom to Begin Anew: Re-imagining Public Reason and Democratic Politics, Receptive Agency: A Philosophy of Music after Adorno (after Cavell)*, and *The Aesthetic Turn in Political Theory*.

TORIL MOI is James B. Duke Professor of Literature and Romance Studies and professor of English and theater studies at Duke University. She is the author of *Sexual/Textual Politics: Feminist Literary Theory, Simone de Beauvoir: The Making of an Intellectual Woman*, and *What Is a Woman? And Other Essays*. She is also the editor of *The Kristeva Reader* and *French Feminist Thought*. Her most recent book is *Henrik Ibsen and the Birth of Modernism: Art, Theater, Philosophy*.

GLENN W. MOST is professor of Greek philology at the Scuola Normale Superiore di Pisa and Professor in the Committee on Social Thought at the University of Chicago. He has published widely on ancient and modern literature, philosophy, and art, on literary theory, and on the reception of antiquity. His most recent books include *Doubting Thomas* and *Hesiod. The Classical Tradition. A Guide*, coedited with Anthony Grafton and Salvatore Settis, should appear in 2009.

STEPHEN MULHALL is fellow and tutor in philosophy at New College, Oxford. His current research concerns Wittgenstein, Heidegger, and Nietzsche. His most recent publications are *On Film* and *The Wounded Animal: J. M. Coetzee and the Difficulty of Reality in Literature and Philosophy*.

GREGORY NAGY is the author of *The Best of the Achaeans: Concepts of the Hero in Archaic Greek Poetry*. Other publications include *Plato's Rhapsody and Homer's Music: The Poetics of the Panathenaic Festival in Classical Athens*. He coedited with Stephen A. Mitchell the second, 40th-anniversary edition of Albert Lord, *The Singer of Tales*, coauthoring with Mitchell the new introduction. Since 2000, he has been the director of the Harvard Center for Hellenic Studies in Washington, D.C., while continuing to teach at the Harvard campus in Cambridge as the Francis Jones Professor of Classical Greek Literature and professor of comparative literature.

MARK PAYNE, assistant professor of Classics at the University of Chicago, is the author of *Theocritus and the Invention of Fiction* and articles on Pindar and Hölderlin, Pindar and Paul Celan, ecphrasis and inalienable gifts, and the idea of poetic childhood in Hellenistic poetry. He is now working on a book about animals in ancient and modern literature.

KIRK PILLOW is dean of the Corcoran College of Art and Design within the Corcoran Gallery of Art in Washington, D.C. He is the author of *Sublime*

Understanding: Aesthetic Reflection in Kant and Hegel and articles on imagination, metaphor, and contemporary art.

FRED RUSH teaches philosophy at the University of Notre Dame. He is the author of *On Architecture* and of a number of essays at the intersection of German philosophy, aesthetics, and political theory. He is also the editor of *The Cambridge Companion to Critical Theory* and coeditor of the journal *Internationales Jahrbuch des Deutschen Idealismus.*

ALAN SINGER is professor of English at Temple University. He publishes on aesthetics and literary theory. His most recently published book is *Aesthetic Reason: Artworks and the Deliberative Ethos.* He has just completed a book on self-deception and aesthetic value.

SUSAN STEWART, poet, critic, and translator, is the Annan Professor of English at Princeton University. Her five books of poems include *Columbarium,* which won the National Book Critics Circle Award in Poetry in 2003, and, most recently, *Red Rover.* Her prose works include *On Longing, Poetry and the Fate of the Senses,* and *The Open Studio: Essays on Art and Aesthetics.* She is a current chancellor of the Academy of American Poets, a former MacArthur Fellow and Guggenheim Fellow, and a member of the American Academy of Arts and Sciences.

PHILIP WEINSTEIN is Alexander Griswold Cummins Professor of English at Swarthmore College. His teaching and his research both focus on modernist literature and philosophy. His writings include *The Semantics of Desire: Changing Models of Identity from Dickens to Joyce, Faulkner's Subject: A Cosmos No One Owns, What Else but Love? The Ordeal of Race in Faulkner and Morrison,* and *Unknowing: The Work of Modernism Fiction.* In 2009 Oxford UP will bring out his latest book, a study of Faulkner's life and work titled *Becoming Faulkner.*

THE OXFORD HANDBOOK OF

PHILOSOPHY
AND LITERATURE

INTRODUCTION

RICHARD ELDRIDGE

I said, "we were not stocks and stones"—'tis very well. I should
have added, nor are we angels, I wish we were,—but men
cloathed with bodies, and governed by our imaginations;—
and what a junketing piece of work of it there is, betwixt
these and our seven senses....

For my hobby-horse, if you recollect a little, is no way
a vicious beast; he has scarce one hair or lineament of the
ass about him—'Tis the sporting little filly-folly which
carries you out for the present hour—a maggot, a butterfly
a picture, a fiddle-stick—an uncle Toby's siege—or an *any
thing*, which a man makes a shift to get a stride on, to cater
it away from the cares and solicitudes of life—'tis as useful a
beast as is in the whole creation—nor do I really see how the
world could do without it.

—Laurence Sterne, *The Life and Opinions
of Tristram Shandy, Gentleman*

As these two epigraphs from *Tristram Shandy* eloquently indicate, human beings
are complicated animals who are freighted with imaginations that range beyond
the senses; they use their imaginations both to escape from life and to find lines of
direction and interest within it. Certain exercises of imagination can seem fruit-
less and strange, yet also compelling and necessary for forming and maintaining
substantial commitments.

Both literature (both its production and the critical study of it) and philosophy
as disciplines have often been seen (sometimes by each other) as embodying either

strange fruitlessness or compelling necessity—sometimes both. As early as Plato's *Ion*, literary works and their authors were cast as divinely inspired, but wayward, uninformed by craft, and useless for the serious business of life. As early as Aristophanes' *Clouds*, philosophy is seen as comically pretentious and ridiculous. With the steady separation of modern science from natural philosophy since the seventeenth century, this impression of philosophy as comical has only widened.

Both literary writers (along with many of those who study them) and philosophers (and those who study them) have long insisted, with considerable force, that they are attending seriously to life, not escaping from it. Whatever their wild varieties of form, the texts that are produced by philosophical and literary writers differ significantly from mere lists of otherwise unassociated words and from sonic word play alone. Some forms of attention and discipline seem to control both philosophical and literary production, even while imagination (beyond sensation, measurement, and calculation) remains central, while which forms of discipline and why and how they control production remain unclear and deeply contested.

In contrast with the focus on material actualities that is typical of the natural sciences (however mediated that focus is by imagination), philosophy and literature as forms of attention focus more on human commitments and passions. At its most abstract and general, philosophy undertakes to specify ideal commitments, or the commitments that it would be most effectively worthwhile to have, even if their fulfillments remain contingent and interruptible. The effort is, inter alia, to specify justice as an ideal form of social life, or morality as an ideal form of personal and immediate interpersonal comportment, or a practice of inquiry as an ideal form of cognitive engagement with the real, or ideal success in formal arrangement. Yet any such effort at least runs a risk of being fantastically ad hoc and empty in relation to empirical details of present material circumstance that remain, in part, hindrances not so easily assimilated to pursuits of the ideal. Tyrannical, sectarian domination may in turn result from attempting to put fantastic ideals into actual practice. Hence, close attention to material circumstances and passions for their own sakes seems necessary to correct abstract ideal theorizing that is always possibly premature. Philosophy seems to need correction by literature's attention to how any commitments might in particular be lived, if it is to avoid comic irrelevance and the rationalization of domination.

Literature, in contrast, focuses on the particular in the universal, undertaking to track what is most likely to come, tragically or comically, of the bearing of particular passions in circumstances that remain always in part intractable. This literary form of attention runs the risk, however, of seeing human beings as caught up only and always in pieces of good or bad luck, failing to discern any genuine universals that human beings might well pursue. Human life may be presented as one damn thing after another, without any clear possibilities either of fruitful emplotment or of evident connections among distinct human lives. Unilluminating particularism is as least a possible fate of close attention to material circumstances and passions, a possible fate that it becomes increasingly difficult to avoid in the wake of the modern disenchantment of nature. Samuel Beckett, for example, favors a form of literature that consists in "the expression that there is nothing to express, nothing with which to express, nothing from which to express, no power to express, no desire to express, together with the obligation to express" (1965: 13). If that is what literature in the end amounts to, then it will be impossible to define, even provisionally and gesturally, and it will become instead a thing of refusals of meaning and resistances to it. As Jacques Derrida puts it, "It's the most interesting thing in the world, maybe even more interesting than the world, and this is why, if it has no definition, what is heralded and refused under the name of literature cannot be identified with any other discourse. It will never be scientific, philosophical, conversational" (1992: 47). Yet if it affords only stuttering, without generalizable meaning of any kind, then the point of the literary work is desperately unclear, however subjectively important it is felt to be by certain isolated intellectuals. Hence, literature seems to need correction by philosophy's efforts to trace universals and to discern and specify ideal forms of commitment, if it is to avoid particularistic emptiness and collapse into light entertainment at best, insignificant word play at worst.

In fact, both philosophy and literature at their bests have engaged with each other to develop forms of attention to human life and to human commitments and passions while avoiding both empty idealism and empty particularism. Philosophy has its particular initiating perplexities and its forms of the emplotment of the progress of an implied protagonist, including at least dialogues, confessions, summas, meditations, essays, treatises, tractates, critiques, phenomenologies, manifestoes, postscripts, genealogies, and investigations, among others. Literature has its forms of appeal to general philosophical terms, as it undertakes to treat the particularities with which it engages, however sotto voce, as significant instances of some more general idea, concept, or theory of the human; emplotment of the plausible is impossible without some more general concept of the probable or necessary. As Asja Szafraniec usefully remarks, "[L]iterature does not exorcise the universal from itself but negotiates an intersection of the singular and universal within itself as a singular work" (2007: 57). Hence, each form of attention—philosophy and literature—both negotiates with and resists the other, engages with and excludes it.

If we focus abstractly on philosophy's concern with ideal, general commitments and literature's attention to particulars as objects of passion, then we might develop something like the following table of opposites:

Philosophy	*Literature*
Universality	Particularity
Reason	(Particularized) Imagination
Ideal Symbolic Order	Primary Process
Detachment	Engagement
Insight	Emotion

Such an abstract set of oppositions has some point in revealing patterns of mutual contestation. But we would do well to remember also that there are, always, engagement and negotiation as well as resistance and repudiation. When we attend to *how* simultaneous engagement and contestation have been played out, we find Socrates, Plato, and Aristotle not quite wholly displacing and killing off Homeric epic, Pindaric Ode, and Sapphic lyric; the modern novel not quite wholly displacing and killing off theological or rationalist philosophy; artistic modernism not quite displacing and killing off more thematized and emplotted philosophy and literature; analytical philosophy not quite displacing and killing off literature; mongrelizing postmodernism not quite displacing and killing off all of philosophy, traditional narrative literature, and more formally unified modernism; and so on.

Both genres and certain central devices of attention (emplotment, characterization, style) then emerge more as ways of registering and coming to terms with continuing tensions between a standing human need for and possibility of reflective orientation under reasonable commitments and a standing absence of completeness of orientation. These tensions are played out within various overlapping spheres of life: social-historical (economic, sociological, political), ethical-familial, developmental-psychoanalytic, moral, formal-aesthetic, and cognitive-scientific. These spheres of life in turn take different historical shapes: the culture of martial honor of twelfth-century B.C.E. Greece is not the same as the culture of cosmopolitan wit in the salons of Berlin circa 1800; the culture of Enlightenment in eighteenth-century Edinburgh is not the same as the culture of capitalism and the image in contemporary Tokyo or Milan; the culture of the nineteenth-century boulevards and arcades in Paris or Vienna is not the same as the cultures of hybridity crossed with fundamentalism in contemporary Cairo, Los Angeles, or Tehran. Oslo is not Abu Dhabi; São Paulo is not Beijing; Mumbai is not Philadelphia; and none of these is Peoria or Surbiton or Yoknapatawpha County or Albogastathir or Banaras. Yet tensions in life between aspiration supported by reflection and the empirically happenstantial remain variously evident, and they are taken up in various and illuminating ways by both literature and philosophy.

Philosophy and literature as forms of attention are then modes of seeking orientation and clarification of commitment and emotion, and both begin within a specific, situated point of view. Focusing on how each form of attention seeks orientation and clarification within a point of view and from a situation of perplexity, R. G. Collingwood argues that they are not, ultimately, distinct:

> Ever since Pythagoras (or so we are told) invented the word philosophy, in order to express the notion of the philosopher not as one who possesses wisdom but as one who aspires to it, students of philosophy have recognized that the essence of their business lies not in holding this view or that, but in aiming at some view not yet achieved: in the labour and adventure of thinking, not the results of it. What a genuine philosopher (as distinct from a teacher of philosophy for purposes of examination) tries to express when he writes is the experience he enjoys in the course of this adventure, where theories and systems are only incidents in the journey. For the poet, there is, perhaps, none of this dynamism

of thinking. He finds himself equipped, as it were, with certain ideas, and expresses the way in which it feels to possess them. Poetry, then, in so far as it is the poetry of a thinking man and addressed to a thinking audience, may be described as expressing the intellectual emotion attendant upon thinking in a certain way: philosophy, the intellectual emotion attendant upon trying to think better.... [But] in so far as each is good, each converges, as regards style and literary form, with the other; in the limiting case where each was as good as it ought to be, the distinction would disappear. (1938: 297, 298)

Collingwood may somewhat overstate his claim: philosophy and literature are at least comparatively distinct from one another, in that philosophy foregrounds result, impersonality, and attention to general discursive and practical commitment, while literature foregrounds process, personal engagement, particularity, and perplexity. Yet philosophy, too, begins in perplexity; and literature, too, seeks at least implicit generalizable significance. Both exist in the space of clarification. As Kantian critique, Dewey on the reflex arc, and Wittgenstein's later criticisms of the *Tractatus* myth of simple objects should have taught us, there is no getting beneath conceptual commitments and ways of taking objects to identify sempiternal, ultimate metaphysical objects, while still retaining a point of view. Point-of-view having lacks any fixed, ultimate ground, and it inherently involves discursive takings that are themselves contestable and freighted with perplexities and emotional opacities. (This should cast doubt on any strict and absolute opposition between a literal language that records the real and a figurative-expressive language that stylizes stance and attitude: representation cannot be absolutely separated from stance, attitude, and expression of interest and mood.) Human subjectivity as such occupies a position of transcendental homelessness that commits it to the seeking of orientation and clarification.[1] This transcendental homelessness may be sensed more sharply in technological modernity and in otherwise fragmented cultures than elsewhere, but there is good reason to think that it attaches in some measure to the bearing of a point of view as such. In mutual engagement and mutual contestation, philosophy and literature as forms of attention arise from within this situation of the human subject.

The most critically astute and historically perceptive general philosophical account of the roles of literature and poetic imagination in human life remains Hegel's *Lectures on Fine Art*. Hegel begins by noting that both literature and philosophy address oppositions, between abstract law, legislative reason, duty, and civic order, on the one hand, and inclinations, sensuous impulses, and somatic responses to an abundance of new phenomena, on the other. These oppositions are natural to human life as such; coherent commitments that would resolve these oppositions never lie fully ready to hand. In Hegel's full history of forms of art, it is these oppositions that function more effectively as a universal that informs human life than does any logic-governed concept of freedom. But while they are universal, these oppositions also take specific shapes in specific historical circumstances; in particular, modernity exacerbates them, as the social division of labor and the need to make a life via specialized skill within a market economy increase.

> These are oppositions which have not been invented at all by the subtlety of
> reflection or the pedantry of philosophy; in numerous forms they have always
> preoccupied and troubled the human consciousness, even if it is modern culture
> that has first worked them out most sharply and driven them up to the peak of
> harshest contradiction. (Hegel 1975, 1: 54)

Though they effectively lack any superintending logic (more so than Hegel's official doctrine would allow), these oppositions can nonetheless be addressed and
worked through partially. One can seek in abstract reflection informed by historical awareness to determine more adequate commitments and practices that
will moderate these oppositions for many to some degree; general philosophical
theories of commitments, practices, and institutions can yield some fruits. Or, and
also at the same time, the work of imagination can recontextualize, emplot, and
redirect commitments that remain significantly tied to particulars, yielding modest routes of orientation via the exemplary. It can take up, elaborate, and clarify
initially inchoate but real emotional perplexities and somatic investments as they
continue to inhabit any form of institutionalized social life.

As Hegel notices, it is poetry that first answers to a standing need for orientation toward the more fit and satisfying exercise of human powers within oppositions. ("Poetry" [*Poesie*] is Hegel's term for all significant imaginative dramatic
literature, including epic, lyric, tragedy, comedy, romance, the novel, and other
related genres and subgenres.) "Man exists conformably to the law of his existence
only when he knows what he is and what his surroundings are: he must know what
the powers are which drive and direct him, and it is such a knowledge that poetry
provides in its original and substantive form" (Hegel 1975, 2: 973). First in epic
and then in further imaginative, dramatic forms, poetry (literature) presents not
material things as they are and may be discerned via impersonal measurement, in
themselves, but rather things as they matter to us, for good or ill, in feeling and
within emplotments of engagements. "The poetic imagination, as the activity of a
poet, does not, as plastic art does, set before our eyes the thing itself in its external
reality (even if that reality be produced by art), but gives us on the contrary an
inner vision and feeling of it" (Hegel 1975, 2: 1111).

The work of poetic or literary presentation is then in general to address and
work through a structure of feeling that has arisen in relation to the lived experience of oppositions, as these oppositions circumstantially take on new shapes
and mobilize somatic investments. Feeling is tested for aptness in relation to its
occasioning perplexities, subjected to complex modulation and development via
emplotment of what is or may be going on, and focused. It is transformed from a
suffered burden deriving from happenstance into an active response of felt engagement, for which both author and reader can then take responsibility, thus making
the continuing of the life of a subject, always caught up in feeling, more bearable.

> [Poetry's] task, namely, is to liberate the spirit not *from* but *in* feeling. The blind
> dominion of passion lies in an unconscious and dull unity between
> itself and the entirety of a heart that cannot rise out of itself into ideas and

self-expression. Poetry does deliver the heart from this slavery to passion by making it see itself, but it does not stop at merely extricating this felt passion from its immediate unity with the heart but makes of it an object purified from all accidental moods, an object in which the inner life, liberated and with its self-consciousness satisfied, reverts freely at the same time into itself and is at home with itself. (Hegel 1975, 2: 1112)

Liberation *in* feeling is not a matter simply of settling on classifications, normative stances, general principles, or policies for future comportment (however important the testing of all these may also be). Instead, it involves animation—more fully achieved ensoulment—within feeling. As Kant puts it, the work of poetic imagination in attending to things is not that of classification alone; rather, it carries out "the addition to a concept of much that is unnameable, the feeling of which animates the cognitive faculties and combines spirit with what would otherwise be the mere letter of language."[2] Without this animation or ensoulment, involving feeling's response to what is unnameable in experience, but feeling then developed, modulated, and brought to poetic expression, human life threatens to be dull, disengaged, dispirited, and evacuated of responsive subjectivity. Or, in Hegel's development of this same point,

[t]he universal and the rational are not expressed in poetry in abstract universality and *philosophically* proved interconnection, or with their aspects merely related together as in *scientific* [*wissenschaftlich*] thinking, but instead as animated, manifest, ensouled, determining the whole, and yet at the same time expressed in such a way that the all-comprising unity, the real animating soul, is made to work only in secret from within outwards. (1975, 2: 973)

Relating the incidents, scenes, persons, thoughts, moods, and feelings that are presented in a literary work of art so as to invite, sustain, and develop emotional engagement, animation, and ensoulment is not, then, the presentation of the merely materially real either enumeratively or theoretically. "In general we may describe poetry's way of putting things as *figurative* because it brings before our eyes...an appearance such that in it we immediately recognize the essence [or what is significant for us within feeling in relation to possibilities of fuller and freer life] through, and inseparably from, the external aspect and its individuality" (Hegel 1975, 2: 1002). Thought, feeling, language, and subject matter remain tethered to one another via figuration, in a sustained act of attention in the furtherance of life.

Given that human subjects necessarily exist in material and cultural situations that are shared at least to some extent, the poetic work of attention and of the working through of feeling must not be uniquely individual. It is a criterion of success for literary and poetic attention that some resonance with the development of the situation in language be achieved with some others. In a thought that Hegel shares with Wordsworth and Collingwood, among others, casual and incidental rendering, as merely happenstantial, must be distinguished from successful attention that deploys the powers of a subject in an exemplary and resonant way:

> In order that this [poetic] expression may not remain a merely casual expression
> of an individual's own immediate feelings and ideas, it becomes the language of
> the *poetic* inner life, and therefore however intimately the insights and feelings
> which the poet describes as his own belong to him as a single individual, they
> must nevertheless possess a universal validity, i.e. they must be genuine feelings
> and meditations for which the poet invents or finds the adequate and lively
> expression. (1975, 2: 1111–12)

How the required exemplarity and resonance are to be achieved remains, however,
deeply unclear, according to Hegel. Whatever the achievements of modern social
institutions may be, there remain enough oppositions in life to provoke manifold
varieties of emotional perplexities and inchoate somatic investments that require
working through. Hence, "the most heterogeneous works count as poetry" (1975,
2: 971); there are no rules of taste, no necessary forms of organization or diction,
no necessary subject matters. Instead, poetic imagination in finding and integrat-
ing appropriate organization, style, and subject, so as to achieve effective working
through, is all.

Hegel's own historical account of the rises and falls of distinct forms of social
life, and so, he argues, of the literary forms appropriate to them, is both excessively, implausibly rigid and yet insightful in its attention to the importance of
social-material circumstances for the practice of literary art. The excessive and
implausible rigidity consist in his supposing that forms of social life are more or
less coherent wholes, not mongrels; that the boundaries between them are more
or less clear; and that their historical succession is governed by a superintending
logic. And yet his insights are penetrating, especially in his account of epic. "Epic
proper," Hegel argues, is "actualized in the most artistically adequate way [only]
by the Greeks" (1975, 2: 1093)—indeed, only by Homer. This is because a celebra-
tory song of accepted heroic virtues (including accepted virtues in conflict with
one another), if it is to do the artistic work of working through an emotionally
freighted point of view that is shared, presupposes a certain social world in which
these virtues are accepted and common attitudes toward them are held. This is
possible only under specific material circumstances:

> The state of human life most suitable as the background of an epic is that in
> which [a universal ethical ground] exists for individuals *already* as a present
> reality but which remains most closely connected with them by the tie of a
> common primitive life.... The relations of ethical life, the bond of the family,
> as well as the bond of the people—as an entire nation—in war and peace
> must all have been discovered, framed, and developed; but on the other
> hand, not yet developed into the form of universal institutions, obligations,
> and laws valid in themselves without any ratification by the living subjective
> personality of individuals, and indeed possessed of the power of subsisting
> even against the will of individuals.... [Man] must still feel himself alive
> in...the means for satisfying his needs: e.g. house and garden, tents, seats,
> beds, swords and lances, ships for crossing the sea, chariots to take him to
> battle, kettles and roasting-tins, slaughter of animals, food and drink...with
> his whole mind and self, and therefore give a really human, animated, and

individual stamp to what is inherently external by bringing it into close connection with the human individual. Our modern machines and factories with their products, as well as our general way of satisfying the needs of our external life, would from this point of view be just as unsuitable as our modern political organization is for the social background required for the primitive epic. (Hegel 1975, 2: 1051–53)

Certain conceptions of human character must further be both commonly accepted and worked into the successful epic text. Inwardness and moralism must have little place. Counsel and freely willed participation—and only these, not statute—hold the Greeks together as a warring body. Hence, Agamemnon's "position as overlord does not become the dry connection of command and obedience, of a master and his servants" (Hegel 1975, 2: 1053), and "Achilles, as an epic character, should not be given moral lectures as if he were a schoolboy" (1068). Hence, if there are modern epics—*Star Wars* or *The Lord of the Rings* or *The Golden Compass*—these must tend strongly toward compensatory escapism rather than objective social description, and they will be set in a time long ago and far away.

We should not, however, suppose that Homer merely describes actual events. The heroic virtues must be developed artistically, presented, for example, through extended, predominantly visual similes[3] and set within plots in which choices about foci of attention must be made:

> But we must not put the matter at all as if a people in its heroic age as such, the cradle of its epic, already had the skill to be able to describe itself poetically....
> The need to make play with *ideas* in such a presentation, i.e. the development of art, necessarily arises later than the life and the spirit which is naively at home in its immediate poetic existence. Homer and the poems bearing his name are centuries later than the Trojan war which counts as an actual fact.... [Yet] in spite of the separation in time, a close connection must nevertheless still be left between the poet and his material. The poet must still be wholly absorbed in these old circumstances, ways of looking at things, and faith, and all he needs to do is to bring a poetic consciousness and artistic portrayal to his subject which is in fact the real basis of his actual life. (Hegel 1975, 2: 1046–47)

Proper to epic, then, as a form of effective high literary art is "the objective presentation of a self-grounded world,... a world to which the poet's own way of looking at things is akin and with which he can identify himself" (1047); absent such a world and wholehearted identification with it, the production of epic as the highest form of literary art is impossible.

Yet beyond this singular case, correlations between social and literary forms are much looser and for some literary forms largely absent. In particular, lyric, unlike epic, "has the advantage of being producible at almost any moment in a nation's history, [and] its contents may be of extreme variety and touch national life in every direction" (Hegel 1975, 2: 1113–14). The task of the lyric poet, as of, later, the modern novelist and writer of shorter forms of artistic prose, all of whom live amidst greater varieties of individualization, is only

> that he shall entirely assimilate and make his own the objective subject-matter. For the truly lyrical poet lives in himself, treats circumstances in accordance with his own poetic individual outlook, and now, however variously his inner life may be fused with the world confronting him and with its situations, complexities and fates, what he nevertheless manifests in his portrayal of this material is only the inherent and independent life of his feelings and meditations. (1118)

A more individualized working through of emotionally freighted point-of-view having, with more uncertain reception, is now the norm. Forms multiply, effectively achieved resonances become more distinctly sectarian, and more markedly individual style and diction become more foregrounded.

Everywhere, and whether one locates its beginnings in fourteenth-century Italy, in seventeenth-century science, or distantly in Hellenic and Roman cosmopolitanism, the modern is marked by awareness of difference, contingency, variability, and the consequent impossibility of the full consolidation of meaningful culture without significant opacities, disenfranchisements, and perplexities. Whatever we make of postmodernity—whether it is something genuinely new and different or rather a late moment of modernity—these awarenesses become yet more prominent. The importance of literature in working through emotions initiated by perplexities becomes all the more significant, in contrast with, say, theology, as both perplexities and felt awarenesses of them increase. As a result, as J. M. Bernstein puts it, "modern works of art are riven with a reflective, critical self-consciousness of themselves as works of art in relation to (postulated, posited, proposed, invented) indeterminate ideals from which they remain forever separate" (2006: 150). They undertake the work of working through, in the hope of achieving the clarification and consolidation of felt interest, while knowing that achievements of fullest clarification, consolidation, and resonance remain elusive. Experimentalism and the marking of literary style as differing from communicative norms become more prominent, as modes of distinctly literary achievement are sought and resought. As new perplexities and consequent emotional burdens are brought into attention, the devices of the Freudian primary process (condensation, displacement, considerations of representability, and secondary revision) jostle against direct communicative intent, too ready emplotment, cliché, and the didactic. Figuration holds open the space of attention to the difficult and emotionally perplexing. Finitude in undertaking to perfect practical and discursive commitments is fully accepted, and the work of literary attending goes on.

And yet address to the perplexing situation of subjects remains possible, even in the absence of the achievement of absolute orientation. In a characterization that may be taken as well to describe the condition of modern literature as such, György Lukács describes "the irony of the novel" as

> the self-correction of the world's fragility: inadequate relations can transform themselves into a fanciful yet well-ordered round of misunderstandings and cross-purposes, within which everything is seen as many-sided, within which things appear as isolated and yet connected, as full of value and yet totally

devoid of it, as abstract fragments and as concrete, autonomous life, as flowering and as decaying, as the infliction of suffering and as suffering itself. (1971: 75)

Engaging with philosophical general terms, yet denying finality in their application, correcting the world's fragility without denying it, and acknowledging and working through perplexities without dismissing them, literature and philosophy as imaginative disciplines are forms of attention both to the generalities and to the difficult particulars of human life.

Given the partly complementary, partly opposed forms of attention to human life that are cultivated in literary and philosophical writing, as they engage with and contest one another, it is not clear that philosophy and literature is a distinct subfield of philosophy, comparable, say, to ethics, epistemology, or the philosophy of science (the subjects of other *Oxford Handbooks*), nor is it clear that it should be. There are numbers of courses with the title "Philosophy and Literature" that are taught in many places, but these courses often do not share any specific readings or organizational scheme with one another. They are generally determined by the interests of a particular instructor, and they generally lie somewhat aslant the main curricula in both philosophy and literary studies.

In thinking about the relations of complementarity and opposition between philosophy and literature, I have taken the "and" in the title seriously. Specifically, I have resisted the idea to organize the collection around the philosophy *of* literature, treating topics such as the definition of literature, fictional objects and fictional worlds, interpretation, emotions about literature, and so forth, as self-standing topics in their own right to be submitted to the normal standards for the treatment of distinctly philosophical problems. Several other collections already exist that usefully collect the most important treatments of these problems. More important, however, this style of normal philosophical problem solving tends to detract from full attention both to the powers and interest of literature and to the uneasy affinities and disaffinities between philosophy and literature as practices. It seeks to understand the work of literature too readily against the background of protocols of knowing that were developed principally within the epistemology of the natural sciences, thus all but inevitably casting literature as secondary, decorative, or deficient.

This collection is also not devoted to philosophy *in* literature; literary works are not to be taken as mere instances of philosophical stances that are more articulately and adequately worked out elsewhere, as one might, for example, take Sartre's *Nausea* as an illustration of *Being and Nothingness*. This approach, too, scants both the powers of literature and the engagements and contestations that bind philosophy and literature to one another as forms of attention and disciplines of culture.

Instead, this collection is organized around considerations of genre, of certain large-scale historical changes in dominant forms of sensibility and expression, of central devices for developing and sustaining literary attention, and finally, of the uses of literature.

Contributors were invited to explore the interests for human life of specific genres of literature, to consider broad modes of attention that have marked off certain large cultural periods from one another and yet may also be available at many times, to trace the workings of certain central devices for achieving attention, and to consider literature as a practice in relation to the practices of inquiry, morality, and politics. As they appeared, the essays developed increasing resonances with one another, as an essay on a given period or device charted its course via comparisons with a neighboring period or device that was the subject of another essay. Various overlapping themes—what words and characters are; how imagination works; the kinds of significances social circumstances have for imaginative literary production; the needs and interests of situated subjects; the distinctiveness of artistic presentation; the fact of style; the significances of Aristotle, Hegel, Nietzsche, Lukács, and Wittgenstein, among others, for thinking about literary practice—became increasingly clear and prominent. It has been both a pleasure and an education for me to work with the contributors who have taken up the invitation to explore philosophy *and* literature with perceptiveness, subtlety, and argumentative cogency that go well beyond what anyone could have hoped for. Given the powers of their essays, I am confident in trusting that other readers will experience similar tuitions and delights.

NOTES

1. György Lukács introduces the notion of transcendental homelessness in order to characterize the situation of the subject in modernity in *The Theory of the Novel* (1920, reprinted 1971: 61). I follow him in thinking of this transcendental homelessness as especially marked in modernity, but reject his claim that it was altogether absent among the eighth–century B.C.E. Greeks.
2. Kant 2000: 194 (p. 316 Akademie edition); translation slightly modified, adding "what would otherwise be" for "*als bloßem.*"
3. On the artistry of visual witness in Homer, see Auerbach (1953), especially chap. 1, "Odysseus' Scar," and Ledbetter 2002: chap. 1, "Supernatural Knowledge in Homeric Poetics."

REFERENCES

Auerbach, E. (1953). *Mimesis: The Representation of Reality in Western Literature* (W.R. Trask, trans.). Princeton: Princeton University Press.
Beckett, S. (1965). "Three Dialogues." *In* M. Esslin (ed.), *Samuel Beckett: A Collection of Critical Essays*. Englewood Cliffs, N.J.: Prentice Hall. (Original work published 1949).

Bernstein, J. M. (2006). "Poesy and the Arbitrariness of the Sign: Notes for a Critique of Jena Romanticism." *In* N. Kompridis (ed.), *Philosophical Romanticism*. London: Routledge.

Collingwood, R. G. (1938). *The Principles of Art*. Oxford: Clarendon Press.

Derrida, J. (1992). " 'This Strange Institution Called Literature': An Interview with Jacques Derrida." *In* D. Attridge (ed.), *Acts of Literature*. New York: Routledge.

Hegel, G. W. F. (1975). *Lectures on Fine Art* (T. M. Knox, trans.). Oxford: Clarendon Press.

Kant, I. (2000). *Critique of the Power of Judgment* (P. Guyer, ed.; P. Guyer and E. Matthews, trans.). Cambridge: Cambridge University Press. (Original work published 1790).

Ledbetter, G. M. (2002). *Poetics Before Plato*. Princeton: Princeton University Press.

Lukács, G. (1971). *The Theory of The Novel* (A. Bostock, trans.). Cambridge, Mass.: MIT Press. (Original work published 1920).

Szafraniec, A. (2007). *Beckett, Derrida, and the Event of Literature*. Stanford: Stanford University Press.

PART I

GENRES

CHAPTER 1

....

EPIC

....

GREGORY NAGY

WHAT is epic? For a definition, we must look to the origins of the term. The word "epic" comes from the ancient Greek noun *epos*, which refers to a literary genre that we understand as "epic." But the question is, can we say that this word "epic" refers to the same genre as *epos*? The simple answer is no. But the answer is complicated by the fact that there is no single understanding of the concept of a "genre"—let alone the concept of "epic."

This is to be expected, since literary genres do not exist in a vacuum. It is not that literature is made up of a fixed set of genres, such as epic and tragedy. Rather, different literatures have different genres. And even the genres we find in any one particular literature may change over time.

Any given genre in any given literature needs to be defined in relation to the other existing genres in that literature (Slatkin 1987). From a worldwide survey of literatures and preliteratures, it is evident that genres exist "in a relationship of interdependence, in which they have complementary functions in conveying different aspects of a coherent ideology or system of beliefs about the world" (Slatkin 1987: 260).

With the advent of modernity, however, the sense of "coherent ideology or system of beliefs" is eroded. Modern critics react to this erosion by expressing a sense of discomfort with mechanical applications of classifications based on genre (see Todorov 1990). One such critic, Benedetto Croce, went so far as to define any great work of literature as something that is sui generis (Croce 1902). So, a great work, to be truly great, has to become a genre in and of itself. It is as if a great work of literature had to transcend its own genre simply because of its greatness.

Paradoxically, Croce's modern formulation applies to the oldest attested genre in European literature: epic. What defined epic was a great work that was in fact considered to be sui generis. The genre of epic as understood by ancient critics was ultimately defined by the greatest work of literature in the general estimation of the ancient Greeks. That work was a combination of two mutually complementary poetic compositions attributed to a figure who was venerated as the greatest of all poets. That figure, who was considered to be so ancient as to be prehistoric even for the ancients, was Homer. And the two mutually complementary compositions attributed to Homer were the *Iliad* and the *Odyssey*.

Looking for testimony from the ancient world, we find the clearest and most accurate overall assessment of these two poems in the *Poetics* of Aristotle, who flourished in the city of Athens in the fourth century B.C.E. This assessment is linked to his view of epic as a genre.

Aristotle compares epic with other genres such as tragedy, dithyramb, and comedy. Epic is the first of these genres to be mentioned at the very beginning of *Poetics* (1447a):

> Concerning *poetic craft* [*poiētikē* (*tekhnē*)] in and of itself, and its *forms* [*eidos* (plural)], and what potential each form has; and how *mythical plots* [*muthoi*] must be put together if the *poetic composition* [*poiēsis*] is to be good at doing what it does; and how many parts it is made of, and what kinds of parts they are; and, likewise, all other questions that belong to the same line of inquiry—let us speak about all these things by starting, in accordance with the natural order, from first principles. So, the *composition of epic* [*epopoiia* = the *poiēsis* of *epos*] and the *composition* [*poiēsis*] of *tragedy*, as well as *comedy* and the *poetic craft* [*poiētikē* (*tekhnē*)] of the *dithyramb* and most sorts of crafts related to the *aulos*[1] and the *kithara*[2]—all of these crafts, as it happens, are *instances of re-enactment* [*mimēsis*],[3] taken as a whole. There are three things that make these instances of re-enactment different from each other: (1) *re-enacting* [*mimeîsthai*] things in different media, or (2) re-enacting different things, or (3) re-enacting in a mode [*tropos*] that is different and not the same as the other modes.

As we learn from Aristotle's subsequent analysis in the *Poetics*, the act of reenactment or *mimēsis* was considered to be an act of *representing* a preexisting something. The various different media used for representation involved various different combinations or noncombinations of recitation, singing, dancing, and the playing of musical instruments such as the kithara and the aulos. In the case of epic in the time of Aristotle, its medium was recitation, without instrumental accompaniment.

As for the mode of making a reenactment or *mimēsis* in the genre of epic, it was basically *diegetic*, which is to say that the actions of characters were being reenacted by way of *diēgēsis*, or narration; by contrast, the mode of making a reenactment in other genres such as tragedy or comedy was *dramatic*, which is to say that the actions of characters were being reenacted by actors interacting with each other or with a singing and dancing ensemble called the *khoros*, or chorus. It is important to add that the act of narrating epic in the time of Aristotle was in its own right an act of reenactment, or *mimēsis*. That is because the narrator of epic was in effect reenacting characters whenever he quoted, as it were, the words spoken by these characters in the act of interacting with each other. It is also because the narrator of the narrative that is epic was in effect reenacting a notionally prototypical master narrative, narrated by a notionally prototypical master narrator, that is, by Homer.

In order to discern more precisely Aristotle's view of epic as a genre, we need to look more closely at the terminology he uses in the statement I have quoted. His word for "genre," *eidos*, is used in a comparable way by his teacher, Plato, in contexts of analyzing the genres of poetry and song making as found in the performances of drama (as in *Laws* 3.700a). But Plato also uses *eidos* in the absolutized sense of "Form" with reference to his Theory of Forms (as in *Republic* 10.596a). For Aristotle, by contrast, an *eidos*, or genre, such as epic is to be defined comparatively in relation to the other genres that he is considering, such as tragedy (Nagy 1999a: 21–32, esp. 29 n. 22). Aristotle's point of view is validated by comparative evidence: as I have already noted, a genre is not something absolute but relative, depending on the coexistence of given genres at a given time and place (Slatkin 1987).

Aristotle's assessment of epic as a genre takes into consideration not only other coexisting genres but also the nature of poetry itself. His key expression is *poiētikē(tekhnē)*, or "poetic craft." The adjective *poiētikē* can be translated as "poetic" simply because it refers to the craft of composing poetry. Similarly, the noun *poiēsis* can be translated as "poetry" simply because it refers to the act of composing poetry. But the more basic idea inherent in these words deriving from the stem *poiē-* is "composition" pure and simple. The verb *poiein*, which means "compose" or simply "make," can refer to the making of any artifact, not only an artifact that happens to be a poem (Ford 2002: 132–39). So the fact that *poiēsis* and *poiētikē* are used exclusively to refer to the making of poetry, not to any other kind of making, shows that *making poetry* was considered to be a most basic kind of *making*. That is why *poiēsis* means not just any kind of making but rather, more specifically, the making of poetry.

Studying the various poetic genres considered by Aristotle in his *Poetics*, we find that the making of poetry is not only a matter of composition but also a matter of performance. Essentially, the genres he considers happen to correspond to two programs of performances that took place at the two greatest festivals of the Athenian state. At the feast of the City Dionysia of Athens, celebrated in the early spring, there were competitions in the performances of tragedies, comedies, dithyrambs, and satyr dramas. At the feast of the Panathenaia of Athens, celebrated in the late summer, there were competitions in the performances of tunes played on the kithara or on the aulos, and of lyric songs sung to instrumental accompaniment by the kithara or by the aulos, and also of epic poetry recited without any instrumental accompaniment (Nagy 1996a: 81–82; see also 26–27 n. 8).[4]

From the wording of Aristotle, it is clear that each of these genres was associated with a distinct *tekhnē*, or craft. That is, the overall *poiētikē tekhnē* (poetic craft) was subdivided into a variety of specialized *tekhnai* (crafts). One such craft was epic.

The term that Aristotle uses to designate the craft of making epic, *epopoiia* (making of *epos*), indicates that the concept of making epic was equated with the most general concept of making poetry, since the word used to designate "epic," *epē*, which is the plural of *epos*, is simply the general word used to designate any kind of poetry produced by way of *poiēsis*, that is, by way of "making" poetry. For example, in the Clouds, a comedy by Aristophanes dating back to the fifth century B.C.E., *epē* refers to the recited "verses" of his comedy (verse 544); in another of his comedies, the *Frogs* (verse 862), *epē* again refers to the recited "verses"—as opposed to the sung "lyrics," which are *melē (melos* plural).

This usage, dating back to the classical period of comedy in the fifth century B.C.E., is most significant. We have already seen that the act of making poetry, *poiēsis*, was considered to be a most basic kind of *making*. Now we see that the act of making epic poetry, *epopoiia*, was considered to be a most basic kind of making poetry itself, since *epē* can refer to any kind of poetic verse that is recited—even the recited verses of comedy as distinct from the sung verses in that genre. In other words, to say *epē* is the most general way of referring to the "verses" of poetry. The linguistic prehistory of *epē* helps explain its ultimate meaning: etymologically, this word means simply "words" or "wording." It is cognate with Latin *vox*, the meaning of which is parallel: *vox* refers to whatever sounds are made by the human voice.

Though the ancient Greeks perceived epic as a most general category in the era of Aristotle, it had a most special status in their civilization. It was considered to be poetry par excellence. The key to this status was the poet par excellence, Homer. This figure was considered to be the supreme poet not only of epic but also of all poetry. As we see from the usage of Plato (*Gorgias* 485d) as well as Aristotle (*Rhetoric* 1.1365a11), to say *ho poiētēs* ("the poet") without any mention of a name was tantamount to saying "Homer." Homer was for them and for all Greeks of their time the poet par excellence.

In the age of Plato and Aristotle, the prehistoric figure called Homer was understood to be the poet who composed two epics, the *Iliad* and the *Odyssey*. Other epics were attributed to figures other than Homer. Those epics, which were classed in a grouping of epics known as the Cycle (*kuklos*), were considered inferior to the two epics attributed to Homer. Aristotle says so explicitly in his *Poetics*, naming two epics of the Cycle as examples, the *Cypria* and the *Little Iliad* (1459a–b).[5]

In order to understand the special status of the Homeric *Iliad* and *Odyssey*, more needs to be said about the actual performance traditions of epic in the time of Plato and Aristotle. By that time, the traditions of performing epic at the festival of the Panathenaia in Athens had achieved a most specialized status. The performers were professional specialists called *rhapsōidoi* or "rhapsodes," as we see most clearly from a dialogue of Plato, *Ion*, named after a celebrated *rhapsōidos* (rhapsode) who flourished in the late fifth century B.C.E., the era of the historical Socrates.

The status of the rhapsode can be reconstructed from the following words of Plato's Socrates (*Ion* 533b–c):

> Here is another thing. As far as I can tell, neither in (1) *playing on the aulos*
> [= *aulēsis*] nor in (2) *playing on the kithara* [= *kitharisis*] nor in (3) *singing*
> *and playing on the kithara* [= *kitharōidia*] nor in (4) *performing as a rhapsode*
> [= *rhapsōidia*] have you seen any man who is skilled at explaining about
> (1) *Olympus*[6] or about (2) *Thamyras*[7] or about (3) *Orpheus* or about (4) *Phemios*
> of Ithaca, the *rhapsode* [= *rhapsōidos*][8]—but who is perplexed about Ion of

Ephesus and is unable to formulate what things Ion *performs* well *as a rhapsode* [= *rhapsōideîn*] and what things he does not.

In this passage, Socrates links the rhapsodes with other professional performers such as *auletes* (aulos players), citharists (kithara players), and *citharodes* (kithara singers). These types of performers correspond to the performers that actually competed at the Panathenaia in the age of Plato, as we learn from an Athenian inscription dated at around 380 B.C.E. (IG II² 2311), which records the winners of competitions in performance at the Panathenaia.[9] We also learn about these categories of competition from Plato's *Laws* (6.764d–e), where we read of rhapsodes, citharodes, and auletes—and where the wording makes it clear that the point of reference is the Panathenaia (Nagy 2002: 38, 40, 42).

The evidence from Plato about these categories of competition at the Panathenaia is supplemented by what we read in the Aristotelian *Constitution of the Athenians* (60.1), where the author refers to these same Panathenaic categories of competition and where the overall competition is specified as the "competition [*agōn*] in *mousikē*."

What does the author mean by *mousikē* here? In Aristotelian usage, this word is a shorthand way of saying *mousikē tekhnē*, meaning "craft of the Muses," that is, musical craft in the etymological sense of the word "musical." It is misleading, however, to think of ancient Greek *mousikē* in the modern sense of "music," since the categories of "musical" performers at the Panathenaia included rhapsodes. The performative medium of rhapsodes in the era of Aristotle was recitative and thus not musical in the modern sense of the word. By "recitative," to be more precise, I mean (1) performed without singing and (2) performed without the instrumental accompaniment of the kithara or the aulos (Nagy 2002: 36, 41–42). In this era, the competitive performances of the Homeric *Iliad* and *Odyssey* by rhapsodes at the Panathenaia were "musical" only in an etymological sense, and the medium of the rhapsode was in fact closer to what we call "poetry" and further from what we call "music" in the modern sense of the word. Still, the fact remains that the performances of rhapsodes belonged to what is called the "competition [*agōn*] in *mousikē*," just like the performances of citharodes (kithara singers), citharists (kithara players), auletes (aulos players), and so on (Nagy 2002: 36, 41–42).

The "musical" performers mentioned in Plato's *Ion* need to be seen in the light of the dramatic moment that serves as the setting for this Platonic dialogue. Ion, a rhapsode from the city of Ephesus, has just arrived in Athens, intending to compete for first prize at the festival of the Panathenaia (*Ion* 530b). Plato's wording makes it explicit that the occasion for performances by rhapsodes at the Panathenaia was in effect a competition or contest among rhapsodes—an *agōn* (*Ion* 530a)—and that the agonistic craft of the rhapsodes is included under the general category of *mousikē* (530a). When Ion says that he hopes to win first prize at the Panathenaia, he adds that he has just won first prize in an *agōn* of rhapsodes at the feast of the Asklepieia in Epidaurus (530a–b) (Nagy 2002: 22, 37–38, 99).

At the *agōn* of *mousikē* held at the Panathenaia, the contests of citharodes, aulodes, citharists, and auletes may have varied in content from one season to the next, but the overall content of what the rhapsodes had to perform was invariable—at least, it had become an invariable by the time of Plato. That invariable was the Homeric *Iliad* and *Odyssey*, performed season after season at the Panathenaia.

Though we know precious little about the Panathenaic performances of Homer by rhapsodes in the age of Plato, there is sufficient evidence for positing three features: (1) the rhapsodes performed in sequence the Homeric *Iliad* and *Odyssey*, (2) each of these two epics was divided into 24 rhapsodic performance units or *rhapsōidiai* (rhapsodies), and (3) the rhapsodes were actively competing as well as collaborating with each other in the process of taking turns in performing sequentially the epic narrative (Nagy 2002: 36–69).[10] There is room for doubt about the specifics of all three of these posited features (Burgess 2004), but there is one overall feature, essential to the argument at hand, that seems beyond doubt: in the era of the Athenian democracy, the repertoire of rhapsodes performing at the Panathenaia was confined exclusively to the Homeric *Iliad* and *Odyssey* (Nagy 2002: 10–12 n. 16).

To advance the argument further, I adduce three interconnected details. The first two come from the *Ion* of Plato, while the third comes from the *Panegyricus* of Isocrates. The first detail has to do with a boast made by the rhapsode Ion: he claims that he is worthy of being awarded the prize of a golden *stephanos* (garland) by the *Homēridai* (descendants of Homer) (*Ion* 530d). The prize that is mentioned here is mentioned again in two other contexts (*Ion* 535d, 541c). In one of these two contexts, the golden garland is associated with the words *thusiai* (feasts) and *heortai* (festivals) (*Ion* 535d). These words are appropriate designations of the festival of the Panathenaia. Piecing together what we learn from all three contexts (*Ion* 530d, 535d, 541c), I infer that the awarding of a golden garland to Ion by the Homēridai is connected with the winning of first prize in the competition of rhapsodes at the Panathenaia.[11] An additional piece of evidence is the inscription I mentioned above (IG II² 2311) concerning the prizes won at the Panathenaia in Athens for the year 380 B.C.E.: the first prize in the competition of citharodes is a golden *stephanos* valued at 1,000 drachmas, which is awarded in addition to a cash prize of silver valued at 500 drachmas. Though the portion of the inscription dealing with the competition of rhapsodes is lost, it is generally agreed that the missing portion indicated that the first prize in the corresponding competition of rhapsodes was likewise a golden *stephanos* and that the amount of cash awarded as first prize to the winning rhapsode was comparable to the amount awarded to the winning citharode (Nagy 2002: 51 n. 16).

The fact that the Homēridai are linked with the performances of Homeric poetry by rhapsodes at the Panathenaia in Athens is relevant to another fact: Homer himself is linked with the performances of the *Iliad* and the *Odyssey* in Athens. Evidence for the linkage comes from myths preserved in the Lives of Homer traditions, especially in the Herodotean *Life of Homer* (*Vita* 1) and in the *Certamen* or *Contest of Homer and Hesiod* (*Vita* 2; Nagy 2004a).[12] According to the *Certamen*, the people of the island state of Chios claimed that Homer was the ancestor of a *genos* (lineage) from Chios who called themselves the Homēridai (*Vita* 2.13–15). According to the Herodotean *Life of Homer*, Homer composed both the *Iliad* and the *Odyssey* in the city of Chios (*Vita* 1.346–98) and planned to perform both epics in Athens (1.483–84), but he died before he reached his destination (1.484–509). In this version, the myth specifies that Homer augments his composition of both the *Iliad* and the *Odyssey* by adding verses that center on the glorification of Athens (1.378–98). Only after he finishes his glorification of Athens does Homer finish composing the *Iliad* and *Odyssey*—only then does he take leave of Chios and set sail to tour the rest of Hellas (1.400), intending ultimately to reach the city of Athens (1.483–84). I infer that these references picturing Athens as the ultimate destination for Homer's would-be performance of his *Iliad* and *Odyssey* are a mythological analogue to the ritual presence of the Homēridai at the rhapsodes' actual performances of the Homeric *Iliad* and *Odyssey* at the Panathenaia in Athens.

I now come to a second interconnected detail in Plato's *Ion*. It has to do with the dramatized circumstances of the Ion's dialogue with Socrates, which happens on the eve of the day when this rhapsode enters the *agōn* of *mousikē* at the Panathenaia (530a–b): Ion will be competing with other rhapsodes in the performance of Homeric poetry, and he expects to win the first prize in that competition.[13] Of special interest here is the term *mousikē (tekhnē)*, which means literally "craft (*tekhnē*) of the Muses." As described above, it would be anachronistic to translate this term as "music," since it applies not only to the craft of singing lyric accompanied by the kithara or aulos, as represented by citharodes and auledes, but also to the craft of reciting epic without any instrumental accompaniment. That particular craft is represented by rhapsodes at the Panathenaia.

The third and decisive interconnected detail comes from a passage in the *Panegyricus* of Isocrates (159), concerning the repertoire of rhapsodes competing with each other in the *athloi* (competitions) of *mousikē* at the Panathenaia:

> I think that the *poetry* [*poiēsis*] of Homer received all the more glory because he celebrated so beautifully those who waged war against the barbarians, and it was because of this that our (Athenian) ancestors wanted to make his *craft* [*tekhnē*] a thing to be honored both in the competitions [of rhapsodes] in *mousikē* and in the education of the young, so that we, having the chance to hear often his [= Homer's] *verses* [*epos* plural], may learn thoroughly the existing hostility against them [= the barbarians], and so that we may admire the accomplishments of those who had waged war and desire to accomplish the same deeds that they had accomplished.[14]

For Isocrates, Homer is the foundational point of reference to what we would call "Western" civilization, in sharp contrast to the "barbarians." In the reference that this contemporary of Plato is making here to Homer, the wording assumes that the epics performed at the Panathenaia were totally familiar to all Athenians. Such epics, in the Athens of Isocrates and Plato in the fourth century B.C.E., can only be the Homeric *Iliad* and *Odyssey*. Even in the general usage of Isocrates (2.48; 10.65; 12.18, 33, 293; 13.2), we find that the term "Homer" refers to no poet other than the poet of the *Iliad* and *Odyssey*. The same goes for the general usage of Plato himself (a case in point is *Ion* 539d).

Also relevant in this passage from Isocrates is the designation of Homeric *poiēsis* (poetic composition) as a *tekhnē* (craft). As we see from his wording, Isocrates links the craft of Homer with (1) the Panathenaic *athloi* (competitions) of rhapsodes and (2) the *paideusis* (education) of the young. In view of the fact that *mousikē* was an appropriate term for designating not only the craft of, say, citharodes performing lyric poetry at the Panathenaia but also the craft of rhapsodes performing the epic poetry of Homer at the same festival, I stress once again that it is misleading to understand *mousikē* as "music" in the modern sense of the word.

Pursuing this idea of the rhapsode as a master of *mousikē*, I return to the passage I quoted above from Plato's *Ion* (533b–c), which lists mythical prototypes corresponding to the categories of performers who compete in the *agōn* (competition) of *mousikē* at the Panathenaia. The correspondences are anachronistic—and revealing in their anachronisms. There is Orpheus, master *kitharōidos* (citharode), that is, one who sings while accompanying himself on the kithara; there is Thamyras, master *kitharistēs* (citharist), that is, one who plays on the kithara but does not sing;[15] there is Olympus, master *aulētēs* (aulete), that is, one who plays on the reed or aulos; and, finally, there is Phemios, master *rhapsōidos* (rhapsode). The key figure in this quartet is Phemios the rhapsode. By contrast with the generic rhapsode who recited Homer in the age of Plato, without musical accompaniment, the prototypical rhapsode Phemios matches an earlier vision of Homer: inside the narrative of the Homeric *Odyssey*, Phemios is not a reciter but an *aoidos* (singer; i 325, 346, 347; xxii 330, 345, 376) who literally "sings" (*aeidein*; i 154, 155, 325, 326, 350; xvii 262; xxii 331, 346, 348; noun *aoidē*, i 159, 328, 340, 351) as he performs his epics inside the epic of the *Odyssey* (at i 326, the epic sung by Phemios is a *nostos* [song of homecoming]), and he even accompanies himself on the equivalent of a kithara (*kitharis*, i 153, 159; elsewhere, his instrument is called a *phorminx* [xvii 262; xxii 332, 340]; verb *phormizein*, i 155).

What, then, is the formal difference in Plato's *Ion* between Phemios the "rhapsode" and Orpheus the "citharode"? After all, Orpheus—just like Phemios—is imagined as singing and accompanying himself on the kithara. The difference is that Phemios, as a rhapsode, is a worthy point of comparison for Homer as the ultimate poet, whereas Orpheus, as a citharode, is not. The "music" of Phemios as a rhapsode is central at the Panathenaia in the days of Plato, whereas the "music" of Orpheus is marginalized. Even as a citharode, Orpheus is mockingly marginalized (Plato, *Symposium* 179d–e).

Let us pursue further the idea that Orpheus, the mythical citharode of Plato's *Ion*, is a specialist in "music" and thus a foil for Homer. The same goes for Thamyras, the mythical citharist, and for Olympus, the mythical aulete: they, too, are specialists and thus foils for Homer.[16] By contrast, Phemios, the mythical rhapsode, is a surrogate for Homer as the ultimate generalist in the "music" of the Panathenaia. Not only the mythical rhapsode but also the contemporary rhapsodes in the days of Plato—as represented by Ion himself—figure as surrogates of Homer in the context of the Panathenaia. As noted above, the performances of Ion and his colleagues at that festival are restricted to the Homeric *Iliad* and *Odyssey*. As surrogates of Homer, the rhapsodes performing at the Panathenaia must be generalists in "music" just like Homer, who is viewed as the generalized embodiment of poetry par excellence in the days of Plato. That is why Homer is known as the *poiētēs* (poet) par excellence and that is why his compositions are known as *poiēsis* (poetry or poetic creation) par excellence.

Thus, the generic rhapsode performing the poetry of Homer at the Panathenaia becomes a generalized representative of poetry as "music": his identity extends from the prototypical singer who sings Homeric song all the way to the contemporary rhapsode who recites Homeric poetry. By extension, Ion the rhapsode may at first seem like a generalized representative of poetry in his own right, for the simple reason that he is a representative of Homeric poetry. To the extent that Homer the poet is considered a generalist, not a specialist, so too the rhapsode who performs Homer may at first seem like a generalist in poetry.

If Ion the rhapsode is a generalist in poetry, then he can be held responsible by Plato's Socrates not only for Homeric poetry but also for all poetry. That is Ion's good fortune, from his own standpoint as the most prestigious rhapsode in his time, "the best rhapsode of the Hellenes" (*Ion* 541b).[17] That is also Ion's misfortune, from the standpoint of the philosophical agenda built into the dialogue named after him. If Plato's Socrates can succeed in discrediting Ion, he can discredit a man who represents the best of all poetry in the days of Plato.[18] In the process, Plato is also discrediting the Panathenaic standard of Homeric poetry, which sets the criteria for what is the best of all poetry.

One way for Socrates to discredit Ion is to show that the rhapsode who performs Homer, unlike Homer, is in fact no generalist in poetry. Plato's Socrates forces Ion to admit that he is a specialist: when Socrates asks Ion whether he is an expert in the poetry of Hesiod or Archilochus, the rhapsode replies that he is not, and that his expertise in Homer is *hikanon* (sufficient; *Ion* 531a).[19] Ion is forced to admit that he is an expert in Homer—and Homer only—but he justifies his non-expertise in other poets on the grounds that Homer is superior to all other poets (531a–32c).[20] This formulation suits perfectly a Panathenaic rhapsode, in terms of my argument that Homeric poetry was the only poetry performed by rhapsodes at the Panathenaia in the days of Plato.

In the context of the Panathenaia, the figure of Homer evolved to the point of becoming the all-sufficient poet, the ultimate generalist in poetry. By the age of Plato, the feast of the Panathenaia could leave no room for any poet other than Homer in the rhapsodic competitions—no Hesiod, no Archilochus—not to mention Orpheus and Musaeus or the poets of the Epic Cycle. Only in the citharodic (and aulodic) competitions at the Panathenaia was there room left for other poets—and these poets had to be nonepic poets, that is, lyric poets, such as Simonides.[21]

And yet, all early poets are linked, says Plato's Socrates, to the single and absolute source of poetic or "musical" inspiration, the Muses. Just as rhapsodes are *hermēneis* (interpreters) of poets, so also poets are *hermēneis* (interpreters) of the

Muses (*Ion* 535b). Below I quote a passage from Plato's Ion where a collectivized concept of the Muses as a single absolute source of all poetry or (music)—in the literal sense of *mousikē* (craft [*tekhnē*] of the Muses)—is expressed by Socrates through the metaphor of the Heraclean or Magnesian stone, that is, the magnet (*Ion* 533d). Poets are imagined as metallic rings directly linked to a prototypical magnet of poetic inspiration, the Muses. Poets, as direct links to the magnet, are the *prētoi daktulioi* (first rings). As we are about to see, Plato's Socrates expresses the direct linkage of the metallic rings to the prototypical magnet by way of the verb *exartân* (link), which I translate as "magnetically link," and he makes it explicit that the poets symbolized by the metallic rings are likewise prototypical, namely, Orpheus, Musaeus, and Homer—in that order (*Ion* 536a–c):

> One of the given *poets* [*poiētai*] is *magnetically linked* [*exartân*] to one Muse, and another poet [*poiētēs*] to another Muse. And we express *this idea* [= auto "it" = passive of *exartân* = "is magnetically linked to"] by saying "is possessed by" [= passive of *katekhein*]. And it [= the idea of "is possessed by"] is pretty much the same sort of thing, since he [= the poet] is literally "held fast" [= passive of *ekhein*] (by the Muse). Then, from these *first rings*, that is, from the *poets* [*poiētai*], each different person is *magnetically linked* [*artân*] to a different poet [*poiētēs*], becoming divinely possessed [= *entheos*]: some persons are magnetically linked to *Orpheus*, some to *Musaeus*, and the majority, to *Homer*; they [= these persons] are *possessed* [= passive of *katekhein*] (by the poets), and they are literally "held fast" [= passive of *ekhein*]. You, Ion, are one of these persons, and you are *possessed* [= passive of *katekhein*] by Homer. When anyone sings the poetry of any other poet, you are asleep and do not know what to say, but when anyone voices the song of this poet [= Homer], then, right away, you are awake and your spirit is dancing and you know very well what to say. For you say what you say about Homer not by means of a *craft* [*tekhnē*] or *expertise* [*epistēmē*] but rather by means of a *god-given legacy* [*moira*] and a *state of possession* [*katokēkhē*]. (*Ion* 536a–c)

Of supreme importance is the image of the first rings (*prētoi daktulioi*) as visualized here in Plato's *Ion* (536b). The first rings are symbols for the three First Poets, named here as Orpheus, Musaeus, and Homer—in that order. It is made clear that the performers of Homer outnumber by far the performers of Orpheus and Musaeus in the era of Socrates. One such performer of Homer is Ion the rhapsode, described as a middle ring in comparison to Homer. By implication, performers of Orpheus and Musaeus are likewise middle rings in comparison to Orpheus and Musaeus themselves, who are first rings like Homer.

A figure like Ion, as a rhapsode, is not a prototypical poet—he is no first ring; he is not even a poet. As a performer, the rhapsode is merely a middle ring linked magnetically to one of the first rings, in this case, to Homer. Performers of epic, like performers of drama, are middle rings in relation to the poets of epic and the poets of drama, who are first rings, whereas the audiences watching rhapsodes performing Homer—who are like the audiences watching actors performing drama in the theater—are the last rings, described as follows by Plato's Socrates: "Of course you know that this person we talked about, the *spectator* [*theatēs*] in the audience, is the *last* of the rings—I mean, the rings that get their power from each other through the force of the Heraclean stone. The *middle* ring is the *rhapsode*—that's you [= Ion]—as well as the *actor* [*hupokritēs*]. And the *first* ring is the *Poet* [*poiētēs*] himself" (*Ion* 535e–36a).

In introducing this passage, I deliberately used a visual metaphor when I said that the audiences of epic and of drama were "watching" the performers, not just "listening" to them. The wording in the passage makes it explicit that the audiences are "spectators" (*theatai*). In using the word *theatēs* (spectator) here in the *Ion* (535e), Plato's Socrates makes no distinction between the audiences who attend performances of Homeric epic at the Panathenaia and the audiences who attend performances of drama at the City Dionysia and other dramatic festivals.[22] The audiences of both epic and drama are the "last" ring. Then there is the "middle" ring, and Socrates places Ion the rhapsode into this category, along with the generic *hupokritēs* (actor) of drama.

In order to discredit Ion, Plato's Socrates has in effect disconnected the prestige of Ion as the performer of Homeric poetry from the prestige of Homer as the notional composer of Homeric poetry. This way, the prestige of Homer is not directly challenged, just as the prestige of Homeric poetry as the premier poetic event of the Panathenaia cannot be challenged. The idea of Homer as the all-sufficient and all-encompassing Poet is a given. It is already a historical reality.

The dominant status of Homeric poetry is not the only historical reality relevant to the argument in Plato's *Ion*. Another reality is the dominant status of the actual craft of rhapsodically performing—and interpreting—Homeric poetry at the Panathenaia in the dramatic time of Plato's dialogues. I say "craft" in view of the explicit designation *rhapsēidikē tekhnē* (rhapsodic craft) as we see it applied by Plato's Socrates at later stages of his argumentation in *Ion* (538b, 538c, 538d, 539e, 540a, 540d, 541a). Thus, the *rhapsēidikē tekhnē* (rhapsodic craft) of the Panathenaic rhapsode is another given—it, too, is already a historical reality.

At the earliest stages of his argumentation, however, Plato's Socrates avoids referring to this *tekhnē* of the rhapsode. Instead, he speaks only about the overall craft of the poet, which is designated as *poiētikē tekhnē* (poetic craft), and he induces Ion to admit that this craft is a *holon*, an integral whole, just like other *tekhnai* (*Ion* 532c). For the moment, I translate *poiētikē* as "poetic craft," but, as we have seen, it is more accurate to render this word as "craft of composition," since the *poiētēs* as "poet" is the composer par excellence.

Then Socrates induces Ion to admit that the craft of painters, *graphikē tekhnē*, is likewise a *holon* (whole; 532e), and that craftsmen are like painters—and sculptors, he adds—in that they need to be experts in the totality of their respective crafts (532e–33b). By the time he speaks about the craft of sculptors, Plato's Socrates has already omitted the word *tekhnē*. This omission facilitates his transition to the passage I have already mentioned about craftsmen such as auletes, citharists, citharodes, and rhapsodes (*Ion* 533b–c). Far from speaking of these craftsmen as representatives of separate crafts, Plato's Socrates groups them together as representatives of a single craft, to which he had referred earlier as that integral whole, the *poiētikē tekhnē*. How could it be, asks Socrates, that any one of these crafts-men—auletes and citharists and citharodes and rhapsodes—could fail to be an expert in that integral whole, in that single craft of theirs, that is, in the *poiētikē tekhnē*? Ion, who has already accepted the premise that the *poiētikē tekhnē* is an integral whole, a *holon*, is now forced to admit that he simply cannot claim to be such an expert; instead, Ion is an expert only in one aspect of that craft, that is, in the poetry of Homer (533c). From the standpoint of a performer's craft, that poetry must be restricted to epic. The poetry of Homer, as far as a rhapsode like Ion is concerned, can only be epic poetry.

Next, Plato's Socrates induces Ion to accept the idea that the rhapsode's profes-sion is therefore not even a matter of *tekhnē* but, rather, a matter of inspiration (*Ion* 533e). By implication, the rhapsode is an expert only in the craft of *mousikē*, the craft of the Muse who inspires poets, not in the craft of the poet himself, that is, in the craft of *poiētikē*. This way, as we have already seen, Ion's authority as a rhapsode can still be validated as "magnetically" linked to the authority of Homer as poet, which in turn is "magnetically" linked to the authority of his inspiring Muse as the ultimate source—the ultimate inspiration. Once Ion accepts this idea, however, his authority as a thinker is thereby discredited: he has in effect admitted that, as a rhapsode, he has no mind of his own and simply speaks the mind of Homer. Only after the rhapsode has accepted the idea that he is an inspired performer does Socrates start speaking openly about the "rhapsodic craft," *rhapseidikē tekhnē*, in his continued dialogue with the rhapsode. By now it is safe for Socrates to speak this way. Since Ion has already been discredited as a thinker, he cannot invoke his prestigious rhapsodic craft as a source for independent thinking. Even the prestige of Homeric knowledge—to the extent that the rhapsode derives it from his rhap-sodic craft—has been diminished: by now the rhapsode's general knowledge seems less impressive than the specialized knowledge that other craftsmen derive from their own specialized crafts.

From the standpoint of a rhapsode, Ion's mistake in the Platonic dialogue named after him is that he missed the chance of asserting, from the very start, that there was indeed such a thing as a "rhapsodic craft," a *rhapseidikē tekhnē*. He also missed the chance of asserting that the prestige of this distinct craft was superior to the prestige of other distinct crafts such as those represented by auletes and cit-harists and maybe even citharodes—at least, at the Panathenaia.

As the craft of rhapsodically performing Homeric poetry evolved in the con-text of "musical" competitions at the Panathenaia, it had reached a level of prestige that overshadowed other forms of performance as they too evolved in the context of competitions at the same festival. I have already quoted the passage where these other forms are listed alongside the premier form, that is, alongside the craft of rhapsodically performing Homeric poetry (*Ion* 533b–c). In this passage, which lists the various crafts of performing various kinds of "music" at the Panathenaia, Plato's Socrates shades over the historical fact that the repertoire of rhapsodes who com-peted at the Panathenaia was by this time restricted to Homeric poetry, whereas the repertoire of, say, the citharodes was not restricted to the poetry of any single master of lyric. Plato's Socrates makes it look like a deficiency that Ion the rhapsode performs—and interprets—Homer and only Homer. Philosophically, this specialization may indeed be a deficiency, but historically, it is a clear indication of the prestige inherent in the craft of performing the epic of Homer in Athens.

In this same passage from Plato's *Ion* (533b–c), the wording shows that any rhapsode who competes at the Panathenaia practices the craft of a performer, not a composer. The same holds for the crafts of the auletes, the citharists, and the citharodes. All such craftsmen are being viewed as performers at festivals like the Panathenaia, not as composers. Moreover, this view extends also to the prototypes of these craftsmen, that is, to Olympos, Thamyras, Orpheus, and Phemios. All four of these prototypical figures are viewed here as performers in their own right, not as composers per se.

The specialization of these four prototypes of Panathenaic performance is most striking in the case of Phemios, who is being equated in this passage with the figure of an archetypal rhapsode. Plato's Socrates exploits this equation to further his philosophical agenda. We have already seen that the rhapsode can perform and even interpret the content of what he performs at the Panathenaia, that is, the epics of Homer, but he is not the composer of this content. Therefore, the rhapsode is not a poet. If Phemios is a rhapsode, then he is not a *poiētēs* (poet) in the literal sense of this word: he is not the "maker" of the content. Only Homer can be said to *poieîn* (make) the content of Homeric poetry.

From what we have already seen about Phemios, we can picture him as a self-representation of Homer in Homer (Graziosi 2002: 25 n. 15, 39–40). And yet, the self that is Homer changes over time. When Phemios is equated with a rhapsode in Plato's *Ion*, this equation implies that Phemios is no longer a poet like Homer, since the rhapsode who competes at the Panathenaia is no composer like Homer but merely a performer of Homer. To equate the Panathenaic rhapsode with the self-represented Homer that is Phemios is to detract from Homer the poet. If Phemios in the Homeric *Odyssey* is merely performing but not composing, like some rhapsode competing at the Panathenaia, then he has no say about determining the content of what he performs. Such a recreated Homer can only say what Homer is saying. And what exactly is it that Homer is saying? According to Plato's Socrates, Homer in turn can only say what the Muse is saying.

Thus, Plato's Socrates exploits the equating of Phemios with a rhapsode by using it as proof for his argument that the rhapsode has no mind of his own when he performs Homer. This argument, however, can be used to discredit the rhapsode only if the craft of the rhapsode has already been discredited. Plato's Socrates has managed to accomplish that by initially eliding the fact that the rhapsode has his own *tekhnē* (craft), the *rhapseidikē tekhnē*. The rhapsode's understanding of Homer, in terms of this *tekhnē*, does not need to be separated from the idea that the rhapsode is inspired by the Muse of Homer. In terms of this *tekhnē*, the professional conceit of the Panathenaic rhapsode is that he reads, as it were, the mind of Homer. The rhapsode's mind has learned the meaning or *dianoia* of Homer (*Ion* 530b–c; Nagy 2002: 29–30 n. 16). The living proof of this conceit is the rhapsode's capacity to perform Homer by heart at the Panathenaia and to be the perfect *hermēneus* (interpreter) of Homer (*Ion* 530c; Nagy 2002: 29 n. 16).

What, then, is the poetry of Homer for the rhapsode? As we saw in the passage I quoted above from Isocrates (*Panegyricus* 159), Homeric *poiēsis* (poetry) is a *tekhnē* (craft) that is activated in two linked contexts: (1) the Panathenaic *athloi* (competitions) of rhapsodes in *mousikē* (musical craft) and (2) the *paideusis* (education) of the young. The wording of Isocrates makes it clear that Homeric poetry is a *tekhnē* in its own right, and that it counts as part of the overall *mousikē* (musical craft) of the Panathenaic *athloi* (*Panegyricus* 159).

Unlike Isocrates, however, who implicitly identifies the craft of the rhapsode with the craft of Homer, Plato seeks to make a distinction between the two crafts. He does this by implicitly making a distinction between the crafts of *mousikē* and *poiētikē*, as if the rhapsode were an expert only in the craft of *mousikē*, not in the craft of *poiētikē*.

Already at the very beginning of the *Ion*, Plato's Socrates had drawn Ion's attention away from Homeric poetry as a *tekhnē* (craft) in its own right by speaking instead about the more general concept of *poiētikē tekhnē* (poetic craft). Once Socrates induces Ion to admit that the *poiētikē tekhnē* is a *holon* (whole) (532c), much like the *tekhnai* (crafts) of painting and sculpting (532e–33b), he has already succeeded in discrediting the craft of performing and teaching Homeric *poiēsis* (poetry). Such performing and teaching is in effect the *rhapsēidikē tekhnē* of Ion. In order to emphasize the universalized importance of Ion's craft, I repeat once again the formulation of Isocrates: the *tekhnē* (craft) of Homeric *poiēsis* (poetry) is coextensive with the *paideusis* (education) of the young. Ion has unwittingly discredited his own *tekhnē* once he admits that he is a specialist in Homer. Moreover, in order to validate his specialty, he is forced to deny that his *tekhnē* is really a *tekhnē*.

Plato's Socrates has forced Ion to make a choice: the rhapsode's authority comes either from inspiration or from the *poiētikē tekhnē*, the craft of poetry. Ion is forced to choose inspiration as the source of his ultimate authority, since that inspiration comes ultimately from the Muse of Homer. Ion is not allowed to claim the craft of poetry as his ultimate authority because he is forced to admit that he is a master in only one aspect of that craft, that is, in Homeric poetry. Moreover, he is a master in only two of three aspects of that poetry, that is, in performing and interpreting it; he not a master in the third aspect, that is, in composing Homeric poetry.

Plato's Ion has to make a choice that a rhapsode need not have had to make, between *tekhnē* and inspiration. Provided the rhapsode insists that his craft is really a craft, a specialized *rhapsēidikē tekhnē* instead of the generalized *poiētikē tekhnē*, he can have his own *tekhnē* and still claim to be inspired by the Muse of Homer. With his specialized craft, he can lay claim to the generalized and even universalized *paideusis* (education) represented by the *poiēsis* (poetry) of Homer, since his *rhapsēidikē tekhnē* is part of the overall *mousikē tekhnē* of performing at the Panathenaia.

The time has come to summarize the distinctions in the meanings of *rhapsēidikē*, *mousikē*, and *poiētikē* as applied to the word *tekhnē* (craft) in the age of

Plato. The *rhapsēidikē tekhnē* is the craft of performing recitative poetry at *agēnes/athloi* (competitions), especially at the Panathenaia. The *mousikē tekhnē* is the craft of performing (1) recitative poetry or (2) song and/or (3) instrumental "music" (in the modern sense of the word) at these same *agēnes/athloi*. The *poiētikē tekhnē* is the craft of composing—but not necessarily performing—in the media of *mousikē tekhnē* and in other media, as well, including tragedy, comedy, dithyramb, satyr drama, and so on. In the opening of Aristotle's *Poetics*, which is, in Greek terms, a discourse about *poiētikē tekhnē*, we saw a definition that validates in many ways the working definition that I have just offered (*Poetics* 1447a8–18).

In Aristotle's catalogue of genres of *poiētikē tekhnē* (poetic craft), we have seen the dimension of performance, not only the dimension of composition. Essentially, his catalogue corresponds to the program of performances that took place at the two great festivals of the Athenian state. At the City Dionysia of Athens, there were competitions in the performances of tragedies, comedies, dithyrambs, and satyr dramas. At the Panathenaia of Athens, as we have already seen, there were competitions in the performances of tunes played on the kithara or on the aulos, and of lyric songs sung to instrumental accompaniment by the kithara or by the aulos, and also of epic poetry recited without any instrumental accompaniment. That is, the overall *poiētikē tekhnē* (poetic craft) is subdivided into a variety of specialized *tekhnai*. Among these specialized *tekhnai* is the composition of epic, which as we know corresponds to the performance of epic by rhapsodes at the Panathenaia.

As we have seen, the term that Aristotle uses for the composing of "epic," *epopoiia* (making of *epos*), indicates a most general concept, since the word used to designate "epic," *epē* (= *epos* plural), is simply the general word for any kind of verbal art created by way of *poiēsis*. And yet, the whole of Aristotle's *Poetics*—and in fact the whole of Aristotle's works in general—operates on the understanding that the only epics of Homer were the *Iliad* and *Odyssey*. So epic as a genre is viewed in a specialized way, even though the wording used to express the idea of epic is expressed in a most generalized way. Even the wording of Aristotle indicates, of and by itself, that the composition of Homeric poetry had achieved the most generalized status as poetry par excellence.

By contrast with the composition of Homeric poetry, we have seen in Plato's *Ion* that its actual performance had achieved a most specialized status as the craft of the rhapsode, *rhapsēidikē tekhnē*. For Plato's Socrates, this craft is no craft at all, and only the overall *poiētikē tekhnē* may be considered as a *holon* (a whole), comparable to the categories of painting or sculpting, each of which is likewise a craft that may be considered as a whole. As a category, the generalized craft of composing poetry cannot have as a subcategory the specialized craft of composing Homeric poetry—let alone any specialized craft of performing Homeric poetry.

This kind of thinking is contradicted by Aristotle's *Poetics*, where the generalized craft of composing poetry is a category that can in fact have as a subcategory the specialized craft of composing Homeric poetry—though this specialized craft is expressed in the most generalized way.

Returning to Plato's *Ion*, I conclude that the discrediting of the rhapsode's craft, the *rhapsēidikē tekhnē*, can be countered by reconsidering it in its own historical context. The prestige of this *tekhnē* is evidently a threat to the philosophical *tekhnē* of Plato's Socrates. As we saw, the rhapsode is not only a performer of Homer: he is also the *hermēneus* (interpreter) of Homer (*Ion* 530c). To speak ably about Homer, says Ion, is the most important aspect of his *tekhnē* (craft) (*Ion* 530c). Homer in turn is recognized as the ultimate source of *paideusis* (education) for the Hellenes (Plato, *Republic* 10.606e).[23] As an exponent of this *paideusis*, the rhapsode is in effect a significant rival of the philosopher.

How, then, can the rhapsode defend himself against the dialectic of Plato's Socrates? In order to maintain Homer as a generalist in the *poiētikē tekhnē*, the rhapsode must insist on being a specialist in the *rhapsēidikē tekhnē*. That way, he maintains a prestige that is coextensive with the prestige of Homer as a universal educator of Hellenes. Since the rhapsode, as a master of the *rhapsēidikē tekhnē*, is a specialist performer but not a specialist composer, he cannot be considered a master of the *poiētikē tekhnē*. Since the rhapsode is a specialist in performing recitative poetry, to the exclusion of other forms of poetry as also of song and music (in the modern sense of the word), he cannot be considered a master of the *mousikē tekhnē*, either.

A qualification is needed here. Though the rhapsode cannot be a master of *mousikē tekhnē* in the restricted sense of the term as used by Plato, things must have been different in an earlier time. I have in mind a prehistorical time—back when the craft of the rhapsode could still be understood in a less restricted sense that matched the literal meaning of *mousikē tekhnē* (craft of the Muses). If the rhapsode of prehistoric time was truly master of the "craft of the Muses," then surely he was capable of inspiration by the Muses, and just as surely, he was also capable of composing as well as performing. Even the etymology of the word *rhapsēidos* (he who sews the songs together) indicates that the rhapsode of prehistoric time had this capability (Nagy 2002: 61–74 n. 11).

To have this capability is to be an *oral poet*. Attested in a wide variety of societies, from prehistoric times all the way into the present, *oral poetry* can be defined as a system of verbal art that enables the poet to compose while performing and perform while composing, though the degrees of composition-in-performance do vary. A classic demonstration is the 1960 book by Albert Lord, *The Singer of Tales*.[24]

To trace the craft of the rhapsode all the way back to an oral poetic phase is to achieve a *diachronic* perspective—as distinct from the *synchronic* perspective achieved by way of analyzing this same craft as the medium of ancient Greek epic in the historical context of Athens in the fourth century B.C.E.[25]

From such a diachronic perspective, ancient Greek epic can be reassessed as a genre (Nagy 1999a: 23 n. 8). When we compare it with forms of oral poetry as attested worldwide in all times and all places, we find a vast array of parallels (Martin 2005: 9–18). A wide-ranging comparison of existing parallels as analyzed in current ethnographic research leads to an equally wide-ranging application of the term "epic" to current forms of oral poetry that exhibit such parallels (Foley 2005: 196–212). Conversely, the analysis of existing parallelisms leads to a broader view of the parameters that define ancient Greek epic as a genre (Martin 2005: 9–19). Such a broadening leads to a refining of comparative methods, which can be divided into three categories: (1) typological, (2) genealogical, and (3) historical. And these methods lead in turn to a refining of such concepts as the "epic hero."[26]

The need to refine is made clear by Lord in this elegant formulation of the problems inherent in using such terms as "epic" and "heroic poetry" in his book:

> The word "epic," itself, indeed, has come in time to have many meanings. Epic sometimes is taken to mean simply a long poem in "high style." Yet a very great number of the poems which interest us in this book are comparatively short; length, in fact, is not a criterion of epic poetry. Other definitions of epic equate it with heroic poetry. Indeed the term "heroic poetry" is sometimes used...to avoid the very ambiguity in the word epic which troubles us. Yet purists might very well point out that many of the songs which we include in oral narrative poetry are romantic or historical and not heroic, no matter what definition of the hero one may choose. In oral narrative poetry, as a matter of fact, I wish to include all story poetry, the romantic or historical as well as the heroic; otherwise I would have to exclude a considerable body of medieval metrical narrative. (2000: 6)

Even the evidence of Greek literature, which is after all the source of our terminology for genres, has its ambiguities. For example, what we reconstruct as the craft of the rhapsode in its prehistoric oral poetic phase cannot even be confined to a single genre, epic. Even in historical times, rhapsodes are known to perform in genres other than epic (Nagy 1996a: 157–60). Moreover, an internal analysis of the primary evidence for epic, which is the surviving text of the Homeric *Iliad* and *Odyssey*, points to a multiplicity of genres (Martin 1989). So instead of saying that these existing genres are "subgenres" of a "genre" that is epic, it is more apt to say that the *framing form* of the epic is a "supergenre" that accommodates other genres (Martin 1997: 138–66, esp. 166).

In short, a comparative approach to epic yields a far broader view of ancient Greek epic as a genre. But such a broadened view does not and, in fact, cannot explain the history of this genre as exemplified by Homer and by the rhapsodic craftsmen who mediated Homer well after Homer, in the era of Plato and Aristotle. Working our way forward in time beyond the era of Plato and Aristotle, we find that the history of the genre becomes ever more problematic. And the greatest problem of them all is the fact that the genre of epic had become equated with Homer himself, as if Homer could exist without his epic tradition—and without the authorized mediation of the rhapsode.

But the hard truth is, the prestige of the rhapsode as an authorized mediator of Homer—let alone poetry in general—was already moribund for intellectuals in the time of Plato. It was in fact moribund even earlier, in the time of Socrates. We see it in the casually disparaging remarks of his contemporaries dramatized in Xenophon's *Symposium* (3.6). It was already a case of terminal prestige.[27]

The fatal blow was struck by Plato himself. In the end, Plato's philosophy killed off the rhapsode as the authorized mediator of Homer. Not only was Homer, along with all other poets, banned from the ideal state of Plato's most definitive philosophical project, the Republic, but perhaps even worse for Homer, his rhapsodic mediators were rendered obsolete. Homer as the poet par excellence now had to speak for himself, through his text, without the authorized mediation of the rhapsodes. The blow struck by Plato was fatal because the cosmopolitan world of philosophers and other intellectuals could no longer be accommodated by the heroic world of Homer as mediated by the rhapsode.

In the wake of Plato, the writings of Aristotle show no trace of any role for the rhapsode in the mediation of Homer—or of epic in general. Now the only person who can speak for epic is the mythologized culture hero Homer, revered as the be-all and end-all for defining not only epic but also Greek culture writ large. And this Homer can speak only through his text, which is by now the only authority that can back up that text. For Aristotle, this Homer is the ideal poet who defines epic.

Aristotle's understanding of epic as defined by the ideal poet is most decisive in the history of literature. Such an understanding leaves as its permanent legacy an overwhelming burden of the past.[28] Even more than that, the burden can be rethought as an all-consuming anxiety of influence.[29]

Here I return to the formulation of Croce, who went so far as to define any great work of literature as something that is sui generis. This formulation, as I noted from the start, applies to the poetry of the Homeric *Iliad* and *Odyssey*. At least, it applies in the sense that the Greeks did in fact view this poetry as something that was sui generis. After all, this poetry was thought to be the creation of the ideal poet. But now the question is, was it really Homer's greatness that made him one of a kind, sui generis?

In addressing this question, I find the formulation of Croce insufficient. In terms of this formulation, as I also noted from the start, it is as if a great work of literature had to transcend its own genre simply because of its greatness. I highlight the phrasing "as if," since I will now argue that the transcendence of Homeric poetry can be explained in relative rather than absolute terms. This poetry transcended the genre of epic only to the extent that its greatness could not be defined in terms of other epics. Instead, this greatness could in fact be defined in terms of another genre. For Plato and Aristotle, that other genre was tragedy.

Both Plato and Aristotle recognized the strongest of affinities between Homer and tragedy. In the second half of the fifth century B.C.E., which is the truly classical period of Greek literature, the ultimate poetic craft or *tekhnē* of poetry was deemed to be not epic but tragedy. One of the clearest examples is the celebrated scene of a grand contest held in Hades between Aeschylus and Euripides in the *Frogs* of Aristophanes (905–1098). What is at stake in this contest is the superiority or inferiority of the old or the current ways of making tragedy, as represented by Aeschylus and Euripides, respectively. And the craft of making tragedy is consistently equated with the craft of making poetry par excellence. Throughout the comedy, there are references to tragedy as the ultimate *tekhnē* (*Frogs* 93, 766, 770,

780, 786, 793, 811, 831, 850, 939, 961, 973, 1369, 1495). The privileged status of tragedy as the craft of poetry par excellence is the one given that is held in respect by both sides in the contest (Herington 1985: 106).

According to Aristotle, the craft of tragedy achieves perfection in its complete and unified structure. And he sees a comparable structure in only two epics, the Homeric *Iliad* and *Odyssey*. In the *Poetics*, Aristotle says explicitly that only the Homeric *Iliad* and *Odyssey* are comparable to tragedy because only these two epics show a complete and unified structure, unlike the epics of the Cycle (1459a–b). This judgment of Aristotle helps explain why he ostentatiously pairs the genre of epic with the genre of tragedy at the beginning of the *Poetics* (*epopoiia...kai hē tēs tragēidias poiēsis*) (Nagy 1999a: 26–27). And he views these two particular genres, epic and tragedy, as cognates (*Poetics* 1449a2–6; see Nagy 1999b: Ch. 14, §§1–5). In the works of Plato, as well, epic is viewed as a cognate of tragedy; more than that, Homer is represented as a proto-tragedian (*Theaetetus* 152e; *Republic* 10.595c, 598d, 605c, 607a).

In the *Poetics*, Aristotle links the existing forms of epic and tragedy to a proto-form of *humnoi* (hymns) and *enkēmia* (encomia, celebrations, songs of praise), and he contrasts epic and tragedy with the existing form of comedy, linking that form with a proto-form of *psogoi* (invectives) (*Poetics* 1448b25–27). More generally, Aristotle reconstructs a prehistoric dichotomy between the ethics of proto-poets who are *semnoteroi* or "more stately" and the ethics of would-be proto-poets who are by comparison *eutelesteroi*, that is, "of less value." According to this construct, poets who are *semnoteroi* are those engaged in the *mimēsis* (reenactment) of actions that are *kala* (noble) and that are performed by those who are *kaloi* (noble), while poets who are *eutelesteroi* (of less value) are characterized by actions that are *phaula* (base) and are performed by those who are *phauloi* (base). Here is the wording of Aristotle: "The *more stately* ones [*semnoteroi*] *made mimēsis* (1) of noble deeds and (2) of the deeds of (other) such stately ones, while the ones who were of less value (made *mimēsis*) of the deeds of the base. In the beginning, the latter made invectives [*psogoi*], while the former made *humnoi* and *enkēmia*" (*Poetics* 1448b25–27).

I restate two points that Aristotle is making here: first, *humnoi* (hymns) and *enkēmia* (encomia, celebrations, songs of praise) are the undifferentiated prototypes of epic and tragedy, and second, both of these prototypes involve *mimēsis* (reenactment) (Nagy 1990: 6§91 n. 7). Of special relevance is a third point that Aristotle makes elsewhere in the *Poetics*: it is not only the prototypical *humnoi* and *enkēmia* but also epic and tragedy that directly involve the *mimēsis* (reenactment) of the noble by the noble, as we see in several passages (1448a1–2, 26–27; 1448b34–36; 1449b9–10, 17–20, 24–28). In these passages, the word for "noble" is *spoudaioi*, meaning literally "the serious ones."

The idea that the *spoudaioi* (serious ones) and the *semnoteroi* (more stately ones) are engaging in *mimēsis* (reenactment) of what is noble is relevant to the use of the word *mimeîsthai* (reenact) in the Homeric Hymn to Apollo (Homeric Hymn 3, verse 163). Here, the performers of *mimēsis* are the Delian Maidens, whose "seriousness" or "stateliness" is a given. And the *mimēsis* is taking place in the context of a *humnos* (hymn). For Aristotle, *mimēsis* takes place in prototypical *humnoi* that have not yet become differentiated into epic and tragedy. Here in the Homeric Hymn to Apollo, we see an approximation of such a model, to the extent that it resembles both epic and tragedy: this hymn is like epic because it has the same meter as epic, dactylic hexameter, and because its diction is closely related to epic diction, while it is like tragedy because it is theatrical, as we see from the usage of the term *hupokrinesthai* ("respond") with reference to the quoted words of the maidens in the hymn (verse 171; Nagy 2003: 21–22). Moreover, the usage of the term *mimeîsthai* ("reenact"; verse 163) is, in fact, explicitly theatrical (Nagy 1996a: 80–81). It can be argued that the use of a theatrical word like *mimeîsthai* in the Homeric Hymn to Apollo (verse 171) reveals an early phase of an ongoing symbiosis of two elements: one was the Homeric tradition as it evolved at the Athenian festival of the Panathenaia, and the other was the theatrical tradition of drama—especially tragedy—as it evolved at the Athenian festival of the City Dionysia.[30]

Aristotle's association of tragedy with Homer, and of Homer with epic, is not merely a matter of literary judgment. By the time of Aristotle, as we have already seen, the only epics performed at the festival of the Panathenaia in Athens were the Homeric *Iliad* and *Odyssey*. These two epics shaped and were shaped by the genre of tragedy as performed at the festival of the City Dionysia. In Athens, ever since the sixth century B.C.E., the genre of epic as performed at the Panathenaia and the genre of tragedy as performed at the City Dionysia were "complementary forms, evolving together and thereby undergoing a process of mutual assimilation in the course of their institutional coexistence" (Nagy 1996a: 81).

By the time of Aristotle, this complementarity of epic and tragedy involved only the epics of the Homeric *Iliad* and *Odyssey*, no longer the epics of the Cycle. This differentiation of the Epic Cycle from the Homeric *Iliad* and *Odyssey* can be linked with the obsolescence of performing the poetry of the Epic Cycle at the Panathenaia. Not only in the fourth century B.C.E., the age of Aristotle, but also earlier in the fifth century, the age of Plato's Socrates, the Homeric *Iliad* and *Odyssey* were the only epics performed at the festival of the Panathenaia in Athens. The epics of the Cycle, by contrast, were excluded from the repertoire of the Panathenaia in the fifth and fourth centuries B.C.E. (Nagy 2004b: 28–30).[31]

Two of the most outstanding epics of the Cycle were the *Thebaid* and the *Epigonoi*.[32] Such alternative epic poetry was absorbed into the tragic poetry of the City Dionysia, as in the case of the *Seven against Thebes* of Aeschylus (produced in 467 B.C.E.), which is evidently a tragic version of the epic *Thebaid* (Nagy 2000).

In the sixth century B.C.E., by contrast with the fifth and the fourth, the Epic Cycle was more broadly conceived. And so also Homer was more broadly conceived. The poetic traditions represented by such epics as the *Seven against Thebes*, the *Epigonoi*, the *Cypria*, and the Little Iliad could be attributed to Homer. In this earlier era, Homer was a master poet who created not only the *Iliad* and *Odyssey* but also the entire Epic Cycle, and the very concept of the Cycle (*kuklos*) was a symbol of a notional totality, the sum total of Homer's poetic creation (Nagy 1996b: 38).

Such an earlier and broader idea of Homer is incompatible with the Homer of later times who had only two epics to his name, the *Iliad* and the *Odyssey*. From the standpoint of Plato and Aristotle, the epic poetry of such an earlier Homer could not be sui generis. Not only that, the poetry of such a Homer would not have been epic. For Plato and Aristotle, only the Homer of the *Iliad* and *Odyssey* defined epic. The epics of the Cycle would not be epic. As Aristotle argues in the *Poetics*, epic is defined by way of its affinity with tragedy, which achieves perfection in its complete and unified structure. Only Homer has that perfection, and that Homer is the poet of the *Iliad* and *Odyssey*. The epics of the Cycle do not have that perfection, according to Aristotle, and so Homer cannot be the poet of these epics, which must have been made by other poets. And they are not really epics, since they are not created by Homer.

Once again, we see that epic must be an ideal genre created by an ideal poet. Once again, we are confronted with the overwhelming burden of the past, with an all-consuming anxiety of influence. Once again, we see that the genre of epic is defined by Homer, and that this genre is therefore sui generis.

How, then, can any new poet recreate epic? The question itself is overwhelming. The only way to recreate this genre is to become the ideal poet. But how can any new poet become the ideal poet? The lack of a clear response leaves the genre of epic stranded in splendid isolation, stranded for good.

That is why the history of epic in world literature is a long-term story of emulating but not reenacting Homer as a perfect model. How well this model is emulated depends on how well it is understood, and the levels of understanding vary over time. In the history of Greek literature after Plato and Aristotle, the most distinguished example of emulation is the *Argonautica* of Apollonius of Rhodes, who flourished in the third century B.C.E. This poetic achievement displays a masterful understanding of Homeric poetry—even of its textual and exegetical history (Rengakos 1994). As poetry, however, it does not replace Homer as a new standard to follow, and the ultimate model remains Homer.

In the history of Roman literature, on the other hand, the most distinguished example of Homeric emulation becomes an ultimate model of epic in its own right. That example is the *Aeneid* of Virgil, who flourished in the second half of the first century B.C.E. The emulation of Homer by Virgil is made most explicit by way of the symmetry inherent in this Roman epic: the first half of the *Aeneid* is clearly modeled on the *Odyssey* and the second, on the *Iliad*.

Virgil's understanding of his Homeric model is exquisite: as a poet who emulates the ostensibly ultimate poet, he achieves in his own right the status of an ultimate poetic model in the overall history of Roman civilization, and this status rivals that of Homer in the overall history of Greek civilization (Putnam 2005: n. 45, 452–75). Even more, Virgil transcends Roman literature, becoming the model of epic for all the world literatures that link to Roman literature as their overall model. For the likes of Petrarch, Milton, Tasso, Camõens, and countless other major poets in the history of European literature, Virgil becomes the new ideal poet of epic (Kallendorf 2005: 574–88).

But now a major question looms: though Virgil becomes the new ideal poet of epic, is his *Aeneid* really an epic? The answer has to be qualified: Virgil is a poet of epic only to the extent that Homer defines epic in the history of Greek literature after Plato and Aristotle. Virgil emulates that Homer, just as he emulates other emulators of Homer, including Apollonius of Rhodes. But his *Aeneid* is not a reenactment of the genre represented by the Homeric *Iliad* and *Odyssey*. That genre is too narrow to suit the *Aeneid* of Virgil. To that extent, Virgil's epic is not really an epic.

The objection could be made that Virgil's *Aeneid* was nevertheless an epic if we think of epic in his terms. It could be said that Virgil's own view of epic transcended Homer, and that his epic model was broader than the Homeric model, which in turn was narrower than earlier Greek models of epic as a genre. As we have seen, the history of Greek literature before Plato and Aristotle indicates a broader view of Homer—and a broader view of what eventually became understood as epic. We can actually observe Virgil's own broader view in his reliance on traditions linked to the so-called Epic Cycle.[33] We can even say that Virgil is consistent in indicating his awareness of poetic formalities that transcended Homer. Nevertheless, this transcendence was for Virgil a matter of emulating a variety of poets in addition to Homer—including the poets of epic in the early Republican era of Rome (Goldberg 2005: 429–39). It was not a matter of actually reenacting the genre of epic as a genre in its narrower or broader forms. At best, then, we can follow C. S. Lewis by referring to the *Aeneid* of Virgil as "secondary epic."[34]

In the end, then, we are left with a paradox. The clearest way for us to view epic as a genre is to keep on looking at Homer synchronically—as he is understood in the historical period of Plato and Aristotle. Our view becomes instantly clouded, however, once we start looking at Homer diachronically. Homer as a model of epic meant too many different things to too many different poets over the ages. And that is because poets emulated not the epic of Homer but Homer himself. Much the same predicament awaited the greatest emulator of Homer, the poet Virgil. When another great poet, Dante, emulated Virgil in his *Divine Comedy*, begun in 1307, his model was clearly Virgil, not the epic of Virgil.

Without the genre of epic, the poet of epic can be emulated at will, without rules, since the poet seems to have no rules. He is simply a genius. Thomas Blackwell, in his *Enquiry into the Life and Writings of Homer* (1736), says that Homer was the ultimate poetic genius because he needed no "rules" for making epic—and because he did not even know any such rules (Grobman 1979: 186–98). Such is the fate of epic as genre—once Plato succeeds in detaching Homer from the authorized transmission of Homer by rhapsodes like Ion.

NOTES

....

1. The aulos was a double reed, most similar in morphology to the oboe.
2. The kithara was a seven-string lyre.
3. Here the word is in the plural, and I render it as "instances of reenactment." In the singular, the basic idea of *mimēsis* is "reenactment"; see Nagy 1990: §1, 46–50.

4. For further elaboration, see Rothstein 2004.

5. For editions of the Epic Cycle, see Bernabé 1987 and Davies 1988.

6. The figure of Olympus is a prototypical master of the aulos; see sources and commentary in Nagy 1990: 3§§7 n. 7, 16–17, 36, 39.

7. The figure of Thamyras/Thamyris is a prototypical master of the kithara in *Iliad* 2 594–600; see commentary in Nagy 1990: §12, 376n.199, 378–79n. 210.

8. The figure of Phemios is a prototypical singer of epic in *Odyssey* i, xvii, and xxii. I will have more to say about him later. On Phemios as a *rhapsōidos* (rhapsode), see Graziosi 2002: 25, 39–40; her interpretation is different from the one I offer in what follows.

9. For further analysis, see Nagy 2002: 38–39, 42 n. 16, 51.

10. For a comparative perspective on the concept of competition-in-collaboration, see Nagy 1996a: 18 n. 11.

11. In one of these contexts (*Ion* 535d), it is specified that Ion already wears a golden garland while he is performing Homer. Perhaps Ion had already won first prize at the Panathenaia on a previous occasion.

12. My citations from *Vita* 1 and *Vita* 2 follow the line numbers in the edition of T. W. Allen, *Homeri Opera V* (Oxford 1912).

13. By implication, Ion was performing Homeric poetry also at the *agōn* of rhapsodes at the festival of the Asklepieia in Epidaurus, where it is said that he likewise won the first prize (*Ion* 530a).

14. For commentary, see Nagy 1996a: 111 n. 24.

15. The nonsinging role of the *kitharistēs* (citharist) may be etiologically connected with a myth about a primal "musical" competition between Thamyras/Thamyris and the Muses (*Iliad* II 594–600). When Thamyris (as he is called in the *Iliad*) challenges the Muses to a duel in singing to the lyre, he is punished for his arrogance by being stuck dumb in the course of the contest, so this proto-citharist is pictured as a citharode who lost his voice.

16. In the case of Thamyras, he is presented by Homeric poetry itself as an implicit foil for Homer.

17. I see no reason to doubt the preeminence of Ion in the historical time that corresponds to the dramatized time of his encounter with Socrates, sometime in the fifth century, when the city of Ephesus was still under the domination of the Athenian empire. In general, it is important to keep in mind that Plato chooses worthy opponents for Socrates. When Plato's Socrates predicts that Ion will win first prize in the Panathenaic competitions that follow the day of their encounter with each other (*Ion* 530b), I have no reason to doubt that this detail amounts to a self-fulfilling prophecy, and that the whole dialogue is predicated on the general success of Ion as a rhapsode.

18. For more on this idea, see Nagy 2002: 9–35.

19. To paraphrase more closely: in *Ion* (531a–32b), when the rhapsode Ion says that he can perform and interpret the poetry of Homer but not the poetry of Hesiod and Archilochus, it is implied that other rhapsodes do indeed perform and interpret the poetry of Hesiod and Archilochus. For further evidence about the rhapsodic performance of Hesiod and Archilochus, see *Athenaeus* 620b–c and the commentary in Nagy 1996a: 159. 162–63.

20. According to Ion, even where Homer and Hesiod overlap in content, they are different in quality (532a). By contrast, Plato's Socrates is represented as an expert in non-Homeric poetry, as well. His expertise in Hesiodic and Orphic traditions is especially to be noted.

21. On Simonides at the Panathenaia, see Graziosi 2002: 225–26.

22. The theatrical mentality of Athenians is ostentatiously deplored by Kleon as "quoted" by Thucydides: *"theatai men tōn logōn…akroatai de tōn ergōn* [spectators of words, audiences of deeds]" (*History of the Peloponnesian War* 3.38.4).

23. See also Plato *Republic* 2.376e–98b and the commentary of Murray 1996: 205.

24. Lord 2000; see also S. Mitchell and G. Nagy, "Introduction to the Second Edition": vii–xxix.

25. On the hermeneutics of *synchronic* and *diachronic* approaches, see Saussure 1972: 117.

26. For a survey of the varieties of epic in world literatures, see Nagy 2005: 71–89; a fuller version is available at http://chs.harvard.edu/publications.sec/online_print_books.ssp/gregory_nagy_the_epic/bn_u_tei.xml_5.

27. For the term "terminal prestige," see McClary 1989.

28. In using the term "burden of the past," I follow the hermeneutics developed in Bate 1970.

29. In using the term "anxiety of influence," I follow the hermeneutics developed in Bloom 1997.

30. Nagy 1996a: 81. The symmetry of the Panathenaia and the City Dionysia as the two most important festivals of the Athenians is evident in a formulation by Demosthenes in the *First Philippic* (4.35).

31. On the concept of a "Panathenaic bottleneck," see Nagy 2004b: 30.

32. For an appreciation of the epic *Thebaid* as an esthetic rival of the *Iliad* and *Odyssey*, see especially Pausanias 9.9.5. The wording of Herodotus 5.67 suggests that the epic themes of the *Thebaid* and the *Epigonoi* may have been the basic repertoire for performances at the festivals of Argos and Sikyon; see Cingano 1985, with reference to Herodotus 5.67. See also Nagy 1990: §1, 22.

33. Such a reliance is typical of Roman epic poetry in general; see Farrell 2005: 425–28.

34. I am grateful to Richard Eldridge for guiding me to this felicitous wording, to be found in C. S. Lewis's *A Preface to Paradise Lost* (1942/1961). His chapter 3 is called "Primary Epic," and it begins with this distinction: "The *secondary* here means not 'the second rate,' but what comes after, and grows out of, the *primary*" (13). Lewis takes Homeric poetry and *Beowulf* as his principal examples of primary epics. Chapter 6 is called "Virgil and the Subject of Secondary Epic," and it begins with this sentence: "The epic subject, as later critics came to understand it, is Virgil's invention; he has altered the very meaning of the word *epic*." The underlying idea is that a subject or theme may be invented by a poet for a new readership. But the distinction seems to trace to Milton's "The Reason of Church Government" (1957: 669–70). The epics of Homer (and of Virgil and Tasso) result, he says, from "the inspired gift of God rarely bestow'd, but yet to some (though most abuse) in every nation: and are of power beside the office of a pulpit, to inbreed and cherish in a great people the seeds of vertu, and publick civility." There is a summary of the distinction in Jenkyns 1992: 55–56, where it is treated as a commonplace among critics.

REFERENCES

Bate, W. J. (1970). *The Burden of the Past and the English Poet*. Cambridge, Mass.: Harvard University Press.

Bernabé, A., ed. (1987). *Poetae Epici Graeci* (Part 1). Leipzig: K.G. Saur.

Bloom, H. (1997). *The Anxiety of Influence: A Theory of Poetry.* Oxford: Oxford University Press. (Original work published 1973).

Burgess, J. S. (2004). "Performance and the Epic Cycle." *Classical Journal* 100, 1–23.

Cingano, E. (1985). "Clistene di Sicione, Erodoto e i poemi del Ciclo tebano." *Quaderni Urbinati di Cultura Classica* 20, 31–40.

Croce, B. (1902). *Estetica come scienza dell'espressione e linguistica generale.* Florence: Sandron.

Davies, M., ed. (1988). *Epicorum Graecorum Fragmenta.* Göttingen: Vandenhoeck and Ruprecht.

Farrell, J. (2005). "The Origins and Essence of Roman Epic." *In* J. M. Foley (ed.), *Companion to Ancient Epic.* Oxford: Oxford University Press.

Foley, J. M. (2005). "Analogues: Modern Oral Epics." *In* J. M. Foley (ed.), *Companion to Ancient Epic.* Oxford: Oxford University Press.

Ford, A. (2002). *The Origins of Criticism: Literary Culture and Poetic Theory in Classical Greece.* Princeton: Princeton University Press.

Goldberg, S. M. (2005). "Early Republican Epic." *In* J. M. Foley (ed.), *Companion to Ancient Epic.* Oxford: Oxford University Press.

Graziosi, B. (2002). *Inventing Homer: The Early Reception of Epic.* Cambridge: Cambridge University Press.

Grobman, N. R. (1979). "Thomas Blackwell's Commentary on The Oral Nature of Epic." *Western Folklore* 38, 186–98.

Herington, J. (1985). *Poetry into Drama: Early Tragedy and the Greek Poetic Tradition.* Berkeley: University of California Press.

Jenkyns, R. (1992). *Classical Epic: Homer and Virgil.* London: Duckworth.

Kallendorf, C. (2005). "Virgil's Post-classical Legacy." *In* J. M. Foley (ed.), *Companion to Ancient Epic.* Oxford: Oxford University Press.

Lewis, C. S. (1942/1961). *A Preface to Paradise Lost.* Oxford: Oxford University Press.

Lord, A. B. (2000). *The Singer of Tales* (2nd ed.). Cambridge, Mass: Harvard University Press. (Original work published in 1960).

Martin, R. P. (1989). *The Language of Heroes.* Ithaca, N.Y.: Cornell University Press.

——. (1997). "Similes and Performance." *In* E. Bakker and A. Kahane (eds.), *Written Voices, Spoken Signs.* Cambridge, Mass.: Harvard University Press.

——. (2005). "Epic as Genre." *In* J. M. Foley (ed.), *Companion to Ancient Epic.* Oxford: Oxford University Press.

McClary, S. (1989). "Terminal Prestige: The Case of Avant-Garde Music Composition." *Cultural Critique* 12, 57–81.

Milton, J. (1957). *Complete Poems and Major Prose* (M. Y. Hughes, ed.). New York: Odyssey Press.

Murray, P. (1996). *Plato on Poetry: Ion, Republic 376e–398b, Republic 595–608b.* Cambridge: Cambridge University Press.

Nagy, G. (1990). *Pindar's Homer: The Lyric Possession of an Epic Past.* Baltimore: Johns Hopkins University Press.

——. (1996a). *Poetry as Performance: Homer and Beyond.* Cambridge: Cambridge University Press.

——. (1996b.) *Homeric Questions.* Austin: University of Texas Press.

——. (1999a). "Epic as Genre." *In* M. Beissinger, J. Tylus, and S. Wofford (eds.), *Epic Traditions in the Contemporary World: The Poetics of Community.* Berkeley: University of California Press.

———. (1999b). *The Best of the Achaeans: Concepts of the Hero in Archaic Greek Poetry* (2nd ed.). Baltimore: Johns Hopkins University. (Original work published 1979).

———. (2000). "'Dream of a Shade': Refractions of Epic Vision in Pindar's *Pythian* 8 and Aeschylus' *Seven against Thebes*." *Harvard Studies in Classical Philology* 100, 97–118.

———. (2002). *Plato's Rhapsody and Homer's Music: The Poetics of the Panathenaic Festival in Classical Athens*. Cambridge Mass.: Harvard University Press.

———. (2003). *Homeric Responses*. Austin: University of Texas Press.

———. (2004a). "L'aède épique en auteur: la tradition des Vies d'Homère." *In* C. Calame and R. Chartier (eds.), *Identités d'auteur dans l'Antiquité et la tradition européenne*, pp. 41–67. Grenoble: Éditions Jérome Millon.

———. (2004b). *Homer's Text and Language*. Urbana, IL: University of Illinois Press.

———. (2005). "The Epic Hero." *In* J. M. Foley (ed.), *Companion to Ancient Epic*. Oxford: Oxford University Press.

Putnam, M. C. J. (2005). "Virgil's *Aeneid*." *In* J. M. Foley (ed.), *Companion to Ancient Epic*. Oxford: Oxford University Press.

Rengakos, A. (1994). *Apollonius Rhodios und die antike Homererklärung*. Munich: C. H. Beck.

Rothstein, A. (2004). "Aristotle, *Poetics* 1447a13–16 and Musical Contests." *Zeitschrift für Papyrologie und Epigraphik* 149, 39–42.

Saussure, F. de. (1972). *Cours de linguistique générale* (T. deMauro, ed.). Paris: Rudolf Engler. (Original work published in 1916).

Slatkin, L. (1987). "Genre and Generation in the *Odyssey*." *MHTIC: Revue d'anthropologie du monde grec ancien* 2, 259–68.

Todorov, T. (1990). *Genres in Discourse* (C. Porter, trans.). Cambridge: Cambridge University Press. (Original work published in 1978).

CHAPTER 2

....

LYRIC

....

SUSAN STEWART

Il existe donc aussi nécessairement une manière lyrique de
parler, et un monde lyrique, une atmosphère lyrique, des
paysages, des hommes, des femmes, des animaux qui tous
participent du caractère affectionné par la Lyre
                    —Baudelaire, "Sur Mes Contemporains"[1]

Philosophy, the love of wisdom,[2] and *lyric*, words meant to be sung to the musical
accompaniment of a lyre, seem, at least etymologically, to have little to do with
each other. Philosophers may even say we make a category mistake in comparing them, since the first term refers to the pursuit of knowledge of truth and the
second term refers to an expressive art form. Yet both philosophers and lyric poets
are solo speakers, and their common material is language—indeed, they share the
same language, for it is not that there are separate tongues for each. Philosophers
and poets are alike in certain actions, as well: they convey intelligible statements;
employ formal structures with beginnings, middles, and ends; and hope to convince or move their audiences, and so incorporate a social view from the outset
(see Preminger and Bogan 1993: 906). Familiar issues of interpretation, making,
and consequence arise whenever we consider the relations between these two
endeavors.

Nevertheless, these shared materials and aims conceal some important differences. The language of philosophy strives for clarity and singularity of reference.
Lyric, in contrast, is always overdetermined; its images, symbols, sounds, the very
grain of the voices it suggests, all compete for our attention and throw us back,
whether we are listening or reading, to repeated consideration of the whole. Philosophy should be paraphrasable and translatable if its truth claims are universal,

but poetry has finality of form, and to paraphrase it is a heresy; to translate it, a betrayal. And whereas philosophy and poetry both involve rhetorical development, their respective attitudes toward rhetoric differ: the philosopher asks for comprehension and often tolerates, even encourages, skepticism; the poet asks for, at least, attention and, at most, appreciation. The differences between intending toward truth, which may involve a process of constant detachment and even alienation from earlier practices, and moving an audience rhythmically and musically, which may produce somatic states of pleasure and pain, further distinguish the obligations of philosophy to clarification and the obligations of lyric to reception. The philosopher convinces; the poet enchants and absorbs. Individual lyrics, like any work of art, must have closure, yet the cultural task of lyric—whether it is the expression of emotion, praise, or a summoning of the originary power of words—is, like philosophy, an incomplete project.

Here, lyric poetry and philosophy can both be seen to stem from traditions of wisdom literature wherein speakers who are *vates* or sages deliver prophecies, oracles, and other powerful utterances that will be deciphered or interpreted by ordinary men and women. Myths as cosmological explanations, and thereby solutions to recurring problems or paradoxes in a way of life, are commonly held and told, frequently in metrically organized form. Myth is at other times broken by song, as in cante-fable form, and song is often a reflection upon a prior framework of myth that provides a vast system of shared references. Shifts from narrative to song reflect the fundamental difference between speaking and singing, a difference that appears in every known repertoire of genres and that neurologists now believe may lie in separate brain functions—one that produces context-bound discursive sentences and another that produces repeatable utterances such as rhymes and "sing-song."[3]

At the core of lyric, effecting both somatic and semantic transport, is the presentation of metaphor: the fusion of feeling and fact, particular and abstraction, one moment transposed to another and compelling recognition. Lyric is in this sense also influenced by such simple gnomic genres as proverbs and riddles, which, too, are measured and rhymed and require a deciphering interpretation.[4] Proverbs are tendered by the elderly and wise and, once grasped, offered up for practical use in the conduct of everyday life. Riddles arise from new experiences—from what we might call experiences of juvenility—since they involve apprehending phenomena beyond the paths of habit. Riddles shift perspectives and create unpredictable combinations of categories. All in all, there is a great deal of redundancy in the content of any genre system, yet each particular genre has its role, and it is in lyric that we find gestures of citing and applying, on the one hand, and breaking up and reforming, on the other—gestures that indicate the relation of individual voice to the contingent propulsions of interior physical states and external social pressures and values.

How did the early fusion of poetic and philosophical language under the categories of wisdom literature eventually, at least in the West, dissolve? To answer this question, we should begin with Plato. In book 10 of *The Republic*, as part of his presentation of Socrates' arguments to Glaucon, Plato contends there is an "ancient quarrel" between poetry and philosophy, one that, for Socrates, stems from the consequences of enigma and inspiration—those very qualities for which wisdom literature traditionally is admired. Under Plato's theory of ideal forms, any work of art, as an imitation of an imitation, and so thrice removed from the reality of ideal forms, is "an indistinct expression of the truth." Plato's criticism thus augments the eighth-century B.C.E. attack on Homer by Hesiod, who claimed a greater obligation than the earlier poet to both truth and usefulness. Heraclitus (c. 540–c. 470 B.C.E.) also suggested that Homer should be "excluded from the contests and scourged with rods" (quoted in Curtius 1991: 204). And Xenophanes (c. 570–c. 490 B.C.E.) mentions that both Homer and Hesiod himself write inappropriately about the scandalous behavior of the gods (Russell and Winterbottom 1972: 4)[5]

Even so, perhaps this quarrel between poetry and philosophy is not as ancient as Plato contends, for philosophy was in many ways being invented by Plato at that moment; he was the first to mention such a quarrel as a traditional one, and he struggled to define his intellectual enterprise against the cultural authority of poets and dramatists (Nightingale 1995: 60–67).[6] Plato's condemnation of epic and tragic poetry in book 10 of the *Republic*, and in his dialogues *Ion*, *Gorgias*, and *Phaedrus*, is part of a larger attack on the cultural role of the poet, who "arouses, nourishes, and strengthens this part of the soul [the passions] and so destroys the rational one … the imitative poet puts a bad constitution in the soul of each individual by making images that are far removed from the truth and by gratifying the irrational part" (Plato 1983, 10: 276). His Socrates says that the poet misleads because he does not really know what he is saying, cannot interpret his own actions, and is bound to lead others astray; implicitly, Socrates is also contending that philosophers enjoy a full consciousness of the sources and connotations of their language and of the consequences that ensue. The fear of loss of control and contagion here is accompanied by a wish for mastery.

Nevertheless, as long as it is not directed toward stirring up and exaggerating emotions that would be better left to cool, lyric poetry is given a somewhat lighter sentence by Plato. He writes, again in the voice of Socrates,

> You can agree that Homer is most poetic and that he stands first among the tragedians, but you must know for sure that hymns to the gods and eulogies of good men are the only poetry which we can admit into our city. If you admit the Muse of sweet pleasure, whether in lyrics or epic, pleasure and pain will rule as monarchs in your city, instead of the law and that rational principle which is always and by all thought to be the best. (1983, 10: 251)[7]

If lyric poets are going to create, beyond their conscious will, forms driven by inspiration and resulting in somatic responses from their audiences, their activities will be judged only by the worthiness of the objects they represent.

Platonism has a continuous, if often subtle, impact on later thinking regarding the relations between philosophy and poetry, leaving us with a division of labor between them. Even so, a closer look reveals that the quarrel between poetry and philosophy is not only a rhetorical convenience, but also quite one-sided—it is a quarrel philosophy has with poetry. Socrates and other thinkers are the butt of jokes in Aristophanes' contemporary *Clouds, Birds*, and a few other ancient texts, but these are lampoons of personalities, hardly sustained critiques of philosophy. There seems to be not a single treatise wherein philosophy defends itself against an attack by poetry, but there is a long history of poetic "defenses" in Western culture—"defenses of poetry" that must protect the form from those heirs of Plato who would argue its uselessness, poor moral influence, and inauthenticity.[8]

The "ancient quarrel," however, is not the only perspective on poetry Plato gives us: his *Symposium* presents another view entirely, one that emphasizes a positive sense of the created dimension of poetic forms. At 205b8–c2, Socrates says "Well, you know, for example, that 'poetry' has a very wide range. After all, everything that is responsible for creating something out of nothing is a kind of poetry; and so all the creations of every craft and profession are themselves a kind of poetry, and everyone who practices a craft is a poet" (Plato 1989: 51). Here Plato is drawing on the Greek sense of *poiesis* as making. In the same text, as Socrates discourses on the teachings of the wise woman Diotima, he argues that there is a coherence between the beautiful and the good—in this sense, *kalos*, the beautiful, fine, right, or noble, is close in meaning to *agathos* as the good, morally good, or beneficial. Here the poet is not a fraud and seducer, but rather a maker of perfect forms; the production of forms and the production of life are linked in the philosophical search for truth as an ideal form of love. The *Symposium*, like the *Republic*, also strictly circumscribes what kinds of forms are ideal: they must have unchanging stability of character; they must be purged of the simultaneous presence of opposites or contradictions; they must be known by the mind rather than the senses—in other words, they must be distinguished from the merely perceptible.[9] Here is an idea of poetic justice or fit—the symmetry, isomorphism, and measured rhythms of poetry all help bring the powers of the daimonic into harmony.

An array of ideas about the systematic exercise of human skill in making informs the philosophy of Plato's pupil Aristotle (384–322 B.C.E.). For Aristotle, essences are produced within and emerge from the natural world, *natura naturata*. Such essences are incomplete and overlain with accidental features, but the poet, who creates an integral or completed form, is able to preserve the essential from the accidental. Within the domain of human action and human values, poetry yields an account of nature's truth by revealing nature's workings and principles. In his *Physics*, Aristotle suggests that the maker partly imitates nature and partly carries to completion what nature has left incomplete (1941c). And in the *Nicomachean Ethics*, he also emphasizes the conceptual origins of art, writing: "[A]ll art is concerned with coming into being...and considering how something may come into being which is capable of either being or not being and whose origin is in the maker and not in the thing made" (1941b: 1025). Aristotle suggests the artist sometimes "errs voluntarily" and that such willed errors are preferable to those made involuntarily; in this regard, artistic decisions are the opposite of ethics, where to err voluntarily is a serious offense, and involuntarily a lesser one (1941a: 1027).

Although Aristotle's *Poetics* is concerned primarily with tragedy, its account of the development of monologue, dialogue, and multiple voices is important for the history of lyric—a form most often expressing a first-person perspective even when it is sung by a chorus or involves group refrains. There is a role for the reflective singular voice in evaluating the meaning and consequences of action that, within the history of poetic forms, lyric speakers continue to assume. Aristotle writes, "Hence poetry is something more philosophic and of graver import than history, since its statements are of the nature rather of universals, whereas those of history are singulars" (1941a: 1464). As the poet imitates the actions of men, he becomes the poet of plots rather than verses alone and finds what is probable and possible in the order of life. In sum, Aristotle places poetry at the center of life and lays the foundation for an argument that poetry is a means of discovery regarding human nature; rather than presenting an imitation of an imitation, poetry for Aristotle is, like all art, a perfected form—an improvement upon nature that penetrates to the principles of nature.

Early Greek melic poetry took the form of either choral odes sung to flute accompaniment or solo songs. The choral works included threnodies or dirges, paeans or hymns, maiden songs, wedding songs, prosodia sung at processions, dithyrambs in honor of Dionysius, enkomia (praise songs), and epinikia (victory songs)—all tied to related rituals and punctuating everyday life with occasions for heightened emotion, reflection, and valuation. The monodies, in contrast, were sung by characters in a tragedy or to a private audience such as a symposium. Sappho (c. 620–c. 565 B.C.E.) and Alcaeus (c. 600 B.C.E.) gave their names to characteristic forms of monody built out of isometric strophes.[10] Whether framed by ritual or solitary performance, the objects of praise, celebration, and lament are individuated and addressed with sustained attention.

In *The Discovery of the Mind* (1982), Bruno Snell makes a sweeping historical argument for the centrality of solo lyric in Greek thought. He regards these "personal lyrics" by Sappho, Alcaeus, Archilochus (c. 680–656 B.C.E.), and Anacreon (570–480 B.C.E.) as significant evidence of the rise of the concept of the individual. Snell argues that in talking of themselves in such lyrics, poets came to be conscious of what was particular or distinctive about their persons. Sentiments such as Archilochus's "each man has his heart cheered in his own way" may universalize the emotion of being cheered, yet they also mark experience as singular. In Anacreon's and Archilochus's poems, individualism is tied to singular choices and values often at odds with those of society as a whole. A separation between internal and external values thus arises. Sappho was, of course, quite familiar with the poems of Archilochus, and Snell argues that what comes to fruition in her work is this distinction between "what others prize and what one's own judgment declares to be essential." The particular fruit she bears is "a new distinction between Being and appearance...since it is understood that love is not a private whim, not a subjective affectation, but an experience of the supra-personal of divine dimensions. The lover cannot but find his way to some reality through the agency of his individual passion" (1982: 53–54).[11]

Snell designates the formal features of lyric—the musical accompaniment that makes the creation of form out of rhythm an analogue for emotional compulsion; the first-person expression evolving under a restriction of intelligibility toward others; the mutual articulation of, and tension between, "interior consciousness" and "external decorum"—and argues that the process of artistic choice, orientation, closure, and reception created incremental changes in consciousness. Snell notes that these poets do not simply express their emotions, but rather always address themselves to a partner, either a deity—especially in prayer—or an individual or an entire group of men, writing, "Though the individual who detaches himself from his environment severs many old bonds, his discovery of the dimension of the soul once more joins him in company with those who have fought their way to the same insight. The isolation of the individual is, by the same token, the forging of new bonds" (1982: 65). The individualism recognized by social sanction that Snell describes in solo lyric is rooted in theology, but extends into the secular deictic "now" of the poem's expression.

Hymn structure remains tied to ritual, and we can see the dynamic of gods, individuals, and audience in the dialectical three-part structure of Pindaric odes, yet Pindar also refers to himself and the unfolding nature of his judgments, and we can trace the continuing force of individual choice in the axiological dimension of all praise poems. In classical tragedy, lyric poetry similarly serves as the foundation for the judgments of the chorus and the closure of lament: action is suspended while the chorus deliberates and draws conclusions. In contrast, the first-person speeches of messengers are based in empirical knowledge and give testimony; they bring the news and model its emotional reception.

The Hellenistic Latin poets took continuity with their Greek predecessors to be paramount, yet there is a fundamental difference in these traditions, for Latin poetry is a poetry of the book. The Late Republican and Augustan poets, Catullus (c. 84–54 B.C.E.) and Horace (65–8 B.C.E.) particularly, exploit the resources of written texts, producing refined brief lyrics that continue to explore the interpersonal ethics of love and friendship that we find in Greek lyric. Horace, Virgil (70–19 B.C.E.), the writer of love lyrics Propertius (c. 50–c. 15 B.C.E.), and the mythographer, epistolary poet, and eventual exile Ovid (43 B.C.E.–c. 17 A.D.) all have ambivalent relations to their imperial patrons, and we discern the ancient role of the poet as vates and judge, as well as the enduring materiality of the book form, beneath the intellectual and emotional freedom the poet begins to claim in this period.

Oral forms emerge in a continuous stream, broken by temporal pauses and the structure inherently provided by repetitions of many kinds. But to read a poem is to project a spatial field in which this stream unfolds. Our sense of the stanza as a room, of closure reflecting back to the closings of individual stanzas, is indebted to the poets of this period, and the basic distinction between stichic and strophic means of organizing lines continues throughout all later poetry to the present. Greek stichic poetry was more discursive than the musical melic poetry organized in strophes. After the advent of written texts and, eventually, printing, the openness of stichic organization often is used as an allusion to oral composition—particularly to the epics and odes of antiquity. Strophic organization often also alludes to songs and other oral forms. Yet strophic poetry also gradually limns spaces within the space of the page, and the stanzas of a poem come to represent units of contemplation.

Between the second and fourth centuries, the material of writing shifted from the scroll to the codex, a radical transformation in the experience of reading and writing exceeded only by the invention of printing in the fifteenth century. In the early medieval period, a supersensible content is joined to a new awareness of these material conditions of literacy. Allegory, moving between material signs and systems of speculative referents, is the appropriate mode of thought for this experience, and there are a number of medieval innovations in the presentation of texts. Many of these aid in the creation of arguments for discussion, abstracting the substance of the text: metatextual structures, such as headings and subheadings, help in such analyses; tables of contents provide an overview of arguments; the use of margins influences a sense of the "aside," and of the spatial bounds of the text, and helps in the summation of arguments, as well (Parkes 1976). Here again, the presentation of paraphrasable philosophical arguments is distinct from the set presentation of hymns and prayers. But other devices, such as the ornamentation of textual beginnings, demand a commitment to absorbed reading that bridges philosophical and poetic works. Of course, these material changes did not simply cause changes in thought and form in poetry and philosophy; they also must be viewed as responses to the needs of philosophers, poets, and their audiences.

Augustine of Hippo's *Confessions*, written in the late fourth century, are divided between the narrative of the first half and the prayerful exclamations of the second half. This split exemplifies a microcosmic relation between universal salvation and the individual's turn away from worldly experience and dramatically illustrates the vertical movement from history to eternity. Poetic forms play a key role in the series of scenes where this turn is evoked. First, in book 8, in the climactic moment of despair when Augustine has flung himself beneath a fig tree and poured out his tears in "sacrifice," he hears the "sing-song voice" of a child, repeating the refrain, "Take it and read, take it and read."[12] What is this sing-song voice, and from where has it come? Augustine thinks "hard whether there was any kind of game in which children used to chant words like these, but I could not remember ever hearing them before" (1961: 177–78). And in book 9, in the period after his mother's death, Augustine describes a scene where the relation between tears and sing-song is reversed. Here he awakens after a sleep that has brought him some relief from his sorrow and remembers Ambrose's "Evening Hymn":

> Deus, Creator omnium,
> polique Rector, vestiens
> diem decoro lumine
> noctem sopora gratia;
> Artus solutos ut quies

reddat laboris usui,
mentesque fessas allevet,
luctusque solvat anxios.[13]

The hymn evokes memories of Augustine's mother, and he is able to release his tears, letting "them flow as freely as they would, making of them a pillow for my heart" (1961: 202).

Medieval hymns indeed provide for Augustine a model of time itself. For example, in book 11, this relation between sing-song, weeping, and reversal becomes a sustained theory of time. Poetic forms are no longer eruptions in the flow of secular time: they now provide a model for the subjective consciousness of time as an eternal present. Realizing that time is "an extension of the mind itself," Augustine writes:

> Suppose that we hear a noise emitted by some material body. The sound begins and we continue to hear it. It goes on until finally it ceases. Then there is silence. The sound has passed and it is no longer sound. Before it began it was future and could not be measured, because it did not yet exist. Now that it has ceased it cannot be measured, because it no longer exists. It could only be measured while it lasted, because then it existed and could be measured. But even then it was not static, because it was transient, moving continuously toward the point where it would no longer exist. (1961: 277–78)

He concludes that "what we measure is the interval between a beginning and an end," yet he realizes that "we cannot measure it [time] if it is not yet in being, or if it is no longer in being, or if it has no duration, or if it has no beginning or end." He returns once more to the beginning of "Deus Creator omnium," with its eight syllables alternately short and long. As "far as" he "can trust" his practiced ear, he can measure these syllables: "It is in my own mind then, that I measure time. I must not allow my mind to insist that time is something objective." Poetry becomes the paradigm for this internal consciousness of time. He describes how silences are measured against sounds in a poem, how poems can be recalled to mind without any voicing, and how an interplay between memory and expectation characterizes the recitation of a poem. Hence, "What is true of the whole psalm is also true of all its parts and of each syllable. It is true of any longer action in which I may be engaged and of which the recitation of the psalm may only be a small part. It is true of a man's whole life, of which all his actions are parts. It is true of the whole history of mankind, of which each man's life is a part" (277–78). Augustine's microcosmic thinking makes a hymn the paradigm for the individual's experience of time and the human experience of eternity.

Philosophical allegory in the Middle Ages thus presented a lasting model for poetry of both narrative and lyric kinds, but lyric has precedence in its relation to hymn and prayer. The shift between narration and prayer, like the shift between linear thought and abstraction and the shift between literal and symbolic meaning, also is indicative of medieval practices that might be viewed as "reading into" and "reading out of": the commentary and meditation. Both these practices may seem at first glance to reify the status of the textual artifact and to indicate reverence toward ideas from the past. But in truth, medieval commentary and meditation are as much riddling as homage, and result in the reevaluation of philosophical and poetic arguments as they also assert the importance of individual emotion, experience, and judgments. Listeners and readers must engage, respond to, and transpose the material of the text as a literal matter of conversion.

Among the most important of early medieval commentaries is Ambrosius Theodosius Macrobius's fourth-century discourse on Cicero's *Dream of Scipio* of 54–51 B.C.E. Latin rhetoricians, including Cicero, had criticized the appearance of poetic fictions such as Plato's "Vision of Er" in philosophical discourse, but Macrobius argues in his *Commentary* that when the poet is speaking of the soul and certain gods, "fabulous narratives" have their place (Macrobius 1952: 84–87). Macrobius marks a turn that we can follow out to the eleventh-century meditations of St. Anselm wherein philosophy becomes a spiritually transformative experience, one concerned not with technical and logical means of solving epistemological problems, but rather with means of self-analysis and self-discipline.[14] Here the early "consolations," or independent and self-focused exercises of the Stoics, are the foundation for a strand of meditation that flowers in the spiritual exercises of later Christian thought, including those promulgated by Bonaventure's thirteenth-century *Itinerarium Mentis in Deum* and the sixteenth-century Jesuit St. Ignatius of Loyola's *Exercitia spiritualia* (Ignatius 1978). Louis Martz has argued for the influence of these exercises on metaphysical poetry of the seventeenth century (Martz 1954),[15] concluding that many of the exercises were transposed directly into experiments with poetic forms in the work of both Roman Catholic and Protestant poets, including Richard Crashaw, Robert Southwell, John Donne, and George Herbert. In the nineteenth century, we find Gerard Manley Hopkins's "desolate sonnets" of 1885 directly following that set of Ignatius's spiritual exercises designed as meditations on sin and hell. Though the spiritual consequences of such exercises were dire for their ancient and medieval practitioners, the sheer imaginative power they required also led philosophers and poets to domains of extended metaphors and fictional worlds that would affect many later forms, from philosophical "thought experiments" to the recurrence of "confessional poetry" well into the twentieth century.

Nowhere is the medieval poetic allegory of the spiritual journey more deeply pursued than in Dante's *Commedia*. In Dante's great poem, the external point of reference is a moral one; it is the ultimate expression of the supernatural and ideal by a figure who lives in a world replete with significances that must be uncovered (Santayana 1910: 79). The recursive structure of *terza rima* embodies a relation between action, interpretation, and understanding that undergirds the poem: interpretation and allegory are required; symbols speak to the hidden significance lying behind all appearances. Dante famously explained the "fourfold method" of interpreting his work in his 1318 letter to his patron Can Grande that accompanied the dedication of the *Paradiso*. Using the Israelites' exodus from Egypt as his example, he described how (1) on the literal level, the Hebrews celebrated Passover and departed from Egypt; (2) on the allegorical level, the members of the Church are redeemed through Christ's sacrifice; (3) on the tropological level, Christians are transformed from sinfulness to grace; (4) on the anagogical level, the soul passes from material bondage to eternal existence. This method is indebted to the practice of Midrash in classical Judaism, where a hermeneutic reading of written scripture casts light on laws and practices of the present, and it draws as well upon typological readings of the New Testament as the fulfillment of indications in the Hebrew Scriptures.

Dante's process follows the spiritual revision of Christian confession. This is not a vague goal of his work, but an actual writing practice; he creates a commentary for his early lyrics by reworking them into the *Vita Nuova*, and there the relation between lyric and philosophy is expressed as a complementary pattern of singing and speaking. He goes on to revise the *Vita Nuova* and later lyrics in the *Convivio*, then revises the *Convivio* in the *Commedia*, and then revises the *Commedia* in *de Monarchia*.[16] In this constantly self-revising and self-perpetuating aesthetics, he reflects patterns of the cosmos; the basic form of this art, like the form of creation, displays the paradox of multeity in unity. Following Augustine's ideas regarding creation, Dante contends that as God fills a finite space/time continuum with a multitude of creatures, so the poet, in imitation of the heavenly maker, creates his literary universe and populates it with an analogous multitude. Numbers provide the necessary extension and variety in the poet's artifact, just as they do in God's cosmic creation.

Much in little, complexity in unity—the purest literary expression of this strain of medieval and early Renaissance aesthetics, however, is not philosophical prose or even philosophical epic, but rather the sonnet, and especially the sonnet sequence. Via such a sequence, the poet creates an illusion of temporal dimension. Under conditions of great formal compression, the sonnet writer is able to create an exposition, turn, and aphorism: the sonnet thus expresses in condensed, miniaturized, form features of argument, dialogue, revision, and summarizing conclusion. It unfolds, with a great deal of novelty, and even surprise, in its sense and a great deal of repetition in its sounds. Whether it is a Petrarchan sonnet with an octave and sestet, a Shakespearean or Elizabethan sonnet with three quatrains and a couplet, or a Spenserian one of interlocking rhymes, it stands balanced on its concluding lines and could not have arrived at that point without its preceding mental work. If it indeed developed out of the agon of Sicilian verbal dueling, it had already by the time of Giacomo da Lentini (1215–1233) incorporated the break between the initial eight and final six lines that would enable the expression of a *volta*, or change of mind, and so two points of view, at the very least, were already incorporated into the form. Classical lyric tended to reify the poet by singling out what was individual to his or her person, but late medieval canzone and sonnet traditions show poetic speakers and the objects of their attention in states of emotional flux and transformation.

By reading a sonnet sequence in its entirety, an experience in durational time, readers come to know fully the object of love, from the mundane to the celestial, as an image of perfection and reflection of divine unity. Michel Zink has explained how medieval writers, especially after the thirteenth century, came to emphasize concepts of truth and fiction when speaking such emotions: "[T]he problem of truth lay at the heart of courtly poetics, which presupposed an identity between the truth of love and that of poetry and made sincerity the touchstone of amorous and poetic perfection" (1999: 62–63). He continues to explain that "at the end of the thirteenth century the need for universality was no less great in personal poetry than in lyric poetry, since in any case its satisfaction was necessary for the audience to be touched by the fortuitous incidents of a particular subjectivity and to recognize itself in them." The very codification of the sonnet, its tendency toward artificiality, led to a possibility of voicing a critique of its emotional stance within the poem. In his *Astrophil and Stella*, composed in the 1580s, Sir Philip Sidney is able to multiply perspectives within the series by fictionalizing the voices of both the speaker and his love; by the 1590s, the epideictic conventions of sonnet writing are so fixed that Shakespeare can use his sonnets to explore not only the complex psychology of the three figures of his series, but also the limits of poetry and metaphor itself. It is as if the fixity of the sonnet and its early conventions of idealization evolved into more and more sophisticated demands for the sincerity of psychological realism.

Thus, through sonnet writing and other activities, late medieval and early Renaissance thinkers value a self-transforming solitude. Petrarch's excursion to the summit of Mount Ventoux was an exercise in Christian self-examination, and his gardening and lonely walks through the countryside of the Vaucluse anticipate the poet-walkers of the eighteenth century and Romanticism. Far from being a troubadour, such a poet is a thinker and contemplative who brings back impressions of nature and the fruits of self-scrutiny as the ancient vates once brought back messages from the gods—not in frenzy, however, but in the face-to-face sincerity of conversation and epistles that imitate conversation.

At the same time, Renaissance poets return to classical culture's concerns with rhetoric and the consequences of poetry for speakers and hearers. The major treatises on poetry revive and continue Plato's "ancient quarrel." Julius Caesar Scaliger (1484–1558) wrote his *Poetics* of 1561 under the influence of Aristotle, of course, but he also discusses Horace and the rhetoric of Cicero and Quintilian. Scaliger emphasizes persuasion and considers the moral effects of poetry to be paramount, but he is given to inflated historical claims and makes little distinction between poetry and verse. Ludovico Castelvetro's commentary on Aristotle's *Poetics*, composed and revised between the 1560s and 1576, proposes that poets should invent their own plots, but then he also praises writers of historical tragedies who successfully employ historical events in their work. Though he, too, worries about the effects of poetry on the "vulgar multitude and common people," Castelvetro illuminates the difference between Plato's model of the poet as a figure infused with divine frenzy and the sense of Aristotle who "did not hold the opinion that poetry was a special gift of the gods, yielded to one man rather than to another, as is the gift of prophecy" (1971: 146).

The most extended and synthetic, if not original, Renaissance argument regarding the relation of poetry to philosophy, however, is Sidney's treatise of 1583, which was not published until 1595, when it appeared posthumously in two versions under the titles *Defense of Poesie* and *Apologie for Poetry*. Sidney wrote his defense in response to an attack on poetry, *The School of Abuse*, published in 1579 by the Puritan Stephen Gosson. Gosson had followed closely, even redundantly, the *Republic*'s claims as he argued that poetry is a waste of time, the "mother of lies," "the nurse of abuse," and that no less an authority than Plato had banished poets from his republic. Sidney drew on Aristotle, Plato, Horace, Cicero, Agrippa, and Erasmus, as well as a range of poetic texts from Greek hymns to the border ballad "Chevy Chase," to formulate his reply. Sidney argued that poetry is a form of education, that poetry is a moral influence upon other domains of culture, that poets are revered by everyone, and, in a nod to Neoplatonism, that poetry is an improvement upon nature, writing "only the poet, disdaining to be tied to any...subjection, lifted up with the vigor of his own invention, doth grow in effect another nature, in making things either better than nature bringeth forth, or, quite anew, forms such as never were in nature" (1970: 14–15). Sidney also follows Aristotle in arguing that poetry is part of action, and not *gnosis*, or knowing, though he considers such action, the imitation of action that produces movement in an audience, as of a "higher degree" than teaching alone. Implicitly, the rhetorical emotional power of poetry is acknowledged, but here turned toward a pedagogical aim. The goal of poetry for Sidney is knowledge of the self, consistent with Neoplatonic self-transcendence.

In Sidney's treatise we see some of the sparks of the quarrel between the ancients and the moderns that will flare in the seventeenth and early eighteenth centuries throughout Western Europe. He in fact notes that the ancient poets "versified" by quantity, but the modern only by number. He is indebted to classical influences and at the same time expects the poet to make new forms, to draw forward out of nature what nature has not yet produced. By the time of the four-way dialogue on the ancients and the moderns in John Dryden's 1668 "An Essay of Dramatic Poesy," the moderns have begun to win. What does this mean? For poetry, it indicates that rather than following a process of imitation and citation and obeying ancient rules of poetic decorum and occasion, the composing poet will be obliged to create new forms for art and speak to the age at hand.

In the early eighteenth century, as both empiricism and the philosophy of feeling give priority to the operations of reason rather than supernatural forces of transcendence and authority, poetry also has an empirical, descriptive cast. The loco-descriptive poets of the eighteenth century, with their underlying moral and social arguments, depart from the meditations of earlier theological poetry by looking outward to nature as teacher. At the same time, they carry forward aspects of the meditative tradition by continuing the perspective of the Petrarchan or Franciscan solitary alone in nature; and, as they so often contrast their view to the cynicism and frivolity of the courts, this solitude is largely moral. Seventeenth- and early eighteenth-century poetry also revives classical satire, criticizing the particular with the universal weapons of common sense and notions of what is "natural" to humankind.

Perhaps I spoke too soon earlier when I suggested that poetry has no quarrel with philosophy, for in many ways late Enlightenment and Romantic poetics are a rebuke to philosophy's claim of cognitive superiority—a rebuke in several senses. At least since Thomas Aquinas's account of beauty in the *Summa Theologica*, the idea of seeing or insight via aesthetic form has a status commensurate to that of other modes of cognition. Aquinas concludes (1981 I, q. 39, art. 8) that beauty involves integrity or perfection, due proportion or harmony (not merely between its parts, but between the object and the viewer), and brightness, clarity, or brilliance. This last quality ties Neoplatonic notions of light as both truth and divine perfection to clarity of thought. The apophatic dimension of Neoplatonic thought is carried over into an interest in the supersensible that includes both that which cannot be said and that which is expressed by silence.

The most prominent proponent of the priority of poiesis over other systems of thought was the early eighteenth-century Neapolitan jurist, rhetorician, and philosopher of history Giambattista Vico. Vico's major treatise, *The New Science* (1744), is rooted in a retrospective myth about the origins of poetry that also links poiesis to an originary anxiety about the absence of form. Here is the story as Vico tells it:

> [W]hen...at last the sky fearfully rolled with thunder and flashed with lightning, as could not but follow from the bursting upon the air for the first time of an impression so violent. Thereupon a few giants, who must have been the most robust, and who were dispersed through the forests on the mountain heights where the strongest beasts have their dens, were frightened and astonished by the great effect whose cause they did not know, and raised their eyes and became aware of the sky. And because in such a case the nature of the human mind leads it to attribute its own nature to the effect and because in that state their nature was that of men all robust bodily strength, who expressed their very violent passions by shouting and grumbling, they pictured the sky to themselves as a great animated body, which in that aspect they called Jove, the first god of the so-called greater gentes [peoples], who meant to tell them something by the hiss of his bolts and the clap of his thunder. And thus they began to exercise that natural curiosity which is the daughter of ignorance and the mother of knowledge, and which, opening the mind of man, gives birth to wonder. (1970: 75–76)

In this account, Vico describes how the earliest humans, living naked in the forest, invented a figure by means of which they could bear their fear of the most powerful forces of nature. He adds, "[T]hey, in their robust ignorance, did it by virtue of a wholly corporeal imagination. And because it was quite corporeal, they did it with marvelous sublimity; a sublimity such and so great that it excessively perturbed the very persons who by imagining did the creating, for which they were called 'poet,' which is Greek for 'creators'" (75). Vico explains that the imagination is moved to represent itself, via onomatopoeia, personification, and other modes of projection, by anthropomorphizing nature and thus giving being to inanimate things. Fashioned from nature as Jove is fashioned by the first humans from their experience of lightning, these "inventions" eventually become narratives (74). And as narratives harden into ideologies, Vico contends that authorization and legitimation give such ideologies ethical force.

Following Vico, we could claim that poetry can be the subject of neither history nor philosophy, for poetry is necessarily prior to these two forms of discourse. Poetry expresses the passage from not-knowing to knowing through which we represent the world, including the perspectives of others, to ourselves and those around us. What is given birth, as "the daughter of ignorance" becomes "the mother of knowledge," is the continuity of a continuously transforming human culture. Language here is pressured to be in some way commensurate to perception and at the same time to be intelligible to others, for, from Vico's viewpoint, the speaking subject as the recipient of the recognition of others is not prior to language: language is the forum within which such a speaking subject emerges. Only when poetic metaphors make available to others the experience of the corporeal senses can the corporeal senses truly appear as integral experiences. The self is compelled to make forms and thereby is transformed into the person of volition and consequence—necessarily a person articulated by speaking and being spoken to. Vico thereby describes the situation of the emergence of subjectivity both ontologically, that is, in general, and historically, that is, in particular. But the reconciliation of this model as a structural problem and a historical practice is not a simple one. Like Hegel's account of the ontology of self-consciousness in his *Phenomenology of Mind* (Hegel 1967: 228–40), Vico's narrative of the origins of poetry and subjectivity is a retrospective fable about our capacity for the fabular. Poetry is both the repetition of an ontological moment and the ongoing process or work of enunciation by which that moment is recursively known and carried forward.

This line of thinking about the founding power of poetry is not merely a critique of the divisions of metaphysics; it is also a critique of a far more pervasive division between matter, including the body, and mind. Many early Greek philosophers practiced an attributive monism wherein one substance, such as Heraclitus's fire and Epicurus's atoms, underlies all forms. Alternatively, philosophers of substantival monism linked mind and matter as the manifestation of a single substance in different states—a single substance variously described as life or nature. For Aristotle, an activity of life joined the soul and body as the universe strives toward perfection; Aristotle thereby promotes an aspiring variety of hylozoism. Spinoza is the most important descendent of this substantival monism. He contended God, who is Nature, is the immanent cause of all things. The contemporary philosopher of action Stuart Hampshire writes of Spinoza's philosophy, "[E]verything must be explained as belonging to the single and all-inclusive system which is nature, and no cause (not even a First Cause) can be conceived as somehow outside or independent of the order of Nature" (2005: 45).

As the Augustinian legacy of elevating human creation as a mirror of divine creation is transposed in Romanticism, poets and philosophers alike take up a monistic view of human creation as one of many powerful creative forces in nature. Through his friendship with Friedrich Jacobi (1743–1819), who had been drawn to Spinoza's philosophy as he also rejected its mathematical rationalism, Johann Wolfgang von Goethe (1749–1832) adopted certain aspects of this variety of monism, especially the idea that the universe contains and expresses a creative force that appears as a duality, but is in truth one. Goethe pursued a philosophy of life wherein "the pursuit of the ideal" is preferable to the ideal itself, and, following Aristotle and Spinoza, he envisions a philosophy of experience and immanence, wherein our powers of representation approach the universal, hence the open-endedness, or episodic quality, of the project of his art (see Santayana 1910: 142).

German Romanticism as a philosophy and artistic practice was a lively forum for discussions of the value of poetry, and perhaps at no other time in history has the practice of philosophy and the practice of an art form been so closely allied and debated. Another friend of Jacobi, J. G. Hamann (1730–1788), claimed "the whole world is the language of God and poetry is therefore nothing but the imitation of this language." Such poetic language archetypally exemplified in myth was for Hamann the paradigm of all knowledge. Johann Gottfried Herder (1744–1803), however, claimed in conversations with Goethe in 1770, and in his subsequent writings on language, that the paradigm for poetry was not myth, but lyric, for the function of lyric is to forge the imagery that is the basic form of language and hence the foundation of all thought. Herder's position regarding the priority of metaphorical poiesis is therefore much like Vico's, though there is no evidence of a direct line of influence. In Herder we find lyric apotheosized as the form that unites all reasoning, perceiving, desiring, and feeling and so best expresses the totality of human life. Those physiological dimensions of lyric expression condemned by Plato are here inseparably bound to psychology and the possibilities of self-knowledge.

Prompting many of these debates about the unity of human experience and the interrelations of sensation, imagination, cognition, and reasoning was the monumental philosophy of Immanuel Kant. Born in 1724, Kant did not publish his *Critique of Judgment* until he was 66, and his writings on aesthetics both drew on, and attempted to resolve, earlier eighteenth-century arguments about beauty, taste, and sublimity—particularly the problems of generalizing from bodily experience to universals. He also sought to reconcile aesthetic judgments with his prior work in epistemology and ethics, setting out a noncognitive and nonpractical basis for the apprehension of beauty in and for itself. In considering the place of poetry in his arguments about aesthetic experience, we can attend to his passing comments on works of art per se and on the relations between composition and sublimity. Kant held that "genius gives the rule to art." Responding to Aristotle's notion that essences are produced within and emerge from the natural world, *natura naturata*, Kant claims that the artist/creator, as opposed to the mere copyist or imitator, uncovers creative principles already hidden in nature, *natura naturans*.

As Kant ranks the various forms of art in his "Analytic of the Sublime," he elevates poetry over music. Here is perhaps the culmination of the discourses on individual originality that can be traced from Longinus's first-century treatise on rhetorical genius to the victory of the moderns over the ancients:

> Among all the arts *poetry* holds the highest rank. (It owes its origin almost entirely to genius and is least open to guidance by precept or examples.) It expands the mind: for it sets the imagination free, and offers us, from among the unlimited variety of possible forms that harmonize with a given concept, though within that concept's limits, that form which links the exhibition of the concept with a wealth of thought to which no linguistic expression is completely adequate, and so poetry rises aesthetically to ideas. Poetry fortifies the mind: for it lets the mind feel its ability—free, spontaneous, and independent of natural determination—to contemplate and judge phenomenal nature as having aspects that nature does not on its own offer in experience either to sense or to the understanding, and hence poetry lets the mind feel its ability to use nature on behalf of and, as it were, as a schema of the supersensible. (Kant 1987: 196–97)

In contrast, music, as an art of tone, "speaks through nothing but sensations without concepts, so that unlike poetry it leaves us with nothing to meditate about." Kant does emphasize, however, that the transience of music makes it "agitate the mind more diversely and intensely" (198).

Central to Kant's concerns in these passages is "the unlimited variety of possible forms that harmonize with a given concept." The concept is limited, but its "exhibition" opens a "wealth of thought to which no linguistic expression is completely adequate, and so poetry rises aesthetically to ideas [of the Reason]." In Kant's system, concepts belong to the understanding. In reflective, as opposed to deliberative thought, as the material of sense intuition is presented by the imagination, the understanding must either create new concepts (as in scientific judgments) or hold concepts either in an unresolved harmony with the imagination (as in the aesthetic judgment of beauty) or in a blocked relation that gives us intuition of the supersensible, indicating the unlimited power of reason itself. Kant finds in poetry a use of symbols that, finite as they are as terms or words, produce a "wealth" of "aesthetical ideas," as he calls them, and thus evoke something like the intuition of reason he finds at work in the experience of sublimity.

It is technically impossible to provide an "example" of Kant's notion of sublimity, as it is technically impossible to provide an "example" of his notion of beauty, since we break the spell of beauty and sublimity once we bring those experiences under concepts, including the concept "poem" and the concept "work of art." Nevertheless, the impact of Kant's philosophy, and of the often-misguided reception of Kant's philosophy by figures such as Samuel Taylor Coleridge, is evident as Romantic poets strive to create sublime effects. The abstract emotions and chanting of Schiller's "Ode to Joy," those "thoughts that do often lie too deep for tears" in the work of Wordsworth, the strings of self-canceling similes in Shelley's "Hymn to Intellectual Beauty," are only a few examples of such efforts. And we might conversely argue that it is from lyric recursivity, that intended progress of speech not brought under the a priori forms of plot teleology, that Kant derives his fundamental notion of art as "purposiveness without a purpose."

In later work by Friedrich von Schiller (1759–1805), the tensions and interrelations between the senses and abstraction, or what he called the "formal" drive, achieved their most harmonious balance in the making of art and in the capacity we have for play more generally (1954: 64–65). In the twelfth of his "Letters on the Aesthetic Education of Man," Schiller suggests that through art we are able both to give reality to the necessity of sensuous experience and to bring a diversity of manifestations into harmony. The creation of form is linked to the affirmation of the individual person in his or her whole humanity:

> When therefore the formal impulse holds sway and the pure object acts within us, there is the highest expansion of being, all barriers disappear, and from being the unit of magnitude to which the needy sense confined him, Man has risen to a *unit of idea* embracing the whole realm of phenomena. By this operation we are no more in time, but time, with its complete and infinite succession, is in us. We are no longer individuals, but species. (1954: 67)

For Schiller, the experience of aesthetic beauty is in this way constantly renewing for individuals and for human life as a whole. Describing how man's humanity is limited or reduced by entering into determinate conditions—conditions of limit posed by our meetings with forces of nature and history, Schiller writes in his "Twenty-first Letter" of the aesthetic as a replenishing counterforce to such determinations: "[Man] possesses this humanity as a predisposition, before any definite condition into which he may come; but in actual practice he loses it with every definite condition into which he comes, and it must, if he is to be able to make the transition to an opposite condition, be newly restored to him every time by means of the aesthetic life." Schiller concludes, "It is, then, no mere poetic licence, but also philosophical truth, to call Beauty our second creator" (1954: 102). The Platonic idea that we saw in Sidney's *Apology*, that the poet has an opportunity to make another nature, is inverted as the creation of beauty endows human makers with new life. The Enlightenment goal of self-overcoming and self-making is not accomplished by reason alone, but is a matter of reconciling the sensual and speculative aspects of the human condition. Poetry, as the abstract art form most closely propelled by somatic forces, has a particular cachet for such a project.

Hegel's 1823–1826 lectures on aesthetics promote a similar view of the relation between the sensible and the thought in poetry:

> [T]he proper element of poetical representation is the poetical *imagination* and the illustration of spirit itself, and since this element is common to all the art-forms, poetry runs through them all and develops itself independently in each of them. Poetry is the universal art of the spirit which has become free in itself and which is not tied down for its realization to external sensuous material: instead, it launches out exclusively in the inner space and the inner time of ideas and feelings. (Hegel 1975, 1: 89)[17]

Yet as Kant's position gives us a clue that the intensity of affect in music might lend something of its emotional force to the sonorous dimension of the poetic, so does Hegel's position stray so far from the reception of particular instances of the poetic that poetry threatens to disappear entirely on its trajectory toward the universal.

An acknowledgment of the material, often agonistic, labor of composition runs as a refrain through Romantic aesthetics and often rescues such theory from overconceptualization. August Wilhelm von Schlegel (1765–1832) claimed that the practice of poetry reenacts on a higher level the creation of language itself, a theory that cannot account for the social and rhetorical demands placed on the reception of poetry, but that nevertheless gives some sense of the sheer effort required to meet Romantic demands for originality and genius. Vico similarly had mentioned the "extremely disturbed passions" at the root of the production of metaphor, and Jean-Jacques Rousseau's theory of the origins of language roots the production of language in contingent emotion (Rousseau 1966).[18]

A similar approach can be found in Coleridge's position on metric as an act of will: in a passage in the *Biographia Literaria*, Coleridge explains that meter arises as an act of mastery or pleasure in the face of an onslaught of passion (i.e., pain):

> This [meter] I would trace to the balance in the mind effected by that spontaneous effort which strives to hold in check the workings of passion. It might be easily explained likewise in what manner this salutary antagonism is assisted by the very state which it counteracts; and how this balance of antagonists became organized into meter...by a supervening act of the will and judgement, consciously and for the foreseen purpose of pleasure.... [There must be] an interpenetration of passion and of will. (Coleridge 1907, I: 50)

His description in this passage should be juxtaposed to Wordsworth's thoughts in his preface to *Lyrical Ballads* on metric and the representation of emotion. Wordsworth contends that "there can be little doubt but that more pathetic situations and sentiments, that is, those which have a greater proportion of pain connected with them, may be endured in metrical composition, especially in rhyme, than in prose" (Wordsworth 1850: 296). And he describes a particular process of composition:

> [P]oetry is the spontaneous overflow of powerful feelings: it takes its origin from emotion recollected in tranquillity: the emotion is contemplated till, by a species of re-action, the tranquillity gradually disappears, and an emotion, kindred to that which was before the subject of contemplation, is gradually produced, and does itself actually exist in the mind. (297–98)

At first glance, just as emotion contradicts tranquility, so does spontaneity seem to contradict recollection. Yet we can see here, and in many of Wordsworth's lyrics of emotional perception—for example, his Lucy poems or a brief work like "Surprised by Joy"—a continuation of a practice of spiritual exercise, a meditation on emotion, that allows for the imaginative contemplation of conflicting emotional states and for their representation in the compelling rhythmic movement of lyric form.[19]

After the nineteenth century, poetic theory remains closely tied to Romantic ideas of organic or autotelic form, particularly in the vein of T. S. Eliot and the American New Critics. The Romantic model of lyric sincerity and originality is both perpetuated and overturned by various efforts to ironize and invert it. Beginning with Charles Baudelaire's 1861 *Les Fleurs du Mal*, with its attack on the piety of romantic natural symbolism and celebration of the artificial, poets have sought fuller accounts of reality, particularly fuller accounts of a modern reality of rapid change and speed. As we can see in the epigraph to this essay, Baudelaire promoted a sense of lyric epiphany in the experience of everyday life. His prose poems led the way for the twentieth-century lyric novel as practiced by Virginia Woolf, Samuel Beckett, and others, just as the long history of lyric interiorization had cleared the path for the appearance of "stream of consciousness" in Tolstoy's *Anna Karenina* and the prose experiments of James Joyce. "To break the pentameter, that was the first heave," Ezra Pound wrote in his *Canto LXXXI*. The practitioners of free verse and prose poetry split themselves from the rhythms and forms of all previous generations of poets/thinkers. Yet by defining their lines against those practices, they also artifactualized the history of poetry, opening it to what Eliot described as a "simultaneity" of all previous traditions.[20]

While twentieth-century philosophy pulls away from philosophy's previous history and refines its field of study to consist of the logical analysis of meaning, both within and independent of contexts of natural language, twentieth-century poetry follows a widely syncretic path. Nowhere is this perhaps more evident than in the ways modern and contemporary poets have incorporated elements of non-Western and archaic traditions into their practices while Western philosophy has split itself entirely from the sage traditions that characterize its own deep past and the concurrent philosophies of other cultures. As science came to claim, from the seventeenth century forward, the sphere of reference and replicability, philosophy became a means of clarifying thought, determining the bounds of thought as the bounds of language. Philosophy continues to see ambiguity as a problem to be overcome rather than a resource for symbolic forms, yet in the early twentieth century, the practice of poetry also comes closer to the practice of philosophy as a concern with sentences, utterances, and speech acts in general begins to dominate analytical philosophy. Gertrude Stein's 1932 "Stanzas in Meditation," for example, can be read as exercises in semantics with a focus quite close to those of Ludwig Wittgenstein's writings on rule following and the impossibility of a private language. Romantic poetry had been preoccupied with the notion of the fragment, but much modernist poetry has an open, unfinished dimension that is close to a Wittgensteinian practice of philosophy as contingent, everyday meditation. Wittgenstein and other twentieth-century philosophers make much of the "thought experiment," and this practice, too, is taken up by poets from the great philosophical modernist Wallace Stevens to living contemporary poets such as John Ashbery and the poet-philosopher John Koethe who use poetry to create "a new reality" (Stevens 1954: 534).[21] For poets of this line, lyrics are fleeting practices that model the passage toward understanding in experience, providing a freedom to reflect upon language beyond the expression of emotion and beyond the disappearance of speech into time and purpose. There is something of the spiritual exercise in this work, since it admits at once of fiction and meditation. And in such a contingent practice, the problem of imitation is put aside—the worlds created in such poems are in and for themselves.

A counter to this analytic tradition is the phenomenological work of Martin Heidegger, whose writing on thinking in particular moves closer and closer to a practice of meditating upon, and eventually emulating, the path of lyric. In his lectures at the University of Freiburg in the winter and summer of 1952, collected in *What Is Called Thinking?* (1968), Heidegger wrote of the inseparability of poetry and thought in the initial, and final, gesture of speaking—that gesture both sensual and requiring hermeneusis. He wrote: "[T]he common view is that both thought and poesy use language merely as their medium and a means of expression as sculpture, painting, and music operate and express themselves in the medium of stone and wood and color and tone." Instead, he suggests that we "get over" regarding art as expression or impression:

> [L]anguage is neither merely the field of expression nor merely the means
> of expression, nor merely the two jointly. Thought and poesy never just use
> language to express themselves with its help; rather, thought and poesy are in
> themselves the originary, the essential, and therefore also the final speech that
> language speaks through the mouth of man. (1968: 128)

Heidegger is here drawing on certain legacies, or threads, of earlier philosophy, among them the distinction between purposeful and contemplative thought in Aristotle's *Nicomachean Ethics*, Kant's vision of the freedom of subjects in the openness of aesthetic judgments, and Friedrich Nietzsche's sense of the calling of the poet/maker. Heidegger is also rejecting all forms of dualism, returning in much of his work to a presocratic monism of flux and transformation. Of all philosophers, Vico and Heidegger are perhaps the most deeply committed to something like a practice of poetics: poetry is the epitome and outcome at once of the originary, founding power of words.[22]

As we explore the historical interrelation of philosophy and poetry, there are certain conclusions we can begin to draw. The "ancient quarrel" between poetry and philosophy, regardless of Plato's motives in claiming it, has some genuine basis in the very means of production of each form. Metaphysics particularly must remove itself from the constraints of individual voice if its claims are to be universal, yet the central tenets of metaphysics remain authored and achieve much of their authority from institutional recognition. Even so, the central questions of metaphysics—questions of knowing, the problem of an exterior world, the question of materiality, the nature of life, the relation between the soul and the body, the possibility of liberty, the question of other minds, the origin of Being, the existence of God—have as well been central not only to the themes of poetry, but also to its methods. We could reframe this list readily from the perspective of poets, for poets, too, have been preoccupied with the subject/object problem, the representation of nature, the materiality of language, the organic sources of form, the therapeutic and spiritual benefits of a practice of poetry, the bounds of traditions and the possibilities of free creation, the intelligibility of poetry for those who receive it, and a sense of ultimate purpose in creation.

Yet in the end, poets and philosophers alike must take a stance against the drawing of conclusions or they will betray what is made possible by their open practices. Creating poems and pursuing truth are human activities that are inseparable from our humanity itself—these actions separate us from other species that can make, but, as far as we know, cannot judge or contemplate their making. Despite its roots in prophecy, lyric, throughout its long history, has rarely been written in the future tense or concerned with the future as a theme. But perhaps this persistent absence indicates something deeper about the free practice of lyric; this very openness may indicate that futurity is nowhere in lyric deixis because it is everywhere. What Baudelaire called "the spirit of the lyre" awakens us to our relation to nature, and to our own natures, and calls us to remember and consider and judge. The fact that our imaginations enable us to picture the future, and the future of our species, roots us more particularly in the sources of life and the possibility of its continuity.

NOTES

1. "Therefore there necessarily exists a lyric mode of speech, a lyric world, a lyric atmosphere, of landscapes, of men, of women, of animals who all delight in the spirit of the lyre" (Baudelaire 1961: 736).

2. Note that "wisdom" in English does not quite convey the range of meanings that *sophia* indicates. For Homer (*Iliad* XV: 412), the skill of a carpenter would be one form of *sophia*. Herodotus (*History* I: 30) suggests that *sophia* is simply a desire to discover, journey, or exercise an intellectual curiosity.

3. Those who suffer from global aphasia, for example, can lose propositional speech (the intended production of context-bound utterances), and at the same time retain an ability to hum previous learned melodies and sing their lyrics, to count, and to recite nursery rhymes and structured bits of language like the days of the week (Damasio 1992: 535).

4. Early English poems demonstrating this connection include the gnomic verses and 95 riddles in the thousand-year-old Exeter Book. Translations of some of these can be found in Alexander 1977: 87–102. The direct line of proverbs can be followed in two of Chaucer's own in his "Proverbs":

> What shul these clothes thus manyfold,
> Lo this hote somers day?
> After grete hete cometh cold;
> No man caste his pilche away.
> Of al this world the large compas

> Yt wil not in myn armes tweyne;
> Who so mochel wol embrace,
> Litel thereof he shal distreyne.

5. This summary comes from Ernst Robert Curtius 1991: 203–04. Curtius himself borrows from Stefan Weinstock 1926: 121 ff.

6. Nightingale 1995 also mentions an attack on poets, who lack "wit" and "understanding" and "take the mob as their teacher," in Heraclitus 64 n. 14, but otherwise argues, following the notes to the 1902 edition of *The Republic* by J. Adam, that the quarrel is largely Plato's invention. Nightingale 1995 focuses on Plato's contested relation to tragedy. For further discussion, see Rosen 1988.

7. Gadamer 1980 attributes this shift toward hymns and deserved praise as part of Plato's educational plan for the guardians. Plato is interested in dispelling the anthropomorphic representations of the gods found in Homer and other writers of a poetry of legends.

8. Ferguson 1983 is the most sustained account of the pivotal defenses of Joachim Du Bellay, Torquato Tasso, and Philip Sidney.

9. Underlying this argument, the etymology of *teknē* as having to do with the bearing and bringing forth of children has a particular resonance. Diotima contrasts the generation and creation of forms by organic means unfavorably to those made by reason, and we see in this passage an important source for the often-oppressive Western division of the labor of making between physical and mental activity.

10. For a précis of the relations between stitchic, melic, and couplet forms in ancient Greek poetry, see Mulroy 1992: 9–11.

11. I discuss Snell's work, and many other issues of lyric history, in Stewart 2003. The discussion of Augustine and Vico that follows also borrows extensively from this work.

12. What he then hurries home to read, through the pagan practice of *sortes virgilianae* applied to the Bible, is a passage from Paul's epistles directing him to turn against "nature's appetites."

13. Augustine 1961: 202 n. 2 provides an 1854 translation by J. D. Chambers:

> Maker of all things! God most high!
> Great Ruler of the starry sky!
> Who, robing day with beauteous light,
> Hast clothed in soft repose the night,
> That sleep may wearied limbs restore,
> And fit for toil and use once more;
> May gently soothe the careworn breast,
> And lull our anxious griefs to rest.

14. The *Proslogium* and *Monologium* are available in Anselm (1962).

15. This path-breaking study emphasizes Roman Catholic spiritual exercises; see also Lewalski 1984.

16. The other side of this process of revision is a willingness to leave works unfinished or suspended. See Robert Hollander 2001: 114 for a discussion of Dante's decision to leave the *Convivio* and *De vulgari Eloquentia* incomplete in order to begin the *Commedia*, as he had left the *Convivio* incomplete while he began *De vulgari Eloquentia* (Hollander 2001: 55). For a discussion of how *De Monarchia* clarifies Dante's positions on the relative power of the pope and emperor, see Hollander 2001: 161–63. Hollander

also discusses Dante's shifts between various lyric modes, which he characterizes as "his inclination to experiment" (2001: 9, 43).

17. Hegel's lectures also discuss the particular subjectivity of lyric verse and the relations between internal feeling, the artistic or universal sense of subjective states, and the "external" support of musical accompaniment. See Hegel 1975, 2: 1111–57.

18. See especially chapter 2, "That the First Invention of Speech Is Due Not to Need but Passion":

> Whence then this origin? From moral needs, passions. All the passions tend to bring people back together again, but the necessity of seeking a livelihood forces them apart. It is neither hunger nor thirst but love, hatred, pity, anger, which drew from them the first words.... [T]he first languages were singable and passionate before they became simple and methodical. (Rousseau 1966: 12)

19. The preface was first composed in 1798, then revised in 1836 and published in 1850.

20. In writing of "the historical sense," Eliot wrote:

> [T]he historical sense involves a perception, not only of the pastness of the past, but of its presence; the historical sense compels a man to write not merely with his own generation in his bones, but with a feeling that the whole of the literature of Europe from Homer and within it the whole of the literature of his own country has a simultaneous existence and composes a simultaneous order. (1919: 4)

21. This phrase comes from "Not Ideas about the Thing but the Thing Itself," the last poem of Stevens's last book, *The Rock* (1954). Here is the poem in its entirety:

> At the earliest ending of winter,
> In March, a scrawny cry from outside
> Seemed like a sound in his mind.
> He knew that he heard it,
> A bird's cry, at daylight or before,
> In the early March wind.
> The sun was rising at six,
> No longer a battered panache above snow...
> It would have been outside.
> It was not from the vast ventriloquism
> Of sleep's faded papier-mache...
> The sun was coming from the outside.
> That scrawny cry—It was
> A chorister whose c preceded the choir.
> It was part of the colossal sun,
> Surrounded by its choral rings,
> Still far away. It was like
> A new knowledge of reality.

Though at first we might imagine it comes from our own minds, this "scrawny cry" has its ultimate source in the sun, as do Plato's ideas. Stevens's extraordinary evocation of the call toward truth arising from nature responds to Paul Valéry's remarks (1958: 52–81) regarding how words acquire a value at the expense of their finite significance; like the opening sounds of music, they reveal that "something of significance is beginning to declare itself." For a discussion of Wittgenstein's thought in relation to modernist and post-modern literature, see Marjorie Perloff (1999). As Perloff acknowledges, Gertrude Stein in fact, did not read the work of Wittgenstein, but Perloff sees his discussion of ordinary and poetic language, and his practice of thinking about words, sentences, and utterances in relation to their context-boundedness and independence as vital to a range of "experimental" literature from the early twentieth-century to the present.

22. See Heidegger (1968: 130):

> [W]ords are not terms, and thus are not like buckets and kegs from which we scoop a content that is there. Words are wellsprings that are found and dug up in the telling, wellsprings that must be found and dug up again and again, that easily cave in, but that at times also well up when least expected. If we do not go to the spring again and again, the bucket and kegs stay empty, and their content stays stale.

Heidegger has a particular interest in the hymn or praise poem because of his focus on the relations between "*denken und danken*" ("thinking and thanking"); as expressed in his 1936 lecture on "Hölderlin and the Essence of Poetry," it is the Romantic poet Friedrich Hölderlin who epitomizes for him the fullest possibilities of poetic thought.

REFERENCES

Alexander, M., trans. (1977). *The Earliest English Poems.* London: Penguin.

Anselm, St. (1962). *Proslogium* and *Monologium. In St. Anselm: The Basic Writings* (S. N. Deane, trans.). Chicago: Open Court.

Aquinas, St. Thomas (1981). Summa theologica (5 volumes). Notre Dame, Ind.: Christian Classics.

Aristotle (1941a). *De Poetica* (Ingram Bywater, trans.). *In* R. McKeon, (ed.), *The Basic Works of Aristotle* New York: Random House.

——. (1941b). *Ethica Nichomachea* (W. D. Ross, trans.). *In* R. McKeon, (ed.), *The Basic Works of Aristotle).* New York: Random House.

——. (1941c). *Physica* (R. P. Hardie and R. K. Gaye, trans.). *In* (R. McKeon, (ed.), *The Basic Works of Aristotle* New York: Random House.

Augustine, St. (1961). *Confessions* (R. S. Pine-Coffin, trans.). Harmondsworth: Penguin.

Baudelaire, C. (1961). "Réflexions sur Quelques-uns de mes Contemporains." *In* Baudelaire, *Oeuvres Complètes.* Paris: Gallimard: 701–52.

Castelvetro, L. (1971). *Poetica d'Aristotele vulgarizzata e sposta* (R. L. Montgomery trans). Excerpted in *Critical Theory since Plato* (Hazard Adams, ed.). San Diego: Harcourt Brace.

Coleridge, S. T. (1907). *Biographia Literaria* (2 vols.; J. Shawcross, ed.). Oxford: Clarendon.

Curtius, E. R. (1991). *European Literature and the Latin Middle Ages.* Princeton: Princeton University Press.

Damasio, A. (1992). "Aphasia." *New England Journal of Medicine* 326(8), 521–39.

Eliot, T. S. (1919). "Tradition and the Individual Talent." *In* Eliot, *Selected Essays.* New York: Harcourt Brace, 1950.

Ferguson, M. W. (1983). *Trials of Desire: Renaissance Defenses of Poetry.* New Haven: Yale University Press.

Gadamer, H.-G. (1980). "Plato and the Poets." *In* Gadamer, *Dialogue and Dialectic* (P. C. Smith, trans.). New Haven: Yale University Press.

Hampshire, S. (2005). *Spinoza and Spinozism.* Oxford: Clarendon Press.

Hegel, G. W. F. (1967). *The Phenomenology of Mind* (J. B. Baillie, trans.). New York: Harper. (Original work published 1807).

——. (1975). *Hegel's Aesthetics: Lectures on Fine Art* (2 vols.; T. M. Knox, trans.). Oxford: Oxford University Press.

Heidegger, M. (1968). *What Is Called Thinking?* (J. G. Gray, trans.). New York: Harper and Row.

Heraclitus. *Die Fragmente der Vorsokratiker* (6th ed.; H. Diels and W. Kranz, eds.). Berlin: Weidmann.

Hollander, R. (2001). *Dante: A Life in Works.* New Haven: Yale University Press.

Ignatius, St. (1978). *The Spiritual Exercises of St. Ignatius: A Literal Translation and a Contemporary Reading* (D. L. Fleming, ed.). St. Louis: Institute of Jesuit Sources.

Kant, I. (1987). *Critique of Judgment* (Werner S. Pluhar, trans.). Indianapolis: Hackett. (Original work published 1790).

Lewalski, B. (1984). *Protestant Poetics and the Seventeenth Century Religious Lyric.* Princeton: Princeton University Press.

Macrobius, A. T. (1952). *Commentary on the Dream of Scipio* (W. H. Stahl, trans.). New York: Columbia University Press.

Martz, L. (1954). *The Poetry of Meditation; A Study in English Religious Literature of the Seventeenth Century.* New Haven: Yale University Press.

Mulroy, D. (1991). *Early Greek Lyric Poetry.* Ann Arbor: University of Michigan Press.

Nightingale, A. (1995). *Genres in Dialogue: Plato and the Construct of Philosophy.* Cambridge: Cambridge University Press.

Parkes, M. (1976). "The Influence of the Concepts of Ordinatio and Compilatio on the Development of the Book." *In* J. J. G. Alexander and M. T. Gibson, (eds.), *Medieval Learning and Literature* Oxford: Clarendon: 115–41.

Perloff, M. (1999). *Wittgenstein's Ladder: Poetic Language and the Strangeness of the Ordinary.* Chicago: University of Chicago Press.

Plato (1983). *The Republic* (G. M. A. Grube, trans.). Indianapolis: Hackett.

——. (1989). *Symposium* (A. Nehamas and P. Woodruff, trans.). Indianapolis: Hackett.

Preminger, A., and Bogan, T. V. F. (1993). *The New Princeton Encyclopedia of Poetry and Poetics.* Princeton: Princeton University Press.

Rosen, S. (1988). *The Quarrel between Philosophy and Poetry: Studies in Ancient Thought.* New York: Routledge and Kegan Paul.

Rousseau, J.-J. (1966). "Essay on the Origin of Languages" (Alexander Gode, trans.). *In* Rousseau and Herder, *On the Origin of Language: Jean-Jacques Rousseau, "Essay on the Origin of Languages and Johann Gottfried Herder, "Essay on the Origin of Language"* (J. H. Moran and A. Gode, trans.). Chicago: University of Chicago Press.

Russell, D. A. and Winterbottom, M. (eds). (1972). *Ancient Literary Criticism.* Oxford: Clarendon Press.

Santayana, G. (1910). *Three Philosophical Poets: Lucretius, Dante, Goethe.* Cambridge, Mass.: Harvard University Press.

Schiller, F. (1954). *On the Aesthetic Education of Man in a Series of Letters* (R. Snell, trans.). New Haven: Yale University Press.

Sidney, Sir Philip (1970). *Apologie for Poetrie* (Lewis Soens, ed.). Lincoln: University of Nebraska Press.

Snell, B. (1982). *The Discovery of the Mind* (T. G. Rosenmeyer, trans.). Mineola, N.Y.: Dover.

Stevens, W. (1990). "Not Ideas about the Thing but the Thing Itself." *In* Stevens, *The Collected Poems of Wallace Stevens*, p. 534. New York: Knopf.

Stewart, S. (2003). *Poetry and the Fate of the Senses.* Chicago: University of Chicago Press.

Valéry, P. (1939). "Poetry and Abstract Thought" (Denise Folliot, trans.). *In* J. Matthews, (ed.), *The Collected Works of Paul Valéry* Princeton: Princeton University Press, 1958.

Vico, G. (1970). *The New Science* (T. Goddard and M. H. Fisch, trans.). Ithaca: Cornell University Press. (Original work published 1744).

Weinstock, S. (1926). "Die platonische Homerkritik und ihre Nachwirkung." *Philologus* 82.

Wordsworth, W. (1850). "Preface to Lyrical Ballads and Appendix." *In* Wordsworth, *Selected Prose.* New York: Penguin, 1988.

Zink, M. (1999). *The Invention of Literary Subjectivity* (D. Sices, trans.). Baltimore: Johns Hopkins University Press.

CHAPTER 3

....

TRAGEDY

....

J. M. BERNSTEIN

Plato's Complaint

....

Tragedy matters to philosophy in part because philosophy at its inception attempts to authorize itself, at least in part, by banishing the tragic poets. Something of tragedy directly challenges philosophy's original self-understanding; some content or manner of tragedy requires either refutation or acknowledgment, but cannot be put aside. In analyzing the relation between tragedy and philosophy, it is tragedy's proximity to philosophy that requires interrogation, rather than, say, the question of "What is tragedy?"—a topic best construed as belonging to poetics or literary theory.

When Plato banishes the poets in book 10 of the *Republic*, it might be thought that the banishment is aiming at all poetry or even all art, that the arts in general in being mimetic and sensible are themselves the proper antagonists for philosophical knowledge. In claiming that art is ontologically deficient, deceptive, and without practical import, however, Plato is doing no more than defining what art is: purposeful artifacts without a practical purpose. If there is a serious criticism of tragedy it must lie elsewhere. In part, art is an appropriate antagonist for philosophy because, with its power of mirroring everything, it may possess a synoptic vision, a vision of the world as a whole. This is also the premise for there being a clash between tragic art and philosophy. What truly concerns Plato, however, "the chief accusation" against the mimetic arts as corrupting and maiming, comes from the contrast between the ultra-stoicism delivered by the deliberative part of the soul, as taught by philosophy, and the lamentation that emerges from the mournful, pitying part of the soul that is the response to tragic performances:

> What is by nature best in us, because it hasn't been adequately educated by
> argument or habit, relaxes its guard over this mournful part because it sees

another's sufferings, and it isn't shameful for it, if some other man who claims to be good laments out of season, to praise and pity him; rather it believes that it gains the pleasure and wouldn't permit itself to be deprived of it by despising the whole poem. I suppose that only a certain few men are capable of calculating that the enjoyment of other people's sufferings has a necessary effect on one's own. For the pitying part, fed strong on these examples, is not easily held down in one's own sufferings. (Plato 1968: 606a–b; see also 426–34)

The question as to whether the theatrical experience of feeling pity for the sufferings of those who do not deserve to suffer weakens one's own ability to endure suffering can be set aside for the moment. What underlies Plato's critique of tragedy is more general: while the tragic (and comic) poets do not know nature in the way science does, they do know what makes people weep (or laugh); they understand the routine and systematic ways in which human action fails, and the multitude of liabilities that all things human bear.

The poets know the causes of human misery, and the fragility of all human goods and practices. Like the philosopher, the poet too has a synoptic vision: tragedy (and comedy) is a view of the world as a whole. The tragic world-view perceives human life as inherently self-contradictory, as continually bound to opposing goods and impossible differences, as bounded by irredeemable loss; what is self-contradictory or seeped in loss cannot be cognitively mastered, but it can, and should be, understood, felt, acknowledged, accepted. In tragedy we understand through feeling, and what we feel, finally, is grief. Tragic knowledge is performative and sensible as opposed to philosophical knowledge that is thetic and intelligible. There is indeed an ancient quarrel between philosophy and tragedy: what Plato finds truly intolerable about tragedy (and comedy) is the thought that such a view of the world be ultimate and final, that human life be lamentable or absurd.

Let me generalize from Plato's complaint. Tragedy is a form of attention best exemplified by tragic dramas. What tragedy attends to are limit situations where the paradigms of civil reason that philosophy seeks to authorize are undone. To borrow a trope from Stanley Cavell, tragedy is not a form of skepticism, but concerns the truth of skepticism, that is, what the skeptical view reveals as requiring acknowledgment: most simply the limits of knowledge and will. Tragedy reveals that life is aporetic, that life is not unconditionally or self-sufficiently rational, consistent, orderly, lovable, intelligible, safe, lawful, or moral. Consider this list of items as collectively comprising what we think of as the achievements of culture and civilization. Tragedy brings into view what the triumphs of civilization—what philosophy rationally celebrates—have sought to repress, dominate, discount, deauthorize, and empty. Tragedy is the return of the repressed. For example, true descriptions of the world are not unconditional: what Oedipus knows is true, but there are other descriptions of the same phenomena. Ignorance shadows knowledge, always. Tragedy reveals the limits of culture: the authority of nature we thought we had left behind returns. Tragedy reveals the limits of freedom: we make the world, but not under conditions of our own choosing. Free action is always subject to interference: contingency and necessity are perpetual enemies of autonomy. So it goes: reason is shadowed by unreason, determinacy by indeterminacy, meaning by the absolute loss of meaning, virtue by murderousness, happiness by suffering, life by death. Tragedy reveals that the relation between the affirmative and its negative shadow is internal, that there is an agonizing intimacy between what we hold dearest and what we most wish to avert.

From the thought that tragedy is a form of attention that brings into view a limiting condition of cultural life, a number of things follow. First, tragedy is relational, not skeptical. Again, what tragedy reveals is that the good at issue—reason, order (cultural or legal or moral), freedom, meaning, authority, progress, and so forth—is indeed good but not unconditionally so. Martha Nussbaum's phrase "the fragility of goodness" (1988) is about right. Fragility, vulnerability, loss, death, irredeemable suffering cannot be outflanked or done away with. But the goods those forces destroy are not less good thereby; for tragedy, the world attains the worth proper to it only through a vision of its transience. Second, what returns in tragedy will depend on what is repressed; this is why tragedy is historical and changing. Third, because tragedy concerns limits, it appears as an interruption of rational culture. Fourth, because tragedy appears as return and interruption, it cannot be held in a steady, firm, unchanging, fully coherent view. Because tragedy grieves it *pulls* at philosophy, even so-called tragic philosophies. Fifth, the form of attention required is that of a reminder, a ritual, a drama, not a thesis or doctrine. Tragic understanding can be performed, but not stated. The limits that tragic attention focuses on are revealed or disclosed, not demonstrated or proven. Sixth—the ultimate rebuke to philosophy—because tragedy concerns the aporetic and indigestible, it makes philosophy's theodicies appear naive, its harmonizing gestures overblown and absolutist. And when philosophy tones down its ambitions by becoming modest and pragmatic, tragedy shows its ameliorations to be self-deceived: the hard truths of human suffering remain.

Arguably, the best philosophical meditations on tragedy know these truths about tragedy, just as Plato knew them, perfectly well, but rather than attempting to disqualify tragedy, each, in its own way, seeks to accommodate tragic thought. In order to gain the measure of these accommodations, I will set in place a dialogue between our two greatest philosophical meditations on tragedy—Aristotle's *Poetics* and Hegel's historicized, modern version of it in his *Lectures on Fine Art*—and three tragic narratives: *Oedipus the King*, *Hamlet*, and the emergent tragic narration of the Holocaust.

ARISTOTLE'S PITY?

Pity is the feeling which arrests the mind in the presence of whatsoever is grave and constant in human suffering and

unites it with the human sufferer. Terror is the feeling which
arrests the mind in the presence of whatsoever is grave and
constant in human suffering and unites it with the secret
cause.

—James Joyce, *A Portrait of the Artist as a Young Man*

At the beginning of chapter 6 of the *Poetics*, Aristotle states that a tragedy is the
imitative representation (*mimesis*) of an action that has weighty and far-reaching
consequences, is of a certain magnitude, and is complete and self-contained; it is
presented through language that has been made sensuously attractive; the mode of
the presentation is through dramatic enactment by agents rather than report; and
through the arousal of pity and fear in the spectators it brings about a catharsis,
an affective working through of experiences of that kind. Equally central to Aristotle's definition of tragedy is the claim that protagonists of a tragic drama should
be admirable persons, better versions of ourselves rather than either demigods or
lowlifes; and in being like ourselves, their character makes them susceptible to acting in untoward ways, the consequences of which are (potentially) disastrous for
themselves and those around them.

Aristotle's definition subtly and powerfully connects an account of the internal logic of tragic dramas with a normative construal of their effects on the viewer.
The formal ingenuity of the account is deepened by the content: the internal logic
of tragedies provides a partial categorical interpretation of the nature and conditions of human action, while its affective impact elicits the constitutive emotions
of the social bonds connecting us to our fellow citizens.

As Hegel will after him, Aristotle conceives of tragedy as an interrogation
of human action: both the form and the content of tragedies are determined by
the nature of action. Aristotle directly tailors the shape of a drama to the unity
of action: a drama is an action that is whole and complete. By "whole" Aristotle
means possessing a beginning, middle, and end. A beginning is an action that does
not presuppose any antecedent events for its intelligibility, but itself gives rise to
further events. An "end," conversely, is something that naturally—all but inevitably—follows from what preceded it but does not have consequential effects. The
"middle" is composed of the ramifying events connecting beginning with end in
a broadly causally coherent manner. Aristotle calls the causal structure binding
beginning to end "plot"; plot, he contends, is the soul of tragedy.

Plots have cognitive and affective force because their shape recapitulates the
unity of a life. In life, of course, there are no absolute beginnings, so the idea of a
dramatic beginning borrows its structural and metaphorical authority from the
fact that each agent is a new beginning, the possibility of there being a new route
through a shared world. Every beginning refers back to an agent's being born, to a
natural birth and a second birth into a particular social world. Equally, in life there
are no significant events that do not lead to further events; hence, every tragic

end gestures toward our final end, our death. And routinely tragedies end with more than a figurative gesture toward death, but with the actual death of their protagonists.

For Aristotle, what binds the intelligibility of action to the unitary arc inscribing a human life is that it is through action that agents achieve, or fail to achieve, happiness. Happiness here refers to the ideal end of human activity, that for the sake of which we pursue any ends whatsoever. It is because happiness and unhappiness, in this strong sense, depend on action that Aristotle urges that dramas be about action and have the unity of action as their norm, rather than being about an individual and having the persistence of that individual through a series of events be the source of unity. Analogously, Aristotle contends that character in drama is for the sake of determining the quality or meaning of an action, and the thought present in speeches for showing the deliberative process leading to a course of action. In drama, all thought and character are for the sake of action, and all action is for the sake of friendship.[1]

It is friendship, *philia*, love in its familial, civic, and romantic forms, that mediates between the structure of a dramatic plot and the feelings of fear and pity that it is to arouse. Plot structures have three components: reversal, recognition, and suffering (*pathos*). Reversal is a change into the contrary of things being done—either a change from good fortune to bad, or from bad fortune to good—in conformity to probability or necessity. Reversals relate to expectations, both the hero's and the spectator's; reversals reveal the true causal chain that has been unfolding. Hence, in tragedy there is a doubleness to all action: on the one hand, action relates to the intentions of the agents; on the other hand, actions are conditioned by forces or have unintended consequences that only slowly emerge and affect the lives of the agents. The power of plotting depends on showing precisely how the two aspects of action are connected, how, for example, the unintended consequences of an action belong to that action, complete it. This is how reversals of fortune are connected to recognition: hero and spectator come to understand the forces and relations that have been forming and deforming their actions all along. But recognition has another aspect: not only does it bring about "a change from ignorance to knowledge," but in so doing it simultaneously brings "the characters into either friendship (*philia*) or enmity, and concerning matters which bear on prosperity or affliction" (Aristotle 1987: 1452a29–32). Finally, by suffering Aristotle intends destructive or painful actions, such as those that cause visible deaths, or excessive torments or woundings.

Aristotle's account of recognition already makes clear that what makes passing from ignorance to knowledge tragic is partially determined by its revealing who is truly a friend (a kin or loved one) and who truly an enemy, so recognition bears upon our happiness or misery through bearing on the fate of our constitutive bonds with others. This argument is pressed further in chapter 14, where Aristotle urges that sufferings are most terrible and hence most pitiable when they concern *philia* relations: when brother kills or intends to kill brother, son kills father, mother kills son, son kills mother, and so on. While the breadth of Aristotle's account of tragedy turns on his attaching tragic form to the contours of human action—and the contours of human action to the shape of a human life stretching out between birth and death—its depth turns on binding the reversals, recognitions, and sufferings that compose a plot to the basis of society and civilization: our *philia* relations (Belfiore 1992: 364–67). This is why in tragedy private misery so irresistibly topples into social chaos, even without kings and queens and the like: in Ibsen's play *A Doll's House*, as Nora slams the door behind her, we can hear a whole society tremble. In tragedy, it is as if what truly binds beginnings and ends are the bonds that hold us together and the forces within each of us and within the nature of the bonds themselves that are bent on destroying them. Tragic ends are deaths that are too soon; their interruption of life is the fact and the sign that the bonds constituting our lives with others have been terribly severed.

In this light, it appears right to say that pity and fear are fundamentally social emotions. Aristotle defines pity as a painful emotion whose object is the undeserved suffering of another. In identifying with the sufferer, we draw close to her, acknowledging that her fate could be our own, that together we "live in a world of terrible reversals, in which the difference between pitier and pitied is a matter far more of luck than of deliberate action" (Nussbaum 1992: 267). Pity is an affective form of recognition, but in recognizing the sufferer in this way, we are both acknowledging and affirming the bond connecting us. In tragedy, pity is a stand-in for the social bond. Conversely, then, fear always speaks to the anticipation of sufferings that token the collapse of the social bond. All this has been beautifully elaborated by Amélie Rorty:

> Just whom do we pity and what do we fear? The tragic hero? Ourselves? Humanity? All three, and all three in one.... Since we are also essentially social and political beings, connected to others by civic *philia*, we treat the welfare of our friends and family as essential to our own welfare. Our *philoi* form a series of expanding circles starting from the closest family and friends, to partners in a common civic project (*koinonia*), and to those who—like members of the human species—share a common form of life. (1992: 13)

If tragedy speaks to the necessity and the terrible vulnerability of the social bond, then Plato's complaint is not altogether wrong: no life is immune to disaster, to the utter destruction of what matters most. These are grounds indeed for repudiating transient, vulnerable life, for seeking stoic self-sufficiency and community with unchanging ideas, for hoping that some god or some therapy or some medical cure will permanently insulate us from such suffering and such loss. For the tragedian, however, to respond stoically to disaster is to deny the depth of its significance: in grief, we howl and lament the loss of what matters most. In *The Trojan Women*, we know Hecuba first as the mother maddened with grief at the murder of her son, set for revenge; at the conclusion, in contrast, we hear an unbearable two-voiced lamentation between Hecuba and the chorus at the final destruction of Troy:

O gods' house, city beloved // alas // you are given the red flame and the spear's iron. // You will collapse to the dear ground and be nameless. // Ash as the skyward smoke wing / piled will blot from my sight the house where I lived once. // Lost shall be the name on the land, / all gone, perished. Troy, city of sorrow, / is there no longer. // Did you see, did you hear? // The crash of the citadel. // The earth shook, riven // to engulf the city. (Euripides 1958: lines 1317–27).

One "of the dark lessons of tragedy is that there are no lessons to be learnt in order to avoid tragedy"(Rorty 1992: 18). But this fact bears on what we are to make of Aristotle's notion of catharsis. In fact, Aristotle would have little time for either Hecuba's maddened vengefulness or her lamentation at the ruin of Troy: the latter is concerned with those who are victims only, not agents, while the former is a collapse into vicious immorality. Aristotle's conception of tragic action normatively demands that the reversals to which tragic heroes and heroines are subject should be a probable consequence of their own doing: it is their error that both explains and rationalizes their fall. And in chapters 13 and 14, where Aristotle schematizes and evaluates types of tragic plot, he praises as best those dramas in which the agent either acts from ignorance and learns the awfulness of his deed afterward (*Oedipus the King*) or, even better, where the recognition of the bonded relation comes in time to prevent the deed being done (*Iphigenia in Tauris*). But this is to say that Aristotle aims to answer Plato, at least in part, by demonstrating how tragedies, as the interrogation of the structures of human action, yield moral insight and promote moral truth.[2] Aristotle harmonizes tragedy with philosophy by providing a normative scheme that promotes tragedies that refine moral understanding and insight, and devalues tragedies in which, as Plato complained, either grief turns into immorality or there is nothing left to be done but lament. Ideally, in accordance with his preferred moral image of the world, Aristotle seeks to apportion pity in proportion to virtue.

But this cannot be quite the whole story since catharsis is not purely cognitive, and it is intimately connected with the experiences of fear and pity. Although it is evident that Aristotle intended his normative scheme to clarify whom we should pity and why, which misfortunes are deserved and which not, the truth is that pity and fear are more generous, expansive, and even promiscuous than Aristotle's moral scheme permits. However horrifying is Hecuba's killing of the sons of Polymestor, we understand how her grief at the murder of her own son might madden her so, driving her to revenge. We understand, too, that revenge is not utterly opposed to morality; on the contrary, revenge "is a desire to keep faith with the dead...the violence it engenders is a ritual form of respect for the community's dead—therein lies its legitimacy" (Ignatieff 1997: 188). We might never act as Hecuba does, but the murder in our hearts is mimetically attuned to the murder in hers. So it is that we pity and grieve for her.

A more generous sense of pity entails a less moralized and less cognitive conception of catharsis. The enduring quality of the pity-fear-catharsis formula, what keeps that formula part of our critical present, is that it captures something of the emotional force of tragedy beyond the confines of Aristotle's moralism. As Jonathan Lear explains, "normal educated people in normal circumstances and outside of the theater seem to have certain beliefs that they do not feel" (1992: 332).[3] Because tragic *mythos* can only be understood through mimetic participation, then tragedy enables us to unify our darkest beliefs with the feelings appropriate to those beliefs, a unification that if continuously present would make ordinary life impossible. Because those beliefs go to the bases of human existence, it is important that at least sometimes we be able to have the feelings appropriate to them without having to suffer the full range of consequences the objects of those beliefs would involve outside the theater. Part of the relief signified by the notion of catharsis is that we are able to feel the truth of our deepest existential beliefs without either moral monitoring or having to suffer their empirical consequences. If the objects of our pity and fear are, also, of irredeemable losses, wild desires, and the power of unassuagable misery, then it becomes necessary to sense in catharsis something akin to the experience of mourning. Does not the experience of tragedy initiate us into the language and work of grief, teach us to count our losses and acknowledge our wounds beyond healing? Is not tragedy a series of fragmented lessons in the acknowledgment of our finitude? We know that the division of labor between the chorus and the protagonists in Greek tragedy refers to the differences between the poetry of the past and the prose of the present, between ancient religion and present politics, between choral lamentation and heroic action (see Vernant and Vidal-Naquet 1988; Loraux 2002). In a sense, Aristotle focuses on action at the expense of lamentation. But the pity-fear-catharsis formula speaks beyond this bias, reminding us of what Aristotle, following Plato, was at pains to repudiate: mournful life.

OEDIPUS THE KING

> Many the wonders but nothing walks stranger than man...
> Language, and thought like the wind
> And the feelings that make the town,
> He has taught himself, and shelter against the cold,
> Refuge from rain. He can always help himself.
> He faces no future helpless. There's only death
> That he cannot find an escape from.
>
> —Sophocles, *Antigone*

Aristotle appears to have written the *Poetics* with both eyes on Sophocles, and especially on *Oedipus the King*. It is thus a constant surprise that the *Poetics* so deftly ignores the theology and piety structuring so much tragic literature. How does Aristotle manage the deflection? How do we? At least in part by hearing gods-talk as primitive, sublimed talk about the forces of chance, history, society, and nature that lie outside the power of intentional action—the very topic that Sophocles is beginning to broach in the ode to man. Again, it is the doubleness of human action—what is within in contrast to what is outside the command of the agent—that tragic plots reveal.[4]

Part of the disturbing power of *Oedipus the King* is how it deploys the simplest and most unavoidable version of the doubleness of action: present provinciality as opposed to retrospective insight. The play is structured around the duality between knowledge and ignorance: Oedipus is driven by the conceits that human suffering is ultimately caused by human ignorance and that he can save the city a second time by discovering the truth behind the curse destroying it. Formally, the forward movement of the play is from ignorance to knowledge, but here, as opposed to the allegory of the cave, each step closer to knowledge is equally a step closer to (private) disaster. It so happens that disaster and saving the city are not separable; hence, what is most awful and what is most precious are not opposites—which is at least one of Sophocles' repudiations of the ambitions of civic enlightenment.[5]

Oedipus does not know the deep facts about his identity, facts that are also integral to the curse plaguing the city. Each episode brings a new epistemic helper—Creon, Teiresias, Jocasta, the messenger, the herdsman—who contributes a clue. But the difference between ignorance and knowledge structuring the plot is also the relation between Oedipus and the audience. Like Teiresias, we already know the truth of Oedipus's identity, yet our godly retrospective knowledge of the whole is useless to us—the stage, like the past, is another (ontological) country. Part of the uncanniness of the play turns on how its movement—the progressive, futural unlocking of the past that allows the play's end to reveal the truth of Oedipus's beginning, hence the truth connecting (every) beginning to (every) end—not only reveals something about the temporal and epistemic provinciality governing action, but does so in a manner that precisely mirrors the relation between play and audience. Because the knowledge necessary for action is routinely unavailable, because we are all temporally provincial, then routinely the knowledge that matters comes too late: we know what we need to know to prevent disaster only through the disaster that arrives. Oedipus suffers his temporal provinciality, but that provinciality is constitutive of human agency.

Exactly what it is that Oedipus knows and does not know is complex. Oedipus is known and knows himself fully in his public, political role; Oedipus as king appears as free from the entanglements of past and family, his rule a consequence of knowledge and leadership. Conversely, as mere man, in his maternal and paternal identity, he knows less than he supposes, and we onlookers know that he is unknown to himself. The standard reading of this situation is backward. For example, Charles Segal opens his account thus: "[Oedipus] lacks the basic information about his origins that gives man his human identity and sets him apart from the undifferentiated realm of nature and the anonymous, unindividuated realm of beasts" (1999: 207).[6] This cannot be correct as stated since Oedipus does know who he is *as citizen*, which is to say, as formed by civilization. What he does not know is not his proper, civil name, but his improper name, his nameless name, his animal nameless belonging to the natural realm. And even were he to know these facts, it is not clear he would or could know fully what they mean; all this is to say that we do not know what our *forever past* natural belonging means. And that must matter because it entails that civilization can never know or therefore never fully overcome its past as nature: the authority of nature is forever surpassed by but continues to haunt civilization: "[P]arricide and incest are poetic metaphors for what human nature does to itself (logically) when it becomes *political*" (Harris 1997: 217).

All this is perspicuous in the play: nature as the gift of life and the power of death conditions the city; it remains an authority, beyond the grasp of meaning and law, which must be acknowledged but can never be mastered—*known*. So the hubris of Oedipus the knower is the hubris of civilization in its departure from the authority of nature. Oedipus becomes king by solving the riddle of the animal with its changing—four, two, three—number of legs, but does not recognize that it applies to himself, or that it inscribes the *natural* arc of a human life. He supposes that his solving of the riddle is his mastery over nature. It is thus no accident that the pollution destroying the city is failed birth: the horrendous and terrifying eruption of the absence of the gift of life. It is this gift that we cannot master and on which civilization depends, absolutely. By coming to know his maternity and paternity, his birth, Oedipus will give birth back to the city. The truth is that every death, every stillborn, every infant mortality, but also every sickness and undeserved pain is *pollution*: unmasterable nature haunting civilization.

Oedipus the knower is the image of the presumption of a synoptic philosophy, self-sufficient and untroubled by the limitations of time and place. Oedipus at the end is blind because he possesses impossible knowledge: utterly natural and utterly political at the same time. The overcoming of the difference between nature and civilization is somehow inhuman: we cannot have synoptic knowledge of the identity in difference of nature and civilization *as agents*, as participants in a civil world. Only in our removal from praxis can we properly acknowledge the connection between civil law and natural law, *nomos* and *physis*. In being blind, lame Oedipus, three-footed Oedipus who was born old, loses even the remnant of uprightness: sight. He is like a hobbling parable of the riddle he solved. In one day a story unfolds that allows Oedipus to attach his end to his beginning: the unity of the plot and the shape of a life are one. The parabola of the story is the emergence out of and return to nature of a being who is constitutively unnatural, civil. The tragic knowledge the play offers is the necessity and instrumental uselessness of the knowledge provided. As tragic knowers we too are blind.

HEGEL'S TRAGIC DIALECTIC?

> Everything tragic is based upon an irreconcilable opposition.
> As soon as a reconciliation sets in or becomes possible, the
> tragic disappears.
>
> —Goethe, Remark, June 6, 1824, reported by
> Chancellor von Müller

With its long backward glance to ancient Greece as a model for overcoming what it took to be the shallow rationalism (or skepticism) of epistemology-dominated modern philosophy and the equally shallow instrumental rationality of modern civil society, German Idealism had Greek tragedy in view even more than ancient philosophy. Recognizing that tragedy elaborated a synoptic vision of its own, the idealists essayed the idea of producing a philosophical analogue of tragedy. Hegel's emphases are those of this tradition: employing, almost always, *Antigone* as his paradigm, Hegel displaces the idea of a tragic flaw, the waywardness of human action, *hamartia*, with opposition, collision, conflict, contradiction, and transgression. Like Aristotle, Hegel thought suffering counted as tragic only if it was the result of an objective obstruction (an objective *pathos*): individuals discover that they can realize a fundamental end (ideal, value, law, orientation) only through transgressing an opposing but equally fundamental end. Antigone can obey the absolute obligation to bury her brother only through breaking the law of the state denying the right of burial to its enemies; in defying the state, she asserts the right of individuality (and the right of the dead) against the ethical demand sacrificing the individual to universal law. (Antigone's clash with Creon thus rehearses another version of the clash between tragedy and philosophy.) Transgressive action actualizes the conflict, manifesting the irreconcilability of the two powers and thus causing the downfall of, at least, the original transgressor, as well as the original harmony between the competing powers.[7] Suffering is the existential reality of social opposition: because we suffer, we acknowledge we have erred.

Conflict is no longer seen as a sign of bias, irrationality, or subjective error; on the contrary, conflict is now accorded the dignity of belonging to the fabric of the world: it reveals either a perpetual surd in the order of human existence (e.g., between the desires of culture and the limits of nature; between the competing demands for universality and generality as opposed to individuality and singularity; between love and law; among essentially incommensurable goods or spheres of culture), and/or becomes the fundamental mechanism through which social learning and historical progress occur. When these conflicts are seen as a *self-division* bringing destruction to its component elements that therefore demand a resolution, reconciliation, then the tragic and the dialectic coincide.[8] Hegel supplements or refines Aristotelian catharsis with the demand for reconciliation. Once the tragic and the dialectic are identified, it follows that tragedies become literary expressions of an existential modality—a modality that nonetheless transpires through action alone, hence the dual treatment of tragedy within the *Phenomenology of Spirit*: on the one hand, Hegel uses *Antigone* as a clue to unlock the fundamental structures governing Greek ethical life and, through Greek ethicality, the logic of the historical processes emerging from its self-incurred collapse; on the other hand, Hegel reads tragedy as the poetic genre proper to Greek ethical life through which it becomes self-conscious about the irreconcilability of the deep structures constituting it.[9]

It is this dual understanding of tragedy—as the intrinsic dialectical movement of society, history, and thought, as opposed to being just one poetic genre among others—that underlies Hegel's contention that, finally, tragedy as a literary genre, like all art and religion, must give way to philosophy as the adequate repository of our collective self-understanding. His *Lectures on Fine Art* provide a perspicuous aesthetic account of the death of tragedy. Hegel conceives of art, religion, and philosophy as the three social forms through which societies become self-conscious about their founding values and commitments; analogously, different forms of art come to dominate under different historical circumstances. In general, art can be the fulcrum for collective self-consciousness only when, for that society as a whole, conceptual understanding and its sensuous realization, meaning and configuration, remain indissolubly bound together. Two specific conditions are necessary for tragedy proper. It must be the case that the standing and fate of morals and justice "should throughout keep an individual shape in the sense that they depend exclusively on individuals and reach life and actuality only in and through them" (Hegel 1975, 1: 184); that is, the heroic individual must appear as the "living instrument and animating sustainer" (1975, 2: 1162) of the universal powers that transcend her. Conversely, it must also be the case that such individuals be incapable of separating themselves from the ethical whole to which they belong. In brief, tragedy can be formative for collective self-understanding when the fundamental forces operative in a society can be represented through the actions of individual agents (however lofty); this is the thought that allows Hegel's historicist aesthetic account of tragedy to rework Aristotle's ahistorical poetics. Conversely, when, owing to its complexity, the rationality of a state can be validated through rational reflection alone, through philosophy rather than aesthetic representation, then tragedy is no longer formative for culture as a whole.

It is precisely in line with these conditions that Hegel distinguishes ancient from modern tragedy, Sophocles from Shakespeare. Because Hegel argues that all art forms have their time of emergence, flourishing, and decay, it is plausible for him to regard modern tragedy as the decay of tragedy. But this cannot be quite correct since Hegel also regards modernity, with its unconditional acknowledgment of the rights of individuality and subjectivity, as breaking from all previous social forms. One might then suppose that Shakespeare, rather than being the degenerated outcome of Greek tragedy (the neoclassical view), would be the initiator of a new, perhaps nondialectical, conception of tragedy. What Hegel cannot quite determine is what the relation is between individuals and universal powers in modern tragedy. He first insists that such a relation is never missing, but because individuals are no longer the charismatic bearers of the universal, their animating source, he must loosen the form of relation. Here is the moment in which the architecture of his argument wobbles and then collapses: "But since now it is not the substantial element in these [real world] spheres which engrosses the interest of individuals, their aims are broadly and variously particularized and in such detail that what is truly substantial can often glimmer through them in only a very dim way; and, apart from this, these aims acquire an altogether different form" (Hegel 1975, 2: 1223). Somehow, dim glimmerings of universal forms seems a wild misdescription of what *King Lear*, for example, has to say about love. Something of tragedy has died for us, but neither the fate of tragic *art* nor the fate of tragic *experience* is adequately thought by Hegel. Philosophy's serene overcoming of tragedy cannot go unchallenged.

Hamlet

Shakespeare "seems to write without any moral purpose."
—Samuel Johnson, *Preface to Shakespeare*

Before examining the death of tragedy issue, Shakespeare's modernity requires outlining if we are to gauge the fate of tragic art. There is a close analogy between Hegel's reading of Descartes and his interpretation of *Hamlet*.[10] While Descartes's method of doubt terminating in the *cogito* frees philosophy from theology, uncovering the founding role of self-conscious subjectivity, for Hegel the Cartesian subject nonetheless remains isolated, homeless, alienated from the world. Hegel reads Shakespeare as, in a sense, elaborating nothing but the tragedy of this new subjectivity: "the progress of a great soul, its inner development, the picture of its self-destructive struggle against circumstances, events, and their consequences" (Hegel 1975, 2: 1230).[11] But precisely because it is only subjectivity—its passions and doubts—that is at stake, and not the founding universals of the society in general, Hegel perceives only alienation. On Hamlet: "But death lay from the beginning in the background of Hamlet's mind. The sands of time do not content him. In his melancholy and weakness, his worry, his disgust at all the affairs of life, we sense from the start that in all his terrible surroundings he is a lost man, almost consumed already by inner disgust before death comes to him from the outside" (Hegel 1975, 2: 1231–32). Hamlet is more antihero than hero; his death is that of a man of doubt, not the founder of a new culture.

Writing nearly 50 years before Hegel, J. G. Herder, replying to classicist critiques of Shakespeare, sees in *Hamlet* a new aesthetic paradigm in which every work, rather than following formal rules, is required to solve *for itself* the question of what it is to be a work of art in an original, nonimitative way—each work depicting its own drama, its own way of being a tragedy. In reflecting a world that is fragmented and divided, the new tragedy displaces the unity of action with event and history—history with all its diversity, complexity, and fragmentariness. In this diverse world, the distinction between genres—comedy, tragedy, pastoral, historical drama—collapses. Speaking of Shakespeare as the educator of "us northern men," Herder writes:

> When I read him, it seems to me as if theatre, actors, scenery, all vanish! Single leaves from the book of events, providence, the world, blowing in the storm of history. Individual impressions of nations, classes, souls, all the most various and disparate machines, all the ignorant blind instruments…which combine to form a whole theatrical image, a grand event whose totality only the poet can survey. (1985: 168–69)

In a Herderesque vein, let me briefly think through the Descartes-Hamlet connection. *Hamlet* concerns the loss of metaphysical morality, the loss of a world of authoritative conventions and norms beyond the will, thought, desire, and actions of individuals. In the same way in which modern philosophical self-consciousness emerges through violence—the threat of the evil demon (Descartes), the state of nature with its threat of sudden and violent death (Hobbes), the battle for recognition between master and slave (Hegel) (see Hoffman 1987)—so Hamlet becomes self-conscious through the violent destruction of his gods: Claudius's killing of King Hamlet and sexing Queen Gertrude. Claudius is the evil demon of Hamlet's world; the death of his father and sexing of his mother produce Hamlet's melancholic doubt: how act in a world in which the very models for coherent action have been destroyed and only further violence on offer? So Shakespeare's play begins with the end of action in its Aristotelian sense, with the overriding sense that passions without the binding of social forms are useless grounds for action: "Purpose is but the slave to memory / Of violent birth but poor validity…. What to ourselves in passion we propose, / The passion ending, doth the purpose lose" (act 3, scene 2, lines 183–190). But this moves too quickly, for in a sense what Hamlet is working through throughout the play is precisely the loss of the father-king and the queen-mother as the last representatives of transcendent ideals that are also, of course, the source from which all our idealizations spring, the source of the very idea of transcendent authority. The father-king and the queen-mother must be destroyed as idealities and as authorities in order to become wholly human, and only if they can be regarded as human can Hamlet claim his humanity, find a way of living it. He never does quite manage the feat.

Arguably, the work of destruction occurs through sexual disgust. Routinely in Shakespeare, woman is represented as a divided creature: the virgin mother and the rapacious whore, goddess and beast. Gertrude's becoming a traitorous whore in Hamlet's eyes does no more than release what is already implicit in the overidealized vision of the mother goddess. Hamlet's raging disgust with his mother's overt sexuality becomes the ground for his disgust at women in general; it is that disgust that is then projected onto Ophelia. If the original images of father, mother, and Ophelia represented for Hamlet his binding to the world, the world being lovable, then in losing them as objects of love, he loses the world as lovable; hence, he loses the world. Hamlet's melancholy is for the ideality of a world now forever lost: this world no longer lovable, or terrible, in the way it once, perhaps, was.

Cavell perspicuously states the upshot of this dilemma:

> Shakespeare's *Hamlet* interprets the double staging of human birth—which means the necessity of accepting one's individuality or individuation or difference, say one's separateness—as the necessity of a double acceptance: an acceptance of one's mother as an independent sexual being whose life desire survives the birth of a son and the death of a husband, a life that may present itself to her son as having been abandoned by her; and an acceptance of one's father as a dependent sexual being whose incapacity to sustain desire you cannot revive, which may present itself to his son as having to abandon him. Hence the play interprets the taking of one's place in the world as a process of mourning, as if there is a taking up of the world that is humanly a question of giving it up. (2003: 188–89)[12]

We might think of this work of mourning, with the perpetual work of memory that is its consequence—Hamlet's last injunction to Laertes "to tell my story" (act 5, scene 2, line 354)—as making explicit the voice of lamentation implicit in Greek tragedy that Aristotelian catharsis and Hegelian reconciliation attempt to suppress.[13] With Shakespeare, tragedy becomes self-consciously the mode in which human spirituality is gathered fundamentally through memory and mourning.

In a sense, Hamlet's dilemma of how to act and Shakespeare's of how to write tragedies are the same: how to continue in the absence of authoritative norms for continuing. What does it mean to say, for tragedy, that each work provides its own accounting of what it is for it to be a work, a tragedy? At least, in part, it involves answering the question of what constitutes the terms of an individual life now that lives are no longer governed by given social roles. Part of what is at stake here involves seeing how external conflicts now become essentially internal, the self for itself now composed of many gods. Shakespeare internalizes the self as emphatically as but more profoundly than Descartes: the conflicts raging within the self are now permanent, regulating the contest between the warring gods within the perpetual work involved in being a self. However, acknowledging and measuring these gods nonetheless requires action, but action of a new kind: each action is now a testing of the meaning of the thought or passion underlying it, and so a staging or dramatizing or theatricalizing of it. We come to know the meaning of our passions and beliefs not through reflective ordering—philosophy's deepest conceit—but through seeing how they *play out* in the world. Hamlet's "antic disposition," his soliloquizing, his putting on of a play, his bantering with Ophelia, his pretense and his sincerity, are the mechanisms through which he might figure himself in relation to himself and the world he inhabits. Hegel eloquently claims that Shakespeare equips his characters with a wealth of poetry, but also he "actually gives them spirit and imagination, and by the picture in which they can contemplate and see themselves objectively like a work of art, he makes them free artists of their own selves, and thereby…can interest us not only in criminals but even in the most downright and vulgar clouts and fools" (Hegel 1975, 2: 1229–30). We might say that it is this new sense of the self and self-fashioning that enjoins Shakespeare's kind of tragic art with its emphasis on scenes, rapid movements from scene to scene, its subplots and minor characters, its continual sense of being improvised, its gripping lifelikeness combined with its great artificiality. Or is it Shakespeare's kind of theater that first gives us the terms for this new conception of the self? Either way, as Cavell states it, Hamlet's extreme sense of theater involves "his ceaseless perception of theater, say show, as an inescapable or metaphysical mark of the human condition, together with his endless sense of debarment from accepting the human condition as his (which is terribly human of him)" (2003: 187–88).

One further issue needs accounting for here. If it is the case that the limit situations of modern tragedy do not directly address the universals governing society as a whole, but only at most their deflection into individual lives, and sometimes not even that, then what are the normative terms of this new art? How do we measure tragic characters, our continuing pity and fear for them, if not through either morality or their connection to universal powers? What now, but really always, governs the breadth of pity? Seeing that Shakespeare's art does not match the terms of Hegel's aesthetic theory, A. C. Bradley offers a compelling response. Tragic art, he avers, provides us with a sense of meaning and significance independent of explicitly moral meaning and significance through providing a horrendous feeling of *waste*; through that sense of waste, we experience the value of all that has been wasted, abandoned, and ruined (1974: 16ff). Hamlet, Lear, Macbeth, Othello, and so on, are neither virtuous nor noble, nor often even decent: Hamlet shows not a drop of remorse for killing Polonius (only disappointment that the wrong person was killed) or for sending Rosencrantz and Guildenstern to their deaths; even in his most empathic moments, Lear sees the suffering of others as only a reflection of his own. Still, in our engrossed, nonjudgmental sense of waste, we sense that their lives matter and that human lives mattering and meaning extends beyond their being simply good or simply evil, virtuous or vicious, that there are terms of meaningfulness and loss that are not explicitly ethical or moral.[14] Bradley goes on to insist that beyond this fact it is equally the case that such mattering is often *akin* to the moral: because they suffer, *we* know they have erred, and hence we know that evil, say, "violently disturbs the order of the world" (1992: 25), even if it is a world in which the good perish and the evil flourish. In a sense, this thought extends Bradley's notion of waste, of what appreciating a life as wasted means. What he is thus pointing toward, however obliquely, is what might be called a "negative" morality, our sense of the uprising of the meaning of the moral through the experience of its emphatic absence. This matters to the fate of tragic thought.

The Death of Tragedy?

After its ceasing to be the repository of our collective self-understanding, tragic art continues in the mode of the ordinary, in the mode of recording how *all* individual lives suffer the collision and conflicts of culture that they feel powerless to transform but must nonetheless find a way through, not just how the existential features of our lives—love, death, friendship, isolation, children, parents—are encountered but even how we as individuals register the absence of connection to the major institutions governing our lives: war and peace. Perhaps we can say that tragic art, on the stage or in novels or films, presents exemplary but not ideal or transformative encounters with the limit situations of everyday life. This is why such art can feel both all important—it goes to the essence of the life we actually lead—and simultaneously marginal, minor, since the terms of society as a whole are not directly engaged or sensed as directly engageable: they continue above or beyond us, behind our backs, and worse, our sufferings and hopes fail to register in its wide counting of what does and does not matter. What is true of tragedy here—private depth and public futility—might be said of culture as a whole.

However, if tragedy is a form of attention to limit situations, then even if it is true that tragic art is no longer the bearer of our collective self-understanding, it seems implausible to believe that the constitutive forms of modern society can avoid encountering their limit situations, and hence that we can manage to address our world fully without tragic knowledge. While art may no longer be formative for society as a whole, might tragic understanding still be? From Georg Büchner's *Danton's Death*, with its bruised tracking of the tragedy of the French Revolution, to the account of tragedy and experience in Raymond Williams's *Modern Tragedy*, through Cavell's Vietnam-inspired lament at the end of his great essay on *King Lear*, the thought has reverberated that tragedy has moved into the world.

Tragedy moves into the world in multiple ways: in the shift from closed world to infinite universe, the fracture or destruction of *philia* relations leading to tragic isolation becomes a constant of ordinary lives; ecstatic efforts of national liberation succeed by installing new forms of tyranny; and nations unsure of their standing or their capacity to join their citizens together dramatize their sense of their mortality through violent acts of aggression that repress it altogether. But there is one case in which Bradley's negative morality joins the experience of attending to a limit situation that seems exemplary for the moral and political present. If anything looks like a limit situation in twentieth-century political experience, it was the policy, construction, and operation of the Nazi death camps in which the extermination of the Jewish people was attempted.

One of the great difficulties involved in thinking about evil is thinking about what it means to suffer evil, what responses to such extreme suffering typically are like, and what responses are open to us. To suffer a great evil is a devastation, and even if people survive such devastation physically, it is common for them not to survive spiritually. The term that has become the most common for talking about the effect of great suffering on those who survive is "trauma." Victims of great evil have been traumatized. Typically, we think that it is individuals who suffer from a trauma, but we are beginning to learn that collectivities, too, can be traumatized, that apart from individual trauma there is also what might be called cultural or social trauma.

Coming to experience an event as culturally traumatic need not mean coming to experience it as utterly paralyzing and debilitating for collective self-understanding. On the contrary—and this is the key argument of Jeffrey Alexander's remarkable essay "On the Social Construction of Moral Universals: The Holocaust from War Crime to Trauma Drama"—coming to experience and recognize an event as an immense evil that has been perpetrated upon our collective social body can be the first step in coming to code that event symbolically as evil, indeed, as the paradigm or archetype of evil. Once we have symbolically interpreted a historical event as a or the paradigm of evil, then in effect we have given ourselves a new moral universal, a new moral understanding of the world since now we have before our hearts and minds a model or emblem of what must not be done, what must never be done to others, what forever is impermissible and morally wrong. In coming to recognize an event as a paradigm of evil, we create or construct a new moral universal, we construct a new baseline for social morality, we construct a pivot upon which our life together now turns. Analyzing how such a recognition takes places is the crux of Alexander's essay; such an analysis is also what draws together the question of the meaning of the Holocaust with the question of the fate of tragedy in our time.

There is one significant difference between individual and collective trauma: collective traumas *become* traumas. In the period immediately follow the Second World War, what we today call the Holocaust did not exist under that description. Rather, from the end of the war through well into the 1960s, the German extermination of the Jews was considered to be an unspeakable atrocity committed upon the Jewish people by a perverse, politically reactionary movement in a nation that was predisposed to extreme anti-Semitism and to following orders. The end of the war was seen as a moment of triumph within a developing history of progress in which the forces of liberal, enlightened modernity were triumphing over pre- or antimodern forms of reaction.

To acknowledge that collective trauma "becomes" is to insist that its coming to be is socially mediated and need not have happened: there would have been no "Holocaust" if either Germany had won the war or, more interesting, if the camps had been liberated by the Russians. Sociologically, the fact that the Holocaust becomes traumatic and thereby becomes an event of exemplary evil means that the question of collective evil is not ontological—not a question of what—but epistemological: a question of understanding and knowledge and experience.[15] To say the question is epistemological is equivalent to saying that it is a question of how the events of the Nazi extermination of the Jews are narrated.

For an event to be narrated as a transformative traumatic evil, it must be understood as attacking the very fabric of a society's collective life. Hence, things construed as exemplarily traumatically evil are not only things thought to be excessively bad or wicked and therefore to be avoided, not done; more radically, they are conceived of as sources of horror and pollution that must be contained at all costs. In order for the Holocaust to become an exemplary traumatic evil, it must be coded as evil (and not just a war crime or an atrocity to anonymous people): it must be weighed as far worse than everyday evils; it must be narrated in a way that makes clear what the traumatizing actions were, who was responsible for them, who were the victims, what were the long-term implications, and what can be done to prevent the same again; and it must make both victims and perpetrators appear as like ourselves. In order to be conceived as an exemplary traumatic evil, the mass killings of the Jews *first* needed to be regarded as a singular event, wholly unlike any event that had ever happened, to be seen as unique. (For some this meant, erroneously, to become mysterious and inexplicable, beyond moral understanding, and hence outside the normal course of history: standing alone, interrupting history.) The coming of this redescription was prepared for in part by the invention, shortly after the war, of the term "genocide" and of the Nuremberg trials coming up with the new idea of crimes against humanity. These two concepts begin to open up the idea that a new, and therefore unknown, type of crime was committed by the Nazis, since it appears not to have been done for any of the traditional reasons: securing political power, or more land, or more wealth, or as a component of a political project to secure these ends in ways that made it a necessary means. The Nazis appeared to want to eliminate all the Jews from the face of the earth for its own sake, and for no external reason. It was in light of this claimed inexplicability that mass murder was renamed "Holocaust" or "Shoah."

Eventually—through the popularity of *The Diary of Anne Frank*, the worldwide reception of the Eichmann trial and Hannah Arendt's account of it, the tarnishing of the image of the United States through its terrible involvement in Vietnam, the massive work of historiography, memorial building, fictional representation, and so forth, of the extermination of the Jews—the Holocaust began to be narrated differently. What replaced the ascending Enlightenment narrative of progress and improvement was now a tragic narration.

Again, a tragic dialectic is one in which contraries are united. What acknowledging the Holocaust as a transformative traumatic event has involved is coming to see modernity itself as tragic, as a movement of enlightenment and progress that simultaneously contains the horrendous powers of destruction displayed by the Holocaust as its own inverted image. Coming to see Nazism itself in the wider framework of modernity means seeing it in the context of the nationalist and imperialist dislocations of the nation-state, through the weakening of moral community and the rise of abstract morality, through the bureaucracy that organized the camps, through the efficiency and technological means through which the exterminations were carried out. Death as a system of production is the black inner lining of modernity itself. Hence, the great atrocities of the twentieth century, from colonialism and its exterminations, through the Holocaust, to the firebombing of Dresden and the bombings of Hiroshima and Nagasaki all belong to the possibilities of modernity. Seeing them in this way is seeing them in the light of the Holocaust as the paradigm trauma drama of modernity.

Once modernity is understood as Janus-faced—like the hero of a tragedy who is noble but has a tragic flaw—then the way is opened to perceiving the events of the Holocaust as terrible but exemplary of modernity at its worst, and thereby to identifying with its Jewish victims as vulnerable and defenseless beings like ourselves. It is just this identification that transforms the moral meaning of modernity: in place of understanding the human through its powers of reason, speech, and free will—collectively the emblems of civil reason—we have come to identify with others through their capacity to suffer, to undergo torment and humiliation; and thus in place of the universality of rational humanity, emerging is the universalism of a solidarity among vulnerable humanity. Tragic solidarity is coming to displace the universalism of reason. What, then, is significant in the account of the emergence of the Holocaust as a moral universal is that it displaces normative justice by exemplary injustice, a progressive narration of modernity with a tragic metanarrative, and a displacement of the Enlightenment paradigm of the rational, autonomous subject with a tragic universalism premised upon fragility and vulnerability. By becoming exemplary, the Holocaust hence becomes a bridging metaphor for understanding major historical events—the extermination of the Herero people, the evil of Stalin's gulags, the Armenian, Cambodian, and Rwandan genocides, and on. The Holocaust's presumed uniqueness is, precisely, what engenders new terms of moral comparability, and so its nonuniqueness. The functioning of this new moral universal is, of course, erratic: it helped generate new international law about genocide, and it was the backdrop to the eventual intervention in Bosnia; too often, however, as in the case of Darfur, it remains like the old voice of conscience—well-meaning, serious, but without effect. It has too often remained as idle in the politics of the present as Euripides' *The Trojan Women* did in his.

Hegel's philosophical program, of which the political philosophy of the present is an echo, was to discover the rose in the cross of the present, that is, to demonstrate the rational authority of the dominant institutions of modernity in abstraction from the slaughter-bench of history producing them and the wreckage of the human surrounding them. The very idea of such a program, like the philosophical programs of Plato and Aristotle, involves a marginalizing and denial of tragedy—only thus is this kind of political thought possible. And I would argue that this philosophical task is necessary and unavoidable if we are to take full rational responsibility for the practices through which we reproduce our life together, in which we ask how we might remove unnecessary suffering, reward virtue with happiness, provide a system of justice fair to all. Philosophy could only begin its authorizing of a rational world by excluding tragedy, or by following the magnificent examples of Aristotle and Hegel, who saw clearly the claim of tragedy and sought to include it within philosophy's serene rational reconstruction of the world. But tragedy—the slaughter-bench and human wreckage—cannot be excluded or included because our disasters and sufferings are not external accretions to our triumphs; as Walter Benjamin puts it, "There is no document of civilization that is not at the same a document of barbarism" (1970: 258). Hence, taking full rational responsibility for our life together demands tragedy's implacable backward look, the acknowledgment of intolerable loss, participation in communal grief. Through the Holocaust we have learned that the paradigms of civil reason require tragic solidarity for their effectiveness and that moral universality must borrow some of its authority from the tragic recognition of evil. Tragic darkness is the necessary complement to the light of reason; tragic lamentation, the constant companion of philosophical hope. As Plato saw, the contest between philosophy and tragedy arises because the vision of each requires an account of the whole. It is neither exactly a philosophical thought nor a tragic one that these two necessary synoptic perspectives on the human are, finally, incommensurable one with the other.

NOTES

My gratitude to the New School for Social Research students in my "Tragedy and Philosophy" seminar in the fall of 2006, and even more to my colleague Paul Kottman, whose Shakespeare made mine possible.

1. The phrase "all action is for the sake of friendship" is the motto for John MacMurray's undervalued 1953 Gifford Lectures, *The Self as Agent*, and *Persons in Relation*.

2. For a pointed critique of Aristotle in this regard, see Freeland 1992.

3. Lear, surprisingly, concludes by urging that undergoing tragic catharsis is coming to realize that the world remains "a rational, meaningful place in which a person can conduct himself with dignity" (1992: 335). I would have thought that tragedy enjoins the thought that with luck we can conduct ourselves with dignity despite the fact that the world is finally groundless, chaotic, etc. Tragic consolation, when it comes, is far tougher and chillier than Lear's sunny conclusion images.

4. In her very fine essay, Nancy Sherman 1992 argues that intelligibility and avoidance are separate for Aristotle. Insofar we can have regret for what we could not have avoided doing, then on this reading Aristotle's scheme is not morally framed in the way I have been arguing against.

5. See Rocco 1997, chaps. 2 and 6, in which Sophocles' critique is shown to be a version of Theodor Adorno and Max Horkheimer's conception of the dialectic of enlightenment (and vice versa).

6. I should say that I regard Segal as our best reader of Sophocles, and this his finest book.

7. This is how to understand the notion of a dramatic beginning: it is the deed that makes manifest the underlying complexity of the situation in which it occurs. How Aristotelian Hegel is can be seen from the fact that his general account of art beauty turns on an account of tragic action. See Hegel 1975.

8. For an elegant tracking of this thesis see Peter Szondi 2002. While Szondi argues that tragedy is dialectic, he acknowledges that not all dialectic is tragic; irony, comedy, and humor are also dialectical forms. The test case for his thesis about tragedy, discussed below, is *Hamlet*. For a pointed reading of Hegel as thinker of the tragic, see Beistegui 2000: 11–37.

9. In Hegel's technical jargon, in the first instance tragedy represents the "in-itself" movement of Greek ethical life, while in the latter case tragedy represents Greek ethicality "for-itself." This technical language has a commonsense translation: what is seen as "in-itself" is perceived as essentially from a third-person, objective perspective, while what is "for-itself" is understood from a first-person perspective. Hegelian speculative knowledge means to join those two perspectives, to track their necessary internal connections; in brief, Hegelian dialectic is structured around the doubleness of action.

10. The argument of this and the following paragraph follows Gjesdal 2004. I should add here that, on the whole, Hegel does not so much misread *Hamlet* as misconstrue the significance of his reading.

11. The "sands of time" thought is central for all of Shakespearean tragedy. Northrop Frye opens *Fools of Time* thus:

> The basis of the tragic vision is being in time, the sense of the one-directional quality of life, where everything happens once and for all, where every act brings unavoidable and fateful consequences, and where all experience vanishes, not simply into the past, but into nothingness, annihilation. In the tragic vision death is, not an incident in life, not even the inevitable end of life, but the essential event that gives shape and form to life. (1967: 3)

12. At the conclusion of his pointed critique of deconstructive readings of *The Birth of Tragedy*, Henry Staten eloquently questions:

> Isn't all of *The Birth of Tragedy* concerned with the problem of giving a face and a voice, or faces and voices, to an absent, deceased, or voiceless entity called Dionysus, who is a figure not of any particular deceased being but decease in general, of all that is already dead or all that lives as already affected by its future death, and thus a sort of transcendental elegy whose figure is *prosopopeia*? (1990: 216)

No matter what else I would have wanted to say about *The Birth of Tragedy* here, I would have concluded with this idea of it being a transcendental elegy.

13. Unless one regards, as I do, Hegel's notion of reconciliation in the *Phenomenology* as itself a cultural form of mourning, what it means to regard the process of history as tragic dialectic.

14. See Frye 1967: 4. Frye thinks this *existential* feature of tragedy is the one that makes it incapable of being absorbed by philosophy.

15. What is an epistemological issue is not that the events of the Holocaust were evil or even radically evil—the Holocaust was a foreseeable intolerable harm produced by culpable wrongdoing—but that their evility was a collective trauma formative of a new moral universal. Even plainly evil events—the massacre of 300,000 Chinese civilians in Nanking by Japanese soldiers in 1938—can fail to become coded as traumatically evil, and hence fail to become radically reformative (refigurative) of prevailing moral

universals. For an interpretation of the "rape of Nanking" along these lines see Alexander 2003: 106–7.

REFERENCES

Alexander, J. (2003). "On the Social Construction of Moral Universals: The Holocaust from War Crime to Trauma Drama." *In* Alexander, *The Meanings of Social Life*. New York: Oxford University Press, 2003.

Aristotle. (1987). *The Poetics* (S. Halliwell, ed. and trans.). Chapel Hill: University of North Carolina Press.

Beistegui, M. de. (2000). "Hegel: or the Tragedy of Thinking." *In* M. de Beistegui and S. Sparks (eds.), *Philosophy and Tragedy*. London: Routledge.

Belfiore, E. (1992). Aristotle and Iphigenia. *In* A. O. Rorty (ed.), *Essays on Aristotle's Poetics*. Princeton: Princeton University Press.

Benjamin, W. (1970). "Theses on the Philosophy of History" (H. Zohn, trans.). *In* Benjamin, *Illuminations*. London: Fontana Books.

Bradley, A. C. (1974). *Shakespearean Tragedy*. London: Macmillan Press.

Cavell, S. (2003). *Disowning Knowledge in Seven Plays of Shakespeare*. Cambridge: Cambridge University Press.

Euripides. (1958). *The Trojan Women* (R. Lattimore, trans.). *In* D. Green and R. Lattimore (eds.), *Euripides III*. Chicago: University of Chicago Press.

Freeland, C. A. (1992). "Plot Imitates Action: Aesthetic Evaluation and Moral Realism in Aristotle's *Poetics*." *In* A. O. Rorty (ed.), *Essays on Aristotle's Poetics*. Princeton: Princeton University Press.

Frye, N. (1967). *Fools of Time*. Toronto: University of Toronto Press.

Gjesdal, K. (2004). "Reading Shakespeare—Reading Modernity." *Angelaki* 9(3), 17–31.

Harris, H. S. (1997). *Hegel's Ladder II: The Odyssey of Spirit*. Indianapolis: Hackett.

Hegel, G. W. F. (1975). *Aesthetics: Lectures on Fine Art* (T. M. Knox, trans.). Oxford: Clarendon Press.

Herder, J. G. (1985). "Shakespeare" (J. P. Crick, trans.). *In* H. B. Nisbet (ed.), *German Aesthetic and Literary Criciticism*. Cambridge: Cambridge University Press.

Hoffman, P. (1987). *Doubt, Time, Violence*. Chicago: University of Chicago Press.

Ignatieff, M. (1997). *The Warrior's Honor: Ethnic War and the Modern Conscience*. New York: Henry Holt.

Lear, J. (1992). "*Katharsis.*" *In* A. O. Rorty (ed.), *Essays on Aristotle's Poetics*. Princeton: Princeton University Press.

Loraux, N. (2002). *The Mourning Voice* (E. Rawlings, trans.). Ithaca: Cornell University Press.

Nussbaum, M. (1988). *The Fragility of Goodness: Luck and Ethics in Greek Tragedy and Philosophy*. Cambridge: Cambridge University Press.

Nussbaum, M. (1992). "Tragedy and Self-Sufficiency." *In* A. O. Rorty (ed.), *Essays on Aristotle's Poetics*. Princeton: Princeton University Press.

Plato. (1968). *The Republic* (A. Bloom, trans.). New York: Basic Books.

Rocco, C. (1997). *Tragedy and Enlightenment: Athenian Political Thought and the Dilemmas of Modernity*. Berkeley: University of California Press.

Rorty, A. O. (1992). "The Psychology of Aristotelian Tragedy." *In* A. O. Rorty (ed.), *Essays on Aristotle's Poetics*. Princeton: Princeton University Press.

Segal, C. (1999). *Tragedy and Civilization: An Interpretation of Sophocles*. University of Oklahoma Press.

Sherman, N. (1992). "Hamartia and Virtue." *In* A. O. Rorty (ed.), *Essays on Aristotle's Poetics*. Princeton: Princeton University Press.

Staten, H. (1990). *Nietzsche's Voice*. Ithaca: Cornell University Press.

Szondi, P. (2002). *An Essay on the Tragic* (P. Fleming, trans.). Stanford: Stanford University Press.

Vernant, J., and P. Vidal-Naquet. (1988). *Myth and Tragedy in Ancient Greece* (J. Lloyd, trans.). Cambridge, Mass.: Zone Books.

CHAPTER 4

COMEDY

TIMOTHY GOULD

THAT comedy is a serious business is—and probably ought to be—mostly over-shadowed by the fact that comedy is fun. Or at least we suppose it is meant to be fun and meant to make us laugh. That comedy is fun, and that it makes fun of things, has tended to keep philosophers at a distance, as if something funny could not, at the same time, yield an insight into something serious, or at any rate, chronic. Another problem endemic to writing about comedy is that, unlike tragedy, comedy quickly lost the definite shapes that it apparently once possessed, having overrun its generic boundaries already in its Greek beginnings. Roman satire, medieval romances, Renaissance anatomies, "The Rape of the Lock," and *Pamela* are further recognizable versions of the comic impulse and modifications of the impulse to drama. By dramatic, I mean nothing more technical than a kind of representation of action occurring on something we now call a stage. The dramatic impulse to comedy can even be taken as helping to create new genres over the centuries. For instance, while the novel is not perhaps essentially bound up with comedy, there are surprisingly few novels possessing utterly no elements of comedy. One need not argue that *Anna Karenina* is full of laughs to see the bitter comedy in the bad timing of Anna's change of heart. In general, the comic impulse seems bound up in forms of narration that grew up around class, sex, money, adultery, and marriage.

Perhaps because of this tendency to infiltrate other genres and even to create new ones (like new families of jokes), philosophers have tended to ignore the roots of comedy in drama. When they do pay attention to these roots, as in John Morreall's useful article in the *Encyclopedia of Aesthetics* (1998), they soon convert the topic into the comic as a species alongside the species of humor and wit. The thought seems to be that we might be able to define comedy as a major portion—perhaps *the* major portion—of the sum of all the things and types of things that make us laugh or smile. Though I have begun with the idea of fun, and of making fun, this essay concerns comedy as a dramatic form, And, risking the charge of committing the genetic fallacy, I continue to imagine that the origin of comedy has something to do with the essence of comedy or, better yet, its grammar. But as in Nietzsche's account of tragedy, there is room for developments and modifications. The idea that both comedy and tragedy begin in something like a religious festival—perhaps even the same festival—is only one clue among several. This clue should be treated with care.

While the roots of the festive and the festival may account for some forms of comedy (as well as tragedy), it is not the case that all forms of humor are festive, and it is also not the case that all forms of the festive become embodied in forms of drama or the dramatic. The topic spreads out even further if, along with the established literary genres of comedy proper, satire, romantic comedy, the comic novel, and so on, we include those harder to classify literary types of spoof, burlesque, parody, pastiche, and vaudeville, as well as an impulse and a form that are harder to name and to characterize that ranges from *Tristram Shandy* to Gertrude Stein, James Joyce, and Samuel Beckett. From Joyce and Beckett and the clowns they admired, it is not hard to find a transition to Buster Keaton, for whom Beckett once wrote a script. And if we include the genres that grew up around Keaton, then we are already next door to Charlie Chaplin's unbelievably inventive genius. Nor should we omit Disney's cartoon *Steamboat Willie* and its homage to Keaton's film *Steamboat Bill Jr.* Of course, we cannot leave out the more sophisticated clowning (among their other forms of comedy) of Mae West, Marilyn Monroe, Rosalind Russell, and Katherine Hepburn—to go no further—and, on the male side, Cary Grant, Jimmy Stewart, William Powell, Tony Curtis, Bert Lahr, and Tom Hanks. Who will find a way to restrict this topic without distorting it? It is inevitable, therefore, to acknowledge at the outset that it is more than a mildly comic task to write about a topic as broad and deep—if sometimes also as shallow and silly—as mannered and sometimes as scatological, as Comedy with a capital C.

I take my bearings therefore not only from a sample of representative cases but from several writers and thinkers and playwrights whose interests intersect with literary or dramatic reflection and by whom I have gained, I trust, some access to the questions of comedy. Nietzsche's *Birth of Tragedy* (1872, 1886), surprisingly, contains a series of clues about the transition from Old Comedy to New.[1] It was much less surprising that Plato's powers of comedy yielded insights into the nature of comedy, most especially as enacted in the *Symposium*. Among modern critics, I have made use of Northrop Frye's *A Natural Perspective* (1995) and Stanley Cavell's *Pursuits of Happiness* (1981), centered on what he characterizes as the Hollywood comedy of remarriage, along with W. K. Wimsatt's (1969) introduction and conclusion to his collection of documents on comedy from Ben Jonson to George Meredith and James Thurber. In the background of this essay is C. L. Barber's *Shakespeare's Festive Comedy* (1959) and its progeny.

It is one of the circumstances under which philosophy makes its tentative contacts with the literary work and its world that literary critics will find this list a laughably small sample of the immense amount of useful work on comedy.

On the other hand, most philosophers will wonder why there is so much literary criticism in the first place. Aristotle's few surviving remarks on comedy do cast their shadow on what follows, but I am less interested than others in fleshing out the bones of structure that he has left to us. The most influential of his thoughts about comedy provides an instructive example. In tragedy, we are told, the protagonist is in some sense higher (more *spoudaios* [serious]) than we are. In comedy he or she is "lower" (less *spoudaios* [serious], more *phauloi* [lazy and good for nothing]). This may fit well enough for Aristophanic and New Comedy, but it is not really adequate to Renaissance comedies, both romantic and the so-called comedy of manners. Taking into account also Rex Harrison or Wendy Hiller or Maggie Smith, or, more generally, the movies, it is certainly hard to think of Cary Grant as someone we look down on, someone whose extrications we find a "lower" version than our own. Within the Shakespearean comedies of Romance, it is hard to think of Helena, Olivia, or even Cressida as someone whose travails we have an obviously higher perspective on. Nevertheless, it is something of a commonplace that comedy can exist in "low" and "high" forms sometimes thought to coincide with the popular (Punch and Judy shows, puppet shows, mime, and vaudeville) and the more literary (e.g., George Bernard Shaw and William Congreve). It is not clear how this is related to Aristotle's point, but some difference between comedy and tragedy is evident in this perception. Hamlet can clown around and put on his antic show, but he cannot actually become a clown.

To begin with the Greeks (where according to legend so much of human culture begins) is not merely a literary convenience. Not quite arbitrarily, my other points of reference are Shakespeare (especially *All's Well That Ends Well*) and some Hollywood movies. To connect these points of reference, I note here that the film *It Happened One Night* is a kind of *Midsummer Night's Dream*, a disruptive idyll of hitchhiking among the mechanized forms of transportation, within a strictly enforced class society. The idyll is a test that pits the hunger of lovers, the temporary hunger of the hitchhiker, and the hunger of the jobless against prevailing social convention, with no end to the adventure. This future, unpredictable and peregrine, cannot be captured on film. The film *Lone Star* is not quite a tragedy or a comedy, but it is about the beginnings of the new that comedy has aimed for. It reminds us that one of the conditions of festivity—and perhaps of the renewal of our cities and our politics—is the now unfestive ability to forget the past. We are to move on, adventurously, into a world without publicly recognizable adventure or festivity. Dramatic comedy is not sheerly the pleasure of laughter at the deformity of our inferiors. Its structure includes the recognition of our own deformities and of our complicity in the pain of others. True laughter is rarely the response to our recognitions and much more often the relief we are granted in the struggle for recognition. Either laughter is on the way to something better, or it is cold comfort indeed.

Since at least the time of Athenian drama, it has seemed natural enough to contrast comedy and tragedy. It is as least as natural as contrasting a happy ending with a sad one, or the solemnity of a death that amounts to a sacrifice with the hilarity and savagery and sheer pleasure that come from transgressing the boundaries of order. Tragedy, we might say, pits the high-born individual against the law of the city, the *polis*, and its relation to eternal justice: both the individual and the city may be shattered, so that the polis can be renewed or somehow survive and the memory of the hero seared into the memory of the people, who will gather to reenact this death and this renewal. Comedy pits the tricky slave, the *eiron*, and the yearning couple, with whom the masses side, against the customs and lesser laws of decorum, so that sexual and political transgression can have their day.

Preliminary Remarks: Of the Genres of Laughter

I follow several procedures in Cavell's *Pursuits of Happiness* in order to untangle a skein of threads, thinking of them not so much as a set of properties as a series of features. One difference from my project is that Cavell's is working out the problematic of the specific genre he characterizes as the genre of remarriage, and I have just been implicitly denying that comedy is or could any longer be considered as such a genre or even as a totality of such genres. Cavell thinks of the genre in question as inheriting certain conditions and as in conversation with the other members of the genre (1981: 28–30). The conditions that the types of comedy I am considering have in common most are that they have some kind of audience and that they present a structure of human incidents as some kind of narrative. The audience may be the audience of a stage, or a movie house, or perhaps the solitary audience of the comic novel. Some comedians—those with a certain flair for storytelling, such as Robin Williams, Whoopi Goldberg, or Richard Pryor—might fit this definition by turning the room they are "working" into a kind of theatrical space. Other comics just as funny—Henny Youngman, Mort Sahl—build their anecdotes to set up their punch lines, and they might not fit this idea of comedy as drama.[2] Here is another reason I cannot, without modification, simply deploy Cavell's notion of compensation as occurring among these features. But if a particular work does not possess the particular features or threads or clues that I am pursuing, there will be consequences in the structure of the work that are unpredictable from the mere inspection of the feature.

I use the term "features" as opposed to properties, but we must grant that the terminology is somewhat arbitrary. It is designed, as Cavell says in the Introduction to *Pursuits of Happiness*, to overcome the idea of the members of a genre (e.g., screwball comedy, Restoration comedy, Old Comedy) as recognizable by, so to speak, inspection, where the idea of inspection is just made to be a companion to the idea of "possessing a property." I have not defined "property" or "genre" any more than I have defined "thing." But if the idea is to oppose the methodological sense that a certain number of comic properties will just add up (so to speak, visibly) to a comic drama, then what are we looking for?

To adumbrate Cavell's use of the idea of feature, I add the ideas of thread and clue. Having no single Ariadne's thread to follow out the mysterious origins of such comedies as *The Clouds, The Birds, The Wasps, Lysistrata*, and *Ecclesiazusae*. I take it as simply worth pondering that comedy was placed by Athenian tradition as following a production of (generally) three tragedies, and that proximity of this kind—in a time of festival—suggests at least some kind of connection between comedy and tragedy. There are elements of oral tradition, cited by Wimsatt, that suggest that, in the beginning, tragedy and comedy were the same. If the connection does not exactly follow from the festivities, then surely there are contrasts and connections that lie close to the nature of the festive. Here is one place where Barber's *Shakespeare's Festive Comedy*, though little noted by philosophers, helped shape the consciousness of at least a generation of American critics. He seems to excavate something about dramatic comedy as such, and not just about Shakespeare's.[3]

Another feature that begins with the Greeks brings us forward to Shakespeare and takes us back to the Greeks. Both in Shakespeare and the Greeks, comedy is at once sexual (or, more broadly, instinctual) and political. The "political" has its roots in the *polis*. If this is not its immediate origin—or if sex is the wrong word to describe the Dionysian sense of the turmoil of origins—then it soon becomes much closer to being the right word. "Sex" is here not the name for genital activities or for the consummation or corruption of the human or political realm by such activities. Sex is the name for one essential condition of the political, or for one realm in which the conditions of human sexuality and its discontents make politics possible—and also necessary.

Comedy's attachment to politics and instinct also speaks to the possibility of language. This means language both in the direction that distinguishes the instinctive cries of animals, human and otherwise, civilized and barbarian, and, finally, those apparently less dramatic distinctions between nations, tribes, sexes, generations, and social classes. Finally, there is the condition of the spectator, or rather, since Nietzsche makes an issue of the spectator as (mere) spectator, let us say rather the "audience"—those out there in the seats, not moving around on the stage. And within this problematic, there is precisely the question of how the audience is related to its presumed status as citizens, as opposed to the status of a mere individual swimming in a sea of nonindividuation or in more modern terms in a kind of dissolution into the mob of human beings and the yet deeper mob of instinct and its conflicts and pains. Within this notion of the audience, we have issues of time, ranging from the freedom to participate in the festival days (a privilege not granted to all) to the time that is created, or secreted, from within the transformative power of the festive spectacle.

The recurrent sense of isolation at the end of a Chaplin movie (though compatible with the presence of a companion) should not be thought of as simply contrary to this feature. Without denying the importance of the drive to unity in comedy, we may notice, for example, that the eloquent stasis—like the masque that Frye speaks of in Shakespearean comedy—gives way to our sense of the importance of Chaplin's walk, and especially the walk down the boulevard at the end of the movie. Surely it is related to the dandy's assertion of individual style. But it is also important that he becomes fully visible in his *departure* and in his discovery of a kind of pastoral exit from the oppressiveness of the city. The visibility of the little man, the tramp, modifies the bragging that always lies just beneath his presence to us. These moments exist in counterpoint to the discovery that Cavell's pairs make, that living together is a kind of adventure rather than a state to be achieved once and for all: Chaplin's exits discover that mere survival is a form of adventure. This speaks not merely of his ability to eat a shoe with something like civility and elegance. It is one way of taking the jauntiness in his less drastic survivals, his sense of accomplishment in just walking away, often alone. This sense of survival as an accomplishment of adventurousness will become important to the features of Cavell's remarriage comedies (especially prominent in *It Happened One Night*). But it is already completely explicit in certain passages granted to Shakespeare's powerful types of the unheroic, from Falstaff, with his "Who hath honor?", to Parolles, with his unforgettable declaration: "Simply the thing I am shall make me live."

NIETZSCHE AND COMEDY'S SPECTATORS

Nietzsche tied the death of tragedy to the birth of what would soon be christened the New Comedy. Greek tragedy, "unlike her older sister arts," committed suicide, most visibly in the work of Euripides:

> What Euripides claims credit for in Aristophanes' *Frogs*, namely, that his nostrums have liberated tragic art from its pompous corpulency, is apparent above all in his tragic heroes. The spectator now actually saw and heard his double on the Euripidean stage, and rejoiced that he *could talk so well*. But this joy was not all: one could even learn from Euripides how to speak oneself. He prides himself upon this in his contest with Aeschylus: from him the people have learned how to observe, debate, and draw conclusions according to the rules of art and with the cleverest sophistries. Through this revolution in ordinary language, he made the New Comedy possible. For henceforth it was no longer a secret how—and with what maxims—everyday life [*Alltäglichkeit*] could be represented on the stage. Civic mediocrity, on which Euripides built all his political hopes, was now given a voice, while heretofore the demigod in tragedy and the drunken satyr, or demiman, in comedy, had determined the character of the language. (Nietzsche 1967: 77–78, emphasis added)

For Nietzsche, this transformation of the height that a character is capable of into the depths of sexuality and conflict and politics into which he or she reaches is reflected first in speech. But this quickly turns out to be a feature of the fact that, whereas tragedy did not originally consist of an audience of spectators, Euripides brought the spectator onto the stage itself. This move brought mere spectatorship into the realm of the represented, and giving spectatorship speech then extended the dramatic realm out into the audience, thus covering over the possibility of access to the Dionysian and creating a new politics for a new polis.

Some of these facts are now taken as well established, and some have been controversial since the opening battles between Nietzsche and Ulrich von Wilamowitz-Moellendorff. I am pursuing Nietzsche's use of history to excavate such concepts as the stage and the spectator, comedy and tragedy, language and instinct that might otherwise drop out of the discussion. I am not concerned to discover an empirical way of determining the history of Athenian drama as a history of degeneration. I am trying to follow such Nietzschean concepts as "degeneration" and the self-reflection of the spectator in the drama as intrinsic to the new forms of comic drama, which have simultaneously displaced the old forms. Nietzsche sees the triumph of the New Comedy as explicitly related to the end of a certain kind of tragedy and to a change in the relation of spectator to what is seen, ultimately in the relation of spectator to citizen, and citizen to spectator.

As a starting point for my potential list of the features of comedy, I want to keep alive the themes of language, politics, spectatorship, sex and sexual instinct, and the ranking and conceiving of the human being in relation to the more and less than human. Within this perhaps itself chaotic set of themes lies the very mark of chaos, the barrier of incest, the boundary marking the realm of family and *polis*, of sex and the social realm, apart from which there is apparently no solution to the question of chaos and order. To invoke these themes is not necessarily to endorse Nietzsche's image of Greek history, but it does suggest the need for some sort of genealogy of comedy, faithful at once to some sense of its origins and of its development over time. When Barber and Frye and Cavell come back to the side of Shakespeare's comedy that Barber calls festive and Frye characterizes as calling for a green world, some kind of problematic can be seen to be working itself out. Cavell makes explicit that the green world may contain some darker forests.

PLATO'S *SYMPOSIUM* AND THE UNITY OF COMEDY AND TRAGEDY

What do we imagine that Plato had in mind when he called for an artist who is capable equally of tragedy and comedy? At the conclusion of Plato's *Symposium*, in the final throes of the drunken party into which the more decorous symposium has degenerated, Socrates is left "trying to prove that authors should be able to write both comedies and tragedies" (223d). That is to say, given Socrates' understanding of workmanship and production, the essence of tragedy and of comedy is either the same or not so far apart as to elude the soul of the artist or workman in both cases.

Plato seems to lack Nietzsche's wish to construct a historical narrative, to enact a portion of that history, and then to dodge its apparently inescapable final act. He remains the first and perhaps the greatest philosopher to enact the kind of thinking he is simultaneously writing out. Here he has clearly constructed a plot that rises like a tragedy and sinks into a chaos of drunkenness and sex. He leaves us with one voice of the conversation still at it, a solitary postlude of a one-man festival of daily life. He leaves us with Socrates, with no one left to talk to, ready to go about his daily business.

What is specifically comic about Plato's vision? If we grant the comedy in the image of dailiness in Socrates' going about his business, then it seems we actually have two images of the comic. We have the comedy of convulsiveness and chaos—precipitated by the intervention of Alcibiades and his unruly love for Socrates—and the comedy of the hero's daily life, seen from the perspective of Diotima's immortal timelessness and the time of the spectator/reader. The other spectators are falling asleep and we are presumably still eager to stay awake, to know the ending that has no real end—none short of Socrates' mortality. That the end is in the future, well off stage, means that the *Symposium* does not possess exactly the shape of Greek tragedy or comedy. *We* know where Socrates will end up: at the dock of Athenian law. If the fate of Socrates is surely at the back of these comic (and philosophical) tours de force, the *Symposium* gestures toward something of the genius or essence of tragedy within these scenes of comedy and daily triumph.

Let us look first at the speech Plato assigns to Aristophanes, the famous speech that returns in its somewhat repressed Hollywood version as the story of the "split-apart" in the Demi Moore film *The Butcher's Wife*. It is there literally presented as a grandmother's story—perhaps you might call it a tale of springtime, told in winter. The ancient grandmother presents the origin of her knowledge as a *critique* of the idea that the story came from Plato. In fact, deliberately or not, the grandmother's claim supports the claim of (the fictional) Aristophanes to be speaking a truth so primordial that it can only be spoken in a myth as deep as the grandmother's folk wisdom. That she passes on her knowledge as one who is out of the sexual game and, moreover, grants this knowledge to her granddaughter out of love demonstrates the power of love to preserve our knowledge of love, beyond the possession of a particular thinker.

The myth of the "split-aparts" requires as its antidote the magic and the philosophy of Diotima—a woman neither young nor old, neither goddess, nor housewife, both a kind of friend and a kind of lover, which is perhaps to say a kind of teacher.

I single out four elements from Aristophanes' story, in order to compare the features of comedy and tragedy, in terms of what Cavell calls their compensations:

1. In the *Symposium* (189d–92b), we are to recognize the physical absurdities or, at any rate, the extreme awkwardness of the original compound humans (man/man, man/woman, woman/woman), and the confidence that these doubled human beings were stronger, and more full of excess or *hubris*, than we are. This physical impediment to satisfaction makes graphic Zeus's mercy in giving us frontal genitality (and hence the possibility of a less haphazard sexual position). As much to Plato's point, if not Aristophanes', is the possibility of seeing the one we yearn for, or perhaps a greater coordination of seeing and yearning. More than one comedy is based precisely on the blindness of sexual yearning to generational differences and the sameness and difference of genders and families. (*Tom Jones* is a more recent example.)

2. The fact of generations carries us further into tragedy, comedy, and indeed, the historical question of royal succession, so incessantly pursued in Shakespeare. In Plato we can be understood as living our lives split apart from the source of our being, our wholeness. After the first generation of (literal) split-aparts, what we are split from is mythically presented as the same "other" half. But comically it is actually some *other* kind of other half that we are yearning for, the result of some other wound, no doubt related to the one that we are striving all our lives to heal. In tragedy, the question of generations is often absorbed into the sheer Greek fact that specific families bear curses, plagues, wishes, or destinies that become the root of the tragic.

3. In Aristophanes' vision, humans are originally more *deinon* (190b: more strange or frightful or, in Heidegger's version, more uncanny and less at home). In the first choral ode of *Antigone*, they are the *most* uncanny: *ta deinotaton*. The fact that they are more *deinon* than we are now does not suggest that to be *deinon* is merely one human attribute among many but that we are to be characterized, essentially, as *deinon*. Whether more or less uncanny at a given moment, our being not at home exceeds the homeliness of the world, its welcome. For the character of being *deinon* is always to outstrip the rest of the world and to be, in essence, overreachers. It is not merely that we were once stronger because of our power of movement and multilimbed capacity for attack. It is from this condition, before we took on our recognizably human form, that we were already subject to a level of *hubris*, itself defined as overreaching, a kind of constantly increasing velocity of excessiveness. Our very being is to drive ourselves forward, upward, but always away from ourselves, away from anything we could call home.

Zeus's splitting us down the middle is less a punishment than a stratagem, making us at once weaker and more profitable (190d). Aristophanes' Zeus presents us with a weaker and more comical human body. Apollo's function is then to let our bodies shine forth, but comically, reminding us, in a kind of parody of philosophical or Oedipal self-knowledge, of our weakness and our previous transgressions.

The absence of the law in this vision—the presence of the sheer power of Zeus to shape our bodies and our destinies, as it were, physically—is the most tangible mode of direct intervention in our lives and our capacity for love. The power of the gods in this dialogue is a comic version of lightning striking, or seas parting, or bushes burning, and it heightens our sense of its presence in Greek tragedy—notably in *Oedipus* and *Antigone*. We are prepared to discern its presence in other comedies, perhaps especially in those of Shakespeare, as seen most unforgettably in Frye's vision of his "problem" comedies and romances. We will return to this.

4. These remarks modify and, I hope, deepen the old idea that tragedy has to do with the destruction or expulsion of the hero. In *Coriolanus*, one right is driven out by another; fire destroys fire. This tragedy's idea of tragedy—part of its idea of itself—is paralleled in Hegel's account of Antigone's loyalty to the family, in the person of her brother, but conceived as the most earthbound source of right. Where the eternal laws that govern the temporal *polis* meet the earthbound polis, there will be force. We still sense the idea of tragedy as an idea in which the fracturing of the polis will allow it somehow to be preserved.

Comedy, in contrast, tends to unify and tends toward a unity most often symbolized by marriage. This unity, on the one hand, represents the lawful union of human drives but, on the other hand, one might say also represents the unity of body and soul that comes out of a unification with another. This points both to the idea of the other as the "other half," but also as a bringing to intermittent peace of what already in Aristophanes is called something like restlessness (*polupragmosune*). Achieving this unity among *different* persons and parts of the self is perhaps more immediately an opposite of the single-mindedness, the wholeness of the tragic hero's mission, which here carries the price of being unable to see the meaning of what he or she opposes until their meanings collide.

A Closer Look at Aristophanes:
The Birds, Love, and Language

Within the aggressiveness of Aristophanes' *The Birds*, human beings are, at several critical moments, characterized by love. Most of this language is probably ironic. Nevertheless, the love in question seems to go beyond the need for some ironic opposite to selfishness and pettiness: it is said to be a love that would share in the kingdom of the birds. Here love means sharing *with* the birds but also refers to a parodic sharing that implies conquering the shared realm. This doubleness of love haunts many of the more interesting comedies of the age. William Arrowsmith's readable (but admittedly not strictly literal) translation provides a line that is not explicitly present in the Greek:

> Their motive is love.
> Love is the burden of their words...
> Love of your life and love of you. (Aristophanes 1961: 47)

The anonymous translator in the Oates and O'Neill translation is closer to the original: "Their love for you and their wish to share your kind of life; to dwell and remain with you always" (1938: 751). This is a pretty fair sketch of what Plato's Aristophanes means by sharing.

Plato's version (192d–93a) tells us that it would take a god to interpret what we want from one another. This suggests that even when we speak the same language, we don't really speak the same language. In particular, as words emerge from the chirps and groans of instinct, they do not, in becoming words, tell anyone (not even ourselves) what we desire. They indicate the traces of where we have come from, not what we are striving to find. The doubleness of language is here portrayed as rooted in the fact that it faces backward to its origins in cries and shouts and forward to the whispers of desire and the apparent unambiguity of our demands. But nothing is unambiguous or beyond the need of interpretation and hermeneutics. Language moves away from its origin in nature and instinct and toward something apparently in its future. It is constructed out of a lost past, something with which we desire to merge and be filled with and something that is out of reach. There is, perhaps, an internal relation between the polysemy of language and the human creature's fatedness to time, to individuation, and to the wish to merge with its own origins, obliterating its own identity.

Let us continue these investigations with a plainer thought: if laughter were not close to an instinctual response, it would not be much of a response to the comic. If laughter were not close to language, articulate speech, something that could be part of a message or of a conversation, or the end of one, it also would not be much of a response to the comic.

Once language becomes full-blown, with all its countless ways of making meaning, blaming, sneering, and putting down, as well as making puns, riddles, jokes, and prophecies, the impenetrability and transparency of names and naming are all part of the comedic, as they are part of language. One could try to trace all language to its instinctual roots or to its more developed lawful, transgressive cousin, Desire, *Wunsch*. But it won't work, or rather it won't play. There is an irreducible element of lawfulness, sense, and exemplarity at the heart of speech, hence of comedy. It can be seen as enacting the function of comedy to test the *polis* and the hearth, from the side of instinct, of language breaking down or breaking up. In short, comedy tests the community of words from below, from the underside that all language must possess.

From Shakespeare to the Movies: The Transformation of Women, the Trial of Words, and the Oracle of the Everyday

Whatever the historical imbalance in leaping from the Greeks to Shakespeare, there is some kind of critical justice to be found in the maneuver. After all, if a vision of comedy could not account for these figures, it would be seriously lacking. And my aim, as I said, is not to arrive at a set of necessary and sufficient conditions for the genre of comedy, but a series of features modifying and replacing each other, whose motions we might regard as the work of the continual (re-)creation of the comic.

Frye pointed out one feature of late Shakespearean comedy and romance that governs the following reflections, albeit in different guises. It is clear enough that at least in some comedies there is an initial problem or perplexity, often a harsh or irrational law, and later a social or sexual tension that does admit of comic resolution, but is not perhaps reducible to something funny. This ranges from the law against fornication in *Measure for Measure*, to the rule of brutishness and retaliation as the news that the newspapers deliver to the bedroom of the film *Adam's Rib*.

Taking off from this insight of Frye's and to the pages that he devotes to *All's Well That Ends Well*, I allow myself to pick up thoughts from a range of Frye's material in *A Natural Perspective*. Frye's lines about this play are a kind of leitmotif throughout the book. To give them an initial summary: In Shakespeare's romances, when the dream of action and time resumes, it is in a different key. Having slipped the bounds of action and time, into the time of trances, spells, and rebirths, the action returns to our time. The drama seems willing to renounce magic and resume the ordinary time in which events occur and babies are born, lost and found, and the time in which audiences sit still for such stuff. But it is not the same audience that first sat down, any more than it is the same characters: both have been transformed, not by magic but by a faith "lawful as eating."

In *All's Well That Ends Well*, while Dionysian chaos and Aristophanic wounding of the human are not quite visible, there is nonetheless a political connection in the shaming of Parolles: as the First Soldier says (after a platoon of Parolles' own camp pretends to take him captive, actually placing him in a captivity deeper than the captivity of weapons):

> If you could find out a country where but women
> Were that had received so much shame, you might begin
> An impudent nation.... (act 4, scene 3, lines 341–44).

I suggest that the idea of an impudent nation is not just a nation composed of shameless people. I hear impudence and shame not only as an idea built on the bodies of ill-treated women and cowardly men, but also as the idea of a nation built over the abyss of shame that underlies all human action and growth. This nation would start where the Greek sense of virtue as the overcoming of shame and dishonor left off—as if the issue forced on us now is that comedy (and tragedy?) begins not from instinctual chaos, sex, and aggression, but rather from repression and rectitude and the concomitant absence of cakes and ale. The resulting disorder, and our ability to get used to it, to live with it, is actually more promising material for the building or rebuilding of community. If this sounds too much like Norman Brown's *Love's Body*, with an Episcopalian overtone, give Frye a moment to expound the consequences and the context.

Frye begins, in a chapter titled "The Triumph of Time," with the relatively mirthless clown Lavache, speaking of the narrow gate to heaven and the broad wide path to fire.

> I am a woodland fellow, sir, that always loved a great fire; and the master I speak of ever keeps a good fire. But since he is the prince of the world: let the nobility remain in's court. I am for the house with the narrow gate. Which I take to be too little for pomp to enter: Some that humble themselves may, but the many will be too chill and tender, and they'll be for the flow'ry way that leads to the broad gate and the great fire. (act 4, scene v, lines 48–56)

What seems remarkable is that these Christian commonplaces contain allusions and associations that would set orthodox Christianity on its head. For example, fire is first of all—at least to a man of the woods—a source of warmth, comfort, and perhaps danger, but not pain and damnation. Thus, the fire that is kept burning by the prince of this world may be part of the temptation of the devil, but it is not yet portrayed as part of our fears of him. The theme of gates too narrow for the proud but accessible to the humble is certainly Christian. But consider that "the many will be too chill and tender," that is, at once too cold to yield to the need for humility and apparently too cold to give up the warmth of the devil's fire, which is still not presented as a thing of pain. And then, after all it is a "flowery way"—as if toward marriage or in a kind of triumphal procession—that leads to "the broad gate and the great fire."

Compare this with the savage truth telling of clowns and fools from *Lear* to *Twelfth Night*: "Who is it will tell me who I am?" "Lear's shadow." "Because thou art virtuous thou thinkst there will be no more cakes and ale." Lavache says next to nothing new, but then salvation is a small thing, too, and Lavache's tropes on these commonplaces suggest how close we are to understanding, and also, as we stand, how far.

Frye puts it this way: "Lavache is simply an old clown with nothing left to him but the privilege of uninhibited speech" (1995: 105). Frye continues: "Uninhibited speech ought to be witty, on Freudian principles, but if it fails to be that it may still be oracular, a quality close to wit, and often used by Shakespeare instead of it" (105). It is part of Frye's irony to describe the oracular as a kind of failed wit: where wit condenses and is barbed enough to penetrate the nature of things, the oracular merely speaks forth the nature of things and hence of the things that lie around us, unseen, the things of our world and the things of which we are composed. What is oracular is not so much Bertram dragged kicking and screaming into a marriage that may yet save him, as Lavache's more encompassing image of human beings rushing toward their own annihilation.

That substitution—like the yoking of wit and the oracular—is Frye's and perhaps Shakespeare's. I cannot find any explicit link in Freud's work between wit and the lack of inhibition. In fact, I would be more likely to suggest that wit is that which breaks through the repressions and inhibitions of civilization, which is not the same as the genuinely uninhibited. The less a child has succumbed to the inhibitions, the less witty is the child's humor likely to be—indeed, the less consciously humorous the child is likely to be. Or put it this way: the humor of children is not likely to be wit. Wit, in our time, does not so much break through the rigidity of repression as momentarily puncture it or subvert it. The child's mind, if it is given over to what attracts it and what repels it, for example, to love and hate or to interest and boredom, is not so much a model of wit as a exemplar of a being who does not need wit.

What Frye finds in this play is not primarily the shameful disorder of Eros, but the blind rush of self-destruction that is the twin of Eros. It is this battle, as Freud put it, of Eros and destructiveness that must be transformed into a dialectic, or drama, of Eros and civilization that is the framework for this most fantastic of Shakespeare's late plays. Finding this, we also find that as the play—that is, the various actions—recede, what emerges into visibility is the drama of Bertram and Helena, hence, after all, the drama of a kind of individual action writ large. The "movement" of the action that Frye finds essential to comedy (perhaps more so than in tragedy) ends by sweeping the high-born but slimy Bertram into the arms of a worthy and immeasurably magical Helena. Unaccountably, she still wants him. And she prepares us for this conclusion with a speech that promises us nothing more than the conditions of life.

But it will not be praise of her man that concludes the play. It is rather the oracular speech—as Frye calls it—near the end, where Helena says this:

> But with the word, the time will bring on summer,
> When briars shall have leaves as well as thorns
> And be as sweet as sharp. We must away;
> Our waggen is prepared, and time revives us.
> All's well that ends well: still the fine's the crown. (act 4, scene 1,
>   lines 38–42)

It would be a mistake to think of this as one more celebration of the "end" crowning the work, a kind of happier version of the "end" justifying what was necessary to achieve it. This is, of course, not an irrelevant reading for a play in which the magical or theatrical strokes are always likely to overwhelm the particulars of the forward motion. In fact, Shakespeare provides his own commentary on these lines, a scant two scenes later at the beginning of act 5. Helena returns to the same formulation, almost the same formula. In counterpoint to The Widow's: "Lord, how we lose our pains" (act 5, scene 1, line 29), Helena finds: " All's well that ends well yet, / Though time seems so adverse and means unfit. / I do beseech you whither has he gone" (act 5, scene 1, lines 24–28). As Frye is constantly reminding us, the musical structure of these late plays is not merely some effect of rhyme, repetition, and leitmotif. The echo of sound is inextricably an echo of sense, and we are encouraged to take this echo as a repetition of a climactic theme and also as a comment on that theme. The idea of "time" as "so adverse" seems to be touched on very lightly.

But if the struggle is between the triumph of time and the adversity of time, this is not merely a slight modification of her original thought, for what "ends" well is not something *out* of time, something to which human means are irrelevant, if momentarily they seem insufficient. It is not just that *this* time is unpropitious or out of joint, *these* means too weak. It is two forms of time that struggle for the play's conclusion, both bound up in language, both partaking of divinity and struggle, both struggling for an ending we can live with. We are partly transformed by the spectacle, and partly untransformed by our participation, with insufficient means, in the struggles of virginity and virtue, language and shame, nobility (hence class) and grace.

My intuition is that both Frye and Cavell are leaning heavily on the idea of transformation itself. We are back, after all, at Nietzsche's few remarks, according to which the depths of human and half-human being turn out to be transformative. Moreover, they are transformative not only concerning the characters—above all, in the later versions, the death and transformation of the woman—but in the power of transformation that the willing audience brings to the powerful enactments. It is the power of ritual, only one step away from magic and religious frenzy, that brings the individual characters face to face with something like identity. In its fragility, its need to be transformed and reborn, identity and its dissolutions are the ground of the transfiguration we aspire to.

Frye singles out the heroine "disguised as a boy"—and especially her transformed possibilities of activity and passivity—as a means of symbolizing the transformations of Romance and its new possibilities of human relationship: "For it is usually the activity of the heroine, or, in some cases her passivity that brings about the birth of the new society and the reconciliation of the old society with it. This activity takes the form of a disappearance and return" (1995: 83).

In Cavell, the woman is not so much disguised from the other characters or from the audience as she is from herself. Cavell is less interested in the possibilities of her physical disguise than in the possibilities of her political and spiritual—her human—transformation, as revealed by the camera. Radical transformation often takes the dramatic form of death and revival, or it comes as close to such a revival as credibility will permit. "It is required of you that you awake your faith," as Paulina says in *The Winter's Tale*, as if the birth, or rebirth, or resurrection of the woman participates fully only in the realm of faith, a passion beyond mortal life and beyond the habits of belief and behavior current in the civilized expectations in the world of men.

This is either a theatricalization of faith, or rediscovery of something like divine possibilities of transformations within the theater. For Frye, the transformation of the woman, her death and reappearance, is the reinsertion of her life into a cycle of birth and death, which participates in a larger circle, neither quite Christian nor Greek, but all Shakespeare.

The spectator is transformed by the willingness to witness and hence to participate in this cycle, which eventually grows to be so all encompassing as to transform heaven and hell into the end foreseen in the knowledge of good and evil.

That is, we are now capable of knowing the tree of life, though we are now barred from it. Comedy is a foretaste of this knowledge of life, achieved not by the sight of angels, standing guard, but within the living of this life.

Walking Away in Time

Cavell engages Frye in a quiet dispute about the nature of time and, for that matter, of the force of Nietzsche's work. For Cavell, Nietzsche is not some avatar of the Greeks or the author of some modern version of a cyclical cosmology. Or at least in Cavell's version, Nietzsche's vision must contain the moment at which the two eternities, or what I called the two modes of time, can meet. And it is the figure of the woman (the new Eve) that replaces the replacement of the old Adam by the new. But Cavell is only rarely interested in the changing of boy actor to girl to boy to girl (as in Shakespeare). Cavell plays on Katherine Hepburn's boyishness (see, e.g., *Alice Adams*), and he provides a revealing discussion of director George Cukor's treatment of gender reversal in *Adam's Rib*. What critics have neglected is the way that Cavell's explorations of comedy continue his explorations of the willingness of (natural) language to repudiate itself, transgress itself. Something in our possession of language makes skepticism possible, from within the fact of our attunement in speech. And something in our need to voice our desires makes comedy possible within the attunements of society.

While this idea tracks the perversity that threatens the couple that has grown up together—forming the threat that corresponds to the inability, especially of the male, to bring together the currents of tenderness and the stream of passion—the parallel of this perversity of language and the threat of incest has not been followed out. Only rarely in Cavell's work does he make it explicit that the sound of quarreling, the happy banter, the silences, and in general the sense that the two streams of drama (of the comedy of comedy and the comedy of philosophy) can rejoin each other naturally because they are the solution to the problem of perversity, in language and in love. What feels natural in comedy is not merely our habituation to the realities around us, portrayed on stage or in film. It is these partial and temporary resolutions of the discord of unnaturalness that show us the path of nature, within our unnatural origins.

This issue of the unnatural naturalness of language—and what this represents in comedy—is one reason, I think, that Cavell spends pages of criticism on Shaw's *Pygmalion* and its revealing failure to achieve the status of a remarriage comedy. Cavell reads it as a kind of positive version of Cukor's film *Gaslight*, where Eliza comes to "proper" speech and to her "proper" self in time to stand up to Higgins and preserve her sanity. But she is not quite in time to resolve the antagonism of speech and the fact that she and Higgins share a mother, so to speak, and must find such resolution as they can consistently live with. Her life with him will be intermittent, a conversation constantly starting and stopping again, whether with his lecturing or her return to silence and thought. In general, in the remarriage comedies, the man does not teach the woman how to speak. (Especially in the film *His Girl Friday*, the one with the riskiest title and the amoralism it might seem to share with Shaw, it is established from the beginning, that she is the better writer, or at least that, while he writes a mean telegram, her words fit the space the newspaper has to print them in. That is: he can write a kind of plea, but she can write the story that makes the plea make sense.) If the man is involved in the woman's education, as Cavell insists, it is because he is the audience of her effectiveness, the survivor of her rejection, and the sometimes hapless object and source of her desire, including her desire for effectiveness.

For Cavell, the visibility of time, the palpability of our struggles in time, and the engagement of the spectator in the spectacle all circle around the death and transformation of the woman. Cavell finds the key to these reeditions of Old Comedy in the rearrangement of emphasis on the heroine (as opposed to New Comedy's emphasis on the man or the tricky slave); what draws Cavell's attention is the transformation of the leading woman into the "new woman." This transformation is a kind of birth, for the woman who now appears before our eyes has never previously been visible or effective in the world we know. The leading woman in these films is born, by the grace of film and the struggles of politics, into the world that she must learn to live in and, by living in it, change it. The first sign of her existence is the camera's assertion of her physical existence, the kind of visibility that the camera cherishes.

But this very visibility, so easily confused with the idolizing or fetishizing of the woman's bodily presence, gives way to her wish to be effective in the world (despite the adverseness of time and the insufficiency of her means). That is, she wants to become real. She wishes to insert herself not only in the order of society that has been denied her, but also in the order of desire and time, which has been waiting for her, waiting for her willingness to be born again.

Frye, on the other hand, ends where we began, with something close to Nietzsche's powerful surmise that "an audience of spectators was unknown to the Greeks" (1872, 1886: 62–63). On the last page of his book, Frye has this to say about what I called the antagonisms of time:

> In the nonexistent world below, time is the universal devourer that has finally nothing to swallow but itself. Prospero's great speech at the end of the masque tells us that everything we perceive disappears in this time. That is, the world of the spectator is ultimately abolished. What is presented to us must be possessed by us, as Prospero tells us. (1995: 159)

To keep this from being simply a struggle of the metaphysics of timelessness against the ordinary time of the spectator requires something like the overcoming of the metaphysics of revenge, of time as the devourer. In turn, what keeps this from being simply a more decorous version of the repetition of the same is that we remain to be transformed, suspended between faith and action. This is something like the state where we made our entrance. Only now the conflict of Apollonian dream world and Dionysian chaos is resolved in a more complex idea of dreaming. "We are such stuff as dreams are made on" now means that we are produced as beings in time, both malleable and inexorable, by the same forces that produce our dreams, beyond time, and must learn to live with the doubleness that makes us up. Our dreams and selves tend back to the medium of that nourishment: our little lives are rounded with a sleep. Sleep is not an emblem of death so much as a mode of experiencing time and desire and image, which is opposed to our normal sense of death as a violent ending and which composes us anew.

In Cavell's vision of film, the movies do not transform the spectators so much as displace them. We are displaced from the stream of action and people by what Cavell first called the "projection" of reality, a projection that leaves the time of these events in some kind of past. (If the stories movies tell had a tense, Cavell once said, it would be the past tense.) This double displacement of place and time leaves room for the kind of absorption we are only rarely likely to know in the other arts. The ground of seriousness in film has had much to gain from this absorption. But perhaps even more powerfully, comedies have still another story to tell and to show: it is the comedy not of moments but of hours and days, the comedy of pleasures light enough to hold the screen, and nourishing enough to keep us coming back for more.

But since there is no happily ever after, no single grand laugh to keep us unappeased and hungry, we are to learn to let go of those human luminaries, those tellers of time, able now and then to tell time for ourselves, and for once to call it quits.

Early in *All's Well That End's Well*, we are presented with a real abhorrence of an imagined incest. But Helena's imagination shows not only the power of her own love for Bertram but the power of his mother's love for Helena at once to create and to annihilate the civilized connections and prohibitions that love must find itself within. The Countess, thinking that Helena is worried about her lowly station in life, insists that she is Helena's mother. Helena shrinks back, saying: "But, I your daughter, he must be my brother?" (act 1, scene 3, line 82). This gives the Countess room to force from her a confession of love and to support her project to go to France. The mother's love has the power to make Helena her own (and to advance the plot) by supporting her projects and her love. But as we shall see, even in a modern age, such powers vie with the power of the law and hence are dangerous.

The sense that love can overcome political boundaries but not the boundary of incest, not even a sort of fictional incest, engendered by a quasi-maternal love may not be exactly funny, but it is the magic of Romance. It is not so much the magic of magic, but the magic of mothers—their humor, as one might say. The mothers' power to support the actions of the young enables them to complete their projects. The mother cherishes these projects as she cherishes her young, uncaring how the world will see it, knowing, however, that a mother's love "hath in it a bond/whereof the world takes note" (act 1, scene 3, lines 172–73). This is a vision of a mother's love that marks our actions as successful, despite what the world calls success, for we are their successors. Using Cavell's terms, we may say that in Shakespeare's romances the couple cannot have grown up together, that the man's particular overcoming of class shows the heroine's ability to solve the puzzlement of our will by the law, by class, by birth.

I close with a glance at a film just outside the scope of Cavell's investigations—though not outside the conceptual frame that he and Frye provide. *Lone Star*, written and directed by John Sayles, is not a comedy, but it walks us up to so many boundaries and taboos that it is hard to see what kind of drama it is. Cavell speaks of the genre of the End of Romance, from which he backtracked into thinking through the structure of the great Romances. If there were a genre in which we learn to survive the end of Romance, the end of tragedy and myth, of the Western, of the army outpost and the drama of generations, that would be a template of Sayles's ambition. The closing of the army base, explicitly an emblem of opportunity for black soldiers and a black colonel (who also figures in one of the "private" generational conflicts), will affect the town's economy. Its Mexican-descended majority is about to assume a more equitable share of the town's power. Various private dramas are played out, adding up to a collective memory, a collective secret or repression of memory, which enables a collective and relatively stable present.

The quest by the sheriff, the son of a legendary sheriff (a quest recalling *Destry Rides Again*), for the truth within his father's legend is matched by the daughter's wish to understand and to evade the fate of her mother, the respectable immigrant owner of a successful Mexican restaurant. The mother's refrain to her workers, "Speak English!!" is an emblem of the pathos of denying your own expressive past and also, finally, a warning to the audience that it does not know the force of its own words and has lost touch with its capacity for making sense. Both mother and daughter represent versions of ethnic political power, the daughter searching for a deeper past of shifting borders and illusory identities, made real by music, politics, and love.

What is brought to an end most graphically is the romance of the drive-in movie in a small town: a small thing, it may seem, compared to those issues of class, race, and sex. But the movie leaves us in front of a boarded-up drive-in screen, after the last of the last picture shows has ended, after a childhood, which is now not the source of their intimacy, but the fulfillment of their actual if unknown incest.

The hero, having given up the search for his father's mythically guilty past, having perhaps hoped to find his own genuine present in the overcoming of that guilty past, stumbles on his father's actual guilt. He discovers a more everyday, more mundane collection of sins, something more in keeping with the structure and the hidden aggressions of class and race: his father took a mistress of a subordinated race. It is a shoddier, less romantic misdeed, but it casts its shadow farther than murder, making the son incestuous after the fact. That this is discovered through letters ("our daughter") and pictures of recreation suggests that the words and pictures of the defunct motion picture theater live on in the motion picture before our eyes. This movie forbids nostalgia, forcing us to decide what to make of our queasiness or our romanticism—should we find ourselves simply on the side of the couple's desires.

In *Lone Star*, the mysteries of birth and power reinstate the boundaries of incest. Love had thought to conquer language and politics and the man's past, and the iciness and "Spanish" *hauteur* of the woman's mother, the illegitimacy not of their own love but of their parents'. In the end, they are suddenly confronted with the past transgression made palpable as the question of whether they have a future. The man answers her explicit question: "That's it?" after a moment's pause. "If I met you today for the first time, I'd feel exactly the same way." Cavell sees the threat to the principal couple as the tinge of incest in "having grown up together." *Lone Star* pictures a couple that literally grew up together, having to imagine themselves as starting from scratch, as if the purity of their feeling is one condition for starting over with each other, in a new time and a new place.

Hence, the question of their unlawful knowledge of each other is subverted by the possibility of the renewal of time. And the woman—this woman of politics and pride in her history and her race—confirms him: "And forget the Alamo." It is something of a question, whether the Alamo can be forever forgotten, for this woman and this man. But for the moment, they move on together, as the camera moves back, in jump cuts that show them alone, still in front of a blank screen. This screen can mean either that we are done with those movies and that past, or that the true movie, the movie of their life in a new present, has yet to begin.

As this particular scene of incest fades to black, along with the past of that politics of race, violence, money, sex, parents, and pain, the questions of politics and color remain off screen, just out of the reach of love. But this love, here and now, withdrawing from the drive-in movie screen, letting go, for once, of the pain of the Alamo (with the echo of its legendary line in the sand; with the exacerbated repetition, in movies and classrooms, of the battle now become the battle cry) settles something: the future is still open. What we are fated to is what we allow ourselves to accept as fate. Both this couple and the mythical place called America are still undefined, still as metaphysical as they are physical or materialistic. If the movie cannot resolve the pain of the politics of race once and for all, as comedy cannot *show* the unity of a marriage, the politics and the comedy of this movie could show us the willingness for mutual love outside the law. And, given that the man has come from a line of sheriffs increasingly renouncing violence for subtler forms of aggression, his lone star stands for the kind of honor that is willing to renounce aggression, and the office of the legitimized uses of aggression.

The woman knows her mother's choice between sexuality and respectability is not her choice. The man chooses the woman's knowledge—and her willingness to forget. He lets go of the legendary murder, and he chooses the everyday misadventures of their lives. This may not be comedy and may not be a laughing matter. But it is a form of art that represents a genuine successor to comedy, choosing the status of love outside the law over the status of aggression under the cover of the law. Choosing to resign the badge of the law for the power of love, it solves the "problem" posed by Frye's concept of the harsh law that shadows the progress of Shakespeare's romance. Like Huck Finn, they light out for the territories, where freedom perhaps still lives. But this time, a couple goes together, presumably where the American *polis* still has a chance to escape from the surveillance of the past and its all too omnipresent parental discontent. So the impulse to comedy and to transgression has returned to one of the oldest stories in our books. The not-so-young couple must evade the strictures of the world of the parents, and the incestuous bond that the parents enabled, if only to forbid it. What is tragic is our politics, where each act of heroism is the grounds for a sacrifice, and no race or tribe or class is left unscathed by the past. What is comic is still the old eros, the old comedian of our lives. It breaks down barriers, but only at the cost of our willingness to leave behind the parental repressions and the shadows of the institutions they created. We leave behind their restaurants and their jails, as well as their badges and their legends, the body as well as the spirit of heroism. And we must leave it for the sake of nothing more—but nothing less—than our transgressive love.

NOTES

1. Coming to terms with this surprise was helped by conversations with Nickolas Pappas and by Pappas 2005: 194ff. Unattributed translations and commentary on the translations should be attributed to Pappas.

2. The drama of ordinary joke telling is part of the drama of ordinary conversation and involves the tension of taking over, momentarily, the attention of the group, singling oneself out. Naturally enough, more attention has been given to the various genres of jokes and stories that more or less naturally command our attention, perhaps even across long intervals of time (compare with Cohen 1999). Joke telling and its genres are perhaps more episodic in nature than other forms of comedy, hence closer to a narrative oral tradition than they are commonly credited with.

3. Here one must also mention Mikhail Bakhtin's influential idea of the carnivalesque, as developed, e.g., in Bakhtin 1984. But it must also be said that while carnivals tend to be festive, not all days of festivity share in the carnivalesque.

REFERENCES

Aristophanes. (1961). *The Birds* (W. Arrowsmith, trans.). New York: New American Library.

Bakhtin, M. (1984). *Rabelais and His World* (H. Iswolsky, trans.). Bloomington: Indiana University Press.

Barber, C. L. (1959). *Shakespeare's Festive Comedy: A Study of Dramatic Form and Its Relation to Social Custom*. Princeton: Princeton University Press.

Cavell, S. (1981). *Pursuits of Happiness: The Hollywood Comedy of Remarriage*. Cambridge: Harvard University Press.

Cohen, T. (1999). *Jokes: Philosophical Thoughts on Joking Matters*. Chicago: University of Chicago Press.

Frye, N. (1995). *A Natural Perspective*. New York: Columbia University Press.

Morreall, J. (1998). "Comedy". *In* M. Kelly (ed.), *The Encyclopedia of Aesthetics*. Vol 1: 401–405. New York: Oxford University Press.

Nietzsche, F. (1967). *The Birth of Tragedy and the Case of Wagner* (W. Kaufmann, trans.). New York: Random House. Original publication 1872; second edition 1886.

Oates, W. J., and O'Neill, E., Jr., eds. (1938). *The Complete Greek Drama*. New York: Random House.

Pappas, N. (2005). *The Nietzsche Disappointment: Reckoning with Nietzsche's Unkept Promises on Origins and Outcomes*. Lanham: Roman and Littlefield.

Plato. (1989). *Symposium*. (A. Nehamas and P. Woodruff, trans.). Indianapolis: Hackett.

Wimsatt, W. K. (1969). *The Idea of Comedy: Essays in Prose and Verse; Ben Jonson to George Meredith*. Englewood Cliffs, N.J.: Prentice-Hall.

CHAPTER 5

....

PASTORAL

....

MARK PAYNE

SOCRATES, in book 10 of Plato's *Republic*, argues that tragedy allows the faculty of pity to grow strong by feeding on the sorrows of others and that comedy, in similar fashion, strengthens the part of a person that enjoys the ridiculous (606b–c). From the perspective of literary history, what Socrates suggests is that the existence of the various genres can be explained by appeal to human nature. They exist to give pleasure and satisfaction to the parts of the soul that take delight in the kinds of actions they portray, and they do so by producing in their audience the same kind of emotional and cognitive events as occur in the world of the representation.

Aristotle takes the hint. Tragedy, he argues, achieves a catharsis of pity and fear in its audience, while the characteristic pleasure of comedy is the amusement of witnessing some act of error or shame that is painless and not harmful (*Poetics* 5–6, 1448a31–49b28). The association of the genres with basic psychic functions goes hand in hand with Aristotle's assertion that their origins are to be located in a dim prehistory. He argues that tragedy's evolution from archaic religious festivals has been documented and that comedy developed in a similar fashion, although the stages in its development can no longer be recovered. While both genres perfected the satisfactions that they offer their audience in the classical polis, their origins lie in the tentative efforts of village life to cater to these same needs.

In this respect, these genres differ from pastoral, which comes into being in the Hellenistic period with the handful of poems about shepherds written by Theocritus, a Sicilian Greek, in the first half of the third century B.C.E. Some questions that suggest themselves, then, are these: If the legibility and persistence of genres is to be explained by their association with fundamental psychic functions, what are these functions in the case of pastoral? How was it that these few poems could found a tradition that came to have the solidity and permanence of genres like tragedy and comedy? What satisfactions did they offer that earlier literature had not, and what did later authors do with them as they refashioned the genre for their own purposes?

In attempting to answer these questions here, I do not offer an exhaustive history. Instead, I examine some decisive moments in the growth and decline of pastoral in the hope that I can identify the characteristic attractions of a genre that was once a canonical element of the Western literary tradition and also suggest some reasons why it eventually fell out of favor.[1]

Spring: The *Idylls* of Theocritus

The bucolic poems of Theocritus have their origin in the reinvention of Greek literature in the Hellenistic period that saw, in addition to bucolic poetry, the creation of the *epyllion,* or short, highly crafted poem on an epic subject; the emergence of what has been called "literary drama," brief dramatic poems for reading, that, unlike the dramatic monologues of the later Western tradition—Robert Browning's "My Last Duchess" is a familiar example—feature more than one speaker; and the spectacular growth of the epigram as a vehicle of self-expression (see Payne 2007).

In the poetry of Callimachus, in particular, there is a new and explicit concern for the ways in which a writer's work can be understood as a manifestation of the self that produced it. Poets no longer present themselves as caretakers of an actual past that shows itself again through their poems, but as creators of the fictional worlds that their poems bring into existence. Aristotle adumbrates the new poetics of the Hellenistic period in the *Nicomachean Ethics* (9.7.3–4, 1167b34–68a4), where he argues that poets are to their works as parents are to their children in that both have conferred upon them the supreme benefit: existence.[2]

It is, then, in a literary and philosophical culture interested in the relationship between fictionality and selfhood that the bucolic poetry of Theocritus makes its appearance. The new genre celebrates its embrace of fictionality in various ways. The herdsmen that give the poems their distinctive protagonists come and go as they please, without masters to answer to or flocks with pressing needs. They spend their time singing, and their surroundings are a pleasure zone of trees, streams, springs, and breezes. Nothing obliges them to act, and the poems they inhabit are largely plotless as a result. The genre in no sense offers a realistic portrait of rural labor, and its characters are not rustic counterparts to the slaves of urban comedy.

At its most aggressive, the manifest fictionality of the poems playfully severs the connective tissue that binds them to earlier literature. In *Idyll* 11, Theocritus refashions the Cyclops of the *Odyssey* as a love-sick herdsman, pining for the sea nymph Galatea. His Cyclops is noncompossible with his Homeric antecedent, and the only way to link the two is by imagining a fiction of our own in which the erotic disappointment that Polyphemus suffers in Theocritus's poem somehow produces the monster of Homer's.

What Theocritus does with Homer in *Idyll* 11, he does with his own creation in *Idyll* 6. Here we find a herdsman by the name of Damoetas pretending to be Polyphemus, but a Polyphemus who now shuns the infatuated nymph who pursues him relentlessly. The revision is carried through to the smallest details: the single eye and hairy brow that in *Idyll* 11 are acknowledged as reasons for his repulsiveness to the nymph have, in *Idyll* 6, become a source of pride for the reimagined Cyclops.

The poem points both to the lability of the bucolic character and to impersonation as the action that defines it. In poem after poem, what it means to be bucolic is to imagine oneself as another bucolic character. The performance by which Thyrsis proves his exemplary status as bucolic singer in *Idyll* 1 is a reenactment of the herdsman Daphnis. The goatherd of *Idyll* 3 introduces a series of legendary bucolic predecessors with whom he endeavors to identify. Comatas in *Idyll* 5 juggles positive and negative models of the herdsman in Daphnis and Melantheus. Lycidas, the exemplary herdsman singer in *Idyll* 7, wishes he could have heard the voice of the famous Comatas.

To have heard bucolic song is to have been inspired with a desire to emulate its leading characters, and dramatic impersonation is one way in which this desire expresses itself. By imagining themselves as others, the herdsmen try out roles from the bucolic repertory, and so stage their own imaginative involvement with the pastoral world of which they are a part. As a result, the characters seldom match up from one poem to the next: the Polyphemus of *Idyll* 6 is constructed point by point for contrast with the Cyclops of *Idyll* 11; the idealized Comatas for whom Lycidas longs in *Idyll* 7 bears no resemblance to the foul mouthed and aggressive Comatas of *Idyll* 5. The more strongly the character is reimagined and appropriated, the happier the impersonator is likely to be. Daphnis and Damoetas in *Idyll* 6 end their songs surrounded by skipping calves; Lycidas, in *Idyll* 7, is able to cure himself of erotic yearning by projecting an idealized Comatas to himself; even Polyphemus, in *Idyll* 11, is able to get remission from his cravings by imagining a strong image of himself as the proprietor of a pastoral paradise.

In occasions of distress, then, the bucolic poems propose mimetic desire as the most effective therapy.[3] Rather than, in Plato's phrase, making lamentation vanish with the medicine of self-examination (*Republic* 604d), the bucolic characters achieve contentment by turning away from themselves through willed identification with their imaginary counterparts. They become bucolic not by discovering a certain kind of self but by imagining and projecting one: this is the characteristic action around which the new genre centers and that takes the place of the unfolding of character in action that for Aristotle is the chief attraction of narrative literature.

The herdsmen's extension of selfhood through identification with imaginary counterparts thematizes the allure of the newly won concept of fictionality of which they themselves are a preeminent example and prepares the ground for the identification of poet with herdsman that will be of decisive importance for the future of the genre. For it is this identification that makes the pastoral world an explicit image of imaginative activity expressed as literary invention.

The relationship between the author and his own pastoral creation is first broached in Theocritus's *Idyll 7*. In this poem, a young poet by the name of Simichidas tells of his meeting with a shepherd by the name of Lycidas. Unlike the other bucolic *Idylls*, which are enacted in a dramatic present, this poem is a retrospective narration with a precise real-world location. It reads like autobiography and was understood as such by ancient readers who identified the young poet with Theocritus. Lycidas, on the other hand, is clearly a bucolic character—he looks like one and sings like one, and his gift of a staff to Simichidas parallels the scene of poetic initiation between Hesiod and the Muses in the *Theogony*.

Inspiration narratives are fairly frequent in Hellenistic poetry, although the encounter with the inspiring being is elsewhere deferred to dreams by the poets of this period. By employing the heteronym Simichidas in *Idyll 7*, Theocritus allows a version of himself to meet his invention Lycidas in a fictional inspiration scene in which this youthful self-representation is inspired by his own creation. By fashioning a poem in which the fictionalized author emulates his own fictional character, Theocritus creates an autobiographical narrative that, elusive as it is, remains faithful to the message of the other bucolic *Idylls*, that we free ourselves to change by identifying with the products of the fictionalizing imagination.

The presence of the author in a fictional world of his own invention, encountering there what is recognizably one of his own fictional creations, is an innovation in literary world building that will be vitally significant to the future of bucolic poetry. For if Simichidas is Theocritus, and Simichidas can meet Lycidas, the poet can be located in his poems in all kinds of guises and disguises. Traces of the interpretive questions this possibility raises can be found in ancient commentary on the poems, and Theocritus's poetic successors respond to the opportunity to place themselves in their poems with imaginative verve.

Most notably, the *Epitaph for Bion* presents a scene in which the historical poet Bion was known to, associated with, and continues to be lamented by his own bucolic characters: "Galatea too weeps for your song, whom you used to delight as she sat beside you on the shore.... Now she sits upon the lonely sands, and tends your flocks till this hour" (lines 58–63). The poem does not merely call a historical poet a herdsman explicitly for the first time (Van Sickle 1976: 27; Alpers 1996: 153). More ambitiously, it posits a bucolic world in which beings from different ontological domains can mingle freely.

The unknown author of the *Lament for Bion* emphasizes his own, and the dead Bion's, allegiance to the bucolic poetry of Theocritus. However, in making the bucolic poem a world in which ontologically problematic content between the realms of myth, bucolic literature, and historical reality can be staged, he goes well beyond the model that authorizes his experiments in this regard. In doing so, he foregrounds the power of the bucolic poet as fiction maker to appropriate entities from all of these realms to create the world of his poems. In the actual world, it is impossible for a poet to meet a character he has invented, although, as the prologue to Hesiod's *Theogony* reveals, he may record his encounters with gods in a way that eludes definitive redescription as either literary trope or autobiographical testimony. For it is widely believed that some kind of interaction between human beings and gods is possible.

Contact between actual and fictional entities is not, however, conventionally accepted, although in bucolic poetry it can be shown. Theocritus, in *Idyll 7*, masks its ontological and cognitive difficulties by inventing the heteronym Simichidas to stage his meeting with the fictional being Lycidas. The author of the *Lament for Bion* is far less reticent. He quite unabashedly asserts Bion's coexistence with his fictional creations and leaves his readers to work out the consequences.

SUMMER: THE *ECLOGUES* OF VIRGIL

As the *Idylls* imagine the transformation of the herdsmen in the image of their own songs, the *Lament for Bion*, like the autobiographical *Idyll 7*, imagines the transformation of a historical poet in the image of his own fiction. The emulation that is characteristic of bucolic poetry is not just poem-internal. Rather, the problematic contact between historical and fictional worlds makes bucolic poetry the genre in which the recursive relationship between literary fiction and historical reality is most clearly staged and investigated: if the dead poet of the *Lament* is represented as a herdsman, this is because he has experienced the same transformation as Theocritus's fictional characters—by singing of bucolic singers he became one himself.

The ease of such transformations is taken for granted in the bucolic poems of Theocritus; the majority of the herdsmen blend without difficulty into their imagined doubles, Thyrsis with Daphnis, Lycidas with Comatas, Damoetas and Daphnis with Polyphemus and his friend. While the goatherd of *Idyll 3* has some difficulty in convincing himself (and us) of his resemblance to his self-elected models, his inability to have the kind of imaginative life he desires lies simply in his failure to imagine this life with sufficient conviction.

Virgil's shepherds, by contrast, are circumscribed by a history and a politics that have the power to suspend this freedom indefinitely. Tityrus, in *Eclogue 1*, may "meditate his woodland Muse on slender reed," but Meliboeus, his interlocutor, is an exile from his country and so incapable of bucolic song. Under such circumstances, continuing commitment to a poetics of fictionality looks like self-deception or willful ignorance. As Meliboeus tells us that Tityrus makes the woods echo the name of Amaryllis, attentive readers will recall that Amaryllis is the beloved of the goatherd of *Idyll 3*, the one Theocritean singer whose grasp of his own genre is manifestly lacking.

As the poem progresses, more details about the exile of Meliboeus emerge. While Tityrus has a protector in Rome who has preserved the tenure of his land for him, Meliboeus's fields are to become the property of an "impious soldier," his dispossession a result of discord among "the wretched citizens" (lines 70–72). The threat that hovered around the opening of the poem takes on a recognizable historical shape: what threatens the herdsmen is expulsion from their land so that this property may be awarded to military veterans, just as land was in fact expropriated for such veterans in the aftermath of the civil wars.

The poem offers a series of analogues between its pastoral fiction and the world in which that fiction is published that cannot easily be worked into a single equation. If Tityrus is an emulator of Theocritus whose land was preserved for him through the agency of a powerful figure at Rome, the suggestion of the ancient commentator Servius that Tityrus is a figure of the poet, whose own land was preserved for him by some such person, seems natural enough. Yet modern scholars have pointed to the impossibility of this identification in other respects—Tityrus is a white-haired ex-slave, and, more tellingly, his conception of bucolic song falls far short of the complex mediation of historical reality and bucolic fiction in *Eclogue* 1 itself (Putnam 1970: 64–75).

In addition to these puzzling coincidences of fictional and historical content, the formal organization of the collection at times conflates historical author with fictional character and at times suspends this conflation. The order of the poems that is consistently observed in the manuscript tradition, and that is generally held to reflect an edition made by the poet himself, shows a clear alternation in mode of presentation: the odd-numbered poems are dramatic, and the even-numbered poems not. While there is considerable variety of both types, Virgil gives a consistent pattern to the diversity of form that characterizes Theocritus's bucolic poetry (Coleman 1977: 20–21; Van Sickle 1978: 19–20).

According to ancient literary theory, the alternation between narrative and dramatic poems ought to correspond to an alternation between poet's speech and character speech. This distinction disappears, however, as the book unfolds. *Eclogue* 2 begins with narrative: "The shepherd Corydon loved the fair Alexis." *Eclogue* 3 opens with unframed dialogue between Menalcas and Damoetas: "Tell me, Damoetas, whose flock is this? Is it that of Meliboeus?" The reader naturally assumes that since *Eclogue* 2 is narration, the speaker who introduces the long speech by Corydon in *Eclogue* 2 is the poet, and that the dialogue between the characters in *Eclogue* 3 is a dramatic fiction from which the poet has absented himself.

In *Eclogue* 5, however, the character Menalcas offers to give to Mopsus the reed pipe "which taught me 'Corydon loved the fair Alexis,' and 'Whose flock is this? Is it that of Meliboeus?'" Either the narrator of *Eclogue* 2 was not in fact Virgil, but the shepherd Menalcas, and the dramatic fiction of *Eclogue* 3 was authored by this same character, or Virgil himself has been an inhabitant of his own pastoral world and while within it gave his pipe to Menalcas, who is now giving it to Mopsus (Hardie 2002: 21; Breed 2006: 354–57).[4] As we wonder about these questions, we face the same dilemma that we face in *Eclogue* 1. Rather than the option to see the bucolic characters as instances of authorial self-projection, a possibility we may freely accept or reject in Theocritus's *Idylls*, Virgil confronts us simultaneously with both the necessity and the impossibility of this identification.

The relationship between Menalcas and the poet is explored at greater length in *Eclogue* 9, a dialogue between the herdsmen Moeris and Lycidas that is carefully patterned on Theocritus's *Idyll* 7. In response to Moeris's eviction from his land, Lycidas recalls his erroneous belief that "Menalcas had saved everything with his songs." Having been corrected by Moeris, the two exchange fragments of Menalcas's works that look back over the *Eclogues* as a whole and trace their resemblance to, and divergence from, the bucolic poetry of Theocritus. Having completed half their journey—they reach the very point at which the Lycidas of *Idyll* 7 makes his appearance as the inspirational genius of bucolic song—they postpone further singing and resolve to go on in silence. Menalcas never appears. Historical reality trumps poetic fiction and the character who is credited with songs that mirror Virgil's achievement in the collection as a whole apparently cannot save Moeris from the same fate as Meliboeus in *Eclogue* 1.

The prospectus of bucolic poetry in the figure of Menalcas is a prelude to the renunciation of the genre in the last poem of the book. Here Menalcas does make a brief appearance among the herdsmen and pastoral divinities that visit the suffering Gallus. Yet this Menalcas is kept at arm's length by the strong authorial voice that tells us at the end of the poem that the poet is hanging up his pipes. The Menalcas of *Eclogue* 5 could hardly be more strongly identified with the poet himself; the Menalcas of *Eclogue* 9 is an echo of the author, his songs a tenebrous double of the *Eclogues* themselves; the Menalcas of *Eclogue* 10, by contrast, is a minor character who is distant from the narrative voice of the poem in which he appears.

The possibility and the degree of identification between Virgil and his herdsmen shift as we make our way through the *Eclogues*. For Servius, Virgil's self-representation as Tityrus is an accommodation to the necessities of patronage at a difficult moment in Roman history. Theocritus, he claims, is always straightforwardly mimetic (his herdsmen are herdsmen and nothing more), but Virgil needed to thank the patrons who had saved his land and so there are moments in his poems when this character stands for the poet. We should not look for such moments everywhere, Servius suggests, but only in passages that deal with this issue. Nevertheless, the presence of allegory is not to be deplored, since it is a sophistication (*urbanitas*) that distinguishes his poems from those of his predecessor (Thilo 1887: 2–3, 33).

We would, of course, prefer to ascribe more ambitious intentions to Virgil's transformation of his models. The poet did not introduce biographical allegory into his poems because his particular situation left him no choice but to vitiate the pure fictionality of his pastoral world with historical references. Rather he chose to do so in order to reveal the ultimate dependence of all literary fictions on the social and political circumstance in which they emerge. Nonetheless, as defenders of Servius have argued, his "principle of discontinuous allegory" recognizes that Virgil does, at moments, identify himself with his characters in a way that

Theocritus does not, and that these moments make art's social and political commitments explicit. While Servius does not explore the more complicated relationship between Virgil and Menalcas, his reading anticipates modern comparisons of the two poets insofar as it is recognizes, and praises, in the *Eclogues* a departure from the "semantic transparency and innocence" of mimetic representation in Theocritus, as a result of which bucolic poetry, for the first time, "becomes a metaphor for something other than itself" (Patterson 1987: 34).[5]

Such a contrast ignores the fundamental role of impersonation and mimetic desire in the bucolic poetry of Theocritus. The doubleness of his herdsmen allows them to be read as figures of authorial self-projection, and it is only by treating the *Idylls* as a foil to the *Eclogues* that this complexity disappears. What is different about Theocritus's herdsmen is neither their simplicity nor their realism, but the fact that, with the exception of *Idyll* 7, their legibility as authorial self-projection is not connected to particular historical circumstances as it is in the *Eclogues*. Reading the self-fictionalizing songs of the characters of the *Idylls* as analogous to those of their author is thus a possibility rather than a requirement, though the emulation of the fictional herdsman Lycidas in the autobiography of the bucolic poet Simichidas in *Idyll* 7 nudges us in this direction.

The *Eclogues*, by contrast, make inescapable, though fleeting, identifications between poet and character, so that we have no alternative at these moments but to read the pastoral world as a figure of the poet's own circumstances. As the *Aeneid* fuses myth with annalistic history, so the *Eclogues* fuse contemporary reality with pastoral fiction, drastically increasing both the number and the transparency of the connections between the pastoral world and the history of the poet's own times. In particular, when real historical events explain the presence or absence of a character within the pastoral world, this world looks inescapably like a way of thinking about the tragedies of history through a darkening of the pastoral fiction.

The overt, robust, and cheerful fictionality of Theocritean pastoral has the form of an invitation. Apart from the problem of unsatisfied desire—not really a problem in any case since it is the membership pass to bucolic society—the only cloud that hangs over the *Idylls* is the poet's melancholy wish, at the end of *Idyll* 7, that he might once again enjoy the experiences we have just heard about. The exclusion that motivates this wish is unexplained, but its effect is to present the world of the poem as effectively closed to its author at the moment of writing. In Virgil such exclusions loom large and make the pastoral world an object of nostalgia even for those within it.

AUTUMN: SPENSER'S *THE SHEPHEARDES CALENDER*

Virgil's prestige ensured that the *Eclogues* became an object of emulation in Latin literary culture. Particularly noteworthy are the *Bucolica* of Calpurnius Siculus (first century) and Nemesianus (third century). Although these poems have not received the critical attention devoted to Virgil, both develop the pastoral genre in innovative ways that repay comparison with Theocritus's Greek successors.

Calpurnius's pastoral double, Corydon, is a rustic praise poet who remains stable as a figure of the author throughout the collection. His changing fortunes allow Calpurnius to develop a subtle account of poetry's dependence upon courtly patronage and the operations of the pastoral fiction in which such dependency is figured (Newlands 1987: 218–31). Ambivalence about the countryside also appears in his extravagant praise of the amphitheater at Rome even as this wide-eyed wonder reveals the panegyric value of the genre: the rustic's innocent eye allows his sophisticated readers to experience their city once again for the marvel it truly is.

The four poems of Nemesianus transmitted with the text of Calpurnius exhibit a formal variety that ranges among the familiar types of pastoral poem, and so, at the end of the tradition, give its salient forms in miniature. All four are beautifully written and display an imaginative handling of the genre's conventions. In addition, the second shows a kind of desperate physical eroticism on the part of its shepherd boys that issues in violence against the love object and differs markedly from the experience of desire in the earlier tradition. Nemesianus, however, eschews the ambitions of the book-length projects of Virgil and Calpurnius; his poems are discrete compositions like those of Theocritus; they make no reference to contemporary history, and their poet does not appear in them in bucolic disguise.

It is, by contrast, the ambition of the pastoral collection and its claims as a cipher of contemporary reality that will particularly appeal to Renaissance pastoralists, and these give characteristic expression to what has been called the "massive incursion of shepherds" into the literature of the period (Iser 1989: 75). While it may seem strange to refer to the first canonical manifestation of such ambitions in English under the rubric of "Autumn," Edmund Spenser (c. 1552–1599) is both heir to the medieval pastoral tradition (Cooper 1976) and a conscious emulator of contemporary continental models (Burrow 2001: 220; Greene 2001: 238). His project strives for a condition of maximum ripeness at a time when the genre attains its greatest prestige.

Three features of *The Shepheardes Calender* are immediately striking in comparison with the pastoral poetry of antiquity: the clear organization of the collection according to the calendar theme, the enormous amount of paratextual material with which Spenser has surrounded his poems, and their extraordinary metrical variety (Alpers 1996: 182; Berger 1988: 319, 327).

Each month of the calendar consists not only of the poem by that name but of a woodcut, an argument, an emblem, a gloss, and a gloss of the emblem. The interpretive efforts of E.K., Spenser's self-inflicted commentator, include, but are not limited to, the identification of rhetorical and poetic figures, notes on literary imitation, revelations concerning the disguised identity of the pastoral characters, and reminders of the mimetic decorum that informs the depiction of rustics. In addition to this line-by-line commentary, there is, at the outset, a synoptic division of the collection as a whole into "three forms or rankes": plaintive, recreative, and moral poems. The hovering interpreter seeks to guide affective as well as cognitive responses, and the world of the work is tightly ringed by hermeneutic imperatives that challenge us to make sense of it even as we are trying to read and imagine it.

The circumscription of the pastoral world by an external interpretive apparatus would of course have been familiar to Spenser from his ancient texts, but it is worth pondering the consequences of his choice to emulate this presentation in the appearance of his own work. In "February," E.K. notes the virtuosity of the poet's description of winter that "may bee indifferently taken, eyther for old Age, or for Winter season." Likewise, in the tale of the oak and the briar, the semantic transparency of the allegorical fable is constantly occluded by the richness of the fabulistic description, as the pathos of the farmer's assault on the oak, and the death of the briar as a result, are given with an animistic empathy worthy of Ovid's *Metamorphoses*:

> The byting frost nipt his stalke dead,
> The watrie wette weighed downe his head,
> And heaped snowe burdned him so sore,
> That nowe upright he can stand no more. (lines 230–33)

Cuddie cuts Thenot off after a couple more lines with a complaint that his long tale contains little of value, and his gesture seems to thematize the reader's likely reaction: the more storylike Thenot's tale becomes, the further it drifts from the hermeneutics of allegory toward the pleasures (or frustrations) of fiction. So, too, in "May," Palinodie responds to Piers's tale of the fox and the goat with the claim that it lacks point—which he promises to supply in his own forthcoming version— and E.K.'s comments on the figure of *fictio* make the gap between the pleasures of invention and the didactic uses to which it may be put all the more apparent.

In "March," Thomalin gives a detailed account of the winged Cupid he has seen entangled in a thicket, and Willye reports that his father, too, once saw him caught in a fowling net "which he for Carrion crowes had set." E.K.'s gloss, that Cupid's appearance is an allegorical representation of the properties of love that should be compared with similar representations in ancient poets, manifestly fails to do justice to the wild blend of the real and the fantastic in the poem itself. Such manifestations of the marvelous in the ordinary English countryside are not so easily assimilated to higher interpretive goals. Likewise, in "July," Morrell's account of the hills of Kent as the resort of "holy Faunes" and "Sylvanes" is not easily reconciled with Thomalin's reverence for these same hills as the home of long dead Christian saints. While E.K. asserts that the former are mere poetic feigning, in the world of the poem no such decision is possible.

To speak, then, of a tension between the represented world and its interpretation hardly does justice to the deliberateness with which Spenser underlines the difference between engaging with his fiction as an imaginative event and interpreting it as a discourse about the world. The emblem to "September" even figures the observer as interpreter in the person of Narcissus and so warns against the dangers of seeing only what we want to see in the world of the poem. For in the case of Narcissus, we learn, "much gazing had bereft him of sence."

So, too, if we pause to marvel at Spenser's metrical virtuosity, we will find ourselves enacting the difference between engaging with the poems as autonomous fictional worlds and appreciating them as artifacts created by their poet. All ancient pastoral, Greek and Latin, is written in the same meter (the dactylic hexameter), and, with a single exception (a later Greek imitation of Theocritus), there are no changes of meter within the poems. Indeed, both Theocritus and Virgil exploit the fact that what within the world of the poems is song, is, at the level of the text, metrically indistinguishable from the dialogue that surrounds it. Nonperformativity is another marker of fictionality and invites the reader to imagine the material difference of the singer's voice that the text does not instantiate.

By contrast, Spenser's metrical variety is palpable and impressive. In addition to differences in meter from one poem to the next, many individual poems feature changes of meter within them that reflect transitions between dialogue and song or between dialogue and fable. The most elaborate is "August," which contains three distinct metrical schemes, one for the framing dialogue, one for the verse-capping song contest, and one for Cuddie's reperformance of a song by Colin Clout, which, not accidentally, happens to be the first English sestina.

The representation of song in this poem's song contest is a closer imitation of actual singing—in its use of nonsemantic vocalization, for example—than anything found in ancient pastorals. In addition, E.K. offers no comment on Colin's sestina, which is lauded by the characters within the poem as the culmination of pastoral song. Is Spenser playing a similar game to the ancient poets here, staging the reader's inability to access the actual sound of vocal performance that, within the world of the poem, sets one singer apart from another? Or should we understand the sestina's complexity as an analogue to the pleasures of the performance, offering a formal satisfaction to the reader that is equivalent to the delight the shepherds take in it as song and that contrasts with the attempt to capture singing mimetically in the song contest that precedes it?

In either case, Spenser's virtuosity is a kind of poetic signature that marks his poems as their author's creation and so in some measure blocks their inhabitability by both his characters and his readers.[6] Reperformance of another character's song is common in pastoral and enables the mimetic emulation at its heart: the herdsmen identify with the singers they imagine in their songs, and these acts of impersonation allow the genre itself to be read as a figure of the imaginative life of its author. However, when Cuddie performs Colin's sestina, there is no sense that he inhabits the imaginary space it offers in this way. Perigot expresses his admiration of Colin's verses and the way in which Cuddie "dolefully his [i.e., Colin's] doole... didst reherse" (lines 190–93).

In addition, we are frequently reminded by E.K. that in the person of Colin "the Authors selfe is shadowed." If Colin is Spenser, then Cuddie would be enacting not Colin's, but Spenser's, virtuosity here and the repeated identification of

Colin with the poet makes E.K.'s lack of comment on the sestina all the more surprising. Once again, the function of the commentator seems to be to underline the
possibility of approaching the fiction in different ways: we may regard the songs as
authored by characters in the poems, or we may read them as transparent demon-
strations of their author's prowess.[7]

E.K. presses his identification of Spenser confidently elsewhere, sifting "poetical fiction" from what is "unfeignedly spoken of the Poete selfe" ("June"; compare
with "September"). Yet this identification can no longer be sustained when his distinctive contribution to the pastoral book, its organization according to a calendar
scheme, is fully realized. For in "December," Colin dies. Indeed, not only does he
die, but he dies with a disavowal of the pastoral project that we are witnessing come
to completion with his death.

What Colin realizes is that human life is not made up of months and seasons.
Looking about him for analogies between his life and nature, he finds he has gone
from spring to winter without the harvest his early years had promised:

> My boughes with blosmes that crowned were at firste,
> And promised of timely fruit such store,
> Are left both bare and barrein now at erst. (lines 103–5)

The failure of the pastoral flowers to bear the fruit of wisdom is further marked by
the absence of an emblem for "December" that would give its character's ethical
aspirations in miniature as the other months do for theirs. Instead, "December"
ends with an epilogue in which the author asserts his distance from his work, now
considered in Horatian mode as a monument of art rather than a projection of
selfhood. "Carefull Colinet" is no longer one with his author.

While renunciation of pastoral for higher forms is a conventional way to end
the pastoral book, Spenser's decision to kill off, rather than simply abandon, his
alter ego is striking—there is no such act of violence in the *Eclogues*—and makes
it all the more remarkable that he should have chosen to bring him back to life
some years later in *Colin Clout's Come Home Again*. Much has been made of pastoral's ability to figure the realities of courtly life under the guise of a protective
fiction (Montrose 1983), and Spenser's second venture into the genre is a splendid
example of these possibilities, as he handles the persons of the court, their accom-
plishments and charms, and even the relative merits of court and country, in a
graceful *poème à clef*.

The Shepheardes Calender is a very different kind of work, however, and the
sort of fiction at which the later work excels operates at best only intermittently
in it (Iser 2006: 78–79). It has none of the knowing, intimate insinuations of the
court insider, and the ecclesiastical controversies of "May," "July," and "September," while unresolved, are as explicit as a writer can be while maintaining any illusion of fictionality. Conversely, Colin's song of "Elisa, Queene of Shepheardes All"
is announced in the Argument to "Aprill" as intended "to the honor and prayse" of
Queen Elizabeth and is, as announced, a fair advertisement of Spenser's promise

as a writer of pastoral panegyric. Yet this song advances Spenser's cause simply by being a "proofe of his more excellencie and skill in poetrie," rather than by reflecting, or reflecting on, anything specific in the world outside the fiction. It is on the perfection of the pastoral achievement itself that Spenser stakes his hopes (see Cullen 1970: 118–19).

WINTER: ARNOLD, MALLARMÉ, PESSOA

One of the ambitions of this collection of essays is to consider for what reasons and under what circumstances a genre ceases to be viable. In the case of pastoral, it is important to note that the genre's exhaustion predates the disappearance of shepherds as familiar figures in everyday life,[8] although this disappearance may make the reemergence of the genre unlikely. To what factors, then, should we ascribe its discontinuation?

It is crucial to pastoral that the poet be able to understand and appropriate the herdsman as a figure of his own imaginative experience and of the practice and potential of imaginative self-projection in human life more generally. Unwillingness to engage in such appropriation is therefore likely to impede the functioning of the genre, as is a more dynamic understanding of the role of the natural world in human development, as an active participant in human formation rather than the "green cabinet" that frames the shepherd's song. Too deep a concern for shepherds as shepherds, and too strong a feeling for nature as such, are, paradoxical as it may at first seem, obstacles to pastoral fiction, and William Wordsworth's preface to the *Lyrical Ballads* contains all the information one needs to understand the obvious antipathy of the Romantics to the genre in its stricter forms.

Wordsworth famously claims to have used "the real language of men" in his poems, avoiding consciously poetic diction,[9] and to have endeavored to illustrate in them "the essential passions of the heart" in the rural circumstances in which they survive uncorrupted by urban culture. He understands his role as poet as "a man speaking to men," communicating his own and others' feelings for the sake of a sympathetic understanding of human life as it really is. Nothing could be further from Wordsworth's intentions than a labyrinth of recreational artifacts that express the poet's capacity for unlimited invention. His is a poetics of service and self-imposed restraint.

"Resolution and Independence" is a powerful manifestation of this antipastoral poetic. Wordsworth describes a walk upon the moors in which he becomes involved in unhappy brooding over the consequences of poets' self-absorption. At this moment of despondency and self-absorption of his own, he comes upon an old man of impressively aged appearance peering into a mountain pool, and he asks him what he is doing in the lonely spot. The man replies that he is gathering leeches, but as he explains his occupation, the poet experiences a kind of sublime alienation from his speech:

> But now his voice to me was like a stream
> Scarce heard; nor word from word could I divide;
> And the whole body of the Man did seem
> Like one whom I had met with in a dream;
> Or like a man from some far region sent,
> To give me human strength, by apt admonishment. (lines 107–12)

Unable to process what is happening to him, the poet recurs to his former fears about poets' self-inflicted isolation and simply repeats his question—"How is it that you live, and what is it you do?"—reenacting in miniature the progress of the poem to this point. The leech gatherer repeats his tale, the poet calms down, and Wordsworth promises himself and us that the man's image will henceforth function as a kind of consolation and self-reproach when he is tempted to feel sorry for himself. The leech gatherer's uncomplaining independence of spirit, we are given to understand, is the opposite of poets' solipsistic tendencies to self-pity.

What in another age might have seemed a promising opportunity for the expansion of the pastoral genre—one can imagine a "Leech-Gatherer Eclogue" alongside other attempts to expand the genre by occupation—here follows an opposite trajectory. Rather than offering himself to the poet for fictionalizing appropriation, the leech gatherer's value to Wordsworth is that, in his lived reality, he rebuffs such efforts at assimilation. His role in the poem is not to be an icon of Wordsworth's imaginative activity as poet, but to enable his imaginative sympathies as an ordinary person, offering a proof of sociality's power to break through the crippling self-absorption that haunts the vocation of poet (see Eldridge 1989: 116–22).

It is against Wordsworth's double disavowal of artifice and fictionality that I want to consider a few last examples of the pastoral impulse, for while the ambition of the pastoral book is no longer to be met with, there are impressive individual efforts to revive the imaginative potential of the bucolic singer, and these last fruits from the old tree are particularly sweet.

Matthew Arnold's most famous statement of his poetics is a declaration of his admiration for Sophocles, who "saw life steadily and saw it whole" ("To a Friend"). The Greek's "even-balanced soul," he claims, "business could not make dull, nor passion wild." So, too, in the preface to the second edition of his *Poems*, Arnold identifies the task of his own poetry as the recovery of sanity: "[T]hat is the great virtue of the ancient literature; the want of which is the great defect of the modern." The literature of his own times, he argues, is characterized by a relentless pursuit of variety and the general intellectual vice of modernity—its addiction to the fantastic.

Arnold's own most successful poetic works are, however, I think it is fair to argue, a brilliant expression of the very emotional and imaginative impulses that he decries in the culture of his age. This is particularly true of his experiments in pastoral poetry, "The Scholar-Gipsy" and "Thyrsis," which are modeled not on the sober classicism of Sophocles (as Arnold saw it), but on the fantastically inventive and emotionally fraught bucolic laments of the later Hellenistic period.

The first of the two, "The Scholar-Gipsy," is a poem of fantasized escape. Addressing his fellow poet and college friend Arthur Hugh Clough as "shepherd," Arnold recalls their walks in the Oxford countryside and the story they shared of a poor scholar who, in an earlier age, fled the university and civic ambition to roam the countryside in self-elected spiritual quest. The pure of heart may still catch a glimpse of him as he haunts the fields and woods, but he shuns all efforts to engage him in conversation. He is above all a figure of flight from the "this strange disease of modern life,"[10] and at the end of the poem he is identified with the refusal of the ancient cultures of the Near East to traffic with the upstart Greeks. In "Thyrsis," the scholar-gipsy is identified with Clough himself, who had died in the meantime, a victim, Arnold suggests, of modernity's enervating and dispiriting dispersal of the self.

In both poems, the richly described landscape is emptied of its human users, not just urban intruders in pursuit of leisure, but also the rural laborers who work its fields, so that the figure of the imagined and imaginary wanderer becomes its sole authentic inhabitant. In "Thyrsis," Arnold himself is tempted by dreams of escape, and his rediscovery of the tree that, in their youth, he and Clough had imagined to be a pledge of the scholar-gipsy's continuing presence in the landscape is enabled by his flight from a party of hunters, which suggests the flight of the gipsy and of Clough himself, who had left England for Italy, disheartened, Arnold claims, by certain egregious social injustices he had encountered in his own country (lines 46–47).

By the end of the poem, however, Arnold has relinquished his claims upon the tree since the possibility of escape it represents properly belongs to Thyrsis/Clough alone and not to himself. He is willing to settle instead for the mere possibility that in the future his friend's voice may yet remind him on occasions of the spiritual ambitions they shared when they were young:

> 'Mid city-noise, not, as with thee of yore,
> Thyrsis! in reach of sheep-bells is my home.
> —Then through the great town's harsh, heart-wearying roar,
> Let in thy voice a whisper often come,
> To chase fatigue and fear:
> *Why faintest thou? I wander'd till I died.*
> *Roam on! The light we sought is shining still.*
> *Dost thou ask proof? Our tree yet crowns the hill,*
> *Our Scholar travels yet the loved hill-side.* (lines 231–40)

Though Arnold feared he had not said enough about Clough in the poem, he has, by its end, become a figure of reproach as effective as Wordsworth's leech gatherer. His power as such derives, however, not from the reality of his life but from the compelling fantasy that Arnold constructs upon it, for the poem is pure fantasy: Arnold believes neither in the mythology of the pastoral and its antique divinities, nor in the scholar-gipsy and the tree that symbolizes his survival. Youth, the countryside, and Clough—all these are really lost to Arnold. But so are the pastoral conventions with which he attempts to console himself for their loss, and it is the very obvious fictitiousness of the reanimated tropology that gives the poem so much of its pathos.

Arnold wills consolation, but his poem is fantastic to its last detail—the whispered voice of the ghostly revenant—and manifests the same inability "to see life steadily and to see it whole" that he laments in the culture of his age. Moreover, the emulation of antiquity that he asserts in his preface as its cure can do nothing to staunch the wound of raw feeling when the beliefs that underpin its literary achievements are presented as manifestly unbelievable. Clough is not "wandering with great Mother's train divine," he is not hearing "the Lityerses-song again," and "Daphnis with his silver voice" is not singing for him. He is simply dead, and modernity, as Arnold understands it and expresses it in his poem, is a condition of nostalgia composed of the desire that it should not be so and the inability to make it otherwise (Lerner 1972: 234–36).[11] This is the limbo of "we" of the "The Scholar Gipsy," we "who never deeply felt, nor clearly will'd, / Whose insight never has borne fruit in deeds" (lines 173–74). It is the condition of those whose imaginative powers are unable to fashion a satisfying solution to their emotional needs. Under such circumstances, the pastoral conventions, and the art language that voices them, can be no more than fictions, which is to say, falsehoods.

The artifice and fictionality that collapse Arnold's pastoral poetry in nostalgia are, in Stéphane Mallarmé's nearly contemporary *L'Après-Midi d'un Faune*, the values that sustain the work and its sylvan protagonist. Mallarmé's faun begins with the question that haunts Arnold's efforts to make use of antiquity: "Aimai-je un rêve?" The faun asserts his desire to "perpetuate" the nymphs that peopled his pastoral vision but wonders if their "incarnat léger" was not perhaps illusory, as it seems to resolve itself into the landscape that surrounds him. He calls for reflection, and wonders to himself, "[S]i les femmes dont tu gloses / Figurent un souhait de tes sens fabuleux."[12]

What the faun learns is that it is the imaginative presence of his visions that matters and not their ontological status (Landy 1994: 60–66). Having calmed the erotic crisis that precipitated his initial outburst, he returns, at the end of the poem, to a state of pastoral lethargy, as he bids farewell to the nymphs and embraces the possibility that they were, in all likelihood, figments of the landscape as he had initially feared: "Couple, adieu; je vais voir l'ombre que tu devins."

The faun's imaginative trajectory exactly parallels that of Theocritus's successful bucolic singers, such as Lycidas and Polyphemus, who are able to quiet their erotic distress by projecting to themselves a vividly imagined version of their own pastoral existence (Walker 1978: 109–12). Likewise, the success of the faun's imaginative exercise is immediately legible as an image of his author's: "[D]roit et seul, sous un flot antique de lumière," the faun is a brilliantly persuasive evocation of antiquity, and the poem asks no more of this vision than that it be fully present to the imagination. Its enactment of fictional presence points toward the famous sonnet that celebrates just this process of self-satisfaction through the willful evocation of an antique landscape:

> Mes bouquins refermés sur le nom de Paphos
> Il m'amuse d'élire avec le seul génie
> Une ruine, par mille écumes bénie
> Sous l'hyacinthe, au loin, de ses jours triomphaux.

Mallarmé's first version of *L'Après-Midi d'un Faune* was intended for the stage, but his desire for performance came to be replaced by an understanding of his literary drama as a kind of ideal theater that gave verbal realization to the multiplicity of selfhood: "A la rigueur un papier suffit pour évoquer toute pièce: aidé de sa personnalité multiple chacun pouvant se la jouer en dedans" (cited in Howe 1990: 100). At this point we have come full circle: the importance of pastoral is understood to lie not in its ability to represent the world in fictional cipher but in its ability, as dramatic poetry, to allow a fictionalizing self-projection on the part of its author. Drama merges with lyric in "le seul théâtre de notre esprit."

So, too, in the work of Fernando Pessoa, pastoral is the sign under which a fusion of dramatic and lyric impulses is enacted. Pessoa spoke of himself as "several different poets at once, a dramatic poet who writes lyrical poems" (cited in Hamburger 1969: 139, 146), and the refusal of the distinction between drama and lyric that resulted in the invention of his heteronymic poets was enabled by his interest in pastoral. He describes the emergence of the heteronyms in a letter to Adolfo Casias Monteiro, a younger contemporary:

> It one day occurred to me to play a joke on Sá-Carneiro—to invent a rather complicated bucolic poet whom I would present in some guise of reality that I've since forgotten. I spent a few days trying in vain to envision this poet. One day when I'd finally given up—it was March 8th, 1914—I walked over to a high chest of drawers, took a sheet of paper, and began to write standing up, as I do whenever I can. And I wrote thirty-some poems at once, in a kind of ecstasy I'm unable to describe. It was the triumphal day of my life, and I can never have another one like it. I began with a title, *The Keeper of Sheep*. This was followed by the appearance in me of someone whom I instantly named Alberto Caeiro. Excuse the absurdity of this statement: my master had appeared in me. That was what I immediately felt, and so strong was the feeling that, as soon as those thirty-odd poems were written, I grabbed a fresh sheet of paper and wrote, again all at once, the six poems that constitute "Slanting Rain," by Fernando Pessoa. All at once and with total concentration.... It was the return of Fernando Pessoa as Alberto Caeiro to Fernando Pessoa himself. Or rather, it was the reaction of Fernando Pessoa against his nonexistence as Alberto Caeiro. (Pessoa 2001: 256; compare the discussion in Paz 1995: 7–8)

What begins as play for Pessoa, a prank upon a younger poet, becomes an unsettling experience of the self-alienation inseparable from fictional invention: this master who has appeared in him is an independent being, such that he can hardly speak of himself as his creator. Caeiro is the sun around whom, in Octavio Paz's metaphor, the other heteronyms and Pessoa himself keep their courses (1995: 10), and he is a pastoral poet, the author of *The Keeper of Sheep* and *The Amorous Shepherd*. His discovery by Pessoa, and his dramatization of this discovery as an inspiration for himself and his poetic work, reenacts two foundational claims of the genre—the advancement of selfhood through willed self-fictionalization and the recursive effect of literary fiction on lived reality—in a disquieting contemporary form.

For Pessoa's heteronyms are not the many modes of a single poet, temporary disguises that can be put on and off at will. There is no one behind the masks, no author behind the personae.[13] Nor is this multiplicity a Whitmanesque abundance of actionable possible selves; it is rather the ontological tragedy of a copresence that somehow falls short of full selfhood: "My dramas, instead of being divided into acts full of action, are divided into souls. That's what this apparently baffling phenomenon comes down to....I subsist as a medium of myself, but I'm less real than the others, less substantial, less personal, and easily influenced by them all. I too am a disciple of Caeiro" (Pessoa 2001: 262).

Plato's division of literature into kinds in the *Republic* according to its narrative mode is coeval with the philosophical project of understanding the self and expressing the results of this inquiry as knowledge. By presenting the speech of literary characters as an illegitimate and untruthful impersonation of actual beings, Plato is able to treat the self's desire for imaginative experience as a craving for falsehood that has no place in authentic projects of self-knowledge and self-development (book 3, 395c–d, 401b–c; book 10, 605c–6b). Through Aristotle's *Poetics*, Plato bequeathed this schema to literary criticism as a strong separation between fictional and nonfictional discourses regardless of how these discourses are valued—Aristotle himself famously prizes successful narrative literature of all kinds as more serious and more philosophical than history because of its ability to image in its plots basic truths about human character that receive full conceptual exposition in philosophy (*Poetics* 9, 1451a36–b32).

On this account, lyric belongs with properly scientific discourses insofar as it is understood as the authentic speech of a poet making genuine claims in his own person, however much these claims may fall short of the conceptual rigor of philosophy. By contrast, fictional discourses—drama and the character speech of epic—however much we may value them for the insights into lived reality they disclose, belong to a special category of simulated or inauthentic speech: "feigning" as Spenser's commentator calls it, in the language of his time.

Pastoral is the genre that challenges this distinction most explicitly. From Theocritus to Pessoa, pastoral asserts the inseparability of fiction from the project of selfhood, conflating dramatic and lyric impulses and dramatizing the role of imaginary experience in the development of the self (see Iser 1993: 22–86). Much energy has been expended on demonstrating the difference between fictional and possible worlds (see esp. Ronen 1994). A crucial difference, we might think, is that the former are unrealized and unrealizable, whereas modal imagining posits outcomes that can be or could have been actualized. Pastoral's charter has been to explore the liminal territory that borders these two kinds of thinking. Its instantiation of a poetics of pure fictionality made it the genre best equipped to investigate the effects of such purified fictions on the self that chooses to espouse them as its project, and it is no accident that Quixote, having failed to become a knight, turns to pastoral as a genre that offers better hopes of success:

> As they pursued their journey talking in this way they came to the very same spot where they had been trampled on by the bulls. Don Quixote recognised it, and said he to Sancho, "This is the meadow where we came upon those gay shepherdesses and gallant shepherds who were trying to revive and imitate the pastoral Arcadia there, an idea as novel as it was happy, in emulation whereof, if so be thou dost approve of it, Sancho, I would have ourselves turn shepherds, at any rate for the time I have to live in retirement. I will buy some ewes and everything else requisite for the pastoral calling; and, I under the name of the shepherd Quixotize and thou as the shepherd Panzino, we will roam the woods and groves and meadows singing songs here, lamenting in elegies there, drinking of the crystal waters of the springs or limpid brooks or flowing rivers. The oaks will yield us their sweet fruit with bountiful hand, the trunks of the hard cork trees a seat, the willows shade, the roses perfume, the widespread meadows carpets tinted with a thousand dyes; the clear pure air will give us breath, the moon and stars lighten the darkness of the night for us, song shall be our delight, lamenting our joy, Apollo will supply us with verses, and love with conceits whereby we shall make ourselves famed for ever, not only in this but in ages to come. (1901: IV, 174)

NOTES

1. For the purposes of this chapter, I consider pastoral as a genre and not a mode, that is to say, in Aristotelian terms, as a literary kind that consists in, and perpetuates itself by, a sustained relationship between form and content. The most adventurous treatment of pastoral as a mode or "process," namely, that of "putting the complex into the simple," is Empson 1935. While there is much to be said for (and still more against) this idea, I look at examples of pastoral whose generic features are readily identifiable.

2. This idea is continuous with Aristotle's position in *Poetics* (9, 1451a36–b32), where he argues that the mythological characters of tragedy are just as much their author's creation as those of comedy, which are universally acknowledged as such. See Ford 2002: 231 and Halliwell 2002: 166–68 on fictionality in the *Poetics* and Vernant 1991: 151–64 and Bakker 2005: ix–xiii on the poetics of Homeric composition and performance.

3. By this I mean the more limited model of mimetic desire as emulation of a literary character advanced at Girard 1978: 3, rather than the generalized model of all desire as essentially mimetic that Girard developed from it.

4. Compare Samuel Beckett's *Trilogy*: in *Malone Dies*, Malone, the narrator of this, its second book, claims to have been the author of the first, *Molloy*, while in the

final volume, *The Unnamable*, the anonymous narrator claims to be responsible for all Beckett's characters from Murphy to Malone.

5. Patterson 1987: 34 does not perpetuate the comparison between the two poets in these terms. Compare Alpers 1979: 204–9, which notes how often comparisons of Theocritus and Virgil replicate, with various degrees of explicitness and sophistication, Friedrich Schiller's antithesis of naive and sentimental poetry.

6. See Grundy 1969: 26: "The world *The Shepheardes Calender* creates exists to be contemplated rather than entered; it presents to us a pure art-image, graceful and remote."

7. I owe this thought to some oral reflections on speeches in Shakespeare by my colleague Richard Strier.

8. An online search for *One Man and His Dog* in fact reveals that, according to Wikipedia, televised sheep dog trials such as this could still attract prime time audiences of more eight million in England in the 1980s.

9. Spenser's early readers already criticize the artificiality of his language in *The Shepheardes Calender* for its failure to accurately represent rural people. For a recent discussion of Ben Jonson's famous claim that Spenser "writ no language," see Maley (2001: 162–79). Artificiality of diction is also a part of Samuel Johnson's well-known dispraise of the genre's mimetic shortcomings: "Surely, at the same time that a shepherd learns theology, he may gain some acquaintance with his native language" (cited in van Es 2006: 121).

10. "Dis-ease," is Arnold's telling rendering of the *neg-otium* that opposes pastoral quiet.

11. An excellent discussion of the relationship between Arnold's nostalgic poetic language and his attitude to scientific modernity is in Riede 1988: 1–29 and (with reference to these poems) 134–56.

12. I will make no attempt to translate Mallarmé's French. See Mallarmé 2006 for English translations.

13. So Hamburger 1969: 138–47 and De Sena 1982: 19–32 distinguish Pessoa's aims and achievement from the persona poetry of Ezra Pound and T. S. Eliot.

REFERENCES

Alpers, P. (1979). *Singer of the Eclogues: A Study of Virgilian Pastoral*. Berkeley: University of California Press.

——. (1996). *What Is Pastoral?* Chicago: University of Chicago Press.

Bakker, E. J. (2005). *Pointing at the Past: From Formula to Performance in Homeric Poetics*. Washington, D.C.: Center for Hellenic Studies.

Berger, H., Jr. (1988). *Revisionary Play: Studies in the Spenserian Dynamics*. Berkeley: University of California Press.

Breed, B. W. (2006). "Time and Textuality in the Book of the *Eclogues*." *In* M. Fantuzzi and T. D. Papanghelis (eds.), *Brill's Companion to Greek and Latin Pastoral*, pp. 333–68. Leiden: Brill.

Burrow, C. (2001). "Spenser and Classical Traditions." *In* A. Hadfield (ed.), *The Cambridge Companion to Spenser*, pp. 217–36. Cambridge: Cambridge University Press.

Cervantes, M. de (1901). *Don Quixote*, 4 Vols. Trans. John Ormsby: Glasgow: Gowans & Gray.

Coleman, R. (1977). *Virgil: Eclogues*. Cambridge: Cambridge University Press.

Cooper, H. (1976). *Pastoral: Mediaeval into Renaissance*. Totowa, N.J.: Boydell & Brewer.

Cullen, P. (1970). *Spenser, Marvell, and Renaissance Pastoral*. Cambridge, Mass.: Harvard University Press.

De Sena, J. (1982). "Fernando Pessoa: The Man Who Never Was." *In* G. Monteiro (ed.), *The Man Who Never Was: Essays on Fernando Pessoa*, pp. 19–32. Providence: Gavea-Brown.

Eldridge, R. (1989). *On Moral Personhood*. Chicago: University of Chicago Press.

Empson, W. (1935). *Some Versions of Pastoral*. London: Chatto and Windus.

Ford, A. (2002). *The Origins of Criticism*. Princeton: Princeton University Press.

Girard, R. (1978). *To Double Business Bound: Essays on Literature, Mimesis, and Anthropology*. Baltimore: Johns Hopkins University Press.

Greene, R. (2001). "Spenser and Contemporary Vernacular Poetry." *In* A. Hadfield (ed.), *The Cambridge Companion to Spenser*, pp. 237–51. Cambridge: Cambridge University Press.

Grundy, J. (1969). *The Spenserian Poets*. London: Edward Arnold.

Halliwell, S. (2002). *The Aesthetics of Mimesis: Ancient Texts and Modern Problems*. Princeton: Princeton University Press.

Hamburger, M. (1969). *The Truth of Poetry: Tensions in Modern Poetry from Baudelaire to the 1960s*. New York: Harcourt.

Hardie, P. (2002). *Ovid's Poetics of Illusion*. Cambridge: Cambridge University Press.

Howe, E. A. (1990). *Stages of Self*. Athens, Ohio: Ohio University Press.

Iser, W. (1989). *Prospecting: From Reader Response to Literary Anthropology*. Baltimore: Johns Hopkins University Press.

——. (1993). *The Fictive and the Imaginary*. Baltimore: Johns Hopkins University Press.

——. (2006). *How to Do Theory*. Malden, Mass.: Blackwell.

Landy, J. (1994). "Music, Letters, Truth and Lies: 'L'Après-Midi d'un Faune' as an *Ars Poetica*." *Yearbook of Comparative and General Literature* 42, 57–69.

Lerner, L. (1972). *The Uses of Nostalgia*. London: Chatto and Windus.

Maley, W. (2001). "Spenser's Languages: Writing in the Ruins of English." *In* A. Hadfield (ed.), *The Cambridge Companion to Spenser*, pp. 162–79. Cambridge: Cambridge University Press.

Mallarmé, S. (2006). *Collected Poems and Other Verse*. Trans. E. H. Blackmore and A. M. Blackmore. New York: Oxford University Press.

Montrose, L. A. (1983). "Of Gentlemen and Shepherds: The Politics of Elizabethan Pastoral Form." *English Literary History* 50, 415–59.

Newlands, C. (1987). "Urban Pastoral: The Seventh Eclogue of Calpurnius Siculus." *Classical Antiquity* 6, 218–31.

Patterson, A. (1987). *Pastoral and Ideology*. Berkeley: University of California Press.

Payne, M. (2007). *Theocritus and the Invention of Fiction*. Cambridge: Cambridge University Press.

Paz, O. (1995). "Unknown to Himself." *In* E. Lisboa and L. C. Taylor (eds.), *A Centenary Pessoa*, pp. 3–20. Manchester: Carcanet Press.

Pessoa, F. (2001). *The Selected Prose of Fernando Pessoa*. New York: Grove Press.

Putnam, M. C. J. (1970). *Virgil's Pastoral Art: Studies in the Eclogues*. Princeton: Princeton University Press.

Riede, D. G. (1988). *Matthew Arnold and the Betrayal of Language.* Charlottesville, Va.: University of Virginia Press.

Ronen, R. (1994). *Possible Worlds in Literary Theory.* Cambridge: Cambridge University Press.

Thilo, G. (ed.) (1887). *Servii grammatici qui feruntur in Vergilii Bucolica et Georgica.* Leipzig: Tevbneri.

Van Es, B. (2006). "Introduction." *In* Bart van Es (ed.), *A Critical Companion to Spenser Studies*, pp. 1–17. Basingstoke: Palgrave Macmillan.

Van Sickle, J. (1976). "Theocritus and the Development of the Conception of Bucolic Genre." *Ramus* 5, 18–44.

——. (1978). *The Design of Virgil's Bucolics.* Filologia e Critica No. 24. Rome: Edizioni dellAteneo & Bizzarri.

Vernant, J.-P. (1991). "From the 'Presentification' of the Invisible to the Imitation of Appearance." *In* F. Zeitlin (ed.), *Mortals and Immortals: Collected Essays*, pp. 151–63. Princeton: Princeton University Press.

Walker, S. F. (1978). "Mallarmé's Symbolist Eclogue: The 'Faune' as Pastoral." *Proceedings of the Modern Language Association* 93, 106–17.

CHAPTER 6

SATIRE

R. BRACHT BRANHAM

When we do philosophy we are like savages, primitive people, who hear the expressions of civilized men, put a false interpretation on them, and then draw the queerest conclusions from it.

—Ludwig Wittgenstein, *Philosophical Investigations*

Upon the whole, I am inclined to think that the far greater part, if not all, of those difficulties which have hitherto amused philosophers, and blocked up the way to knowledge, are entirely owing to ourselves. That we have first raised a dust, and then complain, we cannot see.

—George Berkeley, *A Treatise Concerning the Principles of Human Knowledge*

To ridicule philosophy is really to philosophize.

—Blaise Pascal, *Pensées*

What a satirist does is look at a situation, find the inconsistencies, hypocrisies, absurdities and cut through all the baloney and get to the truth.

—Al Franken, *Lies and the Lying Liars Who Tell Them: A Fair and Balanced Look at the Right*

While satire and philosophy may seem at first glance to be fundamentally distinct forms of discourse, they are in fact fratricidal siblings; like Eteocles and Polyneices, they are destined to be forever at odds but ultimately inseparable. Philosophy and satire claim the same high ground: the right to determine what is to be taken seriously and what is to be laughed out of court, to say just who is the truth teller and who is the buffoon without shame. From Aristophanes and Plato's Socrates to Diogenes, Lucian, Rabelais, Swift, Voltaire, Diderot, Schopenhauer, and Nietzsche—not to mention Aldous Huxley, George Orwell, Woody Allen, Lenny Bruce, and Monty Python—the ancient rivalry between satire and philosophy as to who will have the last word and the last laugh has been profoundly productive not only of satire but also of philosophy. For, as Aristotle reportedly argued in his lost apologia for philosophy, the *Protrepticus*, to reject philosophy is to take up a philosophical position. Hence, the competition is not simply between but also within both discourses. When Jonathan Swift imagines life among serenely rational quadrupeds or Voltaire subjects Leibnizian cosmic optimism to the vicissitudes of picaresque narrative, the satire of philosophy becomes the philosophy of satire. Like the sorcerer's apprentice—who first appears in Lucian—the harder the satirist tries to clean up the mess, to rid us of the fraudulent and mystifying phantoms of philosophers, the more philosophical he becomes. Likewise, the harder the philosopher tries to be an authentic truth teller, to distinguish the honest-to-god philosopher from the legion of imposters to the title, the more he sounds like a true satirist, as do my epigraphs from Wittengenstein, Berkeley, and Pascal. Is there no way out?

Of course there is: we can follow Plato and outlaw satire along with the rest of literature—excluding, of course, Platonic literature! After all, satire, like philosophy, has always been only one step ahead of the law. Consider the facts: don't Rome's most ancient laws, the Twelve Tablets, make *malum carmen*, a satiric incantation or malediction in verse, a capital offense? Didn't the Archbishop of Canterbury ban and burn books of satire (1599), just as Elizabethan poets such as John Donne and Joseph Hall were learning to curse in verse of liars in public places? And didn't Cleon use the laws of Athens to try to silence Aristophanes, as later guardians of public virtue would Lenny Bruce? Is it just an accident that the founding drama of philosophy in the West, the trial and death of Socrates, reveals a similar tension between philosophy and the law? But what do philosophers and satirists have in common? Evidently, the willingness to offend, provoke, and outrage, all in the name of calling a spade a bloody shovel, of telling the awful truth. As Swift observed: "[A] nice man is a man of nasty ideas" (Swift 1727: 654).

Philosophy and satire also share a common cultural genealogy. The literary system of the ancient Greeks was articulated over the centuries through a series of dialogic oppositions between heroic epic and mock epic (Homer's *Iliad* and *Odyssey* vs. Homer's *Margites*), praise poetry and blame poetry (Pindar's epinician odes vs. Archilochus's iambic poetry), tragedy and satyr play, or tragedy and comedy. Underlying all these contrasting but complementary generic pairings is the perennial dynamic of the serious and the comic word. The confrontation between satire and philosophy needs to be seen as another such pairing in the agonistic arena of literary performance, in which each genre stakes its claim to the authority of the word whether "winged" (i.e., voiced) or written. Satire and philosophy may really be opposites, but the kind of opposites that converge. As a way of exploring their dialogic dance, I consider a few defining episodes when their long struggle for identity and self-definition bring them face to face.

Since the terms in my original title[1]—"philosophy" and "satire"—are in contention in this essay, several distinct conceptions of philosophy in its relation to satire emerge. I have been using "satire" in its general, modern sense that goes back at least to John Dryden's classic essay, "The Original and Progress of Satire" (1682).[2] And while the Greeks used a different vocabulary, they produced a wide variety of satiric/comic forms such as mock epic, iambic poetry, the satyr play, the mime, and Old and New Comedy. What all these genres share is a rhetoric designed to produce various forms of *to geloion*—the sources of laughter and the quieter pleasures associated with it.

Distinguishing specifically satiric forms, techniques, or functions from the spectrum of comic arts is a dubious enterprise, since satire is often expressed as a tendency or tone or parodic combination of forms. And it is ultimately how the humor—or *to geloion*—works rhetorically and philosophically that makes an effect, whether of a joke or a literary work, satiric. As one critic has observed, "[C]omedy always has a satiric potential," and "when comedy becomes more purposeful than playful, then it is satire" (Levin 1987: 195). Moreover, the Greek idea of comedy centers squarely on its satiric force: *komoidein* means to lampoon, ridicule, make fun of, put in a comedy—or satirize.

While it may be impossible to segregate the satiric neatly from the comic insofar as both are funny or aim at laughter, only the former is regularly taken to have extralinguistic implications for its audience.[3] Be that as it may, we can say precisely what makes either funny (i.e., *to geloion*), at least in Plato's view, since he gives a concise account of it in his late dialogue on pleasure, the *Philebus*. The burden of the dialogue is to convince us that pleasure almost always entails pain. To understand pleasure in general is to recognize that it is a function of pain—the release from pain. To grasp the nature of a particular pleasure is to identify the pain that precedes it and forms the condition of its existence.[4] To illustrate this theory of pleasure, Plato takes our response to comedy as an example and offers an analysis of *to geloion* as the object and cause of laughter.

A funny character or person, argues Socrates, is one who exemplifies the very opposite of the Delphic motto—that is, one who does *not* know himself, who blithely entertains flattering, inflated ideas of his own virtues. In a word, what makes him funny is the self-ignorance involved in vanity and conceit. The comic figure is a natural *alazōn*, a fraud *malgré lui*. And of all the virtues' that one most often falsely assumed, maintains Socrates, is that of wisdom, *sophia*. Since vanity implies self-ignorance, when we laugh at anyone, according to Plato, we are taking pleasure in his manifest ignorance, and, Plato insists, such ignorance is clearly a bad thing (*kakon*), a misfortune. And while Socrates affirms the conventional Greek view that there is nothing wrong in rejoicing in the misfortunes of our enemies, the envy (*phthonos*) implicit in laughing at our friends' misfortune—their vanity exposed—makes our response to comedy (*to geloion*) a mixture of pleasure (laughter) and pain (*phthonos*/envy) that is ethically suspect. To put Plato's point more positively and plausibly than Plato does, the pleasure of laughter evoked by satire or comedy acts as an antidote to envy (endemic in an egalitarian democracy); the involuntary pain incurred by the thought of others' success (i.e., *phthonos*/envy) is relieved by revealing them to be deficient in the very qualities they most pride themselves on.[5]

As so often in Plato, his brilliant analysis is inextricably tied to his moral (or political) evaluation of what is being analyzed, making the results tendentious. Plato's moral critique of the pleasures of laughter in the *Philebus* depends on a deliberate conflation of the idea of laughing at characters in a comedy with that of laughing at our friends' misfortunes: he begins his discussion with an explicit reference to comedy and tragedy (48a) but concludes by describing our response to comedy as laughing at our friends' misfortunes (49d–50a), as if there were no difference! Yet if we strip away the Plato's moralizing, his analysis of the source of laughter (*to geloion*) gets at something fundamental: what makes us funny is the firm but mistaken belief that we are better and wiser than we are.

The idea that vanity so understood is the wellspring of comic and satiric laughter illuminates many a character from Aristophanes' Socrates to Don Quixote to P. G. Wodehouse's Bertie Wooster.[6] It is surprising, therefore, that while the Platonic account of *to geloion* is specifically offered as a theory of laughter applicable to the stage, it doesn't actually fit the heroes of Aristophanic or Old Comedy very well: their willful disregard of real-world limitations, especially their own, is celebrated and typically ends in a *kōmos* or drunken revel, but it is arguably descriptive of the blocking figures, the comic *alazones*, fakes or frauds, who try to obstruct or exploit the hero's comic fantasy, as Socrates does in Aristophanes' *Clouds*. Be that as it may, *Clouds* is markedly atypical of Old Comedy as a genre insofar as it has a dark ending, in which Socrates' school is set on fire by the father of his pupil. In place of the usual rowdy party, we get arson. (Socrates barely escapes.)[7] But whatever value Plato's account of why we laugh has as a theory of Old Comedy,[8] it fits like a glove Socrates' practice of philosophy as he presents it in the *Apology*.

Before he describes that practice (at his trial on charges of impiety in 399 B.C.E.), Socrates claims to have been a victim of slander and satire and refers to "a comic poet" (i.e., Aristophanes) as one of his old "dangerous accusers" (18c–d). Yet he spends only a paragraph disavowing Aristophanes' caricature, which does seem designed to confound him with pre-Socratics who "study things in the sky and below the earth" and sophists who make "the worse into the stronger argument" (19b). And if we actually turn to the *Clouds* (produced in 423 B.C.E, 24 years before the trial!) expecting a devastating satire of the philosopher Socrates (as we know him), we will be disappointed. Aristophanes' caricature of Socrates seems too broad, silly, and generic to be life threatening. Such eminent targets for satiric treatment as Socrates' divine voice (*daimonion*) and the oracle about him are not even mentioned, nor is his characteristic method of refutation by question and answer—the *elegkhos*—parodied. Yet Aristophanes' Socrates doesn't believe in the gods and does corrupt the young, the very charges Socrates faces in court.

If Socrates does not spend long repudiating Aristophanes' caricature of him, it is because he knows perfectly well that the real source of his remarkable unpopularity is his own relentless and idiosyncratic pursuit of something he ends up calling philosophy (*Apology* 23c, 29c–d)—an activity no less mysterious then than now. To justify this pursuit, he tells a story that a comic or tragic poet could have made up: once upon a time, a friend of Socrates, Chaerephon—who is now dead—asked Apollo's oracle at Delphi if anyone was wiser than Socrates, and the oracle reportedly said that "no one was wiser" (*Apology* 21a). Of course, the utterances of oracles are notoriously ambiguous and deliberately enigmatic. They often serve as a test for the recipient and actually invite misinterpretation: consider how the stories of Oedipus in Sophocles or of Croesus in Herodotus hinge on their misinterpreting an oracle from Apollo at Delphi. The oracle could have meant many things by the answer it gave to Chaerephon: that "no one is wiser" than Socrates need mean no more than that we are all equally ignorant as mortals. It would then resonate with the famous injunction inscribed on Apollo's temple: "know thyself," which is conventionally taken to mean "know your place" as a mortal (not a god) and think mortal thoughts.

Socrates' response is, therefore, astonishing: he assumes he knows what the oracle means—always a rash thing to do—and then attempts to refute it by finding someone else who is demonstrably wiser than himself. He begins by questioning a politician—whom he refrains from naming—who was considered wise by many and "especially by himself." But what he discovers is that "he thought himself wise but he was not"—like a character in a comedy according to Plato. The results of this exchange are inauspicious: "[H]e came to dislike me and so did many of the bystanders" (*Apology* 21c). But Socrates is not easily deterred. Evidently, over many years—he gives no dates—Socrates repeats this performance with the leading politicians, poets, and finally, the craftsmen. Even at the age of 70, he has still not stopped: "I go around seeking out anyone, citizen or stranger, whom I think wise... and show him that he is not wise" (*Apology* 23b).[9]

Socrates could not be clearer: to practice philosophy as he did is to satirize in public anyone with a reputation for wisdom, to show that reputation to be baseless by revealing through question and answer the comic gap (*to geloion*) between self-conception and public performance. Now, we might not call what Socrates did a form of satire if there was no audience responding to it as such, taking pleasure in the unmasking of the supposedly wise. But there was such an audience: "[T]he young men who follow me around of their own free will, who have the most leisure, the sons of the very rich, take pleasure (*khairousin*)[10] hearing people questioned; they themselves often imitate me and try to question others. I think they find a great abundance of people who believe they know something but know little or nothing" (*Apology* 21c). Like any true artist, Socrates inspires imitation. But what exactly are his followers imitating? It is important to remember that the Socratic method of refutation (or *elegkhos*) is purely negative: it does not aim or claim to produce knowledge of any kind, only to rebut a claim to authority by getting the interlocutor to contradict himself on a subject he is supposed to know something about (see Frede 1992). Socrates' development of this method has earned him a reputation as one of the inventors of philosophy, but it would be no less accurate to see him, in Plato's own terms, as the inventor of a form of satire every bit as offensive as the fictions of Old Comedy, one devoted to unmasking in public all those considered wise for the amusement and edification of their fellow citizens.

While the significance of the satiric (or seriocomic) dimension of Socrates— including his satyric appearance and homely arguments—has sometimes been acknowledged as fundamental and is central to Alcibiades' encomium of him in the *Symposium*, it is more typically reduced to "Socratic irony" or to an aspect of Plato's literary representation of him not essential to his philosophy.[11] But the implications of the perfect fit between Plato's account of why we laugh at satire or comedy in the *Philebus* and Socrates' own detailed description of how he conceived and performed his philosophical mission in the *Apology* suggests otherwise. Plato's theory of laughter even helps to explain why Socrates was convicted: perhaps from reflection on Socrates' fate, Plato stipulates in the *Philebus* that such self-ignorance is really only funny in the weak, defined as "those unable to avenge themselves when laughed at"; the same quality in those "with strength and power" is positively scary—"hateful and ugly" (49e). That is why Chaplin has such difficulty making Hitler funny in *The Great Dictator* (1940) and why no form of joking or satire about George Bush ever seems to do justice to the enormity of his folly.[12] Socrates' relentless exposure of the comic self-ignorance of leading Athenians observed no such distinction, landing him in court where he was convicted and sentenced to death.

Implicit in the pairing of serious and comic genres such as tragedy and satyr play or heroic epic and mock epic is the idea that neither the serious nor the comic word can encompass the whole truth on its own. While Plato's satyric Socrates is clearly an attempt to transcend such traditional generic dichotomies, the ancient tradition that acknowledges and embraces this paradoxical notion of truth most explicitly is that of the *spoudogeloios* (or seriocomic) figure invented by the Cynics, whose strategy is to practice philosophy as satire and satire as philosophy.[13] If we ask where the history of philosophy intersects with that of satire to greatest effect, Cynicism must be the answer. The resemblance of philosophic practice to satiric scrutiny persists in Diogenes to such an extent that it is even more difficult than in the case of Socrates to say where philosophy begins or satire ends. If the dialectic of satire and philosophy expresses itself in philosophers who are masters of satire and parody, such as Plato and Nietzsche, and satirists who engage philosophy in the spirit of Pascal's *pensées*, as do Lucian, Rabelais, Swift, and Diderot, no one embodies the terms of the dialectic more paradigmatically than does Diogenes the dog.

It would be a mistake, however, to suggest that Cynicism is simply a further development of the Platonic Socrates, one that happens to give greater scope to humor or satire. Diogenes was not a Socratic and belonged to no school. Indeed, he was not even a citizen but a beggar living in exile in Athens (and Corinth). While it is true that Socrates is capable of comparing himself to Achilles at one moment and to a horsefly the next in the *Apology*—conceding his lowly status as a pest to his fellow Athenians only after making a daring claim to heroic stature—his attempt at persuasive self-definition contrasts sharply with that of the Cynic. Diogenes not only accepts the dismissive and degrading epithet of "dog" but makes it his own by turning it around and comparing himself to various breeds (in one set of anecdotes), which does not stop him from casting himself as a tragic hero elsewhere. But unlike Socrates' comparison of himself to the greatest hero, Achilles about to reenter battle to avenge Patroclos's death (*Apology* 28c-d), Diogenes' *comparandus* is an unknown hero reduced to the pitiful status of a suppliant: "Without a city, without a house, without a fatherland / A beggar, a wanderer with a single day's bread."[14] It is impossible to imagine Socrates as a beggar; in fact, he is convicted precisely because he is too proud to supplicate the jury and beg them to take pity on him, as a defendant on trial for his life was expected to do in ancient Athens (*Apology* 34–35). Socrates says it is beneath his dignity—and that of Athens.

As manifestly different as they were, some ancient traditions nevertheless try to assimilate Diogenes to the Socratic model—and thereby highlight what sets them apart. Since Socrates got his "mission from god" at Delphi, Diogenes too must receive an oracle from Apollo—and so he does: he is told not that "no one is wiser" but that he ought "to deface the currency" (*parakharattein to nomisma*). The wording of the oracle carefully exploits an ambiguity in the word *nomisma*, which can mean "metal currency" (i.e., coinage) or "whatever is sanctioned by current or established usage" (i.e., custom or law); it thereby affirms both Diogenes' original transgression or crime—defacing the coinage of his native Sinope[15]—that effectively launched his career as a philosopher by propelling him into exile, *and* the philosophical mission he discovered as a result of exile. "To deface the currency" became a proverbial metaphor for the practice of Cynicism: to drive out of circulation or replace conventional thinking sanctioned by tradition, with the unshakeable and un-Socratic belief that nature is the sole authority on how to live—not the gods and laws bequeathed by society. Diogenes would have agreed wholeheartedly with J. S. Mill's observation in *On Liberty*: "[B]y dint of not following [our] own nature [we] have no nature to follow."[16] The determination to reject the authority of custom or tradition (*to nomisma*) in the name of nature is the founding act of Cynicism, as basic to it as Socrates' decision to test the wisdom (*sophia*) of his contemporaries is to his—and Plato's—idea of philosophy. It is expressed by Diogenes' adopting a stance of satiric scrutiny toward all forms of received wisdom.

This radical premise sets the stage for the Cynic critique of the prevailing conceptions of the good life, both popular and philosophical, and serves as charter for their active resistance to the "social control of cognition" through fearless acts of truth telling (*parrhēsia*) addressed to those in power (e.g., Alexander the Great) and the improvisation of a seriocomic literature[17] and performance art designed to deface the idols of the tribe: myth, religion, law/custom and, not least, philosophy itself. Diogenes' practice serves to reverse the key terms of Plato's analysis of satire/comedy (*to geloion*) in the *Philebus*: it is society mindlessly enslaved to inherited conventions and unnatural values that does not know itself. Diogenes' quixotic and comical attempt to demonstrate this truth by living out his heterodox philosophy of "life according to nature" in full public view—eating, urinating, masturbating, sleeping, teaching, and begging on the streets of Athens and Corinth—made him both an intellectual scandal and a touchstone of philosophic authenticity rivaled only by Socrates. Indeed, when asked what sort of person Diogenes was, Plato responded famously: "a Socrates—gone mad!" (Diogenes Laertius, 1925: Book 6, Chapter 54).[18]

It is no accident that Plato occurs far more frequently than any other philosopher in the anecdotes about Diogenes. The tradition designates him, the paradigmatic metaphysician and plutocrat, as a kind of antitype to the Cynic. As such, he is a useful tool for defining the Cynic stance by contrast and juxtaposition. Once, after the father of metaphysics had expounded his theory of forms using neologisms such as "tablehood" and "cuphood," Diogenes responded: "Plato, table and cup I see, but your 'tablehood' and 'cuphood'—no way" (*oudamōs*; Diogenes Laertius, 1925: 6.53). This story resembles the occasion when Plato deployed his vaunted method of collection and division to define man as "a featherless biped," and Diogenes produced a plucked chicken as a counterexample, saying, "Here is Plato's man!" (Diogenes Laertius 1925: 6.40). Elsewhere, he dismisses Plato's lectures (*diatribē*) as a waste of time (*katatribē*; Diogenes Laertius, 1925: 6.24) and ridicules the philosopher for paying court to the tyrant Dionysius (Diogenes Laertius, 1925: 6.58), for his aristocratic generosity (in sending him a whole jar of figs when he had asked for a few), and for the vanity of his expensive possessions (Diogenes Laertius, 1925: 6.26). A pivotal theme emerges from this group of anecdotes: the Cynic's distrust of abstract argument is merely the other side of his belief that the test of truth is less a matter of logical finesse than of the philosopher's ability to practice persuasively what he teaches. Plato stands satirized on both counts.

Given that no other figure embodies so clearly the ways in which philosophy and satire can converge in a single discourse, it is worth considering how Diogenes deploys the performance art of satiric provocation as a tool of philosophy. Probably the single best-known story about Diogenes is the one (adapted by Nietzsche in *The Gay Science* in his parable on the death of god)[19] in which he "takes a lamp in broad daylight and walks around saying he is looking for a human being"[20] (*anthrōpos*; Diogenes Laertius, 1925: 6.41): the story comically dramatizes the radical nature of the Cynic attempt to reconceive the human, challenging the traditional hierarchy that defines mankind by placing it in the middle, between gods and animals; it is one of a series of anecdotes in which Diogenes refuses even to acknowledge the conventional application of the word *anthrōpos*, implying that his contemporaries do not warrant the epithet "human," having failed to realize their nature. Far from being midway between gods and animals, the Cynic sees his contemporaries as inferior to both in the respects that matter most—self-sufficiency and happiness.[21]

More notorious—if less often represented in the visual arts—is Diogenes' defense of his habit of masturbating in public: "I only wish I could be rid of hunger as easily by rubbing my belly" (D.L. 6.69). The humor here derives from the fact that Diogenes tacitly rejects the premise of his audience according to which he is violating well-known rules segregating private and public activities; in its place, he has inserted a Cynic premise, the principle of "using any place for any purpose" (D.L. 6.22): natural desires are best satisfied in the easiest, most practical way possible. As far as the body or nature is concerned, one appetite is in principle no different from any other. It is culture that creates a hierarchy of desires and the proprieties governing their tendance. Diogenes' response blandly asserts the claims of nature without even acknowledging the restraints of culture. If he had acknowledged them explicitly, his response would not have been a joke—it would not have been funny. As Umberto Eco has argued, the tacit suppression of the violated norm—the social frame—is essential to the comic (1986: 269–78). Knowledge of it must be supplied by the audience. It is the fact that the audience must simultaneously impose the relevant social frame—the prohibition—and supply the tacit Cynic premise that makes many of Diogenes' jokes work like enthymemes or rhetorical syllogisms. To get their point requires that we collaborate in a process of logical inference from Cynic premises (see Cohen 1983: 120–36). The Cynic premise does not merely violate but contradicts the social frame; hence, the laughter it elicits is tendentious. Indeed, virtually every witticism of Diogenes is tendentious in Freud's sense—hostile, argumentative, and subversive of authority.[22]

Diogenes' deliberate violations of social taboos in the masturbation anecdote—comically enacting the denial of the sacred already explicit in the doctrine of "using any place for any purpose"—is one of a series that exemplify the way he uses humor as a heuristic device, to provoke Cynical thinking from outside the inherited categories. In her classic study of jokes and joking, "The Social Control of Cognition: Some Factors in Joke Perception" (1968), Mary Douglas develops the argument that "the peculiar expressive character of the joke stands in contrast to ritual as such" (368–69),[23] for if we consider the joke "as a symbol of social, physical, or mental experience," we are already treating it as a kind of rite. But what kind? As a spontaneous symbol, Douglas says a joke "expresses something that is happening, but that is all"; it stands in contrast, therefore, to the standardized rite or ritual, "which expresses what ought to happen" and thus, unlike spontaneous joking, is "not morally neutral." Douglas spells out the opposition between joking and ritual as follows:

> A joke has in common with a rite that both connect widely differing concepts.
> But the kind of connection of pattern A with pattern B in a rite is such that
> A and B support each other in a unified system. The rite imposes order and
> harmony, while the joke disorganizes. From the physical to the personal,
> to the social, to the cosmic, great rituals create unity in experience. They

assert hierarchy and order. In doing so, they affirm the value of the symbolic patterning of the universe. Each level of patterning is validated and enriched by association with the rest. But jokes have the opposite effect. They connect widely differing fields, but the connection destroys hierarchy and order. They do not affirm the dominant values, but denigrate and devalue. Essentially a joke is an anti-rite.... The message of a standard rite is that the ordained patterns of social life are inescapable. The message of a joke is that they are escapable... for a joke implies that anything is possible. (369–70, 373)

If this argument is correct, joking in a traditional society organized by myth and ritual tends to set itself in opposition to the prime embodiments of social reason or ideology. The methods of professional philosophers would be one example of such reason; ritual would be a far more important one. If formal philosophical reasoning is the most convention-governed form of thought, ritual is the most convention-governed form of activity.[24] Insofar as Diogenes is an uninhibited opponent of *nomos*—unlike Antisthenes, for example, he never refers even to a *nomos* of *aretē*—we would expect him to be averse to ritual per se (since it embodies and reinforces *nomos*), and he does not disappoint us. Every single reference to ritual activity—sacrifice, prayer, or purification rites—in the *chreiai* is derisive (see Diogenes Laertius, 1925: 6.37, 42, 47, 59–62, 73). Several anecdotes suggest that Diogenes did not believe in the gods of tradition; indeed, it is hard to see how he could have. His ironic response to someone impressed by the quantity of votive offerings in Samothrace comes to mind: "There would have been far more if those whose were not saved had made offerings!" (Diogenes Laertius, 1925: 6.59). The opposition between Cynic jesting and traditional religion continues down to Demonax (Lucian's teacher, second century A.D.), who is put on trial in Athens for not joining the Mysteries, but refuses to take the charges seriously.[25] Where ritual is socially consolidating and conservative, the Cynic *parrhesiast* (frank and candid truthteller) is antiritualistic and disruptive. That Diogenes defends stealing from temples and denies the validity of such fundamental dietary and sexual taboos as those against cannibalism and incest coheres with this antiritualistic stance.[26] The contrast with a philosopher like Socrates is striking and significant. The Cynic's rejection of inherited patterns of conduct makes room for his own improvisations, but where do they derive their authority if, as Douglas also argues, joking "merely affords opportunity for realizing that an accepted pattern has no necessity... [but] is frivolous in that it produces no real alternative, only an exhilarating sense of freedom from form in general" (1968: 365)?

The usual answer to this question would be "nature," but I would argue that Diogenes' authority is conferred by the very mastery of discourse his joking and satiric provocations repeatedly demonstrate in the anecdotal tradition. Even Diogenes Laertius observes that "the man's gift for persuasion was so remarkable that he could easily win over [or defeat] anyone he liked with words [or arguments]" (Diogenes Laertius, 1925: 6.75). If this makes him sound too much like a Socratic or sophistic know-it-all, we need to remember the following anecdote: to someone who reproached him, saying "although you don't know anything, you practice philosophy," Diogenes responded disarmingly, "Even if I do pretend to wisdom (*sophia*), that is to philosophize" (Diogenes Laertius, 1925: 6.64).

If this sounds pointedly un-Socratic, it is. Philosophy for Diogenes, as for Nietzsche, means "living in contradiction to the present,"[27] which now includes the Socratic model of philosophy according to which the opposite of the true philosopher is the pretender to wisdom whose exposure constitutes the Socratic mission. In acknowledging the pretense to wisdom involved in the very attempt to philosophize in his sense—to embody *sophia*—Diogenes refuses to exempt the philosopher from the satiric scrutiny Socrates' mission inspired (in Aristophanes among others)—and failed to refute.[28] Diogenes knows perfectly well that as a talking dog he is socially marginal and the butt of jokes, even as the jesting philosopher is symbolically central and feared for his bite: *cave canem*! When told, on more than one occasion, that most people laugh at him, he does not deny it: "But I am not laughed down!" (Diogenes Laertius, 1925: 6.54).

If the formative moments in the ancient dialectic of satire and philosophy are the trial of Socrates and Diogenes' encounter with Plato and Athens, its final act unfolds in the Menippean satires of Lucian—such as *Philosophers for Sale!* and *Menippus or the Descent to Hades*—in which he renews the Socratic inquest into *sophia* focusing, as had Socrates, on those with a reputation for wisdom, which now means the ancient philosophical schools, more than 500 years old and supported by the state.[29] Writing in the second century A.D., when Greek culture, swallowed up by the Roman empire, appeared to itself as a pale imitation of the greatness of its classical past, the issue of fraudulent or imitation philosophers is symptomatic of a deeper anxiety addressed from many angles in Lucian's satires—the derivative and imitative nature of what passed for high culture in the age of the Second Sophistic (as it is known from Philostratus's *Lives of the Sophists*, second century A.D.). As an interloper from the East, a Syrian writing and performing for Hellenes, Lucian developed a perspective on the Greeks of his day and their obsessive concern with their own cultural origins that only an outsider could acquire. Like Diogenes, he was living a kind of volunteer exile dependent on those he mocked, but unlike Diogenes, he was not even Greek and yet in his work he consistently manages to turn his alien status and standpoint to satiric advantage. The dialectic of satire and philosophy, encapsulated in the idea of the *spoudogeloios*, is translated to the Renaissance almost entirely by means of Lucian's satiric response to postclassical Greek culture.

As Stanley Cavell observes: "[T]he problem of imitation haunts philosophy's establishment in Plato" (2004: 209), and the difficulty of distinguishing the true from the fake philosopher—the pretenders to wisdom exposed by Socrates—only grew as competing philosophical schools emerged and classical traditions calcified into imitations of themselves. In this self-consciously classical culture one question could not be avoided: what makes a tradition—of philosophy or literature or art—authentic and not a mere imitation or quotation or parody of itself? If it is just a copy, what value does it really possess? How can this value be measured or assessed in a publicly persuasive way?

Lucian decided to take up the question of value as it bears on philosophy itself by writing a Menippean satire that asks repeatedly in the most brutal, commercial terms: what is this philosopher worth? Today, when the "free market" is treated much as the Delphic oracle was in Socrates' Athens—as having all the answers however inscrutable—Lucian's premise sounds remarkably contemporary. It is all too easy to imagine a recent secretary of education or an ambitious dean asking the same question, quite literally and seriously, which is exactly how it is posed in *Philosophers for Sale!*[30] in which the founding fathers of the major philosophical traditions of antiquity are put on the auction block for sale as slaves, with Zeus and Hermes presiding as the auctioneers.

It is clearly a work that every student of philosophy should know but probably doesn't. Lucian uses the founder of each tradition to personify what his philosophy had come to represent, for better or worse, in the mind of educated Greeks. The attributes he extracts for each parody serve as seriocomic abbreviations or abstracts of the philosophical preoccupations considered characteristic of a given tradition. In this way, he seems to dodge the question of imitation and focus instead on the nature of the exemplars imitated, but since parody as comic imitation is premised on something already known independently, the truth of the parody is always at issue: does what makes it funny also make it true? This is precisely the question a seriocomic text is designed to pose. If the philosophers' responses are found wanting or patently ridiculous when asked what a slave would be asked when put up for sale—"what do you know best?"—the reader, like the buyer, can draw his own conclusions.

The fictional framework itself—of selling philosophers as slaves—does not mean that the portraits, however parodic, are uniformly unflattering or simply used to deflate the authority of the philosopher in question. When Diogenes is put up for sale in a lost work by Menippus (*The Sale of Diogenes*) and asked what he could do, he replied simply: "Rule men" (Diogenes Laertius, 1925: 6.29). Menippus's aphorism is true to the image of Diogenes as conveyed by the anecdotal tradition, as, for example, when asked what good he had gotten out of philosophy, he replied: "to be prepared for every kind of luck" (*tukhē*; Diogenes Laertius, 1925: 6.68). Lucian's Diogenes, by contrast, satirizes himself by commending the Cynic way of life in revolting terms few could embrace. As the buyer responds, "it's disgusting and not even human" (11). Of course, this is Lucian's point: it's canine. Yet when Lucian has Diogenes describe himself as a "liberator of men" and "an advocate for truth and freedom of speech," he is echoing the very terms he uses to legitimize his own practice as a satirist. Nevertheless, it is fair to infer from the treatment given Epicurus—who does not actually have to submit to questioning and is bought for two minas by someone who promises to feed him such delicacies as Carian figs—that Lucian prefers him to the dirty doglike Diogenes who fetches the lowest price—two obols. (Some legendary philosophers go unsold.) Thus, while each parodied philosopher is funny for different reasons—Pyrrho, for example, cannot but doubt that he has actually been sold, much to his owner's consternation—one theme that recurs is the gap between the buyers' needs and the kinds of things that the philosophers claim to know best.

Here for future reference are the results of the sale:

In order of appearance	Ranked by price
Pythagoras	Socrates: 2 talents
Diogenes	Aristotle: 20 minas
Aristippus	Chrysippus: 12 minas
Democritus and Heraclitus	Pythagoras: 10 minas
Socrates	Epicurus: 2 minas
Chrysippus	Pyrrho: 1 mina
Aristotle	Aristippus: unsold (too drunk to respond)
Pyrrho	Democritus and Heraclitus: unsold (too difficult to understand)
Menippus: notably absent	

Evidently not everyone in Lucian's audience found *Philosophers for Sale!* funny or, if so, knew how to take the joking, which shows that it succeeded as satiric provocation. Just as Socrates' search for *sophia* among his contemporaries landed him in court, so Lucian's satiric representation of the *sophia* of the sages of old leaves him facing an angry jury of those very philosophers led back from the dead by Socrates looking for justice—in his apologetic dialogue *The Dead Come to Life or the Fisherman*. Unlike Socrates at his trial, Lucian does not invoke the Delphic oracle and defend his way of life, but appeals to Philosophy herself and defends his way of writing, casting himself as the personification of verbal license, Parrhesiades or "Freespeaker, son of Truthful, grandson of Exposure," thus identifying himself with a value long associated with Athenian democracy, Old Comedy and the original Cynics. Presenting himself as Parrhesiades allows Lucian to dramatize his underlying affinity with the angry sages who have risen from their graves to stone him to death for his affront to philosophy. Donning this mask, Lucian counters his critics form two traditional angles by implying that he is not really antiphilosophical, since *parrhēsia* is a celebrated Cynic value, and that he is authorized to attack fakes anyway as the heir apparent of Aristophanic or Old Comedy.

This implicit claim is reflected explicitly both in Parrhesiade' protests of solidarity with his assailants and, more important, in the Old Comic structure of the plot: from the attack with stones to Parrhesiades' acquittal, *The Dead Come to Life* is patterned after the famous confrontation between Dicaeopolis and the angry patriots in Aristophanes' *Acharnians* (204–571), who, like the sages, are initially outraged at the hero's treasonous conduct but are ultimately persuaded of his loyalty to their cause.

The Dead Come to Life is allegorical and agonistic like most Old Comedy: it progresses rapidly through a sequence of wildly contrasting parodic structures moving from a paratragic suppliant scene in which Parrhesiades begs for his life by quoting famous bits of Homer and Euripedes, to a trial scene played out before Philosophy and Truth, "the shadowy creature with the indefinite complexion" (Lucian, 1905: Vol. 1, 213). In his formal defense, Lucian/Parrhesiades defines his literary innovation—the satiric-philosophical dialogue—as closer to the pursuit of truth than is contemporary philosophy, which by contrast is a tired imitation of its legendary past. Insofar as Parrhesiades is willing to speak his mind in the old style, to censure the fakery of professional thinkers, he is reasserting the truth teller's role, which is the point of having Diogenes, the most free-speaking philosopher, prosecute him unsuccessfully. Parrhesiades' acquittal by a jury of fabled sages designates Lucianic dialogue as the vehicle for unflattering exposure (elegkhos) that Socratic dialogue, Old Comedy, and Cynic diatribe once were. This claim is given Aristophanic confirmation in the closing scene, in which Parrhesiades fishes for fake philosophers off the side of the Acropolis—using gold and figs for bait! By putting his satiric innovation on trial, Lucian manages to sidestep the fact that in *Philosophers for Sale!* he satirizes not contemporary fakes, as his defense implies, but the leading philosophical schools as personified by their founders. His dramatic vindication of his satiric art as authentically classical and, therefore, authoritative, artfully displaces the problem of contemporary philosophy as anemic imitation, since its truth-telling mission now falls to the satirist on trial, just as it had to Socrates. Too bad that Lucian could not have quoted Goethe in defense of his satiric personification of the philosophical schools: "[A] school of thought is to be viewed as a single individual who talks to himself for a hundred years and is quite extraordinarily pleased with himself, however silly he may be" (1821: 12).

We are now in a position to trace the modern trajectory of the dialectic of satire and philosophy, or the art of the *spoudogeloios*, from its reintroduction to Europe by Erasmus and Thomas More—whose Latin translations of Lucian, *Compulurima opuscula festivissima* (1506), initiated a literary vogue that made him one of the most emulated authors in Renaissance Europe[31]—to the remarkable transformations of the Cynic-Lucianic tradition at the hands of Rabelais, Swift, Voltaire, and Diderot.[32] Instead, I jump to one pinnacle of the modern tradition—Friedrich Nietzsche—who reflected throughout his career on the value to the philosopher of satire and laughter.

Once when Diogenes was reproached for having been exiled from home (Sinope), he replied: "[Y]ou miserable fool, that's how I became a philosopher!" (Diogenes Laertius, 1925: 6.49). Nietzsche could have said the same thing: he went into voluntary exile, to wander and write philosophy, when he resigned his position as professor of classical philology at Basel University. Exile, then, becomes one of his themes: he dedicates *The Gay Science* "to those who have a right to call themselves homeless" (2001a: §377). Not surprisingly, the best way to approach Nietzsche's philosophical response to satire is by way of Cynicism.[33] Cynicism at its core consists of two moments, perhaps induced by the experience of exile: first, the discovery of "the comedy of existence," that is, that the accepted patterns of social life, hallowed by ritual and embodied in *nomos* ("custom" or "law"), "have no necessity," as Douglas puts it; and second, a literary expression of this discovery through the seriocomic forms of philosophical jesting and performance (or exhibitionism), parodic mockery, satiric scorn, and shameless honesty (or speech [*parrhēsia*]) that extends even to the speaker himself, making the Cynic philosopher, as Nietzsche puts it in *Beyond Good and Evil*, a "buffoon without shame" (2001b: §26). The word and the concept of the *spoudogeloios*, or seriocomic voice, speaking from outside the inherited generic dichotomies, as his oxymoronic name suggests, are, as I have noted, a Cynic invention; it is also a philosophic role in which Nietzsche would cast himself increasingly as his thought matured, and as he undertook to speak from outside the confines of those dubious dichotomies that underwrite such conventional value judgments as Good versus Evil.

Let me begin, therefore, with the "comedy of existence." The most famous instance of this insight in Nietzsche is, of course, at the very beginning of *The Gay Science*: it is this recognition that makes *scienza gaya*,[34] that is, that makes the Gay Science possible:

> You will never find anyone who could wholly mock you as an individual, even in your best qualities, bringing home to you to the limits of truth your boundless fly-like, frog-like wretchedness! To laugh at oneself, as one would have to in order to laugh *out of the whole truth*—to do that even the best so far lacked sufficient sense for the truth, and the most gifted had too little genius for that. Even laughter may yet have a future. I mean, when the proposition "the species is everything and the individual is always nothing" has become part of humanity and this ultimate liberation and irresponsibility has become accessible to all at all times. Perhaps laughter will then have formed an alliance with wisdom, perhaps only "gay science" will then be left. For the present, things are still quite different. For the present, the comedy of existence has not yet become conscious of itself. For the present we still live in the age of tragedy, the age of moralities and religions. (2001a: §1)

It is strange, to say the least, that Nietzsche claims that wisdom and laughter have never formed an alliance, that the "teachers of the purpose of existence" (2001a: §1)—the tragic poets, philosophers, and moralists—have never been mocked in toto, laughed at "out of the whole truth," since there is a locus classicus in the Cynic tradition, namely, Lucian's parodic fantasy *Menippus or the Descent to Hades*, where precisely this is done: it is in the encounter of the Cynic philosopher Menippus the only philosopher expressly called *spoudogeloios* in antiquity, with the Theban prophet Tiresias in Hades. Menippus goes to Hades in search of wisdom, to consult Tiresias on the best kind of life for a man, after realizing that the laws contradict the poets and that the philosophers contradict each other and themselves. While crossing the Acherusian plain in search of Tiresias, he discovers that "the individual is always nothing," as Nietzsche put it; all individuality is so completely effaced at death that the legendarily ugly Thersites is indistinguishable from the famously handsome Nireus: "Their naked bones were all alike—ill-defined, unnamed, unrecognizable to anyone" (*Menippus* 15). When Menippus locates Tiresias, the prophet of tragic wisdom, who sees the same things as Apollo in Sophocles, he has been converted to a Cynic perspective: he is laughing and tells the bewildered Cynic to forget the wise men—the teachers of the purpose of existence—and "to go on his way laughing a great deal and taking nothing seriously" (*gelōn ta polla kai peri mēden espoudakōs*) are Tiresias's last words of advice to the philosopher. Only laughter, it seems, has a future: an idea echoed near the conclusion of *Beyond Good and Evil*, where Nietzsche proposes that philosophers be ranked according to their laughter and speaks of a "new and superhuman way of laughing—at the expense of everything serious!" (2001b: §294).

Now Nietzsche had both these voices in him in their original potent forms: the shameless honesty of the Cynic jester unmasking the idols of the tribe with glee, and the prophet of tragic wisdom who would surpass all the other teachers of the purpose of existence, "all earthly seriousness heretofore," announcing "dreadful" truths. His mature work is an unceasing dialogue between his comic and tragic voices. In the end, I think the laughter and shameless honesty of the seriocomic jester prevails, or is it the vatic Zarathustra, Nietzsche's version of "the teachers of the purpose of existence?" Or did he succeed in synthesizing them both into a dialogic version of himself?

However we answer that question, it is clear that the art of the *spoudogelo-ios* becomes even more important for Nietzsche, beginning with *The Gay Science*, which has all the hallmarks of Cynic literature: it is a mischievous combination of the obscene and the prophetic, parodic verse and soaring prose, the personal and the transhistorical, logical analysis and ad hominem caricatures—a comically complex medley of many voices. Its seriocomic qualities are emphatically fore-grounded in the second edition: Nietzsche seems to distance himself from his own portentousness when he rewrites the phrase *incipit tragoedia*, used to introduce Zarathustra in the last book of the first edition, to read *incipit parodia* in the pref-ace, and when he imagines in the last section of book 5 the spirits of his own books saying "with malicious, cheerful, hobgoblin-like laughter" of his "great serious-ness," of his operatic talk in the preceding section of the "destiny of the soul" and "tragedy": "[W]e can't stand it anymore... stop, stop this raven-black music!" (2001a: §383). Their laughter signals a shift in tone in preparation for the ludic "Songs of Prince Vogelfrei," a sort of satyr play appended to the incipient tragedy. Among the poems that frame the five books of prose, at least two can be read as Cynic parodies, most notably §34, "Seneca et hoc genus omne," and the song titled "Fool in Despair." Thus, the very structure of *The Gay Science* registers a serio-comic ambivalence: poems "in which a poet makes fun of all poets in a manner which is hard to forgive" (2001a: preface, §1), framing and inevitably qualifying the effect of five books of virtuoso prose on a huge range of subjects. It thereby raises one of Nietzsche's thematic questions: what can or should be taken seriously? And by whom?

Nietzsche's identification with the Cynics goes a step further in *Beyond Good and Evil*. In section 26 of part 2, "The Free Spirit," to which I have been alluding throughout, he writes:

If he is lucky, as befits a favorite child of knowledge, the philosopher will find real shortcuts and aids to make his work easier. I mean he will find so-called Cynics—people who easily recognize the animal, the commonplace, the "norm" within themselves, and yet still have a degree of spiritedness and an urge to talk about themselves and their peers in *front of witnesses*:—sometimes they even wallow in books as if in their own filth. Cynicism is the only form in which common souls come close to honesty [*Redlichkeit*]; and the higher man must open his ears to every Cynicism, whether coarse or refined, and congratulate himself whenever a buffoon [*Possenreisser*] without shame or a scientific satyr speaks out in his presence.

He concludes this reflection by choosing "the laughing self-satisfied satyr" (i.e., the Cynic) over the angry moralist as the more instructive and the more honest. Later, in part 7, "Our Virtues," he comments at the end of one section that "there is a drop of cruelty in every will-to-know" (§229). He expands on this idea in the next section as follows:

> The sublime tendency of the knower who treats and wants to treat things in a profound, multiple, thorough manner. This is a type of cruelty on the part of the intellectual conscience and taste, and one that every brave thinker will acknowledge in himself, assuming that he has spent as long as he should in hardening and sharpening his eye for himself, and that he is used to strict discipline as well as strict words. He will say "There is something cruel in the tendency of my spirit";—just let kind and virtuous people try to talk him out of it! In fact, it would sound more polite [*artiger*] if, instead of cruelty, people were to accuse, mutter about and praise us as having a sort of "wild (or extravagant) honesty [*ausschweifende Redlichkeit*]"—we free, *very* free spirits—and perhaps this is what our reputation really will be—posthumously. (§230)

The term *Redlichkeit*, translated "honesty" in both these passages, specifically suggests speech, frank and honest speech. Surely Nietzsche knew from Diogenes Laertius that when Diogenes was asked what *to kalliston*, the finest thing in the world, is, he replied with one word: *parrhēsia*. *Parrhēsia* means to say everything or anything on a topic and could be translated as "wild," "reckless," or "extravagantly honest speech," the kind that could, and did, get Cynics flogged, exiled, and even executed. *Parrhēsia* was the "right" of the aristocrat or of a citizen in a democratic state. Anyone else who laid claim to it did so at his peril. That is the point of the stories about Diogenes confronting Alexander and other power brokers—his courage for *parrhēsia*, which in his hands was nothing less than a license to satirize, insult, and unmask.

Nietzsche's seriocomic art reaches its zenith in the works of his last active year, particularly in *Twilight of the Idols: or How to Philosophize with a Hammer*, a book brimming with laughter, malice, and insight, as its witty title, parodying Wagner's apocalyptic *Götterdämmerung*, aptly suggests. To give only one famous example, in a single section titled "How the Real World at Last Became a Myth," Nietzsche manages to give us a Menippean overview of the history of Western metaphysics, which is, as Michael Tanner observes, both "hilarious and unnervingly accurate" (1992: x). Here, humor has clearly become instrumental—and indispensable—to Nietzsche's mode of argument. In *The Case of Wagner*, the last work he would see through publication, Nietzsche actually characterizes his method as seriocomic, or, more accurately, "severo-comic," in his epigraph, adapted from Horace, in which Nietzsche has substituted the word *severum* for *verum*, yielding the phrase *ridendo dicere severum*: "to say something severe with laughter" (2005: 138). In its original form, *ridendo dicere verum quid vetat* (*Sermones* 1.24), Horace was defending his own literary methods in his *sermones* (or satires), asking rhetorically why he could not tell the truth with laughter, thereby invoking the essential Cynic (or seriocomic) idea that laughter (or humor) is a means of perception, an indispensable way of getting at the truth. Or as Wittgenstein observed, "Humor ist keine Stimmung sondern eine Weltanschauung" ["Humor is not a mood but a way of looking at the world"] (1977: 78, 78e). Finally, Nietzsche identifies himself as a Cynic still more explicitly in the postscript when he writes of Wagner's *Parsifal*: "One has to be a Cynic not to be seduced here; one has to be able to bite in order not to worship here. Well then, you old seducer, the Cynic warns you—*cave canem*" (2005: 257). Thus, Nietzsche's interest in Cynicism as a philosophical option, which begins, surprisingly, with its practical ascetic dimension (in the preface to volume 2 of *Human All Too Human*), leads him to embrace the shamelessness of the Cynic *parrhesiast* as a model of enlightened truth telling about the animal nature of man, and ultimately to identify himself literally with the biting laughter of the dog-philosopher—making this paradigmatic Cynic stance all that saves him from the seductions of Wagnerian decadence.

All this leads us to our ultimate question: what did Nietzsche mean when he wrote in his late autobiographical work *Ecce Homo* that his books attain here and there "the highest that can be attained on earth—Cynicism" (2005: 103)?[35] Exactly what he says. Specifically, this refers to his unmasking of the "higher swindle": "Have I been understood? What defines me, what sets me apart from all the rest of mankind, is that I have *unmasked* Christian morality" (2005: 148). Therefore, both his end—the supplanting of traditional morality—and this means, the shameless honesty and seriocomic stance of the buffoon who speaks truths, are deliberately and self-consciously Cynic—with a capital C. This is why he calls himself in *Ecce Homo*, just as he had the Cynic *parrhesiast* in *Beyond Good and Evil*, "a buffoon...and nonetheless...the truth speaks out of me" (2005: 144)—a buffoon because his *ausschweifende Redlichkeit* is applied even to himself. What other kind of philosopher would have admitted in print that the two people he knows best in all the world are also the most serious objection to his most significant idea? "I confess that the deepest objection to the Eternal Recurrence, my real idea from the abyss, is always my mother and sister" (2005: 78)—it's enough to make one a Cynic! If we follow Nietzsche's lead, and rank philosophers by their talent for laughter (2001b: §294, 175), who—aside from Diogenes or Menippus—competes with Nietzsche at this "Olympian vice"?

NOTES

1. This essay was originally titled "Philosophy as Satire/Satire as Philosophy."

2. Our word "satire" comes from the Roman word *satura*, which designates a poetic genre written only by Romans (Freudenberg 2005: 1–30). For Roman satire and philosophy, see Mayer 2005.

3. For the distinction between satire and comedy and related dichotomies (such as *psogos* vs. *to geloion* in Aristotle or "tendentious" vs. "innocent" jokes in Freud), see Branham 1989: 233 n. 70; compare Purdie 1993: 115. For a survey of attempts to distinguish satire and comedy, see Heilman 1978: appendix 6, 270–71; see also Knight 2004.

4. The only exception to this generalization are the pure pleasure that Plato approves of—perceiving pure shapes, colors, notes, or smells—"with no inevitable pain mixed with them" (*Philebus* [1993] 51e). But these are found neither in art nor in nature ("not…of a living being or a picture"; 51a). Plato gives no examples but describes the objects of such perception as if they were forms: "[N]ot beautiful in a relative sense, as others are, but…by their very nature forever beautiful by themselves" (51c). In other words, except for the "pleasures of learning" (51e), all conventional sources of pleasure involve pain.

5. For envy, see Konstan 2006: chap 5.

6. Plato's theory has lived on in many iterations, most notably that of Henry Fielding, who argues in the preface to *Joseph Andrews* that "affectation" is the ultimate source of the "true Ridiculous," (1999: 6) which he traces to two causes, vanity or hypocrisy, extending Plato's insight to his own practice as a novelist.

7. The text of the *Clouds* we have is a revised version, and we don't know how the original ended.

8. Plato's conception of *to geloion* is arguably more applicable to the New Comedy of Menander, which appears in the late fourth century B.C.E.

9. It is true that Socrates concludes from his failure to refute the oracle that it must have meant that he is the wisest of men in that he alone knows that "he is truly worthless in respect to wisdom" (23b). But that does not mean he has relinquished the claim to be uniquely wise. And despite his famous profession of ignorance, he makes dogmatic claims to moral knowledge later in the *Apology* (30b).

10. This is the same word used to characterize the pleasure we take in satire or comedy in the *Philebus*: 49e.

11. Nietzsche is the exception:

> Socrates was the clown who *made himself be taken seriously*: what really happened here?…As a dialectician you have a merciless tool in your hands; dialectics let you act like a tyrant; you humiliate the people you defeat. The dialectician puts the onus on his opponent to show that he is not an idiot; the dialectician infuriates people and makes them feel helpless at the same time. (*Twilight of the Idols*, secs. 5–7; Nietzsche 2005: 164)

12. Or, as Swift observed:

> Satire is reckoned the easiest of all wit; but I take it to be otherwise in very bad times. For it is as hard to satirize well a man of distinguished vices, as to praise well a man of distinguished virtues. It is easy enough to do either to people of moderate characters. (1727: 653)

13. For the concept, see Branham 1989: chap. 1; for the word, see Branham 1989: 227 n. 31; compare Kurke 2006, who argues ingeniously that the carnivalesque figure of Aesop—the ugly, mute, blind slave-savant—lurks behind the Platonic Socrates.

14. Fragment of an unidentified tragedy.

15. This part of the legend is, surprisingly, based on fact: see Branham and Goulet-Cazé 1996: 90 n. 30.

16. Cited and discussed by Cavell 2004: chap. 5.

17. The Cynic classics of the third and fourth centuries B.C.E. by or about Diogenes (or Crates or Menippus) survive only in an anecdotal tradition in which literary fragments are treated biographically, as in our primary source, Diogenes Laertius's *Lives and Opinions of Famous Philosophers* (third century A.D.).

18. Insofar as Diogenes' performance denies the correctness of proper language, he has to be either joking or mad from Plato's perspective (see Purdie 1993: 84). To understand Plato's aphorism ("a Socrates—gone mad!"), it is important to remember that Socrates argues in the *Phaedrus* that some forms of *mania* ("madness") are a source of inspiration and insight not accountable to philosophy. It should also be remembered that ancient tradition records elsewhere that when Diogenes was asked the same question—what he thought of Plato—he responded in kind: "[H]e's out of his mind." And, indeed, from a Cynic perspective, he was.

19. For a brilliant analysis of Nietzsche's adaptation of the anecdote, see Niehues-Pröbsting 1996: 361–62.

20. The more familiar version according to which Diogenes is looking for "an honest man" is not ancient.

21. On this point, see Goulet-Cazé 1996.

22. Compare these two passages from Freud (1960):

Tendentious jokes are especially favored in order to make aggression or criticism possible against persons in exalted positions who claim to exercise authority. The joke then represents a rebellion against authority, a liberation from its pressure. The charm of caricature lies in the same factor: we laugh at them even if they are unsuccessful simply because we count rebellion against authority as a merit. (125)

In the service of cynical or skeptical tendencies [the joke] shatters respect for institutions and truths in which the hearer has believed, on the one hand by reinforcing the argument, but on the other by practicing a new species of attack. Where argument tries to draw the hearer's criticism over to its side, the joke endeavors to push the criticism out of sight. There is no doubt that the joker has chosen the method which is psychologically more effective. (163)

23. Orwell expressed a similar idea in fewer words: "[A] joke worth laughing at has an idea behind it, and usually a subversive idea" (1954: 100).

24. For Diogenes' parody of syllogistic reasoning, see Branham 1996.

25. See Branham 1989: 57–63; for Diogenes' dismissal of the mysteries, see Diogenes Laertius, 1925: 6.39.

26. See Diogenes Laertius, 1925: 6.73; Dio Chrysostom, *Or.* 10.30. There is, of course, a difference between questioning the validity of a taboo and advocating the tabooed activity. Diogenes has sometimes been misinterpreted as engaging in the latter.

27. Once, when entering a theater just as everyone else was leaving, Diogenes was asked why he was doing this. He replied, "[T]his is what I practice doing all of my life" (Diogenes Laertius, 1925: 6.64). Nietzsche as cited in Cavell 2004: 211.

28. For a more complete analysis of Diogene' rhetoric and the role of the body in his performance, see Branham 1996.

29. For Menippean satire, see Branham 1989 and Relihan 1993.

30. The Greek title *biōn prasis* means "sale of lives," i.e., "ways of life" and therefore recalls the question that prompts Menippus's trip to Hades in the *Menippus or the Descent to Hades*: "[W]hat is the best kind of life?"

31. No less important were the fruits of their collaboration on Lucian; they were the first to discover how his essential ingredients—the fantastical journey, the satiric-philosophic dialogue, the paradoxical encomium, and the subtleties of his seriocomic manner—could be made into vehicles of the most original philosophical satires written since antiquity: More's *Utopia* (1516) and Erasmus's *Praise of Folly* (or *Moriae encomium*; 1509–22), the only neo-Latin works to become part of the European canon.

32. The satiric-philosophic tradition receives its most profound expression in dialogue form from Denis Diderot (1713–84) in *Rameau's Nephew*, which he called a satire. Goethe writing to Schiller (December 21, 1804) called it "a bomb that exploded right in the middle of French Literature." (cited in Niehues-Pröbsting 1996: 352).

33. Nietzsche did philological work on our primary source, Diogenes Laertius, and lectured on Lucian in his course on ancient rhetoric at Basel. My understanding of the modern reception of Cynicism is squarely based on the groundbreaking work of Heinrich Niehues-Pröbsting (1980, 1988, 1996).

34. *Gaya scienza* is an oxymoron analogous to *spoudogeloios*, adapted by Nietzsche from the troubadours.

35. "That Nietzsche still used one word, *Cynicism*, and did not distinguish between *Kynismus* (i.e., ancient Cynicism) and *Zynismus* (i.e., modern cynicism) demonstrates the unity [of the history of Cynicism] until the end of the nineteenth century" (Niehues-Pröbsting 1996: 354). See also Branham 2004.

REFERENCES

Branham, R. B. (1989). *Unruly Eloquence: Lucian and the Comedy of Traditions.* Cambridge, Mass.: Harvard University Press.

Branham, R. B. (1996).'Defacing the Currency: Diogenes' Rhetoric and the Invention of Cynicism" In R. B. Branham and M. O. Goulet-Cazé (eds.), *The Cynics: The Cynic Movement in Antiquity and Its Legacy*, pp. 93–94. Berkeley: University of California Press.

——. 2004. "Nietzsche's Cynicism: Uppercase or Lowercase?" In P. Bishop (ed.), *Nietzsche and Antiquity*, pp. 170–81. New York: Camden House.

Branham, R. B., and M. O. Goulet-Cazé, eds. (1996). *The Cynics: The Cynic Movement in Antiquity and Its Legacy.* Berkeley: University of California Press.

Cavell, S. (2004). *Cities of Words.* Cambridge, Mass.: Harvard University Press.

Cohen, T. (1983) "Jokes." In E. Schaper, (ed.), *Pleasure, Preference, and Value: Studies in Philosophical Aesthetics.* Cambridge: Cambridge University Press.

Douglas, M. (1968). "The Social Control of Cognition: Some Factors in Joke Perception." *Man* 3(3), 361–76.

Eco, U. (1986). "The Comic and the Rule." *In* Eco, *Travels in Hyper Reality: Essays*. San Diego: Harcourt.

Fielding, H. (1999). *Joseph Andrews*. Thomas Keymer (ed.). Oxford: Oxford University Press.

Frede, M. (1992). "Plato's Arguments and the Dialogue Form." *In* J. C. R. Klagge and N. D. Smith (eds.), *Methods of Interpreting Plato and His Dialogues*. Oxford: Oxford University Press.

Freud, S. (1960). *Jokes and Their Relation to the* Unconscious. J. Strachey (ed.). New York: W. W. Norton.

Freudenberg, K., ed. (2005). *The Cambridge Companion to Roman Satire*. Cambridge: Cambridge University Press.

Goethe, J. W. (1821). *Own and Adopted Ideas in Proverbial Formulation* (E. Stopp, trans.). *In* Goethe, *Maxims and Reflections* (1998). London: Penguin.

Goulet-Cazé. (1996). "Religion and the Early Cynics." *In* R. B. Branham and M. O. Goulet-Cazé (eds.), *The Cynics: The Cynic Movement in Antiquity and Its Legacy*. Berkeley: University of California Press.

Heilman, R. B. (1978). *The Ways of the World: Comedy and Society*. Seattle: University of Washington Press.

Knight, C. A. (2004). *The Literature of Satire*. Cambridge: Cambridge University Press.

Konstan, D. (2006). *The Emotions of the Ancient Greeks: Studies in Aristotle and Classical Literature*. Toronto: University of Toronto Press.

Kurke, L. (2006). "Plato, Aesop and the Beginnings of Mimetic Prose." *Representations* Spring, Vol. 94, 6–33.

Laertius, D. (1925). *Lives of Eminent Philosophers*, 2 Vols. R. D. Hicks (trans.). Cambridge, MA: Harvard University Press.

Levin, H. (1987). *Playboys and Killjoys: An Essay on the Theory and Practice of Comedy*. Oxford: Oxford University Press.

Lucian of Samosata (1905). "The Fisher." *In Works*, F. G. Fowler and H. W. Fowler (trans.). Oxford: Clarendon Press.

Mayer, R. (2005). "Sleeping with the Enemy: Satire and Philosophy. *In* K. Freudenberg (ed.), *The Cambridge Companion to Roman Satire*, pp. 146–59. Cambridge: Cambridge University Press.

Niehues-Pröbsting, H. (1980). "Der Kurze Weg," *Archiv fur Begriffsgeschichte* 24, 103–22.

——. (1988). *Der Kynismus des Diogenes und der Begreff des Zynismus* (2nd ed.). Frankfürt: Suhrkamp.

——. 1996. "Diogenes at the Enlightenment: The Modern Reception of Cynicism." *In* R. B. Branham and M. O. Goulet-Cazé (eds.), *The Cynics: The Cynic Movement in Antiquity and Its Legacy*. Berkeley: University of California Press.

Nietzsche, F. (2001a). *The Gay Science*. J. Nauckhoff, (trans.). Cambridge: Cambridge University Press. (Original work published 1882.)

——. (2001b). *Beyond Good and Evil*. J. Norman, (trans.). Cambridge: Cambridge University Press. (Original work published 1886.)

——. (2005). *The Anti-Christ, Ecce Homo, The Twilight of the Idols, and Other Writings* A. Ridley and J Norman, (eds.); J. Norman, (trans.). Cambridge: Cambridge University Press.

Orwell, G. (1954). *A Collection of Essays*. New York: Doubleday.

Plato (1993). *Philebus*. Dorothea Frede, trans. Indianapolis: Hackett.

Purdie, S. (1993). *Comedy: The Mastery of Discourse.* Toronto: University of Toronto Press.

Relihan, J. C. (1993). *Ancient Menippean Satire.* Baltimore: Johns Hopkins University Press.

Swift, J. (1727). *Thoughts on Various Subjects.* In Swift (2002), *The Basic Writings of Jonathan Swift.* New York: The Modern Library.

Tanner, M. (1992) "Introduction." *In* Friedrich Nietzsche, *Ecce Homo: How to Become What One Is* (R. J. Hollingdale, trans.). London: Penguin.

Wittgenstein, L. (1977). *Vermischte Bemerkungen* (G. H. Von Wright and H. Nyman, eds.). Frankfurt: Suhrkamp.

CHAPTER 7

···

THE NOVEL

···

ANTHONY J. CASCARDI

IT is a matter of consensus among literary critics that what we call the "novel" possesses no unified generic profile. In a notorious phrase, Henry James said that the novel was like a "loose, baggy monster." The novel is by all accounts a remarkably capacious genre, and it seems able to embrace just about every other literary form within its bounds. Among contemporary genres, only film has a similar capacity, and there are reasons to regard narrative film as the novel's sole legitimate heir. The form of the novel can admit tremendous variation, and even contradiction, sometimes to the point where it can seem maddeningly formless (take *Tristram Shandy* as a case in point). A taxonomy of its subgenres would seem to be limitless. Novelistic subtypes include the stream of consciousness novel, the detective novel, the sentimental novel, and the historical novel, as well as the epistolary novel, the picaresque novel, the science fiction novel, the pastoral novel, the novel in verse, and the spy novel. To these one must add the realist novel, the novel of education and development or *Bildungsroman*, the *roman à clef*, the philosophical novel, the gothic novel, the thriller, and the novel of ideas. The list could well be expanded. (Should the graphic novel, which is wordless in form, be included?) The novel is at one moment starkly authoritative and documentary (*In Cold Blood*), and in the next instance playful and self-conscious (*Rameau's Nephew, Pale Fire*). It can be engrossed in the inner psychic life of its characters (*Crime and Punishment, Lord Jim*), but can also be digressive and errant (*Don Quixote, Joseph Andrews*); it can be realistic (*Bleak House, Old Goriot*), and also magical-realist (*One Hundred Years of Solitude*). But as the account of novelistic types grows longer, the identity of the genre seems only to become less clear. Structural features of the novel such as the presence of a governing narrative voice, or markers of content and style such as the development of seemingly lifelike characters, do not hold universally consistent or true of the genre. This is in part because the novel never fully broke with its ties to the literary past, which was itself remarkably diverse. In its more developed stages, the novel begins by reflecting on the very forms that comprise it. Just as the hero of *Don Quixote* reads the romances of chivalry and attempts to act by them, David Copperfield describes his affinity for the books that his father left in a small home library: "'*Roderick Random, Peregrine Pickle, Humphrey Clinker, Tom Jones, The Vicar of Wakefield, Don Quixote, Gil Blas,* and *Robinson Crusoe,* came out, a glorious host, to keep me company.... [T]hey, and the *Arabian Nights,* and the *Tales of the Genjii*—did me no harm" (Dickens 1999: 53). The novel is an omnivorous, multivalent, and often self-reflective genre. It has continued to incorporate a panoply of preexisting literary forms, including epiclike adventures, letters, popular songs, dramatic dialogue, philosophical monologues, puzzles, culinary recipes, poetry, and journalistic prose.

There is scarcely greater consensus about the circumstances surrounding the novel's historical origins. While some the literary critics (most notably, Ian Watt in *The Rise of the Novel* [1957]) would locate its beginnings in England in the early modern period and would associate its surge in popularity with the rise of individualism in the eighteenth century, others—including Milan Kundera (1988) and Carlos Fuentes (1976)—have claimed that its full range of possibilities was already present in the two volumes of *Don Quixote* (1605, 1615) and that the further development of the genre has amounted mostly to an exploration of the possibilities that Cervantes seemed intuitively to have found. But still others would plead that the origins of the novel are remote, and lie in classical antiquity, and that its roots are to be found either in ancient satire—some forms of which, including so-called Menippean satire, bear little resemblance to what we recognize as the modern novel[1]—or in forms of adventure romance that demonstrate affinities with the novel principally as far as its plot structure is concerned. The novel has also been described as a continuation of the ancient epic, albeit transformed in response to the conditions of the modern world. György Lukács urges this basic point, which is taken over from Hegel, in the *Theory of the Novel*. (I discuss Lukács's theory at somewhat greater length below.)

While I would argue that what is often referred to as the "ancient novel" is in fact a form of Byzantine romance (see Heiserman 1977), it is nonetheless true that the modern novel depends heavily upon its connections to the past. Despite the fact that its name in English indicates something "new," the novel bears witness to the fact that we moderns have arrived late on the historical scene and are, as a consequence, continuously sifting through the accumulated discourses of the past. While the novel may be an artifact of modern culture, it is also an index of modernity's outstanding literary and historical debts. Thus, while the novel may well concentrate on the reality of experience in the present, its engagement with "reality" is invariably tinged with an awareness that the forms of experience are hardly invented anew with the advent of the modern age. Novels are built around the realization that all experience is *historically formed,* and that our consciousness of experience is inseparable from the forms through which it is told. Novelistic narratives may rely on techniques of realistic representation in order to create what

Roland Barthes famously called "reality effects," but they hardly offer direct access to the "real" or an unmediated portrayal of the past (1984: 179–80). Novels that take as their topic the remembrance of the past, such as Proust's *À la Recherche du Temps Perdu*, serve ultimately to show that the past *in itself* remains irrecuperable. Our access to what we call the "past" of personal memory may be dependent on something as circumstantial as the smell of a madeleine dunked in a cup of tea. The novels of writers like Fenimore Cooper and Sir Walter Scott amply demonstrate that our interpretation of the historical past depends directly upon the story-like forms in which it is retold.

Disagreements about the generic identity and historical origins of the novel may well be unresolvable, but they nonetheless register something important for an understanding of its relationship to philosophy.[2] The novel results from a mixing of literary forms within a historical context that is specifically and not unproblematically *modern* in nature. It emerged from a set of circumstances in which many different types of discourse came to contend with one another for legitimacy and influence: prose epic, dramatic tragedy, comedy, romance, and a number of nonliterary genres, including history writing and philosophy. The novel is a genre whose component forms remain strikingly visible and in contention; it is a species of literature in which a final synthesis of forms remains fundamentally difficult, if not impossible, to achieve. This is in part because the novel shares in the modern belief that the world is composed not of fundamental "essences" but of incommensurable particulars and of sometimes divergent constellations of language and experience. Unlike philosophy, which imagines itself as a form of discourse with *privileged* access to the truth, the novel recognizes that there are many forms of speech that can lay claim to the truth, and that the "truth" scarcely exists outside of the languages through which it is formed. Whereas the predominant modern philosophical conception of the truth carries with it an adherence to an accurate account of "the way the world is" and a commitment to telling the "whole story" about the self or the world, the novel operates in a field of obliquely angled fragments and partial accounts; it cultivates a palpable sense of anxiety about the demand for any "true" account to be authoritative and complete.[3]

In *The Theory of the Novel* (1971), Lukács described the novel's refusal to produce a synthesis of forms as involving an internal dismantling of everything from which the genre is constructed. "The composition of the novel," he proposed, "is the paradoxical fusion of heterogeneous and discrete components into an organic whole which is then abolished over and over again" (84). The form of the novel thus counterbalances the propensity to *fix* its own truth-claims, whether by speaking in many voices or by refusing to commit itself to a whole and complete account of the facts. By virtue of its form, the novel stands in opposition to any genre (including philosophy) that is built on the premise that there ought to be only one privileged way of speaking the truth. True, Schopenhauer described philosophy as "a monster with many heads, each of which speaks a different language" (1995: 25), and Descartes drew quite liberally on narrative forms, including travel narratives and autobiography. Indeed, the quest for certainty in his *Meditations* is inconceivable without the invention of a persona whose quasi-autobiographical narration is elaborated in the accompanying *Discourse on Method*. As Descartes himself acknowledges of the *Discourse*, "I am proposing this work as, so to speak, a history—or if you prefer a fable" (1984, 1: 112). In this seminal modern case, the creation of philosophy as a discourse of truth depends upon the invention of an "I" that narrates the process of its awakening from illusions. But even while the *Discourse* is a quasi-autobiography, the project of its subject is to establish itself as the foundation for all possible truths. As for Schopenhauer, neither the admission of the discursive multiplicity of philosophy nor his overarching commitment to the significance of will and idea in determining the world detracts from the view that there is, in the end, "an *object* which constitutes the *basis* of the idea, and which, although different in its whole being and nature from the idea is in all points as similar to it as one egg is to another" (1995: 27–28).

As may be apparent from what I have said thus far, my subject here is not philosophy *in* the novel—the ways in which character and plot reflect the issues and ideas that we have come to recognize as falling within the province of philosophy proper (truth, morality, etc.)—but rather the philosophical implications of novelistic form. The subject of philosophy in the novel has been treated elsewhere at substantial length (see Cascardi 1986; Jones 1975; Nussbaum 1990). Some recent thinkers have also made the case that the narrative style associated with novels affords a richness of insight and a complexity of understanding about topics that professional philosophy tends to view only in schematic terms. Martha Nussbaum's essays in *Love's Knowledge* (1990) are among the best examples of this work. The crux of this argument is that "only the style of a certain sort of narrative artist (and not, for example, the style associated with the abstract theoretical treatise) can adequately state certain important truths about the world, embodying them in its shape and setting up in the reader the activities that are appropriate for grasping them" (6).[4] But whereas Nussbaum concentrates on *style* ("style makes, itself, a statement...about what is important and what is not, about what faculties of the reader are important for knowing and what not" [7]), my concern is with novelistic *form* and with the contrasting ways in which philosophy and the novel respond to the underlying conditions that we identify with modern culture. As I explain in more detail below, philosophy and the novel construct that response through different configurations of subjectivity. Philosophy sustains the view that the "subject" is the monological subject of truth: that truth is *what matters most* to the subject *and* that it is only from the position of the subject that matters of truth can be adjudicated at all. The novel, for its part, reveals that the position of the subject is discursively and historically *formed*.

Radiating out from these very different commitments to the matter of truth are a wider set of implications about what subjectivity entails. As Robert Pippin has cogently explained, the issues at stake in the question of subjectivity range from "questions of self-knowledge, epistemological incorrigibility, first-person authority, and action theory to the nature of autonomy, [to] the scope and basis of rights claims, [and] to phenomenological issues (what it is 'like' to be the subject of one's experiences and deeds, if it is anything at all)" (2005: 10). While the "subject" may coincide with the sociological category of the modern "individual" (indeed, some writers have characterized the invention of subjectivity as a function of "bourgeois philosophy," e.g., Pippin 2005) and may include the affective and reflective registers of consciousness that we associate with romantic "inwardness" (sincerity, authenticity, etc.), subjectivity is premised first and foremost on a posture of skepticism with respect to the preconceptions inherited from the past and of independence with respect to the pursuit of truth. (Descartes's objective in rejecting the wisdom of the ancients is nothing less than to build a new philosophy "upon a foundation which is all my own" [1984, 1: 118].) In philosophical discourse, the posture of the modern subject is determined by a stance in which all dogmatic orthodoxies have been placed in doubt. As exemplified in the *Meditations* and the *Discourse on Method*, the turn away from the beliefs of the past is the prephilosophical basis for modern rationalism. Descartes writes: "I had...given enough time to languages and likewise to reading the works of the ancients, both their histories and their fables...I thought that I could do no better than undertake to get rid of them, all at one go, in order to replace them afterwards with better ones, or with the same ones once I had squared them with the standards of reason" (1984, 1: 113, 117). Of course, Descartes is aware of the need for deferential treatment of those who had continued to hold the formal authority over the truth—most notably, the faculty of theology of the Sorbonne. In the preface to the *Meditations*, Descartes shrewdly attempts to appease "those most learned and distinguished men, the Dean and Doctors of the sacred Faculty of Theology at Paris" (2: 3). But these concessions hardly impede the quest for truth as a form of autonomously established epistemological certainty. Moreover, Descartes's claims to autonomy and his faith in rational certainty serve to reinforce his opposition to the forms of prose fiction that were prevalent in his day. Indeed, Descartes seems to be responding directly to Cervantes when he cautions that fables make us imagine many events as possible when they are not. And even the most accurate histories, while not altering or exaggerating the importance of matters to make them more worthy of being read, at any rate almost always omit the baser and less memorable events; as a result, the other events appear in a false light, and those who regulate their conduct by examples drawn from these works are liable to fall into the excesses of the knights errant in our tales of chivalry, and conceive plans beyond their powers (1: 114). He imagines that his own plan of inquiry will be far more disciplined and methodical than what fictions provide.

Descartes's critique of fiction, including fables and adventure romances, suggests that he was wary of the perspectival refractions generated by the novel's constituent discourses (see Toulmin 1990). By contrast, Cervantes embraced perspectivism as a *response* to the possibility of skepticism, and he saw that it could lead to compromises generated by pragmatic necessity and to agreements to live in asymmetrical and inchoate worlds (see Cascardi 2000). If perspectivism is a philosophy, then the philosophy of the novel is inseparable from the discourse-intensive realms of the social and the political. Indeed, the novel takes "discourse" as fully able to compete with "thought" and with theoretical views about what is true, what is good, and what is just. And because the novel is generated continuously out of many *different* forms of discourse, it is compelled to regard matters of truth, morality, and justice as resistant to any common measure. *Don Quixote* is exemplary of a genre that draws profound philosophical consequences from the fact that none of these discourses is recognized as superior to the others.

The novel thus readily embraces the modern idea that the world is not composed of fundamental, intelligible essences. To this extent, it is consistent with the varieties of modern empiricism that flourished after Descartes. As Roberto Mangabeira Unger explained in his study of British empiricist writing,

> it is possible to divide the world in an indefinite number of ways. No one way
> of dividing it describes what the world is really like.... The modern conception
> of nature and of the relation of thought to nature...denies the existence of a
> chain of essences or essential qualities that we could either infer from particular
> things in the world or perceive face to face in their abstract forms. And it
> therefore insists that there are numberless ways in which objects and events in
> the world might be classified. (1975: 31–32)

Likewise, the modern conception of personality dispenses with the myth of the "given" self; the self is recognized as formed by, among other things, its context. What is *formed* may also be *trans*formed. The result is a view of the self as open to change within the context of a world that can itself be transformed by virtue of human action. Not surprisingly, such ethical and existential interests are coincident with the formation and development of character in the novel. Novelistic characters do not have the appearance of being prefabricated entities, but struggle to fashion themselves as individuals who make value for and of themselves.[5] Indeed, the novel raises the "subject" to the level of a value-question, whether in connection with underlying assumptions about the truth, the demand to synthesize forms, or the striving after cohesive teleologies at the level of character and action.

Although modern philosophy takes up many of these questions explicitly, the novel generally provides a critical counterpoint to what philosophy has to say about them. This is largely because the novel sheds light on the *formation* (discursive and otherwise) of the insights that philosophy regards as achieved and, with that, articulates those things that philosophy tends to leave largely unspoken. To take but one example, it is not just that the European *Bildungsroman* shares some of the aims of Hegel's *Phenomenology of Spirit* or even, as Josiah Royce suggested, that the shape of Hegel's *Phenomenology of Spirit* resembles that of a *Bildungsroman* (see Abrams 1971), but that the *Bildungsroman* imagines character development as fundamentally problematic, as requiring the invention of a form that cannot be presupposed in advance. As Lukács explained, the novel reflects the need to bind "form" and "life." There are passages in the writings of Locke and Hume that demonstrate a bewildering sense of the precariousness of the epistemological claims they hope to establish, but it is only in the novel that the vertiginous world of facts is made problematical in a way that bears on the process and purpose of self-fashioning.

The larger points behind these examples are twofold: first, that philosophy and the novel play contrasting roles with respect to the discursive conditions that underlie the subject and its preoccupations with truth, morality, and meaningful action; and second, that these conditions are historical and discursive. To understand the form of the novel thus requires something other than a "philosophical interpretation." It requires an interpretation that is *historicophilosophical*.

The call for a historicophilosophical understanding of the novel is hardly new. It was in fact a prominent element of one of the central texts of literary-philosophical writing in the twentieth century, Lukács's *Theory of the Novel* (1914–15). Writing in reaction to what he characterized as the petty two-dimensionality of neo-Kantianism and other varieties of positivist thought, Lukács attempted to map large-scale changes in literary form against a broad range of theoretical and historical factors. For this, Lukács took up the Hegelian belief that all aesthetic forms have an a priori ground or "home," and that changes in these forms can be traced according to shifts in the metaphysical beliefs or "transcendental points of orientation" of a given age: "As a result of such a change in the transcendental points of orientation, art forms become subject to a historico-philosophical dialectic; the course of this dialectic will depend, however, on the a priori 'home' of each genre" (Lukács 1971: 40). While Lukács later cast a skeptical eye on some of the methods employed in the *Theory of the Novel*, the fact remains that the work was widely influential; it was read by such figures as Thomas Mann and Max Weber and helped create a space for a historically informed set of philosophical reflections on the novel. Lucien Goldmann's 1965 Marxist work, *Pour une Sociologie du Roman*, depends heavily on it, as does Kundera's account of the historical shifts in fundamental beliefs around which the novel took shape. Here is Kundera in *The Art of the Novel* (1986) in one of his most Lukácsean moments:

> As God slowly departed from the seat whence he had directed the universe and its order of values, distinguished good from evil, and endowed each thing with meaning, Don Quixote set forth from his house into a world he could no longer recognize. In the absence of the Supreme Judge, the world suddenly appeared in its fearsome ambiguity; the single divine Truth decomposed into myriad relative truths parceled out by men. Thus was born the world of the Modern Era, and with it the novel, the image and model of that world. (1988: 6)

What *The Theory of the Novel* was trying to achieve, by Lukács's own lights, was an understanding of the homology between large-scale transformations in history and changes in literary forms. Indeed, in his own later reflections on the *Theory of the Novel*, Lukács said that he was hoping to arrive at an even "more intimate connection between category and history than he found in Hegel himself" (1971: 16).[6] And yet Lukács reached conclusions that are quite different from Hegel's. In Hegel's view, the world of prose is one in which "spirit" has reached a relatively high level of stasis, not only in reflection (thought), but in society and politics, as well. In this world, "art becomes problematic precisely because reality has become non-problematic" (17). The central thesis of *The Theory of the Novel*, while formally similar to Hegel's view, in fact argues the opposite of this. For Lukács, the form of the novel is the reflection of a world out of joint, in which everything is rendered problematic, including art itself:

> [T]he "prose" of life is here only a symptom, among many others, of the fact that reality no longer constitutes a favourable soil for art; that is why the central problem of the novel is the fact that art has to write off the closed and total forms which stem from a rounded totality of being—that art has nothing more to do with any world of forms that is immanently complete in itself.... And this is not for artistic but for historico-philosophical reasons. (17)

For Lukács, the novel is defined by the disintegration of the "rounded totality" of life associated with the epic and by the disappearance of the transcendental certainties that gave such a world its immediate security. So seen, the novel is not just a *modern* form but, in its active reflection on literature's response to these matters, a *modernist* genre. Its sustaining energy derives from the fact that it is the product of a world in which the "rounded totality" of forms is no longer immediately accessible, but is refracted in an oblique fashion.

Whether Lukács's view is historically accurate or is itself a "novelistic" reconstruction of the past is a question well worth pursuing, in part because of what Lukács himself says in a cautionary way about post-epic cultures in relationship to the ancient world: "Henceforth," he writes,

> any resurrection of the Greek world is a more or less conscious hypostasy of aesthetics into metaphysics—a violence done to the essence of everything that lies outside the sphere of art, and a desire to destroy it; an attempt to forget that art is only one sphere among many, and that the very disintegration and inadequacy of the world is the precondition for the existence of art and its becoming conscious (1971: 38).

Following this lead, Jay Bernstein has characterized the relationship between the world of the ancient epic and that of the novel as the result of a process of historical reflection: "The terms 'epic' and 'novel' do not signify for Lukács two unproblematical empirical items which may be illuminated through a contrastive analysis; rather, those terms mark the poles of an act of historical reflection by which the novel can be brought into consciousness in its historical specificity and antinomic complexity" (1984: 48).[7] But the situation may well be more complicated than this account suggests, for in the course of constructing its modern identity the novel participates in the re-creation of the ancient epic as an historical phenomenon, which in turn helps generate the historical distance that our notion of the epic requires. The novel is not merely a "belated" form of epic literature but also, because of its self-conscious modernity, a self-aware form that helps create the epic (as) past.

To grasp the relationship between novel and epic also requires understanding how the historical distance between novel and epic is reflected in the novel's peculiar "inwardness." The novel cultivates inwardness not so much because it is introspective and nostalgic but because it depends, in Hegel's conception, on the recentering of truth within a field that is defined by the subject. By contrast, the epic world can be regarded as "subjectless" because the epic presents *"not the poet's own inner world but the objective events....* This is why the great epic style consists in the work's seeming to be its own minstrel and appearing independently without having any author to conduct it or be as its head" (Hegel 1975, 2: 1048–49, emphasis added). In Lukácsean terms, the epic world is one in which there is no distinction between "form" and "life." The novel, by contrast, has lost this immediacy and integrity and so must struggle to find ways to bind form and life together. It does so just as modern philosophy attempts to come to terms with the division between the empirical and transcendental worlds and with all the dualities that accompany this division.

For Hegel, *Don Quixote* was an exemplary novel because Cervantes' main character demonstrates the "representation of absolute subjectivity as the whole of truth" (1975, 2: 530). In *Don Quixote*, the form of "absolute subjectivity" emerges from the contradictions between "an intelligible self-ordered world" and "an isolated mind which proposes to create this order and stability solely by himself and by chivalry, whereby it could only be overturned" (591). As Hegel went on to suggest, "Don Quixote is a heart completely sure of itself and its business, or rather this only is his lunacy that he is and remains so sure of himself and his business. Without this peaceful lack of reflection in regard to the object and outcome of his actions, he would not be genuinely romantic" (591–92). The spiritual form that corresponds most closely to this form of certainty, with its grasp of its independence and freedom, is not just inwardness, but "absolute inwardness." Indeed, "absolute inwardness" is characteristic of a world where all gods external to the subject have disappeared: "In this Pantheon all the gods are dethroned, the flame of subjectivity has destroyed them, and instead of plastic polytheism art knows now only *one* God, one spirit, one absolute independence which, as the absolute knowing and willing of itself, remains in free unity with itself" (519).[8] Such "inwardness" also corresponds to a world in which characters often turn their attention from the pursuit of great deeds to the trials and tribulations of love. To devote oneself to love and to be open to its fortunes and misfortunes seems to be the fate of many characters who try to act as heroes in a postheroic age.[9] As Leo Bersani wrote of Racine in *A Future for Astyanax*, "Agamemnon, Helen, Achilles: the parents of Racine's characters made history while their children try—unsuccessfully at that—to make love" (1984: 47). The decline that is implicit in the transition from the exalted status of hero to that of lover is already true of the aristocratic world portrayed in a novel like Madame de Lafayette's *La Princesse de Clèves*. In the novels of Stendhal it is all the more valid because the main character of *Le Rouge et le Noir* and *La Chartreuse de Parme*, Julien Sorel, was never anything more than the son of a carpenter. Julien Sorel may spend his time in dreams about taking part in Napoleon's army, but his only worldly resources are deception and hypocrisy. He finds himself in love, and there he is betrayed by his own passions.

The novelistic impulse toward self-fashioning may thus be quite powerful, but there is hardly any guarantee that the self will be successful in any of the projects it undertakes. On the contrary, the form that Lukács described as the "romanticism of disillusionment" seems to be of the essence of novelistic subjectivity as regards both character and novelistic form. As Bernstein has acutely observed, this particular form of "disillusionment" lodges itself in the narrative irony through which the characters and their actions are presented, even while the characters themselves may remain wedded to their illusions.[10] Flaubert's *L'Education Sentimentale* is a case in point. To cite Bernstein,

> [W]e know Frédéric [Moreau] will not be a painter not by our foreknowledge
> of his abilities, but by the circumstances and manner in which Flaubert has
> Frédéric make his decision.... Similarly, we know from the following account
> that Frédéric will fail in his plans to be a statesman.... Frédéric does not know
> that all his dreams must succumb; nor does he attempt to fashion his own life
> by making it a work of literature. That is for Flaubert. Frédéric is a mediocre
> man; the content of his mediocrity is the ironic style which permeates the
> generation of his projects. (1984: 121–22)

In sum, "truth" in the novel is inevitably a function of how the value-laden choices of characters are framed by a narrator, who makes implicit value choices in the process. As Nussbaum has written, "a view of life is *told*. The telling itself—the selection of genre, formal structures, sentences, vocabulary... all of this expresses a sense of life and of value, a sense of what matters and what does not, of what learning and communicating are, of life's relations and connections. Life is never simply *presented* by a text; it is always *represented as* something" (1990: 5). Truth in the novel is always framed; it is contingent on the value-laden speech and actions of characters and also on the narrative voice through which those actions and assertions are represented. It emerges in the presentation of nuance and detail, and in shifting points of view—even to the point where reflection and evaluation may seem to overwhelm the "facts." A novelist like James gives us worlds where every fact and every action, including narrative description and observation, is charged with some value. As epitomized earlier in Nikolai Gogol's *Dead Souls* (1841–46), this leads to the awareness that the voice of the "truth" is but one among many other such value-seeking voices within the novelistic universe. The development of the *style indirect libre* in such novelists as Stendhal and Flaubert—where the narrative voice is not definitively bounded, but where the line between the voice of the narrator and those of the characters is blurred—represents yet another way in which the locus of value and authority circulates in a free and unprivileged way within the novel's inner-worldly domain.

Modern philosophy, for its part, established a new and not unproblematical link to the inner-worldly realm of "experience," which was conceived by empiricist thinkers as coincident with the world of "facts." In particular, the skeptical empiricism of Locke and Hume brought with it a new interest in particulars, together with a turn toward a detailed discourse of "facts" and a commitment to the importance of verifiable "experience." In the introduction to the *Treatise on Human Nature*, for example, Hume writes that, tho' we must endeavour to render all our principles as universal as possible, by tracing up our experiments to the utmost, and explaining all effects from the simplest and fewest causes, 'tis certain *we cannot go beyond experience*; and any hypothesis, that pretends to discover the ultimate original qualities of human nature, ought at first to be rejected as a presumptuous and chimerical. (1969: 44, emphasis added)

There is a related Lockean wish to delimit "experience" by suppressing all "fantastical ideas" (which Locke also calls "chimerical ideas") as having no basis in nature:

Fantastical or chimerical [ideas] I call such as have no foundation in nature, nor have any conformity with that reality of being to which they are tacitly referred, as to their archetypes.... Those [ideas] are fantastical which are made up of such collections of simple ideas as were never really united, never were found together in any substance: e.g., a rational creature, consisting of a horse's head, joined to a body of human shape, or such as the *centaurs* are described; or a body yellow, very malleable, fusible, and fixed, but lighter than common water; or an uniform, unorganized body, consisting, as to sense, all of similar parts, with perception and voluntary motion joined to it. (1964: 234–35)

Locke thus continues the reaction against implausible fictions that began with literary-theoretical reappropriations of Aristotle's *Poetics* in the course of controversies over the fantastical adventures of the *romanzo* in the Italian Renaissance.[11] Indeed, the culture of Enlightened modernity drew liberally upon the Renaissance-inspired desire to secure the truth-claims of philosophy by limiting the representation of fictions and fantasies.

But both Locke and Hume discover that the tenets of empiricism are far less stable than they might have hoped. Certainly the philosophical "discourse" around empiricism is far less simple than is often imagined. There are some breathtaking statements of uncertainty in Locke's *Essay Concerning Human Understanding*, and these are made all the more impressive by Locke's attempts to reach as far as possible to the essences of things. When we come to examine the stones we tread on, or the iron we daily handle," writes Locke,

we presently find we know not their make, and can give no reason of the different qualities we find in them. It is evident *the internal constitution, whereon their properties depend, is unknown to us*. Therefore we in vain pretend to range things into sorts, and dispose them into certain classes under names, by their real essences, that they are so far from our ordinary comprehension. (1964: 287, emphasis added)

As regards the question of whether there can be any true predications, or any other real connection between essences, the *Essay* makes a rather definitive statement:

[E]ach abstract idea being distinct so that of any two the one can never be the other, the mind will, by its intuitive knowledge, perceive their difference, and therefore in propositions no two whole ideas can ever be affirmed one of another.... All our affirmations are only in concrete, which is the affirming, not one abstract idea to be another, but one abstract idea to be joined to another. (297)

The result is a far more precarious world than the standard view of empiricism would suggest.

The *rhetoric* of empiricism nonetheless infiltrates the novel insofar as it supports the desire for a realism of representation, along with forms that bear affinities with history writing and testimonial reports. As empiricism gained cultural prestige, the novelistic adherence to the "eyewitness account" likewise rose in stature and helped secure the novel's claims to legitimacy. And yet to speak of the novel's form as deeply aligned with empiricism would be to misconstrue its intentions. If anything, the novel shows that the very "facts" on which modern empiricist culture came to rely are inseparable from the narrative forms that lend them shape and value. Indeed, the very notion of a "fact" makes sense only in contradistinction to a discourse about "values." The two—"fact" and "value"—stand in an antinomic relationship in much the same way that "form" and "life" do for Lukács. The novel's contribution to the culture of empiricism was to insist upon the narrative value frameworks within which the "facts" could become meaningful.

Indeed, the novel does more than simply reflect or reinforce the antinomies of "fact" and "value." It also strives, through any available means, to give them order—in Lukács's terms, to bind "form" and "life." A work like *Robinson Crusoe* (1719) illustrates that narrative itself strives to be a value-laden form of discourse in a culture that seems devoted to facts. To be sure, *Robinson Crusoe* incorporates various empiricist procedures into this project: direct observations and their recording, the taking of inventories, and the accounting of materials expended and of resources remaining. Daniel Defoe cultivates the practice of experimentation and sustains a pretense of historical veracity. Indeed, the very premise of *Robinson Crusoe* can be taken as an "experiment" in which an ordinary man is placed in a radically unfamiliar context in order to discover, among other things, what is essential about human nature and what is a product of culture. But Defoe's quasi-empiricist strategies, with their commitment to the recording of facts and a discovery of the "truth," are set within a narrative that ultimately casts the "facts" within many different frames of value. The narrative that ostensibly experiments with Crusoe's shipwreck on a desert island can also be read as a spiritual autobiography, as an adventure story, as a mythical account of the foundations of economic society, as an unfiltered personal diary, as an account of the workings of providence in human affairs, and as a grand example of an Oedipal struggle, illustrating the lengths to which sons may go in order to clear free of the authority of their fathers. There is as much consistency among these narrative value frames (or as little) as might be expected of a genre whose form was determined by a crisis in the belief in any single, extraworldly source of authority.

That crisis determines what is sometimes characterized as a denial of the "myth of the given." It is central to the reorientation of transcendental beliefs that Lukács describes in connection with the novel, and it is crucial for an understanding of what Lukács describes as the "productivity of spirit." Empiricists like Locke and Hume encountered the inaccessibility of essences, but Kant's "Copernican turn" reoriented philosophical thinking around the belief that the categories of the mind, and not the world, were responsible for setting the parameters of experience. For Kant, we can truly know only what we make. The mind (spirit) is "productive" in this way: it supplies the categories of any possible experience. Not surprisingly, the more or less local complications that empiricist procedures encountered in attempting to arrive at the truth—the resistance of facts to the procedures of evidentiary validation, for example—do not adequately characterize the role that the "productive spirit" plays in shaping the culture of which the novel was a part.

In *The Theory of the Novel*, Lukács proposed that the cohesion among abstract components of the novel is pure and formal, whereas the principle of "creative subjectivity" implies an ethic that the novel best reveals at the level of content (1971: 84). To invoke the "productivity of spirit" explains why the novel shows human beings endlessly making up their minds, deliberating and deciding, assessing what they can meaningfully take responsibility for, judging whether and how they can claim the world as their own.[12] In the world of the novel, the fundamental Aristotelian question—"How should one live?"—is rendered essentially problematic.[13] Little wonder that philosophical existentialism found the novel such a congenial genre. In the existentialist novel (e.g., *La Nausée*, *L'Étrangère*, *L'Age de Raison*), the act of making up one's mind takes place in a context where there are no preconceived answers. (This is consistent with what Kant meant when he described the self in terms of "spontaneity" [*Selbsttätigkeit*]). But even before existentialism, we have a figure like Joseph Conrad's Lord Jim, who is caught up terrible moral dilemmas, trying to decide not just what to do but how to assess what he has done or failed to do. Even the novels of Iris Murdoch, who was no existentialist sympathizer, are filled with examples of characters who are absorbed in the process of making up their minds. Moreover, her characters are able to change their minds, not just on the basis of the "facts" but on the way in which they come to regard the facts. Her own hope was for a relationship to the facts that mere observation of the world would not allow. In some of her philosophical writings (e.g., *The Sovereignty of Good* [1985]), she describes what it might mean to see *beyond* a way that is subject to the principles of empirical observation. She describes a form of seeing that requires attending to the values that are revealed by the ways in which characters act.

But Murdoch understands the activity of seeing not so much as a value-*producing* enterprise as a source of insight into the way things truly are. She thus strives to reconcile the modern novel with a premodern (Platonic) view of the world. The idea that characters can move from a position of ignorance about the world to one of true insight might even lend some plausibility to the view that character development in the novel owes its greatest debts to Plato's dialogues. And yet there are historical differences between Plato's world and the universe of the novel that Murdoch seems to ignore. Novelistic characters *can* and indeed *do* change, but they do so in a world that is not believed to be fixed one way or another. Indeed, the openness of the world-horizon is fundamental to the most basic interests in telling stories in novelistic ways. If late adolescence and young adulthood are of particular interest in the novel, this is because the novel tends to construe life as having a form in which the full range of possibilities is not given to anyone in advance, but is left up to the individual to produce as a result of maturation. The *Bildungsroman* presents notably complex models of the development of character. It takes seemingly isolated events, including those that mark beginnings and endings, and follows them through an arc that tries to trace meaningful interconnections among them. Jane Austen's novels are particularly illustrative of the philosophical stakes involved in "character development." Alasdair MacIntyre (1981: 222–26) has suggested that Austen's view of character offers one of the few faithful modern interpretations of Aristotle's understanding about the virtues. To be sure, Austen preserves something essential about Aristotle's views of character despite (or in addition to) her inheritance of a non-Aristotelian, Christian outlook on the virtues. And yet the fact remains that Austen is thoroughly modern in just the ways that correspond to Lukács's views about the "productivity of spirit." Her heroines achieve happiness to the degree that they find ways, through their powers of insight, intelligence, and language, to break free from the constraints set by parents or by economic and social contexts. This is the basis of any self-achievement they might attain. The opportunities they have for self-realization are tied to the hope that they can avoid the limiting forms of life that would likely have befallen women in earlier times; in Austen's world, there are new, and newly desired, life outcomes. These are also reflected, *a contrario*, in characters who fail to mature—in Elizabeth Bennet's youngest sibling, for instance, who marries at far too young an emotional age.

But the very reason that the novel concentrates on "creative subjectivity" is that its historical world is neither Platonic nor Aristotelian, but modern. This is, as Lukács argues, the very reason why its form is problematic. The novel is skeptical about the existence of any *necessary* linkage of beginnings, middles, and ends. Indeed, the novel sometimes flouts the very principle of goal-driven behavior, either by subverting expected trajectories of achievement or by refusing to embrace the value of goal-directed action altogether. Self-realization is but one possible pursuit in a world "abandoned by god." Other possibilities include errant behavior (*Don Quixote* again) or forms of activity that are neither profitable nor productive. Novels in this respect stand at an oblique angle to the pragmatic aims that much of modern philosophy accepts. Indeed, Descartes's central purpose in the *Meditations* and the *Discourse on Method* was to find ways of making improvements in very practical matters, to wit, in enabling advances in medical science. This is a far cry from the novelistic awareness that causes and effects relate only contingently to one another, and that "action" is a field that must include various forms of inaction, as well. Consider James's "The Spoils of Poynton" as a case in point. Though technically a short story and not a novel, it is a novelistic fiction that makes a compelling case about the significance of wasteful activity, as if to suggest that modern individuals cannot engage in value and production without also engaging in their opposites.

Indeed, the structures of design and intention at work in the novel often seem to operate in ways that directly contravene Aristotelian ideas about the relationship between beings and the ends that they *ought* to pursue. In the *Poetics*, Aristotle's ethical and metaphysical views were reflected in a conception of plot that required a coherent and goal-driven relationship between beginnings, middles, and endings. The novel, for its part, seems closer to Sigmund Freud's views in *Beyond the Pleasure Principle* (1920), where the activity of the organism is not to achieve "perfection" but to return to an earlier state of affairs, often an inanimate one; it is consistent with an ambition toward undoing rather than achieving, and it involves a dissipation of the very sources of desire that would seem to impel character and action forward. The paradigmatic case, treated by Peter Brooks in *Reading for the Plot* (1984), is Honoré de Balzac's *Wild Ass's Skin*, where the protagonist comes into the possession of a talisman. The conditions of the magical wild ass's skin are that it will fulfill its owner's every desire, but each time at the cost of some remaining portion of his life. The hero can thus do best to try to eliminate all desiring activity. The "story" of the novel is produced as an act of reflection on this grand paradox. To be sure, Balzac creates genuine suspense about what the outcome of the plot will be and sustains a desire to know the end, but the narrative exists only because the end can be delayed. In such circumstances, there is hardly an affirmative binding of "form" and "life," or even a wry reflection on their disjunction, but a higher order production of narrative "movement" that derives from a complete inversion of Aristotelian teleologies.

The further alignment of the novel with such a challenge to philosophy comes from the fact that the novel itself provided a framework that was congenial to Freud's late-modern reappropriation of the ancient myths. Above all, the case histories ("Wolf Man," "Rat Man," "Dora," etc.) have a novelistic cast. They are all instances in which some form of irony, which Lukács describes as the "normative mentality of the novel," is adumbrated as true and strives to assert its validity in light of the fact that the kernel of truth at issue may appear incomplete and obscure, or that access to it is impeded by the subjects themselves. "I begin," writes Freud in "Dora," "by asking the patient to give me the whole story of his life and illness, but even so the information I receive is never enough to let me see my way about the case." And yet he concludes that "the patients' inability to give me an ordered history of their life in so far as it coincides with the history of their illness is not merely characteristic of the neurosis. It also possesses great theoretical significance" (1963: 10). The theoretical significance of this fact—that both conscious and unconscious forgetting are at work—may help explain why "form" and "life" could not possibly be bound together. Both in their theories and in their storylike accounts, the "case histories" confirm something that the novel had already taken to heart: that philosophy's ethical and existential hopes were premised on a notion of the truth that proved inadequate to the modes of discourse and forms of life in which they had come to take root.

NOTES

1. When, in the fourth chapter of *Problems of Dostoevsky's Poetics* (1984), Bakhtin suggested that the novel had evolved from Menippean satire, this was because he saw both as genres in which ceaseless upheavals of perspective and challenges to authoritative standards of truth became established as normative. The principal strategy of Menippean satire, which involves the juxtaposition of differing points of view or *syncrisis*, is not unrelated to novelistic perspectivism. In the words of one recent critic, Menippean satire "is a form that uses at least two other genres, languages, cultures, or changes of voice to oppose a dangerous, false, or specious and threatening orthodoxy" (Weinbrodt 2005: 8).

2. The "problematic" nature of the novel was not always acknowledged to be such. Thus, in "The Art of Fiction" (2004), James could refer to the time when "there was a comfortable, good-humored feeling abroad that a novel is a novel, as a pudding is a pudding, and that our only business with it could be to swallow it." As he goes on to note, however, "within a year or two, for some reason or other, there have been signs of returning to animation—the era of discussion would appear to have been to a certain extent opened" (427). James ultimately presents the novel as a "magnificent" form that offers "few restrictions and such innumerable opportunities" (446).

3. However, the novel may well *mimic* the kinds of truth-claims that pretend to tell the whole truth. The anonymous, proto-novelistic picaresque *Lazarillo de Tormes* is an early example of the novel's invocation of the principle of narrative wholeness.

4. As Nussbaum further argues, in ways reminiscent of Iris Murdoch's writings, fine attention and good deliberation require a highly complex, nuanced perception of and emotional responses to the concrete features of one's own context, including particular persons and relationships.

5. Indeed, when Stephen Greenblatt invoked the term "self-fashioning" in connection with the development of a poetics of subjectivity in the Renaissance, it is largely a novelistic sense of character that is created, regardless of the fact that self-fashioning may have taken place in other genres (poetry, drama, etc.). See Greenblatt 1980.

6. Lukács's complaint about the work, issued several intellectual turns away from the conceptual framework within which it was written, was that the *Theory of the Novel* was insufficiently historical and that its typology of novelistic forms was far too schematic and abstract to be of use: "This method remains extremely abstract in many respects," he wrote; "it is cut off from concrete socio-historical realities. For that reason…it leads only too often to arbitrary intellectual constructs…. *The Theory of the Novel* remained at the level of an attempt which failed both in design and in execution, but which in its intention came closer to the right solution than its contemporaries were able to do" (1971: 17).

7. Bernstein further explains:

What controls Lukács's use of the past is not a utopian philosophy of history, but a methodology. And that methodology is, roughly, a dialectical (critical) hermeneutics…. He denies any desire to proffer a philosophy of history; and he explicitly criticises the idealist tradition for making the epic age into a Utopia. None the less, he must return to Greece for his analysis because the historical identity of the novel, an identity the novel provides for itself, is, in part, constituted by its connection with the ancient epic. (1984: 64–65)

8. It is not just that historical circumstances surrounding the subject are changing and that these changes are reflected in the novel, but that the "novelistic" subject plays a role in resisting belief in external "gods." The matter is thus not just, as Lukács suggests, that the world is abandoned by god, but that the subject has itself played a role in banishing the "gods." Hegel writes:

> This inherently infinite and absolute universal content [of subjectivity] is the absolute negation of everything particular, the simple unity with itself which has dissipated all external relations, all processes of nature and their periodicity of birth, passing away, and rebirth, all the restrictedness in spiritual *existence*, and dissolved all particular gods into a pure and infinite self-identity. (1975, 2: 519)

9. The world of opera—take Wagner's *Tristan und Isolde* as a case in point—is in some important ways more novelistic than epic or dramatic.

10. Compare Michael McKeon's (1987) account of the "theories" of enchantment and enchanters that Don Quixote invents in order to explain his illusions.

11. The Cervantean critique of the excesses of romance in the romances of chivalry was fueled by these earlier Renaissance reengagements with Aristotle. See Forcione 1970.

12. "A human subject is...a meaning-*making* subject (minimally always 'making up her mind' in experiencing and so likewise responsible for what she claims to know), a self-conscious subject, in this active, self-determining relation to itself in all experience as well as in all action" (Pippin 2005: 2).

13. Compare Nussbaum (1990: 23–29), who regards the novel as consistent with this question and as relatively little troubled by it.

REFERENCES

Abrams, M. H. (1971). *Natural Supernaturalism*. New York: Norton.

Barthes, R. (1984). "L'Effet du Réel." *In* Barthes, *Le Bruissement de la Langue; Essais Critiques IV*. Paris: Seuil.

Bernstein, J. M. (1984). *The Philosophy of the Novel: Lukács, Marxism, and the Dialectics of Form*. Minneapolis: University of Minnesota Press.

Bersani, L. (1984). *A Future for Astyanax*. New York: Columbia University Press.

Cascardi, A. J. (1986). *The Bounds of Reason: Cervantes, Dostoyevsky, Flaubert*. New York: Columbia University Press.

——. (2000). "Two Kinds of Knowing in Plato, Cervantes, and Aristotle," *Philosophy and Literature* 24, 406–23.

Descartes, R. (1984). *Philosophical Writings* 3 vols.; J. Cottingham, R. Stoothoff, and D. Murdoch, (trans.). Cambridge: Cambridge University Press.

Dickens, C. (1999). *David Copperfield*. Oxford: Oxford University Press. (Original work published 1849–50.)

Forcione, A. (1970). *Cervantes, Aristotle, and the "Persiles."* Princeton: Princeton University Press.

Freud, S. (1963). *Dora: An Analysis of a Case of Hysteria*. New York: Collier/Macmillan.

Fuentes, C. (1976). *Cervantes o la Critica de la Lectura*. Mexico City: Joaquín Moritz.

Greenblatt, S. (1980). *Renaissance Self-Fashioning*. Chicago: University of Chicago Press.

Hegel, G. W. F. (1975). *Lectures on Aesthetics* (T. M. Knox, trans.). Oxford: Oxford University Press. (Original work published 1835.)

Heiserman, H. (1977). *The Novel before the Novel*. Chicago: University of Chicago Press.

Hume, D. (1969). *A Treatise of Human Nature* (Ernest G. Mossner, ed.). London: Penguin. (Original work published 1739.)

James, H. (2004). "The Art of Fiction." *In* John Auchard (ed.), *The Portable Henry James*. New York: Penguin. (Original work published 1884.)

Jones, P. (1975). *Philosophy and the Novel*. Oxford: Oxford University Press.

Kundera, M. (1988). "The Depreciated Legacy of Cervantes." *In* L. Asher, (trans.). *The Art of the Novel*. New York: Harper and Row. (Original work published 1986.)

Locke, J. (1964). *An Essay Concerning Human Understanding*, A. D. Woozley, (ed.). New York: Meridian. (Original work published 1690.)

Lukács, G. (1971). *The Theory of the Novel*, Anna Bostock, (trans.). Cambridge, Mass.: MIT Press. (Original work published 1920.)

MacIntyre, A. (1981). *After Virtue*. Notre Dame, Ind.: University of Notre Dame Press.

McKeon, M. (1987). *The Origins of the English Novel: 1600–1740*. Baltimore: Johns Hopkins University Press.

Nussbaum, M. (1990). *Love's Knowledge*. New York: Oxford University Press.

Pippin, R. B. (2005). *The Persistence of Subjectivity: On the Kantian Aftermath*. Cambridge: Cambridge University Press.

Schopenhauer, A. (1995). *The World as Will and Idea*. London: J. M. Dent/Everyman. (Original work published 1819.)

Toulmin, S. (1990). *Cosmopolis*. Chicago: University of Chicago Press.

Unger, R. M. (1975). *Knowledge and Politics*. New York: Free Press.

Weinbrodt, H. (2005). *Menippean Satire Reconsidered: From Antiquity to the Eighteenth Century*. Baltimore: Johns Hopkins University Press.

CHAPTER 8

AUTOBIOGRAPHY AND BIOGRAPHY

STEPHEN MULHALL

It seems clear that, of the two literary genres of the life story, autobiography has been more central to the interests and the development of philosophy than biography. It might even be argued that one could write an instructive (even if not exactly exhaustive) history of Western philosophy by concentrating solely on examples of philosophical autobiography; at the very least, such texts as Augustine's *Confessions*, Descartes's *Meditations*, Rousseau's *Confessions*, and Nietzsche's *Ecce Homo* would be pivotal to any attempt to narrate the story of the life of the mind in the West. So the question arises: why should this be the case? Why should such a highly specific mode of writing play such a deeply influential role in philosophy's unfolding and contested conception of itself? And if philosophy can find clarity about itself through a philosopher's attempts to attain clarity about himself, is that in part because any individual's pursuit of self-understanding will find itself drifting or drawn toward philosophical modes of reflection? If philosophical autobiographies are as central to the history and development of their genre as the illustriousness of my examples suggests, perhaps that is because the impulse to take up certain specifically philosophical problems lies at the heart of autobiographical (and hence, biographical) writing as such.

That some degree of philosophical concern for the autobiographical impulse might be appropriate is not in itself controversial. After all, it is one of philosophy's defining characteristics that it seems capable of taking an interest in, even presuming to adjudicate upon, pretty much any and every aspect of human life. We have the philosophy of art and morality, of science and of history, of politics and economics; we philosophize about the mind, the body, language, and logic, about what there is and how we might come to know about it. So it is no surprise that philosophers should take the human business of autobiography to be just as much capable of generating philosophical questions as any other piece of human business, and hence as capable of supporting what one might call "the philosophy of autobiography"—within which one might expect to find a critical investigation of the assumptions and concepts presupposed by any particular autobiographical exercise. But why should these assumptions and concepts—as opposed to those deployed by historian and scientists, or those informing our concerns with aesthetic and moral values—be of any particular, even of an obsessional, interest to philosophers? And why should philosophy repeatedly feel the need to express and to revolutionize itself through essentially autobiographical modes of writing?

An answer to this question might emerge if we reflect upon the peculiar kind of authority that philosophy assigns to its pronouncements. Historians, philologists, and molecular biologists are looked to as authorities concerning their respective subject matters because they have acquired a certain kind of expertise; they know a lot of things about the Second World War, or the vicissitudes of the Romance languages, or the behavior of DNA that most of us do not know, and they have mastered a range of investigative techniques or methods that can, in principle, generate an endless further supply of such knowledge.

Philosophy isn't like that—it has no distinctive subject matter; its peculiar kinds of questions are essentially parasitic upon the existence of other disciplines and domains of human life: they can arise with respect to any of those phenomena, and there is no body of distinctively philosophical knowledge or technique or method that must be mastered by anyone who wishes to try to answer those questions (or at least nothing that is not itself essentially subject to philosophical contestation and questioning). And yet, philosophers continue to claim sweeping authority for their pronouncements; they variously think of the results of their thinking as giving us access to the a priori, as speaking with necessity and universality, as deliverances of pure reason. How is this to be understood?

If we imagine the philosopher, at once gripped by her sense that her insights truly penetrate to a realm of impersonal necessity and yet unable to deny that those insights are unsupported by any impersonally authoritative expertise, I think that we will naturally conjure up a picture of an exposed self, one whose claims to the agreement of others necessarily place her individual existence on the line. In other words, we can picture philosophy as a kind of exemplary self-reliance, a mode of the self's relation to itself in which the individual self is deemed representative of selfhood as such. This does not give up on the philosophical claim to universality; it merely follows Aristotle in thinking that the universal can only be attained through and made manifest in the particular. Without some such picture of oneself as both particular and representative (even if representative only by virtue of one's particularity, which then at least exemplifies the human capacity for individuality—for differentiating oneself from every other human being), why would anyone write an autobiography? And one might then ask whether having such a picture of oneself is inherent to selfhood as such—a condition of being oriented as a subject in (and of) human life.

A picture of philosophical authority as essentially but impersonally autobiographical is detectable throughout the history of the subject, from Socrates onward. Even if we restrict ourselves to the modern period, we encounter Descartes's presentation of himself as subjecting himself to the threat of madness in a search for epistemological purity whose results he invites us to prove by enacting their production ourselves; we find Locke, Berkeley, and Hume acting on the conviction that one individual's discovery of something about his own mind (the absence or presence of an idea) is authoritative for all; and in more recent times, we find Austin and Wittgenstein speaking of what we say when, and thereby establishing how things are in the world, on the basis of their own individual sense of the fitness of words to their contexts of application. Each such inflection of the autobiographical impulse in philosophy obviously invites the charge of arrogance. Its inherent humility may be less obvious, but it is no less real, for, given that the representativeness claimed for the philosopher's individuality is such that any individual can also claim it, it can always be contested or denied. Hence, such self-reliance actually constitutes an important counterexample to the often rather less humble and self-aware modes in which philosophers have claimed authority over others.

If philosophy's peculiar combination of arrogance and humility can in this way be grounded in the self's relation to itself, then philosophy has a particular reason to preoccupy itself with the assumptions and resources of autobiographical writing—that of attempting to achieve not only a clearer understanding of the self, but also thereby a clearer self-understanding. It then becomes a matter of doubled or reflexive significance for philosophy to ask what it betokens about the self that it is capable of an autobiographical relation to itself. And since the idea of a biography is one factor in the meaning of the idea of the autobiographical, we might quickly conclude that this question is not one that we can properly address without also addressing the question of what it betokens about the self that other selves are capable of establishing a biographical relation to it.

Some philosophical accounts of this matter might be read as viewing any idea of the autobiographical as dependent on the biographical as arrived at rather too quickly. Does not Descartes's stance in the *Meditations* discover that, while the real existence of other minds is dubitable, the doubting self cannot doubt the reality of its own existence? And does this not suggest that an autobiographical relation to the self is possible in the absence of the possibility of any biographical relation to that self? But what such an account overlooks is not just the fact that Descartes himself appears to overlook certain constitutive dependencies of the self upon others (in, for example, the meditating self's need to inherit its capacity to articulate its train of thought in words of a common language), but also the fact that Descartes's textual enactment of his capacity to account for himself is addressed to others. And if others can grasp his own account of the life of his mind, what is to prevent them from offering an account of that life themselves (even one that contests his own)?

Could one imagine a situation in which others are in a position to offer an account of the life of an individual when that individual herself lacks any possibility of so doing? The issue here is not best exemplified in cases where someone who once had the capacity to offer an account of her own life comes to lose it (through accident or injury, say); the issue is rather whether, with respect to a creature who is essentially incapable of relating to itself as the possible object of an autobiography, others could regard that creature as the possible object of a biography. In other words, is it internal to our conception of what it is for someone to have or to live a life of which there might be a biography that she be capable of taking an autobiographical stance toward herself? Is our concept of the self such that its distinctive mode of existence must be writable, articulable in thought or speech, from both the first-person and the third-person perspectives?

A familiar line of thought, commonly based nowadays on more or less egregious misreadings of structuralist and poststructuralist philosophers, but also given expression by certain modernist writers, would reject this idea from the outset. To tell a story about oneself is, according to this suggestion, necessarily to falsify oneself; it is to impose a form and structure upon that which, like any aspect of the real, essentially transcends such constraints. Any application of language to reality—being an attempt to confine the particularity of the particular within necessarily general terms, and hence within the identity system of the concept—is a misapplication; hence, any application of words to the human self necessarily misses its target, even when it is the self itself that applies them to itself, even when it simply tries to name itself. As Samuel Beckett's narrator in *The Unnamable* puts it: "I, say I. Unbelieving... I seem to speak, it is not I, about me, it is not about me" (1979: 267).

A. S. Byatt's novel *The Biographer's Tale* (2000) pivots around these kinds of anxiety. Its protagonist, Phineas Nanson, is driven to take a biographical interest in the biographical work of one Scholes Destry-Scholes as a reaction to the ways in which literary theory (in his view) reduces individual texts to mere instances of general structures: "I must have *things*," he wails. "Facts" his supervisor proclaims: "The richness, the surprise, the shining *solidity* of a world full of facts. Every established fact—taking its place in a constellation of glittering facts like planets in an empty heaven, declaring *here* is matter, and *there* is vacancy—every established fact illuminates the world" (4). But even Destry-Scholes is discovered to have recoiled from or, rather, to have reoriented his biographical work in the direction of fictive accounts of the lives of Carl Linnaeus, Francis Galton, and Henrik Ibsen—a taxonomist, a statistician, and a playwright who famously invokes the image of the self as a centerless onion: three debunkers of the inspiring conception of genuinely individual elements of reality, and hence of human individuality. And even here, in these fragmentary, hybrid literary exercises, Destry-Scholes's own self remains absent, withdrawing from the biographer's grasp.

Peter Conradi, invoking a passage from one of Iris Murdoch's novels that expresses an analogous suspicion, draws a moral from it for his own biographical work on Murdoch: "In *Under the Net*, Hugo teaches Jake that 'all stories are lies' because truth is *local and particular*. This was the truth I sought. The biographer must *construct* a story. I decided to tell a *succession* of short stories that might be mutually contradictory, but were each internally coherent, and (I felt) individually truthful" (2002: 6).

But of course, if all stories are lies, then even a succession of internally coherent but mutually contradictory short stories could not (even in principle) be individually truthful. If Hugo is right, then the biographer and the autobiographer alike simply cannot achieve truth, and so cannot coherently seek it; but then we might ask whether Hugo's sense of the inherent particularity of truth really justifies the conclusion that its articulation in language, and particularly in the language of story, must fail. Perhaps truth is not lost the moment a story is constructed for its inhabitation; perhaps its fate rather depends (as Conradi's avowed moral and his biographical practice both suggest) on how one constructs the story—with what degree of particularity. The question of how a constructed story of an actual life may be truthful, even true, could not then simply be shirked.

Pursuing such an alternative line of thought, the philosopher Alasdair MacIntyre has argued in *After Virtue* (1981: 191–6) that the possibility of giving a narrative account of the self is internal to what it is for the self to be a self. He claims that selves are agents and that human actions are necessarily such that they are comprehensible in narrative terms. Actions are not just pieces of behavior, exhaustively describable in terms of physical movements; they are intentional, and hence can be comprehended only by relating them to the intentions, beliefs, and goals of the person performing them, and those intentions can be understood only in terms of the settings or contexts in which they are embedded. I am currently writing an essay; I might also be said to be supporting a university press, furthering my career, following a line of thought from earlier writing and teaching, repaying a debt to one of my colleagues, avoiding domestic commitments, and so on. It is therefore pertinent to ask what I am doing—in other words, to expect me to be able to specify under which of these various descriptions I primarily take myself to be doing what I am doing; and the answer I give will locate my action in a specific setting, which will in turn form part of a larger setting or context. If I am primarily supporting a university press, I am relating my action to the history of a particular publishing institution, and thereby to the particular history of academic philosophical discourse; if I am avoiding domestic commitment, the relevant larger setting is the history not only of the institution of marriage but also of my marriage and its entwinement in my own life as well as that of others. And, of course, I might think of myself as doing both. But however I answer this question, I must do so by implicitly or explicitly embedding my action in a narrative history. I thereby render it comprehensible—that is, recountable as an episode in a set of nested stories—not only to myself but also to others, and in the absence of such embedding, there is nothing that might count as an action to be understood either by myself or others, and so nothing of agency in what I do, only matter in motion. As MacIntyre summarizes the matter:

> I am presenting…human actions in general as enacted narratives. Narrative is not the work of poets, dramatists and novelists reflecting upon events which had

no narrative order before one was imposed by the singer or the writer; narrative form is neither disguise nor decoration....It is because we all live out narratives in our lives and because we understand our own lives in terms of the narratives that we live out that the form of narrative is appropriate for understanding the actions of others. Stories are lived before they are told—except in the case of fiction. (1981: 197)

On this understanding of agency, the identity or unity of a self is the unity of a narrative, a unity of exactly the kind to which autobiographical and biographical stories typically give expression, and since the form such stories give to human lives corresponds to the form that such lives actually have, it must in principle be possible for such stories to capture the truth of a human life (even if practical difficulties of all kinds might prevent its attainment in any given case).

Such an understanding can allow for the possibility that calling a given event or action a beginning or an end confers significance of a kind upon it, and hence can be a matter of debate, since it claims only that the nature of the debate takes for granted the constraints of a narrative tale. It can also acknowledge that individuals are not entirely free to live out whatever story they please—that they are only coauthors of the narrative in which they are their own heroes, insofar as we enter upon a stage that is not of our own design, into ongoing, interlocking narratives that are not of our own making, playing subordinate parts in the dramas of others as well as the central part in our own. It can even allow for the possibility of the most thoroughgoing rejection of the terms in which one's inherited settings inform the narrative options one confronts in living out one's life, for such rejection is simply one extreme way in which one lives out the drama of one's own existence in relation to the other dramatic narratives within which it is embedded. Most centrally, however, it rebuts the charge that to give a narrative account of a human life is necessarily to falsify it—to impose on it an order or form (a structure of beginnings, unfoldings, reversals, achievements, triumphs, disasters, and endings) appropriate to fiction but essentially lacking in reality.

Something like the contrary is in fact the case. Autobiography and biography are motivated by the requirements of truthfulness toward a conception of human life as possessed of narrative form and structure, and this is not because such forms happen to coincide with the way human existence is objectively structured, but rather because the distinctively human form of individual existence is constituted by the exercise of our capacity to tell our own stories. The specific modes of that narrativity may be historically and culturally specific, just as certain forms of self-interpretation (say, those of the Homeric king or warrior) may recede beyond our social grasp only to be replaced by others (say, those of president or spy), but that there are modes or genres of narrative self-interpretation is constitutive of distinctively human life.

MacIntyre's basically Aristotelian approach thus rightly brings the techniques of certain kinds of fiction and those of biography and autobiography into close proximity. It is not clear, however, how well he handles his consequent obligation to show how the two genres might be distinguished (given that they are not to be distinguished by reference to the narrative forms they assume or impose). As we have just seen, he claims that, whereas with respect to real people, stories are lived before they are told, with respect to fictional people it is otherwise; presumably, he does not mean by this that fictional lives are told before they are lived, but rather that they are not lived before they are told—even, perhaps, that the living of them and the telling of them are in some sense one and the same thing. And later, he remarks, "The difference between imaginary characters and real ones is not in the narrative form of what they do; it is in the degree of their authorship of that form and of their own deeds" (1981: 200). Both remarks, however, overlook the distinction between author and character in fictional narratives.

David Copperfield and Sherlock Holmes have exactly the same degree of authorial control over their own actions, exactly the same need to accept the constraints of the settings of their actions and exactly the same responsibility for what they do within those constraints, as did Charles Dickens and Sir Arthur Conan Doyle or, indeed, any real human beings; if they did not, their authors would not have produced a satisfying fictional depiction of human individuals. In particular, David Copperfield certainly lived those events of his life that he is recounting before the event in his life that is his recounting of them: he is remembering his childhood and youth. To be sure, Dickens and Doyle invented Copperfield and Holmes, and hence might be said to be in this sense entirely in control of their creations (although fiction writers are prone to articulate their experience of their characters in precisely opposite terms—as beings who reveal their nature and destiny to their authors, and as alive only insofar as their authors suffer this revelation of their autonomy), but Dickens and Doyle are not characters or forces of any kind in the world in which Copperfield and Holmes live out their lives, the world of the novels in which they are characters.

What this reveals is, I think, an essential confusion in the attempt to illuminate the nature of the real human self's relation to itself by this kind of reference to an author's relation to the characters in a story he has written. For if we say that a human being's relation to itself is that of (part) author of a tale in which she is the hero, then she must be regarded both as a character in the story told by the author and as the author of that story, but these two kinds of relation to the fictional character are not only radically different, but also not obviously combinable. An author of a fictional narrative is (at least according to the model we are considering) at liberty to choose whom to write about, the nature of the world she inhabits, and the events that will make up her life, but as MacIntyre acknowledges, human individuals have no such absolute freedom in relation to the narratives of their own lives. A character in a fictional narrative of the realistic kind (that is, a fictional narrative of the real world) relates to the settings and circumstances in which she finds herself, and to herself, in exactly the way a real human being does; hence her position reiterates that of the real person, rather than contrasting illuminatingly with it.

None of this definitively undermines MacIntyre's core claim that real human lives necessarily have a narrative structure; indeed, insofar as this line of thought depends upon seeing a correspondence between the narrative unity of fictional and real characters as essential to the former's ability to elicit our suspensions of disbelief, it actually reinforces it. What he needs to get more accurately into focus is not any spurious set of differences between a fictional character's relations to her existence and that of a real person, but rather a real and important set of differences between a real person's relationship to another person, and her relationship to a fictional character, for the techniques of realistic fiction can give its readers modes of access to the inmost thoughts and feelings, the most subtle and fine-grained details, of a fictional character's consciousness that are simply unavailable when one is trying to grasp the significance of a real person's thoughts, sayings, and doings. My point here is not that another's most complex thoughts and feelings are beyond expression by that other; if an author can articulate them in a fictional case, there is no reason in principle why a real person cannot convey such things. The point is rather that, with respect to another real person, the sincerity of her self-expressions may be open to question at any given point, whereas when certain fictional techniques are used to convey to us a fictional character's stream of consciousness, we cannot coherently question whether what is thereby conveyed is true.

This point needs careful handling, of course. My claim is not that everything we learn in a work of fiction about a character's inner life—even when it is the character that informs us of it—is trustworthy. The murderer who narrates Agatha Christie's *The Mystery of Roger Ackroyd* does not tell us everything he could, and he certainly does not tell us everything he is thinking, but he never lies, and if he did, his narrative would be unreadable; a completely unreliable narrator—as opposed to one who gives himself away—would not be a narrator at all. Furthermore, the shadow of unreliability in a fictional character's autobiographical narrations is not exactly equivalent to that which hangs over real journals and memoirs. Any biographer must certainly be sensitive to the possible inaccuracies, deceptions, and self-deceptions embedded in her subject's autobiographical writings, but these are controlled or constrained for the reader of a fictional autobiography in ways that the real biographer simply cannot take for granted. It would be essentially pointless, even incoherent, for an author to write a work of fiction taking the form of an autobiography that was largely fabricated by its fictional author, but whose status as a fabrication was undetectable to its readers, whereas a real person's autobiography might well be written with the perfectly intelligible intention of meeting both conditions, and could even succeed in doing so. And the deployment of other fictional techniques similarly excludes certain possibilities of fabrication or deception; for example, when Jane Austen reports Elizabeth Bennet's interior responses to Darcy's letter, there is simply no room for her readers intelligibly to raise the question of whether those responses are what they are reported to be (although they might exhibit certain species of self-deception).

These are the kinds of painstaking comparison and contrast that will truly clarify the differences between our relations to real people and our relations to fictional characters, and the different ways in which these differences emerge in biographical and autobiographical genres. MacIntyre simply does not attend with sufficient patience to these complexities, and as a result, his portrait of the essentially narrative unity of the self can appear to be not only inaccurate but also symptomatic—as if designed to repress something central to the issues with which he is concerned—for his doomed attempt to cross or graft a picture of absolute authorial freedom onto the more familiar, constrained kind encountered both in reality and in realistic fiction strongly suggests that he is tempted to overlook or repress some limit or condition inherent in the way in which human individuals relate to their own existence (and to occlude thereby some limit or condition inherent in attempts by others to narrate that existence from without—to write a biography of the kind of existence that necessarily possesses that kind of relation to itself).

Some suggestions as to what this limit might be can be gleaned from Heidegger's conception of the nature of distinctively human being—what in *Being and Time* (1927) he calls Dasein. On the one hand, Heidegger presents a portrait of human existence that appears to confirm many aspects of MacIntyre's account. For him, Dasein treats its own being as an issue—that is, every moment of its existence confronts it with the question of how to go on with its life, of which among a given range of possibilities it should realize; it thereby projects itself into the future, and does so from a present position that is the result of past such projections, and thereby partly constituted by individual and social factors that either never were or, at the very least, are no longer within its control—a position into which it has been thrown.

This vision of human existence as thrown projection suggests not only that Dasein's mode of being is temporal (more specifically historical), but also that its every element is comprehensible only as a situated transition—a movement within a nest of interlinked narratable structures, an episode in the story of a life. Heidegger reinforces this image by recounting Dasein's temporality in terms of fate and destiny; an individual relates authentically to its life—relates to it as its own, as expressive of its individuality, rather than disowning it—when it recovers from its past a heritage of certain possibilities that it can project into the future as fateful for it, thereby helping to realize (by coauthoring with other Dasein) the destiny of a people.

On the other hand, there are ways in which Heidegger's conception of human historicality can be read as subverting rather than simply reinforcing MacIntyre's emphasis on the necessarily narrative unity of the self. The troublesome term here is "unity," for while Heidegger's talk of Dasein as thrown projection can be understood as emphasizing that Dasein's existence has a necessarily temporal or historical dimension, and hence that its unity is a matter of being a whole articulated in time (as opposed, say, to a Cartesian conception of the self as having the essentially punctual unity of an immaterial substance existing outside time), one can also understand Dasein's temporality as constitutively resisting any idea of human existence as unified or whole.

Take, for example, the projective aspect of Dasein's being—what Heidegger calls its being-ahead-of-itself. This means that, for as long as Dasein exists, it necessarily relates itself to existential possibilities; whenever one is actualized, it is actualized as a situation within which (better, *as* which) Dasein relates to some other, unactualized range of possibilities. This means that Dasein always already relates itself to what is not yet; it stands out into the future, and so there is always something outstanding, something essentially incomplete, in its mode of being. And yet, of course, Dasein does have an end: there is necessarily a point at which every individual life comes to an end—the point of one's death. But, of course, when that point of completion is reached, Dasein is not thereby made complete, for it is no longer there. Dasein's death is not an event in its life, even the last; the point at which it can no longer be said to relate itself to what is not yet actual, and thus to be essentially incomplete, is also the point at which it no longer exists.

MacIntyre seems to think that human mortality straightforwardly confirms his conception of the narrative structure of the self, for when confronted with a critic who claims that life has no endings, and that final partings occur only in stories, he says: "[O]ne is tempted to reply "But have you never heard of death?" (1981: 197). But Heidegger's analysis makes it clear that the human subjection to death in fact introduces an obstacle to narrative understandings of human life, for if my death is necessarily not an event in my life, I cannot grasp it as an episode—even as the final episode—in the story of my life; I may be the hero, as well as the part author, of the story of my dying, but I am necessarily not the chief, or even the sole, protagonist in my death. Hence, Heidegger concludes, I cannot relate to my own death as simply one more possibility of my being, one more possible way of existing that is bound to be actualized sooner or later, for its actualization is my absence, and hence not a possibility of mine, although the life that is mine is marked at every moment by my relation to that impossible possibility. My mortality is not a matter of my life's necessarily having one and only one ending; it is a matter of every moment of my existence possibly being the last such moment, and of my being unable to grasp what that might mean—at least, in the sense in which I can grasp (can understand or imaginatively inhabit) the realization of any other existential possibility or narrative event in my life (such as getting married, or winning the Booker Prize, or mowing the lawn). I cannot grasp it from the inside, as it were (as something that will happen to me), and yet it (what?) looms over and constitutively defines the character of every moment of the life that I do inhabit from the inside, the life that is mine to own or to disown.

How is the self to capture this impossible but necessary knowledge of itself, to articulate autobiographically the way in which its relation to itself in every moment of its existence is marked by its relationship to its own mortality? On Heidegger's view, it is only through an acknowledgment of this relationship that any human being can establish and maintain what he calls an authentic relationship to her life. Grasping the fact that death threatens my existence as a whole, that it cannot be outrun and that no one else can die my death for me, is what will allow me to grasp that my life forms a whole (each choice forming and formed by the overall narrative arc of my existence), that I am ultimately responsible for it, and that I can either take on that responsibility or live in flight from it. Without understanding whether, and if so how, a given person has succeeded or failed in living a genuinely individual life, how can we claim to have understood that person's life, and so that person? But on Heidegger's account, the person herself cannot properly be said to have access to a perspective upon herself from which her own mortality can make narrative sense to her, so in struggling for authenticity, she confronts a constitutive resistance to self-knowledge, a limit to the story of her life—better, to the idea of her life as a story—beyond which her own understanding of herself cannot reach, but it is only in relation to this disruption or dislocation of its narrative structure that her life can attain (and be seen to attain) its individual narrative shape.

And if the self's mortality threatens to subvert the possibility of autobiographical understanding, then how might another self articulate a biographical understanding of that individual? The biographer has the apparent advantage of being able to grasp her subject's death as an event in life—one greeted by mourning, funeral rites, the reading of the will and the unfolding of its legacies (financial, emotional, and cultural). But this is to grasp her subject's death as an event or episode in the lives of others, in the world that the subject no longer inhabits; it is not to grasp her death as hers—in its mineness, as Heidegger would say. Further narrative contexts and consequences come into view from this third-person perspective and provide ways of understanding unavailable to the subject that might expand or subvert certain aspects of her self-conception, but the pervasive opacity—the internal relation to nothingness—that the first person encounters as constitutive of its own mortal identity remains untouched, and to that degree so does the person.[1]

Similar damage is done to the idea of the self as a narrative unity—or rather, the same damaging difficulty appears from another angle—if one shifts emphasis from Heidegger's sense of the self as projective, as being-ahead-of-itself, to his sense of the self as thrown, or being-already (being-always-already). This aspect of his analysis of Dasein's being is in fact made rather more prominent in Sartre's rereading of *Being and Time* in conjunction with his rereading of Descartes, as presented in *Being and Nothingness*. Sartre's starting point is to contest the Cartesian declaration of Alain (Émile Chartrier) that to know is to know that one knows. This is one aspect of Descartes's conception of the self as essentially transparent to itself; the Cartesian mind cannot be in a particular state—for example, that of doubting—without simultaneously knowing that it is in such a state, and hence knowing that it is (i.e., that it exists as doubting). To be thinking and to be aware of oneself as thinking are two aspects of one and the same state of the self; hence, each such state provides the basis for a cogito argument—for the self's certainty of itself, in every punctual moment of its existence, as existing and as existing in a particular state, and ultimately for the self's knowledge of itself as a self-identical immaterial thinking substance.

But Sartre argues that Descartes conflates the self's necessary potential for self-awareness with its actualization, and does so because he occludes the temporality of the self. Sartre stresses that all mental states are intentional—they are directed at something other than themselves: to desire is to desire something in particular, to perceive is to perceive something, and so on. Typically, the self is absorbed in the object of its given state of consciousness; for example, when someone in wartime (subjected to strict rationing) counts the number of cigarettes in his case, he is entirely absorbed in the question of the case and its contents, and entirely unaware of being so absorbed. He can, however, become aware of his absorption; if someone sits down at his café table and asks what he is doing, he can activate the capacity inherent in any genuine self to take any of its own conscious states as the object of its conscious awareness. But in so doing, he actualizes a new state of himself—one whose intentional object is no longer the cigarettes but rather his state of absorption in the cigarettes—and in actualizing that self-conscious state, he is necessarily no longer occupying that state of unself-conscious absorption. To take oneself as one's intentional object is to take up another state of oneself and to relegate the state that is now one's intentional object to one's past. And if one now takes one's self-consciousness of that prior absorbed state as one's new intentional object, one will necessarily no longer exist in that self-conscious state, but in a new state (whose intentional object is one's previous awareness of oneself as having been absorbed in the cigarettes).

In short, one can be conscious of oneself only as one was, not as one is; the self's necessary capacity to direct its attention to itself as well as to that which lies beyond it is realized, and is only realizable, in time, and hence is essentially incapable of bringing the whole of itself (including its present state) into self-consciousness. In effect, then, the phenomenon of self-consciousness does not (as Descartes believed) show that the self is essentially transparent to itself and identical with itself; it rather condemns the self to non-self-identity, to a necessary inability to coincide with itself, to gather itself up as a whole in its own awareness. Heidegger talks of this as an aspect of the self's being-guilty—its inability to have power over its own being from the ground up. Sartre sees it as exemplifying the for-itself's nature as being what it is not, and not being what it is.

Once again, to a certain extent, this conception of the self is congenial to a MacIntyrean analysis of selfhood as a narrative unity—despite MacIntyre's explicit conviction (evident throughout *After Virtue*) that the Sartrean self is the absolute antithesis of his Aristotelian conception. After all, Sartre's conception of self-consciousness precisely allows the self to take up a perspective upon not just its immediate past states, but also its past as a whole, without which the idea of it understanding itself as the hero of an unfolding narrative would not be possible. And further, on Sartre's view, if the self really did coincide with itself, if what it previously was entirely exhausted or determined what it is, then the self would lack freedom; it would lack the ability to be part author of its own narrative as it extends into the future.

Nevertheless, MacIntyre is right to detect a fundamental conflict between his position and that of Heidegger and Sartre, for part of their point is that the self necessarily transcends any narrative it might be in a position to tell about itself, since any such narrative will always fail to include the moment of its own narrating, and the inclusion of that moment will necessarily fail to include the moment in or through which it is included, and so endlessly on. The narrative of *David Copperfield* does not include David's act of writing that narrative as an episode within it, and if it did, what of his act of writing about that act of writing? This may be what the film director John Boorman is trying to get at when he remarks at the conclusion of his recent autobiography that "I suppose the only completely satisfactory ending to an autobiography would be a suicide note" (2003: 301). In fact, however, such a note could not be completely satisfying, since it would remain promissory; to write a suicide note and to commit suicide are two rather different things. William Golding's novel *The Paper Men* (1984), in which an English novelist tells the story of his resistance to an American academic's attempts to write his biography, may actually get closer to Boorman's ideal, although it too fails to attain it, for it ends not so much in midword but in midphoneme, as the scribbling novelist notices that his would-be biographer, frustrated and enraged to the point of violence, is lurking in the woods outside his home: "How the devil did Rick L. Tucker manage to get hold of a gu" (191).

Herbert McCabe makes it clear, in his book *The Good Life* (2005), that this is not simply a point about the complications of being immersed in time; it is another way of approaching my earlier point about the difference between authors of narratives and the characters or personas in them, this time in an explicitly autobiographical context:

> These problems have to do with the fact that "I" cannot function as a proper name. "I tell you" is not part of a story in which "I" is a character; it *is* the telling of a story. It is a sign of authority, of authorship as such (it is, as Aquinas would say, formal not material to the story). My life-story is not the story of "I" but the story of Herbert McCabe, who has become a persona, a persona distinct from I, the author. As Herbert McCabe in the story I have been made flesh and dwell among the other characters. How, then, do we get beyond any story to meet the ultimate author, the ultimate authority? (75)

Certainly not by telling any further story about the author, since that merely presents us with another author-as-character, beyond which again lies the author-as-author, the formal condition for there being a story at all.

Consequently, even autobiography does not and cannot take us to the author it is ostensibly about in the way that an ordinary story takes us to the character in the story; even if the autobiographer's last chapter concerns his writing of this very autobiography, it cannot bridge the unbridgeable gap between author-as-author and author-as-character. But this does not mean that we cannot meet the author; it means that we meet him not in reading about him *qua* character, but just in the form and the fact of the story itself, in the tale and the telling of it—in short, in its authority (the authority it claims, and the authority we cede it).

McCabe illustrates this point by reference to the Bible, understood as the autobiography of God. On the one hand, no one has ever seen or grasped God, and no one ever could; put otherwise, there can be no life story of the eternal God as such, since "eternal life" means "nonnarrative life," which is a contradiction in terms. On the other hand, we are told that the Word has become flesh: God has become incarnate in a narrative, in the character of the Son, over against those of the Father and the Spirit. The Bible (the whole of the Bible, from Genesis to Apocalypse) is the story of the Son; the historical life of Jesus is the Trinitarian life of God played out as history. Hence, encountering God and participating in divine life are possible, but not by directly encountering the author of this narrative as author; it rather involves understanding the narrative as God's story—that is, regarding the historical narrative of the Son as authorized and so authored by God, reading it as in form and fact the authoritative image of the unseen and unseeable Author of all things. It means, in other words, belonging to the community of readers (the Christian community) who acknowledge the Bible as God's Word.

Heidegger and Sartre might baulk at the theological inflection of this example, but they would not reject the fundamental point it registers about the ineliminable difference between formal and material conditions of autobiographical authorship. In their less Thomist terms, it might be thought of as the way in which one's understanding of one's life from the inside involves a sense that one always necessarily comes to understand it belatedly; the self's life is lived before it is understood, and hence, even if it is then understood in narrative terms, the self must also acknowledge that the reach of its story about itself encounters a constitutive limit—a point from which its story as a whole, and each episode within it, must simply be accepted as having begun, beyond any complete recounting (even one that invokes the ongoing, conditioning narratives of other selves or institutional contexts).

In one sense, MacIntyre actually makes this Sartrean point when he explicitly claims that human lives are lived before they are told. But he does not seem to see that this very point determines an internal limit to the cogency of his claim that lives are enacted narratives, or at least to the thought that this fact about them confers a certain kind of unity on those lives. For Sartre and for Heidegger, to exist in time is not only a condition for the possibility of there being a narratable self, an individual possessed of a life of which she can render an intelligible account; it is also an ineliminable obstacle to the completeness or totality of that account.

If the self's autobiography will necessarily fail to include the whole story about that self in this sense, could any biographer of the self do a better job? To be sure, they would not be caught up in their subject's structural inability to catch up with herself; indeed, after the death of the subject, every episode in her life will be available for investigation, as will the nest of other narratives (of other selves, of institutions and cultures) that interlocked with the subject's life, and thereby—so one might think—a far more encompassing conception of her life as a narrative whole. But that way of telling the story of the subject's life avails itself of a perspective essentially unavailable to the subject, and entirely occludes the perspective on that life which the subject of it necessarily occupies, so such a biography would to that extent be false to her subject's relation to her life, and hence false to an essential aspect of her subject's life. One might say that presenting her life as such a narrative whole does not, and could not, tell the whole story of that life.

Suppose one accepts that offering more and more information of the kind available to the biographer (and typically, even necessarily, unavailable to the biographical subject)—contextualizing the life ever more intensively and extensively, in the manner of so many contemporary biographies—can never fill a gap engendered by the constitutive difference between the first- and third-person perspectives on a life. It would not improve matters to imagine that one should instead attempt ever more systematically and penetratingly to adopt the first-person perspective upon that life—to dedicate one's account to the task of imaginatively inhabiting the subject's relation to her own life, for this would be to assume that the subject possesses an understanding of these aspects of her relation to her own life that others lack, whereas the true point of Heidegger's and Sartre's exertions is to show that the first-person perspective encounters a constitutive opacity here just as much as does that of the third person. Neither, however, would it be appropriate to conclude from all this that the very idea of giving a narrative account of the self, or even the idea that the self has a narrative unity, must be given up. The true moral of these analyses is rather that we must reject a certain idea of what it is to conceive of the self as having a narrative unity, and hence of what it might be to articulate that unity in discourse, whether in autobiographical or biographical form. In McCabe's terms, we need to reconceive the way in which we think such narratives acquire and manifest authority; for Heidegger and Sartre, it is a matter of how they, and so we, achieve authenticity.

This is not essentially a matter of authenticating the deliverances of one's memory or the provenance of a document, or of claiming the authority that might flow either from being the central character in a certain sequence of events or from synthesizing the accounts of all involved in it—the familiar (and hardly unimportant) ways of acknowledging any individual's privileged and yet contestable capacity to determine the narrative of her life, and so the most obvious means of securing autobiographical and biographical trustworthiness. What these philosophers are rather trying to argue is that any truly authentic or authoritative exercise in these genres will reflect a conception of the self as simultaneously demanding and resisting subsumption in a unified narrative.

Heidegger's conception of Dasein's relation to its own end and its own beginning as embodying an enigmatic resistance to comprehension precisely assumes (rather than denying) that Dasein's existence must be understood in terms of its relation to beginnings and endings, and hence as having narratable (i. e., that distinctively human mode of temporal and historical) structure. What he wants to avoid is any conception of that narrative structure as inappropriately transparent, self-sufficient, and total—as if the kind of identity across time possessed by human selves could be modeled on that possessed by physical objects or substances, with a capacity for self-understanding in narrative terms simply added on. To exist as self-conscious beings in time is indeed to be committed to understanding ourselves in narrative terms, but it is also to be committed to understanding that our existence simultaneously resists being understood in such terms. The very terms that allow us to make sense of ourselves—terms like beginnings and endings—also disclose dimensions of ourselves as beyond or before such ways of making sense, and it is in this disclosure of their own limits that they disclose a fundamental aspect of our own existence as limited or conditioned, as natal and mortal—in other words, as finite.

A conception of the interrelated genres of biography and of autobiography that acknowledged human finitude in such a way would therefore be one that acknowledged that the individual human life that it was concerned to elucidate was necessarily not such as to be wholly elucidatable, or elucidatable as a whole. It would find ways of bringing its readers up against the enigma residing in any human life, taken in all its individuality. Wittgenstein once remarked: "We say of some people that they are transparent to us. It is, however, important as regards this observation that one human being can be a complete enigma to another.... We cannot find our feet with them" (1997: II, xi, 223e). Heidegger aims to convince us that no human being can be completely transparent, either to others or to itself; his analysis of Dasein begins from the perception that there lies a priori an enigma in the human mode of being, and hence he insists that we can never—whether in philosophy, biography, or autobiography—entirely find our feet with one another, or with ourselves.

Suppose we think of Heidegger and Sartre as concerned to register the enigma of human individuality. Then their concern addresses itself to the heart of what many would regard as the primary motivation for our interest in both autobiography and biography—what Dinah Birch (2003) has described as a "simultaneous hunger for the singularity of a life that has separated itself from the crowd, and an eagerness to identify the values that make that life recognizably human." After all, if individuation is our name for the process whereby one human being distinguishes herself from others, then the capacity for individuation is what connects her to all other human beings. It is to this capacity, and the obligations and opportunities it imposes, that Carlyle may be referring when he claims, "Every mortal has a Problem of Existence set before him...to a certain extent original, unlike every other; and yet, at the same time, so *like* every other; like our own, therefore; instructive, moreover, since we also are indentured to *live*" (cited in Birch 2003).

The Sartrean perspective is also particularly helpful in bringing to prominence another aspect of the interwoven genres of autobiography and biography with which philosophy can and should be interested, and with which I propose to conclude—the degree to which the writer's relation to her subject is not only epistemological (concerning how one might come to know, or fail to know, the other) and metaphysical (concerning the nature of the kind of being to be known), but ethical. Sartre is notorious for arguing in *Being and Nothingness* that being-for-others—relating oneself, understood as a for-itself, to other creatures in one's world possessed of the same kind of being—enacts a power struggle: a struggle for power over another, against another's power over oneself, and against one's desire to have power over others and oneself. Imagining himself seated in a public park, he further imagines seeing another human being pass by. What is it to see him as another man?

> The Other is first the permanent flight of things towards a goal which I apprehend as an object at a certain distance from me but which escapes me inasmuch as it unfolds about itself its own distances.... [T]here is a regrouping in which I take part but which escapes me, a regrouping of all the objects which people my universe....This green grass turns towards the Other a face which escapes me. I apprehend the relation of the green to the Other as an objective relation, but I can not apprehend the green as it appears to the Other. Thus suddenly an object has appeared which has stolen the world from me....The appearance of the other in the world corresponds therefore to a fixed sliding of the whole universe, to a decentralization of the world which undermines the centralization which I am simultaneously effecting.... [T]he world has a kind of drainhole in the middle of its being and it is perpetually flowing off through this hole. (1958: 256)

For Sartre, then, part of the problem of existence set for all individuals is to find a way of acknowledging the otherness of other individuals. He sees us as prone to adopt a variety of strategies to ensure that we deny that otherness, since its acknowledgment entails denying that we are at the center of the universe, which we equate with a denial of our own individual reality in the world. And, of course, our otherness sets the same ethical problem for others. But since biographical writing is one form of the way in which we encounter others in their individuality, it must confront versions of exactly the same ethical problem, and display versions of the same ways of failing to solve or resolve or dissolve it—as two ideas of self-denial cross. Feeling able to ventriloquize one's subject's thoughts at vital moments of her life, feeling compelled to accumulate heaping piles of factual information about the subject's life and circumstance without discrimination, feeling entirely unable to make, or entirely unable to stop making, judgments about the other's actions and thoughts—these would all appear through Sartrean eyes to be not so much technical or generic errors as signs of metaphysical and ethical difficulties—forms of the general failure to find a way of accommodating the individuality of others without seeming to sacrifice one's own.

It is a matter of some controversy whether Sartre allows for the possibility of ever overcoming these spiritual challenges, or whether he defines the human condition as one of suffering the inevitable failure of such acknowledgment. As Ray Monk (2001) has emphasized, Sartre's own biographical practice—understood as driven by, even perhaps driven by the need to validate, his theory of the self—plainly counts as a failure in these terms; in contrast, Raimond Gaita's (1988) biography of his father (a biography that is also, necessarily, an autobiography) exemplifies one way in which these spiritual challenges can be met, with real philosophical profit.

The same difficulties emerge in the course of a fictional attempt to address these problems, and thereby to contribute to what one might call the ethics of biography (which once again appears impossible to separate from an ethics of autobiography). It comes from Byatt's *The Biographer's Tale*, when Phineas Nanson is reflecting on his biographical pursuit of the biographer's biographer, Scholes Destry-Scholes:

I think I was so taken by Destry-Scholes' biography of Elmer Bole precisely because the over-determinism of Literary Theory, the meta-language of it, threw into brilliant relief Destry-Scholes' real achievement in describing a whole individual, a multi-faceted single man, one life from birth to death. I appeared to have failed to find Destry-Scholes himself. I have to respect him for his scrupulous *absence* from my tale, my work. It will be clear that I too have wished to be *absent*. I have resisted and evaded the idea that because of Destry-Scholes' *absence* my narrative must become an account of my own presence, *id est*, an autobiography, that most evasive and self-indulgent of forms. I have tried both to use my own history, unselfconsciously, as a temporal thread to string my story (my writing) on, *and* to avoid unnecessary dwelling on my own feelings, or my own needs, or my own—oh dear—*character*. It will be clear to almost any attentive reader, I think, that as I have gone along in this writing....I have become more and more involved in the act of writing itself, more and more inclined to shift my attention from Destry-Scholes' absence to my own style, and thus, my own *presence*. I now wonder whether *all* writing has a tendency to flow like a river towards the writer's body and the writer's own experience? (214)

Can the flow of that river be reversed, without flowing into the abyss of the other's existence beyond the writer's grasp? Our exploration suggests that the key to these difficulties lies in acknowledging the distinctive way in which the human subject's presence takes the form of a certain kind of absence: to grasp the reality of self-hood, one must grasp that it is beyond the grasp of any narrative account that might be given of it, whether by itself or by another. But if autobiographical and biographical exercises can be genuinely authoritative or authentic only insofar as they make present the self's absence, and so enact a kind of self-abnegation (with the narrating self absenting itself from its account of the narrated self's beyondness to itself), then biography, autobiography, and fiction must be forms of spiritual exercise, and engaging in such exercises must be inherent to becoming, that is being, a person.

NOTE

1. Lee 2005 is sensitive to the exemplary particularity of the difficulties and temptations encountered by biographers when writing of the death of their subjects.

REFERENCES

Beckett, S. (1979). *Molloy; Malone Dies; The Unnamable*. London: Picador.
Birch, D. (2003). "Narratives of Fact." *Times Literary Supplement*, September 19, 7.
Boorman, J. (2003). *Adventures of a Suburban Boy*. London: Faber & Faber.

Byatt, A. S. (2000). *The Biographer's Tale*. London: Chatto and Windus.

Conradi, P. (2002). "Writing *Iris Murdoch: A Life*—Freud versus Multiplicity." *Iris Murdoch Newsletter* 16: 1–8.

Gaita, R. (1988). *Romulus, My Father*. Melbourne: Text Publishing.

Golding, W. (1984). *The Paper Men*. London: Faber.

Lee, H. (2005). "How to End It All." *In* Lee, *Body Parts: Essays on Life-Writing*. Chatto and Windus: London.

MacIntyre, A. (1981). *After Virtue*. London: Duckworth.

McCabe, H. (2005). *The Good Life*. London: Continuum.

Monk, R. (2001). "Philosophical Biography: The Very Idea." *In* J. Klagge (ed.), *Wittgenstein: Biography and Philosophy*. Cambridge: Cambridge University Press.

Sartre, J. (1958). *Being and Nothingness* (H. Barnes, trans). London: Routledge.

Wittgenstein, L. (1997). *Philosophical Investigations* (G. E. M. Anscombe, trans). Oxford: Blackwell.

CHAPTER 9

EXPERIMENTAL WRITING

R. M. BERRY

When I began *The Making of Americans* I knew I really did know that a complete description was a possible thing, and certainly a complete description is a possible thing. But as it is a possible thing one can stop continuing to describe this everything. That is where philosophy comes in, it begins when one stops continuing describing everything.

—Gertrude Stein, "The Gradual Making of
The Making of Americans"

EXPERIMENTATION AND THE LIMITS OF PHILOSOPHY

A philosophical criticism of literature aims to disclose not merely the historically diverse conditions under which literature has occurred, but those conditions we might call necessary or, following Wittgenstein, grammatical. That is, to inquire philosophically into experimental writing would mean to ask what is necessary to anything counting at present as an instance of this concept, to someone's calling a given practice or text "experimental." And this inquiry becomes more complicated if, instead of treating the term "experimental" as descriptive only, we take it to characterize writing that achieves, or seeks to achieve, the seriousness and value of art. Can criticism still be philosophical if it depends on judgments that can no longer, as with Kant, look to a common human sensibility for their stabilization and ground? Nothing would seem more obvious than that experimental writing today appeals to no broad public. After the Second World War, the proliferation of radically dissimilar, mutually contesting, and often short-lived versions of the avant-garde, along with the absence of any widespread agreement about the artistic achievements of these versions, makes a philosophical inquiry into their necessities appear quixotic.

It is some such worry that Theodor Adorno expresses when he begins his *Aesthetic Theory* (1970) with the remark, "It is self-evident that nothing concerning art is self-evident anymore, not its inner life, not its relation to the world, not even its right to exist" (1997: 1). For Adorno, the history of aesthetic experimentation has culminated in an impasse. Art's long struggle for its autonomy, for freedom from external constraints, was originally grounded on "the idea of humanity," which provided an alternative to tradition and state sponsorship. However, as Adorno's *Dialectic of Enlightenment* (1944) recounts, the increasing tendency of modern society to conflate reason, understood as essential to humanity, with mechanistic rationality undermined this alternative. It then became "the idea of humanity" from which artistic experimentation must free itself. This made the task of philosophical aesthetics much more complicated. "Hegel and Kant were the last who, to put it bluntly, were able to write major aesthetics without understanding anything about art. That was possible so long as art itself was oriented to encompassing norms that were not questioned in individual works" (Adorno 1997: 334). In other words, artistic experimentation posed no serious challenge to philosophical reflection as long as it limited itself to "test[ing] unknown or unsanctioned technical procedures" (23). Criticism could still look to established norms in assessing the results: "Fundamental to this idea of experimentation was the latently traditionalistic belief that it would automatically become clear whether the results were a match for what had already been established and could thus legitimate themselves." However, with modernism, artistic experimentation meant "something qualitatively different: that the artistic subject employs methods whose objective results cannot be foreseen" (1997: 24). That is, not just the techniques but the aims themselves became experimental. It then ceased to be clear whether anyone—artists, critics, philosophers, museum curators, publishers, the public—was in a position to determine success or failure.

Given such an anarchic predicament, how can we speak of necessity at all? For Adorno, there is a deep bond between the topic of artistic experimentation, especially in literature, and the possibility of doing philosophy. If, as Adorno claims, the modern tendency toward "aesthetic nominalism"—the belief that aesthetic concepts are extraneous and only individual art works are real—is not an accidental result of historical misunderstandings but "originates in a universal of art" (1997: 201), then experimental writing would seem to mark conceptualization's limit. To try to conceive its necessities, at least in any systematic way, might well mean to repress it, making the crisis of art a crisis for thinking, too. Adorno's famous way out of this impasse was "negative dialectics," a theoretical practice that replaces the logical relations of identity and subsumption with a dynamic reciprocity of concepts and their instances. For Adorno, the recognition "that objects do not go into their concepts without leaving a remainder" (2000a: 57), instead of invalidating philosophical reflection, reveals its ongoing necessity. Only in art's resistance to every preconception—that is, only in uncompromisingly radical experimentation—is art's universal structure disclosed. Aesthetic autonomy, art's demand for freedom from external constraint, simply represents the individual work's refusal to disappear into a prior understanding of it. Instead of a limit case of philosophical reflection, artistic experimentation thus became Adorno's paradigm: "The dialectical postulate that the particular is the universal has its model in art" (1997: 202).

ROMANTICISM AND THE PHILOSOPHICAL EXPERIMENT

How satisfactory one finds Adorno's solution is likely to depend less on the lucidity of his reasoning than on the accuracy and insightfulness of his descriptions of particulars, especially of particular works of art, but regardless of his theory's persuasiveness, Adorno's case against philosophical aesthetics represents a recurrent theme in the discourse about experimental writing. At least one impulse to radical innovation seems bound up with a problem within philosophy itself. Or, to put this more relevantly, the search for new forms of literary practice becomes a necessity only at that moment, both historical and theoretical, when philosophy senses its inability to know literature from any position outside it. According to Philippe Lacoue-Labarthe and Jean-Luc Nancy, this moment occurs in Kant's third *Critique*. In their study of early German Romanticism, *The Literary Absolute* (1978), they recount how Kant's Copernican revolution, his reconceiving of knowledge as the object's conformity to the subject, rests on a paradoxical interpretation of the human subject as simultaneously fundamental and insubstantial, a formal condition of all representation that remains itself unpresentable (1988: 30–31). This formalism secures science at the cost of philosophy: "The first and most fundamental result is that there is no *intuitus originarius*. Whether it was situated as *arche* or as *telos*, within the divine or within the human (as either pure intellectual consciousness in Descartes or pure empirical sensibility in Hume), what had heretofore ensured the philosophical itself disappears" (30). The idea is that, although Kant characterized reason's task in the first *Critique* as self-knowledge,[1] the one who thinks this self-knowledge seems strangely missing: "[A]ll that remains of the subject is the 'I' as an 'empty form'" (30). What seems wanting is some account of the knowing subject's integrity, its relation to itself. Or, as A. W. Schlegel complained in his *Theory of Art* (1798–1803), "[T]he basic defect of the Kantian system [is that it] does not, as true philosophy must, separate in order to connect again, but fixes the divisions of the understanding as insurmountable and posits original separation where there is, rather, unity" (1997: 201).

According to Lacoue-Labarthe and Nancy, this aporia of the subject inaugurates a "crisis" (1988: 29), one that becomes resolvable only with the aestheticizing of philosophy. In early German Romanticism the resolution proceeds along two paths, both of which are prefigured in the third *Critique*. The first, by way of reflection, develops from Kant's account of natural beauty. In his "Analytic of the Beautiful," Kant describes how, in an aesthetic judgment, the reflecting subject apprehends in a beautiful object a formal agreement with the laws of the understanding independent of that object's subsumption under a concept. That is, its form appears right but not as an instance of anything. Although reflection for Kant means comparing, not mirroring, his account already suggests that the subject's pleasure in natural beauty results from the apprehension of its own formal unity:

> If pleasure is connected with the mere apprehension (*apprehensio*) of the form of the object of intuition without a relation of this to a concept for a determinate cognition, then the representation is thereby related not to the object, but solely to the subject, and the pleasure can express nothing but its suitability to the cognitive faculties that are in play in the reflecting power of judgment. (2000: 75–76)

In the proto-Romantic manifesto, the "Earliest Program for a System of German Idealism" (1796), this account of reflection makes beauty a new *intuitus originarius*. As Lacoue-Labarthe and Nancy point out, the crucial step here is the replacement of Kant's subject as "empty form" with "the idea of the subject as self-consciousness" (1988: 33), an idea that makes self and world mutually entailing: "Together with the free, self-conscious being, an entire *world* emerges out of nothingness—the single true and thinkable *creation out of nothingness*" (Kant 1997: 72). The implication is not that self and world just *do* mirror each other, but more nearly that they should or must: "together" each "emerges." Their emergence as a system, what Lacoue-Labarthe and Nancy call "*the System-subject*" (1988: 34), appears in the "Earliest Program" as a struggle between science "weighed down by laborious experiments" and "a general (or greater) physics" which asks, "How must a world for a moral being be constituted?" The answer, at once spiritual and material, is to be found in the aesthetic: "[I]n beauty alone are truth and goodness joined together" (1997: 72). As reflection, beauty ceases to be a formal condition of either subject or object and becomes, in Lacoue-Labarthe and Nancy's phrase, "the subject's self-presentation of the true form of the world" (1988: 33).

According to the second path, that of production, the Romantics' resolution proceeds from Kant's account of fine art. In his "Deduction of Pure Aesthetic Judgments," Kant describes the task of the artist as that of finding material representations that, despite being in excess of anything logically implied by a concept or observable in its instances, will nevertheless combine to form an exemplary presentation of the concept. That is, Macbeth exemplifies a traitor, but from the concept "traitor" one cannot derive Macbeth. What prefigures Romanticism is Kant's idea that, although the artist produces freely, from her own nature, she produces in accord with a rule that her presentation itself is or becomes: "[B]eautiful art cannot itself think up the rule in accordance with which it is to bring its product into being. Yet since without a preceding rule a product can never be called art, nature in the subject...must give the rule to art....[I]ts products must at the same time be models, i.e., exemplary" (Kant 2000: 186). In the "Earliest Program for a System of German Idealism," it is this aesthetic autoproduction that transforms the system-subject from mere reflection into work. As Lacoue-Labarthe and Nancy indicate (1988: 35), key here is the role of presentation (*Darstellung*). What the "Earliest Program" states as its goal, "a complete system of all ideas," is to be achieved through an "act," simultaneously reasonable and aesthetic, in which these ideas are presented mythologically. Little is said about how this is to occur, but what seems clear is that the mirroring of self and world is to result from it: "Then eternal unity will reign among us....Only then will we find the equal cultivation of all powers" (1997: 73). In other words, presentation is not merely a matter of how ideas antecedently known are to be communicated. The manifesto's declaration, "The philosopher must possess as much aesthetic power as the poet" (72), suggests that the "complete system of all ideas" exists only *in* its presentation, in its production-as-rule. Apparently, "the idea that unites all"—that is, beauty—is not there yet. When Lacoue-Labarthe and Nancy conclude that "philosophy must fulfill itself in a work of art" (1988: 35), they are not saying philosophy just *is* art. They are saying that, prior to their exemplary presentation, nobody knows what counts as either one.

Although more work is required to make this strain of Romantic thought clear, its present importance is that it inaugurates a literary necessity exactly as deep as philosophy. Following Kant's third *Critique*, the concepts of art, morality, and science depend for their possibility on a human subject whose endless task will be to present itself. This Romantic subject is free not as the Kantian moral subject is free, by being essentially uncognizable, but as the Kantian genius is free, that is, by producing in accordance with a system that comes into being only *as* production. Theory and practice, taste and genius, thus become inseparable, making literature and philosophy experimental together. When in his lectures on transcendental philosophy (1800) Friedrich Schlegel declares, "Philosophy is an experiment," he means that, instead of comprising a discipline or canon, philosophy must proceed from its origin: "Philosophy is not like other sciences, where one takes what others have already achieved and builds on it. Philosophy is already a self-sufficient whole, and anyone who wants to philosophize must simply begin anew" (1997a: 241). The idea is that philosophy precedes its occurrence, existing in systematic relation with its primordial impulse and, yet, in such a way that no prior presentation is identical with it, ever counts as the whole philosophy primordially is: "Viewed subjectively, philosophy, like epic poetry, always begins in medias res" (1991: §8, 28). To occur at all, philosophy has to occur as development. What Johann Gottlieb Fichte in *The Science of Knowledge* (1794) calls "an inner, self-active force" (1982: 30) is this preexistent autoproductivity in philosophy's origin, the necessity linking whatever something will become to what, in its germ, it already is:

> [Philosophy's] chosen topic of consideration is not a lifeless concept, passively exposed to its inquiry merely, of which it makes something only by its own thought, but a living and active thing which engenders insights from and through itself, and which the philosopher merely contemplates. His role in the affair goes no further than to translate this living force into purposeful activity, to observe the activity in question, to apprehend it and grasp it as a unity. He undertakes an experiment. (30)

To conduct an experiment in this sense is to provoke the origin into life. For the early Romantics, as for Fichte, this is primarily a process of combining (F. Schlegel 1997a: 257), one in which a partial stability is undone and new, more primordial unities generated. The experiment, whether an aphorism or essay or novel, originates with an "individual" (F. Schlegel 1997a: §427, 242), a phenomenon, character, or concept whose individuality appears only against an implicit background of contrasting possibilities. Experimenting means placing the phenomenon, character, or concept into explicit relation with this background and projecting the new wholes that result (Fichte 1982: §22, 188–89). So, in fragment §35 of the "Athenaeum Fragments," Friedrich Schlegel begins with an "individual"—that is, cynicism's customary appearance as base or unprincipled self-interest—and combines it with its contrasting background possibility, that of principled self-negation or disinterestedness: "A *cynic* should really have no possessions whatever: for a man's possessions, in a certain sense, actually possess him." Cynicism, now understood as itself a kind of disinterestedness, forms a new whole, returning the concept of cynicism to its origin in an account of freedom. This more primordial interpretation of cynicism then generates others: "The solution to this problem is to own possessions as if one didn't own them. But it's even more artistic and cynical not to own possessions as if one owned them."[2] As a conjecture or imaginative projection, this kind of experiment retains its connection with science, since it makes explicit the background of possibilities any empirical hypothesis presumes,[3] but in its character as a test or trial, it preserves experimentation's etymological link to "peril." What the experiment imperils is the prior stability of the experimental subject. Its sequence of developing combinations discloses not new information about cynics but a system of relations that, in knowing cynicism at all, the experimenter must have already known. This background, present but unacknowledged from the origin, makes cynicism's partiality a mirror of the subject's: "Aren't all systems individuals just as all individuals are systems at least in embryo and tendency?" (Fichte 1982: §242). In the experiment the subject presents itself as a repressed totality.

Modernism and Necessity: Stein

Two kinds of necessity emerge from this idea of experiment, both of which recur in later accounts of experimental writing. The first, which following Adorno we might call autonomous necessity, constitutes literature as its own origin. In this version experiments are not acts performed on literature by a subject, but rather are presentations, within the writing subject, of the experiment literature already is. As Walter Benjamin has explained, poetic originality thus understood is simply the subject understood as poetically constituted, as a potential for coming to consciousness in the act or medium of writing.[4] Contrary to widespread assumption, the aim of this kind of experiment is not the new or unprecedented but the essential. From the standpoint of literature's autonomy, the present exists as limitation, and the necessity of experimentation is just that literature *be* literature. What performs the experiment, therefore, initially appears as its product or result, making experimentation the self-disclosure of literature's origin, which means the second kind of necessity, namely, historical necessity, is a consequence of the first. This necessity constitutes literature as incomplete, as an experiment whose result cannot be evaluated, not because it has sublimed every criterion, but because it has not concluded yet. The idea, as Benjamin explains, is that self-knowledge is productive, is itself what discloses, in the act or medium of writing, the subject's partiality (Benjamin 1996: 165f). This establishes a fundamentally ironic relation of literature to its presentation (Lacoue-Labarthe and Nancy 1988: 78). What Benjamin interprets as the Romantic theory of the work, of the text as a historically limited totality (1996: 157), Lacoue-Labarthe and Nancy characterize as the experimental genre per se: the fragment. As essential fragmentariness, the writing subject is "the thinking of identity through the mediation of non-identity" (1988: 46), a coming to itself in an encounter with its limit. The literary experiment, therefore, would not be a subversive or exceptional version of a practice alternately known in its normal version. Literature, like philosophy, would have no normal version. Its past would persist only as repression. As historical necessity, then, experimentation represents the insistence of the absolute.

These two necessities receive continuous expression in modernism. Their most familiar versions, both paradoxical, will combine either a demand for change with an underlying wish for recovery or an account of determination with an underlying assumption of freedom. In Gertrude Stein's "Composition as Explanation" (1926), they coexist in formulations that appear nonsensically redundant: "a thing made by being made" (Stein 1990a: 514), "what is seen when it seems to be being seen" (514), "the thing seen by every one living in the living they are doing" (516), and most dizzyingly, "the composing of the composition that at the time they are living is the composition of the time in which they are living" (516). Despite their surface bewilderments, these expressions all reiterate a common Romantic theme: that already being in existence is the condition for originally coming into existence. The idea is that in the experience of a historical present the distinction between creating and discovering breaks down. To live in the present is actively to produce it, but the originality of any productive act is its disclosure of something already there, ongoing. The art that Stein considered modern sought to take this paradox into itself. Its aim was to recover art's essence, its primitive being, through an acknowledgment of art's historical constitution, its essence as changing. Like the shifting viewpoint of cubist painting, Stein's experiments with a "continuous present" (1990a: 517–18) sought to disclose—both through their form and in their compositional procedures—this primordial conditioning of what happens only now.

In Stein's 1907 novella *Melanctha*, art's paradoxical existence appears as a temporal disjunction of words and actions. Melanctha Herbert is a figure of Nietzschean forgetfulness, a young woman who, in her present absorption, appears incapable of recounting anything that has ever happened to her (Stein 1995: 70), while her opposite, Dr. Jefferson Campbell, seems verbally afflicted, much like Stein herself, with a repetition compulsion. Jeff's obsessive topic, both a reform program for African Americans and an ontology, is that self-knowledge should determine experience, not vice versa:

> [H]e believed you ought...to always know where you were and what you wanted, and to always tell everything just as you meant it. That's the only kind of life he knew or believed in, Jeff Campbell repeated. "No I ain't got any use for all the time being in excitements and wanting to have all kinds of experience all the time. I got plenty of experience just living regular and quiet and with my family...." (1995: 81–82)

This effort to make recounting life precede living it looks to Melanctha like alienation. Speaking from experience, she counters that Jeff simply does not know himself: "It don't seem to me Dr. Campbell, that what you say and what you do seem to have much to do with each other...No, Dr. Campbell, it certainly does seem to me you don't know very well yourself, what you you mean, when you are talking" (1995: 82). For Stein, this conflict of self-knowledge and new experience occurs from the origin. In the context of her writing, Jeff and Melanctha function as archetypes, comprising antagonistic versions of what in *The Making of Americans* Stein will call "bottom nature" (Stein 1995: 150). As such, their combination comprises a Fichtean experiment, confronting each with his or her limit and producing a new whole that feels confining to Melanctha but reestablishes Jeff's relation to totality. Although in their early courtship Melanctha exposes Jeff's partiality, she cannot herself rejoin words and acts, but can only occlude words through new acts of daring. As such, she is never present to herself, figuring instead as a tragic realization of Adorno's negative dialectic, the unpresentable remainder of her life's passing. Her position for Stein's modernism remains ambiguous since, as absolute presentness, Melanctha represents the necessity of change, of the self-overcoming modernism is, and yet she cannot herself change. We could say either that Melanctha inhabits the temporal sublime, a momentariness so absolute that, with Lyotard (1989: 197), we can know only that it has occurred, or that she represents history's repression, the never-ending repetitiveness of all who cannot remember: "Melanctha Herbert was always seeking rest and quiet, and always she could only find new ways to be in trouble" (Stein 1995: 62).

By contrast, Jeff seems, for all his stodginess, to represent Stein's modernism itself. His task, like that of Stein—and, in different ways, that of *Four Quartets*, early W. C. Williams, Proust, *Finnegans Wake*, Henry James's Lambert Strether, Woolf, Beckett, Faulkner's Addie Bundren, and innumerable later experimentalists—is simply to become present. When Jeff first meets Melanctha, his talk of "how he wanted things to be with the colored people" (Stein 1995: 82) is an effort to talk over and around what, from their first evening together, stares him in the face: "Melanctha began to lean a little more toward Dr. Campbell" (92). To mean what he says, Jeff must act, must kiss Melanctha (92–93). What seems baffling, however, is that, when Jeff finally does act, that is, when he acknowledges his inexperience (100), falls silent (108), and lies with Melanctha (109), his change resembles more an acquiescence to unchanging conditions—what Stein calls "being" (109)—than an act per se. It is as though, for Jeff, the unity of word and act is to be undergone rather than produced or, better, like the rule of the Kantian genius, is produced precisely *by* being undergone. In the end, Jeff's discovery that self-knowledge requires "suffering" (131–32) replicates the "Earliest Program for a System of German Idealism," culminating in an experience of beauty capable of uniting theory and practice, individual and group: "Jeff always had strong in him the meaning of all the new kind of beauty Melanctha Herbert once had shown him, and always more and more it helped him with his working for himself and for all the colored people" (Stein 1995: 147). How could such timeless, purely subjective immediacy conclude the story of experimental writing?

LUKÁCS AND PRODUCTIVE FORM

This is György Lukács's question. For Lukács, to derive literature's historical necessity, as Lacoue-Labarthe and Nancy do, from autonomous originality and subjective fragmentariness is to make form absolute, a mere abstraction from history per se. Such abstractness, Lukács never tired of repeating, was the mistake of his own early *Theory of the Novel* (1920), where literary forms were imagined to develop from a primordial unity of subject and action, meaning and world. According to this and similar Romantic accounts, modernity figured as a crisis, a disconnection of "the original form-giving principle" from its social and intellectual environment, leaving modern literature "homeless" (Lukács 1971a: 40–41). Afterward, all that remained was a project like Jeff Campbell's, that of discovering as his own subjective essence "the true form of the world" (Lacoue-Labarthe and Nancy 1988: 33). Citing Heidegger's "thrown-ness-into-being" as the exemplary instance of this ahistorical subjectivism, Lukács in his later writings insists that modernism's "experimental gimmicks" (1971b: 37), regardless how shocking, actually represent no change at all: "The only 'development' in this literature is the gradual revelation of the human condition. Man is now what he has always been and always will be. The narrator, the examining subject, is in motion; the examined reality is static" (21). And yet there is something odd, almost perverse, about representing

Stein's modernism in this way. What the examining subject's dynamism is supposed to eliminate, according to Lukács, is "a sense of perspective" (33–34), the critical distance on present conditions afforded by historical consciousness, but as Adorno has explained, critical perspective is precisely what modernism's experiments are meant to achieve (1977: 162), what within a repressive environment the insistence on literature's autonomy maintains. In "Melanctha," the examining subject's dynamism, far from a technical innovation for its own sake, is intended to expose the historical consciousness that in "Composition as Explanation" Stein blamed for the carnage of World War I.[5] By including the composing subject *within* her work, by demonstrating how Jeff Campbell—like Stein's "generals before the war" (1990a: 513)—composes his present as past, Stein provides a critical perspective on, among others, Lukács: specifically, on Lukács's conviction that "the laws governing objective reality" (1977: 38–39), which the realist forms into a narrative, are knowable prior to their narrative formation. In short, her experiment denies to Lukács's philosophy its position *outside of* literature.

According to Adorno, Lukács's blind spot is his tendency to equate a subjective resolution at the level of plot with a purely individualistic meaning of the work as a whole (1977: 159–68). Jeff Campbell's recovered unity of word and act, of his meaning's immanence in service to African Americans, is certainly individualistic in the sense that no one else could have undergone it for him, but this merely comprises Jeff's social representativeness, rather than diminishing it. As Adorno explains, "[T]aken to its logical conclusion, loneliness will turn into its opposite: the solitary consciousness potentially destroys and transcends itself by revealing itself in works of art as the hidden truth common to all men" (1977: 166). To the extent that we find Jeff's initial refusal of Melanctha intelligible, can understand his wanting to avoid suffering by knowing "the laws governing objective reality" prior to undergoing them, we undergo "Melanctha" itself as a new, specifically modern, form of sociality. Lukács's discounting of this social function beyond representation represses not merely the historical significance of experimental works but the historical significance of experimental *form*.

The formal innovation of Stein's early writing, from "Melanctha" through *Making of Americans* and *Tender Buttons*, is her gradual abstraction of narrative context from the event of composition, of present meaning. In "Melanctha" this abstraction, which entails the mirroring of Jeff's spoken idiom by the narrator's discourse, consists of repetition on two levels: first, a repetition of particular grammatical forms in the discourse and, second, a repetition of particular speeches and actions in the plot. The second repetition is produced by the first, specifically, by the narrator's repetition of unelaborated substantives ("trouble," "wisdom"), conditionals ("maybe"), present participles ("wandering"), and imperfect tenses ("was always finding"), which themselves reduce or eliminate the specifications of space and time distinguishing one event from another. In "The Gradual Making of *The Making of Americans*" (1935), Stein explains the significance of such repetitions, characterizing them as a subject's "habits of attention" and saying that they are "reflexes of the complete character of the individual" (1990b: 243), of "every-thing that made them" (242). When Melanctha grasps Jeff's alienation, his habits of attention are what she reads. The idea is that a formative condition normally represented only at the completion of a narrative is actually revealing itself from the outset, is continuously present in every fragment, and it is this prior formation of the subject that produces the narrative.

Following Romanticism, the acknowledgment of these productive forms is how the writing subject presents itself. It is what we call experimental writing. Say-ing that its necessity is our "repetitive compulsion," Lacoue-Labarthe and Nancy elaborate its historical context thus:

> For insofar as we are, we are all preoccupied with fragmentation, the absolute novel, anonymity, collective practice, the journal, and the manifesto; as a necessary corollary, we are all threatened by indisputable authorities, petty dictatorships, and the simplistic and brutal discussions that are capable of interrupting questioning for decades; we are all, still and always, aware of the *Crisis*, convinced that "interventions" are necessary and that the least of texts is immediately "effective"; we all think, as if it went without saying, that politics passes through the literary (or the theoretical). Romanticism is our *naiveté*. (1988: 16–17)

This characterization of our historical condition, that is, of what preoccupies and so goes without saying, both prepares a plan of action and lodges a force-ful critique. The plan is for literature and philosophy—and, insofar as they are politically productive, for freedom and justice—to become practices of the inside, where "inside" does not refer, or not primarily, to individual interiority or a small cadre of the committed, but to the conditions producing practice, conditions both presupposed and brought into existence *by* practice.[6] What Lacoue-Labarthe and Nancy call "the formation of form" is simply the question of this autoproduction as itself what produces modern art: "What was at stake in the question of the formation of form...was indeed the possibility of thinking the 'subject-work,' in other words the becoming-artist of the work or absolute auto-production itself: man as the work of art creating itself, art henceforth identified with the being-artist" (1988: 77), which lodges Lacoue-Labarthe and Nancy's critique. Their hedge, "For insofar as we are," allows that we may not be. What we presently call writing—whether of the left or right, Eurocentric or postcolonial, critical or pop-ular, realist or innovative—may just comprise our effort to talk over or around what stares us in the face. The obvious fact that many of us (many of "us") do not appear preoccupied with fragments, are unaware of an epistemological crisis, and consider writing an instrument of politics, not its formation, simply means, for Lacoue-Labarthe and Nancy, that we ("we") do not inhabit our time. That dwell-ing in the present is neither an unreflecting absorption in what presents itself nor a critical predetermination of its limits is the point that the antagonism of Jeff and Melanctha is meant to bring out. At the level of narrative or plot, this is what Stein's experiment means.

FORM AND THE SUBJECT: BECKETT

The experiment's form, however, is another story. What Adorno recognized about experimental art is that its revolutionary potential is not primarily a function of its content, at least not of any content that philosophy could articulate as a meaning. Samuel Beckett's play *Endgame* (1958) became Adorno's paradigm, not because, like existentialist drama, it made meaninglessness into its meaning, but because it took meaninglessness into its form, its existence as drama. Like every concept in Adorno's writings, the concept of form leads a double life, by turns comprising experience and contradicting it (1997: 138–39), and so, in Adorno's 1961 essay on Beckett's *Endgame*, the work's form derives, first, from "a historical moment" (2000b: 323)—the period following the Second World War—and then, later, from drama's own "immanent dialectic," its autonomous development (338). Far from a mere inconsistency, however, this double life of form, its irreducibility to a context from which it appears inseparable, turns out to be drama's condition of possibility. *Endgame* takes place in what Adorno calls "a zone of indifference" (329), a landscape of Stein-like abstractness from which conceptualization—the difference between inner and outer, self and other, utopia and nuclear holocaust—has all but vanished. This interchangeability ("everything can signify everything" [338]) eliminates the possibility of drama, not because something has repressed it, but because nothing resists it: "What is the *raison d'être* of forms when the tension between them and what is not homogeneous to them disappears…?" (337). Beckett's achievement is to have recognized this apparent lack of resistance as itself our resistance. The idea is that the object of *Endgame* is to inform the present, where present information cannot be conveyed in dramatic form, not because no one accepts it, but because our acceptance would make no difference. The conflict in *Endgame* thus becomes the seeming absence of a problem—the characters' acceptance of their own acts as meaningless forms—a conflict manifest solely in their worry that their problem might *not* be absent, that "something is taking its course" (Beckett 1958: 13). In short, their worry is that they are still in a drama. If drama in such circumstances seems all but impossible to us, then their problem becomes ours, too. Deprived of the spectators' alibi, the claim to be mere products of history, we discover our indifference as *Endgame*'s production.

But whether this means, as Lacoue-Labarthe and Nancy maintain, "that we have not left the era of the Subject" (1988: 16) seems unclear. Unlike Stein, for whom forms manifest the subject's productivity, Adorno regards Beckett's drama as the subject's "final epilogue" (2000b: 336), a residual allegory of the ego's end (346–47). His idea is that the individual as experimental origin has proven historically "transitory" (327–28), rendering incoherent any Romantic theory of art as "subject-work" or autoproduction. What has since Kant worked to present itself now goes missing: "Because no state of affairs is merely what it is, each appears as the sign of interiority, but that inward element supposedly signified no longer exists, and the signs mean just that" (329). In this way, the meaninglessness that comprises

Endgame's historical condition infects its medium, making Beckett's "nonsensical" (339) dialogue the result of subjectivity's attenuation: "With this possibility long since crushed by the overwhelming power of an apparatus in which individuals are interchangeable and superfluous, the meaning of language also disappears" (338). In an essay on *Endgame* written shortly after Adorno's, Stanley Cavell reprises the themes of individuation and Beckett's medium, and like Adorno, Cavell initially pits his modernist reading against Lukács. However, in Cavell's account, the problem posed by *Endgame* is not how to understand it, but how anyone could fail to. In contrast to the critical commonplace that *Endgame* mirrors a "meaningless universe" (Cavell 1976a: 115), Cavell argues that meaninglessness is Beckett's goal, not his given (156): "The discovery of *Endgame*, both in topic and technique, is not the failure of meaning (if that means the lack of meaning) but its total, even totalitarian, success—our inability *not* to mean what we are given to mean" (117). Beckett's technical innovation, what Cavell calls "hidden literality" (119), involves canceling the tacit agreements that uphold this totality, using words in such a way that nothing about their context of use is implied. "The strategy of literalization is: you say *only* what your words say. That's the game, and a way of winning out" (126). But the surprise is that when reduced to their simplest meaning, Beckett's words do not produce a transparent and unequivocal message. They turn opaque.

The difference between Cavell's and Adorno's readings of *Endgame* is not, as Simon Critchley (1997: 177–78) and others have imagined, the difference between Cavell's old-fashioned attempt to establish Beckett's meaning and Adorno's more advanced recognition that, in modernist work, established meanings are the problem. The difference is between Cavell's Wittgensteinian and Adorno's Hegelian understanding of what a meaning is, and this difference has far-reaching consequences for experimental writing. In Wittgenstein's later philosophy, the kinds of sentences that in traditional epistemology grounded meaning—for example, "This body has extension," "That is blue," "Sensations are private," "Red exists," "I know from my own case"—cease themselves to be meaningful as descriptions and instead become part of the linguistic apparatus through which meaning is produced (Wittgenstein 1998: §50). Although previously regarded as models of self-evidence or verifiability, such sentences for Wittgenstein are without informational content, merely making explicit the grammatical conditions with which every competent speaker is familiar. More than once Wittgenstein suggests that we should consider them nonsensical (1998: §252). What misleads readers like Critchley is that, unlike Adorno, for whom nonsensical speech implies nonindividuated speakers and interpretive aporias, Cavell discovers no irresolvable problems of motivation or logical consistency in the dialogue of Beckett's characters. However, it does not follow that Cavell—or anyone—can say what their sentences mean.[7] The uniqueness of hidden literality is that, when it works, it surprises its listeners with a sense impossible to state more obviously. For example,

> CLOV: "Do you believe in the life to come?"
> HAMM: "Mine was always that." (Beckett 1958: 49)

That Hamm's reply is unexpected, and can even provoke a laugh, suggests that the obstacle to understanding Beckett's language is not, as in classic hermeneutics, alienness of meaning, but rather intimacy with it. As Cavell explains, "The words strew obscurities across our path and seem willfully to thwart comprehension; and then time after time we discover that their meaning has been missed only because it was so utterly bare—totally, therefore unnoticeably, in view" (1976a: 119). The idea is that, although Beckett's forms of expression lack nothing necessary to our understanding them, we nevertheless ignore what stares us in the face and look for other meaning instead. For Cavell, as for Wittgenstein, the predictability of this response suggests that our relation to our ordinary language involves repression.

THE EVENT: CAVELL AND LYOTARD

In Cavell's account, Beckett's experimental technique continues the writing subject's effort, following Romanticism, to present itself—but with this difference: instead of acknowledging, as in Stein's early work, productive conditions of the individual personality, Beckett's hidden literality acknowledges productive conditions of the literary medium, of writing's material base. His forms are, like Wittgensteinian forms of life (Wittgenstein 1998: §23), kinds of action, not containers of spirit, and as such, they are fully public, fully social. This provides the motive for repressing them. In Cavell's reading, the problem that hidden literality means to undo is the condition of the world—that is, not just its miserable state, but the condition under which humans have a world or inherit one. That condition turns out to be a curse: "[A]nd moreover the commonest, most ordinary curse of man—not so much that he was ever born and must die, but that he has to figure out the one and shape up to the other and justify what comes between.... All those, however, are the facts of life; the curse comes in the ways we try to deny them" (Cavell 1976a: 122).

To show how our denial curses the world, Cavell follows the procedures of ordinary language philosophy in resituating Beckett's dialogue in circumstances where the world's damnable state ceases to be merely metaphorical. For those on Noah's ark (Cavell 1976a: 137ff), the curse is that they have a world only on condition of injustice. Hamm and Clov have been sheltered; others suffered. They were spared; others died. God's selective mercy, by which Hamm's descendants enjoy life, is a travesty of mercy, making the whole of creation—all the philosophy, art, science, and morality through which, after God's retreat, we try to give our world meaning—just so many attempts to justify the unjustifiable. Instead of acknowledging the violence by which creation comes down to us, creation itself now becomes culpable: its meanings shelter us from the suffering. And so it must end (Cavell 1976a: 151ff).

For Cavell, the goal of Beckett's literary procedures is the same as Wittgenstein's: to disclose our state prior to any attempts to justify it. Only on such a basis is responsible action still possible. The Kantian "crisis" of the subject now takes this form. Living under repression as we do, however, we find such a goal indistinguishable from nihilism: "Where does our investigation get its importance from, since it seems only to destroy everything interesting, that is, all that is great and important?" (Wittgenstein 1998: §118).[8] Lukács is right: experimental writing appears meaningless, aberrant, solipsistic, apolitical. We want to ask why Stein and Beckett don't just come out and *describe* the conditions they mean for us to recognize.[9] In this way, our resistance to works like *Endgame* revives Romanticism's quarrel with Kant: How is the subject's presentation (*Darstellung*) of itself different from a representation (*Vorstellung*) of it?

Frustratingly, Cavell's answer is as indirect as Beckett's or Wittgenstein's. Like Adorno, he knows the goal requires *not* reducing forms to information, so Cavell's literary practice follows Beckett's, depriving readers of shelter, literalizing its own words, asserting as little as possible, until 41 pages into the scenarios of annihilation, Cavell's hallucinating stops at "solitude, emptiness, nothingness, meaninglessness, silence" (1976a: 156). Only after the subject has been emptied of content ("The soul is impersonal" [Cavell 1979:361]) and what differentiates my pain from another's reduces to nonsense (Wittgenstein 1998: §253), can anyone begin "*seeing* what one is filled with" (Cavell 1976a: 156). Everything of value in Beckett's and Wittgenstein's work depends on Cavell's italics. If the competing necessities of overcoming the past and renewing its origin are to coincide, if the formation of form is to become present work and autoproduction realize itself as unrepressing, then the conditions of meaning cannot be meanings themselves. In Cavell's reading, what is taking its course is still the era of the subject, but getting in on the action requires more than refuting Adorno. It "will require passing the edge of madness, maybe passing over, and certainly passing through horror" (Cavell 1976a: 156). At the end of such a passage, Wittgenstein feels inclined to say, "This is simply what I do" (1998: §217). His remark tells us nothing about meaning production, but it reminds us what meaninglessness sounds like. When the subject of writing presents itself, it does not resemble a text. It is an event.

In his writings on experimental art, Jean-François Lyotard has explained the event's priority over meaning as art's attempt to make confronting its end, its potential for nonbeing, the condition for its continuation. The idea is that what every institution, academy, and school tries to repress, precisely by instituting its rules or "regimen," is "the possibility of nothing happening, of words, colours, forms or sounds not coming: of this sentence being the last, of bread not coming daily" (1989: 198). Whether in science, music, philosophy, or politics, the conviction that continuity can be assured by collective agreement protects institutions from radical self-questioning, what Lyotard calls "paralogy" (1984b: 60ff; see also 43). What the event's priority places at issue is this attempt to justify practice by appeals to a social whole: "[I]n the diverse invitations to suspend artistic experimentation, there is an identical call for order, a desire for unity.... Artists and writers must be brought back into the bosom of the community, or at least, if the latter is considered to be ill, they must be assigned the task of healing it" (1984a: 73). For Lyotard, it is this nostalgia for community that motivates Jürgen Habermas's call for limits on aesthetic experimentation, and although Lyotard and Habermas disagree over the liberating or neoconservative consequence, both agree that Wittgenstein's philosophy would make such unity impracticable. For Habermas, what Wittgenstein substitutes for the Enlightenment project of "the rational organization of everyday social life" (Habermas 1983: 9) are heterogeneous "traditions which...are held to be immune to demands of (normative) justification and validation" (14), while, for Lyotard, Wittgenstein's language games model a society of heterogeneous regimens whose conflicts cannot be rationally resolved (Lyotard 1988: xii). For both, the meaninglessness of the artistic event reveals the limits of Kant's *sensus communis*: "That it happens 'precedes,' so to speak, the question pertaining to what happens" (Lyotard 1989: 197). In sum, the conflict between the community and the avant-garde is not that the latter defies the former's rules; it is that, for those facing the possibility of nothing happening, the rules "always come too late" (Lyotard 1984a: 81).

To investigate experimental writing as an event, not a text, is to turn attention away from its meaning and redirect attention to its audience. Key here is that, for both Lyotard and Cavell, the notorious differences of response to experimental art are not explicable by a code or set of norms with which some in the audience are acquainted and others are not. On the contrary, for Lyotard, the spectator's stupefaction before the experimental work results less from any inaccessible meaning than from meaning's near total implication in the work's facticity (Lyotard 1989: 199).[10] We could say that, if what astonishes a spectator is the happening of *this*, then her problem communicating her astonishment will not be that its meaning transcends the *this*, but rather that its meaning and its occurrence appear indistinguishable. I say, "Wow!" You say, "But it's just a urinal." According to Cavell, *Endgame* manifests this division in its audience as a changed relation to its script. Traditionally, what differentiates the actors from the spectators is the former's knowledge of the text, their already knowing, at the instant of each line's occurrence, what motivated it before, where it will lead afterward (compare Wittgenstein 1998: §35). Lyotard calls such familiarity "narrative knowledge" and says it encodes the group's rules (1984b: 18ff). What Cavell observes about Beckett's hidden literality, however, is that such knowledge no longer determines why the lines occur: "It is a matter of our feeling that no one in the place, on the stage or in the house, knows better than anyone else what is happening, no one has a better right to speak than anyone else" (1976a: 158). If I do not know what Clov is asking—"Do you believe in the life to come?"—then Hamm's reply can only remind me. It provides no contextualizing information, or none I don't already have. As a result, the distinction between those in the know (e.g., the actors) and those on the outs (e.g., the spectators) breaks down: "To the extent the figures are not *acting*, but undergoing something which is taking its course, they are not *characters*. And we could also say: the words are not spoken by them, to one another; they are occurring to them.

It is a play performed not by actors, but by sufferers" (158). Nothing before Clov asks his question determines whether what he's saying will occur to me. Agreement reaches its limit. In the event of experimental writing, what of necessity befalls all alike necessarily befalls each alone.

The Promise of Experimental Writing

This paradox—everyone's in the same boat, but if one denies it, "we" is sunk—is what Gerald Bruns has characterized as the anarchic politics of avant-garde groups. As he explains, "[A] poetic community has the structure of a series of singularities rather than a fusion of many into one" (2006: 81), a characterization of communal life that resembles an uprising more than an institution. The idea is not just that these communities are unruly but that they model human solidarity in its most primitive state. In Stein's terms, we could say such communities are *only* continuously present. When the contemporary experimental poet Clark Coolidge writes that "you start with matter, not rules" (Bruns 2005: 24), he expresses what Cavell has called the truth of skepticism: that our engagement with material reality is always more fundamental than our knowledge of it. Avant-gardes can be defined as groups no one enters except in this more fundamental way. The idea is that matter, at least as Coolidge means it, never occurs to anyone unformed, or if it does, that just means nothing is happening, nothing comes, that here and now writing confronts its end. When it *does* happen, however, what makes writing matter precedes anything I can write about what makes it matter. To undergo it is to suffer formation before knowing what that formation means, to allow the public conditions of my subjectivity to materialize before me. In such an event *I* am what's happening. Representation never catches up.

Cavell has described this event as "find[ing] ourselves *within* the experience" (1976b: 84), a locating of the subject that marks passage into the avant-garde group. Comparing it to the self-knowledge sought by psychoanalysis, he differentiates it in two ways from what customarily passes for aesthetic reception. First, it resembles a change of life more than a change of ideas or beliefs, a radicalization of our encounter with texts that finds its best analogy in our encounter with a foreign culture. As Bruns remarks, "In this respect understanding a work is more like understanding a social practice or a form of life than it is understanding a concept, proposition, or the use of criteria" (2006: 92), an explicitly anthropological version of reception for which no technical term is more precise than "getting hip." (Cavell: "It is essential to making an aesthetic judgment that at some point we be prepared to say in its support: don't you see, don't you hear, don't you dig?" [1976b: 93].) And all that makes this anthropological analogy less than exact is Cavell's second emphasis that, unlike passage into a foreign culture, passage into the avant-garde community provides access to no world previously unavailable. On the contrary, experimental writing discloses my ordinary form of life as foreign, as a world that has somehow remained undiscovered by me. In other words, my conviction that such writing presupposes knowledge I lack reproduces rather than describes my outsider's position. By contrast, finding myself within the experience of experimental writing means losing interest in such knowledge. It is, as Lyotard explains, to experience the immediate as itself sublime, as both nowhere and now here. The reason the avant-garde has no popular audience is not that its audience requires expertise, but rather that its goal has from the outset been the elimination of audience. In the community of experimental writing, there is only participation.

The history of experimental writing from Romanticism to the present is the writing subject's progressive discovery of the conditions of its continuing participation within the materiality of writing's medium. In her generically unclassifiable meditation, "Happily," Lyn Hejinian begins a segment with the lines, "The day is promising / Along comes something—launched in context" (2000: 386). It may not appear at first either obvious or especially significant that what we see in these lines as two distinct realities—words and meanings—is simply writing happening. That is, the equivocation of a day both holding promise and making us one is a feature of our colloquial usage that Hejinian can only have discovered, not created—or perhaps we should say that creation here takes the form of discovery, is interpreted by that concept—but the line's promising equivocation is itself something that just comes along. One way of avoiding what stares us in the face is to tell ourselves that Hejinian's writing is about itself, but what is happening on her page is manifestly not *aboutness*, no more than a tree's falling on a roof is.[11] Finding oneself within the experience is being struck, not by the relation of her words to their meaning, but by the emptiness of any attempt to describe that relation. "Along comes something" just means, if anything, along comes something. Her writing's simultaneous intelligibility and barrenness appears paradoxical only so long as we picture it as the relation of something before us—the print on the page—to something absent, something the print's presence ostensibly substitutes for, represents. The fact that we can see nothing wrong with this picture does not mean anything is right about it. The paradox is simply that her lines announce, as though factual, a promise that, unlike performatives, is not made by the one uttering it but that, if it occurs to us, occurs in its announcing. Nothing is being represented, but something quite materially real is taking its course.

In his commentaries on Wittgenstein's later philosophy, Cavell has argued that when skepticism demonstrates that material reality is unknowable, philosophers have erred in concluding that reality is therefore dubious, that knowledge of it is absent or lacking. According to Cavell, what Wittgenstein's engagement with skepticism reveals, by contrast, is that our participation in material reality is conditioned not by our knowledge of it but by our acknowledgment.[12] In other words, our involvement with material reality precedes our reflection on our involvement, implicating the activity of reflection itself in reality's repression. The Wittgensteinian problem, as much literary as philosophical, is how to acknowledge these conditions of our subjectivity without locating ourselves *outside* the experience.

Reflection may not produce suffering, but it reflexively denies it. Hejinian's solution to this problem, like that of Wittgenstein's *Philosophical Investigations* and of experimental writers generally, is to make acknowledgment itself her medium of reflection. That is, what Marjorie Perloff has identified as Hejinian's wordplay (2002: 185) acquires new significance, or perhaps acknowledges a significance the play of words has always possessed, something Freud studied under the concept of parapraxis and Wittgenstein identified with philosophy's depth (Wittgenstein 1998: §111). There is no pun on "promising" in Hejinian's lines, but for those participating in her work, there is a promise—call it sublime—in the event of just these words here and now. It is this impossibility of establishing the conditions of practice prior to practice, of making the knowledge of systems and codes precede action, that Hejinian has in mind when insisting that philosophy and literature are interdependent. What comes along launches a context for reflection to follow. This is the promise of experimental writing. Or its happiness.

NOTES

1. "[R]eason should take on anew the most difficult of all its tasks, namely, that of self-knowledge" (Kant 1998: 101).

2. Fragment §35 consists of these three sentences, the first by Friedrich Schlegel, and these final two by Friedrich Schleiermacher.

3. "Any hypothesis—even the most limited one, if thought through completely—leads to hypotheses about the whole, and actually rests on such hypotheses, although he who uses them may not be conscious of them" (F. Schlegel 1997b: 190).

4. Benjamin develops this idea from Fichte's notion that the "I" does not precede its act of self-realization. In Friedrich Schlegel's early writing, this self-constituting act of the "I" receives an aesthetic inflection: "In the early Romantic sense, the midpoint of reflection is art, not the 'I.'... The Romantic intuition of art rests on this: that in the thinking of thinking no consciousness of the 'I' is understood. Reflection without the 'I' is a reflection in the absolute of art" (Benjamin 1996: 134).

5. "Lord Grey remarked that when the generals before the war talked about the war they talked about it as a nineteenth century war although to be fought with twentieth century weapons. That is because war is a thing that decides how it is to be when it is to be done" (Stein 1990a: 513).

6. When in *Of Grammatology* (1967) Derrida made his notorious statement, "Il n'y a pas de hors-texte" ("There is no outside-text" or, looser but better, "The text has no outside"), I take him to have meant what I have said here: not that texts signify nothing real, but that there is no position from which a reader can say what a text signifies that is not subject to what the text signifies. The critic's judgment of the work, particularly of its limits, makes the critic vulnerable to the judgment of the work. And everything Derrida says of texts holds of our relation to other individuals, groups, and cultures. Reading is an action and, as such, wants justifying.

7. Cavell's account of the limits of paraphrase in "Aesthetic Problems of Modern Philosophy" (1976b) is helpful in explaining what might otherwise seem a paradox

(see esp. 78–81). Also, on the difference between following and interpreting a rule, see Wittgenstein 1998: 82e (§201).

8. Among the many readers who have taken this passage to exemplify a nihilistic attitude on Wittgenstein's part, see Nussbaum 1986: 261–62.

9. "Why doesn't [Wittgenstein] just say what he means, and draw instead of insinuate conclusions?" (Cavell 1976b: 70). Here Cavell means to be mimicking the impatient response to Wittgenstein's indirect style of expression felt by many more traditional philosophers. On Wittgenstein's indirectness, see Cavell 1984: 225ff.

10. Speaking of Stein's *Stanzas in Meditation*, Lyn Hejinian has characterized this immanence of meaning as ordinary or commonplace:

> It is impossible to "explain" *Stanzas in Meditation*. This is not because meaning is absent from or irrelevant to the commonplace but, on the contrary, it is precisely because it is inherent to it—identical with it. When it comes to ordinary things, their meaning is the same as what they are.... In this sense, one might say that things thinging is their achievement of the ordinary, their achievement of the commonplace. (2000: 364)

Heidegger's "thinging of things" reinterprets entities as events.

11. Bruns makes a similar point in saying that experimental poetry

> is made of words but not of what we use words to produce: meanings, concepts, propositions, descriptions, narratives, expressions of feeling, and so on. The poetry I have in mind does not exclude these forms of usage—indeed, a poem may "exhibit" different kinds of meaning in self-conscious and even theatrical ways—but what the poem is, is not to be defined by these things. (2005: 7)

12. The conditioning of knowledge by acknowledgment is the subject of Cavell 1979, most concisely elaborated in part 1 (3–125). However, a helpful short illustration of this conditioning is found in Cavell 1976b: 238–66, esp. 254–58.

REFERENCES

Adorno, T. (1977). "Reconciliation under Duress" (R. Livingstone, trans.). *In* R. Taylor (ed.), *Aesthetics and Politics*. New York: Verso.

Adorno, T. (1997). *Aesthetic Theory* (R. Hullot-Kentor, ed. and trans.). Minneapolis: University of Minnesota Press. (Original work published 1970.)

———. (2000a). "Negative Dialectics and the Possibility of Philosophy" (E. B. Ashton, trans.). *In* B. O'Connor (ed.), *The Adorno Reader*. Malden, Mass.: Blackwell.

———. (2000b). "Trying to Understand *Endgame*" (M. J. Jones, trans.). *In* B. O'Connor (ed.), *The Adorno Reader*. Malden, Mass.: Blackwell.

Author uncertain. (1997). "Earliest Program for a System of German Idealism" (E. Mittman and M. R. Strand, trans.). In J. Schulte-Sasse (ed.), *Theory as Practice: A Critical Anthology of Early German Romantic Writings*. Minneapolis: University of Minnesota Press.

Beckett, S. (1958). *Endgame*. New York: Grove Weidenfeld.

Benjamin, W. (1996). *The Concept of Criticism in German Romanticism* (D. Lachterman, H. Eiland, and I. Balfour, trans.). *In* M. Bullock and M. W. Jennings, (eds.), *Walter Benjamin: Selected Writings* (vol. 1). Cambridge, Mass.: Harvard University Press.

Bruns, G. L. (2005). *The Material of Poetry: Sketches for a Philosophical Poetics*. Athens, Ga.: University of Georgia Press.

———. (2006). *On the Anarchy of Poetry and Philosophy: A Guide for the Unruly*. New York: Fordham University Press.

Cavell, S. (1976a). "Ending the Waiting Game: A Reading of Beckett's *Endgame*." *In* Cavell, *Must We Mean What We Say?* New York: Cambridge University Press. (Original work published 1969).

———. (1976b). *Must We Mean What We Say?* New York: Cambridge University Press.

———. (1979). *The Claim of Reason: Wittgenstein, Skepticism, Morality, and Tragedy*. New York: Oxford University Press.

———. (1984). "Existentialism and Analytical Philosophy." *In* Cavell, *Themes Out of School: Effects and Causes*. Chicago: University of Chicago Press.

Critchley, S. (1997). *Very Little…Almost Nothing: Death, Philosophy, Literature*. New York: Routledge.

Fichte, J. G. (1982). *The Science of Knowledge* (P. Heath and J. Lachs, ed. and trans.). New York: Cambridge University Press.

Habermas, J. (1983). "Modernity—an Incomplete Project" (S. Ben-Habib, trans.). *In* H. Foster (ed.), *The Anti-Aesthetic: Essays on Postmodern Culture*. Seattle, Wash.: Bay Press.

Hejinian, Lyn. (2000). "A Common Sense." *In* Hejinian, *The Language of Inquiry*. Berkeley, Calif.: University of California Press.

Kant, I. (1998). *Critique of Pure Reason* (P. Guyer and A. W. Wood, ed. and trans.). New York: Cambridge University Press. (Original work published in 1781.)

———. (2000). *Critique of the Power of Judgment* (P. Guyer and E. Matthews, ed. and trans.). New York: Cambridge University Press. (Original work published in 1790).

Lacoue-Labarthe, P. and Nancy, J. (1988). *The Literary Absolute: The Theory of Literature in German Romanticism* (P. Barnard and C. Lester, trans.). Albany: State University of New York Press. (Original work published 1978).

Lukács, G. (1971a). *The Theory of the Novel* (A. Bostock, trans.). Cambridge, Mass.: MIT Press. (Original work published 1920).

———. (1971b). *Realism in Our Time: Literature and the Class Struggle* (J. and N. Mander, trans.). New York: Harper and Row. (Original work published in 1958.)

———. (1977). "Realism in the Balance." (R. Livingstone, trans.). *In* R. Taylor (ed.), *Aesthetics and Politics*. New York: Verso. (Original work published 1938.)

Lyotard, J.-F. (1984a). "Answering the Question: What Is Postmodernism?" (R. Durand, trans.). *In* Lyotard, *The Postmodern Condition: A Report on Knowledge*. Minneapolis: University of Minnesota Press.

———. (1984b). *The Postmodern Condition: A Report on Knowledge* (G. Bennington and B. Massumi, trans.). Minneapolis: University of Minnesota Press.

———. (1988). *The Differend: Phrases in Dispute* (G. Van Den Abbeele, trans.). Minneapolis: University of Minnesota Press.

———. (1989). "The Sublime and the Avant-Garde" (L. Liebmann, G. Bennington, and M. Hobson, trans.). *In* A. Benjamin (ed.), *The Lyotard Reader*. Cambridge, Mass.: Blackwell.

Nussbaum, M. (1986). *The Fragility of Goodness: Luck and Ethics in Greek Tragedy and Philosophy*. New York: Cambridge University Press.

Perloff, M. (2002). *21st-Century Modernism: The "New" Poetics*. Malden, Mass.: Blackwell.

Schlegel, A. W. (1997). "Theory of Art" (A. Michel and A. Oksiloff, trans.). *In* J. Schulte-Sasse (ed.), *Theory as Practice: A Critical Anthology of Early German Romantic Writings*. Minneapolis: University of Minnesota Press. (Original work published 1798–1803).

Schlegel, F. (1991). *Philosophical Fragments* (P. Firchow, trans.). Minneapolis: University of Minnesota Press.

——. (1997a). "Introduction to the Transcendental Philosophy" (A. Michel and A. Oksiloff, trans.). *In* J. Schulte-Sasse (ed.), *Theory as Practice: A Critical Anthology of Early German Romantic Writings*. Minneapolis: University of Minnesota Press.

——. (1997b). "Dialogue on Poesy" (A. Michel and A. Oksiloff, trans.). *In* J. Schulte-Sasse (ed.), *Theory as Practice: A Critical Anthology of Early German Romantic Writings*. Minneapolis: University of Minnesota Press.

Stein, G. (1990a). "Composition as Explanation." *In* C. Van Vechten (ed.), *Selected Writings of Gertrude Stein*. New York: Vintage. (Original work published 1926).

——. (1990b). "The Gradual Making of *The Making of Americans*." *In* C. Van Vechten (ed.), *Selected Writings of Gertrude Stein*. New York: Vintage. (Original work published 1935).

——. (1990c). *Three Lives*. New York: Penguin. (Original work published 1907).

——. (1995). *The Making of Americans*. Normal, Ill.: Dalkey Archive. (Original work published 1934.)

Wittgenstein, L. (1998). *Philosophical Investigations* (2nd ed.). Oxford: Blackwell.

PART II

PERIODS AND MODES

CHAPTER 10

....

REALISM

....

BERNARD HARRISON

For words are wise men's counters, they do but reckon with
them, but they are the money of fooles
                                    —Thomas Hobbes, *Leviathan*

The soul looketh steadily forwards, creating a world before
her, leaving worlds behind her.
                                    —Walt Whitman, *The Over-Soul*

I

....

The notion of realism, in its development as a term of literary criticism, is in origin a genre concept. "Realistic" writing is, in that sense, essentially writing that
deals with "low" rather than "high" topics, with the doings of ordinary people
leading everyday lives, rather than with the acts of gods, princes, or nobles; and
deals with them in a "low" style, a style close to the plain language of daily life,
and remote from the "high," poetic diction considered appropriate to the latter.
Erich Auerbach's great book *Mimesis: The Representation of Reality in Western
Literature* (1957) deals exhaustively, through a multitude of examples, with the
gradual emergence of such concerns and styles of writing in literature from late
antiquity onward.

Discussions of realism in nineteenth- and twentieth-century literary criticism and polemic, however, rapidly acquire a moral and political dimension and, in consequence, a philosophical one. Realism in literature, for one thing, becomes associated with claims to "truth," or at least to the truthful "representation of reality." Edmond and Jules Goncourt, in the preface to their 1864 novel *Germinie Lacerteux*, a preface that constitutes inter alia a kind of manifesto on behalf of the French literary realism coming to birth in the period, assert bluntly, "Le public aime les romans faux: ce roman est un roman vrai" ["the public likes false novels: this novel is a true one"] (as cited in Auerbach 1957: 435). A later passage in the preface both forges and explains the connection between an older realism, defined by "low" characters and style, and a newer realism, in France that of Émile Zola and Guy de Maupassant, for example, which adds to these purely stylistic concerns those of social justice and the revelation of otherwise hidden depths in society:

> Vivant au XIXe siècle, dans un temps de suffrage universel, de democratie, de libéralisme, nous nous sommes demandés si ce qu'on appelle "les basses classes" n'avait pas droit au Roman; si ce monde sous un monde, le peuple, devait rester sous le coup de l'interdit littéraire et les dedains d'auteurs, qui ont fait jusqu'ici le silence sur l'âme et le coeur qu'il peut avoir.

[Living in the nineteenth century, in a time of universal suffrage, of democracy, of liberalism, we asked ourselves if what is called "the lower classes" did not have a right to the Novel; if that world beneath a world, the people, must remain under the literary interdict and the disdain of authors who have so far kept silent upon the soul and the heart which it may have.] (1957: 435)

From this point, the line of descent is unbroken to twentieth-century theorists of social realism such as György Lukács (1963) and to a host of writers who consider themselves to be in some sense informing their readers upon, or making present to them, real aspects of their lives and times that would otherwise remain unnoticed and unreflected upon.

Realism in this sense sets up, as realism considered purely as a genre concept does not, one of those linkages, or tensions, between literature and philosophy that it is the business of this volume to investigate. It opens the door, in other words, to a question of one of the standard kinds that professionally occupy philosophers: what could possibly *justify* claims of this sort? If literature is to be, in some sense, an exploration, an investigation, of reality, then some relationship must, presumably, subsist between it and reality. What relationship could that be? As we shall see, pursuing this question very soon involves a second, and perhaps more profound, set of inquiries: Why is literature valuable? Is its value intrinsic or extrinsic to it? To what extent does its value derive from its relationship to reality?

Two answers to the first question, of the precise nature of the presumed relationship between literature and reality, have long been available. According to the first, the relationship is a *mimetic* or *representative* one, and the value of literature consists in its power to represent to its readers, to bring before them, aspects of human life of which they would otherwise remain ignorant. According to the second, the relationship in question is simply *truth*. Great works of literature, on this view, are of value because they "embody" or "express" important *general truths* about human life and society. Both answers are, in their origins, comparatively ancient. The first, that the business of literature, as of all art, is mimesis derives ultimately from Plato. The best recent defense in English of that claim is to be found in A. D. Nuttall's *A New Mimesis* (1983). It swims against the prevailing current of thought, mainly of French origin, associated with the movement known as critical and cultural theory. The view dominant within critical and cultural theory is that the main social function of literature is the dissemination of ideologies—generally reactionary ones, whose function is to sustain one ruling group or another in power. The claim of literature to have any commerce with reality is baseless, since its function is precisely to disseminate an illusory representation of reality. As the following passage of Roland Barthes in "L'Effet du Réel" (1968) affirms, we are dealing, in the case of the purportedly "realistic" details that authors insert in their work, not with reality, but merely with verisimilitude:

> [D]ans le moment même ou ces détails sont réputés dénoter directement le réel,
> its ne font rien d'autre, sans le dire, que le signifier; le baromètre de Flaubert,
> la petite porte de Michelet ne disent finalement rien d'autre que ceci: "nous
> sommes le réel."

[T]hey do not say so, but at the very moment at which these details reputedly directly denote reality, they in fact merely signify it; Flaubert's barometer, Michelet's little door, have in the end only this to say: "we are reality."] (cited in Nuttall 1983: 56)

The second general claim often advanced in favor of realism, that literature conveys valuable general truths, has found a great many modern adherents among writers and literary critics of the past two centuries, though fewer among philosophers. It emerged at least as long ago as the seventeenth century and was already familiar when, in the following century, Samuel Johnson, in *Rasselas*, famously put a version of it in the mouth of the poet Imlac:

> "This business of a poet," said Imlac, "is to examine, not the individual, but
> the species; to remark general properties and large appearances. He does
> not number the streaks of the tulip, or describe the different shades in the
> verdure of the forest.... He must divest himself of the prejudices of his age and
> country...; he must disregard present laws and opinions, and rise to *general*
> and *transcendental truths, which will always be the same*" (1909: 48, emphasis
> original)

Many more recent forms and versions of it are described and critically evaluated in Peter Lamarque and Stein Haugom Olsen's book *Truth, Fiction, and Literature* (1994), which offers an invaluable resource for this branch of the topic. But once again, any such view has long been under threat from philosophers and literary theorists generally. Lamarque and Olsen deploy arguments that leave one deeply skeptical of the idea that any version of realism so founded can be made to stand up to rational scrutiny. They opt themselves for what they call a "no truth" theory of the functions and value of literature, which I address further below.

II

It is nevertheless observable, despite the force of the academic arguments brought against it, that the conviction that great literature has cognitive gains to offer its readers, that it sheds light on "reality" in some sense of that complex and abused term, and that it does so both by "holding up a mirror to nature" and by opening access to otherwise inaccessible insights that it is hard to avoid describing as "truths," retains a far greater hold at present over the minds of intelligent, educated general readers than it does over those of philosophers, literary theorists, and other professionally interested parties. It is open to us, as theorists, to conclude that those outside our charmed circle who cling to such views are simply poor deluded souls swept along in the current of their already outmoded times—times, indeed, that have mysteriously so far failed, as times sometimes will, to yield to the persuasions of currently fashionable versions of historicism, but no doubt will so yield in time. But, on the other hand, it may equally be the case that the deluded masses see something we do not. It is this second possibility that I explore here.

It is best to begin by examining some of the main arguments against the idea that literature has, or could have, any connection with reality. The most obvious, and potent, perhaps, spring from the evident fact that works of literature are created by an author who performs his or her creative task simply by arranging words on a page at the behest of his or her free choice. It can be objected that the production of literary works, at least of those realistic or naturalistic in intention, must to some degree be constrained by the nature of reality. But to this it can be retorted, as in Barthes passage quoted above, that such constraint as is exerted by reality on the creation of the literary text is brought to bear on it, not by the need to achieve truth, but merely by the need to secure *verisimilitude*: to produce, in other words, not so much a faithful depiction of reality as a work *likely to be accepted* by a majority of its readers as a faithful depiction of reality.

In modern philosophy, that simple point has been greatly refined and sharpened, like much else in philosophy, by the work of Gottlob Frege. Frege held that a statement cannot be assigned a truth-value unless the names that enter into its composition can be assigned referents, or *Bedeutungen*. And the names that occur in works of fiction, "Odysseus," for instance, lack *Bedeutungen* precisely because the statements in which they occur—to take Frege's best-known example, "Odysseus was set ashore at Ithaca while fast asleep" (Geach and Black 1952: 62)—are fictional. What follows is not that the statements that figure in works of fiction are false, but something rather worse, that these statements are, as it were, dummy statements, incapable of being assigned any truth-value, either true or false.

A further implication of Frege's point is that, along with the notions of truth and falsity, the notions of confirmation and disconfirmation find no foothold in fictional discourse. It would seem to follow that the entire apparatus of rational scrutiny, the kind of scrutiny to which we subject a statement with a view to determining its adequacy as a description of reality (or "the world," or "the way things stand"), is automatically disabled the moment we pick up a work of literature.

The effect of these arguments is severely to weaken, if not entirely to invalidate, any claim to the effect that literary works might embody any sort of useful or enlightening reflection on the real world, as distinct from the "imagined worlds" that spring from the freedom enjoyed by authors of literary fiction to set, at will, one word after another on a blank sheet of paper. Their tendency is to reserve any actual commerce with reality to putatively factual discourse—the discourse of the sciences, or history. What role does this leave to literature? Plato, on the usual interpretation, at least, credits art with offering us a vision of reality, even if one as inferior to that offered by sensory experience as the latter is inferior to the apprehension of the eternal Forms offered by Reason. The verdict of the empiricist tradition—even less flattering to the poet than Plato's—has tended to be that the business of literature, as indeed of all art, is merely play.

Thomas Hobbes stands at the root of this Renaissance turn in the philosophical critique of literature. He distinguishes four uses of speech:

> First, to Register, what by cogitation, we find to be the cause of any thing, present or past; and what we find things present or past may produce, or effect.... Secondly, to shew to others that knowledge which we have attained, which is, to Counsell, and Teach one another. Thirdly, to make known to others our wills and purposes, that we may have the mutuall help of one another. Fourthly, to please and delight our selves, and others, by playing with our words, for pleasure or ornament, innocently. (1997: 34:)

Literature, presumably, falls for Hobbes into the fourth category, of "playing with words": an innocent form of play, perhaps, but as Hobbes (followed later by Locke, and still later by the entire tradition of critical and cultural theory) at once goes on to say, one instinct with all the potential power of subjectively generated illusion to mislead and, in so doing, to alienate us from the sad actuality that we in fact inhabit.

The power of these arguments, issuing as they do from various philosophical traditions, some frankly antiliterary in character, might lead one to suppose that the main opposition to the idea that literature possesses the power to illuminate reality comes from outside literary studies. That would be a mistake. The idea that literature "holds up a mirror to humanity" and its affairs in any sense analogous to that in which a good geological map of the southwestern United States, say, might be said to "hold up a mirror" to the geological history of that region, comes under critical pressure also from arguments that, given that they question the ability of any such story to offer an adequate account of the value of great literature, might be taken to come from within the tradition of literary studies, that is to say, the tradition of reading and valuing great literature as a serious contribution to our culture.

A striking articulation of this problem has recently been provided by R. M. J. Dammann (forthcoming). Consider, to change genres for a moment, a painting by George Stubbs of a racehorse, Whistlejacket, let's say, and its subject, that very horse. Suppose we say that the painting's value as a work of art lies in the relationship of representation between painting and horse. On the one hand, we seem to have replaced one object, the work of art, with two objects, a horse, and some slabs of pigment adhering to a piece of canvas. Still worse, neither of these objects appears to possess any intrinsic aesthetic interest or value. Similarly, suppose we say that the literary value of *Othello* lies in part in the relationship of representation subsisting between the text of the play and a Venetian general of Moorish extraction. Which general, precisely? Shakespeare's Othello? Or some Othello counterpart presumed to occupy, like Stubbs's subject Whistlejacket, a place among the furniture of nature? If we say the second of these things we replace the single aesthetic object, the text, with two objects: on the one hand, a man; on the other, some words. Now we face again the problem that we faced with the dissolution of Stubbs's painting into a real horse, Whistlejacket, and some equally real patches of oil paint smeared on canvas: neither the words nor the man seem in themselves of any *aesthetic* interest. But if we take the first course, of saying that the general whose tragedy is *represented* in *Othello* is *Shakespeare's* Othello, then talking of representation has brought us no nearer, it seems, to connecting art and reality, since Shakespeare's Othello is a denizen, not of the (one) real world, but of the "world" of Shakespeare's play.

A closely related point to this one of Dammann's is developed by John Gibson. To the extent that we value literature for what it can teach us about the world, Gibson argues, we move the locus of literary value from the literary to the extraliterary:

> We may of course take what we find in a literary text and ask whether it holds true in the real world, whether, if we apply it there, we can acquire a better understanding of worldly affairs. But as soon as we have done this we have left aside literary appreciation and stepped into something more like social science: we are now investigating the world and not the literary work. These questions may be infinitely important to us, …; but they ultimately say nothing about how we experience literary works, and thus they will fail to help us understand the ways in which we can read the literary work of art. (2004: 113)

A further point, common to both Dammann and Gibson, is that literary appreciation, the appreciation of the nature and value of great literature, is exercised entirely about *the language* of the work. Literature is after all, an art *made*, wholly and solely, *out of language*; an art whose works are created merely by arranging words on a page. We seem, as a culture, to experience difficulty with this thought. A particularly fatuous index of the kind of difficulty we feel has lately been provided by the BBC, which put on a series of "modern versions of Shakespeare plays" that kept the plots and the names of the characters but dropped Shakespeare's language. The thought here—the thought that justifies continuing, absurdly, to call these amusing travesties versions of Shakespeare—seems to be that Shakespeare's language cannot be all his work amounts to, cannot be what constitutes his work, because language is—well, just language. And how can *language*, the mere deployment of words, considered just in itself, either be considered *great*—as distinct from, say, resonant, or clever—or for that matter reveal to us anything about anything?

One of the major merits of Lamarque and Olsen's treatment of the topic, also, is their insistence that both literary criticism and our apprehension of the value of literature are exercised about the language, the words, of the literary text, and not about things external to the text to which those words might give access. And I think, moreover, that they are right to see that fact as a further obstacle in the path of those who wish to represent the value of literature as residing in its power either to formulate truths or to "hold up a mirror" to human nature. In any statement that purports to communicate a truth or, to put it more generally, to inform us concerning how things stand in the real world, the language in which it is couched is of value only from the standpoint of communicative efficiency. A given message may be of very great value in that it informs those who read it, let's say, of the sinking of the *Titanic*. But the value of its *language* is relative solely to the efficiency with which it serves to communicate that fact. It would be absurd, in such a case, to suggest that intrinsic value resided in the choice of one form of words over another, or that the message would lose its value *as a message* if any word in it were to be altered. But those are precisely the sorts of things we do say about works of literature. And, since what makes quality of language no more than instrumentally relevant to truth-stating discourse is precisely the relationship in which truth-stating discourse stands to the representation of reality, this does rather suggest that literature lacks, precisely, that—or any analogous—relationship to reality, at least when reality is taken, as it appears we must take it, as something existing independently of, and externally to, language.

It is open to question, though, whether Lamarque and Olsen do not pay too heavy a price for the centrality of this—undoubtedly, at least up to a point, sound—insight to the development of their argument. Forcing too close an analogy between literature and informative, fact-stating discourse undoubtedly makes it difficult, for the reasons just given, to understand why we should ascribe intrinsic value to a literary work, and do so, moreover, in virtue of the quality of its language. It has to be said, however, that to deny literature any relationship whatsoever with reality, as Lamarque and Olsen's "no truth" account does, makes that even more difficult to understand. And that is the direction in which their argument now moves.

Lamarque and Olsen grant, in their chapter "The Mimetic Aspect of Literature," that literature has such an aspect. It has an aspect of "aboutness." And what it is "about" are *themes*. Thus (their example), the *theme* of Euripides' Hippolytus is human weakness in the face of forces beyond our control, coupled with the lack of divine purpose. Euripides' treatment of this theme is built around a number

of thematic concepts, "through which the different features of the play are appre-
hended and related to each other: freedom, determinism, responsibility, weakness
of will continence/incontinence, sympathy, guilt, human suffering, divine order,
purity, pollution, forgiveness, charity, reconciliation" (1994: 401–2).

The thematic concepts that articulate a work of literature are, however, according to Lamarque and Olsen, "by themselves, vacuous. They cannot be separated
from the way they are 'anatomised' in literature and other cultural discourses"
(1994: 403). It becomes clear in context that a rather strong claim is being floated
here, namely, that outside "cultural discourses," including those of literature, such
concepts *find no application*, find, as Wittgenstein would say, no *foothold*. Such
concepts as "divine order," "purity," "forgiveness," "charity," say Lamarque and
Olsen,

> have received a significance *over and above that which they have in everyday use*
> through the role which they play in religious belief, ritual and in theological
> discourse....To point this out is not to suggest that perennial thematic concepts
> receive their definition in philosophical discourse or through the role they
> play in religious practice and are then borrowed by the reader of literature who
> wants to appreciate a work of art. On the contrary, these perennial thematic
> concepts achieve the importance they have within the culture, and receive their
> content, both from the role they play in philosophical discourse and religious
> practice, on the one hand, and, on the other, from the role they play in literary
> appreciation. (407, emphasis added)

In short, the thematic concepts that supply the content of literature not only are not,
but also could not be made, the vehicle of any body of insights concerning the real
world, because they have no application to anything "real" in the sense of *external
to* literature and other "cultural practices" loosely associated with literature.

As radical a divorce as this between the concerns of literature and those of
everyday life is, clearly, required of Lamarque and Olsen by the contention—central
to their "no truth" account of literature—that "whatever the purpose of fiction and
literature may be, it is not 'truth-telling' in any straightforward sense" (1994: 440).
The difficulty it involves them in, however, becomes evident the moment we ask
why literary activity, so understood, should be considered valuable. Why should
we care about the allegedly "mortal" questions [Thomas Nagel's phrase, borrowed
by Lamarque and Olsen] that provide the themes of great literature, or waste time
worrying about the "thematic concepts" in terms of which such questions pose
themselves, if the concepts in question "receive their content" *only* from the role
they play in literature (and a few other, equally rarefied, "cultural practices") and
otherwise have no bearing on the prosaic fabric of life as it is actually lived outside
the covers of books?

It can come as no surprise that Lamarque and Olsen have no answer to this
question, except to say, in the penultimate sentences of their book: "These are simply things we care about and always seem to have cared about. And this is where
the argument stops" (1994: 456).

III

It is time for a new start. Let us return to the simple thought that lies somewhere near the root of the philosophical critique, at least in its Renaissance and modern forms: that since authors create literary works simply by arranging words on a page at their own sweet wills, their works cannot teach us anything about reality. Why not?

The reason cannot be that reality is external to the mind of the writer, for that divorce plainly cannot, and does not, prevent the reality of things from being adequately captured in plain, descriptive prose. The problem is rather that reality is, or is held to be, in every sense, *external to language*. That thought is implicit in Hobbes's typically pregnant aphorism, "For words are wise men's counters, they do but reckon with them, but they are the money of fooles" (1997: 37). The gist of that remark is that words have no meaning that is not derived from correspondence with some item or aspect of extralinguistic reality. It follows that words can, by their arrangement into sentences, compose statements capable of capturing real- ity, *only if their arrangement is dictated by reality*, not if it is dictated by the will of the author. Truthful discourse is discourse transcribed from nature. To abandon the hard work of transcription from nature, and instead to arrange what are, after all, so used, *mere* "counters," into sentences *at will* is therefore merely, as Hobbes says, to play with words, like a child, "for pleasure and ornament, innocently" (1997: 34).

On such a view of language, language has no grip on, no commerce with, real- ity, internal to itself. Its commerce with reality is a purely external commerce, con- ducted via the conventional association of basic terms or sentences with elements of the world; in recent philosophy, for example, Bertrand Russell's individuals, universals, and relations, or W. V. O. Quine's collections of "stimuli."

Is that true? Has language really no inward, internal, commerce with reality? A very powerful and popular argument against saying that it has any such thing is that such talk must lead immediately to linguistic idealism, the thesis that the way we choose to speak has the power to create the reality of which we speak. Tak- ing that route appears to sever all connection between the way we talk and the way things are. Nothing created more animus against the late Jacques Derrida, among English-speaking philosophers, than the latter's remark *Il n'y a pas d'hors- texte*, interpreted, at least in the anglophone philosophical world, as conveying the proposition that there is no such thing as an extralinguistic world against which to measure the success of our attempts to convey its nature in language. Whether or not such an interpretation is fair to Derrida (see Harrison 1985, 1991: 123–43), which is quite another matter, there can be no doubt that the position with which it saddles him is a deeply unattractive one. After all, the connection with real- ity that language seems most paradigmatically to possess, at least in the sciences, runs precisely by way of procedures that are, in an obvious sense, external to itself:

measurement of, and experimentation on, the materially real. I would not wish to go down any path of argument that terminated in a denial of the possibility of that type of entirely external, relationship between language and reality. But is there any other path down which one *can* go, starting from the thought that language has, or might have, an internal relationship to reality, instead of, or possibly as well as, a merely external one?

IV

I think there is. It is the path hacked out by Patricia Hanna and me in *Word and World: Practice and the Foundations of Language* (2004).

One of the central arguments of that book goes, in brief, like this. Frege taught us, among much else, that meaning in a natural language is primarily to be understood in terms of the notions of truth and falsity, and that the prime locus of meaning is, therefore, the statement—in linguistic terms, the sentence. A grasp of the concept of meaning in a natural language therefore requires a grasp of the concept of the *assertoric* or, to put it less tersely, of what it is for a linguistic expression to *assert something*, to be the vehicle of an *assertoric content*—to be, in other words, a suitable candidate for the ascription of the predicates "…is true" and "… is false."

How is the concept of the assertoric to be acquired, or taught? There is, clearly, nothing assertoric to be encountered in the natural world. Assertoricity, if one may speak in that way, is a property not of lakes, trees, or mountains but of linguistic expressions. What it is for such an expression to be assertoric in character has thus to be specified, to be stipulated, if the notion is to get off the ground.

How is that to be done? To explain what it is for a linguistic expression to assert something, to possess assertoric content, is, presumably, to explain its relationship to the conditions that make it true or false. It is tempting to suppose that we might do this, for the statement S expressed by a given sentence Σ, by listing, first, some things or circumstances of which S might be truly asserted and, second, some of which it would be false to assert S. This would be a mistake. Someone who grasps what assertoric content is expressed by a sentence Σ is capable, in virtue of that grasp, to extend indefinitely both the list of things or circumstances of which it would be true to assert the corresponding statement S (call this the T-list) and the list of those of which it would be false to assert S (call this the F-list). From a finite number of items on either list, however, no continuation of the list can be confidently inferred. If I am shown, for example, a finite array of objects of which I am told only that the statement expressed by an English sentence Σ of the form "X is three inches long" is true of each and every one of them, then I am plainly in no position to add a new object to the array, since I have as yet no idea what assertoric content, that is to say, what statement, S, is expressed by Σ, and hence no means of knowing which of the multifarious similarities exhibited by the objects in the array are to be treated as relevant to the truth of S, and which are not. And similarly for any finite array of items presented as exemplifying the class of objects of which it would be false to assert the statement expressed by Σ.

Plainly, there is something that the learner still needs to grasp and does not: something that, if he were to grasp it, would allow him to extend either array with confidence. What could that be? Rather evidently, I suggest, what the learner needs, somehow, to grasp is that the statement expressed by a sentence of the form of Σ is a statement of *spatial dimension*, to be precise, of *length*. If he were to grasp that, he would see how the T-list and the F-list are related to one another. He would grasp that an object belongs in the T-list if its greatest linear dimension has a certain value, but is to be transferred from the T-list to the F-list if its greatest linear dimension has any other value. Grasping that, he would grasp how to set about extending either list in a manner consistent with the principles on which it was constituted in the first place.

But how is the learner to be brought to grasp that the sentence expressed by a sentence of the form of Σ is a statement of linear dimension? We have already seen that there is no way in which we could bring him to that understanding by showing him how to relate sentences of that form directly to classes of natural objects. The only other possibility is that we show him how sentences of that form are related to a certain human practice, namely, the practice of *measuring*. He needs to learn that measurement institutes a standardized system for comparing objects with one another. Our systems of linear measurement, I take it, are built up from the basic idea of taking a small, straight-edged object, M, and seeing how many end-over-end applications of that object it takes to span one edge of a larger straight-edged object, O. The practical utilities of this idea are many. An obvious initial one is that it offers a way of finding out whether a heavy object will fit into a given space, without actually having to move it. The small object M may now become standard in such operations: people in the M-using community begin to ask questions like, "How many M's long must a stone be to fit this space?" Then some unusually astute M-user sees that the business of ascertaining the answers to such questions would be easier if one were to take a rod and mark it out in divisions, each a single iteration of M in length, by applying the object M successively to the rod. "Here"—he says—"I have made an M-stick: use that." As M-stick use spreads and acquires other practical uses—in the measurement of plots of land, say, people begin to need words for what they are doing in measuring. First, they give a name to the length of M: they call it, let's say, "an inch." Then they introduce a word that describes the way in which the object M functioned, and continues to function, in their practice of linear measurement. They begin to say that M served, and serves, them as a *modulus of measurement*.

How is the learner helped, by being thus taught, in practice, what *measuring* is, and how to set about measuring? The problem he faced, remember, was that of discerning any *relationship between* the items composing the T-list and those composing the F-list. He needed, somehow, to grasp that the true and the false are not different *things*, but rather different *aspects* of the same thing, namely, *an assertion*. He needed to see that it is precisely the *assertoric content* of a statement which makes it both true of some things and false of others.

This is the difficulty that is resolved for the learner when, as Wittgenstein puts it, he sees, through learning the practice and the point of measurement, "the post at which we station" (1958: 14e) a sentence like "This is three inches long" relative to the practice. The practice gives him access to a procedure, measuring, by appeal to which he can himself determine whether a given item is to be placed in the T-series or the F-series. He thus sees what it is for the expression "This is three inches long" to be assertoric in form, to convey an assertion, for the essence of what it is to be an assertion is precisely that an assertion can be either true or false.

The moral of this story is, of course, that if meaning in natural languages is, as Frege thought, essentially connected with truth and falsity, and thus with the concept of the assertoric, then the meaning of an expression cannot be explained *merely* by correlating it with some item or aspect of the sensible world. Words are not, as Hobbes thought, merely "counters" by means of which we represent to ourselves the things, "out there" in the world, for which they have been conventionally assigned to stand. On the contrary, the meanings of words are determined internally to language—or better, perhaps, *internally to practice*. Think, for instance, of the ways in which the terms "inch" and "modulus" acquire their meanings in the context of the simple system of linear measurement just discussed. "Inch" is just the name we use for the distance between each mark and the next on the yardstick we make by marking up a rod using the object M. "Modulus" is just the name we give to any object, such as M, used in this sort of way. There is clearly no way, for reasons we have already adduced, in which the meanings of these terms could be explained by ostensively associating the terms with any element of the extralinguistic world. Talk of their meanings is equivalent to, simply amounts to, talk of their relationship to the practice of measurement—to the socially devised and maintained device, the language game, as Wittgenstein would say, in which they find a use.

Does that mean that, since such concepts as "measurement," "modulus of measurement," "length" are not simply markers for prelinguistically existing features of extralinguistic reality ("counters," as Hobbes put it), there can be no possibility of using the corresponding words to frame sentences capable of expressing true statements—statements correctly informing us about how things stand in the extralinguistic world? Plainly not. The statement expressed by the sentence "This book measures six inches by nine inches," uttered with reference to a particular book, manifestly admits either of being true or of being false, and which it happens to be can be easily determined by measuring the book. For it to be possible to use language to say how things stand, or fail to stand, in the extralinguistic world, it is indeed necessary that some relationship should subsist between language and the extralinguistic. But (1) the relationship in question need not necessarily run between elements of language (words, sentences, e.g.), on the one hand, and elements of "reality" (individuals, universals, relations, collections of "stimuli"), on the other. On the contrary, it may, and does, run by way of the relationship between practices and the natural circumstances in which their operations find a foothold, or to put it another way, with which those operations engage. And (2) it need not be identified with the relationship or relationships that determine the meanings of linguistic expressions. On our account, that job is done by the relationships subsisting between linguistic expressions and the practices in the context of which they find a use. What Hanna and I are suggesting in *Word and World*, in effect, is that we should cease identifying what serves to establish the meanings of linguistic expressions with what connects language in general with extralinguistic references existing apart from human practices. Without language, we would still, in a certain sense, "possess concepts." But since, as alinguistic beings, we would be restricted, like animals, to sensual and bodily interaction with the world, such concepts as would remain accessible to us would be concepts only in the rather limited sense of "concept" exemplified by psychological experiments on "concept formation," which in effect concern merely the ability of animals to respond differentially to recurrent patterns of stimulation. The complex interactions, on the one hand, between linguistic expressions and the practices—measurement, for instance—in terms of which we interrogate reality and, on the other, between the latter and the natural features of the world that determine difference of outcome for their operations, equip us with the linked notions of "truth," "falsity," and "assertion," and thus with concepts *in the full, language-presupposing, sense of the term*, that is to say, notions that cannot be entertained without ramifying instantly into a fan of possibilities of sentential occurrence, because to grasp the possibility of using a concept (in the full, language-presupposing sense) in the framing of assertions is (again, in that, full, sense) just *what it is* to grasp, to possess, a concept.

V

The utility for present purposes of the possibility just outlined of thinking about meaning, and about the relationship of language to the extralinguistic, is that it gives us a way of crediting language with a semantic, as well as a syntactic, "interior." The semantic interior of language, on the present view, is constituted by the multifarious interactions of linguistic expressions with the practices in terms of which we interrogate extralinguistic reality.

What sent us down this path, however, was the hope that we might discover some sense in which language might be said to have an internal, as well as an external, relationship to reality. And the argument, which might seem to have left us as far from that goal as ever, states, in effect, that the relationship between language and the extralinguistic runs not by way of the connection of *elements of language* (words, sentences) with anything *simply given,* independently of practices, but rather by way of the establishment, through the operation of the practices in relationship to which elements of language take on meaning, of binary sets of options between which reality can be forced, as it were, to determine a choice, and thus a distinction between the true and the false. If this is right, the connection between language and the extralinguistic runs by way of assertion. And that, it seems, leaves the poet, who as Sir Philip Sidney put it, "nothing affirmeth" (2004: 34) and the writer of fiction, who characteristically makes no assertions about anything outside the "world" of his fiction, still lacking a grip on anything worth calling reality.

But wait—there is one more level of complexity to come. So far, I have been arguing that the involvement of words in practices is necessary to establish the nature of the connection between what is affirmed and what is denied in asserting the truth (or the falsehood) of a given statement. If the argument stands, the involvement of words in practices is what gives us access to the linked notions of truth, falsity, and the assertoric. Seen from that point of view, the function of the internal machinery of language—the machinery constituted by linguistic expressions taken together with their functional modes of insertion into practices of one sort and another—is to make it possible for us to capture, in terms of the truth or falsity of propositions, the nature of a world—the natural world—which is indeed wholly external to language.

There is, however, a second way in which the creation of practices that are in part linguistic in nature bears on our relationship to reality. In the very act of creating the varied practices that found the possibility of propositionally formulated knowledge of the world external to language, we also constitute a second, nonnatural world: *the human world,* a world as *real* as the natural world—the world wholly external to language—but this time a world partly internal to language. Consider, once more, the practice of linear measurement, with its associated notions of "modulus," "length," "measuring rod," and so on. For a society to have access to a commonly understood practice of that kind renders accessible possibilities of social organization, and with them, patterns of feeling, interest, and self-description, that are not accessible to a society without such a practice. It becomes possible to measure land and goods accurately, for instance, and to make exact comparisons of the sizes of fields, or pieces of cloth, say, for purposes of sale, exchange, or inheritance. Such practices very rapidly acquire a moral dimension. Accuracy in measurement very soon becomes one of the parameters of honesty. The merchant or trader who gives good *measure* is an honest man; one whose instruments of measurement have been in some way corrupted or falsified in his own interest, the opposite. Many preindustrial societies have reached the point of having market officials whose duty is to check the accuracy of measuring implements used in commerce: scales, weights, measuring vessels, measuring rods, and so on. It is easy, too, for the connection between accuracy in measurement and honesty to take on a wider moral relevance, so that people begin to think of the moral life itself as, crucially, a matter of observing limits, and of moral intelligence

as accuracy in the measurement of the points at which the free exercise of personal choice ends and moral license begins. Out of these ways of thinking are
born further practices, including law, that are essentially moral in character: at
one and the same time ways of conducting life and also resulting patterns of feeling and response to the events of life, which come to surround our original, purely
utilitarian practices of measurement. Such moral practices give rise, in turn, to
habits of response and corresponding traits of character of the sort immemori-
ally honored with the name of virtues. One such, comparatively little honored
among us nowadays, is the practice of refusing, and the corresponding capacity
to refuse, an *unmeasured* response to the invitations of sexuality. Another is the
practice of refusing, and the capacity to refuse, an *unmeasured* response, not only
to appetite, but also to such essentially unmeasured emotions as anger, including
righteous anger. New collections of terms define themselves through their relationships to these practices, for example, "chastity," temperance," "a short fuse,"
and "self-control." To these we may add also, since virtues have a tendency to
mutate into vices, and vice versa, as circumstances present one or another aspect
of themselves, such expressions as "spontaneity," "decisiveness," "strait-laced,"
and "cold-blooded."

Now for several general points about this situation. A society for which *measure* is a central moral notion, governing a whole family of subordinate moral
notions, is a certain *sort* of society in which certain rather specific sorts of character will predominate and certain rather specific sorts of tension and dilemma be
felt and experienced. That the society in question *is* this way is, I take it, *a reality.*
That it is a society of that specific type, in other words, conducted by persons of
a certain corresponding range of characters and personality types, has as much
right to be regarded as a *real* feature of the world, as part of the "furniture of
reality," as some equally salient *natural* fact, as that the rate of acceleration for a
body in free fall near the surface of the earth is approximately 32 feet per second
per second. The facts about how a given sort of society works, what possibilities
of choice ("living options," as William James would say [1954: 89]) it offers its
members, and what sort of people they become through having been brought
up to inhabit it, are not *natural* facts, in the sense that the workings of the law
of gravity or the structure and physiology of the human body are natural facts.
Rather, they are facts brought into being through the invention and adoption by
human beings of certain specific practices. The society dominated by those practices inhabits, I want to say, a certain *human world* or, to give a new sense to a term
that both Edmund Husserl and Maurice Merleau-Ponty use in related, though
different senses, a *Lebenswelt*.

The relationship in which language stands to the reality constituted by a
Lebenswelt is, I want to say, different from the relationship in which it stands to
the nonhuman, the natural world. The natural world is in no sense *constituted*
by the practices, of linear measurement, for instance, through which we gain
access to the possibility of describing it in propositional terms. A given human
world, a *Lebenswelt*, however, *is* constituted by the very practices in connection

with which a range of associated terms and conceptual distinctions take on meaning. In the case of the human world, or worlds, therefore, the *reality* of how things stand, and the possibilities we possess of *saying* how things stand, possess a common root in the practices constitutive of that reality. We have what we were looking for: a department of reality that, *because* the practices that constitute it constitute *simultaneously*—as it were, *in the very act of* constituting it—a specific, associated body of language, of terms with specific meanings, enshrining specific conceptual distinctions, actually does stand in internal relationship to language.

VI

But how, in practice, does that help, if it does, when it comes to the question of how, if at all, literature can, at times, offer its readers cognitive gains?

It will be best, I think, to arrive at the general answer I want to give to that question by way of a specific and concrete example. Shakespeare's play *Measure for Measure* suggests itself in that role, not least because its language connects it with the kind of examples we have just been discussing. The plot of *Measure for Measure* is simple enough. Vincentio, Duke of Vienna, wishes to restrain the increasing sexual license of the city, whose strict laws against such license have not for some time been enforced. But he does not himself wish to enforce those laws, since having himself allowed them to lapse, he fears to be accused of tyranny if he now has people punished for conduct that he himself allowed to become acceptable. He therefore announces that he will make a long journey, and leaves as his deputy Angelo, a man with a reputation for rigid moral rectitude and sexual purity. In his absence, Claudio, a young gentleman, is arrested for getting with child his betrothed, but as yet unespoused, sweetheart Julia. Claudio is duly sentenced to death by Angelo, that being the penalty for fornication strictly prescribed by the laws of Vienna. Lucio, Claudio's brothel-haunting friend, approaches Claudio's sister Isabella, a postulant nun whose chastity is as renowned as Angelo's, to appeal to the latter for Claudio's life. Her appeal fails, at least on its own terms, but produces the unintended result that Angelo is suddenly seized with desire for her and offers to spare her brother's life if she will sleep with him. She is appalled and refuses. Fortunately, however, the Duke, who set these events in motion, has not left Vienna but has remained there, disguised as a friar, supposedly traveling with a papal commission. The Duke turns the tables on Angelo, by arranging for Angelo's former betrothed Marianna, who has been rejected by Angelo for lack of a dowry, to take the place of Isabella in the sexual encounter with Angelo that Isabella has arranged. Angelo, supposing himself to have slept with Isabella, nevertheless reneges on the deal by ordering

Claudio's execution. This plan, too, is thwarted by the Duke, who finally reappears and reestablishes order.

In one sense, the plot, thus baldly summarized, is an operatic farrago. The characters, similarly, are pure invention. It would seem, then, that the play can tell us nothing about what we are ordinarily inclined to term "the real world"— nothing about the sociology or politics of Renaissance Europe, for example; nothing, either, about "human nature," in the sense of the subject matter of psychology. It may be that the character of Angelo is a rather well-drawn instance of a certain type of anal-obsessive puritan, but even if that were so, it is difficult to see, following Dammann and Gibson, how Shakespeare's success in "representing" a certain sort of puritan character could be relevant to the *literary* value of the play. But in that case, what *is* relevant to the literary value of the play? Shakespeare scholars, echoed by several centuries' worth of common readers, will reply with one great voice: Shakespeare's language! But what exactly is that answer worth? What, for a start, is one saying when one says that it is the *language* of the play that constitutes its value? Is one saying more than that Shakespeare has the gift of creating highly decorative, though entirely uninformative, skeins of words?

It depends what one means by "uninformative." In one sense, indeed, Frege is not mocked. No intelligent reader or hearer of *Measure for Measure* has ever, I suppose, been seriously tempted to assess *for truth* any of the sentences that occur in the text. Rather, readers or auditors of the play assess what they read, or hear spoken, *for meaning*. If the meaning of a word could be identified, as so many philosophers have supposed, with some aspect or feature of the natural world, that is to say, of a domain of reality altogether external to language, then assessment for meaning would be a pointless proceeding, unless its object were simply to determine what, if anything, a given statement asserts concerning that domain. But I have argued that this is not a viable account of language and proposed an alternative, broadly Wittgensteinian one, according to which to attend to what is written or uttered from the point of view of its meaning is to attend to it from the point of view of the foothold that specific words and sentences find in practices, practices that in turn determine in part the shape of a human world, which in turn determines in part the sort of beings we, the inhabitants of that world, have become through living in it, and the kind of dilemmas we face in consequence. When language is used in the ordinary, assertoric way, it neither invites nor allows us to pay much regard to the *constitution* of the human world our practices have created for us, because the functions of the apparatus of assertion, truth, and falsity, even when what is at issue are statements—historical or sociological ones—for instance, concerning the workings of one or another human world, can be brought into play only insofar as the subject matter of the statements addressed can be considered *independently* of any intrinsic relationship in which that subject matter may, at some level, stand to language. Therefore, to bring before us the consequences, in terms of our situation, of the ways in which our practices have devised for us a specific kind of world, the human world, whose nature determines the scope and boundaries of what for us counts as a human life, a tradition of using language nonassertorically is required. That tradition is what we call literature. The poet "nothing affirmeth," as Sidney observed, because if he were to affirm anything he would not be a poet; he would be a deviser of versified philosophy, like Lucretius, or of versified sermons, like the Victorian poet Martin Tupper. It is only by speaking nonassertorically that he can perform his proper function of *showing*, rather than asserting, what the founding practices of the particular human world that we and he inhabit, have made, and make, of us, its inhabitants.

The title of *Measure for Measure* announces the central theme of the play: the balancing of moral debts. The words invoke not only the prosaic practices of linear and volumetric measurement and their uses in commerce, in which the various meanings of the term "measure" originates, but also the extension of that term into the description of morals: "measured response," "measured words," "just—or fair—measure" for instance. The play of meanings here equally immediately invokes the opposite of measure, the unmeasured, that which presses continually against socially contrived boundaries, in the present case, sexual appetite. What the play does, in effect, is explore a range of different responses to this conflict. It does so through the creation of characters. The characters of the play have, clearly, no reference outside the play. Shakespeare is plainly not concerned to offer us a "portrait" of a typical Viennese gentleman of the period, in the way that an Edwardian novelist like Arnold Bennett was concerned to offer his readers "portraits" of typical inhabitants of the Five Towns in, say, 1905. Shakespeare's characters are no more than the situation assigned to them by the plot plus the words Shakespeare puts in their mouths. Nevertheless, as a very long tradition of response, emanating from scholars and common readers alike, assures us, they "live," they are "real." What people who respond in that way are responding *to*, I want to suggest, is the manner in which the words Shakespeare gives his characters invoke features of a human world we share with them, which link our situation to theirs, allowing the emotions associated with the pressures of that common situation to flood from us into them, in such a way, that, viewed in them *as in a glass* (for the specular metaphor has always possessed a certain intuitive force, which it retains in this connection and to this extent), our own situation as inhabitants of, and as the bearers of natures formed by the pressures of, a certain human world becomes in certain respects clearer to us, because surveyable as a whole.

Thus, Claudius, ruefully reflecting to his friend Lucio on the errors that have led to his imprisonment, answers Lucio's question "whence comes this restraint" with the words,

> From too much liberty, my Lucio. Liberty,
> As surfeit, is the father of much fast;
> So every scope, by the immoderate use
> Turns to restraint. Our natures do pursue,

> Like rats that ravin down their proper bane,
> A thirsty evil; and when we drink we die. (2001: I, 2, 11. 113–18)

As with the word "measure" in the title, the words of this brief speech carry with them their modes of insertion in one or more of the many patterns of practice that can frame a human life and, with that, the meanings of contrasting terms. We speak of "surfeit" because we need a word for eating carried to an extreme that produces illness. We need that word because it is in fact possible to make ourselves ill by gorging. The speech simply brings before us the evident possibility that giving unlimited scope to our appetites may result in the loss of our power to satisfy them. We are like rats, says Claudius, that rat poison has made ravenously thirsty but that has also ensured that to drink is death. In a sense, we learn nothing new from this—we knew already what "surfeit" and "ravin" mean: if we had not, we could not have understood the speech. What the speech and the bitter metaphor of the dying rat give the reader or auditor, however, is a sudden sharp sense of what, in another sense of "means," it *means* to have destroyed one's life by giving one's appetites unlimited rein. By the mere force of the words Shakespeare has given him, their power, that is to say, to make familiar relationships rise up before us in a form made newly urgent by the terms of the plot, the nature of Claudio's situation becomes so sharply present that the emotions his words express, of bitter regret and self-blame, become suddenly real to the reader or auditor as well.

As with Claudius, so with the other characters. Each occupies a different situation with respect to the basic dilemma we—and not only Shakespeare's characters—face as beings of potentially unmeasured appetite who also live, and on the whole wish to live, by the light of practices, monogamous marriage, religious chastity, law itself, which all enshrine some concept of measure or boundary. The play offers no advice, no solution to the difficulties we encounter in attempting to square these moral circles. The moral rigorism of Angelo comes indeed to grief, the law he is committed to enforce turning in his hands into a tyranny that reflects the tyranny of his own sexual appetites. In a related way, the moral rigorism of Isabella's chastity stands compromised by its incompatibility with charity toward her brother. But the play's representatives of moral permissiveness, the "fantastick" Lucio and his entourage of pimps, whores, and bravos, fare no better. The Duke's restoration of order in the final scene amounts really to no more than the evasion of a series of impossible choices by means of ad hoc decisions. What, then, have we learned from the play? We have learned, by being given a certain sort of guided tour of certain aspects of a particular human world, a world that we, like Shakespeare's characters, in part continue to inhabit, that the topography of that world is more complex than we might have supposed. We have, in learning that, I suggest, learned something about reality—not, of course, the reality of the natural world, the world altogether outside language; rather, the reality of our world: the—or rather, one possible—human world.

VII

Let me sum up by returning briefly to the questions with which the chapter began. Literature is not about the "real world" in the sense of the natural world, the world wholly external to language. But that does not mean that literature, including great literature, necessarily concerns *fantasy* worlds, worlds made up out of whole cloth, worlds conjured out of the fancy, the mere subjectivity, of one or another writer, in the interests, as Hobbes thought, of amusement or play. Fiction can work like that and serve those ends, but that doesn't *have to be* all there is to it. The "subjectivity" that characterizes the best literature is like the subjectivity that characterizes the work of the best scientists: a subjectivity of personal voice and style only. What, on the other hand, the best literary work, like the best scientific work, is *actually* concerned with is not the "subjectivity" of the writer or, for that matter, of the scientist, but rather reality, the "real world," only, in the case of the former, the department of reality it addresses is not the natural world but the—or a—human world, and the latter considered rather from the standpoint of its constitution, of its roots in *praxis*, rather from the standpoint of its status as subject matter of contingent assertions, true or false.

It is possible to have an art of this kind, an art that is made simply by arranging words on a page, and yet that, at its occasional best, addresses realities, because the realities in question are accessible via the assessment of language for meaning, rather than for truth. They are accessible by this route because the meanings of words are determined by the relationships in which words stand to the practices that in part constitute the realities of a given human world.

Putting things in this way gives the present account, finally, a new grip on those questions of value that turn out, as we saw above, to be inseparable from the question of literary realism. We have come out, in the end, in agreement with the central tenet of Lamarque and Olsen's "no truth" account of literature: great literature *asserts nothing*, either false or true. But we can avoid the conclusion they draw from this thought, namely, that the concepts and themes deployed in literature and other "cultural practices" derive their content internally to such practices and therefore have no foothold in, or relevance to, the prosaic affairs of everyday life, by suggesting, in effect, that "cultural practices," far from being something *added on* to the "everyday life" of human beings, an optional extra, as it were, are, on the contrary, main contributors to the *constitution* of the terms on which any such life is available to be led.

That explains why so many have rightly supposed great literature to be in intimate connection with other aspects of the life we lead. It explains, among other things, how it is that, through reading it, we may be led to all sorts of insights, including, as I have argued elsewhere (see Harrison 1975, 1991, 2001, 2004, 2006), philosophical insights that we are unlikely to have stumbled upon otherwise and that can perfectly well be expressed in indicative statements capable of being assigned a truth-value. That such possibilities exist goes far to explain, I think, why so many minds are so reluctant to abandon the idea that great literature can instruct, can be a source of truths, despite the evident force of the type of counter-argument to that claim assembled by writers like Lamarque and Olsen.

Many of the concepts and conceptual distinctions whose ramifications are displayed by great writers—the sort that Lamarque and Olsen call "thematic concepts"—are moral concepts, and philosophers such as Richard Eldridge (1989) and Martha Nussbaum (1986 and 1990) have begun to take seriously the idea that some of the problems of moral philosophy might be more fruitfully addressed by making literature and literary studies active partners, as it were, in philosophical enquiry. At one point Lamarque and Olsen dismiss this tendency in the following terms:

> [Eldridge] argues as if literature provided answers to serious questions that we
> have to address in our own lives, questions that exist for us independently of
> the existence of literary practice. The trouble with this type of defence from our
> point of view is that it demands a concept of what may be called "true-versions"
> of themes that we have argued in detail cannot be sustained in any substantive
> form. (1994: 451)

The view proposed here makes it clear, I think, why the programs of philosophers like Eldridge and Nussbaum require no such theoretical underpinning: because the "themes" dealt with in great literature are in fact deeply rooted in "our own lives," not through the (admittedly nonexistent) possibility of assigning truth-values to the content of literary works, but through their roots in the practices and forms of life *which* simultaneously (1) determine the content of the concepts in question and (2) constitute the moral framework of whatever human world it is in which our everyday lives are led. In other words, there is simply no such breach as Lamarque and Olsen postulate between the concerns of everyday life and those of literature.

But it also follows, from the position set out here, that the value of great literature does not, as we found Gibson and Dammann rightly insisting, consist in the possibility of being guided by it to such truth-assessable insights as may be derived from reading and reflecting upon it. According to us the power, and the value, of great literature is, just as Gibson and Dammann argue, internal to it, because it resides in the power of its medium, language, to summon up and display—for here the metaphor of mimesis revives and recovers a good deal of the force ascribed to it by writers like Nuttall—through its deployment in the medium of a fiction, the nature of the human practices and choices that found the conceptual distinctions it enshrines, and that simultaneously found, along with them, a world, one that is not only the world in which we live, but a world, and its founding words, made flesh in us: the world that exists only in us, the world of whose values and assumptions we are the living bearers, and that is not, moreover, a static world, but a world constantly in a slow, glacier-like flux of change, one of the motivating forces of which, of course, is great literature. That is why great literature is, or should be, important to us.

That thought suggests a return to our starting point, in the notion of realism as a genre concept. Realism as a genre is, for many literary historians, conterminous with the brief reign of the nineteenth-century realist novel, and passes from the scene with the rise of literary modernism, in the work of such writers as Kafka, Proust, Joyce, Woolf, or Eliot.

The revolutionary character of modernism in literature, as in other arts, is often taken to consist in two main characteristics, both involving a crisis of authority. On the one hand, it is said, modernist writers are painfully aware that, since the book is "only a book and not the world" (Josipovici 1977: 113), and since the claim to capture reality in a fiction is a grandiloquent pretense, the writer cannot rely on reality to authorize what he writes. On the other hand, the recognition by modernists that traditional literary forms and rules of composition are "man-made and not natural" (122), it is claimed, destroys the authority of past literary practice. That double lapse of authority leaves the modernist writer, when it comes to deciding what to write down upon the blank page confronting him, in that state of absolute freedom, at once liberating and angst ridden, that the existentialist tradition, from Kierkegaard and Nietzsche onward, has made it its business to explore.

One way of responding to this situation is to argue, with Gabriel Josipovici (echoing Hobbes, in the passage from *Leviathan* cited above), that it gives to literature, as to art in general, "a greater sense of game, of playfulness, than ha[s] ever been known since the dawn of the Renaissance" (1977: 122). But—and here is the rub—such a stance leaves room for two darker responses: first, that it is a short step from playfulness to frivolity—to an art that no longer functions either as a transmitter or as a critic of cultural stances and values because it has subsided into the self-absorbed pursuit of purely formal "experiments"; and second, that of Thomas Mann in *Doctor Faustus*, that modernism in art, in its surrender of all cultural authority in favor of the naked will of the artist, has a demonic side, a side not without connections, for Mann, with the rise of Nazism.

If the position I have outlined here stands, however, the latter two, pessimistic, responses have rather less to be said for them than might otherwise appear. On the view suggested here, the negative part of the case for modernism advanced by Josipovici and others is sound enough. It is indeed not the business of literature to "describe reality"—even human reality—in the sense in which a *true, literal, indicative* statement "describes reality." No doubt, also, all questions of literary form and technique do indeed fall to the will of the writer to determine. But if we are right, it does not follow that literature is a free field for "play" in the sense of *frivolity*, for the connection between literature and reality does not run by way of the truth or falsity of statements, but by way of deeper linkages, internal to language, between the meanings of words and the practices that constitute human worlds and form the outlook and personalities of their inhabitants. To "play" with these connections, to bring them to consciousness, to criticize them, at times to transform them, is indeed the business of serious literature, including modernist literature. But the "play" in question is serious play, since it affords us one of the few means we have of rising above our habitual acquiescence in the vast fabric of historically accumulated practice, in and through which we live our lives, to a position from which we can, in principle at least, contemplate with a serious eye what that fabric has made, and continues to make, of us.

REFERENCES

Auerbach, E. (1957). *Mimesis: The Representation of Reality in Western Literature* (W. Trask, trans.). Garden City, N.Y.: Doubleday Anchor. (Original work published 1946).

Barthes, R. (1968). L'Effet du Réel. *Communications*, 11, 84–9.

Dammann, R. M. J. *Othello's Language.* Unpublished manuscript.

Eldridge, R. (1989). *On Moral Personhood: Philosophy, Literature, Criticism and Self-Understanding.* Chicago: Chicago University Press.

Geach, P., and M. Black. (1952). *Translations from the Philosophical Writings of Gottlob Frege.* Oxford: Blackwell.

Gibson, J. (2004). "Reading for Life." *In* W. Huemer and J. Gibson (eds.), *The Literary Wittgenstein.* London: Routledge.

Harrison, B. (1975). *Henry Fielding's "Tom Jones": The Novelist as Moral Philosopher.* London: Chatto and Windus/Sussex University Press.

——. (1985). "Deconstructing Derrida." *In* E. S. Shaffer (ed.), *Comparative Criticism* (vol. 7). Cambridge: Cambridge University Press.

——. (1991). *Inconvenient Fictions: Literature and the Limits of Theory.* New Haven: Yale University Press.

——. (2001). "What Are Fictions For?" *Midwest Studies in Philosophy* 25, 12–35.

——. (2004). "Imagined Worlds and the Real One: Plato, Wittgenstein and Literary Mimesis." *In* J. Gibson and W. Huemer (eds.), *The Literary Wittgenstein.* London: Routledge.

——. (2007) "Aharon Appelfeld and the Problem of Holocaust Fiction." *In* J. Gibson (ed.), *A Sense of the World: Essays on Fiction, Narrative and Knowledge.* London: Routledge.

Hobbes, T. (1909). *Leviathan* Michael Oakeshott (ed.). New York: Touchstone. (Original work published in 1651.)

James, W. (1954). "The Will to Believe." *In* A. Castell (ed.), *Essays in Pragmatism.* New York: Hafner.

Johnson, S. (1909). *Rasselas. Prince of Abyssinia.* London: Cassell. (Original work published in 1759.)

Josipovici, G. (1977). *The Lessons of Modernism, and Other Essays.* London: Macmillan.

Lamarque, P., and Olsen, S. H. (1994). *Truth, Fiction, and Literature: A Philosophical Perspective.* Oxford: Clarendon Press.

Lukács, G. (1963). *The Meaning of Contemporary Realism* (J. and N. Mander, trans.). London: Merlin Press. (Original work published in 1958).

Merleau-Ponty, M. (1964). *Signs* (R. C. McCleary, trans.). Evanston, Ill.: Northwestern University Press. (Original work published in 1960.)

Nussbaum, M. (1986). *The Fragility of Goodness: Luck and Ethics in Greek Tragedy and Philosophy.* Cambridge: Cambridge University Press.

———. (1990). *Love's Knowledge: Essays on Philosophy and Literature.* Oxford: Oxford University Press.

Nuttall, A. D. (1983). *A New Mimesis: Shakespeare and the Representation of Reality.* London: Methuen.

Shakespeare, W. (2001). *Measure for Measure.* Oxford: Oxford University Press. (Original work published in 1623.)

Sidney, P. (2004). "The Defence of Poesy." *In* G Alexander (ed.), *Sidney's "The Defence of Poesy" and Selected Renaissance.* London: Penguin. (Original work published in 1795.)

Wittgenstein, L. (1958). *Philosophical Investigations* (3rd ed.; G. E. M. Anscombe, trans.). Oxford: Blackwell. (Original work published in 1953.)

CHAPTER 11

ROMANTICISM

NIKOLAS KOMPRIDIS

In memory of Richard Rorty

[W]hat interests us in romanticism is that we still belong to
the era it opened up. The present period continues to deny
precisely this belonging, which defines us.

—Philippe Lacoue-Labarthe and Jean-Luc Nancy,
The Literary Absolute

UNEXPECTED RESURGENCE

For much of the twentieth century, responding with modernist condescension
to anything that emitted even the slightest whiff of romanticism was simply de
rigueur. After all, romanticism was *so* nineteenth century, an artistically spent cultural force whose obsolete remains have been drained of vitality and meaning. To
succumb to any warmed-over romantic impulses was to risk producing kitsch, or
to make common cause with the forces of cultural conservatism, or to participate
in the ideological distortion of reality.

Theodor Adorno's supercilious and dismissive reaction to the music of
Jean Sibelius is a typical, if extreme, example. Written in the late 1930s during the triumphant spread of European fascism, Adorno's "Glosse über Sibelius" pulls no punches in the name of progressive consciousness. Adorno, the

upright Schoenbergian and understandably anxious modernist, had no doubts whatsoever about what he heard in Sibelius: music of obvious technical infe- riority, produced by a musically backward, conservative hick: "If Sibelius is good, then the perennial standards of musical quality from Bach to Schoen- berg...are invalid" (1982: 251).[1] The general popularity of music of such utterly transparent banality was, for Adorno, a sure sign of undeniable musical and cultural regression. Even worse, the ideological pitch of this music, intoned in the corrupted but comforting language of romantic tonality, rendered it alto- gether too congenial to "blood and soil" nationalism and to antimodern invo- cations of "nature."

Of course, the list of romanticism's various sins can be very long indeed. In addition to its unavoidable reversion to kitsch, its conservatism, its antimodernism, and its ideological distortion of reality, there is also its quietism, its sentimental- ity, its divinization of the visionary powers of the (male) artist, its depoliticization of art, its aesthetic ideology, its masculinism, and, for some (not so long ago), its emasculated, feminine sensibility. Given its many egregious sins, why the resur- gent interest in German and American romanticism? The complex picture of romanticism (and its unrealized possibilities) that one finds in the work of Stanley Cavell, Charles Taylor, Richard Rorty, Dieter Henrich, Manfred Frank, Richard Eldridge, and a number of other important scholars does not seem to conform to the received view of romanticism as an exhausted and suspect set of responses to the modern world.

Perhaps, this resurgent interest in romanticism can be viewed as just another passing academic fashion—in today, out tomorrow. If popular culture can resort to recycling its past when it has nothing new to say, why should we expect things to be any different in the academy? More plausibly, the resurgent interest in romanticism might be a consequence of the decline of confidence in "modernist" modernity, and so an interest in retrieving long neglected or misunderstood pos- sibilities for living modernity's form of life—living it less rigidly, less destructively. The dark side of twentieth-century modernism is rather familiar to us now, not least, the authoritarian and intolerant character of its formalist aesthetic norms, the cocksure aesthetic judgment, and the totalizing (and masculinist) style of criticism.

Surely, one could object, we are not living in a "romantic" age. Whatever might be percolating in the minds of scholars, we are not living in the 1790s, when even the horrors of the French Revolution could not dampen the radi- cal hopes of the young romantics. Our time is not a time anyone is going to look back at nostalgically, as William Wordsworth did in *The Prelude* (1850), and sigh: "Bliss was it in that dawn to be alive / But to be young was very Heaven!" (11: 108–9). To be young today is very different and not a little frightening, despite all the seductive consumer devices offering temporary relief from the intensely felt anxieties of the age. If there is bliss to be had, it may be found only in cultivated ignorance.

The future, too, is different, dramatically less capable of bearing radical hopes, were any to be articulated convincingly. Is romanticism even possible in a skeptical, doubt-ridden age such as ours? The time for romanticism, for better and for worse, has passed. Why not just let it fade into the sunset, move on, dealing realistically with the world *we* face, making the most of the possibilities *our* historical circumstances allow? What need could romanticism answer today?

Well, a *reinherited* romanticism might provide us with a richer evaluative vocabulary than modernism could provide, one that might make it possible for us to say yes or no to modernity, to the present, to the future, in more complex and nuanced ways. And so the resurgence of interest in romanticism could be construed as part of a growing realization that it may be unwise as well as self-contradictory to live modernity's form of life unromantically.

For example, there are certain forms of individual and cultural change that are simply inconceivable apart from our romantic understanding of such change, and our romantic need of it. As long as you aspire to a kind of change in which "[y]ou are different, what you recognize as problems are different, your world is different," then you are bound and answerable to the demands of romanticism (Cavell 1976a: 87). What is demanded of you, despite all the obstacles and constraints, despite the improbability and possible futility of it all, is to find and found new ways of looking at things, new ways of speaking and acting, new kinds of practices, and new kinds of institutions. Anyone who thinks such change is not only necessary but also (improbably) possible, whatever their view of "romanticism," is a hopeless romantic.

Even Wordsworth's disappointment with the French Revolution—its betrayal of its own ideals, not to mention its fervent deification of "naked" reason—did not dampen his faith that such change as romanticism prefigures can be made visible in romantic writing and, when made visible, made realizable.

> ...and I remember, well
> That in life's every-day appearances
> I seemed about this time to gain clear sight
> Of a new world—a world, too, that was fit
> To be transmitted, and to other eyes
> Made visible... (1850, 13: 367–72)

Any critical vocabulary that operates without some (not unassailable) faith in the possibility of "a new world," a faith fostered by "every-day appearances" here and now, would be not only ineffectual *as* a critical vocabulary, but also inconceivable. It would have to treat the aspiration to bring about a change in which "[y]ou are different, what you recognize as problems are different, your world is different" as naive romanticism, and romantic claims such as "all things have second birth" (1850, 10: 83) as mystifications of "real" social change. But then it would leave unanswered the question of how we are to imagine "real" change if it does not lead to, and is not *seen* as leading to, a new world—this world made anew. More important, it leaves unanswered the question of how we are to foresee this new world *without* the help of romantic writing and envisioning. To disclose a "new world" that responds to our genuine needs will require all the resources of romantic writing if it is to be "fit / To be transmitted, and to other eyes / Made visible."

A critical vocabulary that thinks it must renounce romantic notions of change and transfiguration will find itself hugely incapacitated, existentially, not just theoretically. Romantics have given us good reason to doubt that justice without transfiguration is possible. Neither justice nor transfiguration can be achieved merely by providing "good arguments." Conventional arguments, however "good" they might be, cannot cast our problems in a new light, nor can they adjust the light so that we can see ourselves and the things that matter to us in a new way. As Rorty repeated tirelessly, only new vocabularies of description and evaluation will let us do that.[2] By lending themselves to the creation of these necessarily new ways of speaking and acting, both philosophy and literature respond to, and occasionally meet, the demands of romanticism. Having lived through the shortcomings of an unromantic modernism, a modernism that had to suppress its romanticism, might it be that romanticism can redeem modernism? Might it be that we still *need* romanticism?

What *Is* Romanticism?

Before we even venture to answer this question, it might be worthwhile to ask just what would count as a satisfactory answer. If we were speaking of a unified and fully discharged set of artistic and cultural energies that we, owllike, grasp retrospectively in the appropriate categories, we would be entitled to speak of a glorious "early" romanticism and a decadent, politically distasteful "late" romanticism. We would then place it in a historical sequence in which it is eventually superseded by an aesthetically uncompromising modernism, which, having lost its way and our confidence, mutated into a skeptical postmodernism.[3] But if we are of the view that romanticism is not something we are already beyond but is a living, as yet unrealized possibility, then identifying romanticism too closely with its past would construe its meaning and its history (as well as its geography) far too narrowly.

We might also wish to recall Nietzsche's dictum concerning the impossibility of defining anything that has a history. Nietzsche, who could be a ferocious critic of "romanticism," did not try to grasp it in narrow historical categories. Instructively, he applied the concept to a set of expressive responses to the world, the nature of which could be distinguished not according to whether they represented an "early" or "late" form of romanticism, but according to whether their response to the world arose from "the *overfullness of life*" or "the *impoverishment of life*" (Nietzsche

1974: 328). These are hardly uncontroversial criteria, no matter how one construes them; what is of interest to our purpose here, however, is that Nietzsche's very romantic criteria of evaluation (even if Nietzsche could not acknowledge them as such) refer to normatively distinct forms of expressive response, each of which outlines a relation to the world and to ways of life, individual and shared, that these forms of expressive response make visible, as livable possibilities.

In this respect, Nietzsche's approach to the meaning of romanticism is entirely congruent with the approach of this volume to forms as styles of attention to human life, a request that is particularly congenial to my view of romanticism. By treating romanticism as an expressive response to the world, as a form of attention to the possibilities and debilities of human life, we are able to understand it in richer and more comprehensive terms.

That said, we are still left with the problem of determining what constitutes distinctively *romantic* forms of response and attention. Without diminishing the importance or centrality of any historically specific romanticism, determining what counts as distinctively romantic forms of response and attention might require thinking of "romanticism" as a field of problems and concerns, as a field of problematizations, to use a Foucauldian term of art. The "unity" of these problematizations is not to be found in specific theoretical positions or formal procedures but in the family resemblance each bears to the others. Following a first step taken in this direction by Cavell, let us call these problematizations the aesthetic problems of philosophy. Following a second step proposed by J. M. Bernstein, let us treat these aesthetic problems of philosophy as the aesthetic problems of modern society (Cavell 1976a; Bernstein 2003). In doing so, we find that what we are ultimately dealing with is philosophy's *and* modernity's suspicious and anxious relation *to* the aesthetic.

From the perspective of the latter, calling the problems of modern philosophy and modern society "aesthetic" problems typically provokes the suspicion that romantics are in the grip of some aesthetic ideology that cannot but misrepresent and thereby distort problems whose modernity is such that they cannot possibly be captured in aesthetic categories. This was precisely Hegel's point in his lectures on aesthetics: the problems of the modern world were sui generis, and certainly too complex to be grasped in aesthetic categories. Modern social life and modern political institutions simply exceeded the conceptual grasp of aesthetic categories, be they of modern or classical provenance.

Nonetheless, romantics, emboldened by Kant's compelling articulation of the aesthetic problems of philosophy in the third *Critique*, took them also to reveal the aesthetic problems of modern society, problems that had to be grasped in aesthetic categories, for there were no other categories in which they could be grasped. To grasp them in this way was also to see how the aesthetic has become an urgent but repressed problem for philosophy and modern society. This will sound rather unintelligible if, as Bernstein points out, aesthetics is understood as referring to some specialized inquiry into the nature of art, artworks, or beauty, or as having to do with a distinct form of sensuous perception. That there could be a set of problems common to philosophy and modern society, and that these problems signaled the repression (and distortion) of something called the "aesthetic," is an idea that could be intelligible and intellectually urgent only if the "aesthetic" is understood in a way that appears palpably counterintuitive to many—to whit, as belonging to, as having a stake in, the "necessary conditions for cognition, reason, meaning" (Bernstein 2003: 111). To think in this way about the aesthetic is to recognize, as Harold Bloom put it, that the dimensions of the aesthetic are "endless" (Hartman and Bloom 2006).

Once one recognizes this, there is much to be gained by seeking to understand "romanticism" as the self-conscious attempt to confront the aesthetic problems of philosophy and modern society *as* aesthetic problems. To do so successfully would mean, on the one hand, an enlargement of the significance of the aesthetic, confirming the problem-solving power of its semantic and conceptual resources, and, on the other, a new and hopefully more apt response to the problems faced by philosophy and modern society. This is not the place to state these problems, for there is not sufficient space to do them justice.[4] What I can do is take up a few of these problems over the course of what follows, not as part of a systematic treatment of them but to illustrate the romantic response to them.

Conviction Lost and Recovered (and Lost Again)

Already in the closing decades of the twentieth century, Adorno's reaction to Sibelius looked more reactionary than progressive. Composers of very different stylistic and political persuasions found in Sibelius a compelling model for their own compositional practice. In 1984, while lecturing at Darmstadt, the Temple of Delphi of musical modernism, iconoclastic composer Morton Feldman made use of the occasion to point out that distinguishing radicals from conservatives is not as straightforward as modernists typically believe. Sometimes it is the conservatives who are the real radicals, and the radicals who are the real conservatives. To underscore his point, Feldman hummed the theme from Sibelius's *Fifth Symphony* (Feldman 2006: 192). Four decades earlier, and just a decade after Adorno published his diatribe, Arnold Schoenberg, the veritable gold standard of Adorno's modernism, anticipated Feldman's point in the polemically titled essay "Brahms the Progressive" (1947).[5] The point being made here is not the obvious one that our judgments are fallible and liable to future disconfirmation but, rather, that beyond any such conventional fallibilism, there is also a need to reflect on and to acknowledge in our words and deeds the time-bound and time-imprinted nature of our judgments. Through such an acknowledgment, we would be far less tempted to play the (highly seductive) role of the vanguard critic who believes that one's critical practice provides privileged access to "the most advanced consciousness" of one's time (Adorno 1998: 16). The very idea of "the most advanced consciousness" is incoherent, for it must presume epistemic authority over time itself: no on can be in a position to *know* in advance what has a future, what only a past, or to *know* what the next significant turn in human history will be.

Adorno's overconfident (mis)judgment is therefore one more reminder of how intractable is the problem of drawing *firm* distinctions between "modernism" and "romanticism," not least because these categories are mutually entangled and thoroughly permeated by history, a history that is far from over, rendering their meaning far from settled. The multiple, diverse, and contested ways in which these categories are applied evince their semantic elasticity and historical plasticity. No matter how carefully attuned we are to the historical conditions under which we think, judge, and act, the fact that such attunement is fleeting and partial means that all our judgments are inescapably time bound and time imprinted. This does not mean that we have to accept Paul de Man's stoic skepticism about the very possibility of historical knowledge, which skepticism must dogmatically presuppose not that history has come to an end, but that it never began. It does mean, however, that we have to temper our urge to speak in the voice of authority about that over which we cannot claim authority. "Our life is an apprenticeship to the truth that around this circle another can be drawn" (Emerson 1990a: 173). Those of us susceptible to the temptation to speak with authority about that over which we cannot claim authority might wish to heed the "truth" of Emerson's words. These words intend to outline a possible way of life—a way of life in which criticism is compatible with critical uncertainty, with the romantic consciousness of multiple and "infinite" perspectives. As we will see, that would mean changing the orientation of criticism, of theorizing in general.

Before Emerson, Friedrich Schlegel tried to state this romantic "truth" in the terms of his concept of irony; long after Emerson, Rorty tried to restate it in his own version of that concept. Incautiously applied, as though it were a theoretical *truth*, it can easily turn into dogmatic skepticism; alternatively, it can provide us with the opportunity to find another way to live our skepticism, which is what Emerson actually had in mind. The latter possibility depends on paying attention to the idea that this other way to live our skepticism really does involve *apprenticeship*. Apprenticing oneself to this "truth" is willingly to submit to one's possible transformation—to an endless learning process about how to lead such a life, how to articulate it in words and deeds that can be one's own without being authoritatively final. This will involve considerable struggle with and over one's self. It will also involve permanently having to regard oneself as a *beginner*, one who will always have to begin anew, finding new ways to understand and to bear the demands of leading such a life, demands that will necessarily take on new forms each time the circle is redrawn.

The "truth that around this circle another can be drawn" does not entail having to remain silent when we feel called upon to speak in affirmation or in opposition. The possibility that our words will be redescribed and recontextualized in unforeseeable ways, making us look pretty bad in the eyes of the future, is not meant to silence us; rather, it is meant to attune us to how time imprints itself on our words and our deeds. Remaining silent does not alter or mitigate these circumstances, for if what we say is bound to, imprinted by, time, so is our silence. There is no compelling reason why we cannot speak and judge with conviction about the historical circumstances in which we find ourselves, about the things, the objects, with which we surround ourselves and with which we must daily contend. Conviction, as Bernard Williams pointed out, does not require certainty, only confidence (1985: 169–73). Besides, the form of life that we call modernity cannot be lived without engaging in time-diagnostic analysis and criticism. Engaging in these activities is to engage in the project of unsettling our convictions and finding ways to restore our capacity *for* conviction, even when we speak with the "intrepid conviction that [our] laws, [our] relations to society... [our] world, may at any time be superseded and deceased" (Emerson 1990a: 177). We speak, then, as *respondents* and as *initiators*, speaking "second" even when we speak "first," hoping that our speech can inspire or initiate something potentially new, not close a circle around which no other can possibly be drawn. Our apprenticeship to this "truth" is an acknowledgment to others, and to ourselves, that we are leaving open a place, some space of possibility, where someone or something can speak as if for the first time, and we are ready to listen with ears we did not know we had. "There is no virtue that is final; all are initial" (Emerson 1990a: 181).

This transformation and recovery of conviction and its instancing in literary and philosophical modes of expression can thus be seen as one of romanticism's bequests, and one of its standing requests. Is such conviction possible? Well, is it not precisely this possibility that Emerson is trying to capture by the term "apprenticeship"? What would our critical judgments look like, how would they function in the language games of theory and criticism, and how would they change these language games, were our convictions expressed with the awareness that they may be superseded tomorrow, or the day after tomorrow? Would this not make us more attentive, and more responsive, to the *objects* of our judgments? Would we not give these objects more opportunity to talk back, and would that not make us better listeners, and possible initiators of a different practice of listening? And would not all this make us a different, a new kind, of we?

These questions are the central concern of Wordsworth's preface to the *Lyrical Ballads* (1800). Carefully, and with an almost excessive vigilance, he elaborates answers to these questions that revolve around the observation, as much an expression of hope as an observation, that everyday language, the "language really used by men," is the language on which the poet must draw, the language on which she must model her own writing (Wordsworth 1990a: 597). Wordsworth's justification for such an unprecedented break with poetic practice follows from one further observation: it is *in* everyday language that human beings "hourly communicate with the best objects from which the best part of language is originally derived (597).

With this observation, we find Wordsworth circling about an animistic or Adamic view of language, a view of language as arising from a deep intimacy and communion between words and things. It is precisely such a view of language that Walter Benjamin is channeling in his essay "On Language as Such and the Language of Man" (1916). For Benjamin, it belongs to the very "linguistic being of human being to name things" (2004a: 64). In naming things, we are responding to their need for voice, translating "the language of things into that of human beings" (70). When we give things their name, we animate them by acting as their respondents. In responding to things in this way, we do not only bring things into communication with us; we communicate *ourselves* by naming them (64).[6]

Of course, all this supposes, as Wordsworth and Benjamin do, that things communicate with us, and we with them: "[I]f the lamp and the mountain and the fox did not communicate themselves to the human being, how should she be able to name them?" (Benjamin 2004a: 64). To "communicate with the best objects from which the best part of language is originally derived" is to respond to those objects attentively, receptively, which means to "look steadily" upon them (Wordsworth 1990a: 600), abandoning oneself to them in order to bring them to life in words, in just those words, and only those words, which give them life. If a communicative relation between human beings and the things that concern them does indeed obtain or can obtain, then the relation between the "best objects" and the "best part of language" cannot be arbitrary, not if the name that we give to things is what brings them into communicative relation with us. This would then explain why Wordsworth and Benjamin hold the view that it is through the communicative exchange with things that the best part of language is preserved in, and as, semantically rich experience. Absent such communication, the very capacity for experience is threatened, leaving us less capable of seeing things in a new way, less capable of expressive response to things, less capable of seeing their significance for us.

The anxiety that comes to the surface repeatedly in Wordsworth's preface arises from the felt proximity of that threat. All those many times that Wordsworth states that he must bring his poetic language "near to the language of men," that he must "imitate…and adopt the very language of men," he is not just drawing attention to how different is his conception of poetic language from his predecessors and peers. And while we could rightly regard the urgency of Wordsworth's wish to reattune poetic language with everyday language as a proto-Wittgensteinian call to "bring words back from their metaphysical to their everyday use" (Wittgenstein 1958: §116, 48e), we would still be missing something of the anxiety that underlies this call. Without doubt, a part of Wordsworth's anxiety arises from a sense of alienation from the everyday, from the fear that prolonged disconnection from the semantic sources of everyday language impoverishes his own—poetry's own— powers of expression. But felt even more intensely is the fear that prolonged disconnection from the everyday would render its language opaque to him, as though it had become an untranslatable foreign tongue, from whose semantic energies he (and we) would be forever cut off.

Yet another part of this general anxiety arises from Wordsworth's worries about the current *state* of everyday language. Like twentieth-century romantics such as Heidegger, Wittgenstein, and Cavell, Wordsworth understood his own task as a writer as requiring him to bring about a recovery of the everyday by regaining contact with the semantic sources of everyday language and life. Once a writer makes this task her own, she becomes vulnerable to the worry that the semantic sources upon which this recovery depends will become depleted before it can even take place. That worry is fueled, of course, by conditions of (capitalist) modernity that promote a flight from the everyday into the "extraordinary," and an experience of the "extraordinary" that is made possible by the narcotic stimulants of consumer culture. We could call this "the flattening of the extraordinary," and as Wordsworth foresaw, to dwell in it was to risk weakening "the discriminating powers of the mind," reducing it to "a state of almost savage torpor," from which state arises an ever more intense "craving for extraordinary incident" and "outrageous stimulation" (1990a: 599). Although Wordsworth tries to counter the leveling tendencies of the age with a sanguine expression of faith that "the time is approaching when the evil will be systematically opposed," his faith is betrayed by the unstated worry that the time that is approaching might very well be one in which the evil might be systematically braced and unquestioningly embraced rather than systematically opposed. A time might be approaching when the objects with which we daily communicate will not be the best of objects, and therefore the best part of language will be daily impoverished, as will our daily contact with it. A century later, Rainer Maria Rilke noted that this time had arrived:

> …More than ever
> the things that we might experience are vanishing, for
> what drives them out and replaces them is an imageless act.
> An act under a shell, which easily cracks open as soon as
> The business inside outgrows it and seeks new limits.
> (1995: 385, translation amended)

It is surely one of the demands of romanticism that we resist this standing threat to our capacity for semantically rich experience. But how are we to resist? How do we *now* communicate with "the best objects from which the best part of language is originally derived" when those objects, those things we might "experience," might be vanishing? How does the romantic writer do so when she is that kind of writer who must let herself be affected by her time, to let her time imprint herself on her words and deeds? How does such a writer keep from being torn apart by the divided and divisive objects with which she must daily contend, and to which she must remain vulnerably open? How does one actually *live* the demands of romanticism and remain capable of expressive response?

THE REDEMPTION OF THINGS

For modernist critics of romanticism such as Jerome McGann, these romantic questions about everyday language and our relation to everyday things can no longer be our concern since, for him, we are well beyond treating the demands of romanticism as *our* demands. Although romanticism's scattered, stagnating remnants still constitute a part of our contemporary culture, they represent only a "body of illusions" through which we can clearly see when we occupy the right "*critical* vantage" (McGann 1983: 12). That romanticism is something we have definitely surpassed and overcome is a view McGann can assert in epistemologically overconfident terms because he understands the practice of criticism as an illusion-shattering enterprise, a confirmation of its power of unmasking. When grounded in the correct theory (in his case, Althusserian historical materialism), the work of the critic cannot be vulnerable to the illusions it is her task to unmask. The correct theory provides the critic with an epistemic firewall between herself and the ideological processes whose unmasking she undertakes. On principle, such a theory cannot allow "critical uncertainty," for it understands the practice of critique as oriented to truth, to seeing our circumstances correctly, as though there can be only *one* right perspective from which they can be seen correctly.

Romantic criticism, by contrast, aims at *reflectively* disclosing alternative possibilities for going on with our practices differently, at enlarging the space of freedom in which to exercise our agency. Critical uncertainty is a condition of seeing things differently, of going on with our practices in a new way. The very idea of getting our circumstances right, of criticism that tells it like it really is, is an idea that must presuppose that our preferred final vocabulary is *the* final unsurpassable vocabulary of description. Were we ever to have serious doubts about that vocabulary, we would be left without "non-circular argumentative recourse" (Rorty 1989: 73). This is the fatal weakness of ideology critique, a consequence of an overconfident, unreflective trust in its own epistemic superiority.

McGann is not as attuned as he should be to the way in which ideology critique can turn on itself, thereby undermining its own epistemological and historical foundations[7]—and such critique as McGann practices is foundationalist at its core. Ideology critique that does not directly confront this skeptical possibility is also less attuned to alternative ways to live our skepticism. The foundationalist posture it unreflectively assumes cannot but invite the most corrosive forms of skepticism. A critical practice for which conviction requires certainty is a critical practice generally unprepared to recover convictions that have become unsettled, undermined, by the unexpected crises and new challenges to which any practice is subject. Romantics have an awful lot to say about the matter of recovering one's convictions when they have become unsettled or undermined—if we are willing to listen. However, to listen we would have to recognize that we are not beyond the demands of romanticism and have to hope that "the demands of romanticism are not beyond us" (Cavell 1989: 114).

One of those demands is to find a new stance toward the objects of our knowledge, and the things that surround us. Unmasking brands of criticism presuppose an ontology of disengagement,[8] an ontology that places the critic safely outside the object of criticism, unstained and untainted by its ideological effects. The object stands at his disposal, makes itself available to his unmasking purposes. Resistance is useless; talking back is pointless. Under the withering interrogatory gaze of the critic, the object cannot but betray itself, delivering its previously hidden untruth to its remorseless and confident interrogator.[9] This practice of "ruthless critique" (Wang 1996: 15) has been uncritically practiced throughout the late twentieth century, having become the dominant paradigm of critique in the humanities. Perhaps, in light of the morally obscene images of really ruthless methods of interrogation that have become a commonplace in the early twenty-first century, we might now be ready to question ourselves a little more honestly about what we found so appealing about the practice of critique as "ruthless critique," and examine more conscientiously the ethicopolitical as well as epistemic implications of the stance it lets us assume toward the "objects" of our knowledge. We might now wish to be considerably more circumspect before we continue to engage in the practice of critique as though it were identical to the practice of "interrogation," reflecting back to us the violence and violation inherent in "ruthless critique." Unmasking critique must treat all its objects as suspects, including, eventually, its own critical practice. Thus, it cannot but undermine itself, and the very possibility of trust and conviction, without which no human practice is sustainable. As Nietzsche himself realized, it is a very reckless and destructive practice (1974: 35).

So, what might the practices of contemporary theory and criticism look like if they were reconfigured in a different relation to their objects of knowledge, allowing them to talk back, talking us into becoming new kinds of listeners? What would change—in the critic, in the object—if we critics were to exchange the interrogatory stance for a stance of receptivity to the objects of our knowledge? What could objects say to us then? These very questions circulate throughout Jean-Luc Godard's *Two or Three Things I Know about Her* (1967), gathering themselves together at the point in the film when its omnipresent narrator poses the question—"What is an object?" Groping tentatively toward some indeterminate illumination, the narrator proposes the following suggestive answer. "Perhaps it is a link enabling us to pass from one subject to another, therefore to live together." What could be more romantic than to think that objects, *things*, could play this role in *our* lives? It is certainly equally romantic to let this somewhat tantalizing if obscure thought to be immediately engulfed with uncertainty and doubt. One therefore expects it all to end on a note of resignation or despair. Where else could it end once the narrator remarks upon the ambiguity inherent in social relations, the power of thought to divide as much as to unite, and the power of words to do likewise, and then adds to all of this the tendency to reproach ourselves even when we feel blameless, the overpowering force of our objective circumstances, and the inadequacy of our powers of agency to respond to them? Yet, this voice does not invite resignation or despair; rather, it urges a reactivation and intensification of one's capacity for receptivity and connection: " I must listen. I must look around more than ever. / The world—my kin, my twin." Godard's invocation and resignification of the last line from the first poem of Charles Baudelaire's *Les Fleur du Mal* ("—Hypocrite lecteur,—mon semblable,—mon frère") register not only the intimate complicity between poet and reader, or filmmaker and viewer, but also the intimate complicity between one's own condition and the condition of the world. Godard's words thus also resonate with the words from Emerson's "Fate," written just a few years after *Les Fleurs*: "[I]n the history of the individual is always an account of his condition, and he knows himself to be party to his present estate" (Emerson 1990b: 349–50). To acknowledge that one is indeed party to one's "present estate" is implicitly to remove the basis for resenting the world, a resentment that, if Nietzsche is right, is the necessary precondition for a most undesirable kind of "romanticism." Giving an account of one's own contribution to one's "present estate" gives one the chance of a second birth, a new beginning. It gives one the chance to overcome the kind of "romanticism" whose expressive response to the world seeks to revenge itself upon the world, to brand it with the image of one's own suffering (Nietzsche 1974: 330). By contrast, to acknowledge the world as one's "kin" and "twin" is to see that a change in one's own condition is coextensive with a change in the condition of the world—this world made anew. For such a new world to arise as a world that we can realize, it must first be prefigured in "every-day appearances," attentively perceived and made visible:

> Not in Utopia…
> Or some secreted island, Heaven knows where!
> But in the very world, which is the world
> Of all of us,—the place where, in the end,
> We find our happiness, or not at all!
> (Wordsworth, 1850, 11: 140–44)

The movement of reflection from our relation to objects to our relation to the world has been an enduring feature of philosophical and literary practice. What is distinctively romantic is to think of our communication with objects, and their communication with us, as an activity that illuminates the conditions of our existence, conditions whose satisfaction includes meeting the condition that there *be* things that have this kind of thingness. It is as though our intelligibility to ourselves depends upon the presence, or presencing, of things—which is just what Benjamin means when he claims that by naming things we communicate ourselves. Kant thought he had shown definitely that for a world of objects to exist as objects for us, objects had to satisfy the epistemic conditions of human knowledge. But his romantic successors turn the tables on Kant by showing that for objects to be accessible to us we must first become accessible to them; failing that, we suffer from permanent self-inaccessibility. With Cavell, we could say, more dramatically yet, that the problem of how to communicate with objects has become a matter of life and death—the life and death of the world.

Has the question of the possibility of objects ever been posed in a more startling and luminescent way than it is posed in Godard's *Two or Three Things I Know about Her*? Consider the remarkable scene in the café during which the narrator of *Two or Three Things* first poses the question of what an object is. In this scene, it is the objects that are doing the real talking, and it is their perspective we are asked to occupy. That perspective allows us to see not only these things that have become inaccessible to the people in whose presence they are invisibly present, but also how inaccessible, how unintelligible, these people are to themselves. So we witness their concomitant inexpressiveness as it is contrasted with the rich expressiveness of the objects surrounding them. No character in the film conveys the depth and mystery of that uncanny cup of coffee, its black liquid now swirling, now still, framing the world of possibility it opens up. No character receives that intensity of attention, either. Why do objects receive and, more important, why do they respond to, intensely attentive concern? The narrator states: "Objects exist, and if one pays more attention to them than to people, it is precisely because they exist more than these people. Dead objects are still alive. Living people are often already dead."

To romantics, it is not enough to insist on establishing more comprehensively and more globally, a noninstrumental relation to persons (as ends in themselves); we must also establish a noninstrumental relation to the things of the world. Such a noninstrumental relation to things is not only consistent with a nondominating relation to nature; it is also consistent with the quixotic romantic commitment to the redemption of things in general. Part of what underlies this commitment is the need to make sense of our relation to such things as artworks, heirlooms, photographs, and a whole range of significant things, things we treat "in ways normally reserved for treating persons" (Cavell 1976b: 189). Cavell suggests that this tendency might have something to do with the self-conscious persistence of animism in romanticism—that is, the idea that there is a life of things, and it is the romantic writer's obligation to *say* things, to let them speak through us (Cavell 1988: 53):

> Perhaps we are *here* in order to say: house, bridge, fountain gate, pitcher,
> fruit-tree, window—at most: column, tower.... But to *say* them, you must
> understand, oh to say them in ways *more* meaningful than the things themselves

ever could say....And these things that live, fleetingly, understand that you
praise them; transient themselves, they trust us for rescue, us, the most
transient of all. (Rilke 1995: 387, translation amended)

Rilke's animistic image of things as dependent on us for their redemption turns
on an image of romanticism as a practice of redemptive reanimation, thus
satisfying the condition that there be things. This might explain why it is that
romantics—Godard as much as Wordsworth—attend so carefully to things present (and absent) to them, as though, as Cavell puts it, they "prefer things to people" (1988: 66). In giving things a hearing, something they rarely receive outside
literature and art, perhaps we allow them, at the very least, to remind us of our
common fate.[10] Cavell shares with Heidegger and other romantics the thought
that to acknowledge that things are in need of redemption is to acknowledge that
their redemption would mean ours, as well. This acknowledgment of our common fate—that their conditions of intelligibility and possibility are intertwined
with our own—might let us see that romanticism is not a body of illusions to be
deposited in the garbage bins of history but an urgent reformulation of the task of
philosophy and literature.

The redemption of the things of the world is the redemption of human
nature, and chiefly from the destructiveness of its own conditions of existence.
Is this a philosophy of romanticism? If romanticism believes, and is right in its
belief, that things need redemption from the way human beings have come to
think, and that this redemption can happen only poetically, then, according to
Heidegger's essay What Is a Thing?," romanticism would be right in believing
that it is thereby a redemption of human nature from the grip of itself" (Cavell
1988: 55).

For Heidegger, the redemption of things depends on a shift from "representational" thinking [vorstellendes Denken] to a form of thinking that "responds and
recalls" [Andenken]. Such a shift is not like an ordinary shift of perspective, or
change of theoretical paradigm. Certainly, we cannot simply will such a shift, as
though it were a matter of choice and self-control. Any transformative intellectual
or cultural process that is not at our disposal, not controllable by us, and therefore
not something for which we can be held accountable in appropriate ways, is typically regarded as suspiciously mysterious or esoteric, and so unworthy of our trust.
However, the shift from vorstellendes Denken to Andenken is no more esoteric and
mysterious than is the type of learning regarded by Emerson as a form of apprenticeship. It is a type of learning that by its very nature cannot, and therefore does
not, aim at mastery. It belongs to those transformative processes through which we
change our language and our life, our whole sensibility, and that change reposes
upon a change in our relationships to one another and to the objects of our knowledge. Indeed, it is just the kind of learning on which art and literature are based,
the kind that they facilitate and demand. Andenken, the thinking that responds
and recalls, abandons itself to the receptive reflection out of which art and literature arise, and into which they invite us. It is the kind of thinking that brings

romanticism into being, bringing into being the kind of writing that responds and recalls—romantic writing. *Andenken* could be Heidegger's name for romanticism; in giving it this name, he would also pay his debt to it.

Medium Dependence, Receptivity, and Reflection

Wordsworth's reflections on language in the preface to the *Lyrical Ballads*, and in particular on the priority of everyday to poetic language, indirectly convey romanticism's discovery that all our attempts to make sense of the things that matter to us, and thus to *express* their mattering, are radically medium dependent.[11] The meaning of what we are seeking to express can only be expressed in a corresponding medium, from which it is inseparable. "Expressive meaning cannot be fully separated from the medium, because it is only manifest in it" (Taylor 1985: 221).

Romanticism's "expressivist" or "constitutive" view of language, as Charles Taylor has called it, departs completely from the typical Enlightenment view of language that one finds in Hobbes and Locke, and a century later in Étienne Condillac. For the latter, language's primary function is representational and our primary relation to it is instrumental: language is something to be mastered in order correctly to represent states of affairs. If we do not master it, it can master us, thus becoming an instrument of deception, distorting the way things are. Of course, this attitude is in part a function of the atomistic assumptions about language on which this view rests. For romantics, however, to think of language as something to be mastered, as subject to our control, is simply to misunderstand it. In sharp contrast to these instrumental-atomistic conceptions, romantic conceptions of language from J. G. Herder and Wilhelm Humboldt to Heidegger and later Wittgenstein understand language as a holistically structured web of meanings and relationships, only partly, never fully, surveyable. Before we even get to the point of using language as a tool or instrument, language has already disclosed the relationships of meaning, set the conditions of intelligibility, from which the very diverse things we do with words get their sense and purpose.

To concede that we are dependent on language means relinquishing the human claim to autonomy, construed in terms of mastery and self-mastery. Of course, autonomy and self-mastery are not necessarily synonymous. But it has not been easy to think of autonomy without thinking of it in terms of self-mastery. Romantics were the first to explore ideas of freedom and autonomy that were compatible with dependence, which, of course, requires thinking of dependence in new and different ways. For instance, there are some relations of dependence that are inescapable, that are constitutive of human forms of life. One of these relations of dependence is to media of expression that allow us make sense of things, and to express their significance for us. This leads to the realization that not all relations of dependence involve relations of domination (of mastery and slavery). Although our sensemaking possibilities are radically medium dependent, our dependence on a medium is not that of passive, agentless dependence. The medium on which our expressive responses depends does allow us to reshape it. "Reshaping it without dominating it, or being able to oversee it, means that we never fully know what we are doing to it; we develop language without knowing fully what we are making it into" (Taylor 1985: 232).[12]

We could look at this romantic theory of language as a response to romantic worries about the semantically depleted state of language, and then we could see that there are better and worse ways to reshape our inherited language. Although "we never fully know what we are doing to it" or fully know "what we are making it into," we can attune ourselves to the language that we speak, and that speaks us. Such attunement is not to something that has a preexisting and static order, attunement to which requires a passive, mindless surrender of our agency and sub-jectivity. As an *ergon* and *energeia*, language is dynamic and historical, a holisti-cally structured web, to be sure, but the structure is not rigid or unresponsive to those who inhabit it. Attunement means nothing other than *attentive* receptivity. "Language is the place of attention," wrote Maurice Blanchot (1993: 122).[13] Attend-ing to language from a receptive stance allows the thinking that responds and recalls to gently reshape language, listening and—one must say it—obeying, that is, responding to a normative demand that must be met, even if it appears inde-terminate. Notice how naturally one can read Blanchot's description of attention as an elaboration of a remark of Emerson's: "Our thinking is a pious reception" (1990c: 188–89):

> Attention is waiting: not the effort, the tension, or the mobilization of
> knowledge around something with which one might concern oneself. Attention
> waits. It waits without precipitation, leaving empty what is empty and keeping
> our haste, our impatient desire, and even more, our horror of emptiness from
> prematurely filling it in....Attention is the reception of what escapes attention,
> an opening upon the unexpected, a waiting that is the unawaited of all waiting.
> (Blanchot 1993: 121)

That Blanchot and Emerson, separated by more than a century, make receptivity primary is no coincidence. It is, rather, what binds them both to romanticism, for they both see that receptivity is normatively binding for literature and art, and for a certain kind of life, a life of freedom. But since modernism succeeded in making an aesthetic of production primary, and in making production the goal of free activity, the centrality of receptivity in romantic theory and practice has been both neglected and underestimated.[14] Contrary to the claim of Philippe Lacoue-Labarthe and Jean-Luc Nancy's *The Literary Absolute* (1978), romanti-cism is not about the production of something, call it literature, whose primary concern is with "*production*, absolutely speaking." Lacoue-Labarthe and Nancy have been misled by both Kant and Johann Gottlieb Fichte, but especially by

Fichte, and just like Kant and Fichte, their thinking remains captive to figures of mastery and control (even as they seek to escape from their hold). Romanticism must not be misconceived as the instancing of the "truth of production." Its "truth" does not concern "production" or "autoproduction" but receptivity, attentive receptivity.

Receptivity is prior to production, in every sense of prior. It is the condition of possibility of the unexpected, and the new. The unexpected, and the new are not something that can be "produced," since they are not subject to our intentions or our will. That is why at the end of "Circles" Emerson speaks of "abandonment," a self-abandonment. We must be capable of such self-abandonment if we are "to forget ourselves, to be surprised out of our propriety, to lose our sempiternal memory, and to do something without knowing how or why; in short, to draw a new circle" (1990a: 184). And that is why Blanchot also plays a variation on the theme of receptivity as self-abandonment when he writes: "[A]ttention has always already detached me from myself, freeing me for the attention that I for an instant become" (1993: 121). To free ourselves from ourselves through receptive attention to what lies outside us, to what is not us, is a romantic impulse, if there is one, and behind that impulse lies the hope that we can see through the self-centered forms of freedom that remain so powerfully appealing, see through them as forms of unfreedom. I think it was just such forms of unfreedom that Wordsworth was thinking of when he wrote: "Whose mind is but the mind of his own eye, he is a slave, the meanest we can meet!" (1990b: 269). If my eye is ever on myself (altering slightly another phrase of Wordsworth's from "Lines left upon a Seat in a Yew-tree"), I have become an obstacle to the realization of my freedom, which will mean, paradoxically, freedom from myself, for that is just what attentive receptivity demands of me.

Of course, this kind of attentive receptivity is continuous with a certain kind of reflection on oneself and the form of one's life. Similarly, attentive receptivity is continuous with the same kind of reflection when the focus of such reflection is art and literature. Reflection, as Benjamin's monumental essay "The Concept of Criticism in German Romanticism" (1920) first showed, became the key to early German romanticism's concept of art and its concept of criticism. What this involved is precisely a form of attention and of expressive response to transformative possibilities that emerge only through such reflection on the form of things. For Benjamin, early German romanticism did not just take over Fichte's concept of reflection; it greatly extended its application, making it possible to regard art as "a determination of the medium of reflection—probably the most fruitful one it has received" (2004b: 149).

The idea that art might be the most fruitful determination of the medium of reflection will strike some as puzzling, if not absurd, not just because it means treating art as a highly cognitive activity (which of course it is) but because the concept of reflection has traditionally carried connotations of cognitive transparency (which of course art does not). For this reason, but not for this reason alone, it is important to preserve the connection between receptivity and reflection, seeing the latter as a function of the former. Of course, there is also something polemical in Benjamin's assertion. And it just may be that the target of his polemic is Hegel's remark in his lectures on aesthetics that the "modern culture of reflection" has overtaken art, and in so doing has made art itself subject to its higher mode of reflection, as though art would otherwise remain a primitive residue of a superseded stage of reflection. However, if reflection is constitutive of art and, indeed, if it is a distinct form of reflection, then Hegel's attempt to assimilate romantic art to forms of reflection that are in the first instance external to art, was both mistaken and presumptuous—another ambitious but failed attempt at philosophical disenfranchisement.

By the time Schlegel had formulated his theory of art, making art "a medium of reflection and the work a center of reflection" (Benjamin 2004b: 155), it became clear—at least to the genius of Benjamin—that romantics had left behind the traditional concept of reflection, as it was understood from Descartes to Fichte and Hegel. Reflection did not have the status of a cognitive medium that could render its objects fully transparent; rather, reflection operated inside the hermeneutic circle of interpretation, belonging to an "infinite" process of interpretation—infinite not in the sense of "an infinity of advance but of an infinity of connections" (Benjamin 2004b: 126). Now this view of reflection also had consequences for the practice of criticism. Rather than relating to the work of art as an object of possible unmasking, as something to interrogate for its "untruth," the practice of romantic criticism, constrained as much as it is enabled by the hermeneutic circle, consisted not in "reflection *on* an entity," as though from some epistemically privileged position outside it, but in "the unfolding of reflection ... *in* an entity" (151). Criticism is continuous with the same form of reflection as that which is constitutive of art, and thus its task is understood as "a manifestation of the life of works" or an "intensification of the consciousness of the work" (152). To claim, as Benjamin does, that "for the romantics, criticism is far less the judgment of a work than the method of its consummation" (153) is to think both of criticism as radically internal and the internal standards of critique posited in the work of art as radically indeterminate. This calls for a very intimate kind of criticism, one that constitutes a relation of reciprocal interaction and reflection between criticism and art. This is not to say, as Schlegel is wrongly taken to say, that criticism and art are identical activities, but that they are continuous, reciprocally interacting and reciprocally affected activities. Thus, the rather exorbitant and bizarre claim from Schlegel's *Athenaeum Fragments* 1798) that poetry can be criticized only through poetry turns into something very different: "[P]oetic criticism will present the representation anew, will again form what is already formed.... It will complement, rejuvenate, newly fashion the work" (Benjamin 2004b: 154).

THE PROSE OF ROMANTICISM

Among the invaluable insights contained in Benjamin's essay on romanticism, not least is the insight into prose as the romantic "form of forms." Summarizing remarks of Novalis and Schlegel, Benjamin suggests "the idea of poetry as that of prose determines the whole of romantic philosophy of art," making it "so historically rich in consequences" (2004b: 175). It could be said, then, that prose gives romanticism its look and its outlook. As the form of forms prose not only frees poetry from strict rhythmic laws (and rulelike norms), giving it a new look, but also constitutes romanticism's prosaic outlook. Benjamin describes this prosaic outlook as the "antithesis of ecstasy, the mania of Plato" (175) and thereby represents a decisive break with Platonism (which still governs reflection on art today). It also places romanticism more explicitly and more directly in the service of the everyday.

With the ascendance of prose, it is the novel and not poesy that is the ideal romantic art form. If "art is defined as the medium of reflection of forms" (Benjamin 2004b: 165), then of all of its forms it is the novel that is the highest and most capacious medium of formal reflection. The novel can "reflect upon itself at will, and, in ever new considerations, can mirror back every given level of consciousness from a higher standpoint.... [B]ecause the novel never oversteps its form, every one of its reflections can be viewed as limited by itself, for there is no rule-bound form of presentation to limit them" (172).[15]

When later in the nineteenth century Baudelaire dreams of "the miracle of a poetic prose, musical without rhythm and without rhyme, supple and staccato enough to adapt to the lyrical stirrings of the soul, the undulations of dreams, and the sudden leaps of consciousness" (cited in Benjamin 2006: 98), he is unaware that the early romantics already dreamed this idea and made it the centerpiece of their reflections on artistic form. It is an idea historically rich in consequences not only in literature but also in music, as changes in musical form from Wagner to Schoenberg were themselves oriented by an ideal of "musical prose" (see Dahlhaus 1980; Rosen 1996). Schlegel's "[d]eliberate...cultivation...of the smallest detail" (Benjamin 2004b: 176) describes precisely the changes in form and in the normative expectations of formal development that took place in nineteenth- and late nineteenth-century music.

Benjamin and the romantics also anticipated Mikhail Bakhtin's theory of the novel and his concept of "novelness"—that is, a form that can integrate different orders of experience and different forms. In "Discourse in the Novel" Bakhtin reprises the romantic critique of the limitations of poetic rhythm, adding that a unitary poetic language or poetic style shuts out heteroglossia, the critical interanimation and contamination of languages (1981: 296–98).

What we can add to all this is that the critical interanimation and contamination of languages takes place—must take place—at the level of everyday life and language. The prose of romanticism is nothing other than the prose of the world—the everyday world from which we draw meaning and intelligibility, to which we, if we can meet the demands of romanticism, must return with more of the same and something different, too.

NOTES

....

I'm indebted to Richard Eldridge for his patience, generosity, helpful suggestions, and much more.

1. I owe my knowledge of Feldman's heterodox gesture to the illuminating chapter on Sibelius in Ross 2007: 157–77.

2. Rorty's significant contribution to changing our image of romanticism consists in these persistent and persuasive reminders that this is in fact what romanticism tried to teach us.

3. For an example of the conventional story about romanticism still *au courant* among some contemporary scholars, see Sturma 2000.

4. For a more comprehensive discussion of these problems, see Kompridis 2006a, Eldridge 2001, Cavell 1976a, and Bernstein 2003.

5. Schoenberg's reaction to the modernists of his time made the same point in relation to Brahms: "Pioneers of musical progress on the one hand, and keepers of the Holy Grail of true art on the other, they considered themselves entitled to look with contempt at Brahms the classicist, the academician." Through detailed analysis, Schoenberg demonstrates that Brahms, "the classicist, the academician, was a great innovator in the realm of musical language, that, in fact, he was a great progressive" (1984: 401). How many others might this also be true of? What have we failed to see or hear with our "modernist" eyes and ears?

6. "And she names them; *she* communicates herself by naming *them*" (Benjamin 2004a: 64).

7. I am thinking, of course, of Nietzsche, Adorno, and Foucault, among many notable others.

8. The term "ontology of disengagement" is from Taylor 1995.

9. For further discussion of the model of critique, see Kompridis 2000.

10. "The nature of the thing never comes to light, that is, it never gets a hearing" (Heidegger 1971: 170). Compare Descartes's treatment of the piece of wax in the Second Meditation.

11. Here I am disagreeing with Bernstein's otherwise valuable insights into the medium dependence of works of art in Bernstein (2006). The fact of medium dependence is true not just of *artistic* media but of all media—including everyday language, so while it is true that "artistic sense-making is making sense in a medium" (Bernstein 2006: 144), this is just a specific case of the more general truth that *all* sensemaking is making sense in a medium.

12. Thinking of human language as *energeia* not just *ergon*, as Humboldt first suggested, allows us to see that language is a "pattern of activity by which we express/realize a certain way of being in the world, that of reflective awareness, but a pattern which can only be deployed against a background which we can never fully dominate; and yet a background that we are never fully dominated by, because we are constantly reshaping it" (Taylor 1985: 232).

13. Blanchot's "Language is the place of attention" is of course a variation on Heidegger's "Language is the house of being."

14. For various reasons, receptivity does not have a good name. For two complementary views of its significance, see Cavell 1989: 104–88 and Kompridis 2006b: 199–222.

15. Once again, I register disagreement with Bernstein's critique of Jena romanticism. I think Bernstein's critique would have had to take a different direction had he taken into account the fact that it is prose, not "poesy" (with its concomitant commitment to the arbitrariness of the linguistic sign), that is the ideal of romantic art. And as Benjamin points out, this is because the novel is the form of romantic forms because of its capacity to explore and to integrate multiple levels of reflection on form *in* form.

REFERENCES

Adorno, T. W. (1982). "Glosse über Sibelius." *In* Adorno, *Musikalische Schriften IV, Moments Musicaux. Impromptus.* Frankfurt: Suhrkamp.

——. (1998). *Critical Models* (H. Pickford, trans.). New York: Columbia University Press.

Bakhtin, M. M. (1981). *The Dialogic Imagination* (M. Holquist, ed.; C. Emerson and M. Holquist, trans.). Austin: University of Texas Press.

Benjamin, W. (2004a). "On Language as Such and the Language of Man." *In* M. Bullock and M. W. Jennings (eds.), *Walter Benjamin: Selected Writings*, Vol. 1, *1913–1926*. Cambridge, Mass.: Harvard University Press. (Original written 1916, unpublished in Benjamin's lifetime.)

——. (2004b). "The Concept of Criticism in German Romanticism." *In* M. Bullock and M. W. Jennings (eds.), *Walter Benjamin: Selected Writings*, Vol. 1, *1913–1926*. Cambridge, Mass.: Harvard University Press. (Original work published 1920).

——. (2006). *The Writer of Modern Life: Essays on Charles Baudelaire.* Cambridge, Mass.: Harvard University Press.

Bernstein, J. M. (2003). "Aesthetics, Modernism, Literature: Cavell's Transformations of Philosophy." *In* R. Eldridge (ed.), *Stanley Cavell.* Cambridge: Cambridge University Press.

——. (2006). "Poesy and the Arbitrariness of the Sign: Notes for a Critique of Jena Romanticism." *In* N. Kompridis (ed.), *Philosophical Romanticism.* London: Routledge.

Blanchot, M. (1993). *The Infinite Conversation* (S. Hanson, trans.). Minneapolis: University of Minnesota Press. (Original work published in 1969.)

Cavell, S. (1976a). "Aesthetic Problems of Modern Philosophy." *In* Cavell, *Must We Mean What We Say?* Cambridge: Cambridge University Press.

——. (1976b). "Music Discomposed." *In* Cavell, *Must We Mean What We Say?* Cambridge: Cambridge University Press.

——. (1988). *In Quest of the Ordinary.* Chicago: University of Chicago Press.

——. (1989). *This New Yet Unapproachable America.* Albuquerque: Living Batch Press.

Dahlhaus, C. (1980). *Between Romanticism and Modernism*. Berkeley: University of California Press.

Eldridge, R. (2001). *The Persistence of Romanticism*. Cambridge: Cambridge University Press.

Emerson, R. W. (1990a). "Circles." *In* Emerson, *Essays: First and Second Series*. New York: Vintage. (Original work published in 1841.)

——. (1990b). "Fate." *In* R. Poirier (ed.), *Ralph Waldo Emerson*. Oxford: Oxford University Press. (Original work published in 1860.)

——. (1990c). "Intellect." *In* Emerson, *Essays: First and Second Series*. New York: Vintage. (Original work published in 1841.)

Feldman, M. (2006). *Morton Feldman Says: Selected Interviews and Lectures, 1964–1987* (C. Villars, ed.). London: Hyphen.

Hartman, G., and H. Bloom. (2006). "Two Interviews." *Romantic Circles Praxis Series*. July 2006. http://romantic.arhu.umd.edu/praxis/bloom_hartman/.

Heidegger, M. (1971). "What Is a Thing?" *In* Heidegger, *Poetry, Language Thought* (A. Hofstadter, trans.). New York: Harper and Row.

Kompridis, N. (2000). "Reorienting Critique: From Ironist Theory to Transformative Practice." *Philosophy and Social Criticism* 26(4), 23–46.

——. (2006a). "Reinheriting Romanticism." *In* Kompridis (ed.), *Philosophical Romanticism*. London: Routledge.

——. (2006b). "Receptivity, Not Passivity." *In* Kompridis, *Critique and Disclosure: Critical Theory between Past and Future*. Cambridge, Mass.: MIT Press.

McGann, J. (1983). *The Romantic Ideology: A Critical Investigation*. Chicago: University of Chicago Press.

Nietzsche, F. (1974). *The Gay Science* (W. Kaufmann, trans.). New York: Vintage. (Original work published in 1882.)

Rilke, R. M. (1995). "9th Duino Elegy." *In* S. Mitchell (ed. and trans.), *Ahead of All Parting: The Selected Poetry And Prose of Rainer Maria Rilke*. New York: Modern Library.

Rorty, R. (1989). *Contingency, Irony, Solidarity*. Cambridge: Cambridge University Press.

Rosen, C. (1996). *Schoenberg*. Chicago: University of Chicago Press.

Ross, A. (2007). *The Rest Is Noise*. New York: Farrar, Straus, Giroux.

Schoenberg, A. (1984). "Brahms the Progressive." *In* L. Stein (ed.), *Style and Idea: Selected Writings of Arnold Schoenberg* (L. Black, trans.). London: Faber and Faber. (Original work published in 1947.)

Sturma, D. (2000). "Politics and the New Mythology: The Turn to Late Romanticism." *In* Karl Ameriks (ed.), *The Cambridge Companion to German Idealism*. Cambridge: Cambridge University Press.

Taylor, C. (1985). "Language and Human Nature." *In* Taylor, *Philosophical Papers*. Cambridge: Cambridge University Press.

——. (1995). "Lichtung or Lebensform: Parallels between Wittgenstein and Heidegger." *In* Taylor, *Philosophical Arguments*. Cambridge, Mass.: Harvard University Press.

Wang, O. (1996). *Fantastic Modernity: Dialectical Readings in Romanticism and Theory*. Baltimore: Johns Hopkins University Press.

Williams, B. (1985). *Ethics and the Limits of Philosophy*. Cambridge, Mass.: Harvard University Press.

Wittgenstein, L. (1958). *Philosophical Investigations* (3rd ed.; G. E. M. Anscombe, trans.). New York: Macmillan. (Original work published in 1953.)

Wordsworth, W. (1990a). "Preface to the Second Edition of *Lyrical Ballads*." *In* S. Gill (ed.), *William Wordsworth—the Major Works*. Oxford: Oxford University Press. (Original work published in 1800, revised 1802.)

——. (1990b). "Personal Talk." *In* S. Gill (ed.), *William Wordsworth—the Major Works*. Oxford: Oxford University Press. (Original work published 1807.)

——. (1990c). *The Prelude Or, Growth of a Poet's Mind. In.* S. Gill (ed.), *William Wordsworth—the Major Works*. Oxford. Oxford University Press, 1990. (Original work published in 1850.)

CHAPTER 12

....

IDEALISM

....

TORIL MOI

A FORGOTTEN CONCEPT

Idealism is a venerable philosophical term. As a literary concept, however, it has all but disappeared. It is absent from major dictionaries of literary terms.[1] I have never seen it discussed as an aesthetic concept on a par with realism or modernism. At the beginning of the twenty-first century, we appear to have forgotten how important idealism was as a way of understanding art and literature; how strong its hold on nineteenth-century writers, artists, critics, and audiences was; and what a long, slow, and piecemeal task it was for a whole generation—the first generation of modernists—to work itself free of that hold.

In this essay, I use "idealism" as a synonym for "idealist aesthetics" or "aesthetic idealism," understood as an aesthetic norm based on the belief that the task of art (poetry, writing, literature, music) is to uplift us, to point the way to the ideal. Idealists thought that beauty, truth, and goodness were *one*. Artistic beauty therefore simply could not be immoral; to call a work ugly was to question its ethics as well as its aesthetics. Idealism thus seamlessly merged aesthetics and ethics, and usually religion, too, since most (but not all) idealists also believed that God was the highest incarnation of the trinity of beauty, goodness, and truth. Although it could coexist with certain kinds of realism, idealism—at least in Friedrich Schiller's version—required writers and artists to idealize women and sexuality. If they could not be idealized, they had to be demonized. The result was a long line of literary women who sacrifice their life for love, opposed to an equally long line of demonic temptress figures: the madonna/whore opposition is everywhere in idealist works.

By reintroducing the concept of idealism, we can make sense of the long period in literary and aesthetic history that stretches from the end of romanticism as a living artistic movement to the rise of modernism. Much of what is currently lumped together under the general heading of "Victorianism," for example, could be analyzed historically and theoretically as the many-faceted effect of the specifically British appropriation of idealist aesthetics.

The concept of idealism is perhaps even more illuminating when it comes to grasping the aesthetically confusing period from 1870 to 1914, which I see as a moment marked by a great number of different, highly self-conscious aesthetic attempts to *negate* idealism. In this respect, this period can be understood as what Thomas Kuhn would call a period of *crisis*, a transitional period in which one paradigm has broken down and another has not yet become dominant. Kuhn writes that new theories usually emerge "only after a pronounced failure in the normal problem-solving activity" (1996: 74–75). The failure of idealism, its incapacity to deal with modern life and modern problems, became increasingly obvious as the century wore on. For many European writers and intellectuals, the Franco-Prussian War of 1870–71 and the rise and fall of the Paris Commune in the spring of 1871 were events that confirmed the bankruptcy of idealism, filling them with an urgent need to forge something new out of the destruction of the old. The result was aesthetic crisis, and, ultimately, the birth of a new paradigm: modernism.

Idealism's star status in the history of philosophy makes its absence in literary criticism all the more striking. I don't mean to say that literary critics do not discuss idealism; my point is, rather, that when they do, they too have various aspects of philosophical or ethical (as opposed to aesthetic) idealism in mind. Insofar as idealist aesthetics is discussed at all in literary studies today, it is usually under the rubric of romanticism. But if we take idealism to be just another word for romanticism, we deprive ourselves of the resources we need to understand European art and literature after the demise of romanticism as an active artistic movement. We will also fail to understand why the advent of naturalism and modernism provoked the most intense culture wars in European literary history, and why the issues provoked by the death of idealism are relevant today.

This essay, then, is not really about philosophy. Nor is it primarily about literature. It is, rather, about idealism understood as a historically and culturally significant intersection of philosophy and literature, namely, as a set of ideas about art that profoundly affected both literature and the way people thought about literature in the nineteenth century. To write the story of idealism is to chart a glorious rise and an ignominious fall: when idealist aesthetics emerged from German idealist philosophy at the very end of the eighteenth century, it offered the world an ecstatic, revolutionary vision of art as the embodiment of human freedom. A century later, it had become a desiccated, reactionary moralism seeking to make art subservient to church and state.

In this essay, first, I bring idealism back from oblivion and show how important it was to nineteenth-century debates about art, literature, and culture; second, I show that when idealism is placed alongside realism and modernism, it changes the meaning of these terms—that once we realize what idealism was, we also have to rethink our understanding of realism and modernism. Then it becomes apparent that neither realism nor modernism is *one*: just as there are many kinds of realism, there are many kinds of modernism. Seen from this perspective, the widespread tendency to understand modernism as the negation of realism, will come to look too simplistic.[2] The emergence of modernism toward the end of the nineteenth century was a revolt not against realism, but against the principal tenets of idealist aesthetics. Last, I draw attention to the gender norms embedded in idealist aesthetics. To achieve a less sexist and a more modern representation of women and sexuality, writers and painters had to break with idealism. No nineteenth-century author did this in a more convincing fashion than Henrik Ibsen, a playwright whose great women characters still entrance theater audiences all over the world.

Before beginning this work, I need to stress that idealism was not *one*, either. Idealist aesthetics drew on different philosophical sources and was received and practiced differently in different national and religious cultures. It declined at a different pace in different countries. In one essay I cannot hope to do justice to the varieties of idealism that flourished throughout Europe in the nineteenth century. (I draw on material from Scandinavia, Germany, England, and France.) It seems to me that the first and most urgent task is to recover idealism as a literary and aesthetic concept. This essay serves its purpose if it encourages others to look more closely at different aspects of nineteenth-century literary and cultural history with idealism in mind.

Rediscovering Idealism

I owe my own discovery of idealism as a key aesthetic category in nineteenth-century art and literature to Naomi Schor's pioneering 1993 book *George Sand and Idealism*. In the introduction, Schor explains that she first realized the importance of idealism in 1985, when she found a dusty old book in a secondhand bookshop in Hay-on-Wye:

> I flipped to the table of contents to see if [George Sand] was included. It was then that I made an important, indeed a decisive discovery: she was included, but under what struck me as a strange and unfamiliar heading, *Le Roman idéaliste*.... I knew, of course, in a general sort of way—as anyone working on Sand would—that an important idealistic strain existed in Sand's fiction.... But this moldy and outdated study aid suddenly made palpable for me the force of that category and the extent of its disappearance. (1993: 4)

As I was working on my book on Ibsen, I came to realize how right Schor was: idealism was indeed a tremendously powerful aesthetic force in the nineteenth century, and it has disappeared more thoroughly than any other aesthetic category of that century. Refusing to connect Sand's idealism to German aesthetics, Schor focuses on the presence of idealist categories in nonphilosophical contexts, such as reviews, correspondence, and political debates. Following Schor's lead, I started looking for signs of the presence of idealism in the literary debates provoked by Ibsen's plays. The results were spectacular. Not only was idealism everywhere, but it was clear that Ibsen's plays had been important battlefields for the all-out struggle between idealists and anti-idealists. Most important, I also realized that Ibsen's plays explicitly and repeatedly dramatize the questions and assumptions at the heart of idealist aesthetics. (In this essay, Ibsen's works will remain important as examples of the cultural struggles over idealism.)

I think Schor was wrong to leave German philosophy out of her book, for the omission weakens her understanding of what idealist aesthetics was. We have to acknowledge that Kant, Friedrich Hölderlin, Schiller, Novalis, Friedrich Schlegel, Hegel, and others laid the foundations of nineteenth-century idealist aesthetics, and that in the first decades of the nineteenth century distinguished interpreters such as Madame de Staël and Samuel Taylor Coleridge contributed powerfully to spread German aesthetic idealism throughout Europe. But Schor was right to focus on "idealism in action," idealism as it was expressed in French nineteenth-century debates. Truly original and inspiring, this aspect of her pioneering work teaches us to look for idealist aesthetics in places we would not necessarily have connected with German philosophy. In this essay, I follow her lead on this point: I look at letters and newspaper reviews and revisit an institutional practice: the award of the Nobel Prize in Literature.

To put all this slightly differently: around 1800, German idealist aesthetics produced one of the most powerful and inspiring accounts of the nature and purpose of art and literature the world has ever seen. This is hardly news. What *is* news is that *some* version of this account, however debased, diluted, vulgarized, and simplified, shows up practically everywhere in nineteenth-century aesthetic discussions, not just in the 1810s and 1820s, but throughout the nineteenth and well into the twentieth century.

THE IDEALIST VIEW OF ART AND LITERATURE

Idealism is a complex word. It has as much to do with the *idea* as with the *ideal*. Indeed, Plato's ideas *are* ideals: the timeless pattern and archetype of any class of things, as opposed to the lowly imitations we are condemned to live with here on earth. For a long time, *idea* simply meant *ideal*. The Oxford English Dictionary quotes Thomas Browne in 1682: "How widely we have fallen from the pure Exemplar and Idea of our Nature." In everyday usage, we still speak of the idea of a thing in the sense of its general pattern or plan. We are bound, therefore, to concede that actual realizations may always fall short of the idea that spawned them, and thus we find ourselves treading a fine line between the idea and the ideal, and between the ideal and the real. Plato's contrast between the pure sphere of the Idea and the messy realities of ordinary life is only a few steps away.

In contemporary philosophy idealism is often taken to mean the opposite of materialism: idealism is to materialism as Hegel is to Marx. In the late nineteenth century, however, anti-idealism took many forms. Marxist materialism was only one of them. Equally important was the rise of "free thought," that is to say, of secularism, agnosticism, and atheism, on the one hand, and of various forms of scientific determinisms, on the other. August Strindberg's flirtations with Darwinism in a play like *The Father* are perfectly representative of the period.

Let me begin, then, with the German idealists. In 1796 Friedrich Hölderlin— or rather Hölderlin together with his two good friends Hegel and Friedrich Schelling—admirably encapsulated the key ideas of idealist aesthetics in a very short paper titled "Oldest Programme for a System of German Idealism" (1796).[3] Kant's distinction between *freedom* (the realm of reason, of the human will and imagination; the moral and creative world) and *necessity* (the realm of natural laws; the world of science) is as fundamental to Hölderlin as it is to all the other German idealist aesthetes. The world of necessity is the world of material objects, subjected to natural laws that are explained by science. The world of freedom is the world of consciousness, imagination, and the will, the world in which we make moral and aesthetic choices. It is against this conceptual background that Hölderlin goes on to discuss *beauty*, the key term of aesthetic idealism:

> Finally, the idea which unites everyone, the idea of *beauty*, the word taken in the higher, platonic sense. I am now convinced that the highest act of reason, by encompassing all ideas, is an aesthetic act, and that *truth and goodness* are only siblings in *beauty*. The philosopher must possess as much aesthetic power as the poet. Those people without an aesthetic sense are our philosophers of literalness [*Buchstabenphilosophen*]. The philosophy of spirit is an aesthetic philosophy. One can be spiritually brilliant in nothing, one cannot even think about history—without an aesthetic sense....
>
> Thus poetry gains a higher honour, it finally becomes what it was at its inception—*the teacher of humanity*; for there is no longer any philosophy, any history; the art of poetry alone will outlive all other sciences and arts. (Hölderlin 2002: 186)

Echoing Plato, aesthetic idealism considers the *beautiful*, the *true*, and the *good* to be one, but quite unlike Plato, idealism characteristically considers artistic beauty to be the highest expression of this trinity. Because beauty is both sensuous and spiritual—the idea made material through the use of the imagination—it overcomes the split between freedom and necessity and offers us an image of our own lost wholeness. Because truth without beauty remains arid and soulless, a great poet is also a great philosopher, and the greatest philosopher will never be great unless he is a poet, too. (The echoes of this creed reverberated all the way down to the French 1930s, when Jean-Paul Sartre and Simone de Beauvoir thought that literature was a greater and more noble pursuit than philosophy, and Sartre in particular still thought that he could be "saved" by literature.)

Fusing aesthetics with ethics and religion, the idealist program holds out to us all an optimistic, utopian vision of human perfection (see Hölderlin 2002; Schlegel 2003: 263). By advancing such a lofty image of the nature and purpose of poetry (and, to a slightly lesser extent, the other arts), German idealist aesthetics turned poets into prophets and mystics, and allowed artists of all kinds to claim that by pursuing beauty they were serving God. Throughout the nineteenth century, writers would draw on such ideas to defend art in general and theater in particular against the accusation of godlessness.

We have seen that Hölderlin connects ideas (and ideals) to freedom. Freedom is the great theme of Schiller's aesthetics, not least in his masterly little treatise *On Naive and Sentimental Poetry* first published in installments in 1795 and 1796. The ideas contained in this brilliant text circulated in one form or another throughout European aesthetic discussions for the next hundred years. I use it here first to convey both what aesthetic idealism was in its full, romantic, radical, utopian glory and then to draw attention to its inner and ultimately destructive fault lines, which enabled Schiller's glorious vision of aesthetic freedom to be turned into a set of moralistic and deeply reactionary aesthetic norms.

The key idea in Schiller's aesthetics is a utopian vision of human perfectibility. Humankind can become better, freer, more beautiful, more fulfilled. The task of art is to ennoble us, to help us overcome the split between nature and freedom, so that the whole of human nature can find full and free expression. Schiller's "Ideal"—the vision that poetry and art is supposed to convey to us—is an ample and generous one, a picture of a fully harmonious human being, fully free and fully at home in the world.

Long after the death of revolutionary, romantic idealism, this ideal had a strong afterlife in the Marxist tradition. Around 1900, the young Leon Trotsky declared: "As long as I breathe, I shall fight for the future, that radiant future in which man, strong and beautiful, will become master of the drifting stream of his history and will direct it towards the boundless horizon of beauty, joy and happiness" (Deutscher 1954: 54). As late as in the mid-twentieth century, the great Marxist literary critic György Lukács still believed in the advent of the fully "harmonious human being," although he thought that such a perfected creature could only come into being under communism.[4]

Schiller's fundamental starting point is nature. Poets must always be the guardians of nature, he writes, for when we lose touch with nature, "moral and aesthetic degeneracy" follows (1993: 196). Poets, therefore, "will either *be* nature or *seek* the lost nature" (196). From this claim he derives his famous distinction between naive and sentimental poets: the naive poet *is* nature; the sentimental poet *seeks* nature. By nature, Schiller means above all human nature, which he sees as a unique combination of spirit and matter or, in other words, of freedom and necessity, infinity and finitude. The task of all poetry is to "give humanity its most complete possible expression," Schiller writes (201). Poetry is to uplift and ennoble us, to give us concrete visions of a better world with better human beings in it. This is the heart of Schiller's idealist aesthetics.

By mapping the opposition between the naive and the sentimental onto the opposition between the ancient and the moderns, Schiller develops an aesthetic theory balancing finely on the line between neoclassicism and romanticism. Ancient poets, Schiller writes, were at once natural and naive, characterized by an innocence of heart that entirely escapes their modern colleagues. Their task, therefore, was to describe the world as they saw it, as fully and as well as possible. For the naive poet still living in the "original condition of natural simplicity...the most complete possible *imitation of the actual is what necessarily makes someone a poet*" (1993: 201, emphasis original). Naive poets are specialists in realism, in other words.[5]

In the modern world, on the other hand, "nature has disappeared from our humanity, and we reencounter it in its genuineness only outside humanity in the inanimate world," Schiller writes (1993: 194). This gives us a yearning for truth and simplicity unknown to the ancients who had never lost nature in the first place: "They felt naturally, while we feel the natural" (195). Because the modern poet has lost touch with nature, he (all of Schiller's examples are male) cannot convey nature itself, but only the *idea* of nature. "The ancient poets touch us through nature, through sensuous truth, through living presence; the modern poets touch us through ideas" (201). Since modern human beings are no longer at one with themselves, the mere description of reality is no longer poetic: "Here in the condition of culture...the elevation of actuality to the ideal, or, what comes to the same, *the portrayal of the ideal is what necessarily makes the poet*" (201). Schiller's poetic idealism thus emerges out of his historicizing analysis of modern culture.

Because ideas are infinite and nature is finite (the Kantian foundations of Schiller's thought are everywhere apparent), the sentimental poet will always have to face the conflict between the limitations of the actual world and the unlimited soaring of which the imagination is capable. For the modern writer, then, poetry arises when the poet attempts to transcend the limits of the actual world; for the ancient writer, it was enough simply to describe that world.

That these categories were influential in nineteenth-century Europe is beyond doubt. Most important, however, is that they defined art as such. In the late 1860s, the leading Danish critic Clemens Petersen (1865) insisted that Ibsen's *Brand* and *Peer Gynt* were not poetry because they failed to convey "a complete, definite, clear and assured representation of the ideal." The demise of idealism required a completely new understanding of the purpose and meaning of art.

IDEAL FREEDOM AND VULGAR PASSIONS: WOMEN, SEXUALITY, AND SELF-SACRIFICE

Against the "ideal of humanity" Schiller places the "ideal of animality," by which he means the needs of "sensuous nature" alone (1993: 245). Insisting on the contrast between "sensuous nature" and fully free and fully expressive "human nature," Schiller claims that true beauty can be appreciated only by someone who is not in thrall to mere material or sensuous needs: "Beauty is the product of the accord between mind and senses; it speaks to all the capacities of the human being at once. For this reason it can be felt and appreciated only on the supposition of a complete and free use of all the human being's powers" (245). At once sensuous and ennobling, beauty overcomes the alienation (the split) created in human beings by modernity. The incarnation of human freedom, poetic and artistic beauty lifts us up toward the ideal, which is precisely the full and free expression of human nature. In this way, truth, goodness, and beauty are united in the work of art, which itself is the highest expression of human freedom.

In its fullest and most generous formulation, this is an intoxicating vision of human freedom, a utopian vision of the ideal intended to inspire us to battle against all those forces that prevent us from realizing ideal freedom. Yet it is hardly without fault lines. Most prominent is the foothold it provides for narrowly moralistic judgments of poetry and art. Equally pernicious are the difficulties Schiller's reliance on the Kantian opposition between nature and freedom causes for his treatment of sexuality in general and women in particular. Relying on the distinction between *actual [wirkliche]* human nature (which may be bad) and *genuine* or true *[wahre]* human nature (which is ideal, that is to say, always good, true, and beautiful), Schiller declares that outbreaks of sexual passion are always examples of actual and never of genuine nature (1993: 236). Naive poets, who depict nature as it is, therefore often produce vulgar representations of sex and sexuality.

If we wonder exactly what Schiller means by "vulgar," he explains it in a lengthy footnote concerning sex and women, inserted at the very point where he first uses the word. No naive genius, Schiller claims, including Homer and Shakespeare, has ever entirely avoided vulgarity (1993: 237–38):

> If...nature is vulgar, then the spirit...deserts their compositions. For example, in their portrayals of feminine nature, of the relations between both sexes, and of love in particular, every reader with refined feelings must sense a certain emptiness and a weariness that all genuineness and naiveté in the presentation cannot remove....One will hopefully be allowed to assume that nature, as far as that relation of the sexes and the emotion of love are concerned, is capable of a nobler character than the ancients gave it....Here, then, would have been the place for the ancients to render spiritual a material too crude on the outside and to do so from within, through the subject [*Subjekt*]; that is to say, here would have been the place to recover, by means of reflection, the poetic significance missing in the feeling from the outside, to complete nature through the idea, in a word, to make something infinite out of a limited object by a sentimental operation. (237 n.)

It follows that sex and women—in the eyes of Schiller and his male comrades, women, not men, are the bearers of human sexuality—should never be treated realistically. The representation of human sexuality *requires* idealization, or it will be vulgar. In order to become properly poetic, sex must be sublimated, ennobled, and beautified, that is to say, it must be turned into highly idealized love. In order to avoid the coarse and the vulgar, consciousness must transcend the body; morality, duty, and will must conquer mere material nature. This idea explains not only the proliferation of wildly idealized representations of women in nineteenth-century literature, but also the widespread tendency to require that the pure woman prove her purity by being ready to sacrifice her life for love.

Schiller's view of sex is no different from Kant's. Since Kantian morality demands that we elevate ourselves above nature (since moral action is an exercise of freedom, to follow one's natural inclinations can never be a moral act), Kantian morality is extremely cautious with regard to human sexuality. Sex must always have the aim of procreation. If it is used for mere "animal pleasure," even heterosexual intercourse is immoral (Kant 1996: 178). The only thing that can make sex morally permissible is the law, that is, marriage. For Kant, unnatural sexual acts (by which Kant understands anything except procreative sex in marriage) are always vile and self-defiling. But even natural sexual acts may be immoral. If sex has no other aim than pleasure, for example, it turns the other person into a thing, a mere means to one's own enjoyment, and for Kant, it is never permissible to treat another human being as a means and not an end. But it is also immoral to treat *oneself* as a thing, for that is to violate one's duty to one's own humanity. To masturbate, in particular, is to give in to one's basest natural inclinations, to reduce oneself to a thing with the sole aim of pleasure. The resulting act, Kant writes, is so loathsome that it is repulsive even to "call this vice by its proper name" (1996: 179). Kant even thought that suicide might be more morally excusable than such self-defilement (179).

For thinkers like Kant and Schiller, women incarnate human sexuality. In order to lift them above the mere animal stage, poetry and painting need to idealize them far more intensively than men; they need, in short, to create the figure of the *pure woman*, which was to become an icon of idealist aesthetics.[6] When the woman is idealized, the feeling the man has for her can be represented as ideal love, rather than as a base expression of animal nature. If women were to be described as subjected to the same urges and needs as men, the foundation of idealist aesthetics would crumble. Only the extreme idealization of women enables Schiller to continue to believe in the perfectibility of human nature. As we have seen, he believes that this is the sole point on which modern poets always do better than the ancients.

The idea that it is better to sacrifice one's life than to give up one's moral self-respect (one's honor) is everywhere in nineteenth-century European literature. In the case of women, moral self-respect is almost always taken to be identical with bodily chastity. The result is that in a curious reversal of the hierarchy between body and spirit, a woman's honor comes to reside entirely in her sexuality. *A Doll's House* provides a caustic one-line dismissal of this whole tradition of thought:

HELMER: I would gladly work night and day for you, Nora—bear sorrow and deprivation for your sake. But nobody sacrifices his *honor* for the one he loves.

NORA: A hundred thousand women have done precisely that. (Ibsen 1928–57, 8: 362)

By attacking the old clichés about sacrificing life for love, Ibsen hastened the modern deidealization of women and powerfully contributed to the demise of idealism as an aesthetic theory.

IDEALISM AND REALISM

Schiller devotes a long passage to what he calls "a remarkable psychological antagonism between people in a century in the process of civilizing itself," namely, the opposition between idealists and realists (1993: 249). Humankind is divided into two categories: realists who judge only by experience, and idealists who judge only by reason. Realists risk becoming petty-minded positivists; idealists risk taking off into ungrounded flights of fancy, cut loose from every sense of morality. The two types each represent an aspect of ideal human nature, but neither reaches it completely. While it is clear that Schiller considers idealists to come closer to the ideal, he also shows that the "true realist" must ultimately agree with the "genuine idealist" (259).

The same logic applies to the opposition between the naive and the sentimental poet: although the naive poet is a realist and the sentimental is an idealist, both work with the same goal in mind: to give full and free expression to ideal human nature. Schiller's division of sentimental poetry into satire and elegy works in the same way: while satire describes a world in which the ideal is absent, and elegy one in which it is still present, however problematically, the task of both poetic modes is to fill us with the "magnificence of the idea" (1993: 206). What matters to Schiller, in short, is "the manner of feeling prevailing" in the various types of poetry (211 n.). A realist technique is therefore perfectly compatible with idealist aesthetics, for the realist serves the ideal by pointing to the deleterious consequences of its absence. A generation later, the great French realist Honoré de Balzac explained the difference between his own novels and those of George Sand precisely in such terms.

In *Story of My Life* (1854–55), Sand sets out the principles of her own idealist aesthetics. First of all, she writes, a novel should be poetic, not analytical. Just like Schiller, she believes that the passion of love (and therefore also the character who feels it) must be idealized:

> One must not be afraid to endow it [the passion] with exceptional importance, powers beyond the ordinary, or subject it to delight or suffering that completely

surpass the habitual, human ones, and that even surpass what most intelligent people think is believable. In sum, the idealization of a sentiment yields the subject, leaving to the art of the storyteller the care of placing that subject within a situation and a realistic framework that is drawn sensitively enough to make the subject stand out" (1991: 922).

In conversations with Balzac, Sand writes, she learned that "one could sacrifice the idealized subject for the truth of the portrayal, or for the critique of society or humanity itself" (922–23). If this is right, at first glance it is difficult to see what the difference is between Balzac in the 1830s and the naturalists of the 1880s. As Sand continues, however, the difference becomes clear:

> Balzac summed this up completely when he said to me later on, "You are looking for man as he should be; I take him as he is. Believe me, we are both right. Both paths lead to the same end. I also like exceptional human beings; I am one myself. I need them to make my ordinary characters stand out, and I never sacrifice them unnecessarily. But the ordinary human beings interest me more than they do you. I make them larger than life; I idealize them in the opposite sense, in their ugliness or in their stupidity. I give their deformities frightful or grotesque proportions. You could not do that; you are smart not to want to look at people and things that would give you nightmares. Idealize what is pretty and what is beautiful; that is a woman's job." (923)

That Balzac at his best was widely perceived to "combine the ideal and the real," is attested to by French criticism from the 1830s.[7]

Both Balzac and Sand believed that the task of literature was to draw attention to the shortcomings of ordinary human life by exaggeration; both were committed to the fundamental aims of aesthetic idealism: to uplift, ennoble, and transform humanity by filling us with a sense of the ideal. While Balzac chose Schiller's satirical mode, Sand settled on his elegiac mode, sometimes in the form of elegy (as in *Indiana*), sometimes in the form of idyll (as in the postscript to *Indiana*, or in *La Petite Fadette*). As Schor points out, they both subscribe to an aesthetic theory in which idealism is the hierarchically superior and realism the subordinate term (1993: 29).

This may seem an odd claim to make, for from the 1840s to the 1870s intense debates raged between realists and idealists in France. The quarrel started among painters and art critics, and soon spread to literature. Bernard Weinberg, however, has shown that most antirealist critics did not object to the attempt to portray the real world; what they objected to was the absence of the ideal, for without the ideal and the immaterial, they claimed, truth was absent (1937: 141, 192–99). If the realist writers had style (beauty), the critics usually forgave them.

In the 1860s, British critics vigorously debated the respective merits of idealism and realism in the same terms as Balzac had done in his conversations with Sand. Mary Poovey finds that critics at the time were either straightforward idealists or tried to show that realism is compatible with idealism. Among the latter, we find George Eliot. Nobody defends a straightforwardly anti-idealist realism.

Rather, Poovey writes, they "did not precisely prefer realism to idealism but tended to maintain that what critics called realism could also approach higher truths through detailed but imaginatively interpreted descriptions of everyday things" (2004: 443). In Norway, the battle between "realists" and "idealists" turns up in cartoons in the 1880s, after the publication of Ibsen's *Ghosts*.

It is only when the idealist trinity of truth, beauty, and goodness falls apart that realism becomes the outright enemy of idealism. (When critics and writers start thinking that the aim of art is to produce beauty, but not truth, we get various kinds of aestheticism; when they think it is to produce truth, but not beauty, we get naturalism.) Realism, then, is not *one*. The tendency among present-day critics to theorize all kinds of realism in the same way, namely, as "reference" or "representation," obscures the significant differences among Balzac's, Gustave Flaubert's, and Ibsen's realisms. One example of such differences is that Balzac, Flaubert, and Ibsen have a strikingly different relationship to the ordinary. As we have seen, Balzac is highly critical of the ordinary, which he tends to exaggerate, make grotesque, and infuse with melodrama. Flaubert, on the other hand, finds the ordinary indescribably dull, a place where no values, no thrills, no excitement can possibly be found. Ibsen, for his part, turns to the ordinary and the everyday, not as something that has to be overcome, exaggerated, or idealized, but as a sphere where we have to take on the task of building meaningful human relationships. If we fail at this task, the everyday becomes unbearable; if we succeed, it becomes a source of human values.

Truth Undoing Beauty: The War between Idealism and Naturalism

In France, the first signs of an emerging tension within the idealist trinity of truth, beauty, and goodness can be dated to the critical reactions to Balzac's works that surfaced in the 1840s.[8] Truth, however, was not the major issue in 1857, when the French public prosecutor Ernest Pinard took the authors of *Madame Bovary* to court for blasphemy and of *Les Fleurs du Mal* for obscenity. Flaubert won his case and Charles Baudelaire lost his, with the result that six poems of *Les Fleurs du Mal* remained officially prohibited until 1949. The underlying reasons for the prosecutor's outrage were nevertheless very similar in both cases. These works shocked because they appeared to be beholden to no ultimate ethical and religious ideal. Baudelaire's attempt to produce beauty out of evil and Flaubert's nihilistic irony both attacked the very core of idealist aesthetics, and both proposed a new and unsettling understanding of the purpose of art, pointing in the direction of a modern, anti-idealist formalism, and not in the direction of the naturalist crusade for truth. This is why it is the story of modernism, not of naturalism, that starts with Baudelaire and Flaubert.[9] In other words, the development of the modern faith in the "autonomy of the aesthetic" begins when aesthetics is severed from ethics.

The trials of *Madame Bovary* and *Les Fleurs du Mal* are significant because they show that idealists genuinely feared that if truth, beauty, moral goodness, and religion were allowed to come apart in aesthetic works, then the very foundations of the community were in danger. The idealists were right to feel threatened, for once the idealist trinity fell apart, the ground was cleared for all kinds of anti-idealist theories and beliefs: it is no coincidence that materialism, determinism, Darwinism, skepticism, nihilism, "free thought," and atheism were major natural-ist themes and that political movements such as anarchism, socialism, commu-nism, and feminism were all associated with the naturalist onslaught on idealism.

Late nineteenth-century antinaturalist polemics conveys an overwhelming sense that beauty has been blemished, innocence defiled, womanhood dishonored, God defied. Idealists expressed their disgust at the ugliness of naturalism through an unusually insistent and widespread imagery of dirt, manure, sickness, boils, sores, infection, rotting corpses, and sexual depravation. In 1880 the German ide-alist Paul Heyse wrote to Georg Brandes, the Danish critic and intellectual, that he was working on some Provençal stories in order to oppose the modern *Zolismus*, the craze for Émile Zola, which he thought could not last: "Perhaps the world will soon return to the idea that the dirty washing of a courtesan in the long run looks uglier than clean linen and fine silks clinging to healthy and chaste limbs in beau-tiful airy folds" (quoted in von Moisy 1981: 216).

The true inheritor of Schiller's perfectionist aesthetics (and of Sand's idealism, too), Heyse here produces a set of automatic connections between the ugly, the dirty, the sexual, and the "fallen woman," in every respect exemplary of late idealist polemics. Already in 1873, soon after their first meeting, Brandes wrote that Heyse "considers it a kind of duty to depict human beings as better and greater than they on average are; he would like to strengthen everyone's self-respect, give him cour-age to continue to live and hold up for him examples that show that even in a lowly human being there lies much beauty hidden, and that even in a philistine a hero may be slumbering" (reprinted in Brandes and Brandes 1939, 1: 188). In 1882 Heyse wrote a letter to Brandes in which he commented on the work of two Scandinavian novelists, the Dane J. P. Jacobsen and the Norwegian Alexander Kielland:

> When they [the young Danish writers] establish a veritable clinic in which
> the wounds and boils of society are exposed, the eternal stench of disinfectant
> is so shocking that it drives away the unbiased and spiritually free friends of
> humanity, who until now were looking to the fine arts (to which I still think
> the art of writing belongs) to find comfort for the misery of the world....
> I am completely convinced that a single work giving the sunny side of this
> wonderful world of sun and shade its due...would exert a deeper, warmer,
> more stimulating, more reformist influence than all these brilliant studies of
> putrefaction. (quoted in von Moisy 1981: 216–17)

While Heyse's wish for art and literature to represent a kinder, gentler view of the world, his desire to uplift and encourage people through art, may strike us as quaint and naive, it expresses perfectly the feelings of embattled idealists in the 1880s and 1890s. Unlike some of his fellow idealists, however, Heyse was at pains not to dissociate himself from the free-thinking aspects of naturalism—he did not wish to be taken for a reactionary religious spirit; he just believed that works with a more positive outlook on the world would have stronger political and moral effects than the dirt and stench of the naturalists. Lamenting the loss of the good and the beautiful in literature, Heyse continued to give voice to the utopian longings of idealism until he died in 1914.

"A Dunghill at Delphi": Ghosts

No play challenged the idealists as deeply as Ibsen's *Ghosts*, perhaps because it dramatizes the conflict between the competing aesthetic norms that would rage in response to it:

> PASTOR MANDERS: Is there not a voice in your mother's heart that forbids you
>   to break down your son's ideals?
> MRS. ALVING: Yes, but what about the truth?
> PASTOR MANDERS: Yes, but what about the ideals?
> MRS. ALVING: Oh—ideals, ideals! If only I weren't as cowardly as I am!
>   (1928–57, 9: 90)

Throughout *Ghosts*, Mrs. Alving and Pastor Manders embody the conflict between naturalists and idealists, faithfully reproduced and reenacted by outraged or exhilarated reviewers, all of whom deplored the shocking absence of reconciliation and uplift in the play. Ever since the publication of *Catiline*, the Norwegian Hegelian M. J. Monrad had been one of Ibsen's most intelligent and supportive reviewers, but when Ibsen broke with idealism, Monrad broke with Ibsen. Monrad began his 1882 review of *Ghosts* by complaining that idealist aesthetics was being threatened by truth:

> The time is long gone when one turned to creative works in search of what
> one used to call poetry and beauty, when one sought refreshment for the spirit
> and the heart, to be uplifted above the messy, tiring confusion of everyday life,
> to find a reconciled and reconciling view of life. All such things are now only
> considered to be ghost-like matters; what poetry, like every other form of art,
> now wants to offer us, is only what it calls "truth," that is to say the naked, even
> stark naked reality in its most repellent form. It wants to smash all illusions, all
> so-called ideals. (1974: 194).

All *Ghosts* could teach us, Monrad ironically concluded, was that modern society actually requires a "religious foundation," and that the whole of humanity desires to be "liberated from the natural corruption and its consequences of natural corruption" (200).

Elsewhere, the idealist response to *Ghosts* was simple outrage. The kindly Heyse, who had admired *A Doll's House*, wrote to Brandes in December 1881 that when he read *Ghosts*, he felt as if he were sitting in a charnel house, incessantly smoking to keep the stench away, yet nevertheless succumbing to nausea at the abominable mixture of uneasiness, horror, and disgust that Ibsen had arranged with such consummate artistry (von Moisy 1981: 215).

Ghosts, in short, was received as if it were the most horrible expression of naturalism ever produced. This was not least true in Britain, where the culture wars unleashed by the production of Ibsen's plays in the early 1890s laid the foundations for the advent of modernism. After the first London performance of *Ghosts* in 1891, *The Daily Telegraph* devoted a whole editorial to it. In the long article, the writer makes a point of denouncing a claim made by some of Ibsen's English defenders, namely, that *Ghosts* had the purity and simplicity of a Greek tragedy. The passion and the sense of outrage, as well as the language and the themes sounded here, make this article particularly striking and particularly representative of the feelings of the defenders of idealism all over Europe:

> Ay! The play performed last night is "simple" enough in plan and purpose, but simple only in the sense of an open drain; of a loathsome sore unbandaged; of a dirty act done publicly; or of a lazar-house with all its doors and windows open. It is no more "Greek," and can no more be called "Greek" for its plainness of speech and candid foulness, than could a dunghill at Delphi, or a madhouse at Mitylene. It is not "artistic" even, in the sense of the anatomical studies of the Great Masters; because they, in carefully drawing the hidden things of life and nature, did it in the single and steadfast worship of Truth and Beauty, the subtle framework and foundation of which they thus reverently endeavoured to seize....
>
> But Morality, Criticism and Taste alike must certainly draw the line at what is absolutely loathsome and foetid. If Medea could not, according to Horace, kill her children upon the stage, still less can Art allow what common decency forbids. Realism is one thing, but the nostrils of an audience must not be visibly held before a play can be stamped as true to nature. It is difficult to expose indecorous words—the gross, and almost putrid, indecorum of this play of *Ghosts*. Suffice it to indicate that the central situation is that of a son exposing to a mother—herself, in past days, a would-be adulteress—his inheritance of a loathsome malady from a father whose memory the widow secretly execrates while she publicly honors and consecrates it. If this be Art—which word, be it remembered, is but the abbreviation of the Greek name for what is highest, most excellent, and best—then the masterpieces of English literature must be found in such vagaries as Ben Jonson's *Fleet Ditch Voyage*, Swift's mad scurrility, and Congreve's lewd coarseness. (March 14, 1891, reprinted in Egan 1972: 190, 192.)

This passage has it all: the references to dirt, putrefaction, rotting bodies (the "lazar-house"), sexual depravation, and nihilism. This outraged and outrageous article brings out particularly clearly that by the end of the nineteenth century Schiller's aesthetic vision of human perfection had been reduced to a desiccated and moralistic demand for art to be decent, well mannered, simple, and harmonious.

By 1890, then, many intellectuals and artists took idealism to be virtually identical with hypocritical, antiartistic, moralistic conservatism. This is the image of idealism that emerges from George Bernard Shaw's *The Quintessence of Ibsenism* (1891), a book written in response to *The Daily Telegraph*'s attacks on Ibsen (Shaw 1905: 3–5). Shaw's despicable idealists have no connection to Schiller and Madame de Staël; they are simply trying to cover up the unpalatable reality of their own miserable lives. "The idealist...has taken refuge with the ideals because he hates himself and is ashamed of himself," Shaw declares (30).

Because Shaw defends Ibsen by turning idealism into the expression of a personally and politically thwarted psyche, *The Quintessence of Ibsenism* conveys no sense of the illustrious origins of idealist aesthetics, no sense that idealism once had genuine claims to be taken seriously. By reducing idealism to an effect of psychological repression, Shaw accelerated the process that would lead readers and critics of Ibsen to forget idealism entirely. But when we forget all about the idealist tradition in aesthetics, we are no longer able to see that *Ghosts* is not just about family sickness and family secrets, but about aesthetic norms. Paradoxically, then, the death of idealism that Ibsen helped to bring about makes it harder for us to see the aesthetically self-reflective aspects of his contemporary plays more.

Shaw's analysis of idealism, moreover, is entirely based on the opposition between ideals and truth. Realists face the truth of the human conditions; idealists demand that people sacrifice themselves in the name of chimerical ideals. All over Europe, critics engaged in similar polemics. The battles over naturalism were in fact battles over idealism. At the time, it was impossible to avoid taking sides. The moralistic and conservative idealists kept harping on beauty, harmony, and uplift. The naturalists rightly revolted against the increasingly anachronistic, unrealistic, and reactionary demands of idealism. With truth and freedom on their side, they were not in a mood for compromise.

Published in 1886, Nietzsche's *Beyond Good and Evil* is in large parts a response to the debates over naturalism and idealism raging all over Germany. At the time, however, his provocative critique of the starry-eyed belief in the power of truth to set us free could gain him no support from the naturalists, while the very title of his book was enough to ensure that no self-respecting idealist would touch it. If they had opened it, Nietzsche's devastating denunciation of Christian slave morality and European herd morality would have made them throw the book across the room.

By throwing idealists and naturalists together as equally misguided metaphysical moralists, Nietzsche's book far outstripped the cultural debates that surrounded it. The first part of the following passage could have been written specially for Heyse; its second part is directed against naive defenders of naturalism:

Nobody is very likely to consider a doctrine true merely because it makes people happy or virtuous—except perhaps the lovely "idealists" who become effusive about the good, the true, and the beautiful and allow all kinds of motley, clumsy, and benevolent desiderata to swim around in utter confusion in their pond. Happiness and virtue are no arguments. But people like to forget—even sober spirits—that making unhappy and evil are no counterarguments. Something might be true while being harmful and dangerous in the highest degree. (1989: §39, 49–50)

Nietzsche's critique points beyond naturalism, to a kind of art that will reject metaphysics and place itself truly beyond good and evil, an art that understands "the existence of the world is justified only as an aesthetic phenomenon," an art that will "fight at any risk whatever the *moral* interpretation and significance of existence" (1967: 22). This art, of course, turned out to be modernism.

I have defined naturalism as an aesthetic movement obsessed with an anti-idealist quest for truth. Of course, the quest for truth expressed itself in different ways: in a turn toward science, in a preference for critique rather than utopia, and, in general, in a desire for literature to become less ideal and more real. But by the 1870s, realism per se was not unacceptable to idealists. At the beginning of Heyse's *Children of the World* (1873), the reader is slowly introduced to the inhabitants of a boarding house in Berlin, in a manner remarkably (and, surely, deliberately) reminiscent of the beginning of Balzac's *Père Goriot*. When Zola's *L'Assommoir* was published in 1877, a critic in *Le Figaro* wrote that the novel was "not realism, but filth; not crudity, but pornography" (Buss 2000: viii). The problem with Zola, then, was not that he was a realist, but that he was the wrong kind of realist, the kind that refused to deliver beauty and moral uplift to his readers. We have seen that *The Daily Telegraph* drew on the same distinction in order to condemn *Ghosts*. What is missing in objectionable realist works, in short, is reconciliation.

IDEALISM IN ACTION: THE NOBEL PRIZE IN LITERATURE

When Alfred Nobel established the Nobel Prizes in his will of 1895, he specified that the prize in literature should be awarded to "the person who shall have produced in the field of literature the most outstanding work of an idealistic tendency" (Espmark 1991: 1). There has been significant debate about what exactly Nobel meant by "idealistic tendency." Much evidence indicates that he probably wanted to keep faith with the utopian idealism of revolutionary romanticism and, in particular, with the "religiously colored spirit of revolt" of his favorite author, Percy Bysshe Shelley (Espmark 1991: 4–5). But Nobel was out of touch with his time, for by the 1890s, "idealist" no longer meant revolutionary romanticism; it had become the slogan of the antinaturalist, antimodernist, moralizing lovers of uplifting beauty in literature, such as the permanent secretary of the Swedish Academy at the time, Carl David af Wirsén (1842–1912). Because of Wirsén's influence, the first Nobel Prizes in literature allow us to grasp with particular acuity the nature of late idealist aesthetics.

From 1901 to 1911, Wirsén made sure that the Nobel Prize went to works steeped in a "lofty and sound idealism," exhibiting "a true nobility not simply of presentation but of conception and of philosophy of life."[10] In his invaluable study of the aesthetic criteria governing the choice of the Nobel laureate in literature, Kjell Espmark tells us that in the Wirsén era the "literary quality of a work was weighed against its contribution to humanity's struggle 'toward the ideal'" (1991: 10). Atheists and agnostics were automatically disqualified, unless they demonstrated an unusually strong "striving towards higher things and moral responsibility" (12–13). Like most late nineteenth-century and early twentieth-century idealists, the early Nobel committees consistently praised clarity and simplicity, using words like "obscure" and "unclear" as terms of strong disapproval (see 14–15).

The outspoken commitment to rigidly conservative idealist principles explains why the list of the first 10 Nobel laureates in Wirsén's era looks as strange as it does today:

1901	Sully Prudhomme
1902	Theodor Mommsen
1903	Bjørnstjerne Bjørnson
1904	Frédéric Mistral, José Echegaray
1905	Henryk Sienkiewicz
1906	Giosuè Carducci
1907	Rudyard Kipling
1908	Rudolf Eucken
1909	Selma Lagerlöf
1910	Paul Heyse[11]

The first Nobel laureate was an establishment candidate, enthusiastically nominated by the Académie Française. Honored "in special recognition of his poetic composition, which gives evidence of lofty idealism, artistic perfection and a rare combination of the qualities of both heart and intellect," Sully Prudhomme was chosen in preference to Zola, that year's prime reject, whose naturalism was dismissed as "spiritless, and often grossly cynical."[12] In 1902, the German historian Theodor Mommsen was preferred to Leo Tolstoy, "an author who in his otherwise magnificent *War and Peace* attributes to blind chance such a decisive role in the great events of world history…and who in countless of his works denies not only the church, but the state, even the right of property" (Espmark 1991: 17).

Wirsén, who was largely responsible for these decisions, was in fact something of an idealist activist. He had spent large parts of his career as a literary critic praising Bjørnson and panning Ibsen (see the essays on Ibsen in Wirsén 1901). It is hardly surprising, then, that in 1903 the Nobel committee crowned Bjørnson and soundly rejected both Ibsen and Brandes. Brandes' view of life and ethics was unacceptable to the committee, for he was considered to be "negatively sceptical, totally atheistic," as well as far too lax on sexual matters (Espmark 1991: 18). With the explicit exception of *The Pretenders*, *Brand*, and *Emperor and Galilean*, Ibsen's works were criticized for being negativistic, obscure, and generally repellent; about his later plays the committee wrote that their "negative and enigmatic features have repelled even those who would have willingly given the world-famous author a substantial recognition" (18). Bjørnson, on the other hand, was lauded for his poetry, for his freshness of spirit, and above all for his positive and pure idealism in works nobody, not even in Norway, reads anymore.

"On or about December 1910 human character changed," Virginia Woolf famously declared (1988: 421). The Nobel committee begged to differ, for in December 1910 it solemnly awarded the Nobel Prize to Ibsen's and Brandes's old friend Heyse. That year, the committee rejected Thomas Hardy, whose heroines were accused of being lacking in "character," that is to say, in "religious and ethical firmness" (Espmark 1991: 22). Not surprisingly, precisely the qualities that make Hardy's women modern made Hardy unacceptable. Heyse, on the other hand, was praised as the greatest German poet since Goethe. In his presentation speech, Wirsén stressed Heyse's importance as a symbol of the idealist struggle against naturalism:

> Naturalism, which burst forth in the eighties and dominated the scene for the next decade, directed its iconoclastic attack especially against Heyse, its most powerful opponent. He was too harmonious, too fond of beauty, too Hellenic and lofty for those who, slandering him at any price, demanded sensation, effect, bizarre licentiousness, and crass reproductions of ugly realities. Heyse did not yield. His sense of form was offended by their uncouth behaviour; he demanded that literature should see life in an ideal light that would transfigure reality.[13]

Heyse was also praised for his independence, which he had proved not least by disliking *Ghosts* and all the rest of Ibsen's late plays. In his final peroration, Wirsén quotes Schiller, and thus gives full voice to the idealist aesthetics he had defended all his life:

> Aesthetically [Heyse] has been faithful to truth, but in such a manner that he mirrored inner in external reality. Schiller's well known words, 'Life is serious, art serene,' properly understood, express a profound truth which can be found in the life and work of Heyse. Beauty should liberate and recreate: it should neither imitate reality slavishly nor drag it into the dust.[14]

Forlornly seeking harmony in an ever less harmonious world, Wirsén here mixes fragments of Schiller's idealist romanticism with conservative German neoclassicism and mounts a desperate last-ditch defense of the spiritual over the material and—above all—over the sexual.

MODERNISM AND IDEALISM

In 1918 idealism was dead; Heyse was forgotten, and nobody remembered that *Ghosts* had once been a play about aesthetic conflicts. Soon author Bertolt Brecht would deride *Ghosts* as irrelevant to an age that had invented a cure for syphilis.[15] The rise of modernism started the process that was to turn Ibsen into a fuddy-duddy old realist or overly melodramatic symbolist.[16]

The demise of idealism has turned the period from 1870 to 1914 into a puzzle for literary historians. After the horrors of the Franco-Prussian war and the Paris Commune in 1870–71, idealism was decidedly on the defensive in Europe. As we have seen, naturalism was its first prominent enemy. But in the shadow of naturalism, there flourished a plethora of other anti-idealist projects. The closer we get to the ultimate death of idealism, the more hectically different trends and movements flourish and die: symbolism, decadence, neoromanticism, estheticism, fin-de-siècle, and avant-garde are just some of the terms one regularly comes across in discussions of this period.

Despite the proliferation of terms, many of the most important writers of the period remain exceedingly difficult to categorize. It is not just Ibsen who fails to conform to such labels; Oscar Wilde, Hardy, Henry James, and the young André Gide are just as difficult to categorize. Hardy's fascination with the grotesque and the gruesome, his honesty about sex, and his uncanny grasp of women's complexity made his novels anathema to idealists.[17] In 1911, Wirsén's last year on the Nobel committee, James's nuanced, careful, subtle weighing of human motivations, his fascination with the movements of human consciousness was deemed insufficiently clear and concentrated, and the prize went to Maurice Maeterlinck.[18] The very title of Gide's *L'Immoraliste* (1902) would have been enough to make the Nobel committee cringe, and his fascination with transgressive action for action's sake (*Les Caves du Vatican*, 1914) would be completely outrageous to an idealist. (Gide received the Nobel Prize in 1947.)

While finding him entirely alien to his own aesthetic preferences, Wilde admired Ibsen.[19] In fact, Wilde's brilliant paradoxes, his searing indictment of moralism, are as anti-idealist as Ibsen's turn to the ordinary. In its way, *The Picture of Dorian Gray* (first published in *Lippincott's Monthly Magazine* in July 1890) is as preoccupied with the battle between idealism and realism as *Ghosts*. At the very beginning of Wilde's novel, the painter Basil Hallward explains that he is looking for a new aesthetic school, a school he finds embodied in the beauty of Dorian

Gray: "Unconsciously he defines for me the lines of a fresh school, a school that is to have in it all the passion of the romantic spirit, all the perfection of the spirit that is Greek. The harmony of soul and body—how much that is! We in our madness have separated the two, and have invented a realism that is vulgar, an ideality that is void" (1992: 10). Here realism is aligned with the body and vulgarity (as it was in contemporary discussions of Zola's and Ibsen's "naturalism") and ideality with a hollowed-out notion of the soul. Hallward's diagnosis of the problems of contemporary aesthetics turns out to be a perfect description of Dorian Gray himself, for the uncanny paradox at the heart of *The Picture of Dorian Gray* is that Dorian's soul, forever captured in Basil's picture, is as visible, ugly, and material as can be, while his body, engaged in so many mysterious vices, remains perfect, the very embodiment of "void ideality," if there ever was one.[20]

A virulent opponent of idealism, Wilde detested its characteristic mingling of ethics and aesthetics. "There is no such thing as a moral or an immoral book," he declares in the preface to *The Picture of Dorian Gray*. "Books are well written, or badly written. That is all" (1992: xxiii). In "The Critic as Artist" (1890) he reinforces the point: "The sphere of Art and the sphere of Ethics are absolutely distinct and separate. When they are confused, Chaos has come again" (1968a: 393). Unlike Shaw, however, whose anti-idealism turned him into a fairly dry left-wing champion of realism and naturalism, Wilde remained a revolutionary romantic at heart, who adored historical novels full of exquisite and exotic details such as Flaubert's *Salammbô*, Charles's Reade's *The Cloister and the Hearth* ("as much above *Romola* as *Romola* is above *Daniel Deronda*"), and Alexandre Dumas's *The Vicomte de Bragelonne* (Wilde 1968b: 299–300).

Sometimes Wilde sounds like a modernist Schiller, insisting that truth and goodness have nothing to do with beauty, while at the same time believing that "[i]t is through Art, and through Art only, that we can realize our perfection" (1968a: 380). The inheritor of Schiller's idealism, Wilde was a perfectionist sympathetic to socialism. No wonder, then, that in 1888 he praised the stalwart idealist Sand for the spirit of "social regeneration" that is so characteristic of her novels: "This spirit...is the very leaven of modern life. It is remoulding the world for us, and fashioning our age anew. If it is antediluvian, it is so because the deluge is yet to come; if it is Utopian then Utopia must be added to our geographies" (1968c: 87). Wilde, in fact, appears to have found in Sand somewhat of a kindred spirit, a writer of genius fusing a passion for social transformation with a highly self-conscious awareness of the role of art in that transformation. Lauding Sand's "delightful treatment of art and the artist's life," he declares, "What Mr. Ruskin and Mr. Browning have done for England, she did for France. She invented an art literature" (87–88).[21] Like Brandes before him, then, Wilde split the idealist tradition in two, so as to be able to combine the admiration for revolutionary romanticism with the rejection of moralistic idealism.[22]

Once the idealist trinity of truth, goodness, and beauty was coming apart, Wilde chose to cultivate Beauty; Brandes, Zola, and the naturalists who followed them settled for Truth; and Nietzsche and Gide bravely attacked the Good.

The Legacy of Idealism

The demise of idealism furthered the autonomization of art and literature. When idealism disappeared, ethical and religious claims on art lost their legitimacy. Left was politics. There has always been a great deal of tension between formalist modernism and politically committed forms of criticism. In 1871, Brandes called for modern literature to "place problems under debate."[23] The naturalist generation that followed him—the "men of the modern breakthrough" as Brandes himself called them, thus conveniently erasing from his consciousness all the women writers he knew and sometimes even encouraged—took for granted that the purpose of literature was to work for radical social and political change. The idea that art and literature have to serve a political purpose, however, is a successor project to the idealist vision in which the ultimate task of art was to ennoble mankind.

With formalism, the separation of ethics and aesthetics is completed: art is perceived as fully autonomous of all moral, social, and political duties; its task is neither to uplift or improve us nor to change society through its relentless uncovering of truth, but rather to make us think about art. Insofar as naturalism inherited the utopian and perfectionist project of idealism, modernism comes to stand as a negation of both. There is nevertheless an incipient conflict here. If we consider formalist modernism as the ultimate negation of both idealism and naturalism, it represents the final breakthrough of the autonomy of the aesthetic. If this is right, modernism simply can have no political, social, or religious purpose. Yet there has always been a strong political strand within modernism. Marxist modernists such as Erwin Piscator and Brecht spearheaded the twentieth-century quest to combine aesthetic formalism with political commitment.

Inspired by Roland Barthes and Alain Robbe-Grillet, French poststructuralism and its American and European avatars have generated a plethora of more or less sophisticated theories of the "politics of form" or the "politics of the signifier." These are only the most recent attempts to overcome the conflict between utopia and critique, between the desire for a positive project for change and the conviction that all art can do is to avoid, negate, hollow out, or undermine the contaminated, commodified, and fetishized forms of communication characteristic of modern society. Yet it is hard to maintain such artistic purity, for the more art negates and avoids modern society, the easier it is for astute critics to read the gesture of negation itself as a refusal of communication or commodification, thus as a statement of alienation from mass society and a protest against the degradation of art by market forces. It is not difficult, in other words, to turn the formalist negativity of late modernism into a powerful political statement. Here resides an important, but unacknowledged, legacy of idealism: just as Schiller and his friends thought of the artist as a seer, close to God in his understanding of the ideal, late modernism turns the artist, now perceived as a laborer of negativity, into a bearer of purity or authenticity in a corrupted world.

The demise of idealism made it increasingly impossible for artists, writers, and critics (as opposed to politicians, religious leaders, and school board members) to claim in public that art has a duty to promote social ideals, show us the beauty of life, help to uplift us in a difficult world. All these tasks, if they are to be performed at all, have been relegated to the category of entertainment, to the middlebrow and the lowbrow.[24] In the twentieth century, however, idealism did not just live on in the middlebrow and the lowbrow. It also lived on in socialist realism and the fascist cult of "healthy" art. The demise of idealism, therefore, was a fantastic victory for artistic freedom. With the death of idealism, political, religious, and ethical interference in the autonomy of art could no longer find aesthetic justification. Women, in particular, have had everything to gain from the death of the outlandish idealist requirements for the representation of women, sexuality, and love. These gains remain enduring legacies of the victory of modernism over idealism, a victory that owes much to the pioneering, controversial plays of Ibsen.

After modernism, however, critics and writers also routinely take for granted that anyone who reads to be consoled for the sorrows of the world, to be uplifted, to gain a positive vision of what human beings can achieve, has no understanding of literature. Perhaps this is why the formalist, skeptical, ironic paradigms of modernism and postmodernism have come to seem increasingly empty: all they appear to offer is critique bereft of the utopian vision that rightly ought to sustain their critical power. What can they tell us about the task of art in an era dominated by war, genocide, and terrorism? What can art do in an era when secular liberalism, the modern defender of the autonomy of art and literature, is under pressure from militant religious fundamentalisms of every kind? Unless we find answers to these questions, we leave the way open for the return of the death-dealing "claim of the ideal" in ever more pernicious forms.[25]

NOTES

This essay is based on material included in Moi 2006, esp. chap. 3. When not otherwise noted, all translations from foreign languages are my own.

1. "Idealism" or "idealist aesthetics" is not an entry, for example, in Cuddon 1998 or Baldick 2001. In Childers and Hentzi 1995, the entry on idealism is devoted exclusively to idealist philosophy.

2. It is true that the generation of modernists I think of as "high modernists" often thought of themselves as opposing a certain kind of realism. This becomes clear, e.g., in Woolf's superb essays "Mr. Bennett and Mrs. Brown" (1988: 384–89) and "Character in Fiction" (420–38). But if the "high modernists" felt free to elaborate their own views in this way, it was because they were no longer held by the idealist aesthetics that dominated the generation before them. In this way, they build on the achievements of thinkers and writers such as Ibsen, Nietzsche, Émile Zola, Oscar Wilde, the early André Gide, and many others.

3. The fragment is attributed to Hölderlin, but the manuscript version is in Hegel's handwriting, and Jay Bernstein writes that "it is more plausible to regard the fragment as the result of an exchange of ideas amongst the three friends" (2003: 185 n. 1). Eckhart Förster, on the other hand, makes a careful case for Hölderlin as the author; see Förster 2004: 470–75.

4. Lukács's idealist humanism is eloquently expressed in essays like "The Ideal of the Harmonious Man in Bourgeois Aesthetics" and "Marx and Engels on Aesthetic," collected in Lukács 1978.

5. "In terms of reality the naive poet has the better of the sentimental poet" (Schiller 1993: 234).

6. Schott 1988 is a marvelous study of Kant's investment in purity.

7. For the critical reception of French realism from 1830 to 1870, see Bernard Weinberg's illuminating study *French Realism: The Critical Reaction, 1830–1870* (1937).

8. In *French Realism*, Weinberg writes that Balzac criticism became markedly more hostile in the 1840s. I am inclined to interpret this as a sign of the breakup of the union between idealism and realism described in Sand 1991: 32–90.

9. For a succinct overview of the two trials, see LaCapra 1989: 726–31.

10. From the Nobel committee's report of 1905, when the prize went to Henryk Sienkiewicz (Espmark 1991: 9).

11. The web pages of the Nobel Prize in Literature are full of valuable information and documents; see nobelprize.org/literature/.

12. The quotation about Prudhomme is the official Nobel Prize citation for 1901, available from nobelprize.org/literature/laureates/1901/index.html; the quotation about Zola comes from the Nobel committee's internal report cited in Espmark 1991: 17.

13. Presentation speech by Wirsén, available at nobelprize.org/literature/laureates/1910/press.html.

14. See nobelprize.org/literature/laureates/1910/press.html.

15. What Brecht actually wrote, in the 1940s, was this: "While Ibsen was writing *Ghosts*, Ehrlich was working to find a cure for syphilis. The devil that Ibsen painted on the wall for the hypocrites, was wiped out by Ehrlich....The bourgeoisie had become a greater evil than syphilis, its hypocrisy was not interesting because it threatened the bourgeoisie, but because it threatened humanity" (Brecht 1993: 42).

16. This is a reference to a set of attitudes to Ibsen's theater that became particularly widespread in the period after 1945; for more information, see Moi 2006, chap. 1.

17. For an interesting discussion of Hardy's hybrid form, see Daleski 1996.

18. Wirsén complained about James's "lack of concentration" (Espmark 1991: 25–26).

19. Richard Ellmann writes:

Wilde did not underrate his Norwegian rival; he allowed that *Hedda Gabler* was Greek in its power to generate pity and terror. But his own goal, he saw, was to make dialogue as brilliant as possible, while Ibsen confined his characters to ordinary words in ordinary life.... One probed a situation to uncover an infection; the other relied on verbal ricochet, to express a 'conflict between our artistic sympathies and our moral judgment.' For Wilde, unlike Ibsen, the setting had to be in the leisure class, people with time, money, and education, proficient in conversation. (1988: 333)

20. "You were to me such an ideal as I shall never meet again. This is the face of a satyr," Basil says to Dorian when he sees the picture (Wilde 1992: 157).

21. Among Sand's artists' novels, Wilde recommends *Consuelo, Horace, Les Maîtres Mosaïstes, Le Château des Désertes, Le Château de Pictordu,* and *La Daniella.*

22. In Moi 2006: chap. 3 I show that Brandes, in his breakthrough lectures on literature in Copenhagen in the winter of 1871–72, published in 1872 under the title *Emigrantlitteraturen* ("Emigré Literature"), calls for a modern literature that would resurrect the spirit of radical romantics such as Madame de Staël and Schiller.

23. This is the famous catchphrase from Brandes' breakthrough lectures on main currents in European literature delivered in Copenhagen in the winter of 1871–72.

24. The classical work on mass culture as modernism's other is Huyssen 1986.

25. The "claim of the ideal" is my translation of Gregers Werle's incessant harping on *den ideale fordring* in Ibsen's *The Wild Duck.* Another possible translation would be the "ideal demand."

REFERENCES

Baldick, C. (2001). *The Concise Oxford Dictionary of Literary Terms.* Oxford: Oxford University Press.

Bernstein, J., ed. (2003). *Classic and Romantic German Aesthetics.* Cambridge: Cambridge University Press.

Brandes, G., and E. Brandes. (1939). *Brevveksling med nordiske forfattere og videnskabsmænd* (M. Borup, F. Bull, and J. Landquist, eds.). Copenhagen: Gyldendal.

Brecht, B. (1993). *Werke* (vol. 23). Schriften 3: 1942–1956 Berlin: Aufbau.

Buss, R. (2000). "Introduction." *In* E. Zola, *L'Assommoir.* London: Penguin Books.

Childers, J., and Hentzi, G. (eds.). (1995). *The Columbia Dictionary of Modern Literary and Cultural Criticism.* New York: Columbia University Press.

Cuddon, J. A. (1998). *A Dictionary of Literary Terms and Literary Theory* (4th ed.; rev. C. E. Preston). Oxford: Blackwell.

Daleski, H. M. (1996). "Thomas Hardy: A Victorian Modernist." *In* L. L. Besserman (ed.), *The Challenge of Periodization: Old Paradigms and New Perspectives.* New York: Garland, 179–95.

Deutscher, I. (1954). *The Prophet Armed: Trotsky: 1879–1921.* New York: Oxford University Press.

Egan, M., ed. (1972). *Ibsen: The Critical Heritage.* London: Routledge and Kegan Paul.

Ellmann, R. (1988). *Oscar Wilde.* New York: Alfred A. Knopf.

Espmark, K. (1991). *The Nobel Prize in Literature: A Study of the Criteria behind the Choices.* Boston: G. K. Hall.

Förster, E. (2004). "1796–1797: A New Program for the Aesthetic Education of Mankind?" *In* D. E. Wellbery and J. Ryan (eds.), *A New History of German Literature.* Cambridge, Mass.: Belknap Press.

Hölderlin, F. (2002). "Oldest Programme for a System of German Idealism." *In* J. Bernstein (ed.), *Classic and Romantic German Aesthetics.* Cambridge: Cambridge University Press.

Huyssen, A. (1986). *After the Great Divide: Modernism, Mass Culture, Postmodernism.* Bloomington: Indiana University Press.

Ibsen, H. (1928–57). *Hundreårsutgave: Henrik Ibsens samlede verker* (F. Bull, H. Koht, and D. A. Seip, eds.; 21 vols.). Oslo: Gyldendal.

Kant, I. (1996). *The Metaphysics of Morals* (M. Gregor, ed. and trans.). Cambridge: Cambridge University Press. (Original work published in 1797.)

Kuhn, T. S. (1996). *The Structure of Scientific Revolutions* (3rd ed.). Chicago: University of Chicago Press.

LaCapra, D. (1989). "1857: Two Trials." *In* D. Hollier (ed.), *A New History of French Literature.* Cambridge, Mass.: Harvard University Press.

Lukács, G. (1978). *Writer and Critic and Other Essays* (A. Kahn, ed. and trans.). London: Merlin Press.

Moi, T. (2006). *Henrik Ibsen and the Birth of Modernism: Art, Theater, Philosophy.* Oxford and New York: Oxford University Press.

Monrad, M. J. (1974). "Hvad man kan lære af Ibsens *Gengangere.*" *In* T. Christophersen (ed.), *Norsk Litteraturkritikk 1770–1890.* Oslo: Gyldendal. (Original work published 1882).

Nietzsche, F. (1967). "Attempt at Self-Criticism." *In* Nietzsche, *The Birth of Tragedy and The Case of Wagner* (W. Kaufmann, trans.). New York: Vintage Books. (Original work published in 1886.)

——. (1989). *Beyond Good and Evil: Prelude to a Philosophy of the Future* (W. Kaufmann, trans.). New York: Vintage Books. (Original work published in 1886.)

Petersen, C. (1865). "*Peer Gynt,* dramatisk Digt af Henrik Ibsen." Retrieved March 2006 from www.ibsen.net/index.db2?id=229.

Poovey, M. (2004). "Forgotten Writers, Neglected Histories: Charles Reade and the Nineteenth Century Transformation of the British Literary Field." *English Literary History* 71(2): 433–53.

Sand, G. (1991). *Story of My Life: The Autobiography of George Sand* (T. Jurgrau, ed.). Albany: State University of New York Press. (Original work published in 1854–55.)

Schiller, F. (1993). "On Naive and Sentimental Poetry" (D. O. Dahlstrom, trans.). *In* W. Hinderer and D. O. Dahlstrom (eds.), *Essays.* New York: Continuum.

Schlegel, F. (2003). "From *Ideas.*" *In* J. Bernstein (ed.), *Classic and Romantic German Aesthetics.* Cambridge: Cambridge University Press. (Original work published in 1800.)

Schor, N. (1993). *George Sand and Idealism.* New York: Columbia University Press.

Schott, R. M. (1988). *Cognition and Eros: A Critique of the Kantian Paradigm.* Boston: Beacon Press.

Shaw, G. B. (1905). *The Quintessence of Ibsenism.* New York: Brentano's. (Original work published in 1891.)

von Moisy, S. (1981). *Paul Heyse: Münchner Dichterfürst im bürgerlichen Zeitalter. Ausstellung in der Bayerischen Staatsbibliothek 23. Januar bis 11. April 1981.* München: C. H. Beck.

Weinberg, B. (1937). *French Realism: The Critical Reaction, 1830–1870.* New York: Modern Language Association of America and Oxford University Press.

Wilde, O. (1968a). "The Critic as Artist." *In* R. Ellmann (ed.), *The Artist as Critic: Critical Writings of Oscar Wilde.* New York: Random House. (Original work published in 1888.)

——. (1968b). "The Decay of Lying." *In* R. Ellmann (ed.), *The Artist as Critic: Critical Writings of Oscar Wilde.* New York: Random House.

———. (1968c). "M. Caro on George Sand." *In* R. Ellmann (ed.), *The Artist as Critic: Critical Writings of Oscar Wilde.* New York: Random House.

———. (1992). *The Picture of Dorian Gray.* Oxford: Oxford University Press. (Original work published in 1890.)

Wirsén, C. D. af. (1901). *Kritiker.* Stockholm: P. A. Norstedt and Söners Förlag.

Woolf, V. (1988). *The Essays of Virginia Woolf,* Vol. 3, *1919–1924* (A. McNeillie, ed.). New York: Harcourt Brace Jovanovitch.

CHAPTER 13

....

MODERNISM

....

PHILIP WEINSTEIN

Thinking is judged by a standard that does not measure up
to it. Such judgment may be compared to the procedure of
trying to calculate the nature and powers of a fish by seeing
how long it can live on dry land. For a long time now, all too
long, thinking has been stranded on dry land.

—Martin Heidegger, "Letter on Humanism"

There are no classes in life for beginners.

—Rainer Maria Rilke, *The Notebooks of
Malte Laurids Brigge*

One begins by being confused. A cryptic epigram from Rilke, a heady passage
from Heidegger, suggesting that conventional paradigms for "thinking" denature
the activity itself: that's all you have to go on, for starters. In what follows, I propose
two defining dimensions of modernist texts: (1) their initial difficulty (one begins
by being confused), and (2) their experimental departure from earlier conventions
of thinking. To these two dimensions I would add a third: modernist texts involve
less a "judging" than a "trying," in the double sense that they are invested more
in trying things out than in representing according to normative schemas, and
that they are *trying* to read—deliberately so. We do not often like being confused.
(I return later to the notion of "trying" by trying out Franz Kafka's *The Trial* [1925],
a text that Theodor Adorno characterizes as "the trial of a trial" [1983: 268]—a sort
of fish unavailable to dry land judgment.)

Contributors to this volume were invited to take seriously the "and" in its title, *Oxford Handbook of Philosophy and Literature*. I take this to mean that at least two feasible projects are not invited: either a reading of literature as enabled by certain identifiable philosophic positions (literature as a covert rewriting of philosophy), or a reading of philosophy as a species of literature under another name (philosophy's truth-claiming difference disappearing, postmodern fashion, into the subjective maw of literature). Instead, the invitation called for a consideration of philosophy and literature as distinctive genres—or better, "distinctive kinds of attention to human life," literature involving, as philosophy rarely does, acute attention to the representation of *particulars*.

I intend to use particulars for the basic claims of this argument about modernism. I assess neither poetry nor drama here, nor do I say much about the variety of fictional strategies that emerge during the period normally glossed as modernism (1900s to 1930s). Instead of attempting encyclopedic coverage, I consider in some detail the practice of three novelists—Marcel Proust, Franz Kafka, and William Faulkner—with the aim of shedding light on central strategies and powers of modernism.[1] The philosophical company these writers keep includes Freud and the phenomenologists—Martin Heidegger, Maurice Merleau-Ponty, and Emmanuel Levinas primarily—proposed *as* company, not as foundational supports. My project is to show how the formal practices of my novelists, so to speak, *philosophize*, enact a philosophic stance through their particular way of deploying materials. One such way is already before us: modernist fiction's insistence that one begin by being confused alters the traditional genre's way of staging the figure against the ground.

"There are no classes in life for beginners," the fictional Malte writes in Rilke's *The Notebooks of Malte Laurids Brigge* (1910), and he continues: "[I]t is always the most difficult that is asked of one right away" (1964: 80). *The Notebooks* bears out this claim, immersing the reader in Malte's confusing notebook entries for (rather than his developing understanding of) his unmappable Paris experiences. A fundamental difference between life realities and narrative conventions emerges. Life unfolds (the verb is too bland) unpedagogically, while narrative centers on pedagogic development. Narrative seems primordially structured so as to make sense of the human passage through time, to represent it developmentally. To do this, it turns "life" into a "life class." In class, what occurs now ("right away") prepares us (as in narrative) for what is to come. But in life we never exit from a perpetual present tense that may—whenever crisis arrives—return us abruptly to an inescapable first grade. Almost 70 years before Rilke, Kierkegaard emphasized the same radical difference between unpredictable life realities and domesticating narrative conventions: "For my part," Kierkegaard's Johannes di Silentio claims, "I presumably can describe the movements of faith, but I cannot make them. In learning to go through the motions of swimming, one can be suspended from the ceiling in a harness and then presumably describe the movements, but one is not swimming" (1983: 37–38).

SWIMMING AND "SWIMMING"

Swimming as opposed to "swimming": the former occurs only if one is immersed in the water of unrehearsable presence, while the latter is learnable by way of a harness and repeated simulation. Might this correlate to a difference between a kind of thinking (typically hostile to narrative) that occurs in the water, and a kind of thinking (narrative's bread and butter) that takes place on dry land? Heidegger's analogy, like Kierkegaard's, is strikingly spatial, so we need to factor in its no less crucial temporal component. Narrative is fashioned to escape the unknowing of sheer presence—the time frame in which life is actually lived—by providing retrospect, the knowing that graces presence with a perspective available only after presence has passed. In the present, if habit fails, we are suddenly unknowing. To see how this situation might be represented in its modernist fictional particulars, let us try out a scene from the early pages of Kafka's *The Trial* (1925). Joseph K. has awakened to find two strangers in his room, dressed in apparently coded but indecipherable uniforms. They take him into an adjoining room where he is told he is under arrest:

> "You are only under arrest, nothing more. I was requested to inform you of this....That's enough for today, and we can say good-by, though only for the time being, naturally. You'll be going to the Bank now, I suppose?" "To the Bank?" asked K. "I thought I was under arrest?" K. asked the question with a certain defiance, for though his offer to shake hands had been ignored, he felt more and more independent of all these people, especially now that the Inspector had risen to his feet...."How can I go to the Bank, if I am under arrest?" "Ah, I see," said the Inspector, who had already reached the door. "You have misunderstood me. You are under arrest, certainly, but that need not hinder you from going about your business. Nor will you be prevented from leading your ordinary life." "Then being arrested isn't so very bad," said K., going up to the Inspector. "I never suggested that it was," said the Inspector. "But in that case it would seem there was no particular necessity to tell me about it," said K., moving still closer. The others had drawn near too. They were all gathered now in a little space beside the door. "It was my duty," said the Inspector...."I was assuming that you would want to go to the Bank....And to facilitate that...I have detained these three gentlemen here, who are colleagues of yours, to be at your disposal." "What?" cried K., gaping at the three of them. These insignificant anaemic young men, whom he had observed only as a group standing beside the photographs, were actually clerks in the Bank, not colleagues of his—that was putting it too strongly and indicated a gap in the omniscience of the Inspector—but they were subordinate employees of the Bank all the same. How could he have failed to notice that? (1968: 14–15)

What figure-ground relation operates here? How does the passage propose a picture whose caption might read: "What's wrong with this picture?" What conventions for representing the human figure in social space and time have been subverted?

The first subverted convention is the reader's capacity to understand subjects by reliably deciphering their movement through familiar space and time. We absolutely depend on this capacity (in and out of fictions); a good portion of our social intelligence resides in our knowing how to tease out the implications of others' gestures, to catch the false move in an expected sequence. (When, halfway through Henry James's *Portrait of a Lady* [1881], his protagonist, Isabel Archer, glimpses Gilbert Osmond and Madame Merle talking intimately together, he sitting while she stands, Isabel deciphers—and we with her—the legible transgression of a social code. Neither we nor she is wrong in doing so; a shared code for reading human behavior in space and time is operative, and its infraction tells much, tells all.) I have much to say later about the philosophic stance buttressing this assumption so commonplace as to go unnoticed.

The second convention, also sabotaged here, is that represented space is reliably inventoried: not that everything is identified, but that everything *pertinent* to the subject's orientation is identified. The typical narrator silently performs this task of domesticating space in the moment of describing it, making it fit for progressive narrative. Kafka breaks this rule: his text is unpredictably "mined," and the result is (in the Freudian sense of the term) *uncanny*. The three "anaemic young men" eventually surge into recognizability well after K. has already entered the room, and we ask: How did they get there? Do they belong to the Bank or to K.? How can he have "failed to notice" them? (It is more than a question of bad lighting.) In the two centuries of realist fiction that precedes Kafka, there is no room that the protagonist can enter without the narrator—cannily, expeditiously—identifying the pertinent furnishings.

If we resurvey the passage, we note that it is suffused with (what we normally take to be) orientational spatial gestures. The Inspector who rises to his feet, reaches the door, K. who goes up to him, moves still closer, the others who gather together beside the door: all these details that would traditionally facilitate a scene of clarification carry here a tinge of epistemological menace. The orientational assumptions of social life dependent on shared spatial convention—the handshake, the privacy of the bedroom, the meaning of arrest if it does not signify disruption in K.'s ordinary management of space and time—are being sabotaged.

We can generalize this figure/ground further: without orderly space, no orderly time; without either of these, no subject development. K. can learn nothing (see Kern 1983).[2] Later, while discussing his case with the lawyer Huld, the spatial trap is sprung again: "'For example,' Huld says, 'there's a dear friend of mine visiting me at this very moment,' and he waved a hand toward a dark corner of the room. 'Where?' asked K., almost rudely, in his first shock of astonishment. He looked round uncertainly... [a]nd then some form or other in the dark corner actually began to stir" (Kafka 1968: 104). Not so unmotivated this time: K.'s lapse is partially explainable. But the point is that Kafka represents him as *no longer in perceptual control of his space*; he has lost his road map. Other spatial surprises abound—the building (it could be any building) where he enters on the fifth floor and the hearing is being held, the discovery of court doors in Titoretti's apartment, the performance of the Whipper scene within the precincts of the Bank itself. There are no classes in life for this Joseph K., who, despite entering his 31st year, is incomprehensibly returned to the (dis)orientational state of a beginner. His trial unfolds (the verb is too bland) as his being continuously *tried* by everything that happens to him.

What would be at stake in centering modernist narrative on such ongoing distress—a state in which none of one's previous "swimming" lessons has taught one how to swim? To answer this, we need to sketch in the several centuries' history of Western orientational assumptions and procedures that predate Joseph K. and—by privileging canniness—make his sudden incapacity (his being "un-can-ed") so startling. Such assumptions and procedures—constitutive of Enlightenment thought and the realist fiction that body of thought subtends—center on the Western drama of a subject *coming to know*. Although chapter 10 in this handbook focuses on the practice of realism, my argument here must briefly rehearse that prior practice of representation. Only in response to its operative assumptions can we unpack the resonance of modernist *unknowing*.

ENLIGHTENMENT KNOWING

For a subject to *come to know*, an Enlightenment premise of reliable correspondence between the individual and the world must operate. Thanks to the prior establishment of lawful time and uniform space, a subject can learn to map the outer world accurately and, in so doing, achieve inner orientation, as well. Personal identity gets confirmed by way of this achieved knowledge of what is out there. On this model, the subject who would know and the object to be known are assumed to be meant for each other—the latter destined for the former. How did the West come to reconceptualize the outer world so that it might enter these conditions of knowability?

We might best pursue this question by proposing a composite narrative of progress that draws upon four exemplary Enlightenment thinkers: Descartes, Newton, Locke, and Kant. Put too schematically, we can say that Descartes initiates the narrative by conceiving the Western subject who would know. *Cogito ergo sum* gives birth—in pure alienation from parents, siblings, church, state, and culture—to the single knowing subject: *res cogitans*. His opposite number—the outer world now removed from its status as a cosmos of kindred being, and alienated as mere material nature awaiting scientific knowledge—is *res extensa*. Together, *res cogitans* and *res extensa* make a marriage that launches Western science and, later, realist fiction.

The second thinker in this emergent Enlightenment narrative is Newton. His "system of the world" proposes a gravitational model that calculates the movement of matter in both the farthest heavens and an apple falling from the tree. Newton is the Enlightenment's grand mapmaker. Thanks to his theory of gravitational forces, the world—everyone was sure—made rational, secular, knowable sense; it had become a universe of calculable forces. (Not that anyone, including Newton, understood why gravity operated as it did, but few doubted that it did operate as he said it did.)

Descartes conceives the unencumbered rational subject, stripped free of custom and—liberated/liberal now—capable of coming to know. Newton makes available a lawful, material cosmos, conceptually mastered and open to being known. Missing still is a narrative for how Descartes's knowing subject might best learn—in time—to negotiate Newton's knowable world, there before him and awaiting his negotiation. Locke's *Essay concerning Human Understanding* (1690) supplies this narrative, laying out precisely the story of empirical trial by error—of beginning as a blank slate but being capable of knowing more—the story that was to ground Western fiction.

Drawing on representative Enlightenment propositions, we have identified the birth of an unhampered subject who seeks to know (and who knows *how* to know: by way of doubt), and the authoritative ordering of the material universe (from apples to stars) in uniform space and time, its force and motions open to exact calculation. Procedure, subject, and setting are in place. Locke takes these and sets them in motion by way of a plot that has proved to have abiding appeal—launching novels and compelling audiences from his time to our own.

The plot goes like this, moving progressively from dawn to day (but rarely far into the evening): I am born; I learn swiftly that I do not yet know but am capable of knowing; I am not predicated (no inherited schema contains me), but the world I inhabit *is* predicated: knowable by way of trial and error, God-given perhaps but secular in its operations; I can learn to negotiate objects and others in the familiar space and time of this schema, obtaining property as I go; my doing this confirms reflexively my identity as an agent in my own life (property referring simultaneously to what I own and to what is "proper to me," mine alone); I cannot obtain everything, but if observant, prudent, and self-aware, I can get what I deserve. I am, it seems, everyman. I am also white-male-bourgeois-developmental acquisitiveness. Therefore, one last element is required of this narrative: something that will allow it to continue speaking to my projects while at the same time honoring my Judeo-Christian conviction that the systematic career of selfhood is an exercise not of virtue but of vice. The narrative must be effectively moralized, yet without repudiating the earlier givens. This is not only not easy, but probably impossible. Enter Kant.

Kant shows, first (in Paul Guyer's words), "that the validity of both the laws of the starry skies above as well as the moral law within had to be sought in the legislative power of human intellect itself" (1992: 2). Legislative: the moral law within is as rule driven as Newton's obedient comets. Second, despite the fact that, as material phenomena, we are—like all phenomena—unfree, at our unreachable noumenal core we cannot know that we are unfree, and we must therefore, to be human, act as though we *are* free. Thus, Kant arrives at the categorical imperative:

"Act in such a way that you always treat humanity...never simply as a means, but always...as an end" (as cited in Guyer 1992: 322). Others conceive and pursue their ends, even as I conceive and pursue mine. Newton's famous Second Law of Motion becomes moralized. It is no longer that what I do to you rebounds on me, but rather that I am forbidden to encroach on your freedom, even as you are forbidden to encroach on mine, for we each have our own motions in mind.[3]

This Enlightenment narrative is torn by opposed convictions: on the one hand, a story of self-flourishing, as far as one can take it; on the other hand, a story of self-disciplining, treating others as ends rather than means. Others as ends—a tall order for a narrative that has so prioritized the knowing subject, has in fact posited the reality of others and objects as knowable only because answerable to the subject's categories for knowing them. This is a story in which I come first, in which you become recognizable only because you enter into my categories for apprehending you. You reduce to what I know you as. Levinas—a twentieth-century religious thinker and philosopher—repeatedly attacks this story, showing that the subject at its center engages in no real risk; everything I encounter eventually reduces to my categories for encountering it. Levinas calls this master plot of Western discourse "a return to Ithaca," a return to self-sameness in which all my ventures are, thanks to later recognitions, recovered and grounded.

ANATOMY OF REALISM

We may briefly test this Enlightenment narrative—with its contradictory emphases on both my flourishing and my need to respect yours—by developing an anatomy of fictional realism that resembles it, in four parts: introducing the subject, familiarizing the subject, space and time travel, and recognition. Realist fiction introduces the subject by bringing him close-up. Close-up—like Jane Austen's Emma and Charles Dickens's Pip—but not *too* close-up—as Benjy Compson of Faulkner's *The Sound and the Fury* and Stephen Dedalus of Joyce's *Ulysses* are too close-up. *Reliably* close-up, as well: not like Kafka's Joseph K., whom "someone must have traduced, for without having done anything wrong he was arrested one fine morning": a narrative situation putting us in a familiar bedroom with the protagonist all right, but (as we have seen) there's something wrong with that room, something that was never before wrong with it, something we're never going to find out. In realism, we will find out fully what's "on his mind" or "in his path."

Next, familiarizing the subject: the novelistic canvas is immediately peopled with others and their social norms. The protagonist's developing familiarity with these others is doubled by the reader's developing familiarity with them all; the capacity to recognize others proceeds swiftly. Not that realism does not deal in misrecognitions, but it shapes them mainly in the form of mistakes eventually set right—as in Austen's *Pride and Prejudice*, a host of Wickhams in time replaced by

Darcys. Misrecognition in modernism tends to be more stubborn, perhaps irreversible; in much postmodernism it is no longer even pertinent.

Next, space and time travel: in realism, the hero and the reader move around a lot; such moving around is always pedagogic. The realist world of space and time, because lawful, accommodates an incremental series of Lockean trials. Initial sightings prepare for later, reliable ones. As Descartes established doubt to be initiatory, and as Locke stressed ignorance to be the first step toward knowledge, so certain entities on the realist canvas will be misread when first presented, so that they may be, eventually, accurately reread when re-presented. Anyone observing from a neutral position would concur, as though to say, "This is how things are, you need not take my word for it."

Finally, recognition: realism's sublime moments center on recognition. Consider Pip's long-withheld encounter with Magwitch, that stormy night in Pip's chambers. Virtually everyone who matters—Miss Havisham, Estella, Magwitch, Joe, and most of all Pip himself—comes suddenly into a new and disturbing focus. Such recognition scenes appear as crescendo moments of realism—clarifications of an entire life, made possible by coming to know one's world better, and thus oneself better.

How does the realist protagonist manage to rise above the flow of his own life in time and space, and eventually to see who he really is? Such experience becomes fruitful only if the protagonist's identity is assumed to be a coherence sustained throughout time. Time is a disinterested friend of Enlightenment subjectivity; the conscious I of the Enlightenment possesses *reliable memory*. This model of identity is atemporal. Pip has to (and *can*) remember his past accurately, as Maggie Tulliver and Anna Karenina suicidally remember theirs. Memory cannot be evaded; realism launches its recognitions by way of that resource: was blind, but now I see.

This is the bread-and-butter story of Western fiction; it moves with a systolic-diastolic rhythm of eventual progress and enlightenment, of coming to know the territory. Why, and how, do modernist writers refuse this story?

Here are some suggested answers. First, that bread-and-butter story of progress can be unbearably smug—and, second, not just smug but colonizing. It assumes that the rest of the world is somehow just out there waiting for our getting to know it better, to master it better. Its figure/ground model is out of whack: the figure (the individual at the center of the narrative) so large, the ground (all that surrounds him/her) so small. John Maynard Keynes once remarked, "I don't think one realises how very discrete (in the mathematical sense) one's existence is" (as cited in Banfield 2000: 112). One's existence as discrete, infinitesimal within the immeasurable field of countless others: you wouldn't realize this by reading the canon of Western realist fiction. Such fiction is committed, as Virginia Woolf put it in a gender context, to producing mirrors that make the (male) subject look twice his size. Modernism corrects this visual error by puncturing the balloon of male project, reducing its sway. Made smaller, the male subject shares a canvas with others whom he does not succeed in knowing and converting to dimensions of his self-sameness.

As we have seen, the Enlightenment narrative of coming to know assumes lawful time and space as awaiting the mapping energies of a knowing subject. Is this everyone's favorite story because it proposes that we are a species that sustains identity in our course through space and time? (Would we still so believe in the coherence of personal identity if we did not have numberless narratives telling us, "It exists, it really does"?) Western narrative may be shaped primordially to these purposes. As Peter Brooks (1984) puts it, narrative "perverts" time by representing human behavior as a mastering of time by way of achieved self-recognitions: returns to Ithaca. I understand such "perversions" to enact a human fiction at once necessary and without foundation (or, as James Joyce would say, founded on the void). Unlike our nonhuman pets, we do not, and cannot, inhabit a temporality wholly unfurnished with the shapings proposed by narrative. We accommodate time, perforce, by perverting it.

Jean-Paul Sartre describes this trick in his novel *Nausea* (1938): "This is what I thought: for the most banal event to become an adventure, you must...begin to recount it. This is what fools people: a man is always a teller of tales, he lives surrounded by his stories and the stories of others...and he tries to live his own life as if he were living a story. But you have to choose: live or tell" (1964: 39). Live or tell: *live* a life without knowing how it comes out, or *tell* a life from the end-supplied perspective of knowing how it comes out. The binary is, of course, too sharp: a form of *living* uprooted from every retrospective order provided by *telling* is no form at all, but rather chaos or insanity. Yet the binary lets us grasp a central distinction: realism tends to evade precisely this problematic of time, while modernism seeks to take it head on. Realism knows it is returning to Ithaca. It tells its story from the (unannounced) perspective of an Ithaca *already* returned to: the boat is docked before the adventure on the water begins. By contrast, the modernists produce narratives that are difficult precisely because they dislocate the act of "telling" so that it might better represent the unmasterable conditions of "living." The moment of *now*—sheer presence—becomes opaque without the clarifications provided by what went before and that prepare for what comes after. Freud is the theorist of opaque presence, of subjectivity unmoored from its legible becoming in time. He is the doctor of unknowing. For this story in the realm of fiction, we go to Proust, Kafka, and Faulkner.

Modernist Unknowing

We begin with some of Freud's fundamental ideas: defenses and repression as shaping forces guaranteeing that the subject is, at the same time, other than itself; the uncanny as a spatial fault line testifying to ego's "bleeding" into space and warping

it; trauma as the wound to psyche that makes it inhabit a time frame simultaneously then and now (the subject "bleeding" into time). These Freudian *concepts*
emerge in the work of Kafka, Proust, and Faulkner as *narrative forms* (just as realist narrative configures Enlightenment convictions as narrative forms). I do not
propose Freudian readings; rather, I argue that Freud's seminal concepts reemerge
in modernist fictional procedures. Uncanny space turns unlawful; things slip, lose
their familiarity (or are hauntingly familiar even though unknown). Unbound
time forfeits linearity; progress comes to a halt. Modernist narrative involves the
discovery, not of who one is (the drama of knowing), but that one is other. As the
fictional subject's compact with reconfirming space and time founders, a poetics
of knowing cedes to one of unknowing.

One further Freudian term—*anaclisis*—allows us to measure the stakes of a
shattered compact between the subject and the outer world. In seeking to understand the origin of sexual instincts, Freud distinguishes between *anaclitic* and
autoerotic activities.[4] Freud's narrow distinction is between the earliest infantile
instincts that "lean upon" the mother's milk itself, and a later separation/sexual-
izing of these instincts as they move away from any necessary object. (First, the
infant instinctively seeks the life-sustaining milk, and then, more playfully, the
breast that contains the milk but is gradually becoming a sexualized object in
itself, and thereafter any number of potentially sexualized objects unconnected
with "milk"—a trajectory that launches the unplotted history of human sexuality.) The term "anaclitic" has, however, taken on a larger reference. It describes
not the instinct's "leaning," but rather the *infant's* "leaning"—in Jean Laplanche's
terms—"on the *object*, and ultimately *a leaning on the mother*" (1985: 16, emphasis
original). "Leaning on the mother": *anaclisis* figures a sort of elemental socializing
or bonding between infant and mother. More broadly, I read as anaclisis the relation of the subject to *already familiar* space, space previously "leaned on" and made
safe by association, so to speak, with the mother's breast, space located on the path
of ego maturation.[5] Uncanny space, by contrast, is space removed from familiarity,
no longer breast-sanctioned, space you can do nothing with—like the space you
find yourself in, for example, when you've become a noxious insect and your own
bedroom is suddenly a prison.

When the unthinkingly anaclitic pact between knowing subject and familiar world collapses, space and time, "here" and "now," no longer function as lawful, cooperative frames for being. The Enlightenment drama of a subject coming
to know ceases to operate. In such conditions, the subject itself—"I"—alters as
well. A microscopic and ceaseless traffic among all three terms—subject, space,
time—replaces the more easily manageable figure/ground polarity implicit in the
drama of the singular Cartesian subject. In the older Enlightenment model, a fore-
grounded *res cogitans* moves through doubt and learns to gauge accurately a back-
grounded *res extensa*. By contrast, modernism's representational schema draws
on different tenets, produces a different figure/ground—one that might best be
understood as phenomenological.

MODERNIST REPRESENTATION AND
PHENOMENOLOGY

Since my argument centers on the philosophizing enacted through literary form, I only sketch here some basic phenomenological tenets. A range of late-nineteenth- and early-twentieth-century Western thinkers (F. H. Bradley, Henri Bergson, Franz Brentano, and Edmund Husserl among them) were engaged in reconceptualizing the embodied subject's ways of inhabiting and registering the exterior world. Oversimplifying, one may say that, in their work, individual consciousness appears less as the separate subjective lens through which a Hume would despair of arriving at lawful objective conclusions, and more as the participatory "field" within which world apprehension continuously occurs. Consciousness and the world preengage each other, producing in individuals the experience of a lifeworld. Husserl claims that our minds never grasp "the matter straight out," but rather how things "'appear.' For this reason, they are called 'phenomena,' and their most general essential character is to exist as the 'consciousness-of' or 'appearance-of' the specific things" (1973: 50). With Heidegger's publication of *Being and Time* (1927), phenomenology emerges (and for the next two decades remains) as a major current in European philosophy, marking the existentialist thought of Gabriel Marcel, Merleau-Ponty, Levinas, and Sartre.

I make no claim as to influence. (It is likely that, apart from Proust's knowing some of Bergson's work, none of my novelists read these philosophers.) Rather, I seek to disengage some common intuitions that shape my writers' representational strategies, and one leaps into view. In modernist fictional practice things tend (more aggressively than in realism) to enter representation as perceived or "intended" by consciousness. Of course, Enlightenment thought also understands the subject's grasp on the object as phenomenal alone, but subject and object—an immaterial *res cogitans* and a material *res extensa*—remain oppositional terms. By contrast, phenomenology stresses the mental framing of world perception so as to bond inseparably subject and object; subject and world are "hard-wired" into each other.

As Merleau-Ponty puts it, this is, *pace* Descartes, "a philosophy for which the world is always 'already there' before reflection begins—as an inalienable presence" (1973: 72). I am always inserted in the world; all my analyses of it are affected by that preobjective insertion.[6] Merleau-Ponty again:

> It is because it is a preobjective view that being-in-the-world can be distinguished from every third person process, from every modality of the *res extensa*, as from every *cogitatio*, from every first person form of knowledge—and that it can effect the union of the "psychic" and the "physiological." ... We must therefore avoid saying that our body is *in* space, or *in* time. It *inhabits* space and time. (1999: 152, 155)

"Here I am," in phenomenologically oriented modernist fiction, means not that a separate "I" happens to find itself in space and time, but that the (embodied) "I" cannot be responsibly thought apart from the space and time it always inhabits. In this cohabiting, a certain subset of *res extensa*—one's body—gets reconceptualized as the inalienable grounding of *res cogitans*: not alien body but *lived* body. As Heidegger puts it in his study of Nietzsche, "we do not 'have' a body; rather, we are 'bodily'" (as cited in Merleau-Ponty 1999: 124). With a different set of assumptions, Freud arrived at a similar view. The body "speaks" the being, "speaks" it more revealingly, often, than the mind.

"Here I am," an incarnate being moving in space/time. In realism, the subject's capacity for movement is taken for granted; the narrative focuses instead on *res cogitans*'s various projects. In phenomenologically inflected fiction, however, the details of the embodied subject's lifeworld—an array of orientational arrangements prior to, more intimate than, the pursuit of projects—become inexhaustibly pertinent. These writers are more likely to attend to the elemental world-furnishing that makes human being possible. Heidegger writes:

> When we speak of man and space, it sounds as though man stood on one side, space on the other. Yet space is not something that faces man.... Spaces, and with them space as such—"space"—are always provided for already within the stay of mortals.... To say that mortals *are* is to say that *in dwelling* they persist through spaces by virtue of their stay among things and locations. (1977a: 334–35)

Levinas understands this primordial insertion of embodied being into familiar space/time as enjoyment itself—that unthinking orientational confidence that I have been calling anaclitic. Levinas writes:

> Dwelling is the very mode of *maintaining oneself*...as the body that...holds *itself* up and can.... The "at home" is not a container but a site where *I can*, where, dependent on a reality that is other, I am, despite this dependence or thanks to it, free. It is enough to walk, to *do*, in order to grasp anything, to take.... The site, a medium, affords means. Everything is here, everything belongs to me.... The possibility of possessing, that is, of suspending the very alterity of what is only at first other, and other relative to me, is the *way* of the same. I am at home with myself in the world because it offers itself to or resists possession. (1969: 37–38)

If these two passages seem familiar in their claims—however unfamiliar their vocabulary—it means that they reprise an assumption about the subject in space/time already central to realist protocols: that human being is *at home* there. Taken for granted and therefore unspoken in Enlightenment thought, that assumption gets articulated—put into thought—in twentieth century phenomenology, allowing us to see writ large the anaclitic dimensions of our pact with space/time.

Yet a crucial difference obtains in the later schema. The phenomenological model binds *subject*, *space*, and *time* as radically interdependent terms (whereas Enlightenment thought, Cartesian-wise, grasped the subject as essentially free of its setting). No embodied subjects without immersion in space/time; no absolute space/time indifferent to embodied subjects. The terms are wholly correlative. Finally—and this is the point I have working toward—the articulation of subject/ space/time as radically bonded carries with it the possibility of the bond's rupture. In Enlightenment thought neither such a pact nor its rupture is readily conceivable. By contrast, much modernist philosophy and fiction engages this intimate, moment-by-moment pact ("here I am") by way of exploring its rupture. Indeed, the shattering of the subject/space/time bond is the signature event in the modernist fiction under discussion. Levinas has already let us see how this scenario of at-home-ness—furnishedness—sustains itself by converting the alterity of the other into dimensions of the same. What is modernist shock if not the arrival of an alterity that cannot be so converted?

Before resuming that analysis by way of the assaulted modernist subject, let us stay with Levinas's terms a bit longer. Although his concern is philosophical rather than literary, he identifies the logic that drives progressive realist motion through space and time. The wayfaring subject, engaging a set of suspended obstacles (alterity), eventually manages to negotiate these obstacles, converting them into a continuation of the same. In so doing, he returns home. In these terms, realism is the infinitely rewritable story of Ulysses making his way through alterity as he heads toward Ithaca. This drama of turning other into self—of coming to possess it as knowledge, as challenge met and resolved—is, as I argued above, the Ur-narrative of Western realist fiction and Enlightenment philosophy.

Finally, Levinas characterizes not just the logic and the temporality of realist representation, but its seductiveness, as well:

> [We are dealing with] an experience always anticipated and consented to…. The given enters into a thought which…invests it with its own project, and thus exercises mastery over it. What affects a consciousness presents itself at a distance from the first…is represented, does not knock without announcing itself, leaves, across the interval of space and time, the leisure necessary for a welcome. What is realized in and by intentional consciousness offers itself to protention and diverges from itself in retention, so as to be, across the divergency, identified and possessed. This play in being is consciousness itself: presence to self through a distance, which is both loss of self and recovery in truth. (1998: 101–2)

Attended to with sufficient care, this knotty description reveals the temporality of realist plot as an unfolding of experiences anticipated, consented to, accommodated, eventually mastered. Knock, knock; who's there? Realism informs us who, maintains the good manners of announcing the intrusion in advance and providing time for it to be appropriately welcomed. The other then enters the field of intentional consciousness as something partly recognizable in advance (it permits protention), as well as something rewardingly recognized later as slightly different (its retention in consciousness is corrective). Across this divergency—the other's manageable alteration over the time of encounter—the other is "identified and possessed," becoming, for the subject thus encountering it, an event in the career of the same. Finally, this game of the subject's loss and recovery—of consciousness at first inadequate to its encounters but eventually adequate to them—enacts the temporality that "grounds" identity: to lose and then to recover oneself by engaging others in ongoing time just *is* identity. Time—within the anaclitic realm of realism—is the medium in which, encountering others, we (re)become ourselves.

I have entered into this discussion of phenomenology because Enlightenment philosophy—be it idealist or empirical—is typically unprepared to analyze the teeming traffic that occurs at this microscopic level of "here I am." Its epistemological project is focused elsewhere. To recognize what is at stake when this obscure traffic goes awry and orientation *fails*, I have briefly drawn from the work of Heidegger, Merleau-Ponty, and Levinas. Despite his insistence on human furnishing, Heidegger concedes that orientation may fail. "In anxiety, we say, 'one feels ill at ease [*es ist einem unheimlich*].'...We can get no hold on things. In the slipping away of beings only this 'no hold on things' comes over us and remains" (1977b: 103). *Unheimlich*: the reverse of canniness, of the "I can" of intentional identity. David Krell glosses this negative liability in Heidegger as follows: "Such intricate contexts of meaning—which are usually implicit in our activities and become visible only when something goes wrong, when the hammer breaks or the bulb burns out—constitute what Heidegger calls 'world'" (1977: 20).

The broken hammer, the burned-out bulb, the interrupted enjoyment of a "world": when our subject/space/time contract shatters, "here I am" shifts from capacitation to arrest, from orientation to *errance* and obsession. "Obsession traverses consciousness countercurrentwise," Levinas writes,

> is inscribed in consciousness as something foreign, a disequilibrium, a
> delirium....In the form of an ego, anachronously *delayed* behind its present
> moment, and unable to recuperate this delay—that is, in the form of an ego
> unable to conceive what is "touching" it, the ascendency of the other is exercised
> upon the same to the point of interrupting it, leaving it speechless. (1998: 101)

Space here becomes opaque (I cannot name what is "touching" me), time loses its "re-presentational" docility (I cannot catch up with what is marking me and will not release me). Such a subject has exited from the soothing familiarity that Levinas calls "the disappearance of what could shock" (1969: 124). This is the subject who claims our attention in the work of Kafka, Proust, and Faulkner. Wherever he is going, it is not to Ithaca. His distress registers an unknowing penetrated by anxiety, an unpreparedness fraught with fear and trembling.

TIME AND SPACE AS TROUBLE IN MODERNIST FICTION

I indicated at the opening of this chapter that I would proceed, as fiction itself proceeds, by way of compelling particulars. Let us consider now, in uninterrupted slow motion, the particulars of temporal trouble—of trauma—in Proust. Such trauma unfolds (the verb is too bland) as a breaching of the intersubjective bonds we unthinkingly require in order to *be* at all. Reduced to merely oneself, the subject fails to cohere. Lack reasserts itself whenever the anaclitic frame (within which we experience the world outside ourselves as familiar, reliable, breast-sponsored) ruptures. Proust's most moving instance of this dynamic occurs when Marcel, anxious about his grandmother's health, comes upon her unannounced:

> Alas, it was this phantom that I saw when, entering the drawing-room before my grandmother had been told of my return, I found her there reading. I was in the room, or rather I was not yet in the room since she was not aware of my presence, and, like a woman whom one surprises at a piece of needlework which she will hurriedly put aside if anyone comes in, she was absorbed in thoughts which she had never allowed to be seen by me. Of myself—thanks to that privilege which does not last but which gives one, during the brief moment of return, the faculty of being suddenly the spectator of one's own absence—there was present only the witness, the observer, in travelling coat and hat, the stranger who does not belong to the house, the photographer who has called to take a photograph of places which one will never see again. The process that automatically occurred in my eyes when I caught sight of my grandmother was indeed a photograph. We never see the people who are dear to us save in the animated system, the perpetual motion of our incessant love for them, which before allowing the images that their faces present to reach us, seizes them in its vortex and flings them back upon the idea that we have always had of them, makes them adhere to it, coincide with it. How, since into the forehead and the cheeks of my grandmother I had been accustomed to read all the most delicate, the most permanent qualities of her mind, how, since every habitual glance is an act of necromancy, each face that we love a mirror of the past, how could I have failed to overlook what had become dulled and changed in her, seeing that in the most trivial spectacles of our daily life, our eyes, charged with thought, neglect, as would a classical tragedy, every image that does not contribute to the action of the play and retain only those that may help to make its purpose intelligible. But if, instead of our eyes, it should happen to be a purely physical object, a photographic plate, that has watched the action, then what we see, in the courtyard of the Institute, for example, instead of the dignified emergence of an Academician who is trying to hail a cab, will be his tottering steps, his precautions to avoid falling on his back, the parabola of his fall, as though he were drunk or the ground covered in ice. So it is when some cruel trick of chance prevents our intelligent and pious tenderness from coming forward in time to hide from our eyes what they ought never to behold, when it is forestalled by our eyes, and they, arriving first in the field and having it to themselves, set to work mechanically, like films, and show us, in place of the beloved person who has long ago ceased to exist but whose death our tenderness has always hitherto kept concealed from us, the new person whom a hundred times daily it has clothed with a loving and mendacious likeness. And—like a sick man who, not having looked at his own reflexion for a long time, and regularly composing the features which he never sees in accordance with the ideal image of himself that he carries in his mind, recoils on catching sight in the glass, in the middle of an arid desert of a face, of the sloping pink protuberance of a nose as huge as one of the pyramids of Egypt—I, for whom

my grandmother was still myself, I who had never seen her save in my own soul,
always in the same place in the past, through the transparency of contiguous
and overlapping memories, suddenly, in our drawing-room which formed part
of a new world, that of time, that which is inhabited by the strangers of whom
we say "He's begun to age a good deal," for the first time and for a moment only,
since she vanished very quickly, I saw, sitting on the sofa beneath the lamp,
red-faced, heavy and vulgar, sick, vacant, letting her slightly crazed eyes wander
over a book, a dejected old woman whom I did not know. (1981, 2: 141–43)

Freud understands trauma as a breaching of the psyche's defenses sufficiently violent to cause unmanageable distress. The psychic system, overwhelmed, fails to
reorder itself, thus revealing how progressive time itself is dependent on the functioning of the intentional ego. As the ego loses its resourcefulness, so movement
in time loses its linearity. One enters, as it were, a state of fibrillation; purposive
behavior ceases. A trap in the past has been resprung. Proustean trauma arises
otherwise. It involves not a collapse into the suddenly reemerged and engulfing
past, but rather an unbearable recognition of one's *present*. In the space of a single
moment, Marcel sees something traumatizing: what does he see?

First, he sees that seeing itself is reciprocal (a shared pact rather than a private resource), and therefore without guarantee, liable to collapse. All his former
seeings of his grandmother have been unknowingly conditioned upon a reciprocal seeing-back that underwrote their value. Her inestimable value resides in this
mutual seeing; he remains Marcel so long as she remains his grandmother. But her
physical insertion in space and time makes her, at the same time, a being continuously altering and materially unreachable—a situation repressed by the needs of
sanity itself, but unfortunately revealed in this untoward moment. Looking at her
not looking at him, he discovers himself as "the spectator of [his] own absence."
Literally, he is not there in her field of vision; more deeply, he is *not there* unless
sanctioned by her field of vision. Uncorroborated, he gazes at his own absence.
Insofar as all oriented human being depends upon the unthinking sponsorship
of others, Marcel momentarily ceases to be. Need it be said that no realist novel
entertains these quietly terrifying notions, that no realist novel fails to deliver the
drama of coherent individuation? If, as Adorno proposed, modernist art "brings to
light what is infantile in the ideal of being grown up" (1997: 43), Proust reveals what
is grown up in thinking through the aporias of subjective interdependency.

"How could I have failed to overlook...?" Marcel asks, and we remember
Joseph K.'s suddenly distressful "How could he have failed to notice that?" In the
Kafka example, space suddenly becomes opaque, closed to subjective mastery. In
the Proust example, time lurches into view, complicating what had seemed to be
only a familiar entity in space. Marcel realizes that for the longest time now he
has not been seeing his actual grandmother. He has been seeing her as though his
commerce with her in space were time-free; but a photographic lens is ruthlessly
time-focused, on the present. The pathos of the passage resides in the fact that it
takes her not seeing him, for him to see her, for once, as she is. There is no iterative
becoming here, no cozy continuity of being-in-time. Rather, there is a convulsive

alteration, lasting a moment only, and then the curtain drops again. She appears once more as what she used to be. The disinterested camera, capturing only what is actually there, registers (in Proust's model) the world as seen without a self, intolerably up-to-date. More, the inhumanity of this disinterested gaze is potentially Marcel's as well, the camera merely an alibi.

The unfurnished grandmother appears with unmatchable distinctness here, bathed in the estranging and disfiguring medium of time. To see her like this is to recognize all human being in space as continuously time-marked, and to realize that the normal time-coefficient for such seeing is long out-of-date, the act of seeing "an act of necromancy." The passage speaks of "a new world, that of time," which is "inhabited by strangers." Though Proust uses the phrase "êtres de fuite" only for beings in the field of desire, we grasp here its larger resonance. A stranger, his grandmother is being whisked away from him in time, no less than her body will later be (faculty by faculty) taken from her during her illness. In time there are only decomposing strangers headed for unspeakable destinations. The passage's ultimate message is *unknowing*, "a dejected old woman whom I did not know." What bursts forth in Proustean trauma is not the Freudian return of the repressed but the rupture of the time-annealing intersubjective compact.[7] The present breaks through—it breaches—and all is disfigured. Marcel sees that, unknowing, he has all along been seeing the past in place of the present. In this moment he becomes a stranger—to the loved one, to himself—for the new seeing (the past *as* past, the present *as* present) is not bearable (and mercifully not there for long: Proustean subjects falsify time as they falsify space, necessarily, involuntarily). Thus undone, it is Marcel who emerges as "the stranger who does not belong to the house."

The psychic operation in Proustean trauma is eviction from the familiar—a forced relinquishment of the maternal breast. The passage insistently reminds us that, as the pact is mutual, the damage done to her registers in him. The analogies offered—the tottering Academician, the sick man—point to a male subject. Indeed, the sick man whose strategies consist in eluding awareness of his own illness figures less the grandmother than Marcel himself, perpetually buoyed by the reciprocal love of mother and grandmother, ignoring his irreversible physical passage through time. Deprived of his outdated, supportive mirror, he is forced to see himself in uncanny fashion, to catch up with himself: the nose as huge as a pyramid weirdly intimating the momentarily emergent, detested Jew in Proust himself—the Jew otherwise concealed, or projected outward upon Swann, Bloch, and others.[8] Such glimpses, however they differ from each other, imply the same collapse—a falling back upon one's always inadequate personal resources, a return to incurable lack. Indeed, all such Proustean scenes of collapse rehearse the original ejection of Marcel from his mother's kiss, his mother's breast, his mother's womb.

None of this unfolds as realism, for it forfeits the Cartesian premise of *res cogitans*, an independent entity capable (through clear and distinct reasoning) of accurately mapping others in space and time.[9] Proustean time is not a transparent medium within which one progressively pursues one's project. Or, rather, one can do this, one does do this, and the work of the Proustean text is to reveal its terminal inauthenticity. Terminal in the sense of permanent nonarrival: one cannot arrive in Proust (as Tom Jones, Pamela Andrews, Elizabeth Bennet, Eugene Rastignac, and Rodion Raskolnikov all arrive at their appropriate destinations). But one can go back—find out where one has been, even who one has been. In all this we find a rebuke of bourgeois plotting, a repudiation of instrumental achieving—an undermining of the Enlightenment-inspired *projecting* (attempted, failed, revised) that constitutes the main business of Western realism for more than 200 years.

What might Kafkan realism look like (if one could fantasize it)? I suspect it would center on the unfolding career of the Assistant Manager in *The Trial*. This figure—ambitious to rise to the top of his career ladder, unquestioning as to the ends that motivate his effort (focused wholly on the means of arrival)—has no trouble with space, time, or others. His compact is unshakable. Spiritually empty, he embodies his culture's materialist norms, and (if asked) he would say what the chief clerk says to a suddenly disabled Gregor-turned-giant-insect: "[T]his is not the season of the year for a business boom, of course, we admit that, but a season of the year for doing no business at all, that does not exist, Mr. Samsa, must not exist" (Kafka 1995: 77–78). Time as money is the convention within which worldly projects are pursued, attained, failed, or revised. One fine day he will die, but the Assistant Manager will not experience his death until then. His world makes sense, it has a plot, that plot is realism.

As all readers of Kafka know, nothing happens this way. In place of the Assistant Manager, we find figures like Georg Bendemann and Gregor Samsa and Joseph K. Although they themselves are unsurprising (how often they long to become Assistant Managers!), their pathway suddenly becomes a thicket of surprises. Nothing is any longer what it was; even an innocent bank storage room can now house a lurid scene of whipper and victims. It is as though an all-transforming report had been issued off-stage, terminating the successful deployment of habit, career, project. Canniness no longer applies; nothing is any longer reliably familiar.

As for Faulkner, he seems to have taken seriously Nietzsche's remark (which he never read): "I'm afraid we are not rid of God because we still have faith in grammar" (1954: 483). Faulkner invents an entire rhetoric for saying trauma—for wording psyches under assault and immersed in space/time in ways unpremeditated by Newtonian realism. The subject shatters, lives incoherently a scene occurring both then and now. To see how this undoing occurs, let us examine (once more in the uninterrupted slow motion of compelling particulars) young Joe Christmas from *Light in August* (1932)—rushing from a scene of violence at the dancehall to Bobbie's room, thinking to elope with her:

> He knocked. There was a light in her room, and another at the end of the hall, as he had expected; and voices from beyond the curtained windows too....He knocked again, louder, putting his hand on the knob, shaking it, pressing his face against the curtained glass in the front door. The voices ceased....He knocked again...he was still knocking when the door...fled suddenly and silently from under his rapping hand. He was already stepping across the threshold as if he were attached to the door, when Max emerged from behind

it, blocking it. He was completely dressed, even to the hat. "Well, well, well," he said. His voice was not loud, and it was almost as if he had drawn Joe swiftly into the hall and shut the door and locked it before Joe knew that he was inside. Yet his voice held again that ambiguous quality, that quality hearty and completely empty...like a shell, like something he carried before his face and watched Joe through it.... "Here's Romeo at last," he said. "The Beale Street Playboy." Then he spoke a little louder.... "Come in and meet the folks."

Joe was already moving toward the door which he knew, very nearly running again, if he had ever actually stopped.... suddenly he saw the blonde woman standing in the hall at the rear. He had not seen her emerge into the hall at all, yet it was empty when he entered. And then suddenly she was standing there. She was dressed, in a dark skirt, and she held a hat in her hand. And just beyond an open dark door beside him was a pile of luggage, several bags. Perhaps he did not see them. Or perhaps looking saw once, faster than thought *I didn't think she would have that many* Perhaps he thought then for the first time that they had nothing to travel in, thinking *How can I carry all those*. But he did not pause, already turning toward the door which he knew. It was only as he put his hand on the door that he became aware of complete silence beyond it, a silence which he at eighteen knew that it would take more than one person to make. But he did not pause; perhaps he was not even aware that the hall was empty again, that the blonde woman had vanished again without his having seen or heard her move.

He opened the door. He was running now; that is, as a man might run far ahead of himself and his knowing in the act of stopping stock still. The waitress sat on the bed as he had seen her sitting so many times. She wore the dark dress and the hat, as he had expected, known.... And in the same instant he saw the second man. He had never seen the man before. But he did not realise this now. It was only later that he remembered that, and remembered the piled luggage in the dark room. (1985: 555–56)

This is not Kafka's boarding-house room where you perceive only inadequately who is there, yet the subject-space contract operative in realism is no less fundamentally revoked. What in the Kafkan encounter emerges as anxiety registers in Faulkner as velocity and incomprehension. Joe is traveling, as it were, at more than human speed—faster than thought can keep up with—and he runs pell-mell into disaster. Nothing in this space—which nevertheless had earlier been perfectly familiar—answers to his expectations. He encounters, with a vengeance, the "broken hammer" and "burned out bulb." The door opens suddenly, pulling Joe as of its own accord, and Max emerges, dressed for a purpose Joe is too rushed to worry about not understanding. Max's words, with their racist barb, are likewise incomprehensible, but Joe can't attend to them, is moving too fast to register anything accurately. The blonde woman appears and disappears, jerkily, the representation of her movement aligned with Joe's heaving sensory apparatus rather than with her own deliberations. Joe's consciousness may be intentional in the phenomenological sense, but it lacks intention in any other sense. He is unbearably unfurnished. In this definitive moment of his life—Joe's 15 years on the road follow hard on this traumatic encounter—he can get nothing straight, just registers, camera-like, the incomprehensible sense-data coming at him. Why are they dressed this way? How can he carry all those bags? Who is this stranger?

He doesn't so much think these questions as become, fleetingly, penetrated by them one after the other, like events on a speeding movie reel, each one just short of enough repetitions to permit coherent representation. The entire scene is punctuated with "perhaps"; the narrative act refuses to sort out Joe's spatial/temporal experience, to reduce it to retrospective epistemological order. (Retrospective arrangement in Faulkner tends to be ideological rather than accurate.) When the encounter is over, he's on the floor, abandoned and bleeding profusely: he has learned nothing. His final moment will repeat this one: again flat out on the floor, castrated and with his life pouring out of him, still having learned nothing. *Light in August* is fiercely nonpedagogic. Again, the cinema analogy is pertinent: the sound and fury of experience exploding upon the subject (in the subject) in the form of unmasterable encounters, at a pace faster than thought can digest. Consciousness, despite Enlightenment guarantees of accountability, is a defective resource for mapping these spatial/temporal events.

Faulkner's experimental rhetoric savages the decorum of realism's gathered subject-verb-predicate; the reader is hurled unprepared into the nongrammatical turmoil of the text. When, later in *Light in August*, Joe walks toward Joanna Burden's dark house, about to commit the central act of the novel—to slit her throat—he thinks not "I am going to do something" (the basic syntax of agency: subject moving through verb and affecting object), but rather "*Something is going to happen to me*" (1985: 486). "*Something*" is the subject, not Joe. He does not know what he is on the edge of doing; he can conceptualize it only as a shapeless yet monstrous event about to happen to *him*, not *her*. The "central act," I called it, and therefore the act that every reader feels compelled to assess. But an act requires an actor, and Faulkner's syntax represents Joe as acted-upon, not agent: how judge him at this moment?

Faulkner's great work shares with modernist fiction more generally a refusal to indulge in the fatuity, so to speak, of a judgment-centered stance toward its materials. If reason-governed "trial" is a central activity fueling realism—a careful trying of the materials over time, to get them (and thus oneself in relation to them) into finer focus—then it is telling that perhaps the most famous modernist novel turns "trial" on its head. Kafka's *Trial* enacts, as Adorno put it, "the trial of a trial": a trial of the subject's capacity to know, to convert the other outside itself into an adventure of the same. Joseph K. learns no more about his trial, at novel's end, than he knew when it began. Likewise, Joyce's Bloom learns nothing in his 24 hours, Mann's Castorp passes his seven years atop the mountain as in a heady yet personally weightless parenthesis, Proust's Marcel is stuck for several thousand pages in a fluid time zone somewhere between childhood and early manhood. These novels refuse, like Faulkner's, to grant their protagonists the ever more accurate judgments that constitute maturation.

For such modernists, the underlying drama of the subject that countless realist novels deploy and redeploy—yet another story of the "I" of "I can"—has revealed its parochialism. This well-worn story of Ulysses heading home remains enclosed within a self-certainty incompatible with the trial of spirit itself. Such certainty—in Levinas's terms—"remains the guide and guarantee of the whole spiritual adventure of being. But this is why this adventure is no adventure" (1998: 99). To stage an adventure that would really be one, modernists must go beyond the repertory of narrative moves sanctioned by realism, for realism assumes the continuity of cultural norms (norms open to tweaking as a protagonist moves progressively in familiar space/time). It remains *friendly* to its reader: it presupposes a shared and viable world. It is of limited help if, as a writer, you want to make a great deal of trouble.

I conclude by returning to time as trouble. Trouble tends to be mounted in realism so as to be surmounted; it is a distracting force field presented in order to be removed—like dark clouds in a weather mandated as sunny. Realism's insistence on *capacitating* its protagonists is constitutive of the genre. Finally, its Enlightenment conviction that individuality is the priceless condition of humanity, that individuals negotiate their own lives against a complex yet manageable social backdrop, disposes realism toward moralized dramas of individual resolution. Given Sartre's "live or tell," realism chooses "tell" and labors cunningly to make it look like "live."

In a number of courageous ways, modernism chooses "live," and its work is cut out for it. How can you write about "live" without turning "live" into "tell"? Ultimately you cannot, but the heroism of these three writers—a heroism regarded as naive and rarely attempted by postmodern followers—resides in their innovative attempts to do so. In their efforts to return the movement of being from dry land to being's native water—its ongoing and unenlightened present—they brought more of the trouble of life in time and space into their narrative forms. The truth is, we are not knowing in the ways realism proposes. The larger part of our actual experience is uninsured by knowing. Our lives unfold in an unending present that becomes opaque whenever it escapes the grooves of habit or expectation. In reality, we learn slowly in time, by dint of many repetitions. Nor do we own our space except in tentative, provisional, and short-term ways—our relation to the outer world resembles renting (or indeed borrowing) more than it does owning. For many aspects of our lives, we cease, after a certain point, to learn at all. Who is wise in love? Who even becomes wise in love? These are unfriendly truths about life in time and space, and the *work* of modernist fiction is to convey their importance while continuing to honor their unfriendliness. It is the "ungratefulness" of such labor—modernism's putting into narrative what narrative seems designed to repress—for which we should be most grateful.

NOTES

1. A case could, of course, be made for other writers, but I focus on Proust, Kafka, and Faulkner because they are the supremely haunted modernists. They are haunted, not (as in Freud) by repressed sexuality, but more broadly and unpredictably—their texts intimating a sort of underweave of the socially *unworkable*. Among those writers missing from this essay, James Joyce is the indispensable, indeed iconic, modernist, yet Joyce's

texts are not revealingly haunted. The play of consciousness fills the pages of *Ulysses*. He has little interest in repressed psychic materials; Bloomian consciousness is amply "streamed" onto the page. When Joyce wants to access his characters' unacted desires, he invents in "Circe" less a discourse of subject repression than one of fantastic social carnival. Virginia Woolf, likewise, writes a modernist fiction centering on the dance of consciousnesses, not that which lies repressed beneath it. She produces in Septimus Smith a breathtaking case study in psychosis, not a neurotic who reveals symptomatically the psychic disturbances he ignores. One would not align him with the duplicities of a Charlus or Legrandin, the obsessions of a Quentin or Joe Christmas, the blankness of an unreadable Joseph K. Thomas Mann might well have a claim on my argument—his great work is laden with the collapse of exhausted Western norms—yet Hans Castorp (to take a telling instance) has little unconscious. Mann distributes Castorp's possibilities into the array of surrounding characters atop the magic mountain, even as he plays out the implications of Aschenbach's collapse into the surrounding Venetian setting and imagery. D. H. Lawrence, no less than Mann, was creatively attentive to the collapse of the "knowing subject," but he is finally more interested, like André Gide and Hermann Hesse, in representing release than in dramatizing the kinds of arrest that are central here. I omit Robert Musil because his protagonists lack what Proust figures as "infrared"—an interior cathecting energy intimating that what lies beneath the surface is shaping unawares the surface itself. My point is less to disqualify all other modernist candidates than to shore up, briefly, the logic of this particular grouping. I should say, in closing this note, that the claims proposed throughout this essay derive from the book-length argument I make in *Unknowing: The Work of Modernist Fiction* (2005).

2. Stephen Kern draws on Eugene Minkowski (an early-twentieth-century French psychiatrist) to identify the two most prominent subject stances toward the future in this period of technological explosion: "activity" and "expectation." Minkowski aligned "activity" with instrumental, Cartesian man, reshaping the social (and natural) world as never before possible. But, in his psychiatric practice, Minkowski more often encountered "expectation." Its terms are startlingly apt for Kafka: "[Expectation] englobes the whole living being, suspends his activity, and fixes him, anguished....It contains a factor of brutal arrest and renders the individual breathless. One might say that the whole of becoming, concentrated outside the individual, swoops down on him in a powerful hostile mass, attempting to annihilate him" (Kern 1983: 90). Impotence to master future space and time—this emerges as both Kafka's narrative signature and a precise rebuke of Western technological man's unprecedented mastery over space and time in the early twentieth century.

3. I emphasize here the nonnegotiable priority of the (single) subject in Kantian epistemology, but Richard Eldridge reminds me that, on the ethical plane, Kantian autonomy is everywhere doubled by (and weightless without) a larger social project of freedom for all, not just for the (single) subject. These two stances require each other even as, from the perspective governing my argument, the tensions between them are no less telling.

4. As Jean Laplanche has pointed out (1985: 15–16), editor and translator James Strachey's term "anaclisis" is unnecessarily erudite (derived from a Greek term that means "leaning"); Freud's *Anlehnung* is a familiar noun for "leaning" or "propping."

5. Since the term "anaclitic" is an important marker in my discussion of modernist fiction, I need to emphasize two points. First, although the term is Freudian, my usage of it is not. The readings that follow have everything to do with the sudden experience of defamiliarized space, but little to do with scenarios of repressed desire. Second, although

I apply the term to realist practice, the Enlightenment narrative prefers to imagine the questing subject as a free-standing agent immersed in lawful, objective space and time: no "leaning" conceded. The burden of much of my analysis of that narrative was to unearth the "anaclitic" premises that—by making the spatial/temporal world amenable to subjective encounter and exploitation—underwrite realism's progressive plot.

6. The following passage from Kierkegaard reads as presciently phenomenological:

> A system for existence cannot be given. Is there, then, not such a system? That is not at all the case.... Existence itself is a system—for God, but it cannot be a system for any existing spirit. System and conclusiveness correspond to each other, but existence is the very opposite.... In order to think existence, systematic thought must think it as annulled and consequently as not existing. Existence is the spacing that holds apart; the systematic is the conclusiveness that brings together. (1968: 107)

The world, for God, may be a system, but for us who exist in it, it can only be an unsystematic lifeworld. Our constitutive way of inhabiting space and time registers existence as a something "that holds apart," not a "conclusiveness that brings together."

7. If we wish to speak of repression here, it involves not a character's desires but an entire representational schema's will not to know. For realism will not "know" what modernism here grasps: that our compacts are ruptured by an immersion in time no longer domesticated but impersonally hostile to our project of renewed self-sameness.

8. Compare this vignette from Freud's "The Uncanny":

> I was sitting along in my *wagon-lit* compartment when a more than usually violent jolt of the train swung back the door of the adjoining washing-cabinet, and an elderly gentleman in a dressing-gown and a traveling cap came in. I assumed that...he had taken the wrong direction and come into my compartment by mistake. Jumping up with the intention of putting him right, I at once realized to my dismay that the intruder was nothing but my own reflection in the looking glass on the open door. I can still recollect that I thoroughly disliked his appearance. (1955: 248 n.)

9. Heidegger strikingly echoes Proust when he describes (in "Building, Dwelling, Thinking") the space we inhabit as aligned with our psychic investments rather than matching any surveyor maps: "When I go toward the door of the lecture hall, I am already there, and I could not go to it at all if I were not such that I am there. I am never here only, as the encapsulated body; rather, I am there, that is, I already pervade the space of the room, and only thus can I go through it" (1977a: 335).

REFERENCES

Adorno, T. (1983). "Notes on Kafka." *In* S. and S. Weber (trans.), *Prisms*. Cambridge, Mass.: MIT Press. (Original work published in 1967.)
——. (1997). *Aesthetic Theory* (R. Hullot-Kentor, trans.). Minneapolis: University of Minnesota Press. (Original work published in 1970.)
Banfield, A. (2000). *The Phantom Table: Woolf, Fry, Russell and the Epistemology of Modernism*. Cambridge: Cambridge University Press.

Brooks, P. (1984). *Reading for the Plot: Design and Intention in Narrative*. New York: Knopf.

Faulkner, W. (1985). *Light in August. In* J. Blotner and N. Polk (eds.), *William Faulkner: Novels 1930–1935*. New York: Library of America. (Original work published in 1932.)

Freud, S. (1955). "The Uncanny." *In* J. Strachey (ed. and trans.), *The Standard Edition of the Complete Psychological Works of Sigmund Freud* (vol. 17). London: Hogarth Press. (Original work published in 1925.)

Guyer, P. (1992). *Cambridge Companion to Kant*. Cambridge: Cambridge University Press.

Heidegger, M. (1977a). "Building, Dwelling, Thinking." *In* A. Hofstadter (trans.), *Martin Heidegger: Basic Writings*. New York: Harper and Row. (Original work published 1954).

———. (1977b). "What Is Metaphysics?" *In* D. F. Krell (trans.), *Heidegger: Basic Writings*. New York: Harper and Row. (Original work published in 1949.)

Husserl, E. (1973). "Phenomenology." *In* R. Zaner and D. Ihde (eds.), *Phenomenology and Existentialism*. New York: Putnam. (Original work published in 1927.)

Kafka, F. (1968). *The Trial* (W. and E. Muir, trans.). New York: Schocken. (Original work published in 1925.

———. (1995). "The Metamorphosis." *In* W. and E. Muir (trans.), *Franz Kafka: The Metamorphosis, In the Penal Colony, and Other Stories*. New York: Schocken. (Original work published in 1915.)

Kern, S. (1983). *The Culture of Time and Space: 1880–1918*. Cambridge, Mass.: Harvard University Press.

Kierkegaard, S. (1968). *Concluding Unscientific Postscript* (D. F. Swenson and W. Lowrie, trans.). Princeton: Princeton University Press. (Original work published 1846).

———. (1983). *Fear and Trembling* (H. V. and E. H. Honig, trans.). Princeton: Princeton University Press. (Original work published in 1843.)

Krell, D. (1977). "General Introduction." *In* D. F. Krell (trans.), *Martin Heidegger: Basic Writings*. New York: Harper and Row.

Laplanche, J. (1985). *Life and Death in Psychoanalysis* (J. Mehlman, trans.). Baltimore: Johns Hopkins University Press. (Original work published in 1970.)

Levinas, E. (1969). *Totality and Infinity* (A. Lingis, trans.). Pittsburgh: Duquesne University Press. (Original work published in 1961.)

———. (1998). *Otherwise Than Being: Or Beyond Essence* (A. Lingis, trans.). Pittsburgh: Duquesne University Press. (Original work published 1974.)

Merleau-Ponty, M. (1973). "Preface" to *The Phenomenology of Perception* (C. Smith, trans.). *In* R. Zaner and D. Ihde (eds.), *Phenomenology and Existentialism*. New York: Putnam. (Original work published in 1945.)

———. (1999). *The Phenomenology of Perception. In* D. Welton (ed.), *The Body: Classic and Contemporary Readings*. Oxford: Blackwell. (Original work published in 1945.)

Nietzsche, F. (1954). *Twilight of the Idols. In* W. Kaufmann (ed. and trans.), *The Portable Nietzsche*. New York: Viking. (Original work published in 1888.)

Proust, M. (1981). *Remembrance of Things Past* (3 vols.; C. K. Scott Moncrieff and T. Kilmartin, trans.). New York: Random House. (Original work published in 1913–1922.)

Rilke, R. M. (1964). *The Notebooks of Malte Laurids Brigge* (M. D. Herder, trans.). New York: Norton. (Original work published in 1910.)

Sartre, J.-P. (1964). *Nausea* (L. Alexander, trans.). New York: Grove Press. (Original work published in 1938.)

CHAPTER 14

···

POSTCOLONIALISM

···

SIMONA BERTACCO

> Literature, we are told, is vitally engaged with the living
> situation of men and women: it is concrete rather than
> abstract, displays life in all its rich variousness, and rejects
> barren conceptual enquiry for the feel and taste of what it is to
> be alive. The story of modern literary theory, paradoxically,
> is a flight from such realities into a seemingly endless range
> of alternatives.
>
> —Terry Eagleton, *Literary Theory*

This is what one reads in the final chapter of *Literary Theory*. It is not at all surprising that, in 1983, Eagleton decided not to mention the contribution that postcolonial theories were bringing to the field of literary studies. It was in line with his intention to prove that all literary theory is ultimately political, rather than only the most recent and explicitly ideological schools of thought, to which he admittedly acknowledged only a cursory reference. Although he did somehow compensate for the *omissis* in the second edition of the book, published 10 years later, I take the "gap" in Eagleton's work to be interesting as a sign of a generalized "presbyopia" of literary criticism up to the 1980s, meaning that the range of texts actually entering critical analyses were still mostly those belonging to the English canon, from Spenser to Shakespeare and Milton, from Blake to Wordsworth and Coleridge, from Austen to Dickens and the Brontës, and so on. Yet, before becoming a synonym for a supposedly radical theory, "the postcolonial" started its circulation as early as the 1950s—as far as the British context is concerned, slightly later in the American one—as a fast-growing body of writing, coming from around the world but published by "metropolitan" publishing houses.[1] This writing was perceived as "new" for the way in which it handled the English language and fused together stylistics coming from diametrically opposed traditions. Starting with the First World War, such writers as Rabindranath Tagore and Raja Rao (from India), Claude McKay (from Jamaica), and Solomon Plaatje (from South Africa) had started publishing their works in which they took up Western genres and coupled them with indigenous forms, vocabularies, and rituals of narrative transmission. These texts were crammed together under the "commonwealth literature" rubric, considered as a subcategory of English literature and evaluated in relation to the standards of excellence pertaining to English literature "proper": timelessness and universality.

Today we may well stand at the opposite end of the spectrum: it is rare, unless it is the sign of an intentional refusal, to find people totally unacquainted with novels such as *Things Fall Apart* (1958)—possibly the first postcolonial classic—by Chinua Achebe, or *Midnight's Children* (1981) by Salman Rushdie, or *Foe* (1986) by J. M. Coetzee. The extent of the change is visible if we pick any English textbook and browse how works such as *The Tempest, Robinson Crusoe, Jane Eyre*, or *Heart of Darkness* are presented. In terms of literary history, postcolonialism has occupied the space opened by modernism's fascination with the unfamiliar and the primitive. In 1952, Faber and Faber published Nigerian Amos Tututola's *The Palm-Wine Drinkers*, while Editions du Seuil published Martinican Frantz Fanon's *Peau Noire, Masques Blancs [Black Skin, White Masks]*. The former displayed Yoruba culture and an English language visibly uprooted from its British geography and syntax; the latter was a study of black subject formation, pointing to the distinction between the universal man of European Enlightenment and the black man emerging from the historical experience of colonization and slavery. Fanon had written his work in the thick of the Algerian war of independence, at times comparing the need for a struggle for national autonomy to the mental battle to be waged against the canonical texts of the European tradition. The polemic nervousness of Fanon's works derives in large part from the extreme closeness between the text and the world. A similar tension between text and world can be found in many literary works coming from formerly colonized countries. In the hands of what Fanon calls the "Native intellectual," the literary work forces its way into current history and the struggles that define it. It aims at serving a social and pedagogical function, paving the way toward the "decolonization of the mind" that Ngugi wa Thiong'o describes as a way out from the maiming image of selfhood that colonial education has left behind in postcolonial nations after independence.

It should not be forgotten that the rise of English as a discipline occurred during the phase of British High Imperialism, with the 1835 English Education Act defining the study of English texts as instrumental to breed subjects who learned, through the great classics of English literature, "the moral values for correct behaviour and action" (Viswanathan 1989: 93), both within and without the British Isles. In the famous words of Lord Macaulay, in his "Minute on Indian Education" (1835), the goal was to form an indigenous class "English in taste, in opinions, in morals, and in intellect" (1995: 430). As moral *exempla*, the literary texts that were selected aided in establishing the equivalence between English and Christian morality upon which the whole rationalization of colonial expansion rested and gave a clear social function to the teaching and reading of literature that, ironically, has become one of the essential tenets of postcolonialism itself.

If early postcolonial texts were primarily intended to fight in Fanonian terms against the European canon, a countercanon has by now been established and sanctioned, so much so that one has the impression that some of the new postcolonial texts are simply following a formulaic pattern. An understanding of postcolonialism today cannot possibly ignore "the disciplinization of the field" as Deepika Bahri defines it (2003: 37), and its largely pedagogical frame of reference. Postcolonial studies has been, first and mostly, a critical maneuver nurtured in literature departments: it has placed under scrutiny the allegiances of literary texts to the ideological systems that were the backbone of the imperial enterprise, investigating the relationship between literature and society, literature and knowledge, literature and value. What we are dealing with today is a literary postcoloniality,[2] which is a "nervous condition," in Fanon's words, in the sense that while the literary imagination is cherished to the extent to which it contributes to affecting the "symbolic overhaul" (Boehmer 2005: 3) necessary to redress the inadequacies of the past, it is simultaneously cast in an order of existence that is political rather than imaginative.

Caught in the middle ground between the ideological and the aesthetic, the postcolonial text has quite consistently been valued more for its supposed political message than for its formal excellence. Such a hermeneutic stance posits "textuality as endemic to the colonial encounter" (Gandhi 1998: 142) and to its aftermath. The postcolonial outlook on textuality is marked first by a preponderant attention given to the historical conditions of the production of culture—what Edward Said calls the necessary "worldliness" of texts—which reattaches itself to the tradition of cultural materialism. But also and most of all, it is marked by a way of understanding the British Empire in textual terms—looking at the ways in which texts translated the ideology of colonialism into their narratives and forms—mostly derived from poststructuralism via deconstructionism. In Elleke Boehmer's words, the text, as "a vehicle of colonial authority, symbolized and in some cases indeed…performed the act of possession" (2005: 14). If the whole colonial enterprise of taking possession and knowing the new lands was performed textually (through settlers' journals, letters, travel writing, maps, edicts, treaties, etc.), one of the major vehicles of anticolonial struggle could not but be, again, the texts themselves—this time read and written by the colonized subjects. Postcolonial literary theory has therefore favored a notion of subversive textuality whereby the agency of texts—of literary texts in particular—is automatically transposed onto the social and political spheres.

One unavoidable critical voice in the debate concerning textual politics is that of Homi Bhabha, whose *The Location of Culture*—a volume published in 1994 that brings together many of his earlier essays—provided a timely, at times overcharged, vocabulary for the study of the "new" textualities. In a sense, all of Bhabha's thinking originates from a deconstruction—rather than negation—of dualisms in all their forms, not least the one between theory and politics, as a way to respond to the syncretism of contemporary societies and their cultural forms: "[I]f we are seeking a 'worlding' of literature, then perhaps it lies in a critical act that attempts to grasp the sleight of hand with which literature conjures with historical specificity, using the medium of psychic uncertainty, aesthetic distancing, or the obscure signs of the spirit-world, the sublime and the subliminal" (1994: 12).

The erasure of the traditional boundary between theory and politics dispenses both with an abstract notion of theory—which is replaced with a Sartrian and Fanonian theory of/as practical knowledge—and, most important, with the reification of the Other typical of Western critical thought, where the Other is framed and cited as an object of knowledge and, as such, deprived of "its power to signify" (Bhabha 1994: 31). From a postcolonial perspective, the language of critique takes on a political role when it attempts to negotiate the antagonistic affiliations and citations of the postcolonial text, when it consciously locates itself outside familiar traditions and conditions of knowledge, when it stands "at the significatory boundaries of culture, where meanings and values are (mis)read or signs are appropriated" (34). Only if and when critical theory focuses on the problem of the enunciation of cultural difference[3] is the revisionary potential of theory fully exploited.

The import of Bhabha's reflection on textual politics is easily understood if we think, for instance, about using it to enter the complex ambivalence of many apparently imitative works produced in colonial times where the imperceptible variations of both native and colonial models can be deeply engaged in the postcolonial struggle. Yet, precisely because literature has often been used in these contexts as a real weapon against, first, colonial rulers and, then, local regimes, the notion of textual politics has a dangerous side that cannot be overlooked. The many instances one can provide of exiled artists and intellectuals, of writers whose works have been banned or who have been imprisoned because of their writing, such as Nuruddin Farah or Wole Soyinka—or killed, such as Nigerian Ken Saro-Wiwa—reveal the crucially different meanings that the adjective "political" still bears in these contexts. In fact, if, in Bhabha's reading, textuality is to be read and is political agency, the "seamlessness" of such a passage from civil action to aesthetic representation is problematic, to say the least, and it has not gone unnoticed within postcolonial studies itself. The danger that such foregrounding of postcolonialism as a discursive maneuver brings with it is represented by its "slippery political significations" (Shoat 1992: 322), resulting in the loss of the potential for antineocolonial resistance in today's world.

It is from Marxist critics that the most scathing critiques of literary postcoloniality have come. Aijaz Ahmad, for instance, attacks the call to indeterminacy implicit in how the postcolonial is marketed in the late imperial marketplace of our times, an indeterminacy that strips all cultures of their historicity and density and reduces them "to those lowest common denominators which then become interchangeable" (1995: 290). Ella Shoat, as well, demands that more attention be paid to the "politics of location" of the postcolonial phenomena under scrutiny: as "a signifier of a new historical era, the term 'post-colonial,' when compared with neo-colonialism, comes equipped with little evocation of contemporary power relations" (326). Yet this "habit of silence" toward the present is all but politically innocent and risks leaving "no space, finally, for the struggles of aboriginals in Australia and indigenous peoples throughout the Americas, in other words, of Fourth World peoples dominated by both First World multi-national corporations and by Third World nation-states" (327).

Indeed, the number of texts being criticized for failing to bring forward a recognizable revolutionary project has increased, in line also with the flourishing of what Derek Attridge terms "instrumental approaches" (2004: 12) in literary studies. In institutional contexts especially, the postcolonial text is read as a repository of sociological or historical information, and its "aesthetic dimension" put to one side as trivial and not essential to the communication of its social message. Such an interpretive stance seems to contradict the notion of textual politics shaped by postcolonial theory and takes us back to the question of what it means to respond to a work of literature *as* literature, when the postcolonial qualifier enters the picture. Does literature change sides—from the aesthetic to the political—when it exits the "first" or "old" world and enters the "third"?

Postcolonial or Literary?

The peculiar status of postcolonial literature—successful by virtue of its marginality—provides an interesting case study for exploring the import of literature in our times. Not only has, in fact, the literary text been revived by the social function acknowledged to literature in the former colonies, but also the study of literature has been remarkably brought back to prominence in, mostly Western, universities. In the age of information and communication technology, moreover, the visibility of postcolonial literature has been responsible for an unprecedented popularization of literary authors and critics who, like Rushdie and Said, have received a coverage from the mass media hardly common for writers or theorists in our times. Now, if we are to look for at least one crucial change brought about by the impact of postcolonial literatures, it certainly resides in the acknowledgment "that historical, geographical and cultural specifics are vital to both the writing and the reading of a text" (McLeod 2000: 5). In the pages of postcolonial literary works, we can observe how the European notion of literature has been altered by the encounter with native notions. Especially, we can observe how the modes of Western writing have influenced and have been influenced by local modes of orality; we read texts that are written in several varieties of English or that, by mixing English with other languages, break the chain traditionally binding together nation, literature, and language. Postcolonial literature, by casting itself off from literature *tout court*, exposes its supposed nonliterariness: its emphasis tends to be on the political or ideological rather than on the aesthetic, and this view has led the way for the first wave of postcolonial theory preoccupied with dismantling the epistemological violence of the process of colonial "othering" (*sensu* Gayatri Spivak), as Said's explorations of the invention of the Orient for the sake of the Western eye and Bhabha's analysis of the ambivalence and anxiety embedded in colonial discourse have brought to the fore.

Postcolonial literatures intervene right here, upsetting the possibility of building a liberal education today through syllabi still anchored to nineteenth-century ideas of one language per people and of national culture as the expression of the "unified spirit of a people" (Sommer 2003: 4). Postcolonial literary works remind us that many people live day in, day out in more than one culture and more than one language. They accept that what can be said in one language may be inexpressible in another, and they write works that negotiate the irreducible spaces between cultures in a variety of ways: thematically, by foregrounding figures of interpreters and translators, larger-than-life characters living between different imaginative and cultural worlds; stylistically, by developing sophisticated techniques of code-switching, by translating or mixing languages in the same sentence, by letting interferences from one language affect their way of using the other, and so forth. When these techniques are used in literature, language steps out of its ordinary function and becomes exhibitionist and intensive—in other words, unfamiliar. According to Evelyn Ch'ien, the "weird English" of postcolonial literatures (in English) may well be seen as the "new language" of contemporary literature (2004: 6), and I am sure this statement may scare quite a lot of people in literary circles around the world. As readers, we often encounter textualities that are indocile, sometimes secretive, and that make the experience of reading, to say the least, uncomfortable, as I show in the final section of this chapter. The writings the postcolonial has popularized are novel in that they have reworked traditional narrative forms from the multicultural and multilingual contexts they have developed in, but they are also new in the sense that they have provided a point of access into debates that are controversial, yet crucial, not only to rethink the function of the literary in our society, but also to think about the horizons of our knowledge, how we locate ourselves on the world map when we read, and what this entails in terms of taste and of notions of aesthetic excellence. Postcolonial literature attempts to offer a broader, non-Eurocentric, perspective on some traditional questions of theory concerning what is or could be considered literature, what criteria should guide the evaluation of meaning and excellence, and how indebted even these notions are to the Western literary tradition (see Ashcroft et al. 1989: 181).

I turn to a well-known novel, Coetzee's *Disgrace* (1999), and the unflattering staging of the role of a literary education in society that it offers, for an illustration of the working of the postcolonial literary imagination. In the opening of the novel, which is set in Cape Town roughly in the years 1997–1998, a professor of English, pouring quotations from the "classics" of English literature, is turned into a moral monster by his own intoxication with the literary at the expense of the real. David Lurie, a white South African professor, has a crush on one of his female students. He takes her home once and, to the notes of Mozart's clarinet quintet, asks about her literary passions. The rhetorical stance of pertinent questioning and answering that is part of the seduction scene reveals the incommensurability of the cultural worlds they inhabit. He, for whom "as long as he can remember, the harmonies of *The Prelude* have echoed within him" (Coetzee 2000: 13), has to bear with Melanie Isaac's emotionless comment, "I liked the Wonderhorn stuff" (12).

The first four chapters of the novel capture with admirable sharpness the contradictions of the teaching of literature in contemporary postcolonial countries, and not only there. David Lurie is the emblem of the redundant humanist in an educational system struggling to find adequate ways to teach about forgiveness and reversal of fortunes in a way that makes students into responsible citizens of the new Republic of South Africa. The text weaves together an intricate pattern of implied quotations from Baudelaire, Shakespeare, Flaubert, Manzoni, lines taken from Wordsworth, Byron that subtly wink at the Western reader who is "lured," like the naive Melanie Isaacs, to take—even though just for a few pages—his side but who then will feel bad about it for the rest of the novel. Yet the foundations supporting this sophisticated and decadent literary edifice are laid bare as morally gangrened already in the novel's opening when, after a fastidiously precise description of Lurie's affair with a prostitute named Soraya, the truth about his scholarly status is revealed: "Once a professor of modern languages, he has been, since Classic and Modern Languages have been closed down as part of the great rationalization, adjunct professor of communications. Like all rationalized personnel, he is allowed to offer one special-field course a year, irrespective of enrolment, because that is good for morale" (3) He is an academic dinosaur whose upbringing makes him, or so he likes to believe, inappropriate for the role he is to fulfill in society. As a professor, he is cast in the role of the educator.

We follow him in the classroom and observe him while he teaches Wordsworth's *Prelude*.[4] Here again, the contrast between the rhetorical mode of the lecture and the experiential distance of the literary text, on the one hand, and the real aims of the man delivering the lecture (he is trying to capture the attention of his student-girlfriend), on the other, makes the scene emblematic in terms of its metaliterary value. They are reading the stanzas that deal with the poet's trip to the Alps. "We don't have the Alps in this country," admits an increasingly frustrated David Lurie, "but we have the Drakensberg, or on a smaller scale Table Mountain, which we climb in the wake of the poets, hoping for one of those revelatory, Wordsworthian moments, we have all heard about" (23). The *pluralis majestatis* is yet another wink the author gives his model reader: the reference to the Alps, to the archetypes of the imagination, appeal to a European or Western reader—to me—but in his classroom, no one responds or reacts to Lurie's questions. The narrative voice—which speaks David Lurie's own consciousness—translates this clumsy silence in the following terms: "A man looking at a mountain: why does it have to be so complicated, they want to complain?" (21). The wording of the question is interesting: it is not a poet, but a man; not the Alps, but a mountain. In the process of cultural translation, from West to South, something of Wordsworth's poem went lost: the Alps are not, as David and his students know, the Drakensberg or Table Mountain. Together with his students, we are left wondering about what can actually be learned from Lurie speaking of "the great archetypes of the imagination we carry within us" (21): whose imagination is he actually talking about? Whose archetypes? Especially, how are they to speak to the young people living in today's Cape Town?

What went missing in the operation of cultural translation of Wordsworth's poetry that Lurie is rather negligently performing is the poem itself as artistic creation, its ability to say something about the intensity of our response to nature in terms that travel not only across time, but also across geography and culture, and still ring a charming note. Indeed, what this scene offers is an ironic allegory of colonial education: the English poem—the same poem that was used as a moral *exemplum* by colonial educators—is miniaturized, and not because its expiration date is past due, but rather because it is associated with a world, David Lurie's, that has gone sour. The bleak image of literature resulting from Lurie's lectures in the first chapters of *Disgrace* is deliberately juxtaposed against all that has been said and written about the "political energies" of the literary text postulated by postcolonial theory, a notion that—as Coetzee could know only too well—finds in romanticism an important precursor.

If literature does not come out totally undone in *Disgrace*, it is by virtue of *Disgrace* itself being a work of literature, and a fine one, existing not merely as a work of local testimony, but as a work that expresses its tension with that real world through its use of language, its structure, its style—in a word, through its form. *Disgrace* is not a documentary text on life in republican South Africa, and it should not be read that way. Too often postcolonial literature is read and raided anthropologically as an "unmediated text" (Huggan 2001: 39) and used as a substitute for historical or political analyses of national cultures, therefore bracketing any aesthetic value the text may hold in itself. In this sense, *Disgrace* contains one of the most complex lessons in reading one could hope for in order to give substance to what, as a reader of literature, one is doing. By approaching the text as cultural document, we read yet another account of the enormous costs in terms of human lives of the injustice and irrationality that are part of the process of constructing a national community out of a profoundly divided population. By looking at *Disgrace as* literature, by pausing on the rigorous precision of its narrative structure contrasting with the anarchy of the world depicted, by following the gradual disintegration of the literary floweriness of the beginning toward the dry, matter-of-fact syntax of the end, in order to capture the ways in which meaning is layered, one is actually drawn to direct attention to the literariness of the novel, to the subtlety of a textuality that negotiates its thematic concerns with the distressing reality of the new country through an allegorical construction that loses its clarity and faces its impossibility as the story unfolds.

Disgrace is very interesting also in another respect. The relationship between genders, even before that of ethnic groups, is given central stage and treated as emblematic of the complex challenges the new South African society has to meet. In the novel, the relationship between David Lurie and Melanie Isaacs results in Lurie losing his teaching job, which literally undoes his life. Most important, however, it is David's own daughter, Lucy Lurie, who is the one character who accepts to pay for the violence of the past and who will take part in the building of the new society. Lucy is a lesbian. She is raped by a gang of three black men and decides to have the baby resulting from the rape and to become the third wife of Petrus, her black neighbor and assistant as well as the protector of one of the rapists. Her stoicism at the end of the novel is bewildering as well as disturbing. She does not want to go back to Holland to raise the child; she wants to remain in South Africa, but she understands she now has to play by new rules: "Yes, I agree, it is humiliating. But perhaps it is a good point to start from again. Perhaps that is what I must learn to accept. To start at ground level. With nothing. Not with nothing but. With nothing. No cards, no weapons, no rights, no dignity" (205).

In recent years, perhaps the thorniest debates concerning theoretical models within the postcolonial field have concerned the issue of gender in non-Western societies and cultures and its problematic relationship both with Western feminist and postcolonial theories. The idea is that, if the postcolonial is to survive as a viable critical discourse for the future, it will have to embrace the theoretical traditions that are forming in areas as diverse as the Caribbean, Latin America, Africa, and India. In other words, even the current "womanist" phase of postcolonial discourse seems to point toward a new—less metropolitan, more vernacular—postcolonial discourse.

Critics such as Chandra Talpade Mohanti, Trinh Minh-ha, and Sara Suleri—to name but a few—have contributed to this dismantling of the category of the "native woman," the "third-world" woman, as the emblem of oppression, moving away from what is perceived as the imperialism of "first-world" feminism,[5] that deploys homogenizing, and therefore colonialist, feminist criteria to achieve the emancipation of women living at the four corners of the world. In other words, liberal feminism, when it includes women of color in its discourse, seems to deploy the iconic simplification that Said detected in the forms of Orientalism. Mohanti, for example, argues for an analysis "of the discursive construction of 'third world women' in Western feminism" (1991: 172). Despite a superficial similarity, Mohanti points in an opposite direction with respect to Said's theory—which has been criticized for never actually stepping out of the literary and cultural horizon of imperialism—and gestures instead toward a recuperation of the authenticity of lived experience when dealing with postcolonial women. While this "enamorment with the 'real'" (Suleri 1992: 340) has its dangers, namely, a problematic return to forms of essentialism, it might nonetheless be useful to keep an eye on the shifting ground on which, as a European and white woman, I stand as a way of framing my reading of the works by three women writers, from Somalia, Tobago, and Trinidad, respectively.

It is undeniable that, even today, non-Western women often appear as silent silhouettes, mere figures of speech, in current humanitarian and political rhetoric. They are often cast in the role of the seductive but passive objects of the colonial and postcolonial orders. One need only look, however, at the news coming from the "Orient" and the "South" of the world to understand the extent to which Western ideas of emancipation may need some adjusting: the increase in popular esteem that followed Sonia Gandhi's "all feminine" resignation as India's Prime Minister in 2004; the hope for change that led Liberians to choose a woman, Ellen Johnson-Sirleaf, as Liberia's president and Africa's first elected female head of state; and the human rights achievements of the Mothers of the Plaza de Mayo in Argentina are all examples that should make us think, or think again, about the public roles that women are playing outside the West. As much as there still remain gender—as well as ethnic—inequalities in these countries (as well as in ours, one should add), there also are actual wars of attrition being waged by women that, as Hazel Carby argues, risk being "ignored in favour of applying theories from the point of view of a more 'advanced,' more 'progressive' outside observer" (1982: 216).

If the postcolonial embodied, when it first emerged, the need for a revision of commonly held assumptions about central and peripheral nations and cultures, it seems quite natural that the most vexing questions emerging today from within the field demand a further revision of dominant ways of seeing within the postcolonial project itself. Robert Young has identified an analogy between the development of postcolonialism and feminism in political and philosophical terms; in his view, both movements have performed a "conceptual reorientation" toward new "perspectives of knowledges" (2003: 5) developed outside mainstream culture. Yet it is an analogy that does not hold at a deeper level, and in fact yields to one of the deepest fractures within postcolonial studies along the lines that oppose Western women to Native women. In other words, when "the subaltern" is recognized as gendered, a whole new story is about to be told, a story in which postcolonialism and feminism themselves are forced to unveil their biased systems of knowledge—postcolonialism for putting a universal (and male) colonized subject at the center of its inquiry; feminism for presuming to speak for all the women in the world.

In her 1987 essay titled "French Feminism in an International Frame" (less famous than her "Can the Subaltern Speak?"), Spivak puts her own education and personal experience down for scrutiny in her attempt to criticize the conceptual categories of both first-world feminism and male-centered postcolonial theory. At the core of her argument is her own habit, as a young scholar, to approach the works and experiences of "third-world" women through the far too abstract lenses of Western feminist theory. Recalling a childhood memory of two washerwomen arguing with each other over who owned the river in 1949 India, Spivak muses on how "for these withered women, the land as soil and water to be used rather than a map to be learned still belonged...to the East Indian Company" (1987: 135). Those women may well have known nothing of the events that were rewriting Indian politics in those post-Independence years, but they certainly had a clear idea of who the master of the water was. Instead of patronizing them, of wondering, "What can I do *for* them?" the feminist critic should ask herself, "Who is the other woman? How am I naming her? How does she name me? Is this part of the problematic I discuss?" (150). The terms of the problem that Spivak is exploring are engrained in the very constituency of an international or transnational feminism. In her words:

> The academic feminist must learn to learn from them [third-world women], to speak to them, to suspect that their access to the political and sexual scene is not merely to be *corrected* by our superior theory and enlightened compassion....
> How, then, can one learn from and speak to the millions of illiterate rural and urban Indian women who "live in the pores of" capitalism, inaccessible to the capitalist dynamics that allow us our shared channels of communication, the definition of common enemies? (135)

If the colonial subaltern, in Spivak's terms, is in no position to speak, the gendered subaltern will be further removed from any position of enunciation. Where does this leave us vis-à-vis the literary texts "written" by non-Western women? Spivak's deconstructionist method, her way of reading texts "against the grain" in order to find, under the surface, the gaps, the silences, all the things that the text does not openly "say," leave us at a loss, as far as a message-seeking reading of works of literature is concerned. However, there is a lesson in my view that we can take with us: the emphasis on the need *to learn* to listen to the "other woman" in her own terms, even if this entails losing our ground and moving on a foreign territory: "The reader must accustom herself to starting from a particular situation and then to the ground shifting under her feet" (Spivak 1993: 53). She will need to watch her step, to turn to experts for specialist knowledge, to learn, if necessary, a new language.

So much of the experience of reading postcolonial texts has to do with our engaging with them through a Calibanic perspective, yet putting a Calibanic perspective into practice—as Spivak urges us to do—is more easily said than done. If it is true that today postcolonial literature is read much more widely than in the past, it is likewise true that it is increasingly approached within a world literature framework (and often in translation), therefore without the specific sociolinguistic knowledge that would unveil some of its local references. The language of postcolonial literatures is mostly English, or another European language, if we think of the postcolonial in global and discipline-based terms. As a translator, Spivak has a good saying that when studying the literatures of the global South, "you learn the pertinent languages with the same degree of care" (2002: 106) in order to enter the new comparative field that postcolonialism is bound to be. This is wishful thinking, at least for the time being. Postcolonial studies would profit enormously by being cast as the "new comparative literature": by learning also the non-European languages of postcolonial texts, readers would learn to do away with exclusively Eurocentric canons, languages, and cultures by becoming familiar with other textualities, syntaxes, vocabularies. Attention given to the textual, or the literary, would put the postcolonial literary text, at least partially, at bay from the exoticizing anthropological or pseudoanthropological readings whose main preoccupations Graham Huggan sums up in the following terms: "[T]he desire for authenticity, projected onto the screen of a 'real Africa'; the insistence on the documentary value of literary and, especially, fictional sources; the attempt to co-opt [African] literature into a Euro-American morality play centring on the need to understand 'foreign' cultures" (2001: 54).

An illustrative example of the ambivalence of reading (but also of writing) comes from autobiography, the genre *par excellence* of Western individualism, but also one of the major genres through which African women's writing has acquired visibility in the world. As Sidonie Smith and Julia Watson have pointed out, "[T]his autobiographical 'I' is a Western 'I,' an 'I' of the colonizer,…complicit in the West's romance with individualism" (1998: 28), and this creates quite a few problems for the expression of a non-Western sense of selfhood. One need only think of the ethnographic practice of collaborative autobiographies where an often illiterate native informant is helped by a Western interpreter to make the story available and sometimes palatable to large audiences. Who is the author in these texts? How might subjects brought up in the south of the world find a voice through or despite this "I"? How much is it possible to overcome the shadows this "Western I" casts once it is adopted as a point of articulation? And, second, who is the implied reader of these autobiographical accounts? How much does this figure of a model-reader account for the way in which the book is written?

By way of illustration of the complex maze of writing and reading sketched above, I now turn to a novel by Waris Dirie, *Desert Flower: The Extraordinary Journey of a Desert Nomad*, published in 1998 in the United Kingdom, where the writing is the result of a collaboration between the protagonist of the events (the model and U.N. ambassador Dirie) and the American journalist Cathleen Miller. This book is part of its author's active involvement in urging Western nations to punish the practice of clitoridectomy as a crime against the bodily integrity of individuals and to admit it as a reason for political asylum. At the level of close reading, however, the book poses a series of problems to the reader, none of which concern its form. It is on this level that the hand of the Western enabler can be detected in the work done to create a readable text, through the use of clear thematic structure and of catchword titles for each chapter, such as "Becoming a Woman," "Free at Last," or "On the Road," pointing at important icons of Western liberal thought. The story of this woman, delivered through a first-person narrative, is taken as exemplary for Somali women, and the difference of Dirie's cultural background is made acceptable in the terms in which it is filtered through a Western idea of physical and mental emancipation:

> Another benefit of growing up in Africa was that we were part of pure nature, pure life. I knew life—I wasn't sheltered from it. And it was real life—not some artificial substitute on television where I'm watching *other* people live life.…
>
> I *am* grateful that I've experienced both lives—the simple way and the fast way. But without growing up in Africa, I don't know if I would have learned to enjoy life the simple way. (1998: 234, 236)

My reaction to this novel was, first of all, a reaction to a textuality that, as can be inferred from the excerpt above, I felt was closer to journalism than to literature. Yet, this was the text that most of my students (all of them women) actually enjoyed the most out of a reading list featuring more remarkable literary works such as *Nervous Conditions* by Tsitsi Dangarembga, *Beloved* by Toni Morrison, and *The Stone Virgins* by Yvonne Vera: they found it readable and clear; many even went so far as to buy it for their mothers and friends. The diversity of our reactions got me thinking about how much, as a reader of literature, I was less prone to engage myself completely with a text whose authorship I felt was somehow "tainted" from the start. Where did my skepticism arise from? Was I projecting over the text—in its nature as a postcolonial text—an essentialist or, even worse, a purist desire for "authenticity"? Evidently, I cannot exclude this possibility. But the aspect that profoundly disturbed me was actually another. As a woman from a country in which practices of female genital mutilations are banned, yet are illicitly performed in various immigrant communities, and the legal aspects of the matter are all but clearly defined,[6] I could not but react strongly to the message lying at the core of the text and advertised in its final pages: am I competent enough in terms of cultural knowledge in order to understand this issue in terms other than my own?

At the same time, this is one of the central issues to be faced, more and more frequently, in modern societies, and one way or another, one is supposed to form an opinion about it. Shouldn't literary texts be useful tools to put one's own values to the test and, possibly, enlarge one's scope of vision? In Spivak's terms, was my approach suited to hearing the "other woman" speak in her own terms? Was I being too anthropological? Or too literary? Finally, I managed to reconcile myself with my negative reaction to the novel. First, this was a clear example of that formulaic wave that is affecting the postcolonial publishing world: the novel was marketed and sold as literature when it was not meant to be read that way. Second, I could not but feel the shadow of the Western "I" engrained in the genre of autobiography covering, as Woolf wrote in *A Room of One's Own*, quite a few corners of the issue: the story is the account of the flight from a prearranged marriage of the young protagonist from the Somali countryside to Mogadishu, and from Mogadishu to London, and then to New York. Except for the first 84 pages, the whole narrative is taken up by the Western emancipation of the young woman, which coincides with the westward direction of her life journey. Could this be an example of that form of "globalized high-tech feminism without frontiers" (Spivak 2002: 50) under the attack of postcolonial feminists? That was my suspicion in the face of the moral single-sidedness of the book. *Desert Flower* retains its value as part of U.N. ambassador Dirie's humanitarian campaign, and it deserves to be respected for the way in which it makes available for discussion to a large audience an important issue for contemporary multicultural societies; but it also stands as an example of the formulaic patterns into which Western publishers have often filtered postcolonial literature. In the words of Stephen Gray:

> Ever since Joseph Conrad's perennial *Heart of Darkness* (1899) that began the century now closed, British and American readers have seemingly developed a

bottomless appetite for the very untold horrors that Conrad's work was meant to deplore and which the "Dark Continent" appears—at least in the media version—only too willing to keep feeding. (2000: xvi)

Calibanic Texts, Cannibal Readers

Most of this chapter has been dedicated to a questioning of the value of the canonical literary text from a postcolonial perspective. I turn now to two literary examples that, while giving the literary text a crucial role to play in today's society, contribute to broadening the gamut of forms the literary is taking in order to bring my reflection to its conclusion. And by way of a response to the role of Romantic poetry in contemporary South Africa, I return to poetry with the work of two Caribbean writers, both now living in Canada, who attempt to answer the question of what it means to write literature today. Social engagement emerges clearly from their texts, but, as writers, their most radical struggle is the one waged against traditional constructs of womanhood and textuality.

A strong, at times overcharged, deconstructive pull is at work in Marlene Nourbese Philip's poetry.[7] Her work combines a strong metaphorical quality with an equally strong experimentation in syntax and phonetics meant to establish a sustained investigation into the appropriateness of the literary and linguistic tradition to her writing. Hers is an instance of a deconstructive poetics, a poetics that literally chews up the literary vocabularies of different traditions and different places, and articulates, through a physically laborious process that is captured on the page, its own struggle to ground meaning in history and place.

She Tries Her Tongue, Her Silence Softly Breaks (1989) is a difficult book to read, a collection of verses with frequent prose interruptions, a book in which the author faces the problem, for the African artists from the Caribbean, of writing in a language "where the word, their word and the power to name was denied them" (1994: 102). The volume is a radical and at times scathing critique of conventional presuppositions, of all that goes without saying when we approach a literary text, and a poetic text in particular. In the poem "Discourse on the Logic of Language," Philip offers some variations on the theme of natural language and, by recourse to the parental figures of mother and father, creates the central metaphor of the anguish of speaking with a language defined by and as violence. The first deconstructive move the poem enacts has to do with the need for adjustment in terms of reading habits: the reader has to choose whether to read the poem from left to right, or from right to left. Choosing the latter way, the first texts that we find are two italicized fragments of legal edicts concerning the enforcement of language policy in the plantations. Edict I orders the mixing of slaves in heterogeneous linguistic groups in order to disrupt communication among slaves and therefore prevent rebellion. Edict II describes the punishment attending the disobedients:

> Every slave caught speak-
> ing his native language shall
> be severely punished. Where
> necessary, removal of the
> tongue is recommended. The
> offending organ, when re-
> moved, should be hung on
> high in a central place, so
> that all may see and tremble. (138)

History, language, experience come together in this highly convoluted text through the assembling, with a collage-like technique, of various texts within it. The two edicts on the right-hand side of the first and third pages encapsulate the voice and the tone of the "father language," the language of the law and, therefore, of colonialism and slavery that the artist of African descent must necessarily confront. A vertical column placed on the left-hand side of the same pages with the text written in capital letters and going from the bottom to the top of the page, embodies its opposite, the natural, soothing language of the body:

> The mother then put her fingers into her child's mouth—gently
>   forcing it open;
> she touched her tongue to the child's tongue, and holding the
>   tiny mouth open,
> she blows into it—hard. She was blowing words—her words,
>   her mother's words,
> those of her mother's mother, and all their mothers before—into
>   her daughter's / mouth. (138)

The sensuous description of the mother breathing language into her daughter's mouth is placed alongside a slender sequence of words that constitute the lyrical core of the poem, or the poem proper, and that occupy the center of the page that, with a syncopated and repetitive pace, laments the loss of the mother tongue:

> English
> is my mother tongue.
> A mother tongue is not
> not a foreign lan lan lang
> —a foreign anguish (136)

The phonetic pun on the words anguish/language underlines the physical "pain of speaking when one's tongue has been amputated" (Godard 1993: 162). By working intensely on the signifier, Philip writes a poem that embodies the outrage of the violent act: the halting repetition of "lan, lan, lang" is the poem, sung with just the stump of a tongue in one's mouth, of that violation. Realizing that:

> I have no mother
> tongue
> no mother to tongue
> no tongue to mother
> to mother
> tongue
> me
> the speaking I can only conclude that she:
> must therefore be tongue
> dumb
> dumb-tongued
> dub-tongued
> damn dumb
> tongue (Philip 1994: 136)

The more the verbal text invades and expands on the page, is hybridized, its texts and contexts multiplied, the more the poem as a sound creation is made hard to perform, hard to utter, and would seem to move toward its impossibility. Unable to recite the poem, the speaker is left speechless, inarticulate—in a word, dumb. This word, if only for the number of times it is repeated, demands attention. Defined as something or someone "lacking the faculty of speech, therefore silent," but also "someone that is stupid, ignorant, foolish" (*Oxford English Dictionary*), this word in this text suggests another possibility: that she is speaking incorrectly because culturally and cerebrally inferior. And, as a matter of fact, the prose explicatory section on the next page about the neurological processes of speech in the de Broca and Wernicke areas of the brain brings Philip's critique full circle. Puncturing the pseudoscientific discourse with a few lines on its racist undertones, Philip brings to the limelight the inevitable "worldliness" of all forms of discourse, scientific as well as literary.

In a fashion rather typical of postcolonial works, the poetic text is complicated in terms of layout and especially in terms of the interaction of diverse elements within it: by using the "found text" strategy, Philip goes a long way to disrupt the conventional space of the poem and to turn the language of the poem into the embodiment, the written mark, of a very physical pain. As a poem, "Discourse of the Logic of Language" does not read easily, or comfortably, since we have to change our angle of reading, by turning the book sideways, in order to take it all in. By focusing and making us, as readers, focus on literature as embodied experience of writing and reading, Philip is articulating a poetics that recognizes and exploits the sensuous potential of words. The final metamorphosis of language and poetry is in fact mediated through the body, and it is from here that Philip's poetry starts again, from the acknowledgment that "body should speak when silence is" (149). Taking poetry down to its material, bodily existence triggers the final change of the poems at the end of a collection bearing as an epigraph a line from Ovid's *Metamorphosis*: "All Things are alter'd, nothing is destroyed," and moves poetry on:

> That body should speak
> When silence is,
> Limbs dance
> The grief sealed in memory;
> That body might become tongue
> Tempered to speech
> And where the latter falters
> Paper with its words
> The crack of silence;
> That skin become
> Slur slide sussurration
> Polyphony and rhythm—the drum; (149)

Dionne Brand's poetry strikes a different note from Philip's. The sharp barbs of Philip's violent reconstruction of the literary text are bracketed in favor of a poetic sentence that, though ungrammatical for its proselike quality and its use of Trinidadian Demotic English, casts a powerful poetic aura around itself. Brand could be described as one of Canada's most refined writers, but also as one of the most complex and uncompromising voices to be heard in the Canadian literary and intellectual scene. *No Language Is Neutral* was published in 1990 and marked the beginning of Brand's recognition within the Canadian literary mainstream. In it, Brand tells of her early life in Trinidad, the need she felt to escape from there and from its slave mentality, while providing a picture of the Caribbean as a deeply gendered culture. The book's title is taken from a line from Derek Walcott's collection *Midsummer*, and it might be useful to quote the stanza it is taken from in order to shed some light on the operation that Brand is carrying out in her work. These are Walcott's lines from his poem "I heard them marching the leaf-wet roads of my head":

> No language is neutral;
> the green oak of English is a murmurous cathedral
> where some took umbrage, some peace, but every shade, all,
> helped widen its shadow. I used to haunt the arches
> of the British barracks of Vigie. There were leaves there,
> bright, rotting like revers or epaulettes, and the stenches
> of history and piss. (1992: 506)

By choosing Walcott, Brand is inserting her poetry within a West Indian literary tradition, a countercanon in itself, while simultaneously as well as polemically adding to Walcott's idea of the language of poetry the difference of her experience as a woman poet from the same area. *No Language Is Neutral* is divided into four sections: "hard against the soul," "return," "no language is neutral," and "hard against the soul" again, leading the poet along an exploration of her linguistic heritage and of the history that she wants to bear witness to. The texture of the book is, actually, made up of interweaving long poems: lines and stanzas from the various sections keep resurfacing—in a way that is typical of all of Brand's production—throughout the text, repeating images of women, of discovery and engagement with women.

The starting point of the collection recalls the structure of Philip's poetry: the poetic sequence "return" goes back to the past of enslavement and colonization as the necessary acknowledgment of the scar of slavery in order to recuperate the social value of writing. "Blues Spiritual for Mammy Prater" is a poem written, as the paratextual note introducing it makes clear, "looking at 'the photograph of Mammy Prater an ex-slave, 115 years old when her photograph was taken'" (Brand 1990: 17). The whole poem pivots around the act of seeing, of witnessing "her lines and most of all her eyes/and her hands" (17). Mammy Prater had the patience to wait for the time when her experience of enslavement would be told by one of her ideal great granddaughters. The image of stillness provides a new intake of the history of slavery focusing on the forms of silent resistance along the centuries. Brand fully explores this aspect in her novel *At the Full and Change of the Moon* (1999), where she recuperates from "the forgetful places" (18) of history the story of a slave who, in 1802, plotted a mass suicide and died saying, "This is but a drink of water to what I have already suffered." There is an urgency that one can easily follow in Brand's development as a writer to be clear about the social value of literature: poetry is a form of eyewitnessing, bearing testimony to a history the poet has inherited by being born a woman in a Caribbean island. Like Marie Ursule, waiting to plot the suicide for all the members of the rebellious *Convoi Sans Peur*, Mammy Prater comes to perfection by waiting for the poet to catch her gaze and note it down:

> she knew then that it would be me who would find
> her will, her meticulous account, her eyes,
> her days when waiting for this photograph
> was all that kept her sane
> she planned it down to the day,
> the light,
> the superfluous photographer
> her breasts,
> her hands
> this moment of
> my turning the leaves of a book,
> noticing, her eyes. (19)

The title section of the book, "no language is neutral," is made up of a single long poem consisting of the genealogy, in the feminine, of the poetic persona as well as of a revisitation of the native landscape. The opening lines draw us into the scenery and set the relentless rhythm of the long poem as a whole:

> No language is neutral. I used to haunt the beach at
> Guaya, two rivers sentinel the country sand, not
> backra white but nigger brown sand, one river dead
> and teeming from waste and alligators, the other
> rumbling to the ocean in tumult, the swift undertow
> blocking the crossing of little girls except on the tied
> up dress hips of big women, then, the taste of leaving
> was already on my tongue and cut deep into my
> skinny pigeon toed way, language here was strict
> description and teeth edging truth. Here was beauty
> and here was nowhere. (22)

The island's beauty, its sand the color of its people, its almond leaves "fat as women," cannot dissimulate the air that still stinks of slavery, oppression, and hopelessness. The persona's schizophrenic relationship to her native land is further developed in conceptual terms in the analysis of the language echoing in that place:

> To hate this, they must have been
> dragged through the Manzinilla spitting out
> the last spun syllables for cruelty, new sound forming,
> pushing toward lips made to bubble blood. This road
> could match that. Hard-bitten on mangrove and wild
> bush, the sea wind heaving any remnants of
> consonant curses into choking aspirate. (23)

The "they" in these lines are the poet's ancestors who have been drawn with force to abandon their original idioms (*spun syllables*), in order to adopt a new language, made of new sounds, turning their mouths into holes of blood, an image propounding the idea of removal of the tongue as we have seen in Philip's poem even though, here, the syntax of the poem still holds, despite the harsh alliterations on sibilant, plosive, velar consonants, as poetry. It is a poetry that warns us that "no / language is neutral seared in the spine's unravelling. / Here is history too" (23), and meaning can be found only in the interconnection of history, experience, and words. Only after this poetics statement can the poet proceed and write in Trinidadian Demotic in a way that is not belittling or exotic, but poetically necessary:

> Silence done curse god and beauty here,
> people does hear things in this heliconia peace
> a morphology of rolling chain and copper gong
> now shape this twang, falsetto of whip and air

> rudiment this grammar. Take what I tell you. When
> these barracks held slaves between their stone
> halters, talking was left for night and hush was idiom
> and hot core. (23)

These lines mix world-views and cultural orders by simply coupling together abstract nouns and cultural referents that belong to the Western tradition (heliconia peace, morphology, falsettos) with ordinary, monosyllabic words, recording the concreteness of the history of slavery in the West Indies: the morphology of the new idiom is made of rolling chains and copper gongs; falsettos are produced by the sound of whips in the air and a derogatory twang is the rudiment of this grammar.

Brand's writing, because of the analysis it provides of how her received language was formed, and because it is written in that very language, propounds an intense metaliterary reflection that attempts to imagine the place of poetry today as "another place, not here, a woman might touch / something between beauty and nowhere" (34), ushering us into the utopian dimension of the literary text, the ability that art has to have visions to be rendered in a language freed from the burden of mimetic representation. The link this "new country" has with the world is poetry itself, the text struggling to be written in a new language, drifting away from words learned by heart, and longing for new ones, in the realization that

> Each sentence realised or
> dreamed jumps like a pulse with history and takes a
> side. What I say in any language is told in faultless
> knowledge of skin, in drunkenness and weeping,
> told as a woman without matches and tinder, not in
> words and in words learned by heart,
> told in secret and not in secret, and listen, does not
> burn out our waste and is plenty and pitiless and loves. (23)

LITERATURE AND ITS UNFAMILIARS

Unlike in Coetzee's novel, where the social importance of literature is put to the test in a time of intense civic turmoil, poetry is captured by Brand and Philip as "room to live," as offering a utopian space not only for redressing the legacy of the past, but also, and more crucially, for crafting a literary text capable of responding to its social call. In the end, what difference is there between the professor's idea of literature in *Disgrace* and these women's poetries? Nothing much varies in the substance of the texts at hand as literature: they all are written, contain lyrical expansions, and offer a layout that serves its intended—harmonic or caco-phonic—effects. What definitely differs between them is how these texts—Word-sworth's *Prelude* and Philip's or Brand's poems—are offered to the historically specific reader. The issue is not that of good versus bad literature. In Coetzee's novel, Wordsworth's poetry is associated with the ideology of old South Africa: does this affect or diminish its value as a cultural text? As unfair as it sounds, it does, at least in a contingent sense. Literary works are written and read within specific systems of culture that, while fostering a set of styles, issues, materials, and expectations, inevitably deny others. The core of the issue can be summa-rized using Frederic Jameson's words: "The third-world novel will not offer us the satisfactions of Proust or Joyce" (1986: 65). Contained in this observation is not so much the perennial question of the contingency of literary value mistaken for universal excellence as a very honest acknowledgment that in order to name—in Gérard Genette's terms—the figures of a text, the reader has in the first place to be able to see them. And this is still often not the case when literary critics look at postcolonial writing.

The training of the imagination that literary texts are supposed to grant their readers is still deeply implicated in the kind of familiar unfamiliarity that leaves the critics satisfied with their ability to crack the "secret code" of texts. By playing on the principle of creative variation rather than repetition, literature is supposed and expected to puncture ordinary modes of speech. And readers of literature are eager to read and listen to the unfamiliarity resulting from such a process: the more elaborate the text, the greater the pleasure in the achieve-ment of interpretation.[8] However, there seem to be varying degrees in what is considered sanctioned unfamiliarity that explain why an Indian novel such as Rohinton Mistry's *Such a Long Journey* has been criticized for not supplying the non-Indian reader with a glossary of foreign words. I am thinking about a reader advancing the same request in order to read Ezra Pound and T. S. Eliot: how unflattering an image it would provide of the reader's ignorance. There are books that, like *Such a Long Journey*, raise doubts about our competence, lin-guistic and cultural, before literary. And this is part of the experience of read-ing writings emerging out of dissimilar and even opposed legacies of narrative transmission.

The texts I have mentioned in this chapter insist on *not* being read as "the Proust of the Papuans," as Saul Bellow famously put it; rather, they develop a textuality that speaks its message through an intentionally convoluted structure, marking the distance, not only from ordinary language, but also from ordinary readings. This is a central part of the actual experience of reading postcolonial texts, and it deserves more critical attention than it has so far received. When foreign words or unfamiliar varieties of English are used and mixed together in postcolonial texts, they are the graphs of cultural differences, and that difference should be respected, not obliterated by a reading aimed at "saming" the otherness of the text. Missing the pun in a line because we do not master all the languages or the rhetoric of a text is not the end of the world, or the sign of our being unfair to the text; however, casting the blame on the text's supposed unintelligibility or lack of complexity misses the point by far. There are texts that intentionally leave some readers out, thereby raising questions of accessibility that are cursorily dismissed or overlooked by an almost exclusive focus on the thematic content of the literary work. Part of the challenges of reading these works has to do with learning to read them, as we have seen in Philip's poem when an actual choice in the direction of reading is required, or in Coetzee's novel when the microcosm of the novel slowly but relentlessly casts us and the cultural values we represent out of the horizon. We need readings that are textually specific and attentive, also and especially when we are dealing with works of which we do not share either the symbolic or the rhetorical grounds. As with languages, social differences are not always comprehensible or bridgeable, and this aspect of cultures' untranslatability, which indirectly points to the limits of our competence, needs to be acknowledged. In a very literal sense, translation is the model not only for postcolonial writing developing within multiple cultural and linguistic contexts, but also for its critical reading.

NOTES

1. Publishing houses (and, later, literary prizes) played an important role in making the new literatures in English visible as a separate corpus to a larger audience. The British publishing house Heinemann launched its African Writers Series in 1962; its debut novel, written by one of the founding editors of the series was Chinua Achebe's *Things Fall Apart*. Longman opened its Drumbeat Series in the 1970s, and Women's Press its Black and Third World Women Writers Series. For a critical reading of the development of African Writers Series books, see Huggan 2001: 51–57.

2. "Postcoloniality" is a term generally used to distinguish between the intellectual revisionist project of postcolonial studies and the empirical, market-driven life led by postcolonial or exoticized "commodities," on a global scale. It therefore places the emphasis on the commercial context in which all things postcolonial necessarily live and flourish, and on the capitalistic logic regulating the exchanges. Given the counterhegemonic bent that postcolonial theory has taken since its beginnings, the notion of postcoloniality has been produced—resulting in quite different formulations—by theorists themselves as a warning sign against the forms of cultural imperialism hidden under the increasing institutionalization and commodification of the postcolonial.

3. The notion of cultural difference is crucial to Bhabha's attempt to operate a revision of Western critical theory. Bhabha distinguishes cultural difference from cultural diversity. The former is defined as "the process of the *enunciation* of culture as 'knowled*geable*,' authoritative, adequate to the construction of systems of cultural identification" (1994: 34). The latter results from the tendency to abstraction and reification that Bhabha criticizes in Western critical theory, and indicates "culture as an object of empirical knowledge" (34), defined and encased within a comparative view of cultural contents and customs, artifacts, etc. It is through cultural difference, defined as

a process of signification and inhabiting the performative space and time of enunciation, that Bhabha derives his ideas of the ambivalence of colonial discourse, the untenability of claims to cultural purity—hence the necessary hybridity of contemporary metropolitan culture and of the contemporary, postmodern or postcolonial, nation.

4. It should be noted that, especially in early postcolonial texts, the name of William Wordsworth recurs with curious frequency in relation to the psychological alienation produced by colonial education. Wordsworth's "golden daffodils" have often become the objective correlative of a colonial education that, from Antigua to New Zealand, did not question its irrelevance to the native experience.

5. I am aware of the unhappy terminology I am adopting in this section. Both "first-world" feminism and "third-world" woman are, to say the least, unhappy generalizations. However, they are useful in order to direct our attention to the core of the issue that, to put it bluntly, has to do with women trying to fight patriarchy in capitalistic countries vs. women from noncapitalistic countries (in the original sense of third world) having to deal not only with the patriarchy of their social milieus, but also with the effects of colonialism's exoticizing gaze.

6. There is a legal debate going on in many European countries focusing on the issue of rights, bodily integrity, and female excision. Sweden and Great Britain were the first European nations to adopt specific laws on female genital mutilations in the early 1980s, and today such mutilations are legally prosecuted in Finland, France, Germany, Greece, Ireland, Italy, Luxembourg, Portugal, and the Netherlands. In Italy the justice system, under the Berlusconi government, launched an advertising campaign against female genital mutilations. But a legal controversy has arisen around these issues, opposing conflicting versions of human rights and of notions of bodily integrity. In many immigrant communities, in fact, the notion of an individual self is still perceived as foreign and opposed to a collective sense of identity that substantiates itself through the enacting of rituals and cultural habits of the home country.

7. Born in Moriah, Tobago, in 1947, Philip moved to Canada in 1968. Before turning to writing, Philip obtained a degree in Law at the University of Western Ontario, but she soon gave up the practice of law—immigration and family law—to become a full-time writer. Her first book of poetry, *Thorns*, was published in 1980. After that, she published two more volumes of poetry, *Salmon Courage* (1983), and *She Tries Her Tongue, Her Silence Softly Breaks* in 1989. She has published two novels to date: *Harriet's Daughter* (1988), for young readers, and *Looking for Livingston: An Odyssey of Silence* (1991).

8. I have drawn insightful inspiration about the issue of unfamiliar textualities from the reading of Doris Sommer, *Proceed with Caution* (1999), and Bahri, *Native Intelligence* (2003)

REFERENCES

Ahmad, A. (1996). "The Politics of Literary Postcoloniality." *In* P. Mongia (ed.), *Contemporary Postcolonial Theory: A Reader*, pp. 276–93. London: Arnold. (Original work published in 1995.)

Ashcroft, B., G. Griffith, and H. Tiffin. (1989). *The Empire Writes Back: Theory and Practice in Post-colonial Criticism*. London: Routledge.

Attridge, D. (2004). *The Singularity of Literature*. London: Routledge.

Bahri, D. (2003). *Native Intelligence: Aesthetics, Politics and Postcolonial Literature*. Minneapolis: University of Minnesota Press.

Bhabha, H. K. (1994). *The Location of Culture*. London: Routledge.

Boehmer, E. (2005). *Colonial and Postcolonial Literature: Migrant Metaphors* (2nd ed.). Oxford: Oxford University Press.

Brand, D. (1990). *No Language Is Neutral*. Toronto: Coach House Press.

——. (1999). *At the Full and Change of the Moon*. Toronto: Vintage Canada.

Carby, H. V. (1982). "White Woman Listen! Black Feminism and the Boundaries of Sisterhood." *In* Centre for Contemporary Cultural Studies (ed.), *The Empire Strikes Back: Race and Racism in 70s Britain*. London: Routledge.

Ch'ien, E. N.-M. (2004). *Weird English*. Cambridge, Mass.: Harvard University Press.

Coetzee, J. M. (2000). *Disgrace*. London: Vintage. (Original work published in 1999.)

Dirie, W. (1998). *Desert Flower: The Extraordinary Journey of a Desert Nomad*. New York: Virago.

Gandhi, L. (1998). *Postcolonial Theory: A Critical Introduction*. Edinburgh: Edinburgh University Press.

Godard, B. "Marlene Philip's Hyphenated Tongue: or Writing the Caribbean Demotic between Africa and Arctic." *In* Raoul Granqvist (ed.), *Major Minorities: English Literatures in Transit*, pp. 151–175. Amsterdam: Rodopi.

Gray, S. "Introduction". *In* S. Gray (ed.), *The Picador Book of African Stories*. London: Picador.

Huggan, G. (2001). *The Post-colonial Exotic: Marketing the Margins*. London: Routledge.

Jameson, F. (1986). " Third World Literature in the Era of Multicultural Capitalism." *Social Text* 15, 65–88.

Macaulay, T. (1995). "Minute on Indian Education." *In* B. Ashcroft, G. Griffith, and H. Tiffin (eds.), *The Post-colonial Studies Reader*, pp. 428–30. London: Routledge. (Original work published in 1835.)

McLeod, J. (2000). *Beginning Postcolonialism*. New York: Manchester University Press.

Mohanti, C. T. (1996). "Under Western Eyes: Feminist Scholarship and Colonial Discourses." *In* P. Mongia (ed.), *Contemporary Postcolonial Theory: A Reader*, pp. 172–97. London: Arnold. (Original work published in 1991.)

Philip, M. N. (1994). *She Tries Her Tongue, Her Silence Softly Breaks*. *In* C. Morrell (ed.), *Grammar of Dissent: Poetry and Prose by Claire Harris, M. Nourbese Philip, Dionne Brand*, pp. 97–167. Fredericton, Canada: Goose Lane. (Original work published in 1989.)

Shoat, E. (1996). "Notes on the Post-colonial." *In* P. Mongia (ed.), *Contemporary Postcolonial Theory: A Reader*, pp. 321–34. London: Arnold.

Smith, S., and J. Watson. (1998). "Introduction: Situating Subjectivity in Women's Autobiographical Practices." *In* Smith and Watson (eds.), *Women, Autobiography, Theory: A Reader*, pp. 3–43. Madison: University of Wisconsin Press.

Sommer, D. (2003). "Introduction." *In* Sommer (ed.), *Bilingual Games: Some Literary Investigations*, pp. 1–18. New York: Palgrave Macmillan.

Spivak, G. C. (1987). "French Feminism in an International Frame." *In* Spivak, *In Other Worlds: Essays in Cultural Politics*, pp. 134–53. London: Routledge.

——. (1993). *Outside in the Teaching Machine*. London: Routledge.

——. (2002). " 'Breast-Giver': For Author, Reader, Teacher, Subaltern, Historian…" *In* M. Devi (ed.), *Breast Stories* (G. C. Spivak, trans.), pp. 176–37. Calcutta: Seagull. (Original work published in 1997.)

Suleri, S. (1996). "Woman Skin Dip: Feminism and the Postcolonial Condition." *In* P. Mongia (ed.), *Contemporary Postcolonial Theory: A Reader*, pp. 335–46. London: Arnold. (Original work published in 1992.)

Viswanathan, G. (1989). *Masks of Conquest: Literary Study and British Rule in India.* London: Faber.

Walcott, D. (1992). *Collected Poems: 1948–1984.* London: Faber and Faber. (Original work published in 1986.)

Young, R. J. C. (2003). *Postcolonialism: A Very Short Introduction.* Oxford: Oxford University Press.

PART III

DEVICES AND POWERS

CHAPTER 15

....

IMAGINATION

....

KIRK PILLOW

A venerable tradition conceives imagination, for the most part correctly, as far as it goes, as a mental power for making present what is absent through the production of images. Several philosophical disputes are buried in this formulation, and some of these are addressed below. On the whole, however, there is broad agreement that through imagination we exercise a kind of sight for that not currently perceived, and we also visualize alternatives never before seen. The image of an absent loved one, of a treasured or a fabled landscape, of a misplaced heirloom, of a life not pursued—imagination invests absence with significance, but also clothes the present with meaning. Imagining at its most powerful is, I argue here, an interpretive act through which we, more than simply producing images, see things *as* this or that investment of meaning, *as* this or that means of transcending the present toward something else. Imagination, writes Mary Warnock, "enables us to see the world, whether present or absent, as significant, and also to present this vision to others, for them to share or reject" (1976: 196). Literature, taken casually to comprise poetry and narrative fiction, is one of our richest enactments of this imaginative vision. Both in its production and in the exercise it provides its readers for cultivating meaning-making imagining, literature advances seeing *as*.

Both poetry and narrative fiction are acts of creative imagination that stimulate the production of images and the interpretive recasting of what matters. Poetry accomplishes this perhaps more intensively through the evocation of dense imagery via the most economical uses of language, while fiction represents a more extensive mode of expression. The sometimes great investment of time required to read fictions contributes to their imaginative power to "spin a cocoon" around us and hold us within "a containing cosmos" while they do their work on us (Brann 1991: 514). Works of literature generally, or their authors, rather, invite us to "see" things not present and to understand or value otherwise what is present before us by means of the extension of imaginative vision. When fictions bring us to see a character as of a type, to see a course of life as at odds with satisfaction, to see this world as a far cry from something better or worse—then imaginative literature complements, extends, or poses outright challenges to our conventional understanding. Imagination's power to make present what is absent positions it as a means of insight into but, even more significantly, as a source of challenge to the status quo of the "given" world before us. The role of imagination in literary production and reception makes literature a powerful source of pressure placed upon the real to be otherwise. This will lead us to conclusions regarding imagination in literature as a transgressive expression of freedom, regarding the ethical imperatives of imagining, and regarding imagining as the cultivation of a "double vision" (Brann 1991) that not merely shapes fictional worlds but also reshapes our own.

IMAGINING AND PERCEIVING

We will make progress toward appreciating the role of imagining in literature if we first clarify the contrast between perception and imagination. The contrast highlights the distinctive features of acts of imagining and will guide us toward understanding the act of seeing-as.

It has long been observed that imagining is voluntary, or subject to the will, in ways that perceiving is not. One can call up at will an image of home from across town, while one can only directly perceive its kitchen when standing in it. One can invite another to imagine something, but not to perceive something not available for the looking. Percepts are experienced as passively received, in contrast to our voluntary control over images. This contrast holds even if we reject a naive conception of perception as purely a matter of passive reception. Various post-Kantian epistemologies regard perception as an active process of categorization, and a Sellarsian rejection of the "myth of the Given" is a rejection of perception as pure reception of sense-data. But whatever goes into perception, the phenomenologies of perceiving and imagining differ regarding their voluntarism. When observing my desk, I do not choose to perceive a keyboard, even if I can choose what on the desk to attend to. Nor can I choose not to see the keyboard in front of me, except by closing my eyes so as not to perceive visually, or by looking the other way, in which case what I see when looking away is not up to me, either. Percepts "come at us" whether we like them or not, while images can be called up at will and recede as soon as we cease to imagine them. This contrast should not be overstated, however, because there are limits to how subject to willing imagining is (Brann 1991: 159): one can try to call up an image of someone not seen for many years, but fail, and in some cases images come to us against our will or can be recalcitrant to receding once imaged. The contrast holds and is of vital importance nevertheless, because the voluntarism of imagining is, of course, what allows it to serve as a ready alternative to the annoying persistence of the perceived present before us.

The voluntarism contrast exposes several others between percepts and images. The aspects of an image are attention dependent—they cease to exist when one stops attending to them—whereas the details of percepts are there whether one attends to them or not (McGinn 2004: 26–29). When one imagines a favorite pet, the wagging tail wags only as long as one makes it so and exists as part of the image only as long as one wills it. The perceived pet's tail wags, if it does, whether one notices or not. Furthermore, percepts are constrained by the psychophysical structure of the visual field: they must be positioned in space in front of us (22–25). Percepts are situated wherever the eyes are directed, whereas images need not be fixed spatially at all. One can imagine a favorite pet riding in a car in another state, or sleeping in front of one, or standing behind one. Additionally, given the visual and spatial constraints on percepts, they are occlusive of each other, whereas images do not occlude percepts (32–34). One can freely imagine a favorite pet while looking at a computer screen, but one cannot perceive the wall behind the screen while perceiving the screen (without use of a mirror, at least, which will then occlude what lies behind it). Hence, images can be *layered over* objects "translucently" in ways that percepts cannot. This feature of imagining will prove central to understanding seeing-as and its interpretive function.

Images and percepts also differ in what we learn from them. Being largely subject to the will, images are not informative in the way that percepts are, because images contain only what we put into them (Sartre 1991: 11). Close observation of a favorite pet can reveal an infestation of fleas, but an imagined pet has fleas only if one chooses to imagine this; we don't learn anything about the pet by imagining it one way or another. As Wittgenstein puts it, "It is just because forming images is a voluntary activity that it does not instruct us about the external world" (1967: 110). The content of images is *stipulated* by our imagining, and so images have only as much content as we plug into them, whereas percepts are saturated with continuous content. "The object of perception," writes Jean-Paul Sartre, "is constituted of an infinite multiplicity of determinations and possible relations. The most definite image, on the other hand, possesses in itself only a finite number of determinations, namely, only those of which we are conscious" (1991: 21). And because their content is stipulated, images do not require recognition. A favorite pet approaching from a distance has first to be recognized as such when the percept comes into focus, so to speak, but an image of a favorite pet approaching from a distance is just known already to be of the pet irrespective of the limits distance places on recognition (McGinn 2004: 25, 31). We do not come to discover things about our images, because we decided what they were to be when opting to imagine them.

These observations hammer another nail into the coffin of the outmoded "picture theory" of mental images. That theory holds that mental images assume the form of pictures in the mind that refer to what they picture by virtue of a resemblance between picture and object. But unlike mental images, actual perceived pictures can be highly informative regarding their objects, and they require recognition of what they are pictures of. "Images are not pictures," Wittgenstein writes. "I do not tell what object I am imagining by the resemblance between it and the image" (1967: 109). There can be no question of what I imagine via a certain image, because each image *intends its object* directly via the voluntary act of imagining. There can, on the other hand, be a question concerning what a picture pictures, with an answer perhaps in some cases established partly by virtue of resemblances. Sartre, for one, took the intentionality of imagining to undermine not only the picture theory of mental images but even, at least at some points in his *The Psychology of Imagination* (1940), the very notion of mental imagery. On his view, imagination intends its object so directly as to dispense with the mediation of an image. "The imaginative consciousness I have of Peter," Sartre writes, "is not a consciousness of the image of Peter: Peter is directly reached, my attention is not directed on an image, but on an object," Peter himself (1991: 8). To imagine Peter from across town is to "see" Peter rather than an image of him. "There is no image *in* a consciousness which contains it," Sartre adds (19). But this view is unable to make much metaphorical sense of how imagination "sees" what is absent; the view seems to reduce imagining simply to *thinking* of the absent object. Oddly, Sartre does not deny the existence of mental images, so their role in his theory is obscure. To some extent, his ambivalent conception of them is motivated by his commitment to a dubious theory of the transparency of consciousness (6). In any case, the fact that mental images intend their objects directly is sufficient to make consciousness of a mental image a consciousness of its object; we need not deny mental images a mediating role. The production of mental images gives imagination what it visualizes in the mind's eye. Such a conception of imagining can be sustained without suffering from the problems attached to the discredited picture theory of mental representation (for further discussion, see Brann 1991).

The fact that images do not inform as percepts can may suggest that imagining has no educative function. Were this correct, attributing to imagination a vital role in writing and reading literature would seem to derail the sorts of claims for literature that I began by proposing. But first of all, our imaginings surely are educative at least indirectly. The content of images, however stipulated, can remind us of features of objects or situations in ways that inform our judgments and behavior. Further, discovering what we are more or less able to imagine can teach us much about ourselves. More directly to the point, the contrasts described thus far between images and percepts have not shown the full range of what we do with images, and shortly we will see that images serve as powerful tools of interpretation when we engage in imaginative seeing-as. Such a use of imagery will be critical to the experience of literature, and it will secure a profound educative potential for the literary work. Images and texts will be partners in promoting interpretation not merely of the story but of the world. Their ready pairing reflects commonalities of their nature: percepts, as we saw, are saturated with continuous content, while the content of images is limited and stipulated. But much the same is true of fictions: their depictions are stipulated by the author, and even the richest depiction cannot approach the saturated continuity of perception. "The image is like a story in this respect," McGinn writes: "it is constitutionally incomplete" (2004: 25). Far from being a shortcoming, however, this incompleteness inherent to fictions invites the imaginative interpretations through which we fill out fictional worlds and, more important, through which we use fictions to reinterpret and reach new understandings of our own world.

A final contrast between images and percepts reflects my starting point for understanding imagination while also reinforcing the idea that it can yield understanding. Visual percepts, as we know, are of objects present to the visual system of the body, while images are of objects absent to perception. Imagination is a power for making present "to the mind's eye" objects or scenes currently unavailable for perception or even never to be seen. To imagine is to "see" something other than the humdrum present perceptible before us. This standard contrast prompted an observation by Wittgenstein about which I share McGinn's fascination: "While I am looking at an object I cannot imagine it" (1967: 109). Although Wittgenstein intends this remark to reveal differences in our language games regarding perceiving and imagining, rather than as a psychological claim, it does nevertheless seem empirically true. I can perceive a wheelbarrow before me; I can close my eyes or look away and call up an image of a wheelbarrow, but I cannot call up an image of the wheelbarrow before me while staring right at the real thing. It does seem, however, that I can, while perceiving a wheelbarrow, imagine another, or even this one, behind me. Hence the problem with perceiving and imagining the same thing at once hinges on the presence-absence contrast between percepts and images. But note that one can, while perceiving a wheelbarrow, *also* imagine it dancing the can-can in a live revue. Here, one "sees" the wheelbarrow *as* a dancer on stage, and this seeing of the object as something else is not constrained by the perceptual presence of the object in the way that merely calling up an image of the object is. Clearly, some more sophisticated act of imagining is at work in seeing-as, distinct from simply calling up an "uninflected" image of a thing. I turn now to elucidating this imaginative seeing, for this practice will prove central to the role of imagination in our responses to literary fictions.

IMAGINATION AND SEEING-AS

Imaginative seeing, variously called "seeing-as" or "the seeing of aspects," is explored famously by Wittgenstein in *Philosophical Investigations* (1953) by means of the duck-rabbit picture and other devices. Seeing-as is there understood as an operation of imagination distinct from perception, but one that inflects perception when an image "invades" a percept and so motivates interpreting the percept as being or as representing or referring to something other than what it is. This requires some unpacking, first with regard to the distinctness of seeing-as from "basic" perception. " 'Seeing as,' " Wittgenstein writes, "is not part of perception. And for that reason it is like seeing and again not like" (1953: 197). It makes no sense, Wittgenstein thinks, "to say at the sight of a knife and fork 'Now I am seeing this as a knife and fork.' . . . One doesn't 'take' what one knows as the cutlery at a meal *for* cutlery" (195). The taking that Wittgenstein denies to perception is, of course, the take of interpretation. Similarly, some pages later Wittgenstein adds, "I cannot try to see a conventional picture of a lion *as* a lion, any more than an F as that letter" (206). One just sees a lion picture, or sees a lion "in" the picture, without having to interpret the picture as a picture of a lion. Seeing the lion picture for what it is, namely, a picture of a lion, requires the act of recognition typical of perception, but seeing it thus does not, Wittgenstein holds, require interpretation. Now, this is hardly a settled matter among philosophers of mind, hermeneuts, and philosophers of art. Some would argue in a Nietzschean vein that *all* experience is charged with quasi-artistic interpretation, or at least that the comprehension of pictures requires interpretation of an image in light of artificial pictorial conventions. Others would hold, as intimated above, that any Kantian or post-Kantian commitment to the experiential unity of sensory passivity and categorizing spontaneity already entails understanding experience as such as an outcome of interpretation. But even if Wittgenstein were to agree that elaborate, creative, reality-determinative cognitive processes underlie the turning of sense data into the experience of a lion picture, or of an actual lion, he would reject the view that such processes entail seeing the sense data *as* a lion. We just see a lion, whereas seeing a lion picture, or an actual lion, *as* a symbol of royalty or *as* Bert Lahr in costume does involve an imaginative exercise of interpretation. Whether Wittgenstein is correct or not about the noninterpretive recognition of pictures, imaginative seeing is an *interpretive* act in ways that much perception is probably not, however active the process of perception is.

In seeing-as, Wittgenstein writes, "[i]t is as if an *image* came into contact, and for a time remained in contact, with the visual impression" (Wittgenstein 1953: 207). To see a percept as something more or something else involves *layering over* the percept an image by means of which we "read" the percept in one direction or another and so see it differently, despite there being no change in the underlying percept. "The expression of a change of aspect is the expression of a *new* perception and at the same time of the perception's being unchanged" (196). To see a lion as Bert Lahr in costume is to undergo a change of perception, via the imaginative significances one has layered over the percept, even as the initial object of perception has not altered. The lion remains the lion it was, but layers of imagery have altered its meaning for a time. Wittgenstein illustrates this both with the duck-rabbit drawing (194) and with a triangular figure seen in various aspects. One might be shown the duck-rabbit and only ever see a duck; in such a case, one does not see the picture *as* a duck picture, one just sees a picture of a duck. But by prompting or otherwise, it may dawn on one that the picture can instead be seen as a rabbit picture. While seeing the picture as a rabbit picture, one's perception alters as imagination reinterprets it as a rabbit picture, even though in one sense one sees the same old perception all along. Similarly, a figure of a right triangle with hypot-enuse facing and parallel to the bottom of the page can be seen as "a triangular hole, as a solid, as a geometrical drawing; as standing on its base...; as a mountain..., as an overturned object which is meant to stand on the shorter side of the right angle," and so on (Wittgenstein 1953: 200). While it is possible always to see only a duck in the duck-rabbit picture, seeing the triangle as any of these things takes an effort: "[To] take the bare triangular figure for the picture of an object that has fallen over...demands *imagination*" (207).

If imaginative seeing deploys images as an interpretive supplement to percep-tion, we should be able to specify seeing-as further via the differentia between per-cepts and images discussed above (see McGinn 2004: 50–53). Imagining is largely subject to the will, whereas perception is not voluntary. Seeing-as, oddly positioned between the two, is a voluntary act of interpreting perception by means of images. It does not alter the underlying involuntary percept, even while seeing-as alters what we see by investing what is seen with fresh meanings. Images are attention dependent, whereas percepts are not, so what a percept is seen as imaginatively shares the transience of the image: the lion seen as Bert Lahr is altered only for as long as this interpretive attention is paid. Percepts are saturated with continuous content, unlike images, so what the percept is seen as does not appear to us with the saturation of full perception. Seeing a lion as Bert Lahr will be rich with lion perception, but not with the content of actually perceiving Bert Lahr in costume. Again, images, unlike percepts, do not require recognition, because their content is stipulated, so percepts can be misrecognized, but not what we see them as, since we supply the interpretation. Further, because percepts occlude one another but images do not occlude percepts, the images that layer over percepts when we see imaginatively add interpretively to the percept without occluding it. We still see the lion, but we see it as Bert Lahr.

I want to focus more carefully on the remaining contrasts between images and percepts: spatial specificity, presence-absence, and relative informativeness, because it is in these respects that the power and importance of imaginative seeing become clear. Percepts are spatially positioned in front of us, with the consequence that what we see them as imaginatively, when we layer an image over the percept, is seen *as if* before us. To see a perceived lion as Bert Lahr is to see the lion in front of you as Bert Lahr in costume; it is as if Bert Lahr were before you, costumed as the Cowardly Lion. This observation clearly entails a variation in imaginative seeing regarding the presence-absence contrast between percepts and images: the perceived lion is present to the visual system, and what this percept is seen as is presented to us imaginatively as if present, even though what the percept is seen as is itself absent. The key point is that seeing-as involves the "quasi presence" of an imagined object parasitical on the true presence of the object on which one lavishes images. That is, imaginative seeing is a seeing *of* the object via an interpre-tive layer of imagery, rather than merely an imaging in the mind apart from what we see before us. Put simply, to see imaginatively is to see *the object*, or the world, differently, as if other than it is. (Note that this conclusion vindicates Sartre's view of the object-oriented intentionality of imagining, though at the level of seeing-as rather than in the mere calling up of images.) To see imaginatively is at once to see and to interpret something in the world. I argue below that the experience of literature relies upon and promotes an imaginative seeing that is transformative, for a time, of the world before us.

We saw above that images do not exactly share the informativeness of percepts. We learn new things from perception in ways we evidently do not from imagining, especially because the content of images is voluntarily stipulated. Does this mean we have little to learn from seeing-as? Quite the contrary. Seeing-as serves an educative and reflective function in between the involuntary observational content of perception and the voluntary production of images, precisely because when seeing-as layers images onto the perceived world, it accomplishes an investment of meanings into the world. It transforms worldly things at the level of their significance for us, and it does so in the world, not merely in our heads. Warnock conveys this eloquently: "Imagination is our means of interpreting the world, and it is *also* our means of forming images in the world. The images themselves are not separate from our interpretations of the world; they are our way of thinking of the objects in the world" (1976: 194). Imaginative seeing lends a depth to experience that the mere saturation of the percept, however fascinating, cannot provide; seeing-as shows things to be or to mean more than they appear to perception. To practice imaginative seeing is to enact "the belief that there is more in our experience of the world than can possibly meet the unreflecting eye;" it is by virtue of creative seeing-as "that there is always *more* to an experience, and *more in* what we experience than we can predict" (202). But note that while the interpretive function of seeing-as enriches experience, it is also constrained by the world it interprets. Positioned between involuntary perception and voluntary imagining, seeing-as is answerable to the world that it layers over with its image construals. Percepts need to be amenable to specific choices of interpretation; otherwise, seeing-as devolves into idle fantasy. Indeed, fantasy in the pejorative sense, while one outcome of imagining, must be distinguished from the seeing-as that engages constructively with present realities. Imaginative seeing requires informed understanding of the world to make its interpretive recastings compelling or useful.

In sum, seeing-as creatively complicates the image-percept contrast by bringing images into reinterpretive contact with perception. Unlike the simple imaging of something absent, seeing-as is not bound by the Wittgensteinian dictum that "while I am looking at an object I cannot imagine it." While observing an object or the world, one can imagine it otherwise than it appears. One can see the object as something else or as invested with invisible significances. One can see the world other than it is, by the lights of unrealized possibility. To do so is not merely to fantasize some other world, but to see in this world its other potentials. Seeing-as is the power of imagination fully realized, remaking the world and hence granting us a freeing critical distance from the pressing present before us. Aided by imagination, this, too, is what literature does.

INTERLUDE: IMAGINATION AND ROMANTIC GENIUS

The two powers of imagination discussed above—the calling up of images and the more creative seeing-as reinterpretation of things—have a long history in Western discourses of imagining. That history has been studied in depth by many scholars (see, e.g., Engell 1981; Kearney 1988; Brann 1991); here I provide only a brief discussion of romantic theories of imagination as a means to summarize certain themes and to prepare for the remaining claims of this essay. Richard Kearney has identified historical paradigms of imagination, each informed by a different metaphor or figure of its power (1988: 17). The premodern *mimetic* paradigm for imagination employs the referential figure of a mirror capturing images of what we have seen. This reproductive capacity of imagination I outlined in the contrast between perceiving and imagining. The modern *productive* paradigm employs the expressive figure of imagination as a lamp casting a transforming light of creative rethinking on its objects. I have outlined this creativity in terms of imaginative seeing-as. (I do not address Kearney's third paradigm, the "parodic" imagination of postmodernism and its reflexive figure of a labyrinth of mirrors.)

We owe to Kant the most elaborate modern discrimination of the different reproductive and creatively productive powers of imagination. While reproductive imagination is largely limited to calling up the images of phenomena from past perception, Kant invests productive imagination with a range of roles crucial to cognition, aesthetic appreciation, and artistic creation. In the *Critique of Pure Reason* (1781) imagination mediates between sensation and understanding throughout the process of conceptualizing sense data into a coherent experiential structure (1998: 271–77). In the *Critique of Judgment* (1790) imagination is essential to the play of mental powers in which Kant thinks we feel the pleasure of finding something beautiful. Moreover, productive imagination is the guiding power of artistic genius: its "aesthetic ideas" (for Kant, the expressed content of works of art) create "another nature, out of the material which the real one gives" (2000: 192). In artistic genius, imagination "steps beyond nature" (192) by producing a perspective on or interpretation of things that supplements perception with fresh possibilities of significance, as we have seen in the act of seeing-as (see Pillow 2000).

Deeply influenced not only by Kant but by Johann Gottlieb Fichte and Friedrich Schelling, the romantic poets William Wordsworth and especially Samuel Taylor Coleridge made the modern contrasts among imaginative powers central to their conception of poetic creation. In his *Biographia Literaria* (1817) Coleridge distinguished what he calls "fancy," or the mere associative reproduction of images without any unifying structure, from imagination proper (1985: 305). This pejorative fancy is the idle passing of trains of imagery to no purpose but diversion. He divides true imagination into primary and secondary forms corresponding, roughly, to the cognitive versus the aesthetic/artistic powers that Kant had characterized. Coleridge's famous declaration is both fascinating and obscure:

> The primary imagination I hold to be the living Power and prime agent of all human Perception, and as a representation in the finite mind of the eternal act of creation in the infinite I AM. The secondary I consider as an echo of the former, co-existing with the conscious will, yet still as identical with the primary in the *kind* of its agency, and differing only in *degree*, and in the *mode* of its operation. It dissolves, diffuses, dissipates, in order to re-create; or where this process is rendered impossible, yet still at all events it struggles to idealize and to unify. It is essentially *vital*, even as all objects (*as* objects) are essentially fixed and dead. (304)

Primary imagination functions along Kantian lines to imbue perception with conceptual richness. It is, for Coleridge, as James Engell writes, "the agency of perceiving and learning. It is the process of education in the original and general sense: a leading of the mind out into the world" (1981: 343). Secondary imagination, on the other hand, produces ordered structures of rich expression that transcend actual nature into a second nature of organic unity and balance. Coleridge coined the term "esemplastic," drawing on Greek roots, to characterize the power of imagination to "fashion into one" disparate materials ordered for the purpose of conveying something new (Brann 1991: 508). In his poetry, along with Wordsworth in the *Lyrical Ballads* (1798) and elsewhere, Coleridge sought uses of language expressive of a quasi-divine power of imaginative unification.

Throughout its history, from Aristotle onward, imagination has been pressed into the role of mediating between the bodily senses and the rational intellect. Kant's theory of imagination in his epistemology and aesthetics culminates that tradition and grants profound importance to imagining as an agent of cognition and feeling. His theory of artistic genius, and its adoption by the romantic poets and later thinkers, tends, however, to isolate imaginative creativity in a hallowed hall of great and original minds. For Kant, genius is a rare gift of nature more remarkable even than the scientific talents of a Newton (2000: 187). The consequent romantic cult of original genius should be resisted, I believe, for the imaginative seeing characterized above is not the exceptional practice of a gifted few but is instead ubiquitous in the sensemaking practices of interpretive human beings. Acts of seeing-as thoroughly mediate and meld perception and thought wherever we layer image over percept to imbue things and persons with unseen meanings. However correct Wittgenstein may have been that we do not see the cutlery at dinner *as* a knife and fork, we do see them as heirlooms of family tradition, as arranged on the table according to cultural tradition, as one among many cultures' means of dining, as exemplars of a school of design, as embarrassing in their need of polishing, and so on. The imaginative seeing that I have associated with the modern Kantian conception of productive imagination accompanies our experience of the world constantly as an interpretive supplement to more or less all that we see. Artistic talent certainly lies in the organization and expression of emotions and ideas in various sensuous media, and few may be the great poets and artists capable of profound expression in those media. But we are all geniuses of seeing things, through the lens of imagination, as something more or something other than they appear.

The Romantic notion of genius is distinctive of the modern period's emphasis on the individual subject as cognitive agent, aesthetic judge, and political unit. While the capacities of imagining discussed above are hardly unique to the modern subject, they come in modernity to be symbolic of that subject's creative autonomy (about which more below). It takes a culture of individualism to make how each of us differently interprets the world something of defining interest: imaginative seeing-as, it appears, is seen as definitive of the modern self. It perhaps takes that same culture to make the personalities, emotions, choices, and fates of fictional characters maximally of interest, so there is little wonder that modern individualism set the stage for the rise of the novel as an artistic form. The novel's "extensive" mode of expression, the investments of time its appreciation can require, reflects cultural convictions about the fascination of individual lives and what strikes us as a pleasurable use of politically and economically secured leisure. The modern individual is one primed and prompted to make full cognitive and aesthetic use of imagination's seeing-as powers. The endless narrative fictionalizing of modern life is among the richest expressions of this life of imagination.

IMAGINATION AND LITERATURE

In a remark pregnant with significance, Wittgenstein observes in *Philosophical Investigations* that he can see something "in various aspects according to the fiction I surround it with" (1953: 210). To see imaginatively is to clothe something in a fiction that transforms its meaning. This fiction may take the simple form of an image that reinterprets a picture of a lion. It may take the more complex form of a system of images evoked by the language of a poem. Or it may take the form of a fiction proper: an extended narrative relating characters and events, inviting sequences of visualization on the part of the reader, whose imaginative response to the fiction is a kind of seeing and interpreting at once. Reading literature is a process of transforming language into visions, and this process puts imagination as a power of visualization into creative cooperation with language. I noted above that both images and fictions are incomplete: the stipulated content of images falls short of the saturated content of perception; what is described and narrated in a fiction leaves unspecified all manner of details that would be present to perception were the story instead an experience. However profound the power of language to describe events and invite their visualization, language "can never achieve fully determined visibility" (Brann 1991: 473). Neither can imagining, whose products supplement rather than replace perception. Brought into collaboration in the response to literature, visualization and narrative in words take advantage of their similar incompleteness to spark an imaginative seeing in which the stipulation of images by the reader is both encouraged to fill in missing detail and guided by the constraints the narrative poses. "[We] respond appropriately to the statements of fiction," David Novitz argues, "only if we respond imaginatively—that is, [if we] respond by imagining the situations or lives of its fictional characters in terms closely specified by the author" (1987: 81; see also Walton 1990). Just as seeing-as is answerable to perception, the fiction's terms direct our imagining. Even so, the incompleteness of description also frees imagination to visualize well beyond what the language conveys, however short of the saturation of perception its images will remain.

Studies of childhood language acquisition suggest that the development of language skills is closely related to the capacity for imaginative play. Much play entails the acting out of story lines, and playing a tea party or a moon launch requires exiting reality sufficiently to enter into a nonpresent imaginative state of affairs. Paul Harris argues that the understanding and production of narratives, or what he calls "connected discourse," "is only possible for a creature who is capable, temporarily, of setting current reality to one side and constructing a situation model pertaining to a different spatio-temporal locus" (2000: 194). The capacity to invent "situation models" in pretend play, Harris proposes, underpins the sophisticated uses of language in which children and adults describe noncurrent situations. That is, playing at a pretend moon launch prepares the language skills that underlie the ability to understand and describe an actual moon launch one has not witnessed directly. Harris misses the point, however, that the pretend tea party happens in the here and now, not in some other space or time. The hand not actually gloved in white lace, with curled pinky actually distended, is seen as sipping a cup of tea in the present world, not in some other. Seeing-as, we know, transforms things of this world through shifts of interpretation. The imaginative response to literature is a comparable mode of play in which, I propose, we envision our own world differently rather than escaping into some other.

Comprehending a fiction, like playing at tea, indeed requires setting aside, to a degree, current reality so as to envision another. What Colin McGinn calls "fictional immersion," the experience of disappearing into an engrossing story, is made possible by an imagination capable of seeing an image system for a fictional world, sometimes with an intensity to rival perception, even though it never occludes perception (2004: 103). To become immersed in a fiction, we must be able to free ourselves sufficiently from the grip of present affairs, so that we can visualize a narrative of nonpresent events. Imagination makes possible this transcendence of the present, the visual projection of events happening elsewhere, and so our immersion into the story of that world. Now we have seen two principal capacities of imagination: the power to call up images of things absent to perception, and the power to reinterpret things through the layering of images over percepts. Both acts of imagination enrich our response to literature. We visualize the story world through sequences of imagery that fill out its absence. These images hover before the mind's eye and take us out of the humdrum present. This response to literature is an imaginative mode of play akin to fantasy, where fantasy is understood as a hermetically sealed interlude apart from real life, an escapist diversion from reality. Such fantasy has its pleasures as well as its limit of value, for we have seen that the second power of imagining, to see things as other or more than they appear, sustains an "eminent contact with real and daily life" (Brann 1991: 561) that fantasy does not. Full imaginative seeing construes *this* world creatively and invests its objects and scenes with fresh meanings. Imagination enlivens the fictional narrative not merely via the imaging of a fictional world; its more profound service to literature is to bring the fiction to bear on this world through the interpretive work of seeing-as. The things and situations represented in works of literature are intended by acts of imagining directed at this world: they have "substance" not merely in a fantastical space immanent to imagination, but are "intended as external to the imaginer, as imaginations projected into the world" (Brann 1991: 449). When imagination not only "sees" what is absent but also reinterprets what is present, when imagination sees this world as another, or another world in the potentials of this one, it fully serves the interests of literature. Works of poetry and narrative fiction, far from merely calling up isolated sequences of imagery cut off from the pressing real, are fundamentally about the present world over which their images and stories layer. They invite the imaginative seeing of this world otherwise than it is.

This general claim can be further specified in terms of a central device both of imaginative seeing and of literary creativity: the use of metaphor. McGinn calls "cognitive imagination" the entertaining of a proposition, or imagining that p, as opposed to the layering of images in seeing-as (2004: 128). Borrowing his example, when one imaginatively sees the sky as oceanic, percept (sky) and image (ocean) merge into a new perception of the sky under an aspect of watery blue vastness and depth. When one entertains the proposition that the sky *is* oceanic, McGinn proposes, image and belief merge into metaphorical understanding (134–35). These are really sides of the same coin: the imaginative layering of image over percept inspires the metaphorical cognition of one thing as another, and the metaphor expressed in language enlivens imagination's capacity to see the sky as oceanic. Metaphor is essentially the linguistic expression of seeing-as, imaginative seeing pursued in words rather than images. Metaphor distills into language the seeing of one thing in another such that, when successful, it inspires creative seeing-as on the part of its hearer or reader. Now, various philosophers have argued that the structure of works of art, whether linguistic or not, is fundamentally metaphorical (see Hausman 1989): a work functions as a system of metaphors that recast our understanding of something by motivating us to see it not as it is but otherwise. Works of literature often make elaborate use of metaphor internally and invite us to understand characters or events in metaphorical terms or as metaphors for this or that. The larger claim, though, is that the target domain for literary metaphor is the reader's own world. A fiction reshapes our thinking about this world by inviting us to see it under the aspect of an imagined variation or alternative. To take in a fictional narrative is to layer it over the world present before us as a metaphor exposing just how this world is, or as a metaphor for how else, for better or worse, this world might be. Wittgenstein provides the perfect metaphor for the seeing-as that literature prompts: it is "the echo of a thought in sight" (1953: 212). Imagination serves literature by aiding our seeing, both literally and figuratively, and by understanding the world differently through the metaphorical lenses that fictions provide.

The creative flexibility to see one thing as another, to see one thing in another, is intimately linked to the empathic power to see oneself as another, to see in another life the joys and pains possible in one's own. Our responses to works of fiction are often deeply emotional, and while those responses may range across joy, anger, disgust, and admiration, our emotional investment in fictions is secured fundamentally through empathy. Imaginative seeing makes the empathic relation to fictional characters possible. To care about the life and fate of a fictional character is to imagine that life or fate as one's own. "It is only when one responds imaginatively," Novitz writes, "by 'thinking one's way into' the situation of [Anna Karenina]...that one can acquire beliefs about Anna which allow us to feel the urgency, dread, and hopelessness of her situation" (1987: 86; see also Cohen 1999). The empathic power of imagination is accomplished precisely through the imaginative seeing I have emphasized: we see our own lives transformed as into another by metaphorically living out the days and troubles of fictional characters. We have seen that imagining is largely subject to the will, and we know too well that emotion usually is not. Yet the voluntarism of imagination plays a powerful role in helping us "summon emotions and feelings not only as spontaneous accompaniments but even, to some degree, as intentional effects" (Brann 1991: 764). Imagination mediates between the will and the passions, summoning emotions usually out of our hands to concoct; works of poetry and narrative fiction are among the richest means of providing such deliberate exercises of emotional depth. Imagination enriches emotional responses to fiction, but it also informs more broadly the tenor of our desires and what it means when they go unfulfilled. Both imagination and desire are defined, after all, in terms of the absence of their object, though imagination can sometimes partially satisfy desire by making virtually present the absent thing or one desired (Brann 1991: 762)—hence the great appeal of the love story to many of those desiring love.

IMAGINATION AND HUMAN FREEDOM

Imagination allows us to make present through images what is absent from the present world before us. It allows us to reconfigure that world through the image-layering interpretive practice of seeing-as. And in literature, imagination richly realizes its capacity to revise the present world by layering a transfiguring other world over it. In a tradition made gospel by Sartre, these powers identify imagination as a principal source of human freedom. A creature devoid of freedom would be one utterly beholden to the determinacy of the present, unable in any way to escape the clutches of what is the case in each successive moment. The mental horizon of a being without freedom would not extend beyond what is before it. But by making present what is absent, imagination regularly transcends what is the case at present to envision other places, times, and possibilities. By doing so, imagination regularly enacts our free transcendence of present determinacy toward something else. "To posit an image," writes Sartre, "is to construct an object on the fringe of the whole of reality, which therefore means to hold the real at a distance, to free oneself from it, in a word, to deny it" (1991: 266). The voluntarism earlier attributed to imagining, the fact that the calling up of images is largely subject to the will, Sartre understands as definitive of human consciousness as an experience of freedom from present conditions. "For a consciousness to be able to imagine," he writes, "it must be able to escape from the world by its very nature, it must be able by its own efforts to withdraw from the world. In a word it must be free" (267). Consciousness as such is for Sartre an act of setting itself apart from the world, of negating the world through awareness of it; hence, he as much as holds that consciousness is inconceivable without the power and freedom to imagine. At the everyday level, imagination enacts our freedom because the images we call up of absent objects, scenes, or persons open consciousness out into futures of possibility, inform our judgments about better and worse options, and spur us to action.

Sartre emphasizes that however much consciousness negates the present world in apprehending it as not-itself, imagination's freeing production of images always occurs from a determinate perspective on that world:

> [E]very apprehension of the real as a world tends of its own accord to end up with the production of unreal objects because it is always, in one sense, a free negation of the world and that always *from a particular point of view*.... [An] image, being a negation of the world from a particular point of view, can never appear excepting *on the foundation of the world* and in connection with the foundation. (1991: 269)

Our experience of the world is regularly accompanied by imagery of the unreal or the not-present because conscious experience itself negates the fixity of the real and frees imagination to see what is absent or otherwise, what is not real now or yet. But such imaginings always arise from and reflect the subject's place in the world. They have as their backdrop the definite circumstances of the individual consciousness and its awareness not just of any world but of the facticity of this one. This point applies not only to the calling up of images of what is absent, but also to the imaginative seeing in which we reinterpret the world through the layering of images over what is present. Seeing-as is responsive to the definite present; it reinterprets not some fantasy world but the constraining reality of given circumstance. (I take this to be true of many works of fantasy literature; seeing the present world imaginatively does not require a commitment to literary realism or naturalism.) Through its recasting of things of this world, it expresses our freedom to transgress against current understandings of things, while also acknowledging the hold this world has on our points of view. Seeing-as is a worldly act that, while enacting a power to interpret freely and creatively, does not free us of being in the world.

Authors of works of literature attempt the kind of free self-making, the creative shaping of a world that the Greeks called *poiesis*. Poietic works are self-fashioning because, as Richard Eldridge writes, they "are representations of subjects, their characters, their interests, and their possible stances in culture that are made by subjects and that in turn help to make them, insofar as they make available certain routes of self-construal and of action and identity in culture" (1996: 7). Poietic works are expressions of freedom because their production shows that we are "able to articulate and envision, albeit in specific ways, impersonal ideals of free activity and ways of pursuing them" (10–11). They are never creations *ex nihilo*, for they are made from given materials and reflect the situated facticity of the creative subject. But they demonstrate our capacity to transcend determinacy toward fresh possibility. Eva Brann summarizes three aspects of imaginative freedom: "freedom from the compulsions of the present, the freedom to control imaginative vision, and the freedom to show physical competence" (1991: 186). This last is of great importance. It refers in broad strokes to all of our capacities to externalize imaginative products within shareable media of expression, to use physical, mental, and emotional labor to communicate creatively with each other. Not all products of imaginative fancy achieve such communication. A centuries-old tradition associates imagining with madness (see Pillow 2000), especially where imagination devolves into escapist and incommunicable fantasy or delusion. This tradition shows through in the psychologist's alternate definition of *poiesis* recorded in the *Oxford English Dictionary*: "the coining of neologisms, especially by a schizophrenic." To create poietically is to stretch out past given patterns of intelligibility in order freely to express something else and, as such, carries with it the risk of producing nonsense along with the potential for real revelation.

As the truism states, with freedom comes responsibility. The free exercise of imaginative seeing, in both the production and appreciation of literature, entails ethical obligations that raise imagining above escapist play. We have already observed the role of imagination in empathy: our capacity to don the clothes of another's life substantiates our obligation to care about the joys and sufferings of others. Kearney has identified two other ethical functions of imagination: the testimonial and the utopian (1991: 225). Complementary to the more evidentiary practices of historiography, imaginative storytelling records affectively rich testimony about human choices and forms of life. It compels the self-examination that comes from seeing oneself portrayed in an unsavory fictional character, and it exercises our recognition of what should count as worthy lives. The utopian function is really poetical and ethical at once: *poiesis* enacts the imperative constantly to reimagine the world in hopes of something more, for the sake simply of creative transcendence of the present, for the sake of fashioning "products of imaginative power calling to ways of cultural life not yet in being" (Eldridge 1996: 8). But this self-making creativity must be ethically centered in an imaginative seeing that seeks to improve the human condition. The utopian obligation of storytelling does not require a Utopia of every fictional narrative. It does require at least the effort to affect incremental improvement of the human person through the depiction of better and worse choices. It requires depicting the consequences of the presence or absence of kindness, and it requires depicting the courage to achieve, or the cowardice of avoiding, a fresh imaginative vision.

However much it expresses the point of view of the artist from and on his or her foundation in the given world, a work of art is a kind of realized unreality expressed in transgression of that world. While realized in tangible media, the unreality of a poem or a novel lies in its counterpoint to the present world, its challenge to see that world from a critical distance or to see to the world's evolution toward something else. The imaginative seeing that works of literature encourage is fundamentally an act of transgression against the current state of affairs. The "production of unreal objects" that Sartre associated with consciousness of a world poses a continual challenge to the stasis of the status quo. Imagination is our principal means of putting pressure on the real to become unreal. We accomplish this imaginatively by replacing the real with a real perceived otherwise through the lens of seeing-as. When imaginative seeing reinterprets the world before us through its layers of images, it becomes conceivable that the world could or should *be* otherwise. "The possible's slow fuse," Emily Dickinson wrote, "is lit by the imagination" (quoted in Kearney 1988: 370). There is violence in Dickinson's metaphor: imagination lights a fuse to explode the actual so that it may be replaced by the newly possible. But in a sense, this is simply what happens inevitably in the passage of every moment: the possible perpetually replaces the actual with successive actualities as each actuality fades into the past. Indeed, on a Kantian conception of imagination's role in cognition, imagination is responsible for "schematizing" temporally the basic categories through which we structure experience (Kant 1998: 271–77). Imagination puts those categories into time so that they can bear on the passing manifold of sensory input. If, in artistic creation and in seeing-as, imagination lights the fuse of transformative possibility, its role is really to accelerate the pace of change in which it already has a cognitive part.

The distance from the present that our capacity for imagining makes possible, the seeing of present things as something more or something else, and the freedom of self-making embodied therein, all make imagination's sight a critical one, one not beholden to the given state of things. In this respect, as John Whale observes, "imagination is an inescapable and essential element in cultural critique" (2000: 196). Imagination serves literature by affording it the power to intervene sometimes mightily in critical reflection on ourselves. Imagining may generally embody a critical distancing from what is present, but its use especially in the production and reception of works of poetry and narrative fiction can bring its freeing glance of alternative vision to bear fully on transforming the present. My claim has been that imagination works in the service of literature by inviting the seeing-as interpretive play through which poems and fictions call us to revise our understandings of things. My claim may as well have been that works of literature, or their authors, serve imagination by providing the incendiary fuel to make its contrary vision shine most brightly.

IMAGINATION AS DOUBLE VISION

Brann has eloquently summarized the contributions that imagination makes to enriching our lives. Imagining, she writes, "serves our worldly existence by pulling us out of its dumb immediacy, distancing us from an oppressively close present and disqualifying the primacy of the merely real here and now, while according actuality to the absent and the nonexistent" (1991: 798). While Brann does not refer to literature in this passage, my claim has been that imagination and works of literature partner intimately in this enrichment. What she describes imagining as accomplishing for us, literature does, as well. This commonality is not just a happy coincidence but is rather a consequence of the vital role imagination plays in bringing alive the words on the pages of books of poetry and narrative fiction (not to mention the role it plays in getting the words on the page in the first place). Imagination brings words alive by filling in language with imagery responsive to the text but expansive of its significance for us. Imagining accomplishes this by visualizing objects and scenes in the mind's eye, but it enlivens language more profoundly by seeing the world differently, interpreting the world anew through the lens of imaginative seeing-as. At the height of its powers, "the world-revising, world-emending imagination," Brann writes, "projects an inner world onto the external environment and elicits a second appearance from the visible world" (1991: 774). Layering imagination over perception in seeing-as helps us to see more, or other possibilities, than are evident to the perceiving eye. We engage in such creative and interpretive sight when we make sense of the world through metaphor, for example, but we arguably see most imaginatively when works of literature revise our perceptions so as to reveal the world otherwise than customary habits of thought and perception permit. The visual and emotional intensity of the poem and the character exploration and narrative complexity of the novel are efforts of imaginative seeing that, if successful, "elicit a second appearance from the visible world" (Brann 1991: 774). Imagination makes this possible through its powers of visualization, its mediating role with the passions, its interpretive finesse, and above all, its capacity to free us from the pressing present.

Brann calls imaginative seeing a power of "double vision" (1991: 774). In it we continue to perceive the world before us, but that world takes on a different light. We see the contrast between what is the case and the alternate possibilities or meanings that the interpretive layering of images reveals. We see the world doubly: as it is and as something else. Seeing double can be a dizzying experience, and works of literature at their most powerful do make us dizzy with imaginative possibility. The double vision of one thing as another in seeing-as, invited of us richly in poetry and narrative fiction, warrants careful navigation around Wittgenstein's slippery remark: "While I am looking at an object I cannot imagine it." Though literally true with regard to the simple calling up of images, the statement is mistaken with regard to seeing-as. At the figurative level of imaginative seeing, I can imagine an object otherwise while looking at it; I can through image and metaphor transform its significance. This capacity to see otherwise is the freedom of creative transformation that imagining embodies. Works of literature are some of the denser structures of metaphor by means of which we undertake such transformation. They and imagination in concert provide lenses for double vision.

REFERENCES

Brann, E. T. H. (1991). *The World of the Imagination*. Savage, Md.: Rowan and Littlefield.

Cohen, T. (1999). "Identifying with Metaphor: Metaphors of Personal Identification." *The Journal of Aesthetics and Art Criticism* 54, 399–409.

Coleridge, S. T. (1985). *The Collected Works of Samuel Taylor Coleridge*, Vol. 7, *Biographia Literaria* (2 vols.; J. Engell and W. J. Bate, eds.). Princeton: Princeton University Press. (Original work in published 1817.)

Eldridge, R. (1996). "Introduction." *In* Eldridge (ed.), *Beyond Representation: Philosophy and Poetic Imagination*. Cambridge: Cambridge University Press.

Engell, J. (1981). *The Creative Imagination*. Cambridge: Harvard University Press.

Harris, P. L. (2000). *The Work of the Imagination*. Oxford: Blackwell.

Hausman, C. (1989). *Metaphor and Art*. Cambridge: Cambridge University Press.

Kant, I. (1998). *Critique of Pure Reason* (P. Guyer and A. Wood, trans.). Cambridge: Cambridge University Press. (Original work published in 1781.)

——. (2000). *Critique of the Power of Judgment* (P. Guyer, ed.; P. Guyer and E. Matthews, trans.). Cambridge: Cambridge University Press. (Original work published in 1790.)

Kearney, R. (1988). *The Wake of Imagination*. Minneapolis: University of Minnesota Press.

——. (1991). *Poetics of Imagining*. London: Harper Collins.

McGinn, C. (2004). *Mindsight: Image, Dream, Meaning*. Cambridge, Mass.: Harvard University Press.

Novitz, D. (1987). *Knowledge, Fiction and Imagination*. Philadelphia: Temple University Press.

Pillow, K. (2000). *Sublime Understanding: Aesthetic Reflection in Kant and Hegel*. Cambridge, Mass.: MIT Press.

Sartre, J.-P. (1991). *The Psychology of Imagination*. New York: Carol. (Original work published in 1940.)

Walton, K. (1990). *Mimesis as Make-Believe: On the Foundations of the Representational Arts*. Cambridge, Mass.: Harvard University Press.

Warnock, M. (1976). *Imagination*. Berkeley: University of California Press.

Whale, J. (2000). *Imagination under Pressure, 1789–1832: Aesthetics, Politics and Utility*. Cambridge: Cambridge University Press.

Wittgenstein, L. (1953). *Philosophical Investigations* (G. E. M. Anscombe, trans.). New York: Macmillan.

——. (1967). *Zettel* (G. E. M. Anscombe, trans.). Oxford: Basil Blackwell.

CHAPTER 16

....

PLOT

....

ALAN SINGER

PLOT is the means by which human agents negotiate the obstacles that time and worldliness put in the path of our desire to sustain purposeful action. Or, as Aristotle puts it in the *Poetics*, plot is an imitation of actions, not of men: "We maintain, therefore that the first essential, the life and soul so to speak, of Tragedy is the Plot; and that the characters come second....We [therefore] maintain that Tragedy is an imitation of action, and that it is mainly for the sake of the action that it imitates the personal agents" (1450b; 1941: 1461).

Aristotle's clarion privileging of act over character in the *Poetics* tells us in the most compelling way what is at stake in narrative plot: knowledge of the changing self. In his elaboration of the process of plot making, Aristotle makes us intensely aware of the fact that plot instantiates a now self and a then self. This proposition is most articulate in the emphasis Aristotle gives to *peripeteia* or peripety, reversal of fate. Aristotle's precept that the "unity of a Plot does not consist, as some suppose, in its having one man as its subject" (141b8; 1941: 1463) introduces the argument that character is forever knowable only through the vicissitudes of action. As Aristotle goes on to say, "An infinity of things befall that one man, some of which it is impossible to reduce to unity; and in like manner there are many actions of one man which cannot be made to form one action" (141b8;1941: 1463). It is in an action, involving reversals and recognitions (takings of responsibility) over time, that character is not only displayed but also developed. It exists as a responsiveness to variability. In other words, the value of character is inherently a function of character's variability in changing circumstances.

It is not surprising that the occasion for Aristotle's account of plot is the circumstance of human tragedy. Tragedy is a register of human frailty coordinate with the temporal métier of mortal existence. For Aristotle, the link between plot and tragedy seems to be a given: all temporal experience reminds us of our susceptibility to the reversibility of intentional acts. Furthermore, any attempt to come to terms with plot independent of the form of tragedy must reckon with Aristotle's own point of departure for the consideration of plot as a significant subject: the inextricability of tragedy from a more general mimetic impulse. When, in *Poetics*, Aristotle insists that imitation is an instinct of our nature, implanted in man from childhood, he reasons it is because we delight to contemplate: "[T]o be learning something is the greatest of pleasures not only to the philosopher but also to the rest of mankind" (1448b10; 1941: 1457). The universality of the imitative reflex is coherent with the persistence of mind in its pursuit of objects to contemplate over the troublesome course of time. Both constructing and grasping imitations (*mimemata*) are inherently active enterprises, due precisely to the contingent temporal circumstances or situation within which any action or character or life arises.

Because, for Aristotle, the mimetic mode is ineluctable in the human experience of learning, that is, because the task of becoming human presupposes the capacity to imitate, the concept of plot is closely bound up with the more general philosophical ambition of knowing oneself. The concept of plot as a mimesis of human agency bears the burden of self-understanding. Under this description, plot ceases to be merely a subgenre of literary art, of the genre of fiction particularly. We might say that in plot art and philosophy are united. Furthermore, their intimate connection is likely to warrant a rethinking of the terms of human character altogether, rather than a mere subordination of character to typologies or kinds of human action. As I discuss below, while types of plots tend to be associated with types of characters, such generalized thinking invites the very condition of stasis—the constative mode—that is most inimical to Aristotle's focus on activity.

On the contrary, plot must be conceived of as indistinguishable from the project of human agency. This presumption of an active stance toward experience coordinates the concept of plot with norms of behavior and rules for self-justification. Certainly, without these considerations, the goal of self-understanding is a moot proposition. We might even be inclined to think that plot is inextricably bound to tragic knowledge by the responsibility for self-justification per se because tragedy menaces identity. We need only think of how the coherence of self or subject as a continuing source of reasoned expression of character in action is undermined by the abrupt reversals and recognitions that give structural integrity to tragic plot. If nothing else, tragic experience begs for rationalization. Accordingly, we take responsibility for ourselves through the protocols of reason giving. And according to these protocols, we know ourselves to be rational creatures even in the midst of personal catastrophe. The catastrophes of tragic experience are, after all, typically the result of *hamartia*, a form of not knowing. It denotes the condition of not possessing the fullest context of reflection upon one's circumstance. As J. M. Bremer explains in *Hamartia: Tragic Error in the Poetics of Aristotle and Greek Tragedy* (1969), the tragic hero suffers *hamartia* as his "involuntary and inevitable ignorance of one or more of the particular circumstances involved" (26) in an action. In an important way, the sense of error thus associated with *hamartia* is proleptic, soliciting a compensatory knowledge of those "one or two particular circumstances" that otherwise constituted the blind spot of the agent's personal perspective.

For the Aristotle of the *Nicomachean Ethics*, there is always a wider horizon of reflection awaiting human deliberative agency. We might imagine that plot and narrative are thus indistinguishable from the ethical dimension of a character's ineluctably passionate *becoming*, as opposed to the presupposition of a character's dispassionate being. Pathos or the notion of man as *patos mathei* is very much at the heart of plotted narrative precisely because it propels our sense that the intrinsic significance of human temporal experience is the sufferance of personal transformation. Plot is thus a purposive human response to the vicissitudes of temporal experience. It is inescapable given the ethical concept of human nature as both knowing and aspiring to know more from within the grip of temporality.

I

As Peter Brooks has pointed out in *Reading for the Plot* (1992), "Plot is, first of all, a constant of all written and oral narrative, in that a narrative without at least a minimal plot would be incomprehensible" (5).[1] On this account, plot is a form of reasonable engagement with the incomprehensible. If narrative denotes our situatedness in the eventfulness of time, plot postulates something to be known as a result of our observing the interconnectedness of events. This is to say, reasons obtain for our countenancing that events are connected. Plot is the locus of that reasoning. The nature of the reasons is correlative with the principle according to which the events narrated seem to cohere and vary according to the specific nature of the mind contemplating those events. To project the coherence of events in the face of difficulty is to admit the necessity of a mind struggling against incoherence. This is true from the seminal moments of literary plotting. We need only consider the off-stage scene that looms over the plot of Sophocles' *Oedipus Rex*: the episode at the crossroads of Phocis. Here, where Oedipus unknowingly meets his father, he confronts the possibility that his intentions to elude the torment of Apollo's prophecy of patricide and incest may themselves be thwarted. His is an encounter with the Ur-condition of human suffering. He himself may not know what he is doing, or who he is as a result of his doing it. Human intent and human knowledge are revealed here as potential antagonists. When human intent to act and human knowledge of what we have done fall apart, then the very comprehensibility of experience is in jeopardy. Plotting strives to put intent and fact back together again.

This logic of the plotting subject contending with the unknown is perhaps most perspicuously and instructively figured in Joseph Conrad's deviously plotted short novel *Heart of Darkness* (1899). I say this in large part because the conceit

Conrad chooses to epitomize the existential challenge posed to the plot maker is particularly resonant for the question of plot's relation to knowledge. In *Heart of Darkness*, plot is tantamount to a recognition of the necessity "to live in the midst of the incomprehensible" (Conrad 1995: 20). Conrad evokes both plotting character and plotting reader in the figure of a Roman explorer who hails, in a manner of speaking, from the beginning of time, the source of all plotting. Aptly enough, the figure of the Roman legionnaire is the bearer of a civilization that itself stands upon the rationalizing foundation of plot making. But this civilization has tragically overreached the boundaries of its knowledge by undertaking a colonial adventure in the wilderness of a yet unsubdued and therefore incomprehensible alien culture.

In order to reflect the full complexity of the situation adequately, Conrad's plot is famously framed by an unidentified narrator whose protagonist is another narrator, a seafaring purveyor of plots, Marlow. Marlow is in turn obsessed with another protagonist—the Enlightenment savant-cum-savagely avaricious ivory trader, Kurtz. Marlow's plot is aptly *characterized* within Conrad's own text as "not typical" (1995: 18), and yet it is revealed to be exemplary for the practice of the novelist himself. This is what makes *Heart of Darkness* such a vivid emblem of the problematics of plot generally. *Heart of Darkness* is, after all, a narrative unlike that of tales "the whole meaning of which lies within the shell of a cracked nut" (18), that is, where comprehension is a foregone conclusion. Rather, Marlow's plot is a concatenation of episodes whose meaning, according to the most didactic intrusions of the narrator of Conrad's novel, "was not inside like a kernel but outside, enveloping the tale which brought it out only as a glow brings out a haze, in the likeness of one of those misty halos that sometimes are made visible by the spectral illuminations of moonshine" (18). This epitome of Conrad's own plot—a glow within a haze—amounts to an admonition about the centrality of reflective mind to the task of comprehension by which we negotiate the predicament of dwelling in the midst of the incomprehensible, for in *Heart of Darkness* the reflection on the medium of telling becomes an explicit object of the tale. It is widely agreed that plot is a creature of the structuralizing imperatives of human desire, but Conrad makes us acutely aware of the burdens of reflective consciousness that our natural enthusiasm for plotted order too often obscures. Typically, we do not have to accept the relativity of narrative framing as the only available premise of plot knowledge; here we must. When we take up such burdens in *Heart of Darkness*, the simple satisfaction of narrative desire gives way to the perpetuation of narrative desire, the obtrusive presence of reflective mind as an end in itself.

It could therefore be said that Conrad's métier as a narrative plotter acknowledges the problem that made Plato an antagonist of artistic plotters and made Aristotle an advocate. Plato sought to ground human character in the relative stasis of an ontological truth that transcended the shifting ground of appearances. By contrast, Aristotle sought to reclaim the ground of appearances or *phainomena*[2] in the pursuit of truthful knowledge by accepting the epistemological responsibility to choose among them. Aristotle's stance entails the possibility of error and so highlights the discipline of judgment. Plato posits a perfection of character that brooks no errors. For this reason, Plato allows no warrant for pity toward suffering character.[3] Very much to the contrary, in Aristotle's *Poetics* pity is a marker for the fragility of judgment within the framework of changing appearances. In other words, for Plato the manifest order of the world is a counter for a transcendently divine truth and so implicitly a topos of human passivity. For Aristotle, narrative order instantiates an active attunement of human attentions to the world—without which its orderliness and rational truth would remain hidden in the merely perceptible forms of Nature.

Likewise for Aristotle, the vocation of plot, insofar as it entails the mentally reflective labor of choosing and ordering among the disordered difference of *phainomena*, is the attainment of *eudaimonia*. *Eudaimonia* is a modality of *human* happiness as opposed to a modality of divine bliss. For Aristotle, plot is the métier of this human flourishing. But it is not to be confused with timeless happiness, nor is it an illusory refuge of self-indulgent pleasure. If we follow the lead of Martha Nussbaum, among other scholars of ancient Greek philosophical thinking, the term *eudaimonia* implies activity per se rather than constative pleasure, as has often been assumed by Kantians and utilitarians: "Most Greeks would understand *eudaimonia* to be something essentially active, of which praiseworthy activities are not just productive means, but actual constituent parts" (1986: 6).

It is thus fair to say that the enterprise of Aristotelian tragic plot not only describes the world of human labor but also engages the labor of a reader to sort and focus upon the objects of the world with an expectation of their usefulness to us as resources for self-ordering, self-knowledge, and the substantiation of subjective identity. It acknowledges our involvement with the outside world as a condition for positing a meaningful human interiority. It is a touchstone of human goal directedness or what the Greeks termed *orexis*.[4] But it also determines the degree to which our goal directedness exposes us to conditions of risk and self-destruction. Plot is certainly a vehicle of moral learning. It comes at the price of realizing our vulnerability as the paradoxical condition of our prowess as moral agents. It is a testimonial, as Nussbaum has eloquently pointed out in *The Fragility of Goodness* (1986), of "the great power of luck in human affairs" (319). It makes the project of living well incompatible with the Platonist world view according to which the agent always has a firm grip on an external world where uncontrolled events do not pose a significant threat to rational mind.

Such is the case as Plato articulates it in the *Phaedo*, where the vulnerability of the body counts insignificantly by comparison with the self-sufficiency of the soul.[5] In Plato's world, the warrant for reflective mind that seems to be prompted by Aristotelian plot would cease to be an important rationale for moral agency because the vagaries of space and time pose no significant challenge to human existence. For this reason, my equating of plot with reflective consciousness is really a concession to a strong linkage between plot and tragedy that persists beyond the historical instance of Greek tragic drama and the immediate historicocultural circumstance that dictated the operational terms of Aristotle's *Poetics*. And, of course, tragedy in this context does not reduce to fatalism. As Richard Eldridge has affirmed in an important effort to remind us that tragic representations may be our best hedge against the self-delusions of modernist autonomy: "It cannot be that tragedy instructs us only that people like us undeservedly suffer" (2001: 148). Rather, the plottedness of tragedy is the portent of hitherto unrealized explanatory powers that only knowledge of our fateful contingency can make available.

On the basis of these remarks, we can quickly discern that plot passionately— inasmuch as it is pathos driven—possesses an ethical dimension. The mind that must reflect upon itself because events have transpired in a way that defy expectations is already invested in change of state as a hopeful enterprise. One cultivates the hope in order to understand what has happened in terms that even the most rigorously intentional act did not comprehend. Aristotle's notion of the inextricability of *anagnorisis*, or recognition, from peripety, or reversal, directs us to think that tragically plotted action is intrinsically remediable, in the sense that new knowledge entails a positing of new ends.

II

Not coincidentally, Frank Kermode, in *The Sense of an Ending* (2000), his expansive analysis of narrative plot making throughout human history, takes "ends" and the desire for ends as seminal to any full comprehension of how the imperative of emplotment governs in all human affairs. For Kermode, the ultimate end, apocalypse, is the product of failed prophecy, that is, the lack of experiential knowledge adequate to one's sense of purposiveness or cogent beginning. This is to say that we are almost constitutionally creatures who revise our sense of the ending. As Kermode explains it, we fear the end as our own death (2000: 7) and so we are fascinated with the prospect of perpetually ordaining the end. It is an imaginative cooption of what is otherwise a temporal terminus over which we exercise no control:

> Broadly speaking, apocalyptic thought belongs to rectilinear rather than cyclical views of the world, though this is not a sharp distinction; and even in Jewish thought there was no true apocalyptic until prophecy failed, for Jewish apocalyptic belongs to what scholars call the Intertestamentary Period. But basically one has to think of an ordered series of events which ends, not in a great New Year, but in a final Sabbath. The events derive their significance from a unitary system, not from their correspondence with events in other cycles. (5)

End determined plotting is a vicarious escape from the trauma of temporal uncertainty that failed prophecy sustains. The irony of the compulsion to plot in this fashion is that all such attempts to elude the failure of prophetic knowledge are doomed to fail. Only time endures. Kermode himself traces the history of apocalyptic narratives demonstrating the revisionary logic to which they condition us as plot makers. Kermode lets us see how the struggle of the Roman Church to cope with the apocalypse mongering that beset Christian culture with the approach of the first millennium is emblematic of the eschatological burden that plot making can dispose of only by more ingenious plotting. Kermode observes, "The pressure of reality on us is always varying, as Stevens might have said: the fictions must change, or if they are fixed, the interpretations must change" (2000: 24). Or, as Kermode puts it in another passage, the end is no longer "imminent"; it is "immanent" (25) to each moment of time. This is very much in keeping with Aristotle's intimation that peripety lurks in every episodic motion of tragic plot. As *Oedipus Rex* reminds us, each moment of time is pregnant with the revelation of truths that arise out of the improvisational will of the protagonistic hero, or, as Henry James might prefer to say, in every moment of "consciousness."[6] James, who is too often assumed to sacrifice plot to character, nonetheless invests his character with the will to change. With respect to plot in general, this will is explicitly the protagonist's and implicitly the reader's. Aptly, Kermode characterizes our disposition toward an end that is constantly being revised according to a "pressure of reality" that is always varying as a site of "perpetual transition" (2000: 28).

When we countenance the failure of prophecy, in the manner of the early Christian eschatologists, we are forced to reckon with the necessity to improvise new concordances between the episodic moments of our lives and more hypothetical ends. Only in this way does plot keep faith with the enterprise of purposive selfhood swimming against the tide of unpredictable temporal change. Our focus is shifted from a plot whereby the present moment is already reconciled with a future moment, what Kermode designates as "myth," to a plot whereby the end is rendered a speculative proposition based upon the reversals of the moment. The latter prospect entails a speculative enterprise that Kermode designates as "fiction."

I would say that the important point is not so much the distinction between myth and fiction as the ineluctably dialectical play between them. If we now live in an age of "perpetual transition," as Kermode claims, we might see that the discrepancies we discover between our expectations of how things ought to end and our experience of what thwarts those ends forces our recognition that ends are inherently rationalizations. They must therefore be reconciled with normative rationalistic practice. I defend and elaborate the close connection between plot making and protocols of reason giving below. For the moment, it suffices to say that we who live in perpetual transition are always negotiating the meaningless succession of temporal moments that Kermode identifies as *Chronos*—the opposite number of an egotistical mandate for temporal integration that Kermode identifies as *Kairos*. Though Kermode's sources are earnestly theological,[7] construing *kairoi* as qualities of God's time, the very imaginative burden of integration carried by this concept reveals it to be an inherently human and, as we'll see, rationalistic imperative.

III

As Kermode implies, the formal study of literary plot seems to be perpetually caught up in a recognition of the challenge to reconcile temporal differences— or, as Kermode himself puts it, to establish concordance between Chronos and Kairos. The specific arranging or rearranging of discrepant events that plot entails with respect to this goal was probably most influentially theorized in the early and mid-twentieth century by narratologists: Russian formalists (Victor Shklovski, Vladimir Propp, etc.) and French structuralists (Roland Barthes, Gérard Gennette, Tzvetan Todorov, etc.).

The distinction proposed by Shklovski between *fabula* and *sjuzet*, or story and discourse,[8] warrants particular consideration. It proffers an elucidation of the way the existential circumstances of plot makers dovetail with the interpretive mandate faced by all responsible readers of narratives and all hapless human agents caught in the ebb flow of time. While *fabula* designates the order of events as they might happen according to the fact of temporal successiveness, *sjuzet* designates the order of telling those events according to the imperative of human desire. *Sjuzet* expresses the human will to wring intelligibility from the otherwise merely successive and hence unintentional moments of experience, often regarded by Russian formalism as strictly preverbal. As Robert Caserio reminds us in *Plot, Story and the Novel* (1979), the distinction between *fabula* and *sjuzet* is a powerful cautionary against reducing narrative texts to thematic generalities and so a hedge against underestimating the important links between the sensemaking work done by and in plots (7). Caserio scrupulously admonishes us to see that the mere distinguishability of *fabula* and *sjuzet* constitutes a mandate for assuming a perspectivist stance toward the meaning of action. *Fabula* and *sjuzet* constitute something like a ratio of involuntary and volitional acts. While separately they would be understood as divergent accounts of human agency, the narratological pairing of these terms ever more urgently prompts the question: What really happened? It potentiates the perspectivism of reason giving without which no compelling answer to the question is imaginable in the first place.

We typically ask the question "What really happened?" under the pressure of wanting to keep the realms of reality and fictionality discrete. But it may be that, just as plot, in Brooks's words, "cuts across" (1992: 13) the distinction of *fabula* and *sjuzet*, the distinction itself reveals our stake in reason, or reasons, as the essential underpinning of a plotted reality—one that is not merely the antithesis of fiction. If the Russian formalists show us that we must always speak of the elements of story as a seemingly invariable sequence, and that we must always speak of the ordering of the elements of story as a variable of the perspective of the story teller, then we are acknowledging the substrate of plot making to be simultaneously situational and deliberative.

The elements and the order of the elements that make up a plot are thus incipiently dialectical, in the way that acting and thinking are. There is a rough analogy here to Aristotle's explanation of animal movement in the human as a dialectic between physical automata and a scruple of "choice and thinking."[9] Nussbaum emphasizes Aristotle's care to distinguish the merely causal movements of brute animals from human actions that presuppose a "why" and denote an animus of reasons, desires, and beliefs. Any other program (in this case, she glosses Aristotle's differences with Democritus) "would certainly lead to a breakdown of our ordinary distinction between causal explanation and the giving of reasons" (1986: 271). In other words, reason giving is inconceivable without positing the kind of relationality that I'm suggesting the distinction between *fabula* and *sjuzet* prompts us to think about. This is the case even if the theorists of this distinction do not follow the dialectical line of such thinking themselves.

Indeed, I do not believe that narratologists focus enough on the fact that there can be little sense of what constitutes the *fabula* without resorting to a *sjuzet*-like perspective (albeit without hypostatizing human life into something with fixed *sjuzet*). This in turn compels our recognition that all such perspectives are inherently relational. *Fabula* itself is thus rendered a variable of such perspectivism. We are not simply capitulating to relativism with this notion; we are only acknowledging the necessity to relate scrupulously to the existential constraints of emplotment in real time. And once again, the *eudaimonian* pursuit associated with Aristotelian poetics is relevant, for by their very incommensurability, *fabula* and *sjuzet* constitute a warrant for activity—in this case interpretive activity, an elemental protocol of reason giving. The reality that is graspable within the narratological purview thus keeps faith with Aristotelian activity by its implicit authorization of new explanatory powers—even if Russian formalist and subsequent French structuralist methodologies tend toward more taxonomic and static accounts of what kind of knowledge plot can purvey.

Too often, the narratological handling of the *fabula/sjuzet* dyad obscures the reciprocity that obtains between any order of events and its necessary reordering according to the perspective of one who seeks to discern the meaning of its order. That is, if we admit that plots are constructed out of a reflective attitude, distinct from the events related, then every telling is already a retelling and is itself susceptible to retelling. It is worth pointing out that this retelling is conspicuously the burden imposed upon the reader of Conrad's *Heart of Darkness*. The framing device of Conrad's narrative leaves the reader feeling responsible for knowledge of the famous lie that Marlow tells to Kurtz's "Intended." This is a particularly onerous moral encumbrance because the narrator of Marlow's tale remains a silent witness to that lie. We contrastingly are bound to contemplate what it is reasonable to do in similar situations such that we escape complicity with the destructive cycle of history that Marlow's lie succumbs to. In other words, the quandary of how to dispose of the sense of irony that Marlow's lie bestows upon the reader invites us to contemplate the tragic knowledge of living in the midst of the incomprehensible. But Conrad invites us to contemplate the incomprehensible as a spur to normative work, not as a fatal condition of narrative emplotment. In this instance, *fabula* and *sjuzet* are very conspicuously reciprocating propositions.

On the contrary, narratological inquiry tends to treat *fabula* as potentially distinct from *sjuzet*. This practice invites the idea that any narrative order can be made to submit to something like a set of grammatical rules. Attempting to promote itself as a "scientific" study of narrative on this basis, narratology moves increasingly toward an emphasis on the forms of narration at the expense of the act of narrating. Narratology thereby deprives itself of the kind of dialectical perspective I wish to accommodate here. Narratological theorists like Todorov, whose work derives from the structural anthropology of Claude Lévi-Strauss, shifted analytical emphasis to the narrated over the narrating intelligence in his *Grammaire du Decameron* (1969). This work made an effort to equate the narrative object with the object of empirical scientific inquiry by reducing the phenomenon of narrative transformation to a relatively static typology. Todorov saw plot as a programmatic transformation of a predicate term common to the beginning and end of a narrative (see Todorov 1971). Elsewhere, drawing upon the aesthetic stance of Edgar Allen Poe, Todorov insisted that "the tale is characterized by the existence of a single effect, acted upon at the end, and by the obligation all the elements of the tale are under to contribute to this effect" (1975: 87).

Likewise, Propp, in his *Morphology of the Folktale* (1928, translated in 1958), taxonomized the formal elements that are exhibited in manifold combinations or recombinations over the history of Russian storytelling. Propp identified 31 structural functions and gave an equally compendious account of the dramatis personae that reappear under different names to serve repeatable roles: the villain, the hero, the princess, the donor, the helper, and so on. As late as 1973, Claude Bremond offered a *Logique du Récit* in which he identified elementary plot structure with a series of three functions each corresponding to aspects of an unfolding process: an opening possibility, the actualization or nonactualization of that possibility, and the achievement or nonachievement of a deliberate aim that results. In all of these cases—which not coincidentally are based upon a generalized analogy between linguistic system and narrative structure—plot is reducible to relatively static schemata that brook little scope for Conradian incomprehensibility.

French structuralists like Barthes, in *S/Z* (1970) and "The Structural Analysis of Narrative" (1966), present a similar problem. They draw too rigid or static a distinction between *proairesis*, or what Barthes characterizes as the "already done" (1975: 19), the mere sequentiality of events, and the subjective hermeneutics of a subject's having to endure a particular sequence of events. *Proairesis* does imply the meaningfulness of events that constitute sequentiality. But we are mistaken if we imagine, as I believe Barthes risks inviting us to imagine,[10] that proairetic knowledge is in any way separable from the questioning of that meaning; that is, from prompting the question "What really happened?" In other words, the fullest appreciation of *proairesis* requires both that the choice that ordains the sequence of events takes place within matrices of nature and culture that are reasonable *and* that the subject undertake the active work of discerning and contributing to their reasonableness. The subject must question how meaningfulness is specifically available to her or him in this situation. Hermeneutic intelligence specifically licenses this questioning. *Proairesis* understood as mere sequence seems to solicit hermeneutic intelligence, if only by manifesting its own interpretive impoverishment as an intractable finitude. Or, to put it more precisely, under the rule of *proairesis* alone, we are inclined to be less responsive to the essentially hermeneutic principle that I believe governs the Aristotelian understanding of plot in its inducement of reason giving. We become less responsive to the ways in which Aristotle's emphasis on activity always invites the questions "Why did it happen?" and "What must therefore happen next?"

It is telling that according to Roland Barthes the *proairetic* code is best epitomized by the picaresque plot and the hermeneutic code by the detective plot, for these plot types exhibit complementary limitations at their extremes: the picaresque becomes atomistic, inhibiting the posing of large enough questions to produce a peripety with significant conceptual torque; the detective plot reduces all questions raised along the episodic path of plot development to one answer. Sophocles shows us, in *Oedipus Rex*, how the interdependency of the *proairetic* and the hermeneutic codes bestows the greatest authority upon plotted knowledge: such knowledge reveals how character intent and corrective, subsequent self-understanding participate in a drama of learning to dwell in the midst of the incomprehensible—without capitulating to incomprehensibility or irrationality. The persistence of tragedy is the persistence of human activity as Oedipus himself attests by his surprisingly self-conferred power to dictate the terms of his own exile at the conclusion of Sophocles' play. When Oedipus stipulates the conditions under which he will accept his exile from Thebes, Creon's reply, "Do not presume that you are still in power. Your power has not survived you" (lines 1521–22), belies itself, for Oedipus has indeed survived himself, so to speak, by exercising a power of adaptation to new conditions of self-understanding. Contrary to Barthes's apparent understanding that analysis of plot must subsist upon a typological knowledge (1975: 20), which he construes as a programmatic matrix of narrative codes, Sophocles keeps faith with a process: one that sustains human activity, despite what coded fatalism it might seem to portend.

IV

While the Aristotelian insistence upon activity, as I have glossed it, seems essential to a use of plot that would be coordinate with the pursuit of knowledge, we should not conclude that such activity is tantamount to a mere energetics. This is an idea about plot that takes off from principles of Freudian metapsychology. Freudian thought has had fruitful impact on literary analysis of plot. But the literary critic's temptation to construe plot as an impersonal matrix of interlocking dynamic forces, on the model of instinct, ego, superego, is, I believe, no more responsive to the hermeneutic gratifications of plot making than the Russian formalist or

French structuralist taxonomic orders proved to be. Furthermore, the Freudian's emphasis on the conservation of energy as a human end poses an obstacle to fully appreciating the knowledge-producing aspect of emplotment. Specifically, Freud's positing of the "death instinct" or the "death drive" has been taken up by literary analysts as diverse as Walter Benjamin, Jean-Paul Sartre, Brooks, and many Anglo-American Lacanians, as a corollary of the drive toward narrative closure. If, as Freud says in *Beyond the Pleasure Principle* (1990: 6), the instinct is a human need to restore an original state of inertness, then narrative event can be construed as a kind of existential chaos that can be quelled only by mastery of the differences that erupt within it. The narrative drive of plot subsists on the binding of disparate acts to a single purpose. The activity inherent in this binding is paradoxically bound in turn to a principle of cessation. The energetics of balancing difference against resemblance or unity turns out to be as static as taxonomies or typologies of plot, despite Freud's insistence that the modalities of energy and inertia are relational. The flood of stimuli with which the self desirous of death must contend is rendered, ironically, too abstract in the drive toward equilibrium that subsumes it.

Brooks intimates this point in a way that deepens my skepticism about the Freudian model and ultimately my sense of the liabilities that inhere in Brooks's own reliance on a Freudian interpretive matrix: "The organism must live in order to die in the proper manner, to die the right death. One must have the arabesque of plot in order to reach the end. One must have metonymy in order to reach metaphor" (1992: 107). The hypostasis of a principle of continuity between metonymy and metaphor makes the "dynamism" of what Brooks calls Freud's "master-plot" less conducive to the cognitive demands upon human agency that I've suggested inhere in the Aristotelian trajectory of plot. Perhaps the limitedness of the applicability of Freudian thought to a fully ethical comprehension of plot is best indicated in the often-cited "*fort/da*" game from *Beyond the Pleasure Principle*. This is the germ of Freud's close identification of desire and repetition with the death drive.

The anecdote is famously succinct. Freud observes his 18-month-old grandson solacing himself for his mother's absence by tossing a wooden reel—to which a string is attached—from his crib and uttering the word *fort* (gone). The infant then draws the object back within his grip joyfully uttering the word *da* (there). The symbolic recuperation of the absent mother, the reconciling of one moment with another in the grasp of the symbolic object, does capture one aspect of plot: its rescuing the human subject from the chaotic flow of temporal moments. Freud characterizes the child as compensating himself by "staging the disappearance and the return of the objects within his reach" (:1990: 6). And no doubt Brooks is correct in his characterization of the dynamic as a rough corollary of what sets up the tensions within the episodic structure of plot, what he calls "the vacillating play of the middle where repetition as binding works toward the generation of significance, toward recognition and the retrospective illumination that will allow us to grasp the text as total metaphor" (1992: 108). The totality of metaphor denotes something like compensation for the loss of the mother or, more generally, a rescuing of the cogency of resemblance from the irrationality of difference.

So, it might seem that on a descriptive register the Freudian model is reasonably close to the integrative or structural order of plot. But, in the end, Freud's emphasis on the recuperation of knowledge rather than the growth of knowledge compromises its usefulness for understanding plot in a way that embraces plot's farthest reaching work. The Freudian model lacks the speculative momentum that the open-ended work of emplotment sustains: recognition that the plot maker must reason beyond what he already knows in order to give full expression to the productive or *making* self. I am, of course, suggesting in this respect that plot is a kind of *phronesis*. What distinguishes *phronesis* from *sophia* is the practicality of judgment, the constraint of time as an ongoing condition of human activity. I've argued elsewhere that *phronesis* is conditional upon a deliberative process (see Singer 2003: 47–48). Indeed, the practicality of *phronesis* follows from its situatedness in a crisis that demands action.

Aptly enough, Kermode explicates the modern concept of crisis by reference to the punning dimension of the word in Greek: meaning judgment and separation. That is to say, where there is a break in continuity of knowledge, there is a demand for judgment, knitting the act of judging more closely to act qua activity (2000: 25). Or, as I've already noted, the end is "[n]o longer imminent, the end is immanent" (25). Every moment is ripe with the mandate for explanation of its significance in relation to the end. In other words, this end is no longer merely eschatological but now logical. It warrants the assertion of reasons both for positing it and for believing in the prospect of attaining it. Aristotle seems to recognize the importance of this speculative trajectory when he argues that the arts call for more deliberation than the sciences because they take as their field of deliberative activity that which happens when "the event is obscure and with things in which it is indeterminate" (*Ethics* 3: 1112b5; 1941: 971), that is, when the right course is not clearly defined.

Brooks himself betrays a sympathy with this line of thought in his appreciation of a very late essay by Freud titled "Constructions in Analysis" (1937). Here Freud does intimate a significant contribution to the understanding of plot that is compatible with Aristotelian activity, for he characterizes the relationship between the analyst and the analysand in terms that open a deliberative field of play. The deliberative threshold is crossed in Freud's reminder that analysis involves two people, one of whom is trying to bring to light what the other has forgotten. Freud emphasizes the point that the work of the analyst to recuperate what is lost to memory entails a constructive activity. This constructive activity is strikingly analogous to the artifice of plot I have been characterizing here as a deliberative métier. By insisting upon discussing plot in relation to a protocol of reason giving, I am courting the proposition that the discourse of plot itself is charged across the poles of two viewpoints marked as distinct temporal moments. In this respect, it is important to observe with Brooks that for Freud the exchange between the analyst and the analysand requires an alternation, or what I have been teasing out as a dialectical play between interpretation and the production of new knowledge. Brooks points us to Freud's stipulation that when the analysand assents to the analyst's constructions, the gesture has no value "unless it is followed by indirect confirmations, unless the patient, immediately after his 'yes,' produces new memories which complete and extend the construction" (Freud 1964: 262; Brooks 1992: 322). In other words, the analysand goes on by acknowledging previously unacknowledged frameworks of significance. So, despite the essentially conservative trajectory of the death instinct, late Freudian thinking does seem to hold out the prospect for a modality of emplotment that is not merely recuperative or end-stopped in the determination of ends. There is the suggestion that whatever it is on the part of the analysand that "produces new memories which complete and extend the construction" of his discourse therefore portends something like a positing of new ends. It is this Freudian prospect that bears most directly on the ethical dimension of plot making.

V

Earlier in this essay, I suggested that plot is pathos driven. It embodies an exigency whereby the mind must reflect upon itself when events have defied expectations. As a result, I suggested that the plot maker is invested in the subject's change of state as a "hopeful enterprise." It is with respect to this point that tragically plotted action could be said to portend a positing of new ends. This brings us back to a consideration of the way in which plot entails character transformation. The difficulty of possessing character as an intrinsic quality of one's existence in time has been powerfully attested to by St. Augustine in his almost agonizing search for a human orientation to eternity in chapter 11 of his *Confessions*. This meditation has been influentially appropriated by Paul Ricoeur in his magisterial three-volume work, *Time and Narrative* (1984 1985, 1988). Ricoeur reveals how plot and the positing of ends with which we are caught up in the act of plot making broaden the scope of our reflection upon character.

Though one does injustice to Ricoeur's achievement by addressing his text in anything but its threefold entirety, there is some compensatory merit in featuring his concept of a "threefold present," or *distentio animi*. He finds the focus for this project in a single passage from Augustine wherein the saint's meditation on the recitation of a well-remembered psalm reveals an unexpected plot dynamic. Augustine confronts the enigma of time by scrupulously noting that in the recitation of the psalm one seems to move in the medium of a present that is always already past, even as its disappearance into the past depends upon the anticipation of the future. One remembers the psalm. As such, it is already an artifact of the past. But one's recitation brings it back into the future by anticipating what words come next in the act of serving memory. The anticipation is nonetheless an artifact of one's presentness with respect to what has not yet been recovered to memory through speech. The dialectic of expectation, memory, and the attentiveness that marks the presentness of one's act of accommodating the future to the past exhibits a *distention*, what Ricoeur describes as "the shift in, the non-coincidence of, the three modalities of action" (1990, 1: 43).

Ricoeur makes the point that Augustine has exposed a conundrum of human temporality that seems to demand resolution: how does one reconcile the seemingly incommensurable moments of time that are the occasion of our apprehension that time *is*, that is, that time is our passing through it? Augustine himself finesses the problem by concluding that what one wants is a fixed moment or reference point by which one can measure the passage of time as a differential of expectation, memory, and attention. The breakthrough for Augustine comes with the realization that such a fixed point can only inhere in the distended mind itself (Ricoeur 1990: 21). Ricoeur promotes Augustine's insight by observing that in *Poetics* Aristotle has seen that the most significant goal is not to resolve the conundrum of human temporality but to *put it to work* by, as Ricoeur puts it, "producing an inverted figure of discordance and concordance" (41). Ricoeur has in mind the way *making*, emphatically the making of plots, is necessarily a reordering of events independent of any expectation of adequacy to a transcendent systematic order (52).

Ricoeur's/Augustine's orientation to the burdens of emplotment with respect to reconciling differences thus contrasts favorably with the orientation of narratologists, structuralists, and Freudians. Both Ricoeur and Augustine hold out the prospect for character change and the positing of new ends insofar as these are understood to be the salient stakes of the human investment in plot (Ricoeur 1990: 7), for *distentio animi* is acknowledgment that the mind—stretched in three directions at once—necessarily entails a transition from one state to another. This is the underpinning of Ricoeur's strongest assertion of the "primacy of the activity that produces plots in relation to every sort of static structure, achronological paradigm, or temporal invariant" (30). To be fair, Augustine's account defers ultimately to the unachievable concordance of human time with divine eternity. But Ricoeur's Aristotelian inflection of Augustine's meaning with respect to *distentio animi* comprehends the fate of character as roughly equivalent to the slippage between the present of the future, the present of the past, and the present of the present (38).

This slippage for Ricoeur is linked to *muthos*, the activity of composing, which he claims constitutes an inseparable pair with *mimesis* (1990: 30). Imitation is only ever the composition/composing of events into an organizational pattern. Its representational power is indistinguishable from its figurational power. Accordingly, Aristotle's venerable anatomy of the six parts of tragedy (spectacle, thought, song, etc.) in "chapter 6" of *Poetics* is construed by Ricoeur "not as parts of the poem but of the art of composition" (1990: 30). This phenomenological approach to plot perhaps surprisingly refers us once again to the topos of *eudaimonia*, where character is subsumed to activity. Aristotle's rigorous subordination of character to plot now becomes the stage for an ethical project[11] in which personhood is not merely the content of action, a mechanism for the fictional distribution of good persons and bad persons in the world, but an occasion for human self-reflection. It ordains the capacity of "persons engaged in action" (*Poetics* 48A1; Ricoeur 1990: 35) to know themselves better. This, after all, motivates St. Augustine's struggle in relation to the Divine, for the threefold present, or the *distentio animi* of plot, denotes an internalization of dramatic action. It portends a reconciliation with one's differences over time that makes personhood beholden to the necessity of adaptation and change. If, as Ricoeur strongly suggests, Aristotle's marrying of the pair *mimesis-muthos* is the real theoretical accomplishment of *Poetics*, and if Aristotle thereby establishes an equivalence between representation of action and the organization of events (Ricoeur 1990: 30), the idea of character would seem to be devoutly wedded to the practice of self-representation. The task of self-representation would consequently involve a continuous reckoning with the warrant for new reasons or justifications vis-à-vis the actions that accrue to a person over time and without which there would be no compelling pretext for representation at all.

Not surprisingly, the idea that plot has ethical force, by dint of the organizational and structurational capacities of mind, is most strikingly concordant with Aristotle's insistence that plot exhibits intelligence per se. As Ricoeur and many others have attested, this is integral to the proposition that the internal connection of the plot is logical, not chronological. Though the term "logic" does not appear in *Poetics*, precisely because Aristotle's focus is phronetic, not theoretic—the emphasis is always on doing/making—intelligence is the sine qua non of phronetic activity. Or, at least, this would seem to be the case wherever phronesis entails cognizance of a change of state and mandates an accommodation of new evaluative commitments. The evidence for this claim is perhaps even stronger in our acknowledgment of something that Samuel Taylor Coleridge remarked upon centuries later in his own poetics, "On the Principles of Genial Criticism Concerning the Fine Arts" (1814)[12]—that all kinds of realities that would ordinarily be repulsive in our actual experience of them are rendered pleasurable when incorporated to the organizational mandate of the imagination. Or, to put it back in strictly Aristotelian terms, in plot our contemplation of images of the basest animals or putrescent corpses is rendered coherent with "the experience of learning and reasoning out what each thing represents," for example, that "'this figure is so and so'" (1448b12–17, cited in Ricoeur 1990: 21).

Just as Aristotle privileges poetry over history for its emphasis on probable impossibilities rather than possible improbabilities, so the imaginative activity of choosing prospects takes precedence over the prospective knowledge of what choices are known to be possible. In effect, plot is the art of the possible. Or perhaps it would be more precise to formulate its purpose as the art of "making possible," especially in light of Ricoeur's emphasis on the agency of mimesis. Within the scope of Ricoeurian/Aristotelian mimesis, all making—temporally constrained and temporally enabled—makes us ever more scrupulously aware of the fact that possibility itself is a variable of deliberative process. Where our evaluative commitments are challenged by new knowledge/unprecedented circumstance, we must reckon with the mandate for making plans that will prove more compatible with the hitherto unacknowledged contingencies of our situation.[13]

Plotting is planning, but it is planning awry, so to speak. It is a mode of planning that remains cognizant of the reversibility of intentional action and is intentionally or deliberatively responsive to that cognizance. Ricoeur epitomizes its dynamic in the proposal that while plot is always a striving for concordance, particularly in the case of tragedy, the vicissitudes of tragedy in real time constrain us to accommodate a "discordant concordance" (42). This he treats as a counterpart to *distentio animi*. Aristotle, of course, values the quality of completeness[14] in plot action, for which concordance is a correlative principle. And, in this way, he tantalizes us with a prospect for the stability of character achievable through action. But this prospect invites the very mistaken privileging of character over act that Aristotle is so consistently bent upon correcting elsewhere in *Poetics*. The idea that character is the proper end of action would, of course, render discord a punctually resolvable problem of the human experience of time. Alternatively, Ricoeur's discordant concordance keeps faith with a possibility that I believe Aristotle never abandons: that discord is absolutely constitutive of the human experience of time, that is, an ineliminable element of the dynamics of plot. Thus, whatever our idea about character, it is bound to sustain itself through a recognition of its own discordant concord. This is to say that character is not the end of the plot per se. Rather, it is what accrues to the activity of plotting as increments of knowledge.

Within this purview, we should not fail to recognize the conceptual contours of the Conradian predicament of "living in the midst of the incomprehensible," or the relevance of Kermode's notion of human character as living in "perpetual transition" or of Freud's prescription that the sustaining of the relation between analyst and analysand depends upon the production of new memories that "complete and extend" the discourse. Nor should we fail to recognize that each of these glosses on human experience is resonant with the *eudaimonian* spirit of Aristotelian plot that, recall, Nussbaum characterized as "essentially active, of which praiseworthy activities are not just productive means, but actual constituent parts" (1986: 6). In all of this there is the suggestion that if we want to understand the relation of character to plot, we must countenance the dependence of character on what, in the vicissitudes of action, determines the human propensity to ask "Why?"—that is, on what is here, now, not reconciled, recuperated, and already known. We might therefore be prompted to think more broadly of plot as an ongoing response to whatever it is about human activity that determines the interrogative mode.

VI

And yet, at this juncture, one might reasonably ask the question, "Why should we think of plot as having to do with asking why?" After all, given the vast interpretive tradition featuring literary plot as little more than a stage for the exhibition of character, we might imagine that certain plot structures or plot types are programmatically vehicles of characterization. "Who" explains everything. Samuel Johnson's "Preface to Shakespeare" (1765) is the most authoritative exemplar of this tradition. The Johnsonian ideal of "General Nature" prompts us to consider how the hubristic ego determines the plot of tragic suffering in Sophocles or how the lack of the servant's official social power in Plautus determines the plot of his or her wiliness, or how the senility and impotence of the senex in Roman comedy generally produces the perverse marriage plot that threatens an unnatural pairing of the young and the old. Or merely consider how Othello's jealousy dooms him to self-destruction with such compelling logic that we are impelled to generalize that all action is essentially characterological. In such cases, plot seems to illustrate personality and its consequences. As I've already suggested, all of the questions that plot can answer seem to be already presupposed in the nature of character. The "why" of the interrogative mode seems to be mooted as a crux of emplotment.

Of course, we have been repeatedly warned by Aristotle not to trust such appearances, that is, not to treat character type as a cause of action. Such thinking violates the strict priority Aristotle assigns to activity over character. We would fall into the trap of seeing plot itself as effectively *inactive*. And yet it could be argued that this objection, in turn, seems to beg the question of who acts. Despite Aristotle's ample discussion of character and the variety of character types, as if the source of character in activity were self-evidently explicable, he risks a kind of circular logic: he does not clarify how the agency of action is related to the agency of character such that one is clearly anterior to the other. All of this raises a suspicion that the "why" of the interrogative mode is both central to and somewhat incoherent with respect to the meaning of plot when we try to sort out its bearing on character.

And yet, I think the conundrum that emerges here is opportune since it gives renewed urgency for us to see plot and character in some more productively dialectical relation. As I have been suggesting, it is this impetus that reveals most intimately how plot fosters a notion of character as self-investigation, and how this framework for comprehending plot might dovetail with an investment in ethical personhood. The interrogative mode may indeed be countenanced as the motor of emplotment when we understand that activity and personhood are reciprocally determined. After all, the interrogative mode is a pretext for reason giving without which ethical personhood is virtually unimaginable. I have proposed a link between plot and rational practice with an eye toward this condition. Along these lines, it is important to remind ourselves that in the *Ethics* Aristotle affirms that "Reason, more than anything else, *is* man" (1178a). Each person seems to be reducible to his faculty of understanding. Aristotle is grasping the fact that one's sense of one's own protagonistic identity is typically a function of critical distance from oneself.

It is quite true that we implicitly alienate or negate ourselves in taking up a critically reflective vantage point with respect to the actions that hitherto grounded our identity. But Aristotle seems to make the point that one's capacity to reason or understand (without which critical distance is unachievable) follows one across the episodic threshold of one experience after another that is the material substrate of contemplative being. Persistent self-investigation does not preclude the self. In other words, Aristotle preempts the idea, popularized in the wake of poststructuralism, that in crossing such thresholds, gaining new critical vantage points, one has to give up on the proposition that character or subjective identity endures, even and especially through the rigors of peripety. The continuity of understanding through the vicissitudes of experiences that qualify or revise the self we seek to understand would seem to presuppose the interrogative mode. If "Reason, more than anything else, *is* man," his personhood is a continuous inquiry into the springs of whatever action one takes that occasions one's knowing better than to have taken it. This amounts to something like a Kantian apperceptive I, rendered as a métier of learning instead of as an ontological ground.

But it might be even more useful to describe Aristotle's point about the persistence of understanding—the impossibility that understanding could negate itself—as a prescient Hegelian insight. That would certainly help to advance my interest in seeing plot and character in a more dialectical relation, for Hegel's account of self-consciousness, in the *Phenomenology,* and also in his meditations on the tragic, hinges on the way in which the mediations of worldly experience augment self-consciousness. Hegelian negation itself might be said to prompt the interrogative mode if we focus on the fact that Hegelian self-consciousness is plotted, so to speak, by casting doubt on self-certainty. This doubt propels the dialectic of self-consciousness in a way that determines character as based on one's circumstances and the conditionality they embody rather than on some ontological predicate of one's personal nature.

VII

Character is seen to be less typological in light of this dialectic with plot, and it might therefore be more properly characterized as situational and rationalistically pragmatic. Philosophical and psychological theorists seeking to promote an empirically based ethics are frequently disposed to see situationalism as a way out of the labyrinth of psychological groundings of action, thus preempting a view of character as independent of action. Rather than plumbing depth psychology, they have recourse to strategies of "narrative" integration[15] as means of accounting for unconscious motivations. Such unconscious motivations are signaled in the incoherencies that grow out of situations where one's desire to take responsibility for one's self-understanding is frustrated. Situationalists argue that an agent can come to terms with this "unconscious" by reflecting on what motives one embraces when one integrates acts into a coherent story or what reasons one can adduce to support motivational accounts of action.

In *The Possibility of Practical Reason* (2000), J. David Velleman gives us motive for thinking that situational rationality and plot making are complementary activities, by insisting that one's self-knowledge is inescapably a knowledge of what one is doing. For Velleman, the human propensity to ask why can be consummated only in furtherance of the question "What am I doing?" This is consistent with the Aristotelian precept that plotted action is what makes us recognizable to ourselves as significantly human, that is, as distinct from animals. After all, for Velleman, knowing what we are doing is different from simply being able to describe our movements. Rather, "[t]o know what we're doing is grasping our bodily movements under concepts that set them in an explanatory context of motives and circumstances" (2000: 27). He stipulates, accordingly, that the interrogative "What am I doing?" (29) is a prerequisite of acting autonomously. Even more important, it is the condition under which gaining cognizance of a lack of self-knowledge—such that an agent might become aware of the choice to do something else—is originally possible. One is thereby rendered open to the possibility that there are other and possibly better reasons for acting.

What I referred to above as crossing the episodic thresholds of one experience after another potentially yields what we might now call a better story or plot if one understands the reasons for what one is doing as better than other reasons. The ability to discriminate those reasons is in turn dependent upon our ever more scrupulously registering the succession of episodic moments out of which our comprehension that we need motivating reasons in the first place arises. As Velleman puts it: "[R]easons for acting are the elements of a possible storyline along which to make up what we are going to do" (2000: 28).

On this basis, it may be said that as plot makers we are naturally predisposed to respond to the necessity of producing a better story line, one that will always make us more responsive to what will not suffice to convince us that we know what we are doing. That is, a better story line will always be one that makes us more responsive to interruptive incidents that have undermined the authority of a prior story line to reassure us that we know what we are doing. Velleman's sense that knowing what we are doing is "grasping our bodily movements under concepts that set them in an explanatory context of motives and circumstances" intimates how self-explanation, or the kind of self-manipulation that such deliberative reflection prompts, might give us the most illuminating of view of plot as an ethical undertaking. The broader horizon of human reflection to which we are referred when we acquire consciousness of our Aristotelian *hamartia*—our lack of knowledge in unique situations—is encompassed by heeding the interrogative "What am I doing?" as if it were an imperative. The interrogative itself must therefore be countenanced itself as a mode of doing or acting. In this respect, plot commits us to a form of attention to the world.

Unstinting attentiveness is, after all, what Samuel Beckett's Unnamable reckons with as a *going on*, even in the face of a failure of the will to go on: "[P]erhaps they have carried me to the threshold of my story, before the door that opens on my story, that would surprise me, if it opens, it will be I, it will be the silence, where

I am, I don't know, I'll never know, in the silence you don't know, you must go on, I can't go on, I'll go on" (1965: 414). The Unnamable testifies to a form of attachment to the significance of life even before he knows the reasons he might possess to sustain that attachment. The Unnamable's mode of reasoning is one that does not depend upon seeing preformulated reasons as necessary or sufficient to make sense of things, because for him making sense of things is an ongoing and self-sustaining proposition.

Indeed, plot, or the emplotment of narrative experience, produces what might be called a therapeutic effect with respect to the possibility of going on, and perhaps "going on" by way of a better story line, for we have seen how it intimates a capacity to integrate reasons or motives that we may not have "noticed" or paid sufficient attention to in telling a story, but whose significance becomes apparent as the story unfolds. The point can be made even more explicitly. In John Doris's *Lack of Character* (2002), a book that is interested in establishing the situational determinants of character as the basis for an empirical ethics and has no stake in the literary value of plot per se, we nonetheless recognize a striking concordance with Aristotle's privileging of the conditions of action over characterological traits. More important, the author explicitly speaks of plot, predicated on this situationalist view of character, as a form of reasoning whereby we can compensate ourselves for blind spots of reasoning or for our ignorance of motives that we might otherwise need to take responsibility for. As Doris explains, plot, or narrative, potentiates human self-scrutiny, a discipline of taking notice, so to speak. It can show us the evidence of identifications or evaluative commitments that amount to unconscious motives. It does so "even where the narrative's subject disavows the motive in question by illuminating the ways in which the motive expresses operative priorities" (2002: 142). Like Velleman, Doris gives us a reason to think that plot is related to the practice of reason giving, especially where reasons are not spontaneously forthcoming or self-evident. If Velleman and Doris lead us to imagine that plot is in many ways driven by the question "What am I doing?" we might now surmise that the best answer mandates the sustenance of plot making. This is not a mandate for plots to be open-ended as much as it is an admonition to recognize that plots must be studied for the ways they prompt us to pay attention to the world; they foster forms of attentiveness that our already settled characterological dispositions do not allow or entitle us to.

In Velleman and Doris's rationalistic efforts to stretch the capacity of plot making to accommodate unforeseen knowledge, they keep faith with the *eudaimonian* stakes of plot making that Aristotle affirmed for the sake of illuminating a literary enterprise. It is important to remember that the study of plot is originally motivated within the framework of an artistic practice. But it is equally important to realize that it was a philosopher who first took that motive seriously, in large part because the literary enterprise of tragedy was already perceived to be integral to the life of the *agora* where philosophical attitudes joined social practices in the enterprise of human making, the formal arena of human agency. The continuity of philosophical and literary interests is sustained most meaningfully in the kind of recent thinking about plot exampled by Velleman and Doris when it reminds us that as plot makers we are preeminently subjects who wish to interact productively and responsibly with a civil order—one in which human nature can decisively take the initiative of self-justification. The Greek tragedies that served as the warrant for Aristotle's *Poetics* still testify to this aspiration. I think there would be little argument against the claim that self-justification, that is, some small mitigation of Conrad's knowledge that we "dwell in the midst of the incomprehensible," has been the source of our most enduring interest in plot since the time of its most seminal literary progenitors. There is arguably no example of plot that does not bear heavily upon the prospects of humans for sustaining the purposiveness of their being as agents. After all, we are agents in a world where agency is always challenged by the obscurity of human motives, embedded as they are in temporal situation of change and transformation. On this account, plot is perhaps our most trusted compass for finding a human direction in the temporal wilderness of our Natural existence.

NOTES

1. Brooks sees narrative, as distinct from plot, as a uniquely literary or aesthetic proposition. I would not mark the distinction in these terms and would ultimately make less of it.

2. In book 7 of the *Ethics*, Aristotle gives appearances, the "observed facts" (*phainomena*), a methodological status: we can't work through the puzzles of perception and thus attain the truth of beliefs on any other basis. See 1145b1ff.

3. See, e.g., the *Phaedo*, where Socrates does not countenance physical ills as serious liabilities of human existence because they are mere bodily effects.

4. Nussbaum identifies this as "animal activity" (1986: 273).

5. In a famous retort to a natural scientist who would reduce the meaning of an act or event to its rudimentary physical elements, Socrates insists upon "deliberation and rational choice" or intellect as the legitimate basis of learning (*Phaedo* 99A4–5). Nussbaum comments that, given the choice between two patterns of explanation (one by physiology and one by reason or intellect), we see that "only actions...fit the latter...by which he means rational actions understood as the products of intellectual activity, that are said to be inadequately explained by the former" (1986: 272).

6. See the discussion of Rowland Mallet's consciousness in James 1972.

7. See Kermode's reliance, followig James T. Barr, on the Biblical scholars Cullmann, Marsh, and Tillich (2000: 47).

8. French narratological structuralism deploys the terms *histoire* and *discours*. Émile Benveniste explains this subtle shift of emphasis by referencing the fact that French has two systems of past-tense verbs: one designates narration of past events; the other is reserved for oral utterance assuming a speaker and a hearer. See Benveniste 1971: 205–15.

9. Nussbaum 1986: 270 is a useful discussion of the distinction between Democritus's view of animal movement and Aristotle's (in *De Anima*) in order to emphasize Aristotle's stake in some kind of sorting out or focusing on the pieces of the world.

10. Barthes's exposition includes the assertion that the "proairetic sequence is never more than the result of an artifice of reading: whoever reads the text amasses certain data under some generic titles for actions (*stroll, murder, rendezvous*), and this title embodies the sequence" (1975: 19).

11. Of course, the irony, as Ricoeur admits, is that in the *Nicomachean Ethics* (1103a30ff), where ethics is the proper end of the discourse, the subject precedes the action (1990: 37).

12. See the discourse on the beautiful in this essay, Coleridge 1966: 372–77.

13. John Doris, in *Lack of Character: Personality and Moral Behavior* (2002), conducts an extremely interesting investigation into the nature of character on this basis, thereby appreciating how characterological traits might be reconceived as more profoundly situational than natural or constitutional; see esp. 136.

14. Tragedy is deemed to be an imitation of action that is "serious" and "complete" (*Poetics* 49b25).

15. Doris's *Lack of Character* is one example of this style of theorizing. But much of this work arose out of the famous "Milgram situations" and other instances of a longstanding situationist research tradition in experimental social psychology that Doris examines. Researchers in this field wish to demonstrate that, as Doris himself says, "situational factors are often better predictors of behavior than personal factors" (2002: 2)

REFERENCES

Aristotle. (1941). *The Basic Works of Aristotle* (R. McKeon, ed.). New York: Random House.

Barthes, R. (1975). *S/Z*. New York: Hill and Wang.

Beckett, S. (1965). *The Unnameable*. In *Three Novels*. New York: Grove Press.

Beneviste, E. (1971). *Problems in General Linguistics*. Coral Gables: University of Miami Press.

Bremer, J. M. (1969). *Hamartia: Tragic Error in the Poetics of Aristotle and Greek Tragedy*. Amsterdam: Hakkert.

Brooks, P. (1992). *Reading for the Plot*. Cambridge, Mass.: Harvard University Press.

Caserio, R. (1979). *Plot, Story and the Novel*. Princeton: Princeton University Press.

Coleridge, S. T. (1966). "On the Principels of Genial Criticism Concerning the Fine Art." In E.Schneider (ed.), *Selected Poetry and Prose*. New York: Holt, Rinehart, and Winston: 372–77. (Original work published in 1814.)

Conrad, J. (1995). *Heart of Darkness*. New York: Penguin. (Original work published in 1899.)

Doris, J. M. (2002). *Lack of Character: Personality and Moral Behavior*. Cambridge: Cambridge University Press.

Eldridge, R. (2001). "How Can Tragedy Matter for Us?" In Eldridge, *The Persistence of Romanticism*. Cambridge: Cambridge University Press.

Freud, S. (1964). "Constructions in Analysis." In J. Strachey (trans.), *The Standard Edition of the Complete Psychological Works of Sigmund Freud.*, Vol. XXIII. London: Hogarrh. (Original work published in 1937.)

Freud, Sigmund (1990). *Beyond the Pleasure Principle*. (J. Strachey trans.). New York: W W. Norton. (Original work published 1in 920.)

Jackson, J. J., and J. R. J. Jackson, eds. (1995). *The Collected Works of Samuel Taylor Coleridge*, Vol. 11, *Shorter Works and Fragments*. Princeton: Princeton University Press.

James, H. (1972). "Preface" to *Roderick Hudson*. *In* J. E. Miller, Jr. (ed.), *Theory of Fiction*. Lincoln: University of Nebraska Press.

Kermode, F. (2000). *The Sense of an Ending: Studies in the Theory of Fiction*. Oxford: Oxford University Press.

Nussbaum, M. (1986). *The Fragility of Goodness: Luck and Ethics in Greek Tragedy and Philosophy*. Cambridge: Cambridge University Press.

Ricoeur, P. (1990). *Time and Narrative* (Volume 1), In. *Time and Narrative* (3 vols.). K. McLaughlin and D. Pellauer (trans.) Chicago: University of Chicago Press. (Original works published 1984, 1985, 1988).

Singer, A. (2003). *Aesthetic Reasons: Artworks and the Deliberative Ethos*. University Park: Pennsylvania State University Press.

Todorov, T. (1971). "Transformation of Narratives." *In* R. Howard (trans.), *Poetics of Prose* Ithaca: Cornell University Press.

——. (1975). *The Fantastic: A Structural Approach to a Literary Genre*. (R. Howard, trans.). Ithaca, NY: Cornell University Press. (Original work published in 1970.)

Velleman, J. D. (2000). *The Possibility of Practical Reason*. Oxford: Clarendon Press.

CHAPTER 17

CHARACTER

STANLEY BATES

In every agreement to buy or sell, there's also the proviso, acknowledged or not, that says "unless, of course, I don't want to anymore," or "that is, unless I change my mind," or "assuming my yoga instructor doesn't advise against it." The hallowed concept of *character* was invented to seal off these contingencies. But...are we really going to say that this concept is worth a nickel or a nacho? Or, for that matter, ever was?

—Richard Ford, *The Lay of the Land*

Whether the "hallowed concept of character" is a fiction we shall have occasion to consider, but there can be no doubt that there are fictional characters. There are a number of different levels at which character can be considered reflectively, philosophically. One might, for example, reflect on particular styles of the representation of character, and of the character of characters. This could involve a historical account of the development of different modes of representation, such as Erich Auerbach offers in his classic *Mimesis* (2003). One might try to develop an account of why certain fictional/mythical characters seem to develop a presence that exceeds the texts in which they appear—Don Juan, or Faust, or Falstaff, for example. One might also attempt to untangle the relationship between what we believe about the character of actual human beings, and how those beliefs are involved in our relationships to literary characters. I begin at this very general level before moving to some more specific issues.

From a certain, usually unarticulated, philosophical perspective, fictional characters raise a number of puzzling issues. Why do we (those of us who do) concern ourselves with fictional characters? This is an only slightly narrowed version of the question of why we concern ourselves with imaginative literature at all. "What's Hecuba to him, or he to Hecuba?" Why do readers invest their emotions in fictional beings? Why did so many cry at the death of Little Nell? (Oscar Wilde once suggested that one would have to have a heart of stone to read the death of Little Nell without *laughing*.) It would be worth some investigation to try to understand why these questions have been believed to be puzzling. From what perspective is concern for fictional characters found to be paradoxical? Throughout the long history of fictional literature (and drama and narrative fictional film), the vast majority of readers (and viewers) have been emotionally invested in the actions and fates of fictional character. Hence, it would seem more promising to attempt to construct an account of imaginative literature (and drama, and fictional narrative film), which at worst accommodates, and at best accounts for, this vast body of phenomenological data. Any view that implies that there is something impossible, or irrational, or false, or wrong, at the root of the emotional concern for fictional characters must be wrong. What I have just articulated is, of course, an aspect of a "traditional" view of literature—and sophisticated "theories" of the last century and the present have come to challenge it. Kathryn Sutherland quotes A. C. Bradley, a prominent traditional critic of the early twentieth century, as writing of Jane Austen, "It is a great merit, that is, in a story that, besides admiring the characters as studies, you care for some of them as persons, and care very much for at least one." Sutherland then comments:

> The strength of Austen's novels, like Shakespeare's plays is to be found, Bradley argues, in characters who exhibit a habit of life beyond the function of the plot. Hence the conviction that there is more to Elizabeth Bennet, that her textual life is only a part of what is knowable. Though long unfashionable as a professional protocol for reading, the idea of "knowing" or identifying with fictional characters remains important when it comes to explaining why we read novels for pleasure. (2006: 12)

The implication of her last sentence is that a professional protocol for reading at least for the last century or so must have been unconcerned with why we read novels for pleasure. This seems to me more or less accurate. Why should this have been so?

In the professionalization of any field or academic discipline, certain premises about the values of the objects and methods of study will have been built into the construction of that field or discipline. Reflective questions about those premises will generally not be a part of the field itself.[1] Later in this chapter I return briefly to a consideration of what makes possible both postmodernist theories about literature and postmodernist literature. Here, in considering the issues of the role of character and characterization in human fictional constructions, I locate these issues against a wider background of my own assumptions.

SETTING

My own perspective is broadly naturalistic. Literature and, more generally, fictional narratives are human constructions made within a human practice.[2] (This denies a supernatural origin for sacred texts. Sacred texts are created by humans for humans—though, of course, their human creators may believe them to have been inspired by the divine. Hence, if one believes that a text *is* sacred, and not just believed by some to be sacred, my discussion is not intended to be applicable to it.) Why has there ever been a human practice of making up fictional narratives that represent the actions of fictional characters? (From the point of view of certain representationalist theories of language, such narratives are simply lies—intended to deceive.) It seems to me that an answer to this question that operates at the right level, and that is right as far as it goes, is given in the first great work of the analysis of literature in the western tradition, Aristotle's *Poetics*. Before he begins his analysis of tragedy, Aristotle gives a general characterization of "poetry in general"—what we would call literature. Famously, he claims that all the kinds of poetry are forms of *mimesis* probably best translated as "representation" but often translated as "imitation." But then he takes up the issue of *why* there is poetry at all—why do human beings engage in *mimesis*? Aristotle asserts:

> In general, two causes both inherent in man's nature seem to have led to the birth of poetry. Imitation is natural to man from childhood; he differs from the other animals in that he is the most imitative: the first things he learns come to him through imitation. Then, too, all men take pleasure in imitative representations. Actual experience gives proof of this: the sight of certain things gives us pain, but we enjoy looking at the most exact images of them, whether the forms of animals which we greatly despise or of corpses. The reason is that learning things is most enjoyable not only for philosophers but for others equally, though they have but little experience of it....Next, Imitation and melody and rhythm are ours by nature...so men were naturally gifted from the beginning, and progressing step by step they created poetry out of their random utterances. (1958: 7–8)

Aristotle's claim that imitation is natural to human beings seems to be correct. (Any parent involved in the care of a very young child knows this very well.) Of course, in a time when the Darwinian consensus defines biological science, we are required to go further than Aristotle in explaining why imitation and the pleasure in imitative representation is "natural." We must believe that these human capacities have attained their place in human nature through a process of biological evolution. Obviously, these features of human existence have a selection advantage, since they make possible a social transmission of what becomes the body of culture. As Aristotle notes, these capacities are crucially involved in learning, and learning is naturally pleasurable. The human species has a particular need for learning in infancy because of the extended period of dependency of human babies. (Human newborns are at a relatively undeveloped stage compared to what they will eventually be capable of because of the physical limits—set by the size of the birth canal—to the size of the infant head.) This greater period of dependency is compensated for by the greater flexibility of adult human behavior that becomes possible because of the kind of learning of which we are capable.

The acquisition of a native language by a child is a complex process that requires several years, and imitation is the central part of its initial stages. Human parents invariably talk to newborn infants who are, at birth, incapable of understanding any language at all. Human parental figures reinforce certain sounds that are spontaneously produced by babies, usually by themselves making the same sound in order to get the baby to repeat it. Eventually, very young children "catch on" in the vast majority of cases. However, the acquisition of a language is simultaneously the acquisition of a vast amount of information about the world. This is true of the vocabulary we acquire, but it also true of our initiation into various linguistic practices that are associated with our social practices. From very early on, in all cultures most children are told stories—family stories, fairy tales, traditional myths, cartoons, Sesame Street stories, stories in children's books, and so forth. (How the general substitution of television shows and video games for oral transmission, or for reading, affects the development of brain and personality is an ongoing, complicated, and ominous story.) From very early on, children are taught about and understand pretending, playing, "being a horse," "being a mother," and so on. They understand the stories they are presented, and very early on they learn that these are *stories*, that is, that they will not encounter talking groundhogs and mice and rabbits. This seldom diminishes their pleasure in these fictions. A part of the process of learning what stories are is learning the difference between "truth" and "fiction" (whatever the metaphysical status of that distinction is finally judged to be). Stories have always been used to transmit the self-understanding of a culture. Traditional myth, religious traditions, sagas, epics, and eddas involve narrative accounts that explain the origins of a people and of its practices, institutions, and values. I have rehearsed some of these familiar general features of human biology, psychology, and cultural evolution as a context within which we might pursue an understanding of character and characterization in literature as it now exists.

CHARACTERS AND WORDS

Though there are many philosophical and critical references to problems about fictional characters in the history of criticism and the history of philosophical reflection on literature, "character" seems to me be a relatively undertheorized concept in recent work.[3] This might be because a concern for character would seem to betray a commitment to a traditional view of literature and a kind of naive response to it that would be incompatible with a professional protocol of reading. I think that it might also be because the fictional representation of character would seem to be parasitic on some prior conception of character in actual human beings. It might seem that this prior conception needs to come from "folk psychology" (a term for some kind of ordinary human understanding of other people—usually used pejoratively in contemporary philosophy, or the less pejorative term "mind reading") or psychology or psychoanalysis or philosophy. Some more recent theories seem to believe that once we self-consciously reflect on the tautological assertion that fictional characters are fictional, we will understand that they have nothing in common with actual human beings or, alternatively, that the character of actual human beings is itself fictional, illusory, or mythical. The former position is sometimes expressed by the suggestion that fictional characters are "verbal constructions" or made out of words. I examine this presently. The latter position raises, I believe, some interesting issues to which I later return.

In one sense, the claim that fictional characters are made out of words is obviously true. We need some text to provide the locale of a fictional character. I do not want to engage directly the issue of the ontological status of texts, or works of art in general, in this chapter. Almost certainly, there are significant differences between, say, the ontological status of characters in novels, in plays, and in fictional narrative films. The claim that a fictional character is made out of words seems most obviously true in the case of the novel (though the texts of plays, and film scripts, seem to be necessary elements of the characters in those forms). However, the claim that characters are verbal constructions seems often to be accompanied by a "merely." There seems to be an idea that this claim about "words" offers a reductive analysis of fictional characters—a kind of revelation that ordinary readers have been mistaken about them. It is the "merely" that I wish to contest. I believe that it rests on a confusion about what words are. If one mistakenly believes that words are identical with types or tokens of inscriptions, physical markings on a surface, or aural manipulations of sound waves, then it will indeed seem reductive to assert that fictional characters are "made out of words." Words, however, are not reducible to their physical manifestations, any more than human actions are reducible to bodily movements, or money reducible to pieces of metal or paper. Words are what they are because of their uses in a complex system of expression and communication. The many possible uses of language depend upon the complex set of intentions and expectations of the users of the language (and what those intentions and expectations can be are, conversely, inscribed within language). The uses of language involved in fictional narratives about fictional characters will hence depend upon the human intentions and expectations of those who are involved in the practice of fictional literature (of both the producers and consumers of such literature) and, more generally, in the practice of any art that involves fictional characters. I now turn to the originary philosophical/critical discussion of character in Aristotle's *Poetics* to get some sense of literary practice with regard to character as near the beginning of the tradition as we are likely to get.

ARISTOTLE ON CHARACTER

Aristotle's most extended discussion of character in general comes soon after he has presented his definition of tragedy as "the imitation of a good action which is complete and of a certain length, by means of language made pleasing for each part separately; it relies in its various elements not on narrative but on acting; through pity and fear it achieves the purgation (catharsis) of such emotions" (1958: 12). Every part of this definition would need serious discussion in an investigation of Aristotle's account of tragedy. We, however, need it as the background for his presentation of what he calls the elements or aspects of tragedy.[4] There are six such elements—plot, character, diction, thought, spectacle, and music (13). Note that these are all abstractions from tragedy itself, which exists only in actual performance when all of these elements are present together. Most of Aristotle's discussion of the general nature of character (*ethos*) occurs in connection with his argument that plot (*mythos*) is the most important element of tragedy, in particular, that plot is more important than character.[5] His leading argument for this claim is that

> tragedy is an imitation, not of men but of action and life, of happiness and misfortune. These are to be found in action, and the goal of life is a certain kind of activity, not a quality. Men are what they are because of their characters, but it is in action that they find happiness or the reverse. The purpose of action on the stage is not to imitate character, but character is a by-product of the action. (13–14)

We should consider what Aristotle might mean by this claim. What is "action"? In defining tragedy as the mimesis of an action, Aristotle is claiming that tragedy (and, no doubt, epic and comedy) give us a narrative account of some chain of human action (with perhaps an admixture of divine action—famously, the action must be complete, having a beginning, a middle, and an end). Presumably, then, only characters are capable of such actions; the existence of a represented action requires a represented agent—a character. Hence, every tragedy will have a cast of characters. There is, of course, a further step to take to reach the assertion that the character of a represented character must, or ought to, be represented. We might call this the issue of "characterization." Differentiating character from characterization would help make sense of Aristotle's claim that "[w]ithout action there could be no tragedy, whereas a tragedy without characterization is possible. The tragedies of most of our recent poets have no characterization" (1958: 13–14). Obviously, he cannot mean that there could be a tragedy without the representation of agents performing actions. He is referring to the extent to which the character of those represented agents is delineated. But what does Aristotle mean by *ethos*, the term being translated as "character"? It is useful to be reminded that

> [t]he dominant interest in Aristotle (and in most ancient thought and literature) is in analyzing ethically good and bad character, i.e. virtue and vice.... Strikingly absent from the ancient thought-world is the interest in unique

individuality and the subjective viewpoint which figures in modern western
thinking about character. (Hornblower and Spanforth 1996: 317)

In an excellent article, Mary Whitlock Blundell writes, "The interrelation between
ethos, dianoia [the term translated "thought" in Aristotle's list of the elements
of tragedy] and *praxis* [action] in the *Poetics* can only be understood against the
background of the *Ethics*" (1992: 155). This seems to me to be entirely correct, but
we should notice that we are moving from an issue about the representation of
character in a literary form to the issue of the nature of the character of actual
human beings. This is a perfectly natural move to make in considering Aristotle.
As Blundell continues:

> [H]e treats tragic characters as indistinguishable in important respects from
> living people. In the *Poetics* he often speaks of dramatic figures as if they were
> real persons, who must have appropriate qualities of character and intellect in
> order to undertake purposeful action. Conversely in the ethical and rhetorical
> works he regularly illustrates his argument with characters from literature,
> especially epic and tragedy. (156)

I do not attempt here to review Aristotle's *Ethics* in its entirety, but it is useful
to recall that it involves a massive analysis of human purposive action—that is,
exactly what is to be represented in tragedy according to the definition quoted
above. When Aristotle takes up the issue of the good for human beings (*eudaimonia*, often translated as "happiness" but perhaps better translated as "flourishing"),
it is clear, given his understanding of "good," that he must provide an account of
the essential nature of human being. When *eudaimonia* turns out to be "the soul's
activity that expresses virtue," he must produce accounts of both the soul and of
virtue. When "moral" virtue turns out to involve the propensity to choose actions
in accordance with a mean, it follows that he must give account of the human
capacity to choose, to act voluntarily or involuntarily, of the intellectual virtues,
of the role of *phronesis* (practical wisdom) in virtuous action, and so forth. This
simply *is* an account of human character (in the relevant sense of that word in
English).[6] It is clearly implied by Aristotle's account that we should understand the
characters in tragedy, in the same way, and using the same terms, that we understand actual human beings—while at the same time being aware that the characters in tragedy are part of a *mimesis*, that is, a representation of human action.

This becomes even clearer in his subsequent discussion of the appropriate
character of the protagonist of a tragedy. Aristotle considers various ways in which
the good or the wicked can be represented as experiencing a change of fortune, and
he rejects several of them as inconsistent with tragedy. He then goes on, "We are
left with a character in between the other two; a man who is neither outstanding
in virtue and righteousness, nor is it through wickedness and vice that he falls into
misfortune, but through some flaw" (1958: 24). Aristotle is not concerned with
psychological realism in the characterization of the character of the protagonist.
(Indeed, psychological realism in the performance of Greek tragedy would have
been difficult to achieve given the nature of the fairly distant viewing of the action

by the audience, the necessity for vocal projection, and the use of masks for the actors.) Rather, he is concerned with the establishing of the moral character of the protagonist so that that character can be at the center of a plot that achieves a tragic effect. Such establishing may not need to involve much of what we would normally call characterization because ordinary members of the audience bring their ordinary views of character and morality into the theater (of Dionysus, in Athens) with them. Hence, not only characters, but also some expectations and beliefs about the character of those characters, cannot be removed from tragedy. When Aristotle argues for the greater importance of the abstraction "plot" over the abstraction "character" among the elements of tragedy, he writes, "The purpose of action on the stage is not to imitate character, but character is a by-product of the action." This cannot mean that tragedy could dispense with the representation of characters who can be characterized and who perform actions. After all, in the previous sentence he had written, "Men are what they are because of their characters." The explanation of action involves reference to the character of the agent.

Not surprisingly, at least since Nietzsche, discussions of Greek tragedy have tended to focus on its ritual origins, its place in the civic life of Athens, and its distance from our contemporary modes of literature. My remark about the lack of "psychological realism" belongs in this more modern vein. No doubt, there is less interest in the individual's subjectivity in ancient literature than in modern— but it is difficult for us moderns not to bring our ideas of character to our reading of Aeschylus, or Sophocles, or especially Euripides. (Euripides is implicated in the death of tragedy, according to Nietzsche, *because* he aimed for, and achieved, a modicum of psychological realism—he brought the spectator on stage.) Prometheus, and Oedipus, and Medea are representations of suffering, acting, human beings, and it is in their familiarity as well as their alienness that we apprehend them. The literature in which they appear is appropriately designated by Bruno Snell in the title of his classic work *The Discovery of the Mind* (1960). These works represent an early stage in the development of a self-conscious understanding of what it is to be human.

On the Difference between Ancient and Modern Mimesis: Schiller, Hegel, Kierkegaard

Let us now turn to a late-eighteenth/early-nineteenth-century discussion of the relationship of the way in which literature both portrays characters and enters into the formation of character. Along the way, we will consider what might be called the Ur-plot of romantic literature, as an account of the development of the character of the self.

For our purposes, we need not attempt to locate the origin of the modern with precision in the Renaissance, or the Reformation, or the seventeenth-century explosion of modern philosophy and modern science. Presumably, we all know that the hallowed divisions of intellectual periods under such terms as "Renaissance" or "Enlightenment" or "romantic era" are both indispensable and flawed—starting points, and not conclusions, of analysis. Nonetheless, I want to explore a very general way in which a number of philosophers and critics have tried to characterize the difference between ancient and modern literature with reference to characters—in part, because these analyses have themselves entered into the history of modern literature.

Perhaps the best starting point for this discussion is Friedrich Schiller's magnificent essay "On Naive and Sentimental Poetry" ("Über naive und sentimentalische Dichtung," 1795–96). The title in English simply uses English words that are cognates of the German terms used by Schiller. Unfortunately, the normal understanding of the terms "naive" and "sentimental" does not correspond to the distinction about which Schiller is writing. (For instance, both of the words in English normally carry a deprecatory connotation, whereas Schiller uses their German cognates to characterize both distinctions between fundamental modes of experiencing the world and between corresponding modes of poetry.) We should remember that Schiller's essay was an intervention in the ongoing discussion within the emerging German literature and culture in the latter part of the eighteenth century of the significance of ancient Greek literature and culture for Germany.[7] Schiller is not, of course, simply characterizing ancient literature as naive and modern as sentimental. He does, however, find that the dominant mode of surviving Greek literature, especially Homer and the early poets, is naive, and the dominant mode of modern literature is sentimental, and he seeks to explain why this is so.

What then is the "sentimental" mode of experiencing the world? It is first introduced as a way of experiencing nature—nature as contrasted with art. "Nature, considered in this wise, is for us nothing but the voluntary presence, the subsistence of things on their own, their existence in accordance with their own immutable laws" (Schiller 1985: 180). Hence, nature itself *is* naive, but being able to conceptualize nature as naive is a precondition of being able to experience it sentimentally. The naive mode of being of nature and, according to Schiller, of some set of comparatively unreflective and unalienated human beings does seem like a metaphysics of presence, but for us moderns the fall into self-consciousness has already taken place. Schiller stresses that this naive mode is not aesthetic, but rather moral: "*They are what we were*; They are what *we should once again become*" (1985: 181, emphasis original). He distinguishes the naive existence in nature from the sentimental response to it very sharply. It is precisely because we moderns have lost our naive relationship to nature that we can experience it sentimentally. Rather than being in nature, we are able reflectively to make nature an object of our thought and emotion. Why, then, do the modern poets offer tribute to nature?

> It is because nature in us has disappeared from humanity and we rediscover
> her in her truth only outside it, in the inanimate world.... The feeling of which
> we here speak is therefore not that which the ancients possessed; it is rather
> identical with that which *we have for the ancients*. They felt naturally; we feel the
> natural. (190)

Shakespeare is the more recent writer whom Schiller associates with the naive
mode of being in nature that allows for a kind of direct expression in naive poetry.
We do not find *him* in his works despite the inevitable desire, both in Schiller's
time and in our own, to do so. The naive mode of being in the world depends
upon the functioning of a human being "as an individual sensuous unity, and as a
harmonious whole" (Schiller 1985: 193). However, Schiller claims that in a state of
civilization such as his own, this sensuous harmony has been broken. He seems to
mean roughly what T. S. Eliot more recently meant by dissociation of sensibility.
For Schiller, this means that, for the disrupted human being, the correspondence
between feeling and thought that actually existed in the naive mode exists now
only as the goal of her or his striving; hence, it has become ideal. He summarizes
his argument as follows:

> This path taken by the modern poets is, moreover, that along which man in
> general, the individual as well as the race, must pass. Nature sets him at one
> with himself, art divides and cleaves him in two, through the ideal he returns
> to unity. But because the ideal is an infinitude to which he never attains, the
> civilised man can never become perfect in *his* own wise, while the natural man
> can in his.... But... the goal to which man *strives* through culture is infinitely
> preferable to that which he *attains* through nature. (194)

Schiller is among the first of those who adopted a secularized version of the Christian three-stage salvational narrative (innocence in the garden/fall into history/
redemption and salvation). His version of this "natural supernaturalism" adds the
particular twist that the third stage requires an infinite striving and exists as the
ideal but unrealized (and perhaps unrealizable?) goal of that striving.[8] Here, surely,
is one of the earliest formulations of romantic aesthetics.

   I now want to turn briefly to Hegel's use of these ideas in his characterization of the difference between ancient and modern literature (especially tragedy).
Hegel locates the origin of dramatic poetry in Greek culture. He says that in this
classic type of art "individuality is only so far asserted as it directly demands the
free animation of the essential content of human aims. That which pre-eminently
is of valid force in ancient drama, therefore, whether it be tragedy or comedy, is
the universal and essential content of the end, which individuals seek to achieve"
(1962: 60). He goes on to claim that in tragedy "this is the ethical claim of human
consciousness" and that the main interest does not "resolve so much around the
fate of individuals." He contrasts this to modern romantic poetry in which "[i]t
is the individual passion, the satisfaction of which can only be relative to a wholly
personal end, generally speaking the destiny of some particular person or character placed under exceptional circumstances, which forms the subject-matter of all

importance" (60). This priority of the individual over the "universal and essential content of the end" is what Hegel takes to be the defining characteristic of romantic literature. This further produces in that literature an "idiosyncrasy" of action as well as of individual character:

> [I]n contrast to the simple conflicts which characterize more classical dramatic composition, we now meet with the variety and exuberance of the characters dramatized, the unforeseen surprises of the ever new and complicated developments of plot, the maze of intrigue, the contingency of events, and, in a word, all those aspects of the modern drama which claim our attention. (62)

Of course, these remarks of Hegel's would be entirely irrelevant unless we see in them a characterization of the history of narrative imaginative literature that captures something important. Does the rise of the European novel in the eighteenth and nineteenth centuries not require some such explanation? Naturally, like all such generalizations, it will have local exceptions, and we do not need to think of it as a denial of other historical factors that would go into a full account of something as complex as the development of, for example, the novel. And yet, the development of the *Bildungsroman* seems to confirm Hegel's view that a central line of literature will concern the formation and development of an individual consciousness in a variety of contingent circumstances. Hence, character in this kind of literature is both a component and a topic of the work of art. These works are about more than how a given character responds in a particular set of circumstance, those circumstances constituting a fate for him/her. They are representations of how a character is developed and constituted. A general characterization of this plot line is given in the subtitle of Nietzsche's immodestly titled intellectual autobiography *Ecce Homo: How One Becomes What One Is* (1888).

To my mind, the best literary history of the developments noted above is still M. H. Abrams, *Natural Supernaturalism: Tradition and Revelation in Romantic Literature* (1971). This magisterial work is, of course, selective, being mainly concerned with certain lines of English romantic poetry and its relationship to some concurrent developments in German philosophy and, more selectively, to German literature. Nonetheless, Abrams performs an enlightening act of intellectual jujitsu, by reading Hegel's *Phenomenology of Spirit* (1807) as itself an instance of the secularized version of the Christian salvational narrative mentioned above. (Of course, as Abrams notes, Hegel himself acknowledges this connection in his own analysis of the level of "truth" of Christianity.) The *Phenomenology* is not a work of systematic philosophy, as Hegel himself warns. (This may account for the fact that, into the twenty-first century, it continues to be by far the most influential of Hegel's works.) Here is Abrams's characterization of the *Phenomenology*:

> It is organized primarily in accordance with literary principles of structure, and persistently deploys typically literary devices. Hegel's narrative has a protagonist, whom he denominates as *das allgemeine Individuum* or *der allgemeine Geist*—"the general individual" and "the general spirit"; that is, the collective human consciousness figured as a single agent. The story he

tells also applies however, to particular minds, for each reflective individual is able to recapitulate the educational journey in his own consciousness. (1971: 278)

Of course, to recognize the *Phenomenology* as a kind of *Bildungsroman* is not to classify it as novel. It does, however, bring out the way in which the relationship between plot and character is more deeply imbricated in a certain kind of literature than even the usual acknowledgement that both "plot" and "character" are abstractions from actual fictional narratives implies. In this kind of literature, the plot *is* the character—the representation of "how one becomes who one is."

Traditional philosophy, unlike fiction, seeks explicit generalization—and no philosophy more than Hegel's, which claims to achieve the ultimate reconciliation that is the goal of the journey of spirit in an absolute self-reflection of spirit.[9] Kierkegaard, in the *Concluding Unscientific Postscript* (1846), accuses Hegel and modern philosophy of "having forgotten, in a sort of world-historical absent-mindedness, what it means to be a human being" (1968: 109). Fiction, good fiction, anyway, tends to particularize rather than to generalize. This is no doubt why Kierkegaard, in his anti-Hegelian critique, leaves behind the traditional forms of philosophical writing and instead presents works of fiction—with an entire apparatus of fictional authors, editors, and narrators of his so-called "aesthetic" works. Interestingly, it is one of these fictional authors, "A" of the first volume of *Either/Or* (1843), who putatively writes an essay, "The Ancient Tragical Motif as Reflected in the Modern," that takes up the comparison of ancient and modern literature from Schiller and Hegel noted above. As is often the case in Kierkegaard's works, he operates within a Hegelian idiom in his criticism of Hegel. The double-sided nature of the *Phenomenology* seems to make this possible. Here are some of the (unsurprising) contrasts that Kierkegaard (or "A") presents:

> The peculiarity of ancient tragedy is that the action does not issue exclusively from character, that the action does not find its sufficient explanation in subjective reflection and decision, but that the action itself has a relative admixture of suffering [passion, *passio*] .... The reason for this naturally lies in the fact that the ancient world did not have subjectivity fully self-conscious and reflective...in modern tragedy the hero's destruction is really not suffering, but is action. In modern times, therefore, situation and character are really predominant. (1959: 145)

In this essay, the fictional "A" sketches a modern version of the tragedy of Antigone to illustrate his claims. This fiction within a fiction finds the modern Antigone with a secret that she cannot disclose to anyone, which collides with her love relationship, which demands full openness and disclosure to her beloved. As anyone familiar with Kierkegaard's biography would immediately recognize, this situation is the one in which Kierkegaard is believed to have thought himself during his engagement to Regina Olsen. If one accepts this biographical hypothesis, it is

Søren Kierkegaard who is the modern Antigone. In any case, the literary analysis in the passage above is nicely self-referential, since it would apply directly to the text in which it is set forth.

All of this literary analysis by Schiller, Hegel, and Kierkegaard is intended to make sense of the undeniably new developments in European literature, and the reaction of the (partly new) reading public to that literature, in the eighteenth and nineteenth centuries. One thinks of the phenomenon of the supposed poems of Ossian, a phenomenon pictured in Goethe's *The Sorrows of Young Werther* (1774), which was itself a marvel of European literature. Whether or not we accept the mythic claim that Goethe's novel inspired a wave of suicides among the young of Europe, there seems in modernity to be an intensely felt response by the literary public to the accounts of the suffering development of literary characters. The phenomenon of the response to the novels of Jean-Jacques Rousseau has been studied in some detail.[10] Rousseau himself asks to be read in a particular way and gives descriptions of reading practices in, for example, *Julie* (1761) and the *Confessions* (1782). He wanted, and got, emotional identification of his readers with his characters. The novel was, of course, a suspect *genre*, which is why Rousseau said of his *Julie* that it was, and was not, a novel. Robert Darnton says of Rousseau that he "demanded to be read as if he were a prophet of divine truth.... What set Rousseauistic reading apart from its religious antecedents...was the summons to read the most suspect form of literature, the novel, as if it were the Bible" (1984: 252). Rousseau wanted his readers to respond with passionate intensity to his characters and to be brought closer to true virtue by this response—and many of his readers claimed that he had succeeded in this aim. Darnton wrote:

> Something happened to the way that readers responded to texts in the late eighteenth century. How many readers? How many texts? The quantitative questions will not admit of answers. One can only assert that the quality of reading changed in a broad but immeasurable public toward the end of the Old Regime. Although many writers prepared the way for this change, I would attribute it primarily to the rise of Rousseauism. Rousseau taught his readers to "digest" books so thoroughly that literature became absorbed in life. (251)

The accounts of the emotional responses of Rousseau's readers are paralleled by the reports of the responses of Dickens's readers in the nineteenth century—a response perhaps heightened by the initial serial publication of his novels. These are familiar events in the history of literature, and explanations of them will no doubt be complex. However, the setting of this new reading phenomenon, certainly a crucial dimension of the development of romanticism, was against the broad background of the secularization of much of European culture. It is hard to believe that this is a coincidence. From the viewpoint of Hegel, the narrative(s) of Christianity must be understood as fictions conveying a deeper truth. How natural from this Hegelian viewpoint to look self-consciously for the truth about the human condition in what are recognized to be fictions.

SELF-CONSCIOUSNESS AND THE PRACTICES OF ART

It is important to separate several different levels of inquiry about art and literature. Since Aesthetics, as a field of philosophy, began in the eighteenth century, it has been intertwined with the philosophy of art. There are obvious reasons why this has been so: given the new philosophical analyses of beauty (and the sublime) and the new systematization of the "fine" arts (associated perhaps with a new concept of "art"), it was natural to think of the fine arts as activities intended to produce objects that could elicit the response (judgment or feeling) of beauty (or sublimity) in the "spectator" (viewer, listener, reader).[11] It was also natural for many to think that the first important task of the philosophy of art is to give a *definition* of this new sense of "art." Many supposed that such a definition might be useful for understanding art, or for the criticism of art. In a similar way, some have also attempted definitions of the individual arts that make up the "modern system of the arts." I do not attempt to criticize such attempts directly, but I do sketch a different approach to understanding what art and literature are, and have been, and might be. Here, I am guided by Nietzsche's aphorism, "all concepts in which an entire process is semiotically concentrated elude definition; only that which has no history is definable" (1992: 516).

If the view that the modern concept of "art" arose in the eighteenth century is correct, we must still be careful not to draw unwarranted inferences from that fact. It does not mean that we, equipped with that modern concept, cannot identify "art" that goes back to prehistoric times. It is perfectly appropriate, for example, that H. W. Janson should begin his widely read *History of Art* (1978) with cave art from 1,500–10,000 B.C.E. at Altamira and Lascaux (23–24). The necessary implication, rather, is that those who created the cave paintings cannot have thought of themselves as "artists" or as engaged in creating "art," but this seems unsurprising. Even if those creators were influenced by what we would call "aesthetic" considerations, they were engaged in something different from art. Some anthropological theories suggest that "religion" might be the appropriate categorization of their work. However, the term "religion" itself has undergone a history as complex as the history of "art"; we need to think of the "religion" of those cave artists as a comprehensive way of organizing their relationship to the world and to others that was not distinguished from science, philosophy, politics, or art in the way that we would now distinguish them.

Similarly, we could attempt to sketch an account of the development of "literature" that would begin before any self-conscious conception of "literature" had been formed. Of course, such an account, like any account of the origin of language itself, would have to be highly speculative. One thing we can be sure of is that anything we could call "literature" would contain representations of the actions of actors, that is, characters. The tales of a tribe, of its ancestors, of its "history," or its gods develop into what we would call a mythology passed on in an oral tradition.[12]

When we get to the time of the writing down of the legends, myths, and epics of peoples, we are on firmer, well-trodden ground, and what we recognize as histories of literature can be written from the surviving evidence and works of literature, tracing the developments of the various genres. Throughout this process, we are dealing with the development of a complex and varied human practice. Here I adapt Alasdair MacIntyre's sketch of what is involved in a human practice. MacIntyre deploys this account of "practice" in his development of the concept of "virtue" in *After Virtue* (1981):

> By a "practice" I am going to mean any coherent and complex form of socially established cooperative human activity through which goods internal to that form of activity are realized in the course of trying to achieve those standards of excellence which are appropriate to, and partially definitive of, that form of activity, with the result that human powers to achieve excellence, and human conceptions of the ends and goods involved, are systematically extended...the range of practices is wide: arts sciences, games, politics in the Aristotelean sense, the making and sustaining of family life, all fall under the concept.
> (1984: 187–88)

Of such a practice, one can always raise the question: Why did human beings engage in it? The answer will have to be given in terms of a conception of human nature and of the already existing whole body of human practices that are rooted in fundamental human forms of life. For our purpose, Aristotle's account of why there is mimetic literature (fictional narrative whether dramatic or epic) seems satisfactory. This is, remember, meant to be an account of why human beings develop literature as what we call "art" (as opposed to writing and narrative for utilitarian, or economic, or business, or war waging, or religion). Aristotle, we can recall, gives two reasons: human beings are naturally mimetic, learning from mimesis, and they take pleasure in mimesis. Notice that these claims, if correct, would be used to explain the emergence and development of the practice of a literature consisting of the fictional representation of the actions of represented characters. The theorizing about this practice begins, in the West, at least as early as the work of Plato and Aristotle in the fourth century B.C.E., but the practice itself was already very old by that time.

The usefulness of MacIntyre's account of a "practice" given above is that it allows us to distinguish the question of origin from the particular questions about the variety of ways in which the representation of fictional characters can be accomplished, and for what purposes they may be used. Nietzsche draws this distinction in his discussion of the fallacy of attempting to account for the origin of the practice of law with punishment in terms of its present purpose:

> The "purpose of law," however, is absolutely the last thing to employ in the history of the origin of law; on the contrary, there is for historiography of any kind no more important proposition than the one it took such effort to establish but which really *ought to be* established now: the cause of the origin of a thing and its eventual utility, its actual employment and place in a system of purposes, lie worlds apart; whatever exists, having somehow come into being, is again and again reinterpreted to new ends, taken over, transformed, and redirected by some power superior to it. (1992: 513)

The crucial point in MacIntyre's account is the idea that practices extend the range of possible human aims and goods. Practices may have both external and internal histories. In their beginning periods, whatever brought them into existence—now to be thought of as external to the practice itself—determines the nature of the practice. However, in the complicated historical development of any complex practice, new purposes and ends may emerge for it. A certain class of games might have emerged because they amused and interested children and provided them with some physical exercise that was thought to be healthy. Later, perhaps, some games might have been thought to be useful because they modeled the social value of competition within rules. However, the excellences that can be achieved in the playing of games include those that have no purpose outside of the playing of the game itself—excellences that are determined relative to the internal nature of the game. Another example might be the stylization of human movement that becomes dance. It may have begun as a component of the fixation of ritual, or perhaps earlier, out of the mating behavior of our ancestors, and it may have therefore served some external purpose, However, the excellence of, for example, a performance of Balanchine's ballet *Agon* is determined by standards that are internal to the developed practice of dance.

Let us return to the practice of a literature of fictional narration of the actions of represented characters. In this chapter I have already indulged in some speculative consideration of its origins, and have tentatively accepted an Aristotelian account of why such a practice could have come into being—what preexisting (or "external") human purposes it would have served. However, what could or would be made of this practice can only be described historically, and that history will involve both of what I have called "internal" and "external" factors. In general, as a practice is developed the standards for evaluating actions taken, or objects created, in accordance with that practice develop with it. The "essence" of a human practice is always temporary and provisional, subject to inevitable change. Such changes cannot be predicted in accordance with any general laws of social science.[13] Though such change is inevitable, such change presupposes some continuing identity of the practice—without such continuing identity nothing could count as "change." The descriptive and normative are necessarily connected in the concept of a practice, but neither can be captured in timeless rules or specifications.

All of this implies that there are no general truths about the function of character in literature, about methods and styles of characterization, about

the way in which fictional characters relate to, and affect, a reading (or viewing) audience. There are, of course, generalizations that can be made about
historical literary movements, or literary styles—these are commonplaces of
criticism. Such generalizations depend neither on abstract definitions of literature nor on social scientific claims about human character. They depend
upon careful reading of historically and culturally particular texts. Thus, the
historical example I gave above about the new way of reading for (a part of)
the audience for literature at the end of the eighteenth and the nineteenth century does not give us a general truth about "literature" but, rather, the exact
opposite—an account of particular works and of a particular audience at a
particular time.

The existence of a practice of the narration of fictional actions of represented characters initially depends upon a representation of them as exceeding
the bounds of the fiction. (Of course, they do not literally exceed the bound of
the fiction, but that is the illusion that is sought. In general, the reader knows
that it is an illusion, but that knowledge does not dispel the illusion. There is a
"willing suspension of disbelief." Thus, in a limited sense the default position of
traditional literature is a kind of realism. This is not the claim that characters
have to be "realistic"—rather, that they have to be representations of imagined
persons who are also imagined as having a "reality" that extends beyond the
narration.) There are many purposes for works of fiction. They can be used
to amuse, to educate, to provide models of virtue, to instruct about the possibilities of character, and so on. The traditional defenses of poetry stressed the
capacity to provide moral instruction, but since the development of the modern
senses of "art" and of "belles lettres" in which the autonomy of art has been
supposed to be established, such defenses have become rarer. Indeed, the relationship between literature (or, more generally, art) and morality has become
mightily vexed, even up to the present time.[14] One might argue for a kind of
minimal defense of traditional literature that it encourages and instructs the
human capacity to "think of oneself as another"—the capacity that underlies
the possibility of morality and sociality in human beings.[15] Human selfhood is
always already developed in a social context, and the sociopathic incapacity to
recognize the selfhood of others results in the impoverishment, indeed mutila-
tion, of the self. A number of recent writers have stressed imaginative fiction's
capacity to help develop the empathetic sense of other selfhoods that is necessary for the development of one's own selfhood.[16] The argument is not that all
literature contributes to the creation of "good" or "virtuous" people, but that
at least some literature (and, perhaps, most of what has been thought to be the
best) opens up the moral dimensions of life to readers, makes them aware of the
existence, and the difference, of others, shows them the possibilities and varieties of love and heroism, gives them an understanding of the nature of human
desire and human suffering. (Naturally, the claim is not that all imaginative
literature does this, but that it is this capacity of the practice that gives it an
important place in human life.)

LITERATURE WITHOUT CHARACTERS—OR
WITHOUT CHARACTERIZATION?

Once we have an autonomous practice of fictional narratives of the actions of represented characters, that practice is subject to internal developments that may move it away from even the default "realism" that I mentioned above. The histories of all of the arts are histories of change, and some of the change is driven by the desire of new generations of artists to challenge the traditions of the practice of their arts. This is perhaps most obvious in the visual arts, and in music, but it is also true for literature. This has become an acute issue, variously in the different arts, in modernity. If we take Hegel's work as a rough summation of lines of thought that had been growing strong during the eighteenth century, we might take it also as a rough marker of the time of a self-conscious awareness of one's artistic tradition as historical—as containing change, and even "progress." Kant's formulation, in the *Critique of Judgment* (1790), of the necessity of "genius" for artistic creation, could be seen to be realized in Beethoven, the nineteenth century's paradigm of an artistic genius capable of originality, and the exact contemporary of Hegel. There had, of course, always been originality in the history of art (and, no doubt, lack of originality), but it seems not to have been a self-conscious requirement for an artist before the late eighteenth century. When we consider, for example, Beethoven's relationship to Haydn and Mozart, we must think that he was moved to surpass them (not, of course, to obliterate them). Similarly, Wordsworth thought himself called to be a bard, in the tradition of Milton, but in a new time when the traditional Christian *mythus* no longer sufficed.[17]

One line that is opened up for an artistic practice with a history is to produce work that is, as it were, concerned with the artistic practice itself. In the case of the practice of fictional narration, this possibility might be realized in what have been called "metafictions." Such fictions might very well reject what I have called the minimal realism of traditional fictions. They might self-consciously undercut the illusion of the reality of characters, calling attention in the work itself, to the author's creation of the fictional characters. (This would be roughly equivalent to a form of painting that calls attention to the work as a painting rather than concentrating on the represented subject and striving to make the technique of representation invisible. This characterization needs to be formulated carefully for it might seem to assume, incorrectly, that all painting had aspired to the condition of *trompe l'oeil*.) Perhaps one might want to say that almost all of the moves of metafiction are already present early on in the history of the novel. Laurence Sterne's *Tristram Shandy* (1759–69) is often given as an example. However, the prime examples cited are usually more recent. Some of the novels of the *nouvelle roman* in France, for example, those of Alain Robbe-Grillet, Michel Butor, Claude Simon, and Nathalie Sarraute, work against traditional modes of characterization, though they do not dispense with characters. In American fiction, the inventions of John Barth and Donald Barthelme can be cited. Another kind of example would be characters lacking in "depth," that is, without affect, deliberately inscrutable, depsychologized. Some of the early works of Ann Beattie represent characters who are as lacking in depth as cardboard cutouts. The fiction of Paul Auster often challenges traditional conceptions of character. Some of the genres of modern fiction retain characters without pursuing issues of identity or character formation. The traditional English detective story, because the form is so tightly defined, restricts what can be done with characters. For example, in an Agatha Christie story, because any of the main characters might turn out to be the murderer, the readers cannot be given a lot of characterization. Famously, Christie's use of an unreliable narrator in *The Murder of Roger Ackroyd* (1926) outraged aficionados of the genre. Science fiction can utilize nonhuman characters—machines, aliens, galactic clouds—but these must always be attributed powers of thought, perception, decision, and action to some extent to be conceivable as characters: they must be anthropomorphized.

Interestingly, in the periods of modernism and postmodernism the most radical formal innovations (characterized by José Ortega y Gasset as "dehumanization") have been in the visual arts and music. Perhaps this is because the use of language is optional or peripheral in these arts. The novel, poetry, drama, and narrative film drama are much more closely tied to language and the structure of meanings that it makes available. Of course, there are formal innovations and experimental traditions in recent literature. Indeed, a characteristic feature of modernism in all the arts has been great formal innovation. James Joyce in *Ulysses* (1918–20; 1922) engaged in a large number of literary experiments. In his decisions about the overall structure of the novel, and in his adoption and adaptation of a variety of literary techniques and styles for different parts of the book, he can be seen as perhaps the greatest formal innovator in the history of the European novel. But think of the rich, richly specific, characters he created in this work. There are no more thoroughly "real" characters (in the minimal sense of realism that I specified above) than Leopold and Molly Bloom and Stephen Dedalus. At first, *Ulysses* was incredibly hard to read, for a general public. Joyce's literary reputation, based on *Dubliners* (1914) and *Portrait of the Artist as a Young Man* (1914–15; 1916), was very high with a limited but elite group of literary figures, so his work was taken seriously. Gradually, after issues of obscenity were resolved and the work became widely available, it entered into the canon of modernism. At the turn of the twenty-first century, when the Modern Library editorial board constructed its list of the 100 greatest novels in the English language of the twentieth century, *Ulysses* topped the list (Lewis 1998).[18] The point is that *Ulysses*, which probably did not look like a novel at all to most readers when it became widely available, is now at the center of the idea of an artistic work of literature. It is widely studied in English Literature courses, and it continues to sell. Compare this to Joyce's final work, *Finnegan's Wake* (1939). There are Joyceans who revere and study the book, but it has never found the general, high literary audience that *Ulysses* has. In addition to the formal and linguistic experimentation of Joyce's writing in this book, he experiments with the concept of character to a very high degree. Perhaps it is still an open question whether this kind of experiment can be shown to be a successful narrative fiction in the way that *Ulysses* is. How much of an audience does a novel need? One incontestably great twentieth-century writer, Samuel Beckett, in his latest works in pursuit of nothingness, eliminated traditional elements of character to as great an extent as he could. Whether these works succeed would have to be investigated in an act of criticism. It seems to me that these works need to be read in conjunction with the whole body of his work, to understand their significance in the light of the trajectory of his development as a writer. Whether they succeed as individual works is more problematic.

Perhaps the closest literary experiment to the complete abstraction achieved by painting in the twentieth century would be the dada and surrealist experiments with "automatic writing." The issue is not whether any of their productions can be counted as "works of art" or as "poetry." Of course they can—the twentieth century has taught us that anything can brought under those rubrics. The issue is whether any of these works can count among the high achievements of literature. There is no a priori argument that they cannot. The issue can only be engaged at the level of criticism of specific works. Such criticism is necessarily involved in a version of the hermeneutical circle, since it will depend upon assumptions about the nature of the practice of literature that the work in question may reject. The only point to be remembered is that such rejections are not guaranteed "success"; the would-be artist is not the sole determinant of the quality of her or his work. What it means for a work of literature to "succeed" may change because someone is able to make a new kind of work in a new way, and it can be accepted by some audience as a genuine work. In the case of a particular work, one looks for a kind of critical appreciation in which it can somehow be shown how *this* work succeeds. Another possibility would be to take what seems to be a work of literature to be a work of some kind of new graphic art. Again, such a claim cannot be ruled out a priori, but one would have to engage in an act of critical appreciation in considering the experiencing of such a new art form to see if such a claim could seem plausible. For a long time in the twentieth century, it seemed implausible to most people, and to many serious critics, that film or photography could be new art forms. Presumably that question has been settled by the work that has been done in those media.

The obverse of the possibility of a depsychologizing that calls attention to the fictionality of a character would be the phenomenon of characters who seem actually to exceed the works in which they are represented. For figures like Don Juan and Faust and the Wandering Jew, this is almost certainly because they were already legendary before they were represented in their most famous literary incarnations. No doubt an analysis of the specific mythical background of these characters can help explain their cultural resonance at particular moments. They exemplify great themes of human possibility and human limitation. Some of Shakespeare's characters seem to exist at this level, too, and though he used historical and traditional sources for his stories, his characters so far exceed their prototypes in the sources that they seem entirely to be his inventions. Hamlet,

Falstaff, Othello, and Prospero (and others) are inventions who seem almost to justify Harold Bloom's attribution to Shakespeare of the "invention of humanity." In any case his characters have proven useful "to think with," to use the anthropologist's phrase.

Indeed, the sociological or anthropological perspective might be useful in considering the ways in which some literary characters interact with the social reality of the audience of literature. MacIntyre discusses dramatic traditions with a stock of fixed characters in developing a concept of character in relationship to social reality that he distinguishes from social role. Here is the passage:

> [Certain] characters partially define the possibilities of plot and action. To understand them is to be provided with a means of interpreting the behavior of the actors who play them, just because a similar understanding informs the intentions of the actors themselves; and other actors may define their parts with special reference to these central characters. So it is also with certain kinds of social role specific to certain particular cultures. They furnish recognizable characters and the ability to recognize them is socially crucial because a knowledge of the character provides an interpretation of the actions of those individuals who have assumed the character. It does so precisely because those individuals have used the very same knowledge to guide and to structure their behavior. *Characters* specified thus must not be confused with social roles in general. For they are a very special type of social role which places a certain kind of moral constraint on the personality of those who inhabit them in a way in which many other social roles do not. I choose the word "character" for them precisely because of the way it links dramatic and moral associations. (1984: 27)

Characters in Literature and Life

The question of which comes first—the character (in MacIntyre's sense) or the literary representation of it—is not decidable since both the character and the various representations (or incarnations) of it emerge from the same interactive process. That process can be understood only retrospectively, and since it is one of mutual influence, there will be no clear foundational moment for either. The interesting thing for us about MacIntyre's discussion is that he finds examples of such characters both in sociological accounts of contemporary reality and in fiction. The "bureaucratic manager" he finds portrayed in Max Weber's sociology. The character of the "rich aesthete" is realized in two characters, Ralph Touchett and Gilbert Osmond, in Henry James's *Portrait of a Lady* (1881). This doesn't mean that Henry James invented the "rich aesthete" and then some individuals modeled themselves on his invention, nor that James simply represented realistically what he found in his contemporary society. It means that James most significantly discerned and represented, in fictionally "real" individuals, an emerging form of social life and brought it to his and his reader's self-consciousness. The fictional representation of, say, Ralph Touchett is not an abstract moral proposition but a representation of the way an individual life, moved by particular desires and possibilities, can go.

In general, it seems that the products of the practice of narrative fiction can offer readers ways of conceiving the range of human possibilities, as well as the specific pleasures internal to the practice of reading and writing fiction. All of this corresponds roughly to Aristotle's claim that we learn from mimeses and that we enjoy them. There need not be any general conflict between these utilitarian and aesthetic features of the representation of characters in fictional narratives. The relationship between the "external" effect of a work of fiction and its "internal" literary, aesthetic nature is not to be captured by any exceptionless general truths. It would require an argument based on a wide-ranging survey of the history of the European novel to show that the greatest fiction helps form our character or enlarges most our view of the world. Similarly, it would require a critical argument to attempt to establish that the greatest literature need not do this sort of thing. Again, there can be no a priori arguments based on definitions or universal principles about what art or literature can accomplish.

If it is the case that literature (or, more broadly, any art that represents the actions of characters in fictional narratives) is a historically specific social practice that is related to the whole body of social practices, then it seems obvious that it will provide a major example of human self-understanding. Our understanding of who we are as human beings will be partly constituted by our literature—both for the cultural community and for the individual. It is not clear that there is an "ordinary" conception of human character that exists independent of the representation of characters in fictional narratives. Philosophical attempts to give an account of the "true" or "real" nature of the human self have often attempted to abstract entirely from social practices to find some core entity that the self really is. These attempts have been complicated by being involved in metaphysical and religious issues that arise within any framework that draws a sharp ontological distinction between the soul and the body, or the mind and the body.[19] Among philosophers as diverse as Hegel, Marx, Nietzsche, Peirce, James, Dewey, Heidegger, Sartre, Wittgenstein, Cavell, Rorty, Derrida, and many others, there is a general agreement that such attempts must fail. The point of noting this is that if this philosophical consensus (which, of course, is not universal) is correct, then we need to attend both to our ordinary concept of character and the variety of ways in which it can be represented, and also to the ways in which these representations affect character as we see it embodied in other human beings and ourselves. If fictional representations of character can affect the actual character of human beings, we may need to attend more thoughtfully to the general cultural phenomena of what the representations are (on television, in video games, in the tabloid press, in films) that are most powerfully present today. Often these representations of character are replacing those of literature and traditional storytelling.

How does all of what I have been claiming comport with the supposed insights of postmodern critical theory? Though I haven't room to try to answer this question in any systematic way, I do want to make a comment on it in relation to the "deconstructionist movement."[20] In literary criticism, this "movement" was inspired by the early work of Derrida. Richard Rorty draws a clear distinction between Derrida's own philosophical writing and the literary theory that took itself to be inspired by that work. Rorty reads Derrida as extending the antimetaphysical line of modern thought, with an engaging self-awareness of the difficulty of rejecting metaphysics without falling into metaphysical assumptions or claims oneself. Nietzsche thought he could manage such a rejection, but Heidegger finds that Nietzsche is still captured by metaphysical categories. Heidegger in *Sein und Zeit* (1927) thought he could manage it, but Derrida finds that he, too, fails. "Derrida thinks of Heidegger's attempt to express the ineffable as merely the latest and most frantic form of a vain struggle to break out of language by finding words which take their meaning directly from the world, from non-language" (Rorty 1995: 172).

Notice that all of this involves either traditional philosophical issues—the question of being, the nature of human being, the relationship of language to the world—or the "metaphilosophical" issue of how philosophy can encounter those issues. Derrida is often taken to have presented views about the general nature of language; for example, he is supposed to have rejected the possibility of a transcendental signified, a presence outside of language that is the guarantor of meaning. Whether or not Derrida actually held this view and whether this view is correct are not my concerns here. The question is, what implications does this general view have for literary criticism? Once again, I state what seems to be the obvious truth. Anything that is true of all language cannot yield principles of literary criticism useful for understanding particular texts, or ways of representing character, or groups of texts, or literary movements. (The exception might be texts that attempt general characterizations of language.) What we know in advance about all texts cannot help us in understanding the individuality of any particular text. Hence, if there are brilliant deconstructive readings of particular texts (as I believe there are), they cannot be based on some general thesis about language.

Derrida's views seem to belong to a familiar strain of postmodern philosophy (where the phrase "postmodern" means roughly "since Kant"). This is antimetaphysical, above all in being antifoundational. The idea is that language, knowledge, and morality are not secured by some reality that is independent of all of our human practices. Philosophers as various as Hegel, Peirce and Nietzsche, Heidegger and Wittgenstein, Davidson and Derrida might all agree on that. Such a conclusion does indeed mean a rejection of a great deal of the tradition of Western philosophy. Plato and Aristotle, and their inheritor traditions, and modern rationalism and empiricism can all be read as seeking the kind of foundation that this postmodern philosophy denies. However, this does not undercut the possibility of language being meaningful (since it obviously is), nor does it show the impossibility of knowledge (though perhaps what Descartes thought knowledge had to be is impossible) or of morality.[21] If one were to accept Derrida's famously formulated early claim that there is nothing outside the text, what follows is that we would need to redescribe all of the traditional dichotomies (fact/fiction, reality/appearance, true/false, belief/knowledge, writing/speaking, etc.) in terms of our actual human practices, since these are all meaningful contrasts that we do, in fact, use. Recognizing that they may not have the nature that some philosophers have thought does not undercut them. Any view that implied that the role of literary characters in human life is, in general, based on a mistake must be based on a mistake.

NOTES

1. Often, such reflective questions will be pursued under the rubric of "the philosophy of ___." (An exception to this generalization must be made for the field of philosophy itself, which will always include reflection on its own nature.) Physics, for example, does not generally deal with the issue of why we might want to know the truth about the nature of physical reality. The development of the modern university curriculum, hence, incorporates a vast number of assumptions about the values of what is to be studied and how it is to be studied, and these values are usually self-consciously considered (and then only partially) at infrequent moments of curricular revision. Of course, there have been much more frequent occurrences of such occasions in the past 50 years or so in literary studies, and in the humanities more generally, with varying assaults on the "canon" or on "canonicity" and with the importation of literary theory into British and American university departments of literature.

2. I discuss the idea of a "human practice" in some detail below.

3. E.g., in the immense *Literary Theory: An Anthology* (2004) edited by Julie Rivkin and Michael Ryan, though many of the pieces are relevant to issues about character, there is no entry for "character" in the index.

4. One can consult such a discussion, e.g., in Kaufmann 1992.

5. For an extended discussion of Aristotle's view of plot, see chapter 16.

6. *The Oxford English Dictionary* (1971) lists 8 literal and 12 figurative senses of the word "character." The 11th of these 19 senses is the "sum of the moral and mental qualities which distinguish an individual or race, viewed as a homogeneous whole; the individuality impressed by nature and habit on man or nation; mental or moral constitution." The 16th (also figurative) sense is a "person regarded in the abstract as the possessor of specified qualities; a personage, a personality." The 17th (also figurative) sense is a "personality invested with distinctive attributes and qualities, by a novelist or dramatist; also, the personality or 'part' assumed by an actor on the stage."

7. E.g., Nisbet 1985 includes essays by Winckelmann, Lessing, Hamann, Herder, and Goethe, in addition to the Schiller essay. It was to this ongoing conversation that Nietzsche's *Birth of Tragedy* (1872) was a contribution.

8. The quoted phrase is Carlyle's, famously used by M. H. Abrams as the title of his study of European romantic literature. This book is discussed in the text that follows.

9. For a detailed discussion and critique of this Hegelian view, see Bates 1996.

10. See Darnton 1984, whose notes contain numerous references to the literature on the eighteenth-century reader response to Rousseau.

11. Some of these matters are discussed in Kristeller 1965.

12. Oral language always precedes written language. Presumably, Jacques Derrida was acquainted with this well-known fact and was criticizing what he took to be illegitimate philosophical inferences from it that had privileged "speaking" over "writing" because of a presumed guarantee of linguistic reference by the "presence" of the referent. We need not make that presumption.

13. For an extended series of arguments in favor of this claim, see MacIntyre 1984, chap. 8.

14. There is no space to review the past two centuries of debate on this topic with contributors such as Marx, Flaubert, Tolstoy, Lukács, Sartre, Camus, Iris Murdoch, and dozens of others. There has been an explosion of interest by analytical philosophers of art in the topic of the ethical criticism of art and literature. This has been nicely described in Carroll 2000.

15. An interesting discussion of this can be found in Ricoeur 1992.

16. Here I am thinking of such works as Eldridge 1989 and Nussbaum 1992 and 2001. In my view, the most insightful work on the understanding of fictional characters and their relationship to their audience is in Stanley Cavell's two books on genres of Hollywood film, *Pursuits of Happiness* (1981) and *Contesting Tears* (1997). His recent publication of *Cities of Words* (2004) provides a specific linking of particular films with particular central texts of the Western philosophical tradition—many of the same films that are discussed in the genre books are given extended discussion.

17. Harold Bloom has famously identified this as the anxiety of influence, and he reads it in Freudian terms. Such readings may be persuasive when critically articulated in particular cases, but if the thesis is generalized to all poets or writers, it becomes unpersuasive unless it is converted into a tautology by using it to pick out "the" tradition.

18. Of course, the idea of such a poll is somewhat bizarre, and it was used as a kind of advertising ploy for Random House. The point, though, is that the result of the poll, even for those who disagree with the ranking, could not be unexpected or totally inappropriate. Compare that outcome to the results of an online reader poll organized at the same time that found three of Ayn Rand's novels to be among the seven greatest of the twentieth century.

19. A very useful account of the development of ideas about the self in European modernity is given in Taylor 1989.

20. This phrase is itself problematic. I adapt it from Rorty 1995. Insofar as there was such a movement in literary criticism, it took itself to be inspired by the work of Derrida, who claimed neither to have invented a "theory" nor to have established a movement. I use a number of Rorty's characterizations of Derrida in what follows since I am not dealing with Derrida directly but rather with the issue of what can be properly inferred for literary criticism from what were widely regarded as his views on language and textuality.

21. Here I join what Rorty (1995: 175) calls a "somewhat milder line of criticism of Derrida"—milder, that is, than that of those who take him to be a linguistic idealist. In

fact, I take this milder line not necessarily to be criticism of Derrida at all, but rather to be critical of how he has been interpreted. I think this despite the fact that John Searle, whom Rorty presents as the example of this line, did indeed have many substantive criticisms of Derrida.

REFERENCES

Abrams, M. H. (1971). *Natural Supernaturalism: Tradition and Revelation in Romantic Literature*. New York: Norton.

Aristotle. (1958). *On Poetry and Style* (G. M. A. Grube, trans.). Indianapolis: Library of Liberal Arts.

Bates, S. (1996). "The Mind's Horizon." *In* R. Eldridge (ed.), *Beyond Representation*. Cambridge: Cambridge University Press.

Blundell, M. W. (1992). "*Ethos* and *Dianoia* Reconsidered." *In* A. Rorty (ed.), *Essays on Aristotle's Poetics*. Princeton: Princeton University Press.

Carroll, N. (2000). " Art and Ethical Criticism: An Overview of Recent Directions of Research." *Ethics* 110, 2 (January), 351–87.

Darnton, R. (1984). "Readers Respond to Rousseau: The Fabrication of Romantic Sensitivity." *In* Darnton, *The Great Cat Massacre*. New York: Basic Books.

Eldridge, R. (1989). *On Moral Personhood: Philosophy Literature, Criticism and Self-Understanding*. Chicago: University of Chicago Press.

Hegel, G. W. F. (1962). *Hegel: On Tragedy* (A. Paolucci and H. Paolucci, eds.). New York: Harper.

Hornblower, S., and A. Spanforth. (1996). *The Oxford Classical Dictionary* (3rd ed.). New York: Oxford University Press.

Janson, W. H. (1978). *History of Art* (2nd ed.). New York: Prentice-Hall and Harry Abrams.

Kaufmann, W. (1992). *Tragedy and Philosophy*. Princeton: Princeton University Press.

Kierkegaard, S. (1959). *Either/Or* (vol. 1; H. A. Johnson, ed.; D. F. and L. M. Swenson, trans.). Princeton: Princeton University Press. (Original work published in 1843.)

——. (1968). *Concluding Unscientific Postscript* (D. F. Swenson and W. Lowrie, trans.). Princeton: Princeton University Press. (Original work published in 1846.)

Kristeller, O. (1965). "The Modern System of the Arts." *In* Kristeller, *Renaissance Thought II: Papers on Humanism and the Arts*, pp. 163–227. New York: Harper.

Lewis, P. (1998). "*Ulysses* on Top among 100 Greatest Novels." *New York Times*, July 20.

MacIntyre, A. (1984). *After Virtue* (2nd ed.). Notre Dame: University of Notre Dame Press.

Nietzsche, F. (1992). *The Genealogy of Morals*, Section 13, "Second Essay." *In* W. Kaufmann (ed. and trans.), *Basic Writing of Nietzsche*. New York: Modern Library. (Original work published in 1887.)

Nisbet, H. B., ed. (1985). *German Aesthetic and Literary Criticism*. Cambridge: Cambridge University Press.

Nussbaum, M. (1992). *Love's Knowledge*. Oxford: Oxford University Press.

——. (2001). *The Fragility of Goodness* (2nd ed.). Cambridge: Cambridge University Press.

Ricoeur, P. (1992). *Oneself as Another.* Chicago: University of Chicago Press.

Rorty, R. (1995). "Deconstruction." *In* R. Selden (ed.), *The Cambridge History of Literary Criticism* (vol. 8). Cambridge: Cambridge University Press.

Schiller, F. (1985). "On Naive and Sentimental Poetry." *In* H. B. Nisbet (ed.), *German Aesthetic and Literary Criticism*, pp. 180–232. Cambridge: Cambridge University Press. (Original work published in 1795–96).

Sutherland, K. (2006). "On Looking into Chapman's *Emma.*" *Times Literary Supplement,* January 13, 12.

Taylor, C. (1989). *Sources of the Self: The Making of Modern Identity.* Cambridge, Mass.: Harvard University Press.

CHAPTER 18

......

STYLE

......

CHARLES ALTIERI

If my remarks do not bear a stamp which marks them as
mine,—I do not wish to lay any further claim to them as
my property.

—Ludwig Wittgenstein, *Philosophical Investigations*

Artists never fail to resent the fact that they have a style.
(Which is not to say that they wouldn't also resent the
allegation that they didn't have one.)

—Richard Wollheim, "Style in Painting"

Foregrounding the "how" invites the grammar of "as."
"Style as the Man"

—Charles Altieri[1]

I do not think anyone in the heyday of modernism could have imagined how little
style matters now as a topic in academic discourse in the arts and in philosophy.[2]
Of course, they also could not have imagined that ideals of impersonality would
become "the death of the author" or that ideals of intuition and resistance to universals would become a demand that works of art honor every mode of otherness
and resist hierarchy at all costs. Nor could they have imagined having to figure
out why the concept of style might still matter—for literary study, in particular,
but also for how literary study might influence the application of the concept in
other disciplines. But given current trends in criticism, it is imperative now to ask

the Wittgensteinian question, What do we lose if we are blind to style or unable to establish a workable concept of style as an aesthetic means of individuation? What would we not be able to appreciate, and therefore what concepts and models would be lacking to us, when we try to characterize the values at stake in the arts?

I am overgeneralizing. Not all concepts of style have gone out of style. Style as fashion retains a strong hold on contemporary imaginations—but as something embraced and as something that dominates the individual agent. But by some academic version of Gresham's law, these concepts have had the power to drive out other work on style. They either deny the significance of individual agency or reduce that individuality to stylization while ignoring the more complex and elaborate modes of individual purposiveness that style constitutes in ambitious literary work as well as work in the other arts. Now, according to an article in the *Wall Street Journal*, capitalism's endless inventiveness has produced "lifestyle designers" who advise about "lifestyle goods" such as jewelry and furniture, help "those who have made unexpected business fortunes and don't have the time or natural inclination to conquer the basics of gracious living," train persons in the visible choices that will earn them kudos for stylishness, and plan events where one can exhibit those choices and the character traits that are designed for them. The *Journal* reports that "the pressure to be stylish has reached the point where even some ordinary working professionals are hiring designers," and it lists five of those designers with their hourly rates (Hughes 2005).[3]

While fashion is probably the most important feature making it difficult now to talk about style as a distinctive feature of high art and ambitious writing, it is decidedly not the most important one in creating internal difficulties for anyone foolhardy enough to turn to that topic. Those difficulties emerge largely from the fact that such discussions follow a period in which the study of style flourished in both philosophy and the arts. If we take up the topic, we have to account for why decades of intense labor left us only with this contentious and confused mélange of concepts incapable of producing adequate agreement except on the impossibility of agreement. So it is not surprising that even critics today who are willing to learn the necessary linguistics tend not to be interested in the study of literary style because they have no operating concepts they can trust.[4]

The flourishing I refer to occurred in the United States after the Second World War until about 1990 as such German writers as Leo Spitzer and Erich Auerbach became available and as linguistics went through several stages of seeming to offer the humanities new paradigms for speculative work. As one measure of the age, three major anthologies on literary style came out within three years, 1967 to 1970 (Chatman and Levin 1967; Love and Payne 1969; Freeman 1970). Other measures might be art historical work by such figures as Meyer Schapiro, Ernst Gombrich, and David Summers and the theories of style produced by philosophers such as Nelson Goodman, Arthur Danto, Berel Lang, Jenefer Robinson, and Richard Wollheim. Since this heritage still affords the only framework for contemporary engagements with the topic, I spend considerable time here outlining why I think the lines of reasoning explored there have not born much fruit. Only then can

I even try to propose an alternative approach to literary style that may avoid some of the difficulties pervading this heritage by developing two basic claims—that style be seen as purposive activity inseparable from the aesthetic shaping of the work as a whole, and that the best way of modeling this activity is to take the foregrounding of style as what I shall call "a demonstrative speech act." The demonstrative is a category describing what can be achieved by foregrounding individual activity within language, and so it contrasts with J. L. Austin's performatives that accomplish something by invoking institutional practices.

In all the relevant disciplines, theory of style after the Second World War had as its first priority to establish significance for the artists' individual manners of making meaningful work. This, after all, was the great age for ideology stressing the individual. For the first half of the twentieth century the prevailing models had been Hegelian. What mattered then were the differences making possible what Schapiro called "a manifestation of the culture as a whole, the visible sign of its unity" and "the inner form of collective thinking and feeling" (1998: 143). Each age and each culture had dominant forms of expression, and one culture in each epoch would most fully realize the possibilities of spirit that could appear in its stage of development. In literary history, there were groundbreaking studies of the differences between the Ciceronian styles that dominated the Renaissance and the plain style accompanying the scientific revolution, with its preference for paratactic rather than hypotactic syntax and its efforts to supplant rhetorical afflatus with concrete description. Even more influential was the work of art historians such as Heinrich Wölfflin, who developed five compelling general indices of differences in style between "the [classic] art of the Cinquecento and the [baroque] art of the Seicento": "the development from linear to painterly," "the development from plane to recession," "the development from closed to open form," "the development from multiplicity to unity," and "the absolute and relative clarity of the subject" (Wölfflin 1932).[5] Wölfflin even took these categories as a reason to break with the Hegelian model of the spirit's progress. Instead, he took a hermeneutic position honoring each culture's distinctive possibilities and regarding normative comparison between cultures as "arbitrary."

When this generalizing work prevailed, the promise of illuminating forces and patterns basic to cultural life made it seem trivial to insist on paying careful attention to what distinguished an individual style from others within the same general dispensation. But the excitement could not be sustained. Critics soon emerged to accuse such work of being merely taxonomic and so, in the words of Louis T. Milic, stuck in "specious and minor similarities among authors"; such work takes us away from "what is really significant, the author's own peculiarity, his difference from his contemporaries, which is what is truly his style" (1973: 450).[6]

But calling for attention to individuality is very different from putting that study on secure grounds. Studies of individual style face two obvious problems. First, how central a role will one give stylistics—the analysis of style on the basis of principles developed within linguistics—in determining what claims we make about the manner of the author's work in producing a distinctive aesthetic experience?

Linguistics and aesthetics give quite different accounts of authorial agency and have quite different disciplinary constraints about what counts as significant interpretation. Second, exactly how does a writer characteristically manipulate his or her medium? That is, how does the writer make local choices and produce variants capable of sharpening or realizing some particular experience?[7] But having names for these features does not help a great deal in deciding how to characterize any particular aspects of writing. Linguistics affords statistical or formal models that are simply not equipped to characterize the modes of intentionality that characterize individual purposiveness.[8] But without specifying and analyzing repeated linguistic elements, we have no way to determine which features of a text's language count as significant in shaping a style for the work and for the author. Linguistic patterns by themselves may be empty, and aesthetic judgment vain, without a foundation in systematic description.

These problems affect any discourse on style. They were exacerbated by the fact that in this postwar period three major models emerged for determining what counts as the force of style in particular literary works, and all three raise serious problems.[9] Most studies of individual style early in this period were based on the idea of deviance. Writers were seen as breaking norms and making such breaks the basis of effects that were unavailable within the norms. But what makes either a linguistic norm or its breaking count aesthetically? Did most people have to use the expression to make it a norm, or was a norm determined by a society or moment in time? Or perhaps the authors themselves established norms from which they could then break with significant force. And does the breaking of a norm count as a stylistic device or as a means of sharpening content—since style and content have a way of folding into each other? Then there is the persistent problem that if we try to make the relevant distinctions on an ad hoc basis, we in effect admit that we are only impressionistic critics rather than linguists seeking a coherent theory.

The next two waves in studies of literary style turned to more flexible linguistic principles more sensitive to aesthetic interests, but ironically, they also selected more difficult linguistic methodologies that critics were reluctant to take on without firmer guarantees about their value for aesthetic and for existential questions. First, there were several ways of shifting away from deviance as the determination of style to a stress on how the writer deployed patterns and also strategically broke from them. Roman Jakobson provided what would become the motto for these approaches when he defined the poetic function in language use as projecting "the principle of equivalence from the axis of selection into the axis of combination" (1966: 358). The axis of selection determines choices exclusively by considering their effect on the message conveyed. When agents want to create a work that has a distinctive body or materiality in its own right, they turn to the axis of combination, mining these resources for internal relations that it affords. But while Jakobson's method considerably thickened our sense of what style is, it did little for the ability of stylistics to deepen our appreciation of the uses to which style was being put. As is evident from his classic essay with Claude Lévi-Strauss on Baudelaire's "Les Chats," the axis of combination affords virtually infinite possible connections. So stylistics still has to be supplemented by claims about purposiveness that pull against the purity of sheer linguistic description and, again, that license charges of impressionism.

The third powerful of model of stylistic analysis was more promising because it relied on transformational grammar and hence could focus on two distinctive levels of style: deep structure and surface structure. This focus concentrates on features that from the start are basic units of meaning; one does not have to project significance on to linguistic elements that typically do not function semantically. Because there are deep structures to sentences, and variations on how to employ those structures, the choices composing a style are active selections that directly shape how one forms meanings. The deep structure might be noun phrase, adverb, verb, and noun phrase: "John quickly finished his work." Repeated variations on this kind of structure, say, passive constructions or more elaborate adverbial structures, would reveal particular habits of thinking that constitute how a person handles the axes of selection that language affords. Studying such selections "implements" better stylistic descriptions, "better in that they isolate more fully, economically, and demonstrably the linguistic features to which a perceptive reader responds in sensing one style to be different from another" (Ohmann 1970: 268). And by demonstrating how meanings get made, theorists such as Richard Ohmann could insist that style is not ornament but a display or refinement of "conceptual orientation, a preferred way of organizing experience" (1970: 271). With transformational grammar, one could use formal models rather than impressionistic ones to do much of the interpretive work of explaining how works cultivate distinctive styles.

But does it suffice to treat style in terms of the cognitive orientations providing preferred ways of organizing experience? One might notice that this model will have difficulty distinguishing dispositional from occasional aspects of style. That means it will have difficulty identifying the most dramatic or climactic individual passages. And that means there will always be a substantial gulf between the study of style that explains how experiences are organized and those that explain how writing intensifies and deepens those experiences. Ohmann's cognitivist orientation makes style too pragmatic by emphasizing only cognition and ignoring how it can involve other values not directly cognitive, such as rhythmic values or modes of engaging affect. He is not interested in reasons for making that pursue aesthetic rather than cognitive values. And he fails to provide a significant dramatic context for such individual makings because he proposes no threatening other, no sense that an individual style is always at risk of becoming merely *a* style and so involves struggles to establish agency that extend well beyond the cognitive.

While all these models specify useful ways to look at uses of language, none of them seems to me to provide a sufficient picture of the kinds of acts individuals perform by foregrounding what style can do. While they tell us how style works, they fail to articulate sufficiently why we might care about that working. We have to look to philosophy for full engagement with issues of how to value what agents do with the medium.[10] Consider, for example, the difference that is established by Lang's elemental definition of style as "the instance of an act that manner qualifies" (1998: 318; see also Lang 1983). He concentrates our attention on the actions that provide purposiveness for what language shows, and therefore he can establish ways of moving beyond lists of stylistic traits to a dramatic notion of style as the manner modifying what might count as matter for an audience.

But what are the sources of dramatic manner, and what is its value? To address these questions, we need deeper accounts of human subjecthood and subjectivity, so I explore probably the two most representative ways of talking about individual style in philosophy so that I can sketch a third alternative: I contrast Danto's emphasis on style as the presentation of a way of seeing, with Wollheim's case for style as ultimately a way of demonstrating feelings that have "psychological reality." Then I argue that neither pays sufficient attention to how artists and writers emphasize sheer self-reflexive mastery of the medium as the vehicle for a wide variety of purposes. I want to connect the simple fact of having to struggle for recognizable stylistic effects not swallowed by cultural generalizations to the deployment of manner to modify the matter in many registers. For the basic problem with prevailing views of style is that they are not sufficiently abstract on how style achieves the force it does to allow themselves sufficient variety on the uses to which that force can be put.

I begin with Danto because his is the most straightforward version of seeking individuality and because his is the most egregious effort to align the individuals with their cultures without acknowledging any dialectical struggle. His argument begins with what seems a useful separation of style from mere "manner," so that he can cast style as a distinctive way that individuals address history from within (1981: 200). Then, it seems, he has a choice: he could say that style is a way of employing the resources of manner, or he could try to stress aspects of style that are quite separate from manner. He chooses the second, with unfortunate results, for this denial of dialectic requires him to argue that "style is what is done without the mediation of art or knowledge" (201). And that decision forces him to associate style with something that is not based on traditions of making or modes of thinking. This, I think, is the logic that underlies his identifying style with seeing how one is seeing: "What, then, is interesting and essential in art is the spontaneous ability the artist has of enabling us to see his way of seeing the world—not just the world as if the painting were like a window, but the world as given by him" (207). We are back with Ohmann's cognitive orientation, but without the formal method.

This emphasis on the individual spontaneously making visible his way of seeing allows Danto two advantages. He can easily equate his agent, stripped of art and thought, with other historical agents in the same period. The stress on seeing in a certain way makes it feasible to identify individual manner with general manner while being confident that there is something left to individual difference. And because style becomes inherently self-reflexive, he can make style the measure of value. He can turn to the famous statement "style is the man himself" and flesh out how "the structure of a style is like the structure of a personality":

> It is not merely what a man represents, but it is the way in which he represents it, which has to be invoked to explain the structures of his mind....Of course we speak as well of the style of a period or a culture, but this will refer us ultimately to shared representational modes which define what it is to belong to a period. The conceptual structures of periods and persons are, I proposed above, sufficiently similar that we may speak of a period as having an inside and an outside, a kind of surface available to the historian and a kind of inwardness belonging to those who live in the period in question, which is pretty much like the inward and outward aspects of the human personality. (1981: 207, 205)

"The greatness of the work" becomes "the greatness of the representation the work makes material. If style is the man, greatness of style is greatness of person" (207).

But if style is the man, style affords only a thin and depleted version of the man when it is based only on seeing, especially on seeing that is "without the mediation of art or knowledge." The structure of style is not the structure of personality but, at best, the structure of chosen constructs of personality. Compare Danto on style is the man to Wittgenstein's treatment of the same topic: " 'Le style c'est l'homme,' 'Le style c'est l'homme méme.' The first expression has cheap epigrammatic brevity. The second, correct version opens up quite a different perspective. It says that a man's style is a picture [*Bild*] of him" (Wittgenstein 1980: 78).

Danto wants to naturalize style by rendering it as fundamental to experience as a way of seeing might be. But at best, this claim is circular: all style has to be configured to what can be claimed as a kind of seeing. To get that claim to work, Danto has to neglect how style can establish modes of hearing and feeling and thinking. Wittgenstein, on the other hand, wants to distinguish two aspects of individuality—the way we identify the agent and the way we project the agent identifying self-reflexively with the possibility of willing or affirming that agency—hence his stress on the significance of the reflexive "meme." That second model entails not separating style from the mediation of art and knowledge but rather treating style as the mediation by which art and knowledge take concrete distinctive shape.

Danto's limitations create the challenge of our having to characterize style as something more capacious and differently self-reflexive than making visible one's own ways of seeing. This is precisely what Wollheim offers, at least for painting, so I turn to his work as providing almost the opposite case for how individual style might be envisioned. Wollheim does not locate style in any specific model of mental activity like Danto's seeing (which is doomed to vacillate between literal and metaphoric uses). Rather, the fundamental feature of style is that a variety of activities all have a distinctive "psychological reality." What matters is how artworks make specific investments in particular intentional states and corresponding attitudes explicit. I am not sure quite how to translate what Wollheim means by "psychological reality," but I am sure that this reality emerges because style manifests a commitment on the part of a subject to what is being created. That is why Wollheim is such a virulent opponent of any taxonomic approach to style, since that kind of approach can cannot handle the affective intensities and corporeal specificity that individual manner produces as thematizing intentions.[11] "Individual style has reality" because its possession makes a difference for a painter. The reality that difference makes is psychological because "the difference that having a style makes is a difference in the mind of the painter....An individual style is acquired through being formed..., not learnt" (Wollheim 1995: 41). Learning may play a part in that formation, but the artist is individual to the degree that he or she does something with that learning.

Viewers can locate this individual psychological reality by tracing the emergence of two distinctive practical capacities: the first, the "schemata of the artist's style," consists in segmenting or conceptualizing the elements of painting in a certain preferred way; the second "consists in evolving rules or principles for operating with those schemata" (1995: 42) in order to give shape to them and to form internal relations for those shapes. Taken together, these capacities "encapsulate" style in how the artist's body appears in the work as the fine-tuning of the eye. Style, then, "puts within reach of a painter the fulfillment of his intentions" (1995: 43). Fulfillment is not merely making work that is "*suggestive of*, or *evidential for*, his intentions" (1995: 43). Rather, it affords the kind of realization that allows us to speak of the expressive force possessed by the work. Style brings to bear "figurative elements: that is, elements that not only require for their detection seeing in [which is the process by which visual art represents aspects of the world] but are then identified through concepts" (1995: 44) that involve tonalities and hence expressive force. Style is what allows the particular work exemplary status as the actual manifestation of a particular way a mind can be invested in a segment of the world.[12]

But Wollheim pays a considerable price for giving style this kind of psychological reality, for either style reinforces the strict identity conditions established by the artist's schemata, or it encounters traumatic conflict where its ability to pervade bodily manner creates total crises for that identity. Such conflict emerges when a painter's style becomes threatened by a fascination with another foreign but powerfully inviting style. When Titian submits to the muscular style of Michelangelo or when Picasso enters another stage in his metamorphoses, "[t]he artist's own style and those around it will be conceptualized as bits or parts or products of the body, and by this stage the scene is set for any one of the great dramas of projection, introjection, projective identification that deep crisis precipitates" (Wollheim 1995: 49). Only psychoanalysis then possesses the necessary methodological resources to explain the damage and make efforts to repair that damage.

Wollheim is reduced to these two options because he insisted "one artist, one style" (1995: 49): "[T]he characteristics associated with individual styles do not alter," even if art historians "will come up with formulations that fall short of this ideal" so they differ among themselves in describing those styles (1987: 26). Cases when one is tempted to challenge that equation fall for Wollheim into one of three categories: instances of the prestylistic, the poststylistic, or the extrastylistic (29–32). So, when differences emerge, the critic has either to posit crises or to argue that the case is a case of the failure of style to emerge at all. Such moves obviously tempt one to circular arguments, since it is tempting to treat any problem with one's own account—of style and of identity—as the result of style not being fully present.[13]

The result is an approach that can be as reductive as Danto's equating style with a stable mode of seeing. Wollheim's need to populate the art world with "non-styles" derives primarily from two features of his argument—one involving too strong an assertion of identity, and the other a relatively inflexible psychology. Unlike Danto, he can capture the moi-même that makes style self-reflexive and perhaps involves something like will. But because he needs to base identity on something as persistent as schemata, he repudiates the possibility that style can actually become a means of imaginative flexibility, allowing or even encouraging experiments in what manners one can identify with. He treats changes in habits of investment as only causes for a sense of crises. The work of style has to adapt long-standing investments rather than provide a sense of discovering new possibilities in scenes and objects that call upon somewhat different dispositional traits and libidinal economies, or that call on letting the making dictate what dispositional traits emerge. For Wollheim, schemata shape what making can be, thereby blocking the possibility that style itself can adjust to concrete questions about how best to realize an experience or produce distinctive affective force.

Danto's style as seeing provides cognitive force but cannot account for any individual psychological factors, while Wollheim's emphasis on style as psychological reality traps artists within schemata and minimizes the force of the occasional adjustments they make in that very sense of identity in order to realize specific aspects of experiences they care about. Therefore, a third alternative is necessary that can be flexible about the modes of purposiveness—practical and psychological—that can be embodied by the foregrounding of labor made visible as style. In my view, this flexibility can be created if we are highly abstract, or perhaps metapsychological, about the basic satisfaction for a writer or artist in developing a style for a given work, for then we can acknowledge several different ways this satisfaction can be produced, and we can indicate some of the values realized by adapting manner to matter. So, I propose going to the level of abstraction characterizing Wittgenstein's version of the "moi-même" that attention to style allows an agent. This moi-même factor points to how individual style can function as the self-conscious celebration of the dialectical work of making a manner that cannot be subsumed under general styles. And dwelling on this level of self-consciousness seems to distinguish having a style from merely displaying linguistic habits, because style becomes an aspect of an authorial act with shaping intentions and with a sense of effects the style might produce in its audience.

In addition, Wittgenstein's formulation helps us see how the manner of a work can incorporate something like a willing, a self-reflexive taking of responsibility for how art links to life. The relevant means of making can range from various ways of producing the surprise of defamiliarization to emphasizing how the art medium can produce vivacious and precise renderings of experience. Taking of responsibility then extends that activity in two ways. Obviously, it stages the self as feeling that its concerns are represented within the manner displayed. Then, because the manner becomes objective through the making, style becomes a force that takes on a kind of social existence. The taking of responsibility is not a mere subjective claim but an accomplished fact because it enacts what ownership of one's actions entails. Style makes ownership not an abstract claim to a right but an overt exemplifying of a path for realizing values for anyone who cares to identify with it. Conceiving the topic in this way also allows us to move from painterly to literary examples as the strongest evidence for the complex judgments style invites of its audience.

Danto and Wollheim both seem to me to naturalize style. That is, they directly connect it to certain cognitive or psychological traits that become conditions of experience antecedent to the work. Therefore, these philosophers cannot sufficiently attend to the sheer madeness, the sheer production of the differences from ordinary practices that make art and artifice such strikingly different phenomena from other kinds of experiences, yet they clearly are right that style is not just artifice. Individual style has at least two complex continuities with the world available for experience: it has qualities of giveness, and hence of limitation, that it shares with how we experience our bodies and our situations in the world; and it has qualities of expansiveness of spirit, of making available a purposiveness that distinguishes, concretizes, realizes, and intensifies what is available for experience. How can we conceptually capture both dimensions?

First, we have to recognize that individual style in art involves the moi-même because it is a fundamentally second-order phenomenon. Style is a mode of realizing particular first-order qualities. It is also a mode of taking second-order responsibility for how those qualities are realized. Speaking of style as a mode of making helps us to account for this taking of responsibility because it avoids collapsing style into a feature of the content of the work and insists on the author's purposive activity. Style becomes a dramatic phenomenon in its own right. We set terms like purpose and purposiveness against terms for the difficulty that these terms face—difficulties caused by the limitations of the medium, or by the triumphs of past practitioners in the medium, or by what it takes to defamiliarize or otherwise surprise audiences in relation to the experience being addressed.[14]

Let me describe individual style, then, as the statement by the artist that "this is what I can make to bring about the kind of presence for the object so as it to give it expressive force in the world that goes beyond art." The expressive force is established by equating style with specific powers of seeing, or cognizing, or realizing one's way of making investments. But if we see that these first-order relations have the task of fleshing out a second-order domain established simply by the overt madeness of the object, we can both honor the sheer labor of style and recognize the variety of terms that are required to establish how that labor affects what we can experience through the made object. Style is not just seeing or cognizing, but the objectifying of possibilities of seeing that a person wants to convey as mattering for an audience.

The best way I know to keep visible both first- and second-order dimensions of literary style is to develop the possibility that there is a significant category of speech act that theorists have yet to elaborate, primarily because it gets subordinated to the performative. I refer to what I will call the "demonstrative," a concept that applies not only to style but to a variety of ways that we deal with showing how things are possible or how things might be accomplished. Let us take as demonstratives those speech acts that refer to themselves as displaying something significant that can modify behavior or instruct about the resources of a model.

Typical demonstrative speech acts include instances of the following language games (that can occur by gesture as well as in actual speech):

"This is done like this."
"Try it to perform the piece in this way."
"The story of that can be told in this way."
"In this kind of situation I am likely to respond in this way."
"In this language the phrase is usually used in this way."
"This is what I can do when I get a chance."
"It hurts here not there," or more generally, "this is how I feel."

These examples function in one or more of three related ways—to emphasize how actions can be accomplished, to clarify various uses of things (especially uses of language), and to provide a means for agents to display various capacities, especially capacities for feeling and for making. Demonstratives do not propose assertions that something is true but instead show that something is happening or is possible.[15] The fundamental demonstrative claim is that I am showing you how I do something so that you can do it or at least understand how it is done. Style, then, becomes the display of possible uses of a medium—as innovation in relation to tradition and as shaping possible ways that manner effects matter.

Why not just treat style as evoking a performative speech act, and so as the performative dimension of imaginative activity? The idea of performativity gives a rationale for attending to manner and, more important, marks a crucial difference between activity that is essentially geared toward description or argument and activity that is aware of what can accomplished by an emphasis on the doing. But there are at least two reasons for rejecting this model. First, Austin's treatment of the performative emphasizes social functions that are almost the exact opposite of anything one might want to claim for style. The performative matters less as a model of doing or making in its own right than as a model for how that doing might be "felicitous" and so satisfy certain social conditions that make the speech act count in an official or at least in an interpersonal context. Saying "With this ring I thee wed" is a paradigm for doing something in language if one meets the appropriate conditions. In such situations, it is crucial that what one intends simply does not matter. If you satisfy the conditions and speak the words, you are married.

Therefore, my first reason is negative—Austin's concept of the performative has insufficient scope to handle many of the things we do with language, especially the things that individualize utterances. My second reason is positive: if we call attention to demonstratives as speech acts, we can substantially reduce the burden on the concept of the performative to cover all emphases on what an activity does rather than on what meanings describe. And then we can see such philosophers as Jacques Derrida and Judith Butler who complain about Austin's narrowness as if they were reenacting how Kant's heirs responded to his speculations about the thing-in-itself. Kant's heirs were convinced that such a powerful notion could not just be a limit concept but had significant positive ontological and religious work to do. In both cases, the contemporary and the romantic, the eagerness to make concepts do too much work ends up substituting vague and ambiguous concepts for ones that are extremely useful precisely because of the constraints that could be put upon them. Positing the demonstrative allows us means of characterizing two contrasting ways of acting in language, and hence two ways of framing the constative assertions concerned with observation and description. One way of acting manages affairs by means of acts in language; the other makes particular displays offering examples of what can be done with words.

The demonstrative is irreducibly a term stressing an action being carried out for a purpose or, in the case of aesthetic orientations, for a display of what purposiveness can establish. Where the performative defines an agent as satisfying certain conditions, the demonstrative presents the deed of making or offering a model. Affectively, one demonstrates what one is feeling; semantically, one provides a model for how some aspect of the language can operate; and stylistically, one exemplifies possible powers of a medium to intensify or realize what the agent is engaging. By using the category of the demonstrative, we show how intentional qualities can be attributed to making and how that intentionality can be conveyed so as to afford possible identifications. And we can at least introduce questions about how and why responsibility is taken for what style accomplishes.

Finally, stressing the force of the demonstrative also clearly connects style in art with the values people have placed on style in other domains—from Baudelaire's dandy to the craftspeople idealized by William Morris. The demonstrative makes clear the possible connection style affords between pleasure and labor. Labor becomes a means of making articulate the purposiveness of a given activity, so labor becomes the necessary means for various kinds of satisfaction that communication and personalization afford. More specifically, most acts of foregrounding style promise a distinctive mode of being within social space because pleasure becomes wound up in the activity itself rather than only in any practical results the activity might produce. In talking about style in art, we are perforce talking about how the making of objects foregrounds what subjects can do to shape the very objects that display their powers. And we are examining how that shaping invites our taking on possibilities of seeing in, seeing as, and seeing otherwise. The work demonstrates the making of differences that can make a difference, if only in the attitudes we take toward the experiences engaged by the artist.

This theorizing begs for examples, so I illustrate the utility of my model by exploring three quite different ways poets invite us to attribute purposiveness to what is foregrounded about the making of the text. These examples should at least show why it matters for theory to stress how making is clearly a second-order operation that then leads us to examine and test what is being demonstrated. (I do not take any examples from prose fiction or drama because they would take too long to develop. But to the degree that such texts emphasize the labor of making, they also function as similar demonstratives—either locally in specific paragraphs or structurally to give the entire narrative demonstrative force.)

My first example, from Alexander Pope, highlights the possibility that the manner of a work need have nothing directly to do with the psychological reality of a specific person, and everything to do with sharpening or realizing of what is asserted as content. Pope identifies style with purposive thinking, and he treats purposive thinking as necessarily turning the empirical subject into a subject completely invested in producing "[w]hat oft was thought, but ne'er so well expressed" (2001: line 298). The other two examples will become progressively more expressive of distinctively subjective processes—the first as an elaborately self-conscious identification with traditional lyricism put to expressive purposes, and the second as an effort to have style serve as affirming the power of will within an overall representation of utterly bleak conditions. In each case, the moi-même of individual style opens into an invitation for all to see and think as the artist does in articulating what certain choices make possible.

The first example literally speaks for itself by demonstrating what it also asserts. These lines are from Pope's "Essay on Criticism" (1711):

> While expletives their feeble aid do join
> And ten low words oft creep in one dull line
> While they ring round the same unvaried chimes
> With sure returns of still expected rhymes... (2007: 14, ll. 346–49)

On one level, these lines can be read as instances of Pope's basic disposition toward style. Pope accepts the heroic couplet as period style. But that mode takes on in his hands a characteristic swiftness of association, intricacy of balance, and precision of phrase, all delivered as vehicles for a biting wit. And he is an absolute master of varying the couplet to emphasize different weights of words and phrases, so that moments of flat sing-song iambics are almost nonexistent. Yet to remain with such generalizations is to ignore how Pope rises to individual occasions by having his making sharpen our focus.

Each line seems to choose a different aural key, especially in the contrast between the *e*'s dominating the first line quoted and the sonorous *o*'s marking the center of the next one. Then there is the semantic register. "Do" in the first line exemplifies the addition of expletives; the "ten words" in the second literally creep in one dull line because the line is uncharacteristically without internal variety; and the last two lines provide the expected rhymes they refer to, although they also stage those rhymes within elegantly balanced phrases. In other words, the triumph of style here in how Pope makes the language refers to itself, to its own manner of making choices about diction. This rhetoric exemplifies exemplification. Yet at the same time as the rhetoric exemplifies the vices to which it refers, it also insists on the power of poetry to contain such criticism while celebrating its own absolute opposition to the world of hackneyed expression.

This sense of poetry's triumph over the spirit of dullness tempts me to invoke the concept of will. Style clearly moves us out of the empirical order of description into the order of avowals. Yet these avowals cannot be treated as simply the expressions of affective attitudes toward habits of verse making. Rather, they self-consciously celebrate what is involved in being able to treat an attitude as one's own while literally confining the self to sheer miming. Will here is the affirmation of the ability to render common sense uncommon without denying the responsibility to orient that freedom to public use.

William Butler Yeats's "A Drinking Song" (1910) puts style to work in another kind of situation where it is asked both to realize and to transform a quintessential popular form:

> Wine comes in at the mouth
> And love comes in at the eye;
> That's all we shall know of truth
> Before we grow old and die.
> I lift the glass to my mouth,
> I look at you, and I sigh. (1983: 93–94)

Ironically the popular nature of the form provides the substance for an acutely self-conscious affirmation of the artist's adapted manner. It is almost as if no one before has quite heard the potential for form within the drinking song. And it is almost as if once one does hear that potential, one's response cannot but appropriate the very form itself for a metaphoric level capable of bringing out the full sadness perhaps at the core of most song.

Notice how the song structurally depends on a powerful contrast. The fifth line converts the opening reference to wine into a kind of action. But then the correspondences change because that same kind of conversion for the second line takes only four syllables of the last line. This is enough to seduce into trying to figure out how the remaining elements fit this possible structural motif of matching actions to states: after all, "I sigh" parallels the other transformations of non-human subjects into human actions. This figuring out is not difficult—the poem, after all, is "only" a drinking song. Yeats breaks standard symmetry in order to emphasize how the expansive third and fourth lines produce the simple corresponding action of the "sigh"—as if that were the only action that might correlate with such verbiage. All those words not only provoke the sigh but explain it. What else can one do with the temptation to let the language of despair take over except find the one physical gesture that can at the same time interpret and mock the pathos. This sense of pathos may even be the underlying cause of the desperation provoking the drinking song. But this sense also provides a way of valuing how the poem fills out the triple rhyme. The "sigh" becomes a measure of power as well as of pathos, since in fact it does correspond to discursive language, in the same way that lifting the glass and looking at you respond to the sentiments that provoke them. Through self-conscious manner, this poem transforms the drinking song into a surprising affective register, all the more striking by its recuperation of a distinctive formal symmetry.

My third example is somewhat more elaborate since I want to concentrate on how style might negotiate what can be done with negation—as a linguistic and as a psychological phenomenon. In the late work of Wallace Stevens, such negotiation does not take place in the typical way of simply finding a positive assertion to contrast with the negative. Rather, Stevens manipulates the processes of negation so that he can render what can be affirmed within the very consciousness elaborating the negations. This is his "The Plain Sense of Things" (1954):

> After the leaves have fallen, we return
> To a plain sense of things. It is as if
> We had come to the end of the imagination,
> Inanimate in an inert savoir.
>
> It is difficult even to choose the adjective
> For this blank cold, this sadness without cause.
> The great structure has become a minor house
> No turban walks across the lessened floors.
>
> The greenhouse never so badly needed paint.
> The chimney is fifty years old and slants to one side.
> A fantastic effort has failed, a repetition
> In a repetitiousness of men and flies.
>
> Yet the absence of imagination had
> Itself to be imagined. The great pond,
> The plain sense of it, without reflections, leaves,
> Mud, water like dirty glass, expressing silence
>
> Of a sort, silence of a rat come out to see,
> The great pond and its waste of lilies, all this
> Had to be imagined as an inevitable knowledge,
> Required, as a necessity requires. (1997: 428)[16]

These quatrains closely echo in style much of Stevens's late poetry. Gone is the "essential gaudiness" of his early work as well as the speculative dazzle and scope of his extended meditations on such themes as the imagination and major man. This is the unadorned world rendered in a basically simple referential mode where simple quatrains try to make peace with everything that causes this sense of impoverishment.

But the greater the simplicity, the greater the burden on style—both to elaborate the significance of this plain sense of things and to mark how the subject can care for this world. Here I want to concentrate on the force of one figure, the "rat come out to see," as an emblem for what Stevens seems to think style has to accomplish in order to serve as a significant force in the poet's confrontation with everything in modern life that threatens to make "desire…too difficult to tell from despair" (Stevens 1997: 286). Almost all of Stevens's late poems provide figures for the "mind of winter" capable of bearing witness to this bare scene. But this particular choice of the rat both extends and transforms the negatives shaping the poem in deep and exciting ways. First, let us count the negatives defining this plain sense of things. The scene is sad; the great structure has become "a minor house"; there is "no turban" walking across the "lessened floors"; and there is a sense of failure everywhere reinforced by the awful thought that every negation is only a repetition of what seen from distance seems only "a repetitiousness of men and flies." Above all, the sense of that "we have come to the end of the imagination" cannot stand by itself but seems condemned to issuing the further negations that conclude the first stanza.

Yet Stevens is keenly aware that at some point excessive negation has to turn into something else. The basic question here is not whether the poem will shift gears but how it will shift gears without having both the buildup and the conclusion seem self-indulgent fantasy. He responds to that challenge in three elemental ways. First, there is something odd about the reference to "no turban walks across the lessened floors" because, unlike the other details, this is not a standard image for depression: no one would expect a turban to walk across those floors. So we have not quite come to the end of the imagination. Then there is the explicit demand that opens the fourth stanza: "Yet the absence of imagination had / Itself to be imagined." Here simple negation will no longer do because the poet insists that he cannot rest in isolated observations. The poem must establish another level on which it synthesizes what the negations have wrought. Here, then, the sense of absence of imagination becomes the imagination's feel for its present situation, and the poem must take responsibility for its own analogizing.

But how will it do that? Deploying the rat provides Stevens's answer. After the generalization opening the fourth stanza, the poem returns to what seems a concrete situation. Yet "the great pond" in fact hovers between an additional detail of the scene and a metaphor for how the absence of imagination can be imagined. Projected description and self-referential metaphoric reach become strangely identical. This strange identity then evokes the "rat come out to see." The rat's task is to observe the actual plain sense of things while also serving as the mind's figure for its own pushing itself on the scene so as to find ways to figure the absence of imagination. The rat parallels the mind's uncomfortable but somehow fated presence as witness to this desolation, and as one more feature of the desolation that has to be imagined. Now, though, "imagination" is no longer an abstract term. It becomes just what enables the poet to identify with how this rat emerges in this situation. The rat suggests that, confronted with this scene, the most the mind can do is compose an emblem for its own estrangement in a bizarrely intimate way. By having a figure of consciousness that is also a figure of nonidentity with the self, the poem can encompass the scope of the poverty it confronts. This scope then turns to include not only the plain sense of things before the mind but also the necessity that makes this such a challenge for the mind: "all this / Had to be imagined as an inevitable knowledge."

It seems that only imagination can establish the theatrical terms by which there can be figures for the viewing of this poverty. And only imagination can bring to bear a sense of this poverty as inseparable from our destiny as human beings. Needing to pursue a plain sense of things in this most unplain way is the price we pay for having the investments we do in recognizing and appreciating our situations. But this price seems worth paying, as long as we can imagine imagining a quasi identification with this rat as a basic aspect of that poverty. Such imagining provides an instrument for coming to terms with a fatality too comprehensive and abstract to be engaged by discursive reasoning. Figures prove absolutely necessary for dealing with the plainest possible sense of things. And figures require a version of agency capable of directing what they present—both cognitively and affectively—hence the role that the second-order considerations about consciousness have to play in the poem.

This is why the concrete figure of the rat gives way to the purely syntactic power of the "as" as the ultimate example of the imagination's power. The repeated invocation of "as," that grammatical figure for figures, brings to bear a range of interpretive contexts that seem inseparable from the process of self-reflection, even as they become sufficiently abstract to prevent any single image of the self from taking form. First, there is the simple assertion of what we might call a mode of vision: all this had to be imagined in the mode that necessity requires. But this sense of necessity cannot be encompassed by description. We have to reflect on what is afforded by the series of "as" expressions as they connect the contingent and the necessary. Our thinking and our figuring all become aspects of our recognizing that we are not so much describing the absence of imagination as ritually manifesting where we are positioned when we make that attempt. We have to align entirely with necessity, but at a distance, in another tree, provided by everything that our ability to use "as" makes visible.

Such use proves most important for its giving substance to the "we" that begins as only a hopeful assertion in the poem's first stanza. This "we" evokes a transcendental ego's power to adjust to necessity, and it embodies the power to feel what one shares with others even as one is most sharply confronted with one's own isolation. The power to generalize proves inseparable from the second-order power to see that it takes generalizing in order to stage the absence of imagination in its full theatrical presence. (One's own absence of imagination would be banal in comparison.) Yet for all this generalization, this power can only be realized by the individual's accepting the condition of our fully fleshing out the worlds that "as" produces—namely, that each of us align with the sense of necessity. "All this" in the last stanza provides in elemental form the necessary synthesis. Then the final figures can give the feeling for what the scene had lacked—not as a fiction but as a bleak assessment that satisfies because it raises the level of transparency that can be taken into intimate being. That may be all that is left viable as a concept of the will, and it may suffice.

I think what ultimately matters in all three examples is how treating them as demonstrative acts makes clear how art objects elicit and reward identifications. Style constitutes a process by which the subject pervades the situation and makes the situation inseparable from the qualifications (what I call the "as-ness") by which it becomes articulate. For the artist, concern for this as-ness makes the manner inseparable from the matter, and it allows the work to suggest that it establishes certain possibilities of enactment as elemental features of the empirical world. And for audience participating in the work, the demonstrative force of style can modify their sense of possible attitudes that can be taken toward the material. Style in Pope's lines suffuses a critical commonplace with a witty presence opening into a world where instruction and pleasure can fuse. Style in Yeats's poem manages to find in the most banal rhetoric a powerful expression of pain that is inseparable from understanding the banality. And style in Stevens's poem exemplifies the imaginative energy it takes to align what a subject demands as a condition of feeling its own vitality with how objects can elicit the withdrawal of all the illusions that typically nourish this mode of feeling.

Therefore, one can argue that style matters, in art and life, because if we fail to establish manner as substance, we have only picture thinking. And if we are reduced to picture thinking, we lose any language either for the variations in intensity afforded by aesthetic experiences or for the capacity to make discriminations that having that repository of examples might afford. The danger of reducing style to fashion, or to evidence of *a* style, is that style then becomes only something to be pictured: style loses all its roles as a demonstrative act. And the audience loses all the subtle ways that consciousness can respond to what can only be shown and not said.

NOTES

1. One reason I include myself in my epigraphs is to call attention to a dilemma often facing older critics. I have to assume that I was invited to write this essay because of two other essays I have written on the concept of style (Altieri 1989, 1995). I must have had something useful to say then; now I put myself in a position where my alternatives seem repeating myself or arguing extensively with myself (or both)—none of which is appealing. So I subscribe still to the detailed arguments I made there while treating this essay as a more general treatment of the topic within which my earlier arguments might be contained with a little recasting.

2. My Google review of this critical literature on style over the past 10 years turned up two books, very few essays on the general concept of style, and not much more on style in relation to individual authors or artists. But I have to mention a very recent essay by Richard Neer (2005), which begins with the same gambit I do about "the relative neglect of stylistics in recent historiographic work." However, it turns out that connoisseurship is not a very good model for stylistics because it has to emphasize "the inference of an artifact's spatial and temporal point of origin on the basis of morphological (stylistic) criteria" (3). "Possession of a style on the one hand, and the status of being an artifact are synonymous" (5). However, I treat individual style as different from possessing "a style" because individual style indicates not only point of origin but also the point of the originating. Neer is not concerned with intentionality or

purposiveness because he sees the primary task of the connoisseur as establishing causal evidence for attributions of provenance, so the individual is an analytic construction "which is not necessarily the same as a particular human subject" (12). I see the critic's interest in style as establishing evidence for how and why particular choices are made within the individual work.

3. Taken by itself, this example might be trivial, but it indicates a dilemma for those who want critical leverage from the concept of style against such mainstream aspects of cultural fashion. There is always the possibility of drawing on the theorizing of the Frankfurt School to show how mainstream capitalist culture continually absorbs what had been concepts with critical potential into narcissistic logic that produces a "near-perfect circuit of production and consumption." As Hal Foster puts it, "this 'designed subject'" might be "the unintended offspring of the 'constructed subject' so vaunted in post-modern culture": "Contemporary design is part of a greater revenge of capitalism on postmodernism—a recouping of its crossings of arts and disciplines, a routinization of its transgressions" (2003: 18). But then, it is difficult to escape the charge that such criticism only follows academic fashion and so reduces to a kind of grumbling about change. The more we use the past for critical leverage, the more we might be encouraging in younger critics the sense that, rather than turning on mass culture, they should embrace it and treat style only in its terms. The other alternative is to find other concepts not so corrupted by nostalgia.

4. These critics are not likely to get any help from the poststructural models in philosophy that are still the most influential on literary study because these philosophers are not willing to countenance any form of idealization in which such concepts as mastery play a part. The entire conceptual field of such philosophy pulls against honoring the energy and labor it takes to make one kind of object stand out as an exemplary act of overcoming both the indifference of nature and the ways fashion allows us to conceal that indifference.

5. My remarks have been substantially influenced by the case made in Summers 1998.

6. Wollheim offers richer, more penetrating critiques of parallel taxonomic movements in art history. He shows convincingly that these generalizing categories are only ideal entities that have no reality, no particular images or verbal formulations that allow increasing depth and richness to a given analysis. This model of style developed for the visual arts "cannot explain why paintings in a given general style look as they do"; "on the contrary they are in whatever general style they are in because of how they look." (1995: 47). Generalizing theory cannot even begin to explain the difference we commonly make between being in a style and having a distinctive style. And because the characterizations are ideal constructs, they allow no dialectic, no way of having attention to individual examples change the repertoire of cultural terms.

7. Wollheim (1987: 42–43) uses "schemata" and "principles" or "rules" to describe the same difference, but his choice is costly because none of these terms allows for the flexibility that the notion of occasion provides.

8. My favorite essay on literary style, Watt 1973, is terrific on the tensions between linguistic and literary explanation of style and on what it takes to justify an aesthetic approach.

9. In his great "Generative Grammars and Literary Style" (1970), Richard Ohmann identifies 12 critical approaches to stylistics.

10. To engage the philosophers, one must be willing to focus on visual art and be content to extrapolate what one can for literary cases. All but two of the influential

philosophers engaging questions about style work exclusively on visual art because it is probably easier to focus on the action that manner qualifies. Everything about the visual medium seems to manifest style, whereas in writing, attention to the instrument is likely to be torn what the meaning is and how that might be qualified by style. Of the two exceptions, only Robinson works on literary examples; the other, Lang, concerns himself with how philosophers rely on manner to challenge the primacy of impersonal method that is an aspect of the Cartesian heritage in philosophy. To be concerned with individual actions for Lang is necessarily to set them in resistance to everything that can be handled in impersonal terms. Literary critics, on the other hand tend, to assume that what matters is the individual and then go too quickly to specific questions about how language per se reveals that individuality, without worrying about how language can be the vehicle for distinctive actions.

11. I am combining two of Wollheim's treatments of the concept of style. The idea of thematization on several levels is brilliantly worked out in *Painting as an Art* (1987: 21–25), while the list of attributes claimed for style is developed in "Style in Painting" (1995: 41–44). I should note that in the later work, the essay, Wollheim is careful to say that style is "psychological only in the way in which vision or language-competence is psychological. It interacts with other psychological phenomena at some level" (48). But then, on the very next page (which I take up in a few moments), he offers his version of how the body gets involved in style, and that provides a clear link between psychological and psychoanalytic. It is this link that justifies my treating Wollheim within a language of expression and investment that he does not explicitly sanction.

12. Specifying style depends largely on l'ésprit de finesse because it is always a matter of reconciling two somewhat different concerns. Stylistic descriptions analyze given works, while style descriptions clarify the schemata and the rules that govern an individual's style in general. For in any given work, the artist's style is not likely to be "employed in its entirety," while from the style description there is no way to predict what shape individual works will end up taking.

13. But such determinations will be circular because they depend on deciding from the start what will count as style. For example, Wollheim argues that Cézanne had a long period where he did not develop a style because a lack of confidence forced Cézanne to be emphatic and so he could not "allow his work to be tentative" (1987: 29). To make his point, he compares the panoramic and "prestylistic" *View of Auvers* (1874) with the "fully stylistic" *View of Medan* (1880), with its dense, abstracted relation among shapes and color units. But if we expand the definition of style to include attributes other than "tentativeness," the earlier painting is clearly signed by Cézanne: the very high vantage that in turn brings the background up and forward and forces constant adjustments in our sense of place. More important, if we turn to other paintings like *Lutte d'Amour* from the 1860s, we find a characteristic violence that Cézanne's later work struggles to put to work as an intensity of apprehension. In other words, personal style need not be just a listing of attributes but can comprise a characteristic mode of struggle in which one's past gets taken up and transfigured. Attributions of nonstyle simply avoid the challenge an artist might present, even to himself or herself, of finding ways to carry on conversation within various stylistic features.

14. I follow Kant in treating "purpose" as following the rules of understanding and "purposiveness" as "a thing's harmony with the character of things that is possible only through purposes": purposiveness is what the reflective power of "judgment prescribes not to nature ... but to itself," a law for its reflection in nature (1987: 20). Then I use Wittgenstein's distinction between following a rule and the condition where an

unstatable intentionality in an object keeps intimating where I have to go. See Kant 1987: 20, 21–22, 28–29.

15. In making these attributions about the demonstrative, I am trying to work out a way to elaborate one of Wittgenstein's central ideas—that a great deal of discourse is not in the language games of making observations and forming propositions but is about evaluating samples supplying the framework of language for what they can and cannot make possible for practical use. See Wittgenstein 1958.

16. There is another version of this reading in Altieri 2005.

REFERENCES

Altieri, C. (1989). "Style as the Man: From Aesthetics to Speculative Philosophy." *In* Richard Shusterman (ed.), *Analytic Aesthetics*. Oxford: Basil Blackwell.

——. (1995). "Personal Style as Articulate Intentionality." *In* C. Van Eck, J. McAllister, and R. van de Vall (eds.), *The Question of Style in Philosophy and the Arts*. Cambridge: Cambridge University Press.

——. (2005). *The Art of American Poetry*. Oxford: Basil Blackwell.

Chatman, S., and S. R. Levin. (1967). *Essays on the Language of Literature*. Boston: Houghton Mifflin.

Danto, A. C. (1981). *The Transfiguration of the Commonplace*. Cambridge, Mass.: Harvard University Press.

Foster, H. (2003). *Design and Crime*. London: Verso.

Freeman, D. C., ed. (1970). *Linguistics and Literary Theory*. New York: Holt, Rinehart and Winston.

Hughes, J. (2005). "Who Did Her Personality?" *Wall Street Journal*, July 7, W1–W5.

Jakobson, R. (1966). "Closing Statement: Linguistics and Poetics." *In* T. A. Sebeok (ed.), *Style in Language*. Cambridge, Mass.: MIT Press.

Kant, I. (1987). *Critique of Judgment* (W. S. Pluhar, trans.). Indianapolis: Hackett. (Original work published in 1790.)

Lang, B. (1983). *Philosophy and the Art of Writing*. Lewisburg: Bucknell University Press.

——. (1998). "Style." *In* M. Kelly (ed.), *The Encyclopedia of Aesthetics* (Vol. 3). New York: Oxford University Press.

Love, G. A., and M. Payne. (1969). *Contemporary Essays on Style*. Glenview, Ill.: Scott Foresman.

Milic, L. T. (1973). "Against the Typology of Styles." *In* G. T. Polletta (ed.), *Issues in Contemporary Literary Criticism*. Boston: Little Brown.

Neer, R. (2005). "Connoisseurship and the Stakes of Style." *Critical Inquiry* 32, 1–26.

Ohmann, R. (1970). "Generative Grammars and Literary Style." *In* D. Freeman (ed.), *Linguistics and Literary Theory*. New York: Holt, Rinehart and Winston.

Pope, A. (2007). *An Essay on Criticism*. London: Dodo Press. (Original work published in 1711.)

Schapiro, M. (1998). "Style." *In* D. Preziosi (ed.), *The Art of Art History*. New York: Oxford University Press.

Stevens, W. (1997). *Collected Poetry and Prose* (F. Kermode and J. Richardson, eds.). New York: Library of America.

Summers, D. (1998). " 'Form,' Nineteenth Century Metaphysics, and the Problem of Art Historical Description." *In* D. Preziosi (ed.), *The Art of Art History*. New York: Oxford University Press.

Watt, I. (1973). "The First Paragraph of *The Ambassadors*." *In* G. T. Polletta (ed.), *Issues in Contemporary Literary Criticism*. Boston: Little Brown.

Wittgenstein, L. (1958). *Philosophical Investigations* (3rd ed.; G. E. M. Anscombe, trans.). New York: Macmillan.

———. (1980). *Culture and Value* (P. Winch, trans.). Chicago: University of Chicago Press. (Original work published in 1977.)

Wölfflin, H. (1932). *The Principles of Art History* (M. D. Hottinger, trans.). New York: Holt.

Wollheim, R. (1987). *Painting as an Art*. Princeton: Princeton University Press.

———. (1995). "Style in Painting." *In* C. Van Eck, J. McAllister, and R. van de Vall (eds.), *The Question of Style in Philosophy and the Arts*. Cambridge: Cambridge University Press.

Yeats, W. B. (1983). *W. B. Yeats: The Poems* (R. Finneran, ed.). New York: Macmillan.

CHAPTER 19

EMOTION, MEMORY, AND TRAUMA

GLENN W. MOST

I

In the very first scene of Salman Rushdie's novel *Fury* (2001), the central character, "Professor Malik Solanka, retired historian of ideas, irascible dollmaker" (3) goes out one hot summer day, foppishly dressed, for his customary afternoon walk on the Upper West Side of New York, and is asked by a beautiful young neighborhood woman in a friendly, teasing, certainly rather nosy, but also slightly flirtatious way, why it is that he is always walking alone and where he is going. This is his reaction: "Sudden anger rose in him. 'What I'm looking for,' he barked, 'is to be left in peace.' His voice trembled with a rage far bigger than her intrusion merited, the rage which shocked him whenever it coursed through his nervous system, like a flood. Hearing his vehemence, the young woman recoiled, retreating into silence" (5).

Irascible indeed—Rushdie is careful to point out that although the girl's intrusion might well have legitimately provoked *some* degree of irritation, it does not seem worthy of the fury that is now welling up in Solanka's spirit. Nor is this an isolated incident: as Rushdie indicates, this is a repeated occurrence in Solanka's psychic life, and it shocks him every time it happens—although each shock does not prevent it from happening again. Over and over, something is happening, to him and within him, and he can recognize its effects but cannot understand their causes or control them. We might say that he is at odds with himself, that he is the locus of a discord that is his only because it is no one else's, but with which he cannot identify himself and that therefore strikes him as alien and frightening.

Only a few pages later, Solanka is returning to his apartment building from another walk and encounters in the lobby a copywriter who wants the advice that he, as a genuine Englishman, can be supposed to be able to give him about a proposed advertising slogan. Solanka tries to fend him off with banalities, but the advertiser insists. And then:

> Professor Solanka felt huge irritation rise up in his breast. He experienced a strong desire to screech at this fellow with the damn-fool alias, to call him names and perhaps actually smack him across the face with an open hand. It took an effort to restrain himself.... Then he hurried into his apartment, shut the door with his heart pounding, leaned against the wall, closed his eyes, gasped, and shook.... [W]here was all this anger coming from? Why was he being caught off guard, time and again, by surges of rage that almost overwhelmed his will? (36)

Solanka has good reason to be alarmed: he is repeatedly reacting with excessive anger to trivial annoyances, and his reactions are slipping further and further out of his control. He is thrown out of a café because he has been yelling angry obscenities without even being aware of it; his cleaning lady tells him that he has fired her in a violent rage, but he has no recollection of this whatsoever; when he walks through the park with a beautiful woman and a young man approaches to compliment her:

> A great roaring rose in Malik Solanka's breast. It would be good now to tear this young man's tongue out from that vile fleshy mouth. It would be good to see how those muscled arms might look when detached from that highly defined torso. Cut? Ripped? How about if he was cut and ripped into about a million pieces? *How about if I ate his fucking heart?* (147–48)

Wanting to eat his enemy alive—should this not remind us of someone?

What is more, all around him, New York seems to be repeating on a larger scale his own paroxysms of rage. The Islamic taxi driver in whose cab he is riding suddenly starts screaming foul racist insults against Jewish drivers. And somewhere in the city, a nameless serial killer is murdering nice young women one after another by bashing their heads in with pieces of concrete. As we learn in the course of the novel, the refined, highly cultivated Professor Solanka had fled his English home because one night he found himself standing above the bed of his sleeping wife and child, holding a murderous carving knife. Now, uncontrolledly furious, recurrently amnesiac, compulsively peripatetic, can he be entirely certain that this terrifying anonymous murderer is not in fact himself?

Rushdie's novel was published in 2001 and has a sophisticated, complexly ironic relationship to the Western literary tradition of which it is one of the most recent products. That tradition begins for us with the *Iliad*, and the *Iliad*, too, opens with a scene of suddenly ignited, swiftly proliferating, and almost uncontrollable anger. Rage is named as the poem's very first word, *mênis*, and different forms and degrees of wrath skip at its beginning like a rapid brush fire from character to character, from Apollo, who "quaked with rage" (*Iliad* 1.44; Homer 1990: 79) because Agamemnon has scorned his priest, to Agamemnon himself, who reacts wrathfully to Calchas's advice that the god be appeased by returning Chryseis to her father—"furious, his dark heart filled to the brim, blazing with anger now, his eyes like searing fire" (1.103–4; 1990: 81)—to Achilles, in whom Agamemnon's decision to take Briseis makes the ambient fury rise to a terrifying climax:

> anguish gripped Achilles
> The heart in his rugged chest was pounding, torn...
> Should he draw the long sharp sword slung at his hip,
> thrust through the ranks and kill Agamemnon now?—
> or check his rage and beat his fury down?
> As his racing spirit veered back and forth,
> just as he drew his huge blade from its sheath,
> down from the vaulting heavens swept Athena.
>
> (1.188–95; 1990: 83–84)

No human being could possibly assuage a wrath as fierce as Achilles'—by introducing Athena as *dea ex machina* to swoop down and calm him, Homer can both allow his hero to go to the very furthest limits of his anger without, boringly, having to yield to the considerations of common sense, and at the same time can save him from the inevitable consequences of succumbing to that emotion. This time Athena will indeed succeed in placating Achilles' wrath, but he will remain subject to various forms of that emotion, directed to various objects, throughout the poem almost until its very end—indeed, at one point he will notoriously say to the dying Hector, "Would to god my rage, my fury would drive me now / to hack your flesh away and eat you raw" (22.346–47; 1990: 553).[1]

II

We might say that both Solanka and Achilles are reacting to situations with inappropriate emotions. In both cases there is an unpleasant external stimulus, in the form of a disagreeable modification in their world caused by the intervention of some other person, and they react to this stimulus, but they do so inappropriately. We can distinguish three kinds of theoretically possible inappropriateness that might be involved: they might feel the emotion in the total absence of any stimulus whatsoever (they might be fully delusional); they might react to a real stimulus with the wrong emotion (e.g., with fear instead of anger, or love instead of envy); or they might react to a real stimulus with the right emotion, but in the wrong quantity (too much or too little). In all three cases, but especially in the latter two, what counts as inappropriate will, of course, vary widely from period to period, from culture to culture, and even among different segments of the same culture.

In the two texts we are considering, it is evidently above all the third case that is in question: Achilles and Solanka are reacting to the right kind of stimulus with the right emotion, anger, but with the wrong quantity, too much of it. The stimuli involved are ones that none of us would be likely to find agreeable; Solanka's causes for anger are admittedly quite trivial, but we can certainly understand that we ourselves might well be somewhat irritated, too, if they happened to us, while, as far as Achilles goes, if Agamemnon's public humiliation of him did not indeed make him very angry, we would surely think there was something wrong with him (and, in fact, the evidence suggests that many ancient Greeks failed to recognize that Achilles' reaction was at all inappropriate). But the crucial point is that Solanka and Achilles react to these stimuli with an excess of anger: nothing in the banal New York situations Rushdie describes justifies the intensity of Solanka's rage, as he himself recognizes (indeed, daily life in New York is made up in large part of precisely such minor irritants, and the city would become far more difficult to enjoy if its inhabitants tended to react to them with murderous rage), while it takes only a minimum of reflection to recognize that for Achilles to attempt in his fury to kill Agamemnon is the worst possible way for him to try to keep Briseis and to secure his standing in the Greek army.

We may hazard the generalization that much, though not all, of ancient Greek philosophy, especially as represented by Plato, at least some Stoics, and probably Epicurus, tended to oppose all kinds and degrees of emotion per se as a dangerous factor that interfered destructively with the rational capacities that they considered to be man's noblest feature.[2] For recent philosophical investigation of the emotions, this radical approach has not proved to be very productive: the emotions are simply too deeply embedded within human nature for us to be able to rid ourselves of them, and too importantly involved in much of what we consider best about human beings for us to wish to try to do so. Hence, most of the recent work on the philosophy of emotions that has reconsidered the ancient roots of this discussion has tended instead to focus on a broadly Aristotelian approach that considers emotions to be reactions, often reasonable ones, to certain kinds of situations.[3] For such an approach, the question of inappropriate emotions is particularly interesting, in that it raises the issue of the degree of correspondence, or lack of correspondence, of the reaction to the stimulus that provokes and, in the best of cases, justifies it.

Given that, of the three kinds of inappropriateness distinguished just now, the former two (absence of any stimulus at all and reaction with a qualitatively wrong emotion) seem obviously pathological, it is not surprising that it is the third kind of inappropriateness (too little or too much of the right kind of emotion) that has attracted most attention—and this applies not only to the increasing number of recent philosophical analyses of emotion, but above all to the many literary treatments of emotions suitable and unsuitable. Authors of literary texts, after all, want us to empathize to some degree with their characters, and if these are simply delusional or radically pathological in some other way, our interest in identifying with their vicissitudes and our capacity to do so will be much reduced.[4] To be sure, authors are also interested in telling stories that are new and interesting, and a story about someone who reacted to some real stimulus with exactly the right quantity of just the right emotion would surely be no less boring than a detailed and extensive narrative about a perfectly happy marriage. So we might be inclined to dismiss the existence of stories about inappropriate emotion as a merely literary phenomenon, one that tells us more about our tastes in fictions than about the makeup of our emotional life. Yet that would be a mistake: people like stories for many reasons, but also because these tell them, indirectly, about certain features of their own lives, and of the persons who matter to them, which they are particularly eager to think they understand more fully than they feel they can on their own; and conversely, people often understand their own lives in large part on the basis of the stories they have heard about people, themselves and others, real, fictional, and otherwise. What is more, in the case of successful and influential authors such as Homer and Rushdie, the stories they tell about their fictional characters seem plausible to us not only because they correspond in their general ethical structure to the ideas that we already had about the behavior of human beings before we came to their texts, but also because their fictions have helped to shape the ways we understand ourselves and one another even before we encountered them: they are not only canny observers of the social world, but also important contributors to its self-understanding. It might be said that we moderns live in a world that is Rushdiean, at least in part (which of course does not mean that Rushdie's novels, including this one, have not been the subject of vigorous criticism for all kinds of reasons), but also, to a certain extent, still somewhat Homeric, whereas the Greeks lived in a world that was largely Homeric and not at all Rushdiean. So Homer and Rushdie may both be writing what we (but not the ancient Greeks) would regard as fictions, yet their fictions both document and help to create social realities. Perhaps, then, considering how Homer and Rushdie deal with the inappropriate anger they contrive for their heroes may teach us something about the larger differences between Homer's world and ours.

III

We have already seen Professor Solanka asking himself in anguish, "Where was all this anger coming from?" Solanka sees obvious and terrible effects, but he cannot easily discover their hidden causes; not understanding the causes makes him find these effects even more worrisome, in part because this ignorance implies a troubling opacity of the self to itself, in part because to know the causes might help him to remove them and thereby to abolish their effects. So where *is* all his anger coming from? The question is not one that we can imagine bothering Achilles very much, and in fact, one of the main differences between Rushdie and Homer in this regard is that Rushdie, unlike Homer, treats his protagonist's excessive anger as a kind of illness that ought to be liable to diagnosis, etiology, and therapy and appears to consider it part of his duty as storyteller to do his best to provide these.

I return to this important difference further below; for the moment I focus instead upon Rushdie's presentation of Solanka's "case history." Solanka's outbreaks of excessive rage are the counterpart to a diminishment of his libido; his acute bouts of "too much" in an aggressive direction balance a chronic "too little" in an erotic direction; in both cases he seems to be considering something external as a menace to his well-being and trying to protect himself against exposing himself to it. Yet the present threats that he thinks he perceives in his actual day-to-day life, when measured against any kind of realistic standard (of the sort he is quite capable of adopting in his more lucid moments), turn out to be far too trivial to explain the extremity of his reactions. But what other kind of threats might be disturbing him? The only hint that Rushdie supplies us is that Solanka becomes particularly distressed whenever a woman with whom he is erotically involved takes hold of his head, especially during the sexual act: under such apparently trivial (or perhaps even, for some people, rather agreeable) circumstances, the sudden increase in his rage entirely blocks what is left of his diminished libido. Though Solanka wishes to cure his mental ailment, he refuses the two remedies that (at least in New York) are the standard ones, psychotherapy and chemotherapy; instead, he prefers, heroically, to combat his demons himself, but he does not seem to be having much success in doing so—until, that is, he is rescued, not for the first time in world literature, by the love of a good woman. At the most furious moment of a violent altercation between Solanka and his lover Neela, she suddenly reaches out and caresses his forbidden hair: "The spell broke. He laughed out loud. A large black crow spread its wings and flew away across town, to drop dead minutes later by the Booth statue in Gramercy Park. Solanka understood that his own cure, his recovery from his rare condition, was now complete. The goddesses of wrath had departed; their hold over him was broken at last" (219).

The intersection of mythical and therapeutic language here is extraordinary: it is clearly intended to mark this scene as a climactic moment in the novel. And indeed, immediately after, Solanka can go on finally to tell Neela, and us, and himself, his "true" story: how as a child he had repeatedly been abused sexually by his stepfather, Doctor Sahib, who had dressed him as a girl and made him perform fellatio upon him while he held the child's head. Any trace whatsoever of the painful memories themselves had apparently vanished altogether from Solanka's consciousness, but their indirect effects had lingered on (in his passion for doll making, in his sexual difficulties, and in his bouts of rage), and their devastating pain had remained quite undiminished in their domination of his psychological makeup—until, by the very act of telling his "story" (219) and making his "confession" (223), he somehow manages to free himself—suddenly, entirely, definitively—from their tyranny. Now, we think, we understand: we can diagnose Solanka's excessive anger as the result of a childhood trauma that he had repressed rather than working through; now his recognition of its cause has permitted him to free himself from it once and for all by narrating it in a talking cure.

IV

I return later to the structure and history of the kind of account Rushdie provides for Solanka's ailment. But first consider once again the ancient case that certainly is like it in some ways but no less certainly is vastly different in others: Homer's Achilles. Some (not all) ancient Greeks and Romans were able to recognize that, at least in certain regards, Achilles' anger was sometimes excessive and hence inappropriate, but no one in antiquity ever seems to have suggested that Achilles was simply ill. What is more, no one in antiquity ever even hinted that Achilles' notoriously excessive anger might have been the result of his having had an unhappy childhood—indeed, the very notion that some Greek or Roman might have even imagined making such a suggestion seems just as ludicrous to us as such a suggestion would doubtless have seemed to them.

And yet, if people had sought to explain Achilles' behavior as an adult by linking it with the experiences they could have supposed he had as a child, Greek myth would in fact have supplied ample material to support all kinds of plausible diagnostic hypotheses.[5] Achilles' parents, Thetis and Peleus, had a famously unhappy marriage: Thetis never reconciled herself to Zeus's forcing her to marry a mortal, and many sources report that she first transformed herself into every possible shape in a desperate attempt to foil Peleus's courtship and then, having failed to repulse him, abandoned her husband soon after Achilles' birth. According to the author of the archaic epic *Aegimius*, attributed to Hesiod or Cercops, Thetis had the disagreeable habit of throwing the children she bore Peleus into a cauldron of boiling water, presumably in order to find out whether they were immortal or not (i.e., whether they took after her, in which case they would survive, or after him, in which case they would not); eventually Peleus became annoyed at this behavior, and so he intervened, stopping her just as she was about to drown Achilles and thereby saving him. Once he managed to survive infancy, Achilles did not have a much easier childhood: he was raised not by his father (let alone by his mother), but by the centaur Chiron in the wilds of Mount Pelion, and what little socialization he acquired he owed to a tutor who, though certainly far gentler than his ferocious fellow centaurs, was nonetheless half horse. During his adolescence, when Thetis concealed him among the daughters of Lycomedes of Scyrus in order to save him from the military service in the Trojan War, which she knew would be fatal to him, he indulged in a bit of transvestitism, wearing a girl's dress, until Odysseus found him out by offering him splendid weapons, a boy's toys. And he was painfully aware, for much of his brief life, of just how brief that life would be.

For eyes that can see, all the materials necessary in order to construct Achilles' psychoanalytic family romance are abundantly available: we can easily envision how the parents' acrimonious marriage and their neglect and maltreatment of the child, compounded by his upbringing at the hooves of an inhuman centaur in the desolate wilderness of Thessaly, by his uncertainties about his sexual identity, and by his obsession with his own mortality might well have created psychological traumas resulting in the extraordinary mixture of narcissism, uncontrollable rage, lack of self-restraint, vindictiveness, violence, unswerving loyalty to his friends, and boundless pity for himself that make up the charming personality of Achilles as an adult.[6] To be sure, it is the very same corpus of Greek myth that tells of Achilles' adult character that also offers these materials about his childhood, and, to be sure, Achilles' childhood was often imagined in ancient artistic representations, especially in later antiquity. Yet no ancient Greek or Roman, as far as we know, ever made this specific causal connection between Achilles' childhood sufferings and his adult personality. Instead, when they imagined Achilles as a child, they imagined him as being just like the adult Achilles, only rather smaller. The most extensive and detailed portrayal extant of Achilles as a child is provided by Statius in his *Achilleid*,[7] and however delicately ironic and subtle the interplay is between the childish Achilles, on the one hand, and the foreshadowings of his future greatness, on the other, it is evident that Statius conceives even the childish hero as being in essence only a somewhat diminutive version of the adult one. Chiron tells Thetis that his fellow centaurs often come to complain to him about how baby Achilles has devastated their homes and flocks and driven them in flight across the fields and rivers, setting ambushes for them and waging precocious warfare against them (*Achilleid* 1.152–55), and when Thetis sees her child approach, even she turns pale in fear—he is covered with sweat and dust, for he has just killed a lioness and, having left her body behind, he is carrying her whelps with him and is playing with their claws (1.158–70).

V

If Statius sees little Achilles as being just like big Achilles, only somewhat smaller, the reason is not that he lacked the mythic information that would have enabled him to envision a different kind of childhood for the irascible hero, but instead that he had a very different conception of the relationship between childhood and adulthood from Rushdie's. Let us call Statius's model of imagining Achilles' childhood *continuous*. Throughout antiquity, the adult Achilles was thought to have had a fixed and unmistakable character—as Horace puts it in his advice to the aspiring poet, "celebrated Achilles" must be depicted as being "*inpiger, iracundus, inexorabilis, acer* [tireless, wrathful, inexorable, ferocious]" if he is to be at all recognizable as Achilles (1999: 99–101). On the basis of this personality structure of the adult Achilles he knows so well, Statius imagines what kind of child such an adult must have been like, and he is guided in his imaginative reconstruction by principles of *resemblance* and *continuity*: baby Achilles must be supposed to have been as similar to adult Achilles as possible, so that the development from child to adult can be gradual, linear, and uninterrupted. What makes baby Achilles baby Achilles is that at this tender age he already possesses, to a much larger extent than normal babies do, all the natural capacities that he will later display as adult Achilles—only that he does so in a somewhat reduced degree, as befits, more or less, a child.

We may presume that the ancients usually had little or no authentic information about what those who later became their great men (or, rarely, women) had really been like as children. Hence, they had to reconstruct such childhoods imaginatively if they wished to envision their heroes as children, and the continuous model told them how to do so, encouraging them to find the very same traits in the child that made the adult so remarkable—as it were, for them, if not in Wordsworth's sense, the child was father to the man. Statius's baby Achilles, the ferocious lion-slaying tot, is of a par with the many other miraculous infants who populate the imaginary kindergarten of ancient culture. Homer, already as a small boy, we are told, surpassed all the other children in the grammar classes taught him by his teacher Phemius, and he soon reached the level of Phemius himself, so when the teacher died, he left everything he possessed to his star pupil—not surprisingly, given that it was Homer's poetry that was required reading in grammar classes throughout the Greek world. When Hesiod was an infant in his cradle, a swarm of bees came to settle in his mouth, either because his breath was already so sweet or because his singing would one day be so (and exactly the same miracle was later reported of Lucan, in whose ancient biography this story about Hesiod is found). When Pindar was a boy, he went hunting near Mt. Helicon and fell asleep from exhaustion; as he slept a bee landed on his mouth and built a honeycomb there. Plato was born on the 7th of Thargelion, the traditional date of Apollo's birth on Delos, and while he was an infant bees came and either sat on his lips or made honey on them. And so forth, down to the miracles ascribed to the baby Jesus in apocryphal gospels and infancy accounts, and well beyond.

Of course, in all such stories, the point is not to explain the specifics of adult misbehavior by linking it in some causal way to some particular negative childhood experience, but rather, in more general terms, to establish a connection consisting of a larger continuity between exceptional adult capacities (whether positive or negative) and exceptional childhood ones. But it seems undeniable that these tales all participate in the same structural model identified just now. Their similarity to accounts of the miraculous infancies of the Greek gods—for example, the Hermes of the Homeric Hymn, who still in his swaddling clothes can outwit his big brother Apollo, or the Apollo of the Callimachean Hymn, who can utter prophecies while still unborn in his mother's womb—is evident, though we should be careful not to consider these biographies of mortals to be mere secularizations of the divine accounts; rather, both kinds of story are products of the same continuous model. Even in political biography, like Plutarch's (1914–26), where, despite the importance given to education in forming character, surprisingly little attention, if any, is paid to the great man's childhood, what little evidence we are supplied invariably adheres to this continuous model. Already as a child, Philopoemen is the consummate soldier: "For from his very boyhood he was fond of a soldier's life, and readily learned the lessons that were useful for this, such as those in heavy-armed fighting and horsemanship" (X, 261). By contrast, little Themistocles is already the perfect politician:

> However lowly his birth, it is agreed on all hands that while yet a boy he was impetuous, by nature sagacious, and by election enterprising and prone to public life. In times of relaxation and leisure, when absolved from his lessons, he would not play nor indulge his ease, as the rest of the boys did, but would be found composing and rehearsing to himself mock speeches. These speeches would be in accusation or defence of some boy or other (II, 5).

Little Cato the Younger is already the stern Stoic sage:

> We are told that from his very childhood Cato displayed, in speech, in countenance, and in his childhood sports, a nature that was inflexible, imperturbable, and altogether steadfast. He set out to accomplish his purposes with a vigor beyond his years, and while he was harsh and repellent to those who would flatter him, he was still more masterful towards those who tried to frighten him. It was altogether difficult to make him laugh, although once in a while he relaxed his features so far as to smile; and he was not quickly nor easily moved to anger, though once angered he was inexorable. (VIII, 237).

Alcibiades, finally, by contrast, was already displaying on the playground the very same mixture of charm and vice that made him notorious as an adult:

> He was naturally a man of many strong passions, the mightiest of which were the love of rivalry and the love of preeminence. This is clear from the stories recounted of his boyhood. He was once hard pressed in wrestling, and to save himself from getting a fall, set his teeth in his opponent's arms, where they clutched him, and was like to have bitten through them. His adversary, letting go his hold, cried, "You bite, Alcibiades, as women do!" "Not I," said Alcibiades, "but as lions do" (IV, 5–6)

VI

Doubtless, it may seem tempting to dismiss these observations about the continuous model as trivial or self-evident. A biographer may be pardoned for citing evidence from childhood that seems to confirm his diagnosis of the ethical character of the adult, and as for his sources, we can readily imagine how easily, once a man of a certain sort became famous, his relatives, teachers, and childhood friends might have colored their fading memories of his early years by projecting back onto them the vivid impressions that his adult virtues and vices made upon them. Even in our own days, the secular hagiography of an Albert Einstein, a Marie Curie, or a George Bush tends to run along similar lines. Yet the fact that this continuous model is not a monopoly of the ancient world but continues to remain viable in certain contexts even in our modern one does not mean that we can afford not to take it very seriously, for this ancient biographical tendency is in fact deeply complicitous with some very basic views about the nature of human beings that seem to have been quite widespread in the ancient world and that are anything but self-evident.

Above all, for the most part human beings seem in antiquity to have been thought to be equipped at birth with a fixed natural endowment consisting of a set of ethically relevant capacities and weaknesses; it was the business of education to enhance the capacities and to minimize the weaknesses, to detach the child from his pursuit of the satisfaction of his immediate appetites, and to point him in the general direction of society, reason, and the good. The specific practical details concerning the methods of education, and the overarching metaphysics of the human soul, that Plato provides in the *Republic* and *Laws*, and Aristotle in the *Nicomachean Ethics* and *Politics*, are no doubt significantly at variance with the realities of most Greek pedagogy, and deliberately so; but their fundamental view of the relation between nature and education is in fact an attempt to conceptualize systematically views on this topic that we have every reason to believe were deeply entrenched and widely disseminated in their culture. Surprises could happen; people, sometimes, could change. But most people seem to have been thought to have received their character dealt to them like a hand of cards at birth; then, education gave them a single chance to better their hand by weeding out their poorer cards (and whether they were able to take advantage of this opportunity depended in part upon social class, family, and luck, in part upon the very same ethical cards they were already holding)—after that, their success or failure was due to the interaction between this natural endowment, modified by education, and the chances of life. In short, for the ancients, circumstances were contingent, but character was not; for us, character, too, can be contingent.

This does not mean that the ancients were quite indifferent to reports about childhood character or experiences, only that they do not seem to have been inclined to cite and analyze such reports as sources of information in order to shed causal light on the hidden wellsprings of adult personality and behavior: either the extant childhood data simply confirmed the adulthood findings by their similarity to them, *per miraculum* if in no other way, or else they seem to have been invoked merely as curiosities, as a form of gossip. Suetonius is a good example of this very general tendency. His biographies of the 12 Caesars are remarkable for the amount of detailed attention he pays to the adult behavior (or, more usually, misbehavior) of his subjects: he is prepared to report the most extraordinary excesses of vice or crime, and even sometimes small deeds of relative kindness or moderation, and he also not infrequently applies general moral categories to explain imperial personalities by fitting them into the standard lists of vices and virtues. Along the way, he sometimes also provides potentially interesting information about their childhoods—but while we ourselves might want to inquire into how the specific events of that particular childhood might have led to the specific deeds and characteristics of that particular adulthood, Suetonius never displays even the slightest indication of wishing to do so himself. The childhood episode remains, in explanatory terms, a foreign body within his account, isolated and inert: it may be of interest for itself, but it does not serve to explain anything at all. Suetonius describes Augustus's nursery but does not tell us what happened there (§6; 1957: 53), and he tells us that Augustus lost his father at the age of four but does not wonder what effect this loss might have had upon the child or upon the adult (§8; 1957: 54); later in his biography, Suetonius begins the section of his account dedicated to Augustus's "private life, his character, and his domestic fortunes" not with any information about his childhood, but with the loss of his mother when he was 20 and of his sister Octavia when he was 54 (§61; 1957: 84). The only incidents reported from his childhood are three miracles that foretell his future greatness (§94; 1957: 101–2): as an infant he vanished from his cradle and climbed a tall tower to face the sun; when he was learning to talk he told some frogs to stop croaking, and since then, according to the locals, no frog had ever croaked again; and one day when he was eating lunch on the Appian Way, an eagle swooped down, stole some bread from his hand, carried it off—and then flew back in order to restore to him what it had stolen. When he comes to Tiberius, Suetonius tells us that "his childhood and youth were beset with hardships and difficulties, because Nero and Livia took him wherever they went in their flight from Augustus" (§6; 1957: 112); of Caligula, that he suffered from epilepsy as a boy (§50; 1957: 174); of Claudius, that "nearly the whole of his childhood and youth was so troubled by various diseases that he grew dull-witted and had little physical strength" (§2; 1957: 183); of Nero, that he lost his father at the age of three and, despite inheriting one third of his estate, lost it all to Caligula and grew up in poverty (§6; 1957: 212); of Otho, that "his early wildness earned him many a beating from his father" (§2; 1957: 256); of Domitian, that his youth was "poverty-stricken and rather degraded" (§1; 1957: 295). In all such cases, surely at least some modern readers are tempted to try to establish some form of causal connection between the child and the adult, in order to attempt to explain later monstrous behavior as in some way motivated by episodes or patterns of childhood suffering.[8] But Suetonius himself, who is the very one who provides the information, shows not the slightest interest in using it for that purpose: he registers such details about childhood no differently from facts about clothing, or diet, or sexual behavior, and moves on.

As the case of Suetonius suggests, the ancients, in considering the relation between child and adult, seem either to have subscribed to the continuous model or to have had no other alternative model available. On the continuous model,

Achilles' rage as an adult is due to his having been born with an especially fierce natural disposition and to his parents' having failed to mitigate this defect adequately by means of education. Aristotle's words in the *Politics* could easily apply to him: "Again, those who have too much of the goods of fortune, strength, wealth, friends, and the like, are neither willing nor able to submit to authority. The evil begins at home; for when they are boys... they never learn, even at school, the habit of obedience" (1295b14–17). When Achilles imagines one of his Myrmidons complaining behind his back, "your mother nursed you on gall!" (*Iliad* 16.203; Homer 1990: 419), his point is much the same: according to his imagined critics, who subscribe to the continuous model, his mother should have mitigated his innate ferocity by giving him gentle milk; instead, his inhuman savagery as an adult proves that it must instead have been fierce bile that she put into his baby bottle, thereby enhancing the natural cruelty of his character.

In a certain sense, then, the unsatisfactory explanations for character lamented by many readers of Plutarch and the other ancient biographers is built into the very structure of the continuous model, for by deriving character from the natural endowment at birth and giving education only one chance massively to modify it, this model in effect forecloses the very possibility of detailed and highly specific explanation, by locating the cause immediately in a realm of necessity that it is impossible for us to inspect and assess. "Why was A as an adult x?" "Because A was already x at birth." Or, alternatively, "Because A was born as y, but education made him x." Neither answer provides much scope for further investigation.

VII

Rushdie's presentation of Professor Solanka's curious psychological condition could not be more different. Rushdie apparently is convinced that it is important to find a precise and comprehensive explanation for his character's bouts of fury, and he seems to believe that it is possible, in principle, at least, to discover such an explanation and, in fact, not only one and just one explanation but also precisely the right one. But the most evident difference between Rushdie and the ancients, at least in this regard, is that the model that Rushdie uses to guide his investigation is in certain crucial regards not at all like the continuous one.

We might term Rushdie's model, instead, a *traumatic* one. How does Rushdie explain Solanka's anger? It is not difficult to imagine many possible explanations that he might have proposed—perhaps the most plausible in such cases being a quite recent accumulation of entirely unrelated minor irritants that explodes when some particularly annoying (or particularly safe) incident finally provides a sufficiently effective catalyst. Instead, Rushdie's traumatic model presupposes that, whatever some person's initial makeup at birth, his character as an adult comes to be decisively influenced by some terrible psychic injury that he has suffered as a child and whose consequences continue to haunt him, and to make him, for the rest of his life. For Rushdie and his readers, not only are circumstances contingent; character is, too. If the ancient view of human character is like a game of poker—you are dealt your hand, you get one chance to improve it, and after that it is up to you to make the best of the opportunities that chance affords you—Rushdie's model seems to be much more like a game of 52 pickup: whatever the cards you have been dealt, some terrible disaster can sooner or later throw them all in confusion onto the floor, and if so, you will end up spending the rest of your life trying to bring them into some kind of order, if possible and necessary, with the help of a professional psychoanalyst.

Obviously, Rushdie's model is not just Rushdie's model. The plot of *Fury* is certainly bizarre in many regards—though it must be admitted that Rushdie's analysis of Solanka's anger forms one of the weakest aspects of what is, all in all, a quite interesting novel. And there is no doubt that the fictional nature of *Fury*, its novelistic requirement of enhanced intelligibility and closure, leads to a certain degree of artificial oversimplification in the presentation of Solanka's case and of his cure—indeed, precisely this drastic reductiveness makes the novel particularly transparent and hence useful for the purposes of this argument, for this renders all the more striking the fact that Rushdie's rather crude account of Solanka's quite strange psychology is likely to seem intuitively plausible, if not to all readers, then at least to many.

If so, this is probably because *Fury* deploys psychological concepts and devices in a way that ultimately goes back to Sigmund Freud's work on hysteria and neurosis but that has gone on to become a vague and all-pervasive psychoanalytic *koine* typical of much of our contemporary culture. Freud had begun his psychoanalytic work with Josef Breuer in the 1890s, working especially on cases of hysteria—mostly young women, to be sure, rather than men, and mostly involving phobic fear rather than furious rage, but all the same, no less obviously cases of inappropriate emotions (too much of an emotional reaction to the right, if trivial, stimulus) than Homer's *Iliad* or Rushdie's *Fury*. Freud's young patients were overreacting badly—with deep phobias, with furious aggression, with acute bodily pains, with threatened and attempted suicide—to the most banal events: a boy who touched her hand during dinner, an off-color joke. Freud discarded the hypothesis that these young women simply had some inborn disposition to become hysterical—that is, he considered the continuous model as a mode of explanation but decided to reject it—and instead developed the theory that they had been the subject of some form of sexual abuse during their very earliest years of childhood, long before their reproductive organs had matured and they could have any idea of what was happening to them. So traumatic and so incomprehensible had such an event been that it had been repressed altogether from consciousness—and thereby had been consigned to the unconscious, where it did not vanish at all but went on to fester for years in an intermediate period of latency. Finally, when the girls' sexual maturity developed as they reached puberty, some new slight incident could release all the dire energy that had been stored up during the intervening years, and what had been repressed could return, with an explosive violence that was quite inexplicable if one took account only of the most recent, paltry event that had acted as catalyst.

Over the years, to be sure, Freud modified his initial hypothesis in a number of crucial regards, in particular, coming to doubt the reality of at least some of the scenes of childhood seduction whose existence he had once postulated as necessary, and coming to attribute to even the smallest children a much more lively and sophisticated sexuality than he had first imagined. Nonetheless, three basic concepts determined his thinking on this subject from the beginning to the end of his working life:

1. Repression (*Verdrängung*): A trauma is not forgotten but repressed. It is removed from consciousness, yet does not in the least thereby cease to exist. Instead, it persists in the unconscious, continues to produce effects, and can be called back into consciousness, though not without difficulty, at a later time. For Freud, nothing that has become part of the unconscious ever dies.

2. Deferral (*Nachträglichkeit*): Events produce effects not only when they occur, but also much later. A childhood experience may completely escape the child's conscious understanding at the time, but it remains latently powerful and can produce neurotic symptoms decades later. In the end, the events themselves can matter less than their memory traces, which can cause effects many years later.

3. Overdetermination (*Überdeterminierung*): As a result, no event in psychic life has only one effective cause. For any effect to happen, a multitude of partial causes must concur to produce it. The task of the psychoanalyst is to move from the manifest causes to the latent ones: only when the very last of these has been brought to full consciousness, by means of a second, therapeutic return of the repressed, is the work of psychoanalysis complete and the patient cured.

Even in the first years of his work, when Freud was treating an extraordinarily small number of cases of extremely unusual hysteria (only about a total of 13 cases by the mid-1890s), he was still inclined to consider his patients as being typical of much more widespread psychic structures rather than as being anomalous or exceptional—this was one reason he sought to explain their ailments not in terms of some exceptional hysterical predisposition but as a result of childhood sexual experiences of whose frequency he was, oddly, fully convinced. As time went on, Freud broadened the scope of his explanatory model until, with his introduction of the Oedipus complex, he came to locate the origin of neurotic ailments in sexual conflicts characteristic of apparently healthy children as well as of sick ones; and in his later, even more ambitious writings, such as *Beyond the Pleasure Principle* (1920) and *Civilization and Its Discontents* (1930), he sought to locate these irreconcilable conflicts in the universal founding structures of the human psyche and of all human civilization.

VIII

One convenient measure of just how profoundly the post-Freudian understanding of the importance of traumatic childhood experiences in helping to shape adult human character differs from the pre-Freudian one can be found in the contrast in this regard between tragedies written by the ancient Greeks and tragedies on the same mythic subjects written by twentieth-century authors who stood under the influence of Freud and had studied his works. After all, it was Greek myths and tragedies that provided Freud with some of his most important labels for various widespread psychic phenomena—the Oedipus complex, the Electra complex, narcissism[9]—and, given the manifoldly dysfunctional families that populate Greek tragedy, it is hard not to imagine that children raised in the peculiarly difficult circumstances of the house of the Labdacids, the palace of the Atreids, or in other unhappy dynasties would have grown up to manifest signs of all kinds of psychic distress. Imagine having Atreus as your grandfather and Thyestes as your second cousin, or Clytemnestra as your mother and Iphigenia as your sister; or imagine having Oedipus as your father, and brother, too, and Jocasta as your mother, and grandmother too—might you not be expected to grow up, if at all, with all kinds of neuroses crying out for psychoanalytic treatment?

And yet there is not a single passage in all of Greek tragedy in which the psychological suffering of a child is used to explain the later behavior of that child when he becomes an adult. For that matter, there are very few passages in all of Greek tragedy where a child's psychological suffering is ever mentioned.[10] When children suffer in Greek tragedy, it is usually not because they get abused but because they get killed and, sometimes, eaten; and if so, they are not likely to grow up to become adults at all, let alone troubled ones. And when, as happens very frequently, characters in Greek tragedies are shown to have been traumatized by their experiences—Orestes above all, but also Electra, Hecuba, or Medea, to name only a few—it is the traumas of adulthood from which they suffer, not those of childhood.

Even at those rare moments when the characters in Greek tragedies seem to come closest to thinking about their childhoods in a way somewhat like our own, the difference that separates them from modern attitudes is unmistakable. Thus, the aged Oedipus in Sophocles' *Oedipus in Colonus* takes great pains to justify his notorious actions, and in so doing he even refers in one passage to what his parents did to him as a child:

> And yet, how was I evil in myself?
> I had been wronged, I retaliated; even had I
> Known what I was doing, was that evil?
> Then, knowing nothing, I went on. Went on.
> But those who wronged me knew, and ruined me.
>
> (Grene and Lattimore 1959: 91, ll.270–74)

Oedipus's point here is precisely not that what he suffered as a child was what led him to do what he did and to become who he was as an adult—on the contrary, Oedipus means that, on the one hand, he himself bears no blame for having slain his father Laius at the crossroads, partly because he was acting in justifiable self-defense, partly because he was quite ignorant of who the old man was; whereas on the other hand, his parents, who had exposed him as an infant on Mount Cithaeron, had known full well who *he* was and therefore could be excused by no mitigating circumstances. Oedipus is precisely *not* saying that he was punishing his parents for what they did to him when he was a baby or that his character as an adult was a consequence of his sufferings as an infant; he uses this episode not to provide a causal account of his actions or personality but to illustrate axiologically what he sees as the enormous difference in moral value between his own qualities and those of his apparent victims. Oedipus sees himself as responding with perfect legitimacy to the outrage committed upon him as an adult by his father at the crossroads; if anyone in his story is evil, he is suggesting, it is not he, but his parents, who exposed him when he was a baby. The childhood incident, like the one in adulthood, exposes moral qualities; there is no causal link between them. How close Oedipus seems to come here to suggesting that as an adult he was avenging himself, consciously or unconsciously, for the fact that his parents exposed him at birth—and yet he does not at all actually say this, and in fact how absurd it would have been if he had!

In the case of Oedipus as in general, ancient Greek tragedy leaves no room, between adult payback and primordial curse, for childhood trauma as an explanation for adult suffering. How different matters are when we turn to tragedies on Greek themes written by modern dramatists who cannot help but read Greek myths through the lenses provided them by Freudian psychoanalysis: now adults are haunted by childhood memories, blame their parents for sufferings that express themselves in all kinds of neuroses in later life, seek therapy, and, at best, find catharsis. Hugo von Hofmannsthal's *Elektra* (1903) emphasizes far more explicitly and prominently than do the play's Greek models the heroine's absorption in her past, which makes it impossible for her to live fully in the present. Twice, arguing with her more normal sister Chrysothemis, she claims that she, unlike brute animals, is incapable of forgetting (1954: 20–21); and when she confronts her mother, she gives voice to an obsessive terror and hatred fueled by fantasies of her earliest infancy:

> I know in the whole world
> Nothing that makes me shudder, like thinking
> That this body was the dark gate out of which
> I crawled to the light of the world.
> On this lap I lay, naked?
> To these breasts you raised me?
> So indeed I crawled out of my father's grave,
> Played in diapers on my father's place of execution. You are

Like a colossus, out of whose bronze hands
I have never leaped forth.

(26–27) [11]

Indeed, so much is Elektra trapped in the sufferings of her past that she cannot
survive Orestes' vengeance, which, by slaying Clytemnestra and Aegisthus, might
have been supposed to put an end to them—at the very end of the play, when her
past dies, she collapses and dies, too.

The concern with childhood traumas is even stronger in Eugene O'Neill's
adaptation of the *Oresteia, Mourning Becomes Electra* (1929–31). Here the domi-
nance of the past over the present, which in Aeschylus had been limited to the conscious action of vendetta and the theological dimension of curse, comes to fill the
conscious and unconscious life of the characters in the form of obsessions, com-
pulsive repetitions of their own and of their most hated enemies' actions, and all
kinds of adult resentment, anger, frustration, and helplessness. Brant cannot free
himself from his memories of childhood violence and humiliation, and as an adult
he seeks only to avenge himself on those who had abused his mother and himself
when he was a child. Lavinia (Electra) tells her mother Christine (Clytemnestra),
"So I was born of your disgust! I've always guessed that, Mother—ever since I was
little—when I used to come to you—with love—but you would always push me
away! I've felt it ever since I can remember—your disgust! (*Then with a flare-up of
bitter hatred*) Oh, I hate you! It's only right I should hate you!" (1959: 249). As for
Orion (Orestes), he was always susceptible to fantasies of his past—at one point he
and his mother lovingly share a morbid, detailed memory of the ferocious Oedipal
tensions between baby Orion and his parents (300–1)—and in the last play of the
trilogy, Orion retreats altogether into what Lavinia calls his "incessant brooding
over the past" (352), devoting all his time to writing a history of the family (354),
asking his sister once, "Can't you see I'm now in Father's place and you're Mother?"
(356), and eventually, out of obsession with the past and incapacity to accept the
present, shooting himself (367).

In such cases, as in other modern tragedies, one cannot help suspecting that
early and systematic application of a vigorous program of family counseling and
psychoanalytic therapy might well have spared these characters a considerable
amount of unpleasantness.

IX

This is not the occasion to examine in detail the complexities of the development
of Freud's thought, or the variety of interpretations, schools, and approaches to
which it has given rise. Nor is it necessary, since my argument has been pitched at
a sufficiently high level of generality, to show in what ways the traumatic model of

a Rushdie or an O'Neill or a Freud is significantly different from the continuous model that appears to have been so widely diffused in the ancient world. In conclusion, I can point out some of the most obvious of these differences in a very summary fashion.

The continuous model proposes a basic unbroken connection between the child and the adult beginning from birth, while the traumatic model generates a narrative of ruptures and breaks, during the course of which the roles and characters of the various figures involved shift radically. Hence, in dealing, for example, with excessive emotion, the continuous model locates its source in a strong innate natural capacity that has not been sufficiently modified by education, while the traumatic model explains it as the consequence of repressed childhood suffering that finds a compromise expression in later life. As a result, the continuous model assigns the responsibility for these faults of character to a presocial nature, while the traumatic model lays the blame on the structure of family or society and the operation of other persons. Or, to put this another way, the continuous model praises socialization as a good and necessary process without which we remain animals and cannot become fully human, while the traumatic model sees socialization as an infliction of violence and a cause for suffering.

Another fundamental difference between these two models resides in the fact that the traumatic model is ultimately directed toward diagnosis and therapy, the continuous one merely toward instantiation. The childhood experiences narrated by the traumatic model are indispensable causal factors without which the adult personality structure would remain unintelligible; those told by the continuous model are merely one example among others that reveal a particular character, if they were left out, no one would notice. The continuous model does not really explain inappropriate emotion but merely moves the *explanandum* back one step from the adult to his inborn nature, whereas the traumatic model takes great pains to find the specific causes for what it takes to be such ailments, since it hopes to derive a cure for them from their recognition. If the continuous model seeks at all to cure excessive emotion, then it can only do so by bringing the adult to recognize the truth of certain universally valid philosophical doctrines, whereas the traumatic model tries to bring to consciousness, in the form of a detailed narrative of the self, the specific contents of the patient's repressed memories of his individual childhood experiences. As a consequence, the continuous model tends in the direction of generalization, trying to teach people to subsume their case under a universal rule, while the traumatic model tends in the direction of particularity, teaching them to recognize and understand the most specific and individual circumstances of their personal history. It is not surprising, then, that the traumatic model has achieved widespread currency in the age of the realistic novel and cinema, which have elevated the detailed account of the vicissitudes of unique individual experience to the highest form of art.

In conclusion, I am well aware of just how rough and crude some of these distinctions are. I can only hope that my readers will not suspect that this chapter was designed as some sort of fiendish psychological experiment to stimulate feelings of excessive rage among them by reminding them of the scenes of their most painful suffering as children. I should emphasize that it has not in the least been my intention to suggest that these two models, which I have called the continuous and traumatic ones, are at all as monolithic or as undifferentiated as, in this brief chapter, they may seem, or that our society as a whole is in any simple sense a Freudian one (indeed, Freud himself strikes many of our contemporaries as being very outdated in crucial regards, and all kinds of post-Freudians and non-Freudians are waging battle with one another nowadays), or that the kind of analysis sketched out here is in any way self-sufficient and would not benefit greatly from extension to other cultures (especially Asian and African) and to other periods (especially the Middle Ages). Instead, it is my hope that readers will find these reflections useful in helping them to see not only how peculiar the ancients were in their understanding of human beings, but also how we ourselves are no less peculiar and may, in fact, be far more so. A culture like ours, in which astonishingly many people are convinced that their problems as adults are in large measure due to events that they believe happened to them as children but the real existence of which they can never obtain any kind of proof—a culture in which astonishingly many people suppose that the way to cure the problems they have as adults is to immerse themselves in the details of what might or might not have occurred during their earliest years and to put the blame for their afflictions upon their nearest relatives and friends: this is a culture that the ancients, and not only they, would most likely have found very strange indeed. A story like that of Professor Solanka would probably have completely baffled them. How strange that it does not seem so strange to us.

NOTES

1. On the development of Achilles' anger and its relation to pity, see Most 2003.

2. Excellent recent surveys of ancient philosophical views of the emotions and their later transformations are provided in Sorabji 2000 and Knuuttila 2004.

3. Two representative authors are David Konstan (see, e.g. 2001, 2006) and Martha Nussbaum (see, e.g., 2001).

4. A very interesting recent exception is MacEwan 1997, which explores a case of egregiously inappropriate emotion in which all three kinds of inappropriateness seem to be involved, in a complex and perplexing mixture.

5. Of little help in this regard is Latacz 1995.

6. MacCary 1982 provides a remarkable psychoanalytic analysis of Achilles' character but does not really touch upon the questions of childhood trauma that I focus upon here. Shay 1994 thinks that Achilles' personality problems derive from his battlefield experiences rather than from his childhood.

7. See, on this remarkable poem, Heslin 2005.

8. Precisely this kind of psychological and explanatory approach is one of the features of most modern novelistic treatments of ancient celebrities, including the Roman emperors; see, e.g., Graves 1934; Yourcenar 1951. It would be an interesting exercise to examine in detail how such novels make use of their ancient sources to modern ends.

9. On Freud's use of Greek myth, and of the myth of Narcissus in particular, see Most 2002.

10. See Sifsakis 1979. Usually, children's psychological suffering in tragedy is designed to increase the pathos of the physical sufferings of adults, e.g., in Euripides' *Alcestis*.

11. "Ich weiß auf der Welt / Nichts, was mich schaudern macht, als wie zu denken, / Daß dieser Leib das dunkle Tor, aus welchem / Ich an das Licht der Welt gekrochen bin. / Auf diesem Schoß bin ich gelegen, nackt? / Zu diesen Brüsten hast du mich gehoben? / So bin ich ja aus meines Vaters Grab / Herausgekrochen, hab gespielt in Windeln / Auf meines Vaters Richtstatt! Du bist ja / Wie ein Koloß, aus dessen ehernen Händen / Ich nie entsprungen bin."

REFERENCES

Graves, R. (1934). *I, Claudius: From the Autobiography of Tiberius Claudius, Born B.C. 10, Murdered and Deified A.D. 54*. New York: Haas.

Grene, D., and R. Lattimore, eds. (1959). *The Complete Greek Tragedies*, Vol. 2, *Sophocles*. Chicago: University of Chicago Press.

Heslin, P. J. (2005). *The Transvestite Achilles: Gender and Genre in Statius' Achilleid*. Cambridge: Cambridge University Press.

Homer. (1990). *The Iliad* (R. Fagles, trans.). London: Penguin.

Horace. (1999). *Ars Poetica*. In H. Fairclough (trans.), *Satires, Epistles, and Ars Poetica*. Cambridge, Mass.: Harvard University Press.

Knuuttila, S. (2004). *Emotions in Ancient and Medieval Philosophy*. Oxford: Oxford University Press.

Konstan, D. (2001). *Pity Transformed*. London: Duckworth.

———. (2006). *The Emotions of the Ancient Greeks: Studies in Aristotle and Classical Literature*. Toronto: University of Toronto Press.

Latacz, J. (1995). *Achilleus: Wandlungen eines europäischen Heldenbildes*. Stuttgart: Teubner.

MacCary, W. T. (1982). *Childlike Achilles: Ontogeny and Phylogeny in the Iliad*. New York: Columbia University Press.

MacEwan, I. (1997). *Enduring Love*. London: Cape.

Most, G. (2002). "Freuds Narziß: Relflexionen über einen Selbstbezug." In A.-B. Renger (Ed.), *Narcissus. Ein Mythos von der Antike bis zum Cuberspace*. Stuttgart- Weimar: Metzler.

———. (2003). "Anger and Pity in Homer's *Iliad*." In S. M. Braund and G. Most (eds.), *Ancient Anger: Perspectives from Homer to Galen*. Cambridge: Cambridge University Press.

Nussbaum, M. (2001). *Upheavals of Thought: The Intelligence of Emotions*. Cambridge: Cambridge University Press.

O'Neill, E. (1959). *Three Plays: Desire under the Elms, Strange Interlude, Mourning Becomes Electra*. New York: Vintage.

Plutarch (1914–26). *Lives*, 10 Volumes. B. Perrin (trans.). London: Heinemann.

Rushdie, S. (2001). *Fury. A Novel.* New York: Modern Library.

Shay, J. (1994). *Achilles in Vietnam: Combat Trauma and the Undoing of Character.* New York: Atheneum.

Sifsakis, G. M. (1979). "Children in Greek Tragedy." *Bulletin of the Institute of Classical Studies* 26, 67–80.

Sorabji, R. (2000), *Emotion and Peace of Mind: From Stoic Agitation to Christian Temptation.* Oxford: Oxford University Press.

Suetonius (1957). *The Twelve Caesars* (R. Graves, trans.). Harmondsworth: Penguin.

von Hofmannsthal, H. (1954). *Elektra. In Gesammelte Werke in Einzelausgaben. Dramen II.* Frankfurt am Main: Fischer.

Yourcenar, M. (1951). *Mémoires d'Hadrian,* Paris: Plon.

PART IV

CONTEXTS AND USES

CHAPTER 20

....

LITERATURE AND KNOWLEDGE

....

JOHN GIBSON

It is common to claim that in works of literature we find some of the most powerful representations of reality our culture has to offer. This claim is central to the general humanistic conception of the value of the literary work of art: it is at least partly in the business of revealing to readers something of consequence about the nature of their shared world. According to this view, the literary perspective (and the artistic perspective more generally) is the definitive *human* perspective: the standpoint from which we are best able to bring to light the range of values, desires, frustrations, experiences, and practices that define the human situation. On this view, works of literature, at least when they live up to their promise, represent cognitive achievements: they embody ways of *knowing* the world.

But in developing a literary tradition, we have come to devise a rather curious way of going about revealing our world. As the saying goes, literature is "the book of life." And what is curious, simply put, is that when we open this book we find it to be filled with *fictions*. That works of imaginative literature—the sort of literature I discuss here—speak about the fictional rather than the real is hardly news. To be sure, one would think that literature's use of the creative imagination constitutes rather than refutes its claim to cognitive value: it is the tool with which literature builds its vision of our world. But the challenge the philosopher of literature faces is one of explaining just how this may be. How is it, exactly, that a textual form that speaks of fictions can tell us something of consequence about reality? Why is it that we have come to find that writing about fictions can be a powerful way of opening up a window on our world? We tend to think that it can be, of course. But as with all philosophical challenges, explaining this with a respectable degree of sophistication turns out to be a difficult affair.

The problem runs deeper than literature's interest in the imaginary and the unreal. It is not only that when we look between the covers of a novel we find descriptions of fictions. We also notice a conspicuous absence of all those tools, devices, and techniques we commonly take to be essential to the search for truth and knowledge: argumentation, the offering of evidence, the setting forth of "the facts," the proffering of premises, the derivation of conclusions, and so on (see Stolnitz 1992; John 1998; Lamarque and Olsen 1994; Diffey 1988). Needless to say, the ways in which works of history, philosophy, and science—paradigm cases of works of *inquiry*—make use of these devices and techniques vary considerably. It may even be the case that they are all, like literature, irreducibly narratological in form—this is a fairly popular claim in contemporary postmodern culture (see White 1978; Fish 1980). But works of inquiry weave their narratives in ways very unlike literature, and it is the particular way a narrative is woven that makes the difference here. Literature standardly constructs *fictional* narratives that have *dramatic* structures; works of inquiry standardly attempt to construct *factual* narratives that have *argumentative* (or evidentiary) structures. This would seem an important difference. And the challenge is to show that literary works can have a claim to cognitive value in the *absence* of those features of writing commonly taken to be the stuff of the pursuit of knowledge. For in their absence, precisely what aspect of literary works do we point toward that justifies treating them as players in the pursuit of knowledge? What do we find *in* works of literature that even entitles us to think that they wish to be read for knowledge? Again, we tend to think that there is something, but identifying precisely what is the challenge.

It is also now generally understood that to call into question the view of literary works as vehicles of knowledge is not thereby to embrace a form of literary philistinism, namely, the picture of literary works as entertaining but ultimately trivial playthings. Since the rise of various brands of literary formalism and aestheticism in the past century, philosophers and literary theorists have done much to show that there is a powerful alternative to this so-called "cognitivist" tradition of speaking about literature, one that has an equal claim to being a defense of the value of literature, of why we take literature so *seriously*. Philosophers and literary theorists of an anticognitivist bent do not deny that literary representations are very often profound, perceptive, awe-inspiring, and so forth. The thought is rather that while we will have a very hard time accounting for this profundity (etc.) in cognitive terms—say, a profundity of insight—it is altogether easy to do so in aesthetic terms. It is also likely more natural, for literary works are, after all, works of art. Indeed, an aesthetic view of literature can even urge that it is to commit what Gilbert Ryle would call a category error to try to account for the value of literary representations in cognitive terms: it amounts to a silly desire to carry over to aesthetic domains terms meant to account for the value of representations in philosophical and scientific domains.

Whether or not one quite agrees with this, it does have a certain intuitive appeal, for we have a vocabulary that works perfectly well for talking about works of art—an aesthetic vocabulary—and it is not altogether ridiculous to think that to apply the vocabulary we use to account for the value of works of inquiry also to literature is simply to misunderstand the nature of what we are talking about. At any rate, the possibility of offering a fully aesthetic theory of literature marks the presence of a more direct, and certainly less challenging, way to account for the value of literature. It is hard to imagine a literary cognitivist who has not at one time felt its appeal, who has not at least for a moment thought that she may have taken the wrong route to arrive at her defense of the value of literature.

This is the challenge I address in this chapter. I hope to give a sense of how powerful the arguments against the cognitivist view of literature are, but also to bring to light how the philosopher beholden to it might respond to them. More precisely, I argue that we must accept that literature's particular manner of engaging with reality is *sui generis*, so much so, in fact, that it constitutes its own form of cognitive insight. This implies, among others things, that we abandon what we might call the *philosophy-by-other-means* view of literature, and in general any defense of literary cognitivism that attempts to model literature on a theory of how *other* sorts of texts can have cognitive value (e.g., by showing them to mimic philosophical works, perhaps by being a thought experiment in literary guise, a sort of dramatic "proof," an exercise in moral reasoning by example, and other like things we in no obvious sense find when we look inside the majority of literary works). I also hope to show that literature's cognitive achievements are intimately bound up with its aesthetic achievements. The humanist need not turn her back to the aesthetic dimension of literary works when defending the cognitive value she believes many of them store. Rather, the humanist must embrace it, for it is here that literary works effect their particular enlightenment.

Before beginning, note that the debate on the cognitive value of literature does not concern a mere epistemological puzzle. It begins with this, but it brings something much more important to the attention of the philosopher of literature. It opens up a discussion of the general *cultural* significance of the literary work of art. Perhaps the issue of whether literary works can offer a precise sort of knowledge is not even what is really at stake in this debate. In asking whether works of literature can offer knowledge, we are asking to have the *worldly* interest we take in art vindicated. What is at stake here is our ability to articulate what amounts to a satisfactory account of the interplay of art and life itself. I do not attempt anything as grand as this here. But I do hope that what I say about the epistemological issue will give a sense of how one can use it as a tool for exploring the variety of ways in which literature and life take an interest in one another.

THE TEXTUAL CONSTRAINT

We can learn any number of things from works of imaginative literature, though many are trivial and of little literary relevance. From a master stylist, I might learn how to write with wit and grace; from an Elizabethan drama, I can gain insight into the English of an older age; from a novel of dazzling inventiveness, I can acquire knowledge of possibilities of description and conceptualization. The list is nearly endless. If the problem of literary cognitivism were simply one of identifying something—*anything*—we can learn from literature, it would be a very dull debate, for it is impossible to imagine how one could fail to arrive at a positive response to the question. But the challenge is not merely to find a way of showing that we can leave our literary encounters with "more information," so baldly put. We do, in countless ways. Rather, the challenge is to reveal literary works *themselves* to have as one of their goals the offering of a form of understanding, and this is a quite different and much more difficult matter. The claim to cognitive acquisition on the part of a reader is of little literary relevance if not tethered to a complementary claim to the effect that what the reader has learned is a lesson the literary work actually puts on offer. It is only in this sense that the question is a proper *literary* one, that is, a question that stands to reveal something about the nature of the literary work of art.

This is not always as appreciated as it should be. One finds much ink spilt on how works of literature might help improve our faculty of imagination (Currie 1998; Harold 2003), develop our cognitive skills (Novitz 1987), discover what we would think, feel, or value if in another's shoes (Walton 1997; Currie 1998), become more sympathetic and adept moral reasoners (Nussbaum 1990), and so on. These are genuine cognitive achievements, and literature can certainly help us in our pursuit of them. But, like the above examples, they tend to say too much about readers and too little about literary works. Since literary works are for obvious reasons rarely *about* the imagination, cognitive skills, or emotions of their readers, to gesture toward these things in an attempt to defend the thesis of literary cognitivism is to gesture toward the wrong thing. The question is primarily textual: it concerns the nature of the literary, of what we find of cognitive significance when we look *inside* a literary work. It is only about readers—about the ways in which their minds and morals can be improved through their encounters with literature—in a secondary, derivative sense.

Consider a classics student who, having been asked to read Plato's *Symposium*, returns to his teacher and claims to have learned much from it. The teacher asks the student to explain exactly what he has learned, to which he replies, "a considerable amount of Attic Greek and some fine metaphors for drunkenness." He very well may have learned this—one can find all of this in Plato's dialogue—and he might be all the better for it. But naturally the teacher will think that the student has missed the point of the assignment. The student has learned something, but he has not learned it from *Plato*. This is because what he claims to have learned makes no reference at all to what we might describe as the *cognitive labor* of Plato's dialogue, to the lesson it wishes to impart, to the insight it struggles to articulate—assuming, as I am, that Plato intends in that dialogue to illuminate the nature of love and not the grammar of Attic Greek or our capacity to speak in metaphors. Indeed, the student's response fails to show an *understanding* of the text, which is what we expect a claim of cognitive acquisition to reveal.

Likewise, responses to the problem of literary cognitivism that put all of the emphasis on how readers might become more successful imaginers, emoters, and reasoners are, in the end, much more sophisticated versions of the mistake of the classics student. It is valuable to have accounts of how engagements with the literary affect readers in morally and intellectually positive ways. We do live in a culture in which art is at times thought to be of no more significance than its ability to amuse, and these accounts do much to counter literary philistinism of this brand. But as a response to the question of whether literary works themselves have cognitive aspirations, they are not very satisfying. In fact, they are largely silent on this matter.

It is true, as Berys Gaut argues, that we are able "to apply the imaginative world of the fiction to the real world, and thereby to discover truths about the world" (2006: 123). We do this often when moved by a work. We turn from it and find ourselves now capable of seeing the world in its light, and this can be an important source of cognitive insight. After we read George Eliot's *Middlemarch* or Shakespeare's *Henry IV*, for example, we find ourselves able to identify all the Casaubons and Falstaffs who inhabit our world. These characters are, in their proper literary mode of presentation, creatures of pure fiction and so without any intrinsic cognitive value. But we can use these characters as tools for approaching reality, treating them as lenses through which we can attempt to perceive human character more clearly. This, in turn, can open up a way of acquiring truths about human nature, of coming to discover something about it. But while this may be a significant feature of what we do with literary works, it is not a particularly good strategy for a defense of literary cognitivism. If the acquisition of truth depends on the reader *applying* aspects of a fictional world to the real one, then presumably that truth is not given expression in the work itself, and so the work cannot quite put it on offer. We may come to learn about the world when we do what Gaut claims we do. But we haven't quite come to learn about the world *from literature*. And this is what we want answered: Can literature *itself* record, document, or bear witness to something about our cognitive relation to reality? We miss the point if we try to explain this by describing ways in which readers rather than literary works perform the cognitive labor here.

This is a problem with many popular versions of the so-called propositional theory of literary cognitivism (for a discussion of its history, see Lamarque and Olsen 1994). In an influential and clever defense of this, Peter Kivy writes:

> Now if one thinks, as I do, that part of the reader's literary appreciation consists in confirming and disconfirming for himself the general thematic statements he perceives in fictional works he reads, sometimes unaided, sometimes through the help of literary critics, one will see why it is quite compatible with the Propositional Theory that such confirmation and disconfirmation are part of appreciation, and that *appreciation* is the job, if I may so put it, of the reader, not the critic *qua* critic. The critic's job, *qua* critic, is, among other things,

to make available to the reader whatever hypothesis the fictional work may, directly or indirectly, propose. It is the reader's job to appreciate them, in part by confirming or disconfirming them for himself. (1997: 125, emphasis original; see also New 1999: 116–20)

When we find ourselves struck by a literary representation, we tend to find a *suggestion* in it, a clue as to how we may view the real world. Though the characters we find in a literary work are fictional, the particular ways in which an author invests their lives with meaning, their actions with urgency, their relationships with consequence, always suggest to the reader a way of regarding actual human affairs. The production of these visions and suggestions is typically a matter of literature's thematic rendering of its subject, say, the way in which a certain work configures "suffering," "jealousy," or "joy" as *this* sort of experience. Through the force of its thematic representation of a region of human concern, literature is able to hold up for appreciation a finely wrought *vision* of human experience and circumstance. And we tend to have an interest in subjecting these visions to cognitive scrutiny, in asking whether our world is *really* like that, or whether it would be better if it were. Much of this is surely right, and to this extent positions such as Kivy's capture an important dimension of our appreciation of literary works.

Note, however, that Kivy (and this line of thought more generally) accepts that literary themes are of no intrinsic cognitive significance. To build the bridge to truth, we have to engage in an activity that is rather suspicious from the literary point of view. We (or the critic) must *convert* a literary theme into a philosophical claim, a "hypothesis"—this is the act of rendering a theme in propositional form— which we can then go on to scrutinize for truth (e.g., by casting the representation of jealousy in *Othello* in terms of a claim to the effect that "jealousy can destroy what we hold most dear"). If this is so, it is hard not to be left with the feeling that the process of conversion that is the mechanism of cognitive acquisition here illicitly replaces literary content with philosophical content, and that in so doing, it moves the object of appreciation from the text to what is ultimately outside it. We do *not* in any literal sense find these "hypotheses" in literary works, and thus our appreciation of these hypotheses, though occasioned by our encounters with the literary, cannot itself be properly literary. When we convert a theme into the form of a hypothesis (or proposition), we are already once removed from the work, and when we begin scrutinizing this hypothesis for truth, we soon find ourselves twice removed. It seems clear that the labor put into forging the connection to truth is, again, performed almost entirely by the reader rather than by the work, and thus we face the old problem.

What these reflections bring to view is a basic constraint on what can count as a response to the problem of literary cognitivism. We might call it the "textual constraint" and treat it as telling us that a satisfactory account of a proper feature of a literary work requires that whatever property we attribute to a text—say, the property of being cognitively valuable—be an actual property *of* the text: something we come into contact with when we explore the interior of the work. It must be a part of its *content*, broadly construed. So if a certain point or insight is not *in* the work, then, according to this textual constraint, we cannot claim to have learned that point from the work. Of course, novels, at least good ones, make us think. But the important question from the literary standpoint is *what* we think about when we think about a work. And if it is something not quite in the work, then that something cannot be invoked to explain a value *of* that work. If we fail to respect this, we are ignoring the text, much as the classics student ignored Plato. We are merely commenting on how we can enlist the text in our personal intellectual pursuits and ultimately saying nothing about how the literary work of art itself might embody knowledge of the world.

THE LOSS OF THE WORLD

It is here that the problem begins to take the form of a proper philosophical challenge. According to the textual constraint, we must limit our search for cognitive value to the work itself, looking inside rather than away from it. And what we find is that virtually all the resources contemporary philosophy has given us for describing the "inside" of literary works appear to make impossible the claim that we can find in them something sufficiently real to give support to the thesis of literary cognitivism.

Prior to the twentieth century, the tradition of broadly humanistic philosophizing about art—beginning with Aristotle and extending through the German and English romantic traditions—was canonical, though always with the occasional detractor. When philosophers spoke of art, there was, in addition to compulsory observations on the nature of beauty and other aesthetic features of art, almost always an important word offered on art's general cultural significance, on the ways in which works of art articulate an insight into our capacity to achieve freedom, attain moral selfhood, reveal the universal implicit in the particular, find meaning in a world without much of a point, and so forth (see Davis 1996; Weston 2001).

But when philosophy took its initial steps toward the so-called "linguistic turn" of the twentieth century, discussions of the nature of literature began to focus on the semantic and referential features of literary language rather than on its power of cultural articulation, and a very different habit of speaking about literature began to emerge in philosophical circles. Perhaps the decisive first step in this shift was Gottlob Frege's 1892 publication of "Über Sinn und Bedeutung" [On Sense and Reference], in which we find the following claim:

> In hearing an epic poem we are…interested only in the sense of the sentences and the images and feelings thereby aroused. The question of truth would cause us to abandon aesthetic delight for the attitude of scientific investigation. Hence it is a matter of no concern for us whether the name "Odysseus" has reference, so long as we accept the poem as a work of art. (1970: 63)

What we find announced here is a view of the language of literary works that has the consequence of severing whatever internal connection we once thought might exist between literary works and extraliterary reality. Works of imaginative literature retain the "sense" of our terms, and thus the words we find in them preserve their standard meanings. Literature and what we might call "world-directed" texts (e.g., historical works, which attempt to refer to or otherwise represent reality) share the same language, generally put; they both participate in the same *Sinn*. But literary language stays on the level of *Sinn*, whereas in its standard (empirical) uses, language takes the extra step of applying these words to the actual world. Thus, literature is, if not quite self-referential, at least not interested in referring to anything real, to anything beyond itself. And if this is so, then, as Frege puts it, the "question of truth," central to so much of the humanist tradition, is barred from our appreciation of literature.

There are few Fregeans around today, but the very general orientation toward literature we find in "Über Sinn und Bedeutung" is still with us. Frege's view of literature as a sort of pure "sense" language has not aged well. (In fact, it may not even be Frege's view, since it is often argued that there can be no genuine sense without reference on Frege's model, but this is how contemporary literary aesthetics has received him.) Literature does, on many views, have truth and reference, just of a rather deviant sort. What we find in the tradition that arose after Frege is that the notions of truth and reference have been relocated to the *fictional* dimension of literature, in order to explain the ways in which works of literature function to generate and state "truths" about fictional worlds. Thus, these notions no longer serve the traditional humanistic purpose of marking the means by which literary works speak about reality. In this respect, while philosophers have recovered from Frege a notion of "literary reference," the wedge Frege drove between literature and truth is very much still in place. The consequence of this, of course, is that literature is made mute about the stirrings of extraliterary reality.

To give a sampling of prominent recent theories of fiction, in so-called speech-act approaches it is argued that writing a work of fiction is a form of nondeceptive pretense in which authors pretend to state as fact what is known to be untrue (Searle 1974–75; Beardsley 1981). In this sense, literature speaks, simply with a wink, about what is not, and so, while not in the business of telling lies, does not go about stating worldly truths. Or we find accounts that claim that literary works project a special class of *possible* worlds, namely, fictional worlds (Lewis 1978; Pavel 1986; Doležal 1998). The problem of fiction in literature here becomes somewhat like the problem of counterfactuals in the philosophy of language, a matter of describing the mechanism that allows a writer to describe actions and events that never actually occurred (or allows a reader to understand statements made about them, e.g., how we are able to make truth-valued and referential statements about nonactual states of affairs). And we have the extraordinarily influential "make-believe" account of fiction (Walton 1990). Here it is argued that just as children use sticks and stones as swords and bombs in a game of make-believe, when adults read literature they use words in much the same way. We do not *believe* what we read in a work of imaginative fiction, since we cannot believe a sentence (or a text largely composed of sentences) we know is not true. But we can *make-believe* them, and so we treat the descriptions in a literary work as props for our imaginative involvement in the story line, using nonepistemic attitudes (e.g., "imagining that") to ground the possibility of appreciating a fiction as a something though we know all the while that it is really nothing at all. (For a survey of contemporary theories of fiction, see Davies 2000.)

One should notice that none of these theories proposes the patently absurd idea that works of imaginative literature speak exclusively about the imaginary and the unreal, a claim that would imply that when William Faulkner wrote *As I Lay Dying* he invented not only Addie Bundren but also Mississippi, wagons, and death. The picture we get from these theories is that the bits and pieces of reality we find woven into works of fiction play a *nonepistemic* role in these works. They are used to give texture to the fictional world of the work rather than to represent or state truths about actual states of affairs. We do criticize a novel that uses, for instance, New York as its setting yet fails to get straight the difference between Downtown and Uptown. But this is a critique of the setting's accuracy, and it is done along the lines in which we criticize a set in a play rather than an argument to the effect that the literary work attempts to make truth-claims about the world and fails in so doing. Saying so much—claiming that accuracy of worldly background and setting in works of imaginative fiction is straightforwardly truth-functional or referential— would be akin to saying that the set in a production of *A Street Car Named Desire* functioned to make truth-claims about New Orleans, which is plain silly.

What we find in this shift in twentieth-century literary aesthetics from traditional humanistic concerns to an overriding interest in the logic and semantics of fictional discourse is that philosophy has developed a vocabulary for speaking about literature that has made it even more difficult to give sense to the thesis of literary cognitivism. There are other theories of fiction around than those just surveyed. But in virtually all of them we see a commitment to the old Fregean move of denying that literature has real-worldly truth and reference. The consequence is that it gives an air of nonsense to the idea that literary language might actually be able to *tell* us something of cognitive significance about the world. For if it does not speak about reality—if it sends its words and description to fictional rather than real addresses—how could it possibly be revelatory of reality? In this respect, the problem for the literary cognitivist is not merely that literary works refuse to use the tools of inquiry to build support for their claims, as discussed above. *Literature does not even make claims*, so there is really nothing for it to support.

This is likely one of the reasons that attempts to defend literary cognitivism such as Gaut's and Kivy's are so prominent. At first glance, the sort of insight they argue works of literature can offer may seem odd from the literary point of view, arguing as they do that readers rather than literary works perform the lion's share of cognitive labor. But given the notion of fiction with which so much contemporary philosophy operates, we can also see why moves such as theirs are so alluring. If what we have to say about literary fiction is that it concerns possible worlds, or that it casts the content of a literary work as an object of make-believe, then the idea of finding reality disclosed *through* a literary work is made utterly mysterious. If this is so, then it appears obligatory to look outside the text to establish a connection with truth and knowledge.

And so we arrive at the heart of the problem: according to the textual constraint, we *must* look within the work to ground literary cognitivism, and this seems to be precisely what we cannot do. Literary language has no declarative power, and thus it is not in the business of telling us about the nature of our world. It is true that works of fiction can embody a vision of aspects of human experience and circumstance: *Bartleby the Scrivener* is among the most potent representations we have of alienation; *Othello*, of jealousy. But visions are, from the epistemic point of view, just that: mere pictures, representations of life that are often powerful, moving, even beautiful, but for all that, cognitively neutral. Thus, something outside the work must be invoked to build the bridge between these visions and worldly truth. But the moment we look outside the work to build this bridge, we have implicitly conceded the defeat of literary cognitivism. We might console ourselves by remarking on the ways in which we can enlist literary works in our extraliterary cognitive pursuits—as we saw above, this is rather easy to do—and so we needn't fear that literary philistinism is a consequence of this. But given what philosophy tells us it means for a text to be fictional, for a use of language to be literary, it is hard indeed to see how we might give life to the thesis of literary cognitivism.

Moving the Debate Ahead

Those of us who still feel drawn to the idea that literary works are sources of worldly illumination will likely think that in all of this something crucial has been left unmentioned, and that this something is essential to the thesis of literary cognitivism. I think that this is right, and for the remainder of this chapter I try to identify just what this something is.

What should strike one as initially suspicious in the way the problem is set up in the debate is that it seems to make the case for literary cognitivism hang on whether we can apply to literature the vocabulary we have for explaining how works of inquiry illuminate reality. Though this is rarely made explicit by the major players in the debate, one does have a sense that the discussion gets afoot by looking at standard sorts of text with cognitive value—scientific, philosophical, and so on—and then wondering whether works of art can do what they do, at least at some level and to some extent. This is a questionable way of approaching the matter. I assume that painting is a paradigm case of art. But I also assume that no sensible person would try to account for the artistic value of *music* by asking whether what we find in paintings can also be found in symphonies. We are likely guilty of a similar sin if we hear the question of whether literary works have cognitive value as asking us solely whether they can offer truth and knowledge. What I think we see in the above arguments for anticognitivism is the poverty of the vocabulary of truth and knowledge when applied to literature (for similar critiques see Lamarque and Olsen 1994; Lamarque 1996, 2006). But perhaps the literary cognitivist does not need this vocabulary.

Yet what is meant by "truth" and "knowledge" here? What these anticognitivist arguments deny that the literary work possesses is a standard (and significant) sort of knowledge. This standard sort is often called "propositional" or "conceptual" knowledge, depending on the particular spin one gives it. If literature were able to offer us this sort of knowledge, then the story we should be able to tell about it would be something like the following. If we were to acquire what appears to be a potential candidate for knowledge from Fyodor Dostoyevsky's presentation of, say, suffering in *Notes from Underground*, then this work would in one way or another have to *assert* something about *what suffering is*. This would be done by offering a proposition—implicitly, in the case of works of art—to the effect that suffering, or a species thereof, is "thus and such a thing," say, a condition of mind in which one's world and one's self appear at once alien and revolting. If this happened, we would then be given epistemic access to a new *concept* of suffering or, at any rate, a refinement of the one we already possess. Literary works, however, lacking declarative power, and much else in addition, are not in the business of articulating truths of this variety, and thus they cannot be (or do not wish to be) vehicles of the sort of propositional-conceptual knowledge tied to it.

In recent years there has been a steady proliferation of philosophers who have noticed that art has an important power to offer forms of insight that in no obvious way rest upon the proffering of knowledge of this standard sort—in fact, that do not consist at all in the stating of truths about the way our world is. And this, I think, offers the literary cognitivist an important clue. Metaphors, as Ted Cohen has argued, can give expression to a new way of feeling and thinking about a familiar subject of human concern. When I offer you a successful metaphor, the metaphor holds in place a certain cognitive and emotional *orientation* toward the world (rather than states a truth about it), and it thus functions to "invite you to join a community with me, an intimate community whose bond is our common feeling about something" (Cohen 2004: 236). Noël Carroll has argued that the ethical value of art is a matter not of its offering a body of moral knowledge but of its capacity to enrich the knowledge we already possess: "[I]n mobilizing what we already know and what we already feel, the narrative artwork can become an occasion for us to deepen our understanding of what we already know and feel" (1998: 142). And Richard Eldridge has argued at length for art's capacity to present to us "materials about which we do not know exactly how to feel and judge" (2003: 226). Works of art do not resolve this material—say, a striking representation of a morally ambiguous practice—into a proposition that tells us *what* to feel and think about it. The force of their presentation of this material resides in the very act of working through it, for in so doing works of art bring to light the "complex texture of our human lives" (230). (For a similarly spirited accounts, see Graham 1995; John 2003; Harrison 1991; see also chapter 10 this volume.)

There is much to admire in these positions. In each of them the insight is tied to an artwork's *aesthetic* handling of its content. Works of art, thus conceived, illuminate the world not by pausing from their artistic pursuits and mimicking a work of inquiry (e.g., by arguing, acting as a thought experiment, or dealing out claims about the nature of this or that). Rather, this illumination is inseparable from the metaphoric and narratological dimensions of works of art. These philosophers urge that if we look deep enough, we can discover a certain cognitive force *in* these features of art, which has the attractive consequence of showing us how to allow art to be just that yet find ground upon which to build an account of its cognitive value. Like Carroll, I want to argue that literature's cognitive value resides in its ability not to offer knowledge but rather to act upon the knowledge we already possess. And like Eldridge and Cohen, I want to claim that the form of insight we get from this concerns not truth, properly so-called, but a certain cognitive orientation toward the "texture" of human experience and circumstance. Like all three, I hope to show that literature's ability to do this resides in the work itself, in the power of the visions of life it holds in place.

Before I can explain how this is so or precisely what this means, I need to introduce the sort of understanding I shall argue that literature is especially able to offer. The intuition I want to exploit is that there is much more to "understanding" than the possession of knowledge of the propositional or conceptual variety. This is perhaps obvious: there is a great variety of ways of understanding and knowing the world that cannot be captured exclusively in terms of conceptual knowledge (knowing-how is one example). But I have a specific sort of understanding in mind. It is not an alternative to conceptual knowledge. It is rather a sort of understanding that must be added to it if we are to understand certain aspects of our world *fully.* The aspects I have in mind are of a broadly moral import. They are those that designate sorts of human practice and experience in which questions of value, of response, of feeling, come into play: joy, jealousy, suffering, love, as well as racism, exploitation, self-fulfillment, trust, and the like—many of the things that are given expression in literary works of art. Let me explain.

UNDERSTANDING AND MERELY KNOWING

To hurry my discussion along, I offer a few examples, all rather far-fetched, but I will bring them down to earth in a moment. Each of the examples concerns a certain failure of response. These failures in turn raise a question about the conditions under which we are willing to attribute genuine understanding to an agent.

Imagine that you are crossing a busy midday intersection when a large bus speeds past the red light and into the crowd of people directly in front of you. Bodies are thrown and lives are lost; quite a few people are clearly in a bad way. Next to you is a man who quickly produces a cell phone. He begins to dial. A sense of relief, if that is the right word, begins to wash over you: help will soon be on its way. But when the person the man has called answers, you hear the man say, "Hey Pete, I just saw the *damndest* thing…" Now imagine the same scene, but after the accident the man turns to you and says, in absolute sincerity, "someone *really* should call for help." But he starts walking off, intently navigating his way round the wounded, his cell phone tucked securely in his pocket. Last, imagine not the accident but the moment before it. You and this odd man see the bus approaching. There is just enough time. You rush to push the people ahead of you out of harm's way. The man, however, pulls you back to safety and says, with a hint of tough knowingness, "it ain't worth it." You reply, "Of course it is!" But it is too late. In all three cases, assume, the man does not strike you as fully aware of what is wrong with his responses. When he notices the look of disgust on your face, he appears not embarrassed (or defiant or amused) but genuinely nonplussed. His expression is one of, "What?"

There are many things wrong with this man. Most are of the standard moral variety: he is likely in possession of a rather vicious character; he seems not to care much for what one should care for greatly; he turns a tragedy into an anecdote—and much else besides. But while these examples raise moral issues, my interest here is not quite in their moral dimension, narrowly conceived. Rather, I am especially interested in how the moral failure here suggests a certain *cognitive* failure. It is a failure of moral understanding, to be sure. But it is the issue of understanding itself that I wish to explore.

The first, perhaps obvious, point is that in each of these cases the failure we find in the man is not a failure of *knowledge*, at least in the minimal sense in which we ascribe knowledge to someone. He, like you, *knows* what has happened. If he did not know this, his responses would have been of an altogether different nature. He would have done nothing instead of an odd thing. He knows that there has been an accident, that there is a question as to whether one should risk one's safety to help others, that those suffering are not actors or automatons but people made of flesh and blood, and so on. If these are among the "truths" of the matter, then the man is in possession of these truths. If you were to put them to him in the form of propositions ("Do you see that there are people who are hurt, that they require help…?"), then he would assent to them. He knows, in this basic epistemic sense, what you know.

The question we naturally want to ask is this: *Given* that the man knows all this, *how* could he respond as he did? The strangeness of his response, of his particular way of acknowledging the knowledge he shares with us, gives us a reason to think that the difference between you and this man is not only moral but also intellectual: there is something he just does *not* get (or that the two of you get very differently), for if he understood the event as you did, he would have responded to your look of disapprobation not with confusion but a snarl, a mischievous grin—*something* that would have revealed that he is aware of how one should act in such a moment and that he just did not care to act thus. But this is precisely what you do *not* find in him. In a crucial respect, he seems *oblivious*, over and above the respects in which he appears simply callous. His failure to lead his knowledge though the appropriate channels of response suggests that at some level there is a significant divergence in cognitive orientation toward the *same* event. He either does not understand something you do, or he understands it in a way that is fundamentally different than you do. Either way, there is something in your mind that cannot be found in his. What might it be, exactly?

There are many ways one could explain this, and I do not want to wander off into arcane corners of epistemology and cognitive philosophy in search of them. For the sake of simplicity, I distinguish two basic sorts of understanding this example suggests, with the hope that they will suffice in a general way to bring to view an interesting point about cognition. Each form of understanding concerns a grasp of what, one might say, "counts" (in this and the following, I draw from Mulhall 1994 and especially Cavell 1969).

In the first sense, call it the *criterial*, to know is to know what counts as an *instance* of something: one thing a stone, another a table, that an expression of suffering, this of joy. Understanding in this sense is made evident by our success in extending our concepts out into the world and correctly placing particulars under their scope. This sort of understanding records a facility with dividing the world up accurately and correctly describing its particulars, a grasp of "what something is" as a success of identifying this as that sort of thing. It is a matter, simply put, of the individuation and identity of the bits of the world before us. The man's behavior meets this condition for ascribing understanding to him. He shows by his elementary success of identification—that what you and he witnessed is of the kind that it is, that the wounded are in the state that they are, and so forth—that he is in possession of this sort of awareness.

But the example also gives us reason to think that, without supplementation, this form of understanding is decidedly incomplete. Indeed, there is something rather "mere" about it. It is necessary, of course, for without the capacity to represent the world aright, we have no chance of responding to the world as we should. As a designation of a form of cognitive awareness, this criterial understanding marks one of the most basic orientations we can have toward our world, that of simply being able to identify its furniture correctly. To meet this condition for counting as a knower, all one must do is reveal that one is in possession of the relevant concepts and that one can relate them to the world in a certain way. We expect much more from a knower than this. To count as genuinely understanding what one knows in this "mere" sense, one must grasp something else.

To borrow an ugly term from ethics, for a moment at least, we might call the second sense in which understanding is linked to a notion of what counts *axiological*. It is in this respect that the odd man does not quite understand what you do. Here "counting" is, broadly put, a matter of value—of how something counts as an object of concern, as a site of significance, of how and why it *matters*. If the criterial sense emphasizes our ability to represent the world correctly, the axiological sense highlights the capacity to see the consequence of those aspects of the human world so represented. This sort of understanding designates an awareness of what is *at stake* when we represent the world in certain ways; it reveals a grasp of how an object or event should function to *engage* us with the world when we describe it as thus and such. To this extent, it is a distinctly cultural form of understanding, for it has as its target not merely "objects" and their identity conditions but also the values, cares, and concerns that define the character of our particularly human practices and experiences.

Understanding is never value-neutral, is never merely conceptual, at least not when it concerns human reality. To count as possessing full understanding of something, we must reveal not only that we have the relevant concepts and representational capacities. We must also show that we are *alive* to those patterns of value, significance, and meaning that are woven into the aspects of the world we otherwise "merely" know. We do this not by revealing that we are in possession of the right propositions or descriptions, say, by asserting, correctly, "an ambulance is needed" or "these people are in pain." In fact, when we attempt to elaborate this sort of understanding, to bring into full view just what it is, we tend to do so by depicting not what one says but what one *does* when one knows something. We offer examples of how one *invests* oneself in the particular scene one knows (or refuses to, e.g., in characters such as Bartleby). That is, we describe a type of response, a kind of gesture, that embodies this understanding. We give an account of how one *acknowledges* what one knows, of how a piece of knowledge should function to configure the knower as certain sort of *agent*. And for this, a picture, a vision, of human activity is necessary, not the elaboration of a concept or principle.

Note that a moral response, an act of acknowledgment, is a kind of *dramatic* gesture and that the understanding it embodies itself has a certain dramatic structure. An act of acknowledgment is a way of giving life to what it is that we know, of bringing it into the public world, not unlike the way in which an actor gives life to a character, or an artist manifests an inner emotion through a perfectly rendered expression. Indeed, understanding, if fully possessed, establishes a type of dramatic relation between a knower and the world. It places us in the world as agents who are responsive to the range of values and experiences that are the mark of human reality. Recall that the term "drama" itself comes to us from the Greek for "action" or "deed" (*drama*; adj. *dramatikos*), and "dramatic" has in its more contemporary usage the sense of doing something with a certain emotional investment or charge (see Shusterman 2001 for a discussion of this). These are, in effect, the markers of the form of understanding I have tried to outline here.

Literature and the Embodiment of Understanding

So what does all of this allow us to say about the thesis of literary cognitivism? How might this offer a foundation for developing our intuition that literary works, while not in the business of stating truths about the world, still have much to show us about it?

I think that the first thing we should want to say is this: what literary representations are able to do especially well is take the concepts we bring to our reading of a work and present them back to us as concrete forms of human engagement. When we read *Notes from Underground* or *Bartleby the Scrivener,* we see suffering and alienation presented not as mere "ideas" but as very precisely shaped human situations. And this contextualization of these concepts, this act of presenting them to us in concrete form, is literature's contribution to understanding, the particular light it has to shine on our world. Literary works do not embody conceptual knowledge, if by this we mean that they offer an elaboration of the nature of some aspect of our world, delivered, as it were, in a propositional package. Nor need they, if they are to have a claim to cognitive value. If they embody a form of understanding, it will consist in a more literal act of embodiment, namely, in the capacity of a literary narrative to give shape, form, and structure to the range of values, concerns, and experiences that define human reality.

The vision of life we find in literary narratives shows us human practice and circumstance not from an abstracted, external perspective but from the "inside" of life, in its full dramatic form. And if the argument I gave in the last section is convincing, we can now see how this dramatic presentation of life might be a very important cognitive achievement. This achievement does not consist in the stating of truths or the offering of knowledge of matters of fact. It is rather a matter of literature's ability to open up for us a world of value and significance and of all that this implies about our capacity to understand fully the import of various forms of human activity. Literary works' mode of engaging with the world is never narrowly or purely cognitive. Literature would not be *dramatic* if it were. But it is precisely this drama we need if we are to have a textual form that is capable of documenting our particular way in the world. And this is not a minor accomplishment from the cognitive point of view. It shows literature to be among the richest, most potent media we have for the articulation of cultural understanding.

When literary works are successful dramatic achievements, it is always in part because they fashion a sense of what is at stake in the specific regions of human circumstance they represent. In this respect, there is an interesting parallel between literary narratives and moral responses. Just as a moral response does not so much convey knowledge of an event as it gives expression to an agent's awareness of its significance, literary works, rather than stating truths about our world, bring to light the consequence, the import, of those aspects of reality they bring before us. Put differently, literary works represent ways of acknowledging the world rather than knowing it (see Gibson 2003, 2008; Cavell 1969). A literary narrative is in effect a sustained dramatic gesture, a way not only of presenting some content or material but also of responding to it. What we see distilled into the narrative perspective is a vision of how and why this content *counts*, the precise respects in which it might matter.

These patterns of significance, value, and meaning we find in literary works are patterns to which we tend to have no cognitive access in our in less dramatic, quotidian lives. We simply do not see what Eldridge felicitously calls the "complex texture of our human lives" with such precision of detail and depth of vision in our everyday encounters with the world. We very likely knew what racism is, or that a lynching is among its most brutal manifestations, before reading James Baldwin's short story "Going to Meet the Man." But unless we have engaged in the very practices Baldwin depicts in his story—and one would hope that few of us have—we have not been granted an understanding of the form they may take as specific types of human activity. Baldwin's manner of representing the desires, repressions, pursuits, and relationships of the characters he imagines for us—indeed, the precise manner in which he develops racism as a theme that structures the story itself—is itself a way of acknowledging what racism is. That is, it constitutes an attempt to render explicit its significance and import in the context of our cultural practices. And in following the story, we too are forced to acknowledge something about the nature of racism, for instance, that it can have its source in something other than just hatred and ignorance, contrary to what we were often told in school. It might reside in something much more primitive and pervasive, something that reaches all the way to the core of our social and sexual natures. For this reason, Baldwin's story forces us to see racism as more complex, and so more terrifying, than we had once thought, or were willing to think.

Literature does not treat the world as an object of knowledge but as a subject of human concern. And this itself is a cognitive accomplishment, a way of bearing witness to the world. Indeed, this gives us reason to speak of literature as engaged in a form of worldly investigation, just of a sort that is markedly different than we find in works of inquiry. It is a dramatic investigation. But human life itself is dramatic in nature, and thus literary works, in their uniquely literary form, are perfectly built for its exploration. Literary works needn't cast aside their literary pursuits and mimic works of philosophy if they are to engage in this form of investigation. They simply need to go about their usual business.

If this is so, then we can respect the textual constraint when defending literary cognitivism, for the form of insight literature trades in is bound up with the internal structure of a literary work—in fact, it is inseparable from it. The insight into life we find in a great novel is the novel itself. It is woven into the fabric of the story, the specific ways in which it configures and gives dramatic expression to its subject matter. Thus, we should not ask whether literary works might be able to do what standard works of inquiry do if we wish to defend literary cognitivism. They do not, nor should we wish them to. We can leave them be as they are, without worrying that we will thereby make them cognitively trivial on account of it.

Instead of asking whether literary works might be able to offer us what other works of inquiry do, a more interesting way of putting the matter is to ask what aspects of our world would be left undocumented, unaccounted for, if we had no literary works. If we think of texts as archives in which we store the various accounts we have to offer of the nature of our world, what would be missing if there were no literary works? The question itself is likely imponderable, for if literary works play an important role in the articulation of cultural understanding, then our sense of our world is itself at least partly literary in origin. At any rate, what we would lack without literary works (and works of art more generally), what would be missing from our archive, is not a body of knowledge but a certain perspective. It would be, of course, the human perspective, that purchase on the world that reveals not what we know about it but how we go about living in it. Without this, we really wouldn't have much to show for ourselves.

REFERENCES

Beardsley, M. (1981). "Fiction as Representation," *Synthese*, 46, 291–313.

Carroll, N. (1998). "Art, Narrative, and Moral Understanding." *In* J. Levinson (ed.), *Aesthetics and Ethics: Essays at the Intersection*. Cambridge: Cambridge University Press.

Cavell, S. (1969). "Knowing and Acknowledging." *In* Cavell, *Must We Mean What We Say? A Book of Essays*. New York: Charles Scribner's Sons.

Cohen, T. (2004). "Metaphor, Feeling, and Narrative." *In* E. John and D. Lopes (eds.), *Philosophy of Literature: Contemporary and Classic Readings*. Oxford: Blackwell.

Currie, G. (1998). "Realism of Character and the Value of Fiction." *In* J. Levinson (ed.), *Aesthetics and Ethics: Essays at the Intersection*. Cambridge: Cambridge University Press.

Davies, S. (2000). "Fiction." *In* B. Gaut and D. Lopes (eds.), *Routledge Companion to Aesthetics*. London: Routledge.

Davis, T. (1996). *Humanism*. London: Routledge.

Diffey, T. J. (1988). "Art and Meaning." *In* Richard Woodfield (ed.), Proceedings: XIth International Congress in Aesthetics. Nottingham: Nnottingham Polytechnic Press.

Doležal, L. (1998). *Heterocosmica. Fiction and Possible Worlds*. Baltimore: Johns Hopkins University Press.

Eldridge, R. (2003). *An Introduction to the Philosophy of Art*. Cambridge: Cambridge University Press.

Fish, S. (1980). *Is There a Text in This Class? The Authority of Interpretive Communities*. Cambridge, Mass.: Harvard University Press.

Frege, G. (1970). "On Sense and Reference." *In* P. Geach and M. Black (eds. and trans.), *Philosophical Writings of Gottlob Frege*. Oxford: Oxford University Press. (Original work published 1892).

Gaut, B. (2006). "Art and Cognition." *In* M. Kieran (ed.), *Contemporary Debates in Aesthetics and the Philosophy of Art*. Oxford: Blackwell.

Gibson, J. (2003). "Between Truth and Triviality." *British Journal of Aesthetics*, 43, 224–37.

——. (2008). *Fiction and the Weave of Life*. Oxford: Oxford University Press.

Graham, G. (1995). "Learning from Art." *British Journal of Aesthetics*, 35, 26–37.

Harold, J. (2003). "Flexing the Imagination." *The Journal of Aesthetics and Art Criticism*, 61, 247–58.

Harrison, B. (1991). *Inconvenient Fictions: Fiction and the Limits of Theory*. New Haven: Yale University Press.

John, E. (1998). "Readiing Fiction and Conceptual Knowledge: Philosophical Thought in Literary Context." *The Journal of Aesthetics and Art Criticism* 56, 331–48.

——(2003). "Literary Fiction and the Philosophical Value of Detail." *In* M. Kieran and D. M. Lopes (eds.), *Imagination, Philosophy, and the Arts*. London: Routledge.

Kivy, P. (1997). *Philosophies of Arts: An Essay in Differences*. Cambridge: Cambridge University Press.

Lamarque, P. (1996). *Fictional Points of View*. Ithaca, N.Y.: Cornell University Press.

——. (2006.) "Cognitive Values in the Arts: Marking the Boundaries." *In* M. Kieran (ed.), *Contemporary Debates in Aesthetics and the Philosophy of Art*. Oxford: Blackwell.

Lamarque, P., and S. H. Olsen. (1994). *Truth, Fiction and Literature*. Oxford: Clarendon.

Lewis, D. (1978). "Truth in Fiction." *American Philosophical Quarterly* 15, 37–46.

Mulhall, S. (1994). *Stanley Cavell: Philosophy's Recounting of the Ordinary*. Cambridge: Cambridge University Press.

New, C. (1999). *Philosophy of Literature: An Introduction*. London: Routledge.

Novitz, D. (1987). *Knowledge, Fiction and Imagination*. Philadelphia: Temple University Press.

Nussbaum, M. (1990). *Love's Knowledge*. Oxford: Oxford University Press.

Pavel, T. (1986). *Fictional Worlds*. Cambridge, Mass.: Harvard University Press.

Searle, J. (1974–75). "The Logical Status of Fictional Discourse." *New Literary History*, 6, 319–32.

Shusterman, R. (2001). "Art as Dramatization" *Journal of Aesthetics and Art Criticism*, 59, 363–72.

Stolnitz, J. (1992). "On the Cognitive Triviality of Art." *British Journal of Aesthetics*, 32, 191–200.

Walton, K. (1990). *Mimesis as Make-Believe*. Cambridge, Mass.: Harvard University Press.

——. (1997). "Spelunking, Simulation, and Slime: On Being Moved by Fiction." *In* M. Hjort and S. Laver (eds.), *Emotion and the Arts*. Oxford: Oxford University Press.

Weston, M. (2001). *Literature, Philosophy and the Human Good*. London: Routledge.

White, H. (1978). *Tropics of Discourse*. Baltimore: John Hopkins University Press.

CHAPTER 21

....

LITERATURE AND
MORALITY

....

TED COHEN

THE idea that art has or can have something to do with morality is an old and enduring idea, beginning at least as early as the disagreement between Aristotle and Plato over the moral acceptability of fiction. In the current literature, the idea appears in at least two continuing discussions, and these are the topics of this chapter. Some other topics are mentioned but left largely unexamined.

The two continuing discussions revolve around two questions: (1) Does or can acquaintance with works of art have a moral effect upon an audience? (2) Is the moral character of a work of art relevant in its "aesthetic" assessment?

I

....

It may be thought that literature is an aid to morality in the sense that appreciative reading of literature makes one a morally better person. As plausible as this may seem, surely it is dubious. Taken as an empirical claim, it collapses immediately under the weight of anecdotal evidence. University and college departments of literature are full of people skilled and practiced in the reading of literature, and it is obvious that these people are morally no better (or worse) than other people. It is perhaps just as obvious that those philosophers who specialize in ethics also tend to be morally no better or worse than other people. (Perhaps it is true that those who spend much time reading have less time in which to do bad things, but it is then equally true, one supposes, that they have less time in which to do good things.)

Suppose it is true that reading literature at least *can* be morally uplifting and improving, presumably by exposing readers to human situations—their complexities and necessities—that they would otherwise not be aware of. If so, then it must also be true that reading literature can be morally degrading. If one might learn, say, from Charles Dickens's *Hard Times* that unrestrained capitalism is morally vicious, then one might learn that free-market capitalism is essential to the elevation of the human spirit by reading Ayn Rand's *Fountainhead* or *Atlas Shrugged*. If one can learn the horrors of racism and the need for tolerance by reading Harriet Beecher Stowe's *Uncle Tom's Cabin* and Richard Wright's *Native Son*, then one can learn of the unredeemable and implacable depredations of the Jews from T. S. Eliot. If one can acquire sympathy for the plight of women in the modern world from Henrik Ibsen and Gustave Flaubert, then one can learn of women's deep need for sexual subjugation from Pauline Réage's *The Story of O*.

In the cases of some significant works, it is far from clear what is to be learned. From Joseph Conrad's *Heart of Darkness* (1899) do we learn the obtuse and culpable racism found in it by Chinua Achebe, or do we learn that the arrogant sophistication of white Christian Europeans has robbed them of that morally essential instinct for *restraint*, an instinct still alive in native Africans? And in Mark Twain's *Adventures of Huckleberry Finn* (1885), what do we learn from Huck's argument with Jim about the acceptability of a Frenchman's failure to speak English, an argument in which Huck has the right conclusion but Jim has the better logic, an argument Huck leaves, saying, "I see it warn't no use wasting words—you can't learn a nigger to argue. So I quit"? (2005: 74).

Plato's seeming objection to fiction is that it has nothing to do with knowledge, and thus Aristotle's reply includes the assertion that one can learn from such "imitations." The Platonic reply to this, surely, is that there is no guarantee that what may be "learned" is the truth. Should we chance it, hoping for the best? John Rawls once noted, in an informal lecture, that as a very rough characterization one might think of a conservative as someone who, despite acknowledging current imperfections, is so troubled by how much worse things might be that he refuses to initiate changes without a strong guarantee of what will result from change, while a radical is so appalled by the present situation that he is willing to exchange it for virtually anything. The Platonist, thus, is so worried by fiction's capacity to "teach" the wrong things that he would prefer not to risk being taught by fiction at all. And, of course, it may be not that the author-teacher happens to be wrong, but that he may intentionally purvey what he takes to be false. He might be like the author of this poem:

> They asked me: Wise one, who is it who doesn't
> distinguish between what's right and wrong,
> and sings in praise of his day's elect
> while his heart has long seen through his song?
> And I answered them: My friends, it is I—
> I am the poet who lies.
>
> (Meshullam Depiera, "The Poet,"[1] in
> Cole 2007: 230)

Still, the idea that literature at least *can* be morally beneficial is an idea of long standing, and some have thought literature even more effective than philosophy in this regard. Thomas Jefferson, for instance, wrote this:

> Moral Philosophy. I think it lost time to attend lectures on this branch.... State a moral case to a ploughman & a professor. The former will decide it as well, & often better than the latter, because he has not been led astray by artificial rules. In this branch [moral philosophy] therefore read good books because they will encourage as well as direct your feelings. The writings of Sterne particularly form the best course of morality that ever was written. (1984: 901)

If literature *can* affect a reader's morality—whether for better or for worse—how does this happen? There seem to be at least two ways. The first was described by Aristotle in his claim that dramatic literature—specifically tragedy—can present human life and action exhibiting a kind of necessity, a necessity not always conspicuously exhibited in human affairs when those affairs are simply confronted in ordinary life or presented in nondramatic historical narration. Thus, an ancient Greek tragedy, or perhaps any work of fiction, might teach us that when a man or a woman acts in certain ways, there will be consequences for which that actor is responsible. It will do this by presenting the acts and their sequels as linked by what Aristotle calls necessity, and this will reveal the implicit moral significance of those acts, something the audience might not otherwise have realized.

But even if literature can exhibit the moral dimensions of human life, presumably by firing the imagination of its audience, the question of how the audience will itself then behave will remain open. One sees this in a remark of Virginia Woolf's: "The reason why it is easy to kill another person must be that one's imagination is too sluggish to conceive what his life means to him" (quoted from Woolf's diaries in Sittenfeld 2005). Surely this is right as an explanation of the ease with which some can kill, but it fails utterly to recognize that it may be exactly one's ability to imagine the cost to another that makes it possible to wish to kill him. Thus, if a literary work made clear to a reader just what someone's life might mean to him, this could lead to murder as well as to compassionate restraint. My desire to kill someone might well be increased by my imagining that he will then be unable to enjoy his grandchildren or to profit from his pursuits. And, of course, I might think I will relish the pain it will cause those who love him.

Perhaps the right moral to draw from this is the one Peter Kivy has drawn when writing of the possible moral effects of music: "Of course a *human* life guarantees neither a good life, nor a happy one. The best that we can hope from music, it seems to me, is that it help to *humanize*. Happiness and goodness we will all have to work out for ourselves" (1993: 31). Similarly, then, if literature *can* enrich one's imagination and sensibility, it remains an open question just what actions that might lead to.

Just how is it that literature achieves a morally significant effect, if it does? Perhaps it is that some moral distinctions are so fine that they may go unrecognized in real life and thereby lose what ought to be their felt significance. Literature can have the power to bring these distinctions forward and induce a sense of their moral urgency. A reader of Herman Melville's *Billy Budd* (1924) who is careless or too quick to judge springs to the conclusion that Captain Vere is right to effect the execution of Billy. Or he is sure that Vere is wrong to do it. Either way, such a coarse reader is obtuse. Is it right that Billy is hanged? Yes. And no. Who is responsible and perhaps to blame for Billy's fate? No one. And everyone. But how can this be—how can there not be what Kant thought of as a virtual formula for calculating moral rights and wrongs, or a utility principle that would do the same? Perhaps *Billy Budd* teaches us—if "teach" is the right word—that, given a good man in an imperfect and imperfectable world, the unavoidable and inescapable moral agony of Vere awaits every human being with the moral wit to rise to it.

It is useful to have a closer look, if a brief and oversimplified one, of how *Billy Budd* presents its terrible vision, taking note of how exquisitely and poignantly Melville creates the moral dimensions of his situation. When provoked or attacked, Billy's response is to strike out, and thus he kills Claggart. A singularly ill-conceived response, one supposes (although it is not clear that Billy has done any "conceiving"), and yet, when Billy served on the merchant ship *The Rights of Man*, this was exactly how Billy responded to provocation, and that response was a great success. So one cannot easily indict Billy for a failure to learn from experience. Things are different on the warship, however, one says, and when Billy joined that ship he entered a different kind of society. Yes, but remember that Billy did not *join* the crew of the warship: he was conscripted, whereas presumably he had earlier freely joined the crew of the merchant ship.

It is not easy to exonerate Billy, but nor is it easy to condemn him. The person who must decide whether Billy is to be condemned, or exonerated, or have his punishment mitigated is the captain of the warship, Vere. What is Vere to do? It is commonly supposed that Vere's reason and justification for having Billy executed are roughly this: the relevant naval regulations prescribe capital punishment for a crew member who strikes a superior. They do this because any lesser penalty might be insufficient to deter mutinous activity. Mutinous activity must be deterred because such activity obviously would be detrimental to the success of the British Navy. And, of course, the success of the British Navy is vital to the very sovereignty of Britain. More could be said, but this is enough to suggest the apparently utilitarian justification for Vere's decision to have Billy hanged.

To pay respect to the subtlety and complexity of Melville's work, it should be noted that this reasoning may or may not represent Vere's reason for killing Billy. It is through this reasoning that Vere persuades the drumhead court to deliver a death sentence, but that does not establish that it is Vere's personal conviction. Perhaps Vere has another reason for thinking Billy must die. But we will not go into that, for this chapter is not concerned with the depths of interpretation of literary works.

Let us suppose that the reader of *Billy Budd*, intent upon finding moral significance therein, is led to entertain this reasoning. Does he find it compelling? Billy is killed to forestall a mutiny, or so the junior officers of the court believe, and yet the one and only occasion upon which the crew show signs of disobedience is when they have been summoned on deck and apprehend that Billy is about to be hanged.

The officers must consider two propositions:

P1. Let Billy get away with killing Claggart, or at least not hang him here and now, and this crew (and possibly others, hearing the news) will be more likely to disobey.

P2. Undertake to hang Billy and this crew will protest violently.

In deciding what to do with Billy, is it thus just a matter of deciding which proposition is more likely to be true? This seems an unspeakably vulgar way of understanding the moral question of whether to kill a man. But is it?

Now, of course, if you believe in the completeness and consistency of Kant's categorical imperative, or of the utility principle advanced by J. S. Mill and his followers, then you may think that what *Billy Budd* teaches is not a truth. That is exactly as it should be, for, as noted above, if literature is capable of casuistry or assertion, or otherwise able to affect the imagination and motivation of a reader, that capacity as such is neither good nor bad, and can lead to either, and the literature itself gives no moral assessment.

It may be that actions and judgments of moral significance require being able, as it were, to see and feel from the point of view of another. This need can be realized easily when one considers the inadequacy as a major moral principle of the so-called golden rule. When I consider doing something that will affect another person, if I ask myself only how I would like having that thing done to me, I may well indulge my own eccentricities and idiosyncrasies. Thus, as the saying goes, from the standpoint of the golden rule, a masochist is justified in indulging in sadism.

What seems to be required of me is not that I sense how I would feel if the action were perpetrated upon me, but how the actual recipient will feel. For instance, suppose I contemplate making a joke at Jack's expense. Will I be (morally) acceptable if I do that? If I ask myself only how I would feel and judge if the joke were made at my expense, I may fall short of an accurate appraisal. What I need to know is how Jack will feel if I make him the butt of a joke.

Now if this is right, then morality requires what might be called "empathy," and however that term is understood, it might be argued that the capacity for empathy, for empathic understanding, can be augmented by experience in dealing with literature. Fictional literature, after all, virtually invites, requires, and facilitates such "identification," such efforts to grasp the experience of others.

Surely there are other ways of amplifying people's capacity for empathy—if there were not, then nonreaders would invariably be morally incompetent—but even if the reading of fiction were the only way, such reading would be a best a necessary condition for moral competence. It certainly would not be a sufficient condition because, as noted above, the capacity fully to appreciate the consequences to another person of one's action might lead to dreadful acts precisely because the agent has a vivid sense of the pain he wishes to cause.

Still, one should not underestimate the critical need for empathetic understanding and the capacity of fiction to stimulate this capacity. It seems to do so by presenting characters and their situations so vividly and unignorably as virtually to compel the reader to "feel" what it would be to be such a character in such a situation—no small achievement, and one of no small moral significance, especially if one's experience of fiction can be thought of as a kind of exercise whereby one's capacity for interpersonal understanding is strengthened and then activated in the contexts of real life.

There is an oddity here, what might be thought of as a paradox of moral instruction. Suppose that some fictional work displays a subtlety or complexity of moral relevance, and that it might profit someone to have an experience of this work. How much moral acumen is required of a reader to discern this content? If it requires a great deal, then any reader is either one already capable of bringing a heightened moral sensibility to matters in his real life and thus has no need of this work, or he is morally obtuse and is thus incapable of benefiting from the work.

If the moral significance of a fiction were exactly as difficult to apprehend as the moral significance of matters in real life, then the fiction would be either useless or superfluous. It seems to follow that in order for the fictional work to be efficacious, it must be accessible to someone currently unable to respond adequately to events as they unfold in real life but still able to react competently to the work. It is as if the work must present, as the saying goes, real life but with better lighting. And perhaps that is how some fiction does its work of moral instruction.

II

The second topic of this entry is the question of whether morally objectionable features of a fiction count against its aesthetic merit. If *Billy Budd* or *Atlas Shrugged* or *Heart of Darkness* is morally reprehensible, is it a lesser work for that reason?

It is extremely difficult to formulate this question with enough precision and specificity to permit even a coherent answer. In the first place, it is unclear how a fiction can have a moral dimension. It is commonly complained of various works that they say that Catholics are superstitious, that black people are innately incompetent, that Jews are mendacious, that war is a good and noble undertaking, that homosexual behavior is disgusting and dangerous, and that women are best satisfied when they are dominated by men. Such complaints, obviously, are based on the conviction that these assertions are false. But even if it were possible to credit the idea that fictions *say* anything, it would be almost unaccountably mindless to blame a fiction for saying something false. A *fiction*, virtually by definition, is exactly a collection of falsehoods. If we should object to falsehoods as such, then how can we avoid rejecting "Vere was the captain of a British warship," "Charley Marlow piloted a steamboat up the river into the Belgian Congo," and

"Huckleberry Finn was born in Hannibal, Missouri, and grew up with a friend named Tom Sawyer"? We would reject such statements as false only if we did not know what a fiction is.

Questions regarding the truth-value of fictional sentences and regarding the possibility of linking a fictional work to any assertion whatever (as if a fiction might assert something) have no place in this chapter, but it will be assumed that the question of the morality of fiction cannot usefully be addressed in terms of "fictional truth."[2] There remains room for a moral dimension in fiction if, as considered above, fiction can induce in its readers a heightened moral sensibility, an awareness of subtle significances, perhaps a new conviction about the rightness or wrongness of something, and possibly even new or altered forms of behavior. If a work of fiction could do those things, then should that fact count in an assessment of the work's literary merit?

If a literary work has a moral component, even a casuistic one, does that fact, regardless of just what the morality is, itself count for or against the work? The history of literature, constituted by both writers and critics, shows different opinions about this, as noted in a recent review: "'We hate,'" wrote John Keats, 'poetry that has a palpable design upon us;' but Stowe was born into the age of Dickens and the Brownings, when high imagination and a moral message were felt to be compatible" (Bromwich 2007: 51). The question is whether the moral characteristics of a literary work count in assessing the work's literary or artistic merit. That is the question, and it sounds like a clear, answerable question, whatever the correct answer may be, and yet asking the question brings up another question whose answer is hard to find.

The late Frank Ramsay offered a suggestion for dealing with long-standing philosophical debates in his *The Foundations of Mathematics and Other Logical Essays* (1931). When philosophers are positioned on both sides of a debate that has stood unresolved for a long time, Ramsay counseled looking for something both sides agree to, and denying that. Is its morality relevant to the literary, aesthetic merit of a work of fictional literature? Some philosophers (and others) have said yes, some have said no, and some have pronounced, with nuance, sometimes and in some ways yes, otherwise no. The positions and arguments of these thinkers have been canvassed fairly, diligently, and accurately by Richard Eldridge (see 2003: chap. 9). Virtually all participants in this debate must suppose there to be some at least tolerably serviceable distinctions, on the basis of which one might take the true statements that can be made about a fictional work and sort them into a group of statements concerning the work's morality, another group that concern the work's literary merit, and, no doubt, a number of other groups (e.g., statements concerning the work's genre, or its provenance, or its author). And then the question is whether members of the first group belong in, or entail members of, the second group. Whether there is such a distinction is the question that has been, so far, ignored.

The question inspired by Ramsay, then, is this: How reasonable is it to suppose that the moral-relevant statements can be distinguished from other statements about the work and, in particular, from nonmoral relevant statements that concern the work's literary merit? One might think that surely there are features of a literary work that are exclusively of aesthetic or literary significance and have nothing to do with morality, and among those features, perhaps, are ones having to do with what, broadly, is called "style." But even these features are not so obviously morally innocuous. Apart from questions of grammar and syntax, consider simply the question of word choice. Is there no moral significance in the author's choice of a lexicon?

Commenting on Ernest Hemingway's prose, William Faulkner famously (or notoriously) said: "He has never been known to use a word that might send a reader to the dictionary." Whether or not this is a fault in Hemingway's writing, it seems a fair description, as exemplified, for instance, in the opening lines of *A Farewell to Arms* (1929):

> In the late summer of that year we lived in a house in a village that looked across the river and the plain to the mountains. In the bed of the river there were pebbles and boulders, dry and white in the sun, and the water was clear and swiftly moving and blue in the channels. Troops went by the house and down the road and the dust they raised powdered the leaves of the trees. The trunks of the trees too were dusty and the leaves fell early that year and we saw the troops marching along the road and the dust rising and leaves, stirred by the breeze, falling and the soldiers marching and afterward the road bare and white except for the leaves. (1995: 1)[3]

Compare this kind of writing with that found in the works of Vladimir Nabokov. In his short novel *Pnin*, which runs to fewer than 150 pages in the 1996 Library of America edition, one finds these words: pyrographic, felted, downcome, amphoric, vagitus, volitation, mangosteen, skiagrapher, cathetus, tumefied, scholiast, glabella, soubrette, calvity.[4] Such writing surely sends a reader to the dictionary.[5]

Certainly there are good questions about these two very different kinds of literary achievement. In Nabokov we find an exuberant, nearly ecstatic joy in the fabulous riches of the English language. His strange, wonderful words stand out like the sound of an oboe in a full orchestra. In Hemingway, by contrast, we find only common, pedestrian words, although their composition is stunning. The occurrence and recurrence of the words "troops," "dust," and "leaves," for instance, figure in a kind of polyphonic pattern resolved in the phrase "except for the leaves," where the final word also suggests the ending of the paragraph itself. A student of literature could work on these texts with profit, trying to understand how language works in each, whether one linguistic practice is somehow better than the other, and whether they simply appeal to different sensibilities. These would all be matters of literary or aesthetic merit, presumably, and would have nothing to do with morality.

But is this true? Does the question of lexical proclivity have nothing to do with ethics? Might one argue that Hemingway's prose is far more democratic, that indeed the term "demotic" is made for such prose, while Nabokov's lexicon of arcana is elitist? The meaning of many Nabokovian sentences is simply inaccessible to any reader who does not either already possess an incredible vocabulary or find access to reference materials—and at that, he will need far more than common dictionaries: nothing short of the *Oxford English Dictionary* will turn up all of them, and even that will leave some doubt about a few.

One distinguished philosopher who thought there to be a connection between art and morality and, indeed, that the making of art is itself a moral activity was R. G. Collingwood (1938).[6] He argued that successful art—all art, and certainly including literature—succeeds in telling the truth about oneself, one's feelings, and the world. He often writes as if failed attempts to do this were moral failings— an extreme idea, no doubt, and an extravagant one, but well worth going into.

It is sometimes argued that the full aesthetic achievement of Leni Riefenstahl's movies is available only to those viewers with at least a tolerance for myths of Nordic beauty and superiority, and that tolerance seems a matter of moral significance.[7] Then isn't Nabokov's literary achievement likewise available only to those with a fondness for, or at least a tolerance of language that escapes the ken of the vast majority of English speakers?

If even something as seemingly innocuous as word choice can have a moral bearing, then perhaps even the most isolated, formal characteristics of literature are available for moral appraisal, and if that is so, then in the continuing debate over the aesthetic relevance of moral concerns, both sides have been assuming a literary/moral distinction that itself is either dubious or question-begging. There will be no clear distinction between one set of sentences all of which refer to a work's moral quality, and another set whose members refer only to literary features of the work, and thus no question as to whether members of the first set are aesthetically relevant. Instead, there will be just one set, those sentences referring to the work, and the question will be, for instance, whether the morally elitist character of Nabokov's prose affects the aesthetic quality of the work. It will take at least some literary or aesthetic awareness to detect the oddity of Nabokov's lexicon, and then a decision will be required as to whether this is a matter of moral significance, and then, finally, a newer aesthetic question, namely, whether that moral matter itself is relevant in appraising the literary quality of the novel. I take no stand on these matters, but hope only to have made them somewhat clearer.

NOTES

1. This poem was written about 700 years ago.
2. For the question of whether fiction can have anything to do with the truth, see chapter 20 this volume.
3. A very useful meditation upon the paragraph is found in Didion 1998.
4. The words can be found, respectively, on pp. 312, 312, 320, 326, 330, 349, 362, 367, 377, 388, 396, 409, 421, and 424. A less than laudatory note about Nabokov's use of such words is in Stern 1993.

5. A typical computer spell-checker finds only three of them in its dictionary. The small, paperback version of the *American Heritage Dictionary* lists none of them.

6. A slight introduction and guide to a part of this work is Cohen 1989.

7. An excellent discussion of this topic, with specific attention to Riefenstahl, is Devereaux 1998.

REFERENCES

Bromwich, D. (2007). "The Fever Dream of Mrs. Stowe" [a review of *The Annotated Uncle Tom's Cabin*]. *New York Review of Books*, October 25, 51–53.

Cohen, T. (1989). "Reflections on One Idea of Collingwood's Aesthetics." *Monist* 72(4)., 581–85.

Cole, P. (2007). *The Dream of the Poem: Hebrew Poetry from Muslim and Christian Spain, 950–1492.* Princeton: Princeton University Press.

Collingwood, R. G. (1938). *The Principles of Art.* Oxford: Oxford University Press.

Devereaux, M. (1998). "Beauty and Evil: The Case of Leni Riefenstahl's *Triumph of the Will*." *In* Jerrold Levinson (ed.), *Aesthetics and Ethics: Essays at the Intersection.* Cambridge, Cambridge University Press.

Didion, J. (1998). "Last Words." *New Yorker*, November 9, 74.

Eldridge, R. (2003). *An Introduction to the Philosophy of Art.* Cambridge: Cambridge University Press.

Hemingway, E. (1995). *A Farewell to Arms.* New York: Scribner. (Original work published in 1929.)

Jefferson, T. (1984). "Letter to Peter Carr, written in Paris, August 10, 1787." *In* Merrill D. Peterson (ed.), *Thomas Jefferson, Writings.* New York: Library of America.

Kivy, P. (1993). "Music and the Liberal Education." *In* Kivy, *The Fine Art of Repetition.* Cambridge: Cambridge University Press.

Sittenfeld, C. (2005). "Review of *Virginia Woolf: An Inner Life* by Julia Briggs." *New York Times Book Review*, November 20.

Stern, R. (1993). "*Pnin*'s Dust Jacket." Reprinted in Stern, *One Person and Another.* Dallas, TX: Baskerville. (Original work published in 1957.)

Twain, M. (2005). *Huckleberry Finn.* Cheswold, DE: Prestwick House. (Original work published in 1885.)

CHAPTER 22

······································

LITERATURE AND POLITICS

······································

FRED RUSH

PHILOSOPHICAL discussion of the topic "literature and politics" can take many forms. For instance, one might be concerned to argue for or against the claim that literature must be understood as a product of the social and political forces that are at work when it is produced. Or, one might be concerned to assess the claim that literature is a form of political critique, perhaps even a preeminent form of it. Or, one might argue that literature can induce political change, that is, can be revolutionary—perhaps that it should be. Further questions involve how political and aesthetic properties interact in works. Does the presence of both sorts of property in a work create difficulty for aesthetic judgment? If one thinks that aesthetic judgment requires separating aesthetic from political properties in some strict way, the presence of political properties in the work will be problematic for aesthetic judgment. The problem might go as well to the heart of artistic production—that is, formalism of various stripes holds that one isn't "really" creating art, if one is creating political "art." Or one might be concerned that political and aesthetic properties are so intertwined that strongly negative or positive political judgment might spoil aesthetic judgment. Recent cases in the literature often are drawn from music or cinema, for example, Richard Wagner's *Ring* and *Parsifal* and Leni Riefenstahl's *Triumph des Willens*, which are admired by some for their technical innovations and formal composition but reproached for their political content. Many questions of this sort have been asked about literature, as well—to take, again, the standard cases of Shakespeare's *The Merchant of Venice*, Mark Twain's *The Adventures of Huckleberry Finn*, Louis-Ferdinand Céline's *Voyage au bout de la nuit*, and Knut Hamsun's *Hunger*.

Typically, issues of the political nature of art center on conceptions of artistic *content*, even where content is considered in relation to aesthetic form. In this chapter I focus instead on the idea that literary *form* itself is political. More specifically, I investigate claims that literature can criticize and alter political belief by being experienced in terms of its form.

I

Dating the inception of modern literature with any claim to exactness is foolhardy. But a strong indication of its onset is when writers and critics begin to think of themselves in contradistinction to "the ancients" or what is "classical." This coincides roughly with the time when writers begin to produce literature that is formally reflexive.[1] What I mean by "formally reflexive" literature is literature that takes the conditions for its own possibility to be thematic and that makes questions of its basis part of its own formal constitution. That is, one of the main ways to reflect these conditions within the work is to make the formal nature of the work difficult to take for granted—to make form thematically "problematic" for the work. Modern literature is especially aware of its conventions and willing to embed this awareness in works quite explicitly. "Formal," as it is often used in discussions of aesthetics, pertains to perceptual properties of an object. Restricting "aesthetic" in this way is certainly arguable, but let it stand for now. While some formal properties of modern art are undoubtedly of this sort, many are not.[2] It is not stretching the term "formal" too much, I think, also to admit to its extension structural properties of works that otherwise "make them possible." For instance, the structural properties of a work that allow for the recognition of narrative relations of beginning and ending might count as "formal," even though the awareness of them is complex and not a matter of "mere perception."

Self-reference or even reflexivity in literature, then, does not originate with the high modern literature of the mid-nineteenth through mid-twentieth centuries. *Parabasis* was a standard element of Attic "Old Comedy"; internal narrative self-reference, essential to *Don Quixote, Tristram Shandy*, and so forth. Nor, at the other end of things, is self-reference sufficient to divide modern literature from literature often thought to be reacting to deficiencies in modernism, for example, "postmodern" literature of various sorts. One might say that what is singular about high modern literature is that it takes formal self-reference to be almost a requirement on art worth the name—that is, to make formal self-reference constitutive of what literature at the cutting edge consists in. Innovation in narrative technique in Joyce, Proust, and Woolf or the exploration of phonetic value in Stéphane Mallarmé are exemplary. Still, there is probably no sustainable hard-and-fast distinction between modern and postmodern on this score. Inventing new forms of formal self-expression is less pressing in the "metafiction" of postwar America, for example, in Thomas Pynchon, John Barth, and Don DeLillo. Yet, one might consider the envelope-pushing prose and poetry of, for example, Georges Perec's lipogrammatic novel *La Disparition* (1969) or, for example, Paul Celan's "meridi-nal" verse to be modern in spirit. Is Cormac McCarthy's *Blood Meridian* or Toni Morrison's *Beloved*, almost certainly the two most important works of fiction in English over the past quarter century, premodern, modern, or postmodern? It is probably not possible to tell.

The claim that aesthetic form has the power to influence belief is also not new with modernism. That has been a potent idea from the beginning of the history of philosophical reflection on art. The problem with *mimēsis* for Plato is not merely that "likenesses" are cognitively inferior to "knowledge." It is also that likenesses can cause beliefs and actions to imitate *them*. Likeness begets likeness for Plato, which is never a good thing in the abstract. Indirect discourse should be favored over direct address in poetry; otherwise, the identification of *rhapsode* and audience with what is said is much more immediate and potentially problematic. Even so, there is an increase in concern over the intersection of politics and the formal properties of works of art in the modern period. This is understandable, given that modern art makes its own formal nature thematic.

One particularly interesting modern strand of thought at this intersection is one that focuses on the claimed power of formal *innovation* to change political belief. This claim was pressed mainly by a group of Marxist critics operating in Central Europe beginning in the 1930s and is put in its most complex and compelling form by two of them, Walter Benjamin and Theodor Adorno. I discuss the views of both Benjamin and Adorno, but treatment of Benjamin comes in and out of the analysis, not because Benjamin's views are not interesting in their own right—Benjamin is pertinent for this chapter to the extent that he provided the young Adorno with important components for his views on the interconnection of art and belief. But Adorno, simply put, is the thinker who most rigorously pursued the idea that interests me here, that literary form is political in itself, and is so because of its cognitive effects. Although one would not want to treat Adorno as the last word on this, understanding his version of this claim is unavoidable.

Cleaving to the standard meaning of "form" mentioned above—that is, as having to do with perceptual awareness—one way to discuss aesthetic experience historically has been in terms of its connection to "preconceptual" or "nonconceptual" experience.[3] These terms admit of all sorts of interpretation. The first thing to notice is that they are not synonymous or, at least, they needn't be. There might be all sorts of nonconceptual experiences that are not anterior to conception. But, in fact, the two concepts have been conflated in traditional treatments of aesthetic form. Moreover, since Alexander Gottlieb Baumgarten inaugurated philosophical aesthetics as a discipline, what interpretation one adopts of preconceptual experience will depend in great measure on what account of conceptual experience one opposes to it. If one is a sense-impression empiricist, where concepts enter one's experience after an initial unmediated reception of the data of that experience, what is preconceptual will be a brute, unstructured (by human means) continuum of sensation. This means that preconceptual experience will be a species of feeling with no conceptual import in itself. Emotivism in aesthetics results from such views. It is not very interesting from the point of view of the question posed here. The most that one can say is that literature can enflame (or cool) political belief.

II

But appeal to the inchoate, churning push-pull of sensation is not the only avenue open to interpret the category of the "preconceptual." Benjamin and Adorno favor an entirely different tack, one that has its roots in Kant's epistemological and aesthetic writings. Kant holds that aesthetic experience is "preconceptual" in the special sense that it implicates processes of concept and belief formation. That is, it involves processes antecedent to the actual formation of a concept or belief (or to its actual application in a judgment), but ones that are necessary for the emergence of the concept or belief in question. I cannot fully go into the technicalities of Kant's account of how this is so, but I canvass some general features of the Kantian picture of aesthetic, preconceptual experience that are important as a contrast for Benjamin's and Adorno's views on aesthetic form. Benjamin and Adorno argue that the experience of form can interrupt and reconfigure belief formation processes logically prior to their being "locked into" accepted understandings of the social and political roles of the concepts in question. They hold, with Kant, that art is experienced most properly as being conceptually indeterminate. "Indeterminate" here does not mean entirely without structure or amorphous; it means, rather, "undetermined" by concepts, where "determination" by a concept would be to "fix in meaning" in terms of the concept in question. And, thus, "preconceptual" does not mean "prior to any conceptualization," but rather "without conceptual fixity." That is still vague, and I qualify it a bit later, but let it stand here unqualified for expositional reasons.

For Kant, beliefs are results of predicative judgmental processes, most of which are, psychologically speaking, implicit or unconscious, which require the unification of two or more concepts. All experience of objects, in the broadest sense of "object," involves judgment; therefore, concepts figure at every level of experience (or, at least, at every level of experience of which one can be aware). Kant differentiates two basic "powers" of judgment: "determining" (*bestimmende*) and "reflecting" (*reflektierende*) (Kant 1908: 180). Determining judgment subsumes particulars under concepts already at hand. Some of these concepts may be quite precise, perhaps even stipulated or defined, as one often finds in mathematics or the physical sciences. Empirical concepts are not so exact; in fact, Kant denies that they can be given a definition *sensu stricto*. Even so, they categorize the world in relatively fixed ways. By so doing, determining judgment orients one in the world by grouping things according to their shared properties. This orientation might be called "instrumental," not in any necessarily pejorative sense, but rather to mark the fact that orienting oneself in the world conceptually is a precondition for discovering regularity in the world and for making the rational predictions that underwrite successful pragmatic interventions in the world. It is best to think of concepts, then, as being on a continuum—no empirical concept is wholly determinate (it can always be adjusted by subsequent judgment), and none is so amorphous that it lacks all categorial force. Because judgments functionally relate concepts, they may be thought of along similar lines.

Determining judgment takes empirical concepts at their face values and is therefore not in the business of adapting such concepts, discarding old ones, or forming them anew. Kant arrogates this later function to reflecting judgment. When it reflects, judgment looks to itself and to imagination, to search out among the multiplicity of experience unity where none is pregiven and to form new ways of thinking together particulars. Reflecting is much closer to what Aristotle called *phronēsis* (Aristotle 1986: 1104a7–10) and to what Kant calls *Mutterwitz* (Kant 1990: A133/B172), that is, a capacity to search for and discover affinities and differences among particulars that provide the logical building blocks for concepts. Kant argues that reflecting judgment has many important and even necessary uses, but the one that concerns the question of the political salience of literary form is aesthetic judgment. Aesthetic experience is "preconceptual" for Kant in the same sense as reflective judgment is. It is a synthetic process in which particulars are put in comparative relations without any one relation being determinative. This is *not* nonconceptual experience because being conceptually indeterminate does not mean being outside the ambit of concepts—any way of grouping things, even if it is so highly defeasible or multivalenced that it can be called indeterminate, is still indeterminate *conception*. The issue, to repeat, is conceptual pliancy, not the lack of concepts altogether. The core idea here is that there are innumerable ways to categorize any given array of particulars. Aesthetic experience is the experience of, simultaneously, that multiplicity and its cognitive potential. Any deploying of concepts aesthetically in a work of art will leave vastly underdetermined any specific ways that the work can be interpreted. This does not mean that "anything goes"—there can be constraints that operate within interpretative plurality—but works that promote this special sort of response must leave the plurality in place.

Adorno's main idea, one that he takes over almost without alteration from Benjamin's early writings, is just this Kantian one—that is, that the experience of aesthetic form does not require and, indeed, is defeated by too much conceptual fixity.[4] The conceptual indeterminacy of the work of art will allow the inherent particularity of things to precipitate out of its multivalence. Accordingly, the work of art does not show the particularity qua particularity "nakedly"; it is rather that the impossibility of definitive understanding of the work displays particularity by that fact that there is always an aspect of the work that cannot be rendered, as yet, generally. Again following Benjamin, Adorno calls the conceptual nexus that is the work of art as it stands in relation to its interpretations a "constellation." The "idea" of the work, in contrast, is what always outstrips potential interpretation and can only be approached conceptually asymptotically. Following Benjamin, Adorno chooses the term "constellation" to denote the sort of systematicity that a work of art possesses in order to emphasize the dependency of form upon human interpretative intervention.[5] There *are* no constellations of stars, if what one means by that is natural groupings of them. There are stars that can be arranged in various ways—for mythological purposes, in order to navigate, and so forth—but these arrangements are human inventions, subject to change or reordering, given different human needs or desires. To "constellate," if that is not too precious a way to put it, is to conceive of a group of particulars under a description, which, like the idea of a constellation, wears on its sleeve the fact that it is not a fixed, systematic rendering of phenomena that tracks their inner natures.

This understanding of the fundamental ontology of the work of art allows for two complementary ways to characterize the experience of aesthetic form relative to concepts. The first I have already stressed: works are preconceptual and bases for potential coeval interpretations. That is, works are preconceptual because their use of concepts reflects, at a conceptual level, protoconceptual indeterminacy and multiple interpretability. One brings one's prior experience to a work and, if it is "serious" art, the work transforms that experience by re-presenting those concepts "prismatically," that is, in new contexts or with new connotations that encourage one to question the content of the concept in question, as well as the way the concept might figure in emergent alternative ways of thinking. A second way to gloss the relevance of concepts to aesthetic experience is to say that such experience is "superconceptual." Because there are so many ways to conceptualize a work of art, none of which can lay claim to the sort of verification native to more fixed forms of conceptualization, one might say that the work of art presents an excess of meaning: works of art are works in which the base-level requirements of generic conceptualization are so exceeded that their effect is due to this fact, that is, that they exceed run-of-the-mill conceptualization. Calling aesthetic experience superconceptual may sound like it is at odds with aesthetic experience being "preconceptual," but it is not. As long as one does not make the error of identifying preconceptual with nonsynthetic or entirely noncategorical experience, the two formulations amount to the same thing: aesthetic experience of form is experience of the irreducibility of the aesthetic object to any single category.

Benjamin and Adorno's candidate for the base preconceptual state in terms of which aesthetic experience has implications for belief formation and revision— "mimesis"—is quite different from Kant's. And their analysis of the structure of modern art is also a radical departure or, perhaps better, a radical reworking of the idea of organic form—or, even more classically, unity in multiplicity—that lies at the base of Kant's account of beautiful art. Kant identifies a number of synthetic processes short of full conception that allow for similarity to be registered subjectively. One thing that unites these various processes is the idea that subjective cognitive "labor" on what is given to synthesis proceeds according to the demands of form and not of what is formed. Matter is responsive to synthesis and not the other way around. For Kant, these base states, from which fully conceptual states evolve, are constructive and minimally reflective, that is, such states are always quasi judgmental. For Adorno, however, basic human orientation in the world of objects is much more reactive and not representational. And, in that sense, mimesis is only qualifiably a type of "imitation" (1970–86, 7: 109). Adorno conceives of mimesis at its early stages somatically, and he stresses a continuum between this capacity on the part of other animals and humans. In particular, here following Benjamin, Adorno finds such a capacity at work in children's play make-believe.[6] Humans in the first instance respond to environments in terms dictated by what are to become objects for them. Encountering a thing *as an object* presupposes having partly withdrawn from one's immersion in the world. In virtue of mimesis, a subject differentiates herself from an object by attempting to form itself according to the form of the object (1970–86, 7: 169; see also 1972–86, 2.1: 204–13). The cause for this minimal distancing is self-preservation; mimesis is thus a kind of cognitive camouflage in which an encounter with "an other" is neutralized by submitting oneself to it by becoming more like it.[7] Mimesis is also invested with conative as well as cognitive aspects. As mimesis becomes more complicated and evolves under social and natural pressures into determining judgment, the cognitive dimension gains the upper hand. But the conative dimension—what one might call the expressive rather than the representational dimension of mimesis—is never lost altogether. There are perhaps senses in which mimesis at this base level is intuitional, but it is, nevertheless, rational. It is precisely because of its inherent rationality that Adorno can hold that mimesis is what makes art a unique form of "cognition" (1970–86, 7: 88). The idea that intuition itself is rational is an inheritance from late-nineteenth-century neo-Kantianism, many forms of which were familiar to Adorno (see Rush 2004).

Adorno does not, at least in his better moments, think of mimesis entirely atavistically. Within this state one has one's most immediate experience of the particularity of the thing, although that state is still mediated, as it were, by the minimal distance required for the initial reaction of self-preservation. Even base-level mimetic mediation can be social and is at least incipiently "instrumental." It is not supposed to be a pristine, unfraught relation to things. But the fact remains that, for Adorno, what I am calling base-level mimesis is the closest one comes to encountering things with minimal human cognitive overlay. That said, mimesis is also not atavistic for Adorno because it is not paradisaical; that is, mimesis is not an irrational Eden that one might work oneself back to by stripping away conceptual thought, and once that is done (if it could be done), all would be well. While mimesis is minimally invasive in relation to a thing's particularity, it is also the beginning of the cognitive control that undercuts an experience of particularity. So, in some moments of utopian speculation, thinkers like Adorno will not so much yearn for a return to Edenic or infantile mimesis as much as wish mimesis had never taken place at all. Synthetic subjective processes and concepts proper enter at a later cognitive stage where, in a compensatory moment, the subject is in a position to reinterpret the distance resulting from the initial differentiation between subject and object in terms that allow for more instrumental control of the thing at hand in terms of categories. But—and this is crucial for Adorno—concepts always contain within them traces of the prior noncategorial, noninstrumental mimesis.

This is Adorno's version of Kant's claim that art always outstrips actual conceptualization, here broadened to an assertion about all things. Aesthetic form preserves this balance between concept and mimesis at the conceptual level; Adorno is even more intent on not falling into noncognitivism in art than is Benjamin. This is the epistemological basis for Adorno's claim that art can engage audiences without conceptual "hardening" in order to suggest other ways to understand a given array of phenomena conceptually. This is the way that experience of aesthetic form is more true to the particulars, not because it affords an immediate window upon things beyond description, but because it allows one to experience a thing in terms of its being a possible object of reexperience.

The status of mimesis vis-à-vis art is oddly two-faced. On the one hand, as the core of human responses to things "other," it is both alienating and the staple for technology and other instrumental orientations in the world. To that extent, mimesis is not something ulterior to instrumental or "identity" thinking that can be developed artistically into a way to avoid instrumental thought. It is the problem, not the cure. Max Horkheimer seems especially to have registered this "negative" element of mimesis, writing that the struggle for freedom was the, in some sense, impossible task of becoming nonmimetic[8] (1974: 115–16), and Herbert Marcuse (1978: 47), at the polar extreme, urges that freedom is id-like and "beyond mimesis." On the other hand, mimesis in its earlier stages is less instrumental than its developed forms just because it has not undergone systematic socialization in favor of "judgment." In this way "childlike" or "primitive" mimesis preserves as much of the particularity of the thing that is its object as is possible consistent with a slight categorial distance from it. In this vein, mimesis holds open to the artist ways of making objects that do not ask for univocal judgment.

Adorno's debt to romanticism means that he does not think that one can discursively limn such a state. Rather, the "purely" mimetic is shown as a kind of "shadow effect" of progressively modern art. It is the lag between "the new" in art and its formal convention, appearing for but a moment before being assimilated into instrumentally based art. Much like the Kantian category of "the sublime" or the romantic one of "the absolute," the mimetic is experienced as a residue of the effect of a thing that has superseded definitive conceptualization. Art is the tension between the conceptually indeterminate potential of mimesis and what Adorno calls "spirit" (*Geist*), that is, socialized categorization. The way that this is so—the cognitive structure in virtue of which that tension is present in the work—is a kind of second-order, reflective representation of that potential. That is, the only way to represent mimesis *qua* nonrepresentation at the conceptual level is to reconstruct it conceptually by emphasizing what is most mimetic at the conceptual level— that is, the radical underdetermination of the work by its possible interpretations (1970–86, 6: 14). This is perhaps why Adorno rarely averts to the term "preconceptual" to denote the mimetic component in an artwork. He prefers instead the description "nonconceptual." This word resonates historically with similar uses in early German romanticism, for example, in Novalis and Friedrich Schlegel. But the point of using "nonconceptual" instead of "preconceptual" is, presumably, to make clear that nondetermining mimesis is present even after concepts have taken hold. It is what concepts seek to exclude, which, ironically perhaps, is their own enabling conditions.[9]

Having to add so many qualifications to the uses of the terms "preconceptual" and "nonconceptual" may make one wonder why I retain the terms at all. The main property of the states or processes to which those terms refer is the degree of fixity of conceptualization and not conceptualization *tout court*, so why not put the point in terms of fixity and pliancy within conceptualization? My answer has expository and conceptual dimensions. On the expository side, Adorno and Kant express their accounts in those terms, and it is important to track their language. Second, and more important, retaining the terminology, with appropriate qualification, captures that these states and processes *are* antecedent to more full-blown "theoretical" uses of conceptual capacities, even though they need not eventuate in those more articulated forms of experience. Deploying the standard terminology helps to keep this structure front and center. This is especially important because, according to Adorno, what is reflected in the sort of art that arrogates to "primary," conceptually indeterminate mimesis a central role is precisely the slippage between lower and higher "levels" of conceptual fixity.

III

As it stands, this account of mimesis may seem too ahistorical to be a view that Adorno would embrace. But Adorno does not think that the reflection of something like "mimetic residue" in art is an attempt to graft onto discursive experience a *soupçon* of the nondiscursive that is not itself a product of socialization. Perhaps in the case of the child, this might be so, but even there Adorno can see through the Proustian gloaming in which Benjamin bathed his memories in his *Berliner Kindheit um 1900* (1938). Adorno is committed to the position that historical and cultural constraints impinge on even initial mimesis. Keeping this in mind helps to explain why Adorno is overwhelmingly concerned to explicate the political function of artistic form in terms of modernism. Modernism is the current state of play in which Adorno writes. One must assess the continuing cognitive prospects for art, including its political wherewithal, against this background. Adorno is extraordinarily pessimistic about the prospect of art or anything else telling one the way the world affirmatively should be. This attitude is rooted in Benjamin's messianic form of Marxism, which prohibits the idea that redemption of any sort, political or otherwise, can be achieved in the secular sphere.

History for Benjamin is a squalid accretion of suffering that itself cannot yield reconciliation; it can, however, in its very morbidity express a potential kind of salvation apart from history. History does this by consisting in social products— for example, artwork—that hammer home the abject baseness of the secular. This is why Benjamin prizes the neglected genre of the Baroque *Trauerspiel*. Drama in this tradition is not important because it is "great"; both Benjamin and Adorno grant that no modern art can really compare in greatness to Homer, Dante, or Shakespeare. Rather, such art is important art because it is banal. The *Trauerspiel* is such a hollow stand-in for real ethical or religious value that it provides a powerful negative indicator of how unthinkable salvation is in history and of a barely imagined possibility that profane salvation is not the only salvation there is. Allegorical works such as these deploy correspondences between finite and infinite realms that are, unlike symbolic works, fungible. This fact underlines the utter, profane distance at which this world stands from any world suitable to human freedom. Modern art, for Benjamin, therefore, functions *negatively*. It displays in its form the ruination and fragmentation of the world and is itself, since part of the world, a ruin. But the work of art, now understood as itself a formal fragment, also has a *positive* function. In the world of shard-signs of the holy that admit many interpretations just because humans are too distanced from unsullied original particulars to be able to reconstruct their Adamic "names," the fact that works are multivalent can be marshaled in order to achieve a second-best reconstituted meaning for art and society. Somewhat confusingly, since he has just claimed both that it is impossible to redeem oneself in a secular world and, thus, one would suppose, in art, Benjamin calls this sort of criticism "redemptive." What he means, however, is not that criticism adds to the fragmented work some extra component that vaults it into the realm of nonfragmentary social product. Rather, interpretation is a matter of the conceptual dismantling of what is left of the semblance of unity in the work. Criticism is then a process of decomposition that "redeems" the work as the ruin that it is. In doing so, one not only shows that work to be the fragment that it is and the society that it is expressive of as equally disjoint, but also partly reconstitutes the work in a particular way. Because any work of art, perhaps more than other cultural products, will bear traces of its original particularism no matter how bankrupt it has become, interpretation of the work, if pushed far enough, will limn meanings of the work that would be repressed both by the instrumental conditions under which the work was produced and by standard modes of instrumentalized criticism.

The question naturally becomes: What is "enough"? Benjamin favors an almost unbridled interpretative scope, under the view that the more outlandish an interpretation may seem, such an interpretation, by juxtaposing itself starkly with the accepted status quo understanding of the work, will liberate new meanings of the work. Adorno would come to have doubts about this view of the scope of permissible criticism; it seemed to him to leave no room open for *judgment* of art. Adorno nevertheless accepts the basic idea that criticism and art go hand in hand as reciprocally reinforcing components in the modern experience of art, where that mutual reinforcement is not meant to shore up the idea of stable aesthetic form but is rather set upon making aesthetic form problematic while retaining the idea that form is indispensable. For some Marxist critics, literature can seem to have a merely symptomatic value: contradiction in the text is emblematic of larger cultural forces and thus valuable as data for social theory, but is not valuable *as art*. This is just another way of saying that, for many Marxist critics, the category of "the aesthetic" is essentially bourgeois. In contrast, Benjamin and Adorno do not subject the idea of aesthetic form to criticism in order to dispense with it. They think that the critique of aesthetic form must be immanent. This means (1) that the idea of form cannot be dismissed as a potential vehicle for freedom and (2) that the social meanings of artistic form must be explicated in terms of the problem of form itself.

IV

The term "content" is often used in everyday discussions about art, as well as in the philosophy of art, to denote something like "thematic" or "narrative" elements in the work of art. This is the way I have been using this concept thus far. This does not rule out that there might be formal elements of art that constitutively relate to contentful elements. Indeed, it is probably impossible to make a bright-line test for a division between such elements, but the distinction surely is possible between, for example, a fictional event of Buck Mulligan shaving (story-content) and the way Joyce interweaves this episode with the rest of *Ulysses* (narrative form). Adorno's terminology does not track this distinction very precisely, and unless one is careful to make some distinctions between different senses in which art has content for him, the way he deals with issues of the relation of form, content, and politics will be lost.

Adorno is perfectly willing to use the term "content" (*Inhalt*) to refer to thematic content or the political "message" of a work. But, if he were a bit more sensitive to everyday usage, he would stress more than he does that "content" in this sense is but a kind of content for him or, better yet, a particular way that content is present in a work. At a deeper philosophical level, Adorno deploys the concept of content to refer to whatever flows into the work via the artist from the world. In many ways this is a terribly inexact formulation, but the concept of content for Adorno's aesthetic theory is so basic that it is hard to be more precise. Perhaps a slightly better way to attempt to come to grips with it is to list the sorts of matter that can make up content: social surroundings, biography, relation to prior art history, unconscious experiences, involuntary memories, and so forth. In effect, content is one of two main components of mimesis in art. It is the unruly and conceptually outstripping expression of experience by means of art. The other element of mimesis is form. It is the way in which content hangs together in the work, however precarious (and Adorno thinks that all art worth the name is somewhat precarious in this way). Form is not supposed to be a subjective mental contribution to art, as it would be, in a special sense, for Kant. It is rather whatever unity is brought to content through the artist's intervention. Form, too, is social; artists don't operate as creative surds for Adorno. Forming is a human act that has a history, and this history is the basis for the history of formal aesthetics. So, content and form are dialectically related in this way. The tension that results from their interrelation is also what Adorno calls its "content" (*Gehalt*). It is this second sense of "content" that is closer to the everyday use of the term in connection with art for him.[10] But it is still not coextensive with it. "Content" here means "dialectical content," which is a very abstract way to talk about the general structure of *any* work of art. *Gehalt* is the work as it holds together a certain volatile relation of the uptake of the artist (*Form*) with a certain mimetic "content." This radically underdetermines possible "content" of particular works, that is, their themes. To repeat: there are three distinct senses of content relevant to discussion of Adorno's philosophy of art:

(A) Mimetic content (*Inhalt*)—what of the world the artist, in her art, receives in her making of the art

(B) Dialectical content (*Gehalt*)—what the artist does in that making, that is, how *that* making is *hers*

(C) Thematic content (*Inhalt*)—what "happens" in the work, what the work or the artist "says," and so forth[11]

Adorno cannot consider (A) and (B), that is, mimetic or dialectical content, to be problematic counterparts to form, since there must be "content" of a work in order for there to be a work at all. It is the relation of form to (C), that is, thematic content, that is at issue.

Given this rehearsal of Benjamin and Adorno's main claims concerning the ontology of the work of art, the standing importance of the category of aesthetic form and the role of criticism in engaging that form, how does the experience of the artistic form of truly modern literary works amount to political criticism? Here Benjamin and Adorno diverge. Benjamin holds that the commodity form can be harnessed to produce politically critical art and, in some ways, may even be tailor-made for that purpose. Commodity form is already divorced from inherent value. While Benjamin sided with Bertolt Brecht on the issue of whether explicitly political art is revolutionary, Adorno never abandoned the dichotomy between artifact and commodity. This is another way of saying that "autonomy" is an important category in the philosophy of art for Adorno, whereas for Benjamin it is not.

Adorno charts the progression of modern form-reflective works in terms of two related arcs: (1) in terms of continued innovations in self-reflective form that are disorienting to the status quo, and (2) in terms of an increasingly shrinking margin of "the new" from which such innovation can be drawn. As late capitalism becomes even more efficient, a good part of its efficiency consists in the capacity to appropriate and reintegrate what is new into what is expected, thereby robbing what were once innovations of whatever aesthetic and political potential they might have once had. Adorno holds that the lapsed time between true innovative art and its rendering into ersatz commodity versions of "the new" is nearing zero, and he is openly concerned with the available resources for true formal innovation, as well as about the production of illusory versions of innovation (e.g., "independent film," now entrenched as a genre concept and marketing vehicle).

Adorno claims that it is aesthetic form that registers and expresses the contradictions of late bourgeois modern life with heightened impact. Dickensian preachiness or Orwellian hectoring is not as effective a device for changing political outlook as is the fractured musical undertow of a late modern lyric. For Adorno, the formal properties of the modern artwork are under the same social pressures as its content. The technical formal devices that Joyce deploys in *Ulysses* are products of social forces just as much as are his characterization of Molly and his use of myth as a framing device for the novel. Now, on the face of it, there would not seem to be a problem with insisting that a work of art (1) have political content and (2) revitalize the imagination in the way Adorno takes the experience of avant-garde literary form to enable. Nor is it any argument against explicitly engaged literature that formal innovation is the *best* vehicle for aesthetic inclusion into political belief, unless, that is, one holds that explicitly engaged content nullifies or blunts the formal impact on belief. Works might do best on this score when they push formal boundaries and upset general formal expectations, but they might usefully supplement this with political themes. What, precisely, is Adorno's objection to "engaged" art (1965, 3: 109–35; 1970,-86 11: 409–30)?

The political import of Adorno's conception of aesthetic form depends on the relationship he holds form to have with the emergence of concepts and beliefs. Art of any period reflects both formally and as a matter of content the conventions of its day. This does not mean that art merely represents such conventions as a matter of "superstructure," as some more traditional Marxist critics held. Rather, art *expresses* these conventions and thus is a base constituent of how humans understand their social being at different points in history. Much, if not most, art is highly conventional. If it is highly conventional, art can suffer from the same conceptual fixity that hamstrings the political potential of instrumental thinking. The structure of conventional art, that is, precludes the kind of "open texture" that would implicate imaginative and interpretative encounters with it, which encounters might open up new ways to think about conventional social life. While all art has some level of conceptual fixity, and thus begins to work within conventional modes of artistic production and expression, only art that transforms those conventions has progressive political potential. For Adorno, "serious" art effects this transformation by breaking down conceptual fixity while remaining attentive to it. But even serious art does not offer determinate political answers. Prima facie, this may seem like pretty weak tea; the political effect of art via its form is very indirect and ephemeral. Although there is a temptation either to deny the indirectness or to dismiss the political effect of form as minimal at best, the temptation should be resisted—at least it should be resisted as a temptation, for Adorno's point is that the political effect of serious art in virtue of its form *is* indirect and the effect may also be quite difficult to pin down in individual cases. But that is the nature of the phenomenon and is not particularly a problem—that is, it is not a problem unless one expected a more direct and directly traceable political effect from literary form. Adorno's view, however, is that it is wrong to expect that. It is, after all, *art* that is in question, not a bunch of political arguments. Adorno's analysis of just this point—of the indirect and negatively critical nature of the transformation of political concepts and beliefs through formally innovative literature—is wed to his discussion of the role that "truly" modern works play in preserving art's critical edge.

V

....

For Adorno, modern literature truly begins with Charles Baudelaire. Following a line established in Benjamin's essay "Über einige Motive bei Baudelaire" (1972–89, 1.1: 605–54), Adorno celebrates the author of *Tableaux parisiens* as a thoroughly social poet, who is perhaps the first writer to be in a position to register formally a uniquely modern alienation, one that is torn between the extremes of the illusory unity of bourgeois life and its disintegration (1961, 2: 162; 1970–86, 11: 260). Samuel Beckett is the culmination and state of the art in expressing by aesthetic indirection how far this core modern experience has "progressed" (1961, 2: 188–236; 1970–86, 11: 281–321). Adorno places great stake in the stuttering near-speechlessness of characters in works like *Fin de partie*. Even more important to him, however, is the character of hope in the face of hopelessness that he alleges finds unparalleled expression in much of Beckett's work.

Adorno's defense of the political potential of aesthetic form is honed against two main adversaries, both of whom at one time Adorno counted among his intellectual allies. The most important case is György Lukács. Two of Lukács's early works, *The Theory of the Novel* (1920), written while he was still an adherent of Wilhelm Dilthey, and the collection of essays *History and Class Consciousness* (1923), the book that virtually invented humanistic Marxism, were seminal for Adorno. Lukács had in the meantime renounced his earlier work and embraced more materialistic forms of Marxism, reformulating in the bargain his philosophy of art along Soviet party lines. There will likely always be a difference of opinion about the degree to which Lukács actually embraced these views, but no matter what sort of allowances are made on his behalf, it is difficult to read the prefaces to many of his works collected in *Werke* and not cringe. It was certainly difficult for Adorno. But Adorno's reactions to later Lukács go well beyond disappointment in a heroic figure from his youth. Lukács's views are seriously misguided, according to Adorno, precisely because they extolled the revolutionary potential of literary content over modernist form.

Neither Adorno nor Lukács holds that there is any promise for politically progressive art in adapting the structure of commodity objects in artistic ways. Both are also quite wary of the idea that socialist revolution could emerge from the proletariat. Art, if it is to be politically progressive, must hold itself above both commodity form and common taste. Lukács's much cited reproach that Adorno had taken extended residence in the "Grand Hotel Abgrund," from whence one could take rarified, sublime enjoyment in the shipwreck of modern times, is *not* a scolding administered from a "man of the people" to an aesthete (Lukács 1971: 16). It is rather a charge from mandarin to mandarin concerning the question of the standing of the category of aesthetic form. The immediate provocation for Adorno's negative assessment was a series of lectures Lukács gave in 1956 on the subject of the "contemporary significance of critical realism" (1971:4, 457ff.)[12] Lukács argues that literary modernism is nothing but an extension of late capitalism that shrinks from true critique back into a shell of self-implicating "idealistic" subjectivity. The central progressive strand of literature is found instead in "realism." Realism in this sense is not naturalism—which Lukács holds merely reflects the surface degradation of modern social life—but rather a depiction of the forces behind that degradation in terms of the narrative content of the work. For Lukács, bourgeois literature can be realistic and critical to a degree, which accounts for his endorsement of the critical potential in a writer like Honoré de Balzac, who is for Lukács a kind of nonmelancholic Giacomo Leopardi—a royalist who, nonetheless, witnesses with resignation the implacable passing away of the nobility. It is the *haut bourgeois* novelist, Thomas Mann, who is the *terminus ad quem* of Lukács's tale of critical realism. Mann, who had nontrivial connections to both Lukács and Adorno,[13] is important because he is the same kind of transitional writer, in this case marking time between the ultracultured *Großbürgertum* of Wilhelminian Germany and the advent of its dissolution. Mann's *Buddenbrooks* (1901) and, especially, the novella *Tonio Kröger* (1903) thus are cardinal instances of the sort of realism that Lukács has in mind. An author like Franz Kafka, crucial for both Adorno and Benjamin, is lumped into the category of "regressive irrationalism" that Lukács further develops in his *Destruction of Reason*.[14] This emphasis on critical realism might have been enough to set Adorno's formalist teeth on edge, but it must have been Lukács's insistence that what he calls "socialist realism" is the paramount type of politically progressive literature that most exercised him. Lukács cites Maxim Gorky as the key figure here.[15] Socialist realism builds into itself a historically accurate portrayal of life in capitalism combined with a basic optimism for univocal politically progressive change and exhortation to such change. Embracing such literature reflects Lukács's basic view that Hegel was correct that one can under the right circumstances fully specify and realize the requirements for freedom. Put more abstractly, Lukács holds that "totality" (*Totalität*) is an indispensible critical concept. Adorno rejects this outright. Any "totalizing" literature is for him stipulative, propagandistic, and, in effect, regressive. Moreover, such literature is easily reabsorbed by the cultural status quo. This is not just because the message of such literature can be soft sold or otherwise contorted to the aims of mass culture, although Adorno no doubt holds that as true. Rather, such works are dangerously malleable because they can be ignored dialectically. Unlike progressive form, which operates at much more incursive preconceptual levels and much more immanently, directly thematic works are generally superficial and foreordained to operate at the margins of social change.

A second target of Adorno's claim that explicitly political content spoils the political impact of literature is Brecht. Brecht's plays promote a certain relationship between actors, play, and audience. Classically, at least if one takes the dramatic theory of Aristotle, A. W. Schlegel, and Friedrich Schiller to be "classical," drama has its effect on an audience either by arousing certain emotions in them or in virtue of a metaphysical effect provided by the interplay between the knowledge that the action is fictional and the discounting of that knowledge in "identifying" with aspects of the play.[16] Brecht contrasts this "dramatic" approach with his own "epic" theater.[17] The Brechtian *Verfremdungseffekt*, though hardly practiced univocally across his many works, destroys this delicate balance, which Brecht treats as indicative of traditional dramatic art. The audience is meant to realize starkly that the action on the stage is real, and this is brought about by a number of techniques. Some have to do with literary structure, for example, plot interruptions (e.g., in *Die Elefantenkalb* (1926), where the actors walk offstage and order drinks), montage effects, direct address (e.g., offstage narration in *Der kaukasische Kreidekreis* (1944), opening address to the audience in *Die Mutter* (1931), *Die Dreigroschenoper* (1928) and other plays, etc.). Others involve acting technique, for example, delivering dialogue as reportage (Frau Yang in *Der gute Mensch von Sezuan* [1943]), use of nonprofessional actors, and so on. And still others have to do with stagecraft; for example, in the early days of the Berliner Ensemble, Brecht required stage lighting to be full up, even directing that the apparatus be visible to the spectator.

While some of his works might be classified as propagandistic and even "realistic" in Lukács's sense of the term,[18] most of Brecht's theater is not jam-packed with political tirade. From his theoretical writings, it is fairly clear that Brecht denies that political *messages*, indirectly delivered from playwright to audience, are goals of his theater. The aim of Brechtian theater seems to be, rather, getting people to reflect critically by experiencing the action of the play as the characters experience it, that is, self-consciously.[19] That is—and this is a feature of Brecht's practice that, curiously, often goes unremarked—epic theater invites a kind of identification of the audience with the characters (or even a kind of empathy with them), but this identification is not passive, because the characters whose experience the audience is meant to share are already at a critical remove from the narrative events of the play. So, the alienation effect is not or, at least, not always promoted by prohibiting all types of identification or affective response on the part of the audience.

So, why is Brecht's theater insufficiently formal for Adorno? The commonplace that Brecht put aesthetic faith in the proletariat while Adorno did not does not go very far in explaining the source of Adorno's complaint. Nor does the formalism/antiformalism debate illuminate the scene, as it did in the case of Lukács. What Benjamin, for instance, saw as revolutionary about Brecht's theater was precisely its formal innovation. Adorno does not disagree that Brecht's concerns are formal. One aspect of the problem from Adorno's perspective is that the result of Brecht's formal innovation, if it works at all (and Adorno believes it sometimes does not work), only manipulates belief intellectually. Brecht's work is simply not "aesthetic." But this is not all. Adorno's overall aesthetic project is to allow nonintellectual determinants to mingle with intellectual components of world-views without lapsing into the dreaded "irrationalism," which would argue for formative, intuitional, and univocal aesthetic effect in political life that is not subject to rational critique. Brecht's formalism is not only overintellectual, but also overdeterminate. Only if form leaves content radically underdetermined does art produce interpretation, which is, in many ways, the basic epistemological category for Adorno. Autonomous art for Adorno is not art that intends to change political belief in one way or another. It is essentially negative—it shows the tension between the unity of society as it is, as that is expressed in the work in terms of form (and content) and the form barely being able to contain the disintegration of that world. Like Socrates' *daimonion*, autonomous art does not say "do this or that," but rather cautions simply "not this" (*Apology*, 1903: 31d). As Adorno puts it, perhaps a bit dramatically, artwork shoulders the "burden of wordlessly asserting what is barred to politics" (1965, 3: 135; 1970–86, 11: 430).

VI

The idea that there is an important connection between formal aesthetic properties of art and political belief merits further investigation. More precisely, the claim that art is uniquely political because it is useless deserves philosophical attention. This idea runs contrary to both the typical claims of formalism (i.e., art, in its highest vocation, is useless and therefore not political) and didactism (art in its highest vocation is useful and useful politically). Up to this point, Adorno has developed most systematically these ideas, but his formulation of the problem is in many ways idiomatic. As is appropriate whenever one encounters a treatment of a particular issue that is embedded in a heavily systematic philosophical framework, it is worth asking what one can take away from Adorno's account by abstracting from technical questions involved in the interpretation of his overall aesthetic theory. I cannot undertake that task here; I have tried merely to clarify and reconstruct some of Benjamin's and Adorno's basic thoughts in nontechnical ways as a preface to such work. I can indicate, however, three areas for further consideration. Adorno and Benjamin are interested in how art enters into the process of emerging order, political among other sorts. One aspect of Adorno's account that may seem unsatisfactory is that he offers no independent argument for the conclusion that the presence of express political content necessarily defeats the power of aesthetic form to trigger political imagination, even if that power is, in some way, superior to the power of express political content to effect such change.

In my view, Adorno's most important insights survive this failure. Nothing conceptual hangs on what I have called the "exclusionary claim." What requires discussion, then, is how formal aesthetic imagination can be politically relevant in works that may or may not also have political content. Awareness of the danger of conceptual fixity (i.e., "identity thinking") is one thing, but it must be balanced critically against a stifling immersion of art into extravagant subliminalism.

Second, even if one grants that formal innovation can allow for revision of political belief by allowing for alternative conceptions of the political at basal conceptual levels, there is nothing about formal innovation in itself that guarantees that such changes will be changes for the better. Political conservatism, not to say fascism, is well represented in the history of the avant-garde in Europe, for example, futurism, the *Georgekreis*, Pound, and Eliot. Perhaps ironically, this is especially true of forms of modern avant-gardism that share Benjamin and Adorno's substantial connections with romanticism. Reactionary primitivism is just as much in need of liberated imagination as is socialism. Something more has to be added to the idea of aesthetic innovation—something that gives it a progressive direction—even if, like Adorno, one wishes to be very careful about prescribing particular reforms through art. For Adorno, this is achieved by application of a suitably "humanized" Marx; that may be a very good resource indeed. But the issue of the formal impact of art on politics will be a good deal more interesting philosophically if Adorno's own brand of Marxism is not a prerequisite to development of the idea. Third, one will have to decide whether the issue of the formal political impact of art requires accepting something like a standing role for a generally modernist conception of the significance of art. The challenge comes directly from Adorno's pessimistic account of the possibility of continued innovations in the face of ever-shrinking margins of what can count as "new"—one might call this the "problem of disappearing form." Is Adorno more-or-less correct about this or not? Is most mass art not "autonomous"? And should that matter?

To the analytically minded philosopher of art, the issue of cognitive form and especially the complex and speculative treatment that Adorno gives it, may seem like quite a lot to take on board. This is entirely understandable, but if one is to take the idea that the formal elements of art may be a source for its political effect, as Plato certainly appreciated, one will have to have an account in place of art's general cognitive form. Moreover, one will have to take seriously, or at least seriously investigate, claims that some art has a unique cognitive force that is not rule-governed that is proper to it, and perhaps to it alone. This need not commit one to essentialism about art, or even about "serious" art. Art, and literature, no doubt plays many roles. But, it may commit one to the position that some literature has important political ramifications that are passed over if the literature in question is not formally innovative. And, no matter how one precisely comes down on the question of the political potential of aesthetic form, at some point complexity is likely to take hold and force one's speculative hand.

NOTES

Many thanks to Richard Eldridge, Lydia Goehr, and Gregg Horowitz for their very helpful comments on an earlier version of this chapter.

1. In this chapter, I use the terms "modern" and "modernism" roughly in the way that literary theorists use it, i.e., to refer to a period in the history of literature and its criticism that begins in the mid-nineteenth century after romanticism. I am not using the term as it is used in the history of philosophy, where the seventeenth-century Descartes would count as "modern," or as historians of science use the term to refer to Galileo and Bacon.

2. In this chapter, I use the terms "form" and "aesthetic form" interchangeably. This should not be taken to commit me to the idea that "aesthetic" means "perceptual."

3. This, of course, also tracks the meaning of the Greek word "αἴσθησις'" from which the term "aesthetics" is formed.

4. See Buck-Morss 1977: chap. 1 for a good account of Benjamin's early influence on Adorno.

5. Adorno tends to understand the term "idea" in a more Kantian way than does Benjamin.

6. For Benjamin's views, see 1972–89, 2.1: 210–13. Halliwell 2002: 178–79 and nn. 4–5 points out that Aristotle had a similar understanding, a point that is not often appreciated.

7. Compare Nietzsche's remarks in *Die fröhliche Wissenschaft* §§ 354–55, 1873: 590–95. What I mean by "self-preservation" here is obviously *not* preservation of oneself *as* a self. The idea of a discrete self is a product of the distance, not its cause. I also do not mean "self-preservation" in the much more conceptually developed sense that Max Horkheimer and Adorno think is basic to various forms of modern moral philosophy (see Horkheimer and Adorno 1969: 113ff). All I mean by "self-preservation" here is the minimal idea that humans, once buffeted by natural forces in ways that cause them to recoil from sensual immediacy, overcome that dislocation at first by somatic reassimilation. One might canvas the same idea in terms of the concept "suffering," as Horkheimer sometimes does.

8. Adorno certainly allowed that certain other base-level human aspects of human experience are nonmimetic, nonreactively somatic, but this category does not play a major role in his aesthetic theory.

9. This is why "conceptual art" need pose no barrier *as a matter of principle* for Adorno (although there may be other reasons for rejecting some of it).

10. It is difficult to capture the difference in force in German of the words *Inhalt* and *Gehalt*. Ordinarily, they both mean simply content. But it might be argued that *Inhalt* is a "container" term that refers to what is held inside a structure. *Gehalt*, it might also be argued, is an "orientation" term that refers to the way a thing stands in relation to its environment, i.e., how a thing "holds forth."

11. In his writings on music, Adorno contrasts form with "material" (*Material* or *Stoff*) (see Paddison 1993: 149–52). This brings up the question of whether material is "content" in one or more of the three senses I have distinguished or whether it is a fourth category of content. "Material" means something like "prior musical practice," and "form" means the inventing, on the basis of that past practice, of novel musical expressions.

12. The lectures were first published in 1957 as *Wider den mißverstandenen Realismus*. Lukács had engaged in a similar debate over expressionism with Ernst Bloch in the 1930s, which, Lukács characterizes, with a certain saturnine resignation, as "something of a grotesque situation in which Ernst Bloch polemicized in the name of *The Theory of the Novel* against the Marxist Georg Lukács" (Lukács 1971: 12).

13. It is well known that Mann consulted Adorno on technical musical points in the preparation of *Doktor Faustus* (1947). But not even Adorno could claim a turn as a character in a Mann novel. This Lukács might have done; he was the model for the fanatical priest Naphta in *Der Zauberberg* (1924), who spouts pseudo-Nietzscheanisms, challenges the humanist Settembrini to a duel, and, when the latter fires into the air, shoots himself in petulant satisfaction of "the Will." Of course, no one would want to claim the honor of such a portrayal, and it seems that Lukács never recognized himself (at least publically) in the portrait.

14. "Irrationalism" was something of a brickbat du jour back then; many critical theorists, most prominently Horkheimer, also deploy it.

15. Russian literature, and especially the modern Russian novel, is a rather special case for Lukács. Fyodor Dostoyevsky, for instance, is a figure who survives remarkably intact in Lukács's critical estimation from his early expressivism in *Theorie des Romans* (1920) into his later systematic aesthetics. The polar opposite of Lukács in this sphere would be the patrician Vladimir Nabokov, who had no time at all for Dostoyevsky and for whom Nikolai Gogol was the measure.

16. Bentley 1946: 256–57 usefully points out the Wagnerian idea of the *Gesamtkunstwerk* as a foil for Brecht. Put another way, *Die Dreigroshenoper* is "Oper" in Wagner's own sense of the term and not "Musik-Drama."

17. For classic statements, see Brecht 1957: 13–28, 60–73. Adorno puts particular emphasis on statements in what many consider Brecht's main theoretical work, "Kleines Organon für das Theater" (1957: 128–73). Adorno seems to have taken Brecht's theoretical works very seriously, demanding from them a good deal of philosophical rigor and coherence. This is probably not the most promising way to approach Brecht's dramaturgy. Brecht was no philosopher and seems to have had a very healthy appreciation of the "loose grain" of his ideas. He was primarily concerned to promote a certain type of theatrical *practice* and not with theory as such. He can thus be excused for his myopic understanding of Aristotle's views on *katharsis*, for instance. What is important for Brecht is the kind of general foil Aristotle can become for modern epic theater, and selectivity of his reading of Aristotle is part of that "casting" decision. In any event, *episch* is a good deal less genre-specific than the English "epic." *Das Epische* includes the novel and narrative poetry, as distinguished from lyric poetry and drama. Much that Brecht means to flag by the distinction between "dramatic" and "epic" theater simply is that the former is "dramatic" in the everyday sense of "exciting" or "arousing," while the later is not, allowing for distance and reflection.

18. I have in mind pieces like *Die Maßnahme* (1930) or *Die Ausnahme und die Regel* (1937), written during Brecht's time in Moscow. It is impossible to divide Brecht's work into chronological periods on the question of whether the plays are propagandistic. The two above are fairly clear cases, I believe, but are written in the same years that one finds some of Brecht's more nondidactic works. Even a work as savaged on this score as *Die heilige Johanna der Schlachthöfe* (1932) hovers complexly between didacticism and alienation-effect. The best general rule in the periodization of Brecht's theater is perhaps to treat the plays up to *Die Dreigroschenoper* (1928) as "expressionistic" and thus in some sense as nonepic and somewhat didactic. The didacticism bleeds over into Brecht's work from 1930 to 1945 in some plays, but not all. Work including and after *Leben des Galilei* (1943) seems to instantiate Brecht's ideal of epic theater most comprehensively.

19. Brecht was not entirely consistent in his views on the superiority of reflection over affect. See, e.g., the remark: "ein schlechter zuschauer im theater: wer zu viele und zu genaue meinungen über das hat, was auf ihn wirkt" (Brecht 1973: 797, lowercase nouns original).

REFERENCES

Adorno, T. W. (1961, 1965). *Noten zur Literatur* (Vols. 2 and 3). Frankfurt am Main: Suhrkamp.

——. (1970–86). *Gesammelte Schriften* (R. Tiedemann, ed.). Frankfurt am Main: Suhrkamp.

Aristotle. (1924). Aristotelis Ethica Nicomachea (I. Bywater, ed.). Oxford: Oxford University Press.

Benjamin, W. (1972–89). *Gesammelte Schriften* (7 vols.; R. Tiedemann and H. Schweppenhäuser, eds.). Frankfurt am Main: Suhrkamp.

Bentley, E. (1946). *The Playwright as Thinker*. New York: Reynal and Hitchcock.

Brecht, B. (1957). *Schriften zum Theater*. Frankfurt am Main: Suhrkamp.

——. (1973). *Arbeitsjournal* (W. Hecht, ed.). Frankfurt am Main: Suhrkamp.

Buck-Morss, S. (1977). *The Origins of Negative Dialectic: Theodor W. Adorno, Walter Benjamin, and the Frankfurt Institute*. New York: Free Press.

Halliwell, S. (2002). *The Aesthetics of Mimesis: Ancient Texts and Modern Problems*. Princeton: Princeton University Press.

Horkheimer, M. (1974). *Eclipse of Reason*. New York: Continuum. (Original work published in 1947.)

Horkheimer, M., and T. W. Adorno. (1969). *Dialektik der Aufklärung*. Stuttgart: Fischer.

Kant, I. (1908). *Kants gesammelte Schriften* (Vol. 5; Königlich Preußischen Akademie der Wissenschaften, ed.). Berlin: de Gruyter.

——. (1990). *Kritik der reinen Vernunft* (3rd ed.; R. Schmidt, ed.). Hamburg: Meiner. (Original works published 1781 [A] and 1787 [B]).

Lukács, G. (1971). *Werke* (Vol. 4). Darmstadt: Luchterhand.

——. (1971). *Die Theorie des Romans*. Darmstadt: Luchterhand. (Original work published in 1920.)

Marcuse, H. (1978). *The Aesthetic Dimension*. Boston: Beacon Press.

Nietzsche, F. (1973). *Sämtliche Werke. Kritische Studienausgabe* (Vol. 2; G. Colli and M. Montinari, eds.). Berlin: de Gruyter.

Paddison, M. (1993). *Adorno's Aesthetics of Music*. Cambridge: Cambridge University Press.

Plato. (1903). *Apology* (J. Burnet, ed.). Oxford: Oxford University Press.

Rush, F. (2004). "Conceptual Foundations of Early Critical Theory." *In* F. Rush (ed.), *The Cambridge Companion to Critical Theory*, pp. 6–39. Cambridge: Cambridge University Press.

INDEX

Abrams, M. H. 167, 403–404, 417n8

Achebe, C. 323, 343n1, 487

Acknowledgment 72, 78, 82, 91, 189, 196, 209, 216, 217, 218n12, 253–254, 261, 337, 339, 383, 481–483

Adorno, T. W. 91n5, 200–201, 204, 208, 210–211, 213, 247–248, 252–253, 267n7, 298, 313, 317, 498–513, 514n4, 514n5, 514n7–11, 515n13, 515n17

Aeschylus 36, 400

Ahmad, A. 325–326

Alain 190

Alcibiades 451

Alexander, J. 88, 93n15

Alexander, M. 65n2

Allegory 51, 52, 505

Allen, T.W. 41n12

Alpers, P. 120, 125, 136n5

Altieri, C. 420, 437n1, 440n16

Anselm, St. 53, 66n14

Aquinas, St. Thomas 57

Aristophanes 4, 22, 36, 48, 97, 99, 100, 102–105, 142–143, 149, 151–152

Aristotle 6, 14, 35–40, 55, 56, 58, 59, 81, 82, 85, 90–91, 119, 140, 151, 157n3, 175, 178n11, 181, 185, 358, 372, 377, 379, 380, 387–390, 390n9, 407, 408, 414, 415, 416n5, 445, 452, 473, 486, 487, 488, 511, 514n6, 515n17

  Nichomachean Ethics 48, 64, 118, 371, 381, 390n2, 391n11, 399, 500

  Poetics 20–23, 33, 37–39, 48–49, 73–78, 97, 117, 134, 135n1–2, 172, 176, 360–370, 373–374, 375, 383–386, 391n14, 395, 397–400

  Politics 454

Arnold, M. 130–132

Ashcroft, B. 327

Attridge, D. 326

Auerbach, E. 223, 224, 393, 421

Augustine, St. 51–52, 54, 180, 382–383

Austen, J. 175, 187, 304–305, 394

Auster, P. 411

Austin, J. L. 182, 422, 430

Autobiography 120, 124, 164, 173, 181–197, 333, 334

Autonomy 72, 165, 166, 186, 262, 319n3, 359, 374

  Of art, the aesthetic 200–201, 205, 208, 283, 292, 293, 409, 507

Bach, J. S. 248

Bahri, D. 324, 344n8

Bakhtin, M. 115n3, 177n1, 266

Bakker, E. J. 135n2

Baldick, C. 293n1

Baldwin, J. 483

Balanchine, G. 408

Balzac, H. de 176, 280–282, 287, 294n8, 510

Banfield, A. 305

Barber, C. L. 96, 99, 101

Barth, J. 410, 497

Barthelme, D. 410

Barthes, R. 164, 222, 226, 292, 376, 378–379, 391n10

Bate, W. J. 42n28

Bates, S. 417n9

Baudelaire, C. 45, 63, 64, 259, 266, 282–283, 423, 431, 509

Baumgarten, A. G. 498

Beardsley, M. 474

Beattie, A. 411

Beckett, S. 5, 63, 96, 135n4, 183, 207, 210–215, 388–389, 412, 509

Beistegui, M. de. 91n8

Belfiore, E. 76

Bellow, S. 342

Benjamin, W. 91, 205, 217n4, 255, 264–266, 267n6, 380, 498–502, 504–507, 509, 512–513, 514n4–6

Bennett, A. 240

Bentley, E. 515n16

Benveniste, E. 390n8

Berger, H., Jr. 125

Bergson, H. 308

Berkeley, G. 139, 140, 182

Bernabé, A. 41n5

Bernstein, J. M. 12, 169, 171, 177n7, 251–252, 267n4, 267n11, 268n15, 294n3

Bersani, L. 170

Bhabha, H. K. 324, -325, 327, 343n3

Birch, D. 195

Blackwell, T. 40,

Blanchot, M. 263, 264, 268n13

Bloch, E. 514n12

Bloom, H. 42n29, 252, 413, 417n17

Blundell, M. W. 399

Boehmer, E. 324

Bogan, T.V.F 45

Boorman, J. 192

Bradley, A. C. 86, 87, 394

Bradley, F. H. 308

Brand, D. 338–341

Brandes, G. 283, 289, 291, 292, 295n22, 295n23

Branham, R. B. 157n3, 158n13, 158n15, 158n24, 158n25, 159n28, 159n29, 159n35
Brann, E. T. H. 349–350, 352, 357, 358, 359, 361, 362, 364, 366
Brecht, B. 290, 292, 294n15, 507, 510–512, 515n17–19
Breed, B. W. 122
Bremer, J. M. 370–371
Bremound, C. 378
Brentano, F. 308
Bromwich, D. 492
Brooks, P. 176, 306, 371, 376, 380, 381–382, 390n1
Browne, T. 274
Bruns, G. L. 215, 218n11
Büchner, G. 87
Buck-Morss, S. 514n4
Burgess, J. S. 24
Burrow, C. 125
Buss, R. 287
Butler, J. 430
Butor, M. 410
Byatt, A. S 183, 196–197

Capitalism 6, 332, 421, 438n3, 487, 507, 510
Carby, H. V. 331
Carlyle, T. 195, 417n8
Carroll, N. 417n14, 477–478
Cascardi, A. J. 165, 166
Caserio, R. 376
Castelvetro, L. 55
Catharsis 74, 77–78, 81, 85, 117, 398, 515n17
Cavell, S. 72, 86, 98–99, 101, 102, 109, 112, 113, 149, 158n16, 158n27, 211–216, 217n7, 218n9, 218n12, 248, 249, 251, 256, 258, 260–261, 267n4, 268n14, 414, 480, 482
    Disowning Knowledge 85, 86
    Pursuits of Happiness 96, 98–99, 100, 110–111, 417n16
Celan, P. 498
Céline, L. -F. 496
Cervantes, M. de 135, 163, 166–167, 170, 175, 178n11, 497
Cézanne, P. 439n13
Chaplin, C. 96, 99–100, 144
Character, characterization 6, 11, 20, 74– 75, 86, 109, 119, 369–370 372, 385–387, 397–418, 452–461, 483
Chatman, S. 421
Chaucer, G. 65–66n4
Ch'ien, E. N.-M. 327
Childers, J. 293n1
Christie, A. 187, 411
Cingano, E. 42n32
Coetzee, J. M. 323, 327–330, 341–343
Cohen, T. 115n2, 147, 362, 477–478, 495n8
Cole, P. 487
Coleman, R. 122
Coleridge, S. T. 60, 62, 274, 357–358, 384, 391n12
Collingwood, R. G. 6–7, 9, 494

Comedy 141–144, 151, 157n3, 164
Conrad, J. 174, 335, 371–372, 377, 378, 385, 487, 491
Conradi, P. 183–184
Coolidge, C. 215
Cooper, H. 125
Critchley, S. 211
Croce, B. 19, 36
Cuddon, J. A. 293n1
Cullen, P. 129
Currie, G. 470
Curtius, E. R. 47, 66n5

Dahlhaus, C. 266
Daleski, H. M. 294n17
Damasio, A. 65n3
Dammann, R. M. J. 228, 239, 243
Dangarembga, T. 334
Dante 40, 53–54, 505
Danto, A. C. 421, 425–426, 428–429
Darnton, R. 405, 417n10
Davidson, D. 415
Davies, M. 41n5
Davies, S. 475
Davis, T. 473
Defoe, D. 173
DeLillo, D. 497
de Man, P. 253
Depiera, M. 487
Derrida, J. 5, 217n6, 231, 414–416, 417n12, 417n20, 417n21, 430
Descartes, R. 83, 84, 85, 164–167, 175, 180, 182, 188, 190–191, 201, 265, 267n10, 302–303, 305, 308, 415, 439n10
De Sena, J. 136n13
Deutscher, I. 276
Devereaux, M. 495n7
Dewey, J. 7, 414
Dickens, C. 163, 186, 192, 304–305, 487, 492, 508
Dickinson, E. 365
Didion, J. 494n3
Diffey, T. J. 468
Dilthey, W. 509
Diogenes 144–152, 155–156, 158n17, 158n18, 158n20, 158n25, 158n26, 158n27, 159n28
Dirie, W. 333–334
Doležal, L. 474
Doris, J. M. 389–390, 391n13, 391n15
Dostoyevsky, F. 477, 515n15
Douglas, M. 147–148, 153
Doyle, Sir A. C. 186
Dryden, J. 141

Eagleton, T. 322
Eco, U. 147
Egan, M. 285
Eldridge, R. 42n34, 130, 243, 248, 267n4, 319n3, 364, 374, 417n16, 477–478, 483, 492

Eliot, G. 281, 471
Eliot, T. S. 63, 67n20, 136n13, 206, 244, 342, 402, 487, 513
Ellmann, R. 194n19
Emerson, R. W. 253–254, 259, 261, 263, 264
Empson, W. 135n1
Engell, J. 357, 358
Epic 6, 8, 10–11, 19–42, 47, 134, 140–141, 163–164, 169–170, 177n7, 396, 407
Espmark, K. 287–288, 294n10, 294n12, 294n18
Euripides 36, 90, 100–101, 229–230, 400, 462n10

Fanon, F. 323, 324, 325
Farah, N. 325
Farrell, J. 42n33
Faulkner, W. 207, 299, 306–307, 311, 315–317, 318n1, 475, 493
Feldman, M. 252, 266n1
Feminism 283, 330–32, 334, 344n5
Ferguson, M. W. 66n8
Fichte, J. G. 203–204, 263–264, 265, 357
Fictionality 118, 120–121–124, 126–127, 130, 132, 133, 134–135, 135n2, 175, 185–188, 196–197, 226–231, 242, 244, 305–306, 349–350, 359–362, 365, 370, 376, 383, 393–395, 397, 404, 406, 407, 409–410, 412–414, 446, 467–468, 471–472, 474, 475–476, 486–488, 490–492
Fielding, H. 157n6
Figuration 9, 12, 57–58, 427
Fish, S. 468
Flaubert, G. 171, 282–283, 487
Foley, J. M. 35
Forcione, A. 178n11
Ford, A. 135n2
Ford, R. 393
Förster, E. 294n3
Foster, H. 438n3
Foucault, M. 267n7
Frank, M. 248
Franken, A. 139
Frede, M. 144
Freeland, C. A. 91n2
Freeman, D. C. 421
Frege, G. 226–227, 232, 239, 473–474, 475
Freud, S. 12, 147, 157n3, 158n22, 176, 306–307, 314, 318n1, 319n4, 319n5, 329n8, 379–382, 455–457, 458, 459–460, 461, 462n9
Freudenberg, K. 157n2
Frye, N. 92n11, 92n14, 96, 100, 101, 106–109
Fuentes, C. 163

Gadamer, H.-G. 66n7
Gaita, R. 196
Gandhi, L. 324,
Gaut, B. 471, 475,
Genette, G. 342, 376

Gibson, J. 228, 239, 243, 482
Gide, A. 290, 291, 293n2, 319n1
Girard, R. 135n3
Gjesdal, K. 92n10
Godard, B. 336
Godard, J.-L. 258–259, 260, 261,
Goethe, J. W. 59, 81, 152, 159n32, 289, 405
Gogol, N. 171
Goldberg, S. M. 40
Golding, W. 192
Goldmann, L. 168
Gombrich, E. 421
Goncourt, E. 224
Goncourt, J. 224
Goodman, N. 421
Gorky, M. 510
Goulet-Caze, M. O. 158n15, 158n21
Graham, G. 477
Graves, R. 462n8
Gray, S. 334–335
Graziosi, B. 31, 41n21
Greenblatt, S. 177n5
Greene, R. 125
Grene, D. 457
Grobman, N. R. 40
Grundy, J. 136n6
Guyer, P. 303–304

Habermas, J. 214
Halliwell, S. 135n2, 514n6
Hamann, J. G. 59
Hamburger, M. 133, 136n13
Hampshire, S. 58
Hamsun, K. 496
Hanna, P. 232, 235
Hardie, P. 122
Hardy, T. 289, 290, 294n17
Harold, J. 470
Harris, H. S. 80
Harris, P. L. 360
Harrison, B. 231–232, 235, 242, 477
Hausman, C. 361
Hegel, G. W. F. 7–12, 14, 58, 61–62, 73, 74, 81–83, 85, 86, 90–91, 104, 163, 167, 168–170, 178n8, 251, 265, 274, 275, 294n3, 387, 402–405, 410, 414, 415, 422, 510
Heidegger, M. 64, 68n22, 103, 188–190, 191, 193–195, 207, 218n10, 256, 261–262, 267n10, 268n13, 298–299, 308–309, 311, 320n9, 414, 415
Heilman, R. B. 157n3
Heiserman, H. 163
Hejinian, L. 216–217, 218n10
Hemingway, E. 493
Henrich, D. 248
Hentzi, G. 293n1
Herder, J. G. 59, 83–84, 262
Herington, J. 37

Hesiod 27, 41n19n20, 47, 120, 121, 448, 450
Heslin, P. J. 461n7
Hesse, H. 319n1
Heyse, P. 283–284, 285, 286, 287, 288, 289, 290
Hobbes, T. 84, 223, 227, 231, 234, 242, 262
Hoffman, P. 84
Hofmannsthal, H. von 458–459
Hölderlin, F. 68n22, 274–276, 275–276, 294n3
Hollander, R. 66n16
Homer 10–11, 20, 22, 24–40, 47, 119, 140, 278, 401,
    443–444, 446, 448–450, 454, 455, 505,
Homelessness, Transcendental 7, 167–170,
    173–174, 178n8
Horace 156
Horkheimer, M. 91n5, 503, 514n7, 515n14
Hornblower, S. 398–399
Howe, E. A. 133
Huggan, G. 329, 333, 343n1
Hughes, J. 421
Humboldt, W. 262, 267n12
Hume, D. 167, 171–172, 182, 201
Husserl, E. 237, 308
Huyssen, A. 295n24

Ibsen, H. 76, 273, 274, 277, 279–280, 282, 284–286,
    289, 290–291, 293, 293n2, 294n15, 294n16,
    294n19, 295n25, 487
Ignatieff, M. 77
Imagination 3–4, 61, 204, 275, 277, 342, 353–367,
    384, 394, 409, 428, 434–437, 450, 468–471, 475,
    483, 488, 490–491
Iser, W. 125, 134
Isocrates 25–26, 32

Jakobson, R. 423
James, H. 175, 177n2, 207, 290, 294n18, 301, 375,
    390n6, 413–414
James, W. 237, 414
Jameson, F. 342
Janson, H. W. 406
Jefferson, T. 488
Jenkyns, R. 42n34
John, E. 468, 477
Johnson, S. 83, 225, 386
Jones, P. 165
Josipovici, G. 244
Joyce, J. 63, 73–74, 96, 207, 304, 317, 318n1, 342,
    411–412, 497, 506

Kafka, F. 244, 298–302, 306–307, 311, 315–317,
    318n1, 319n2, 510
Kallendorf, C. 39,
Kant, I. 7, 62, 64, 200, 210, 213, 214, 217n1, 260,
    263–264, 274–275, 277–279, 294n6, 302–304,
    319n3, 354, 373, 387, 415, 431, 489, 490,
    499–504, 506

The Critique of Judgment 9, 59–61, 201–203,
    207, 251, 357–358, 410, 438n14, 499–500
The Critique of Pure Reason 174, 217n1, 365, 500
Kaufmann, W. 416n4
Kearney, R. 357, 364, 365
Keaton, B. 96
Keats, J. 492
Kermode, F. 374–376, 381, 385, 390n7
Kern, S. 301, 319n2
Keynes, J. M. 305
Kierkegaard, S. 244, 299–300, 320n6, 404–405
Kivy, P. 471–472, 475, 488
Knight, C. A. 157n3
Knuuttila, S. 461n2
Kompridis, N. 267n4, 267n9, 268n14
Konstan, D. 157n5, 461n3
Krell, D. 311
Kristeller, O. 417n11
Kuhn, T. S. 272
Kundera, M. 163, 168
Kurke, L. 158n13

LaCapra, D. 294n9
Lacoue-Labarthe, P. 201–203, 207, 209, 210, 247,
    263–264
Laertius, D. 146–150, 152, 155, 158n17, 158n26,
    158n27, 159n33
Lamarque, P. 225–226, 229–230, 242–243, 468, 471, 477
Landy, J. 132
Lang, B. 421, 424–425, 439n10
Laplanche, J. 307, 319n4
Latacz, J. 461n5
Lattimore, R. 457
Lawrence, D. H. 319n1
Lear, J. 78, 91n3
Ledbetter, G. M. 14n3
Lee, H. 197
Lerner, L. 132
Levin, H. 141
Levin, S. R. 421
Levinas, E. 299, 304, 308–311, 317
Lévi-Strauss, C. 378, 423
Lewalski, B. 66n15
Lewis, C. S. 40, 42n34
Lewis, D. 474
Lewis, P. 411
Locke, J. 167, 171–173, 182, 227, 262, 302–303, 305
Loraux, N. 78
Lord, A. B. 34–35, 42n24
Love, G. A. 421
Loyola, St. Ignatius 53
Lucian 140, 149–152, 159n31, 159n33
Lucretius 240
Lukács, G. 12–13, 14, 163, 164, 168–171, 173–176,
    177n6, 177n7, 178n8, 207–208, 211, 213, 224,
    276, 294n4, 509–511, 514n12, 515n13, 515n15
Lyotard, J.-F. 206, 212, 213–214, 216
Lyric 6, 11–12, 21–22, 45–68, 133, 134, 432, 508, 515n17

Macaulay, T. 323–4
MacCary, W. T. 461n6
MacEwan, I. 461n4
MacIntyre, A. 175, 184–186, 188–189, 191, 407–408, 413, 417n13
MacMurray, J. 91n1
Macrobius, A. T. 53
Maeterlinck, M. 290
Maley, W. 136n9
Mallarmé, S. 132–133, 497
Mann, T. 244, 317, 319n1, 510, 515n13
Marcel, G. 308
Marcuse, H. 503
Martin, R. P. 34, 35
Martz, L. 53
Marx, K. 275, 414
Marxism 168, 275, 276, 292, 325, 498, 504–506, 508–509, 513
Materialism 257, 275, 283, 324
Maupassant, G. de 224
Mayer, R. 157n2
McCabe, H. 192
McCarthy, C. 498
McClary, S. 42n27
McGann, J. 257
McGinn, C. 351, 353, 355, 360, 361
McKay, C. 323
McKeon, M. 178n10
McLeod, J. 326
Melville, H. 476, 489–490, 491
Memory 382–383
Merleau-Ponty, M. 237, 299, 308–309, 311
Metaphor 28, 29, 49, 53, 55, 58, 59, 62, 74, 80, 90, 124, 134, 145, 212, 240, 241, 243, 335, 357, 361–362, 365–367, 380, 433, 435, 477–478
Michelangelo 427
Milic, L. T. 422
Mill, J. S. 145, 490
Milton, J. 39, 42n34, 410
Mimesis 20, 37–38, 56, 124, 127, 223–226, 370, 383–384, 391n14, 395–396, 398–399, 407, 414, 483, 498, 501–504, 506
Minh-ha, T. 330
Minkowski, E. 319n2
Mistry, R. 342
Mitchell, S. 42n24
Modernism 6, 63, 200, 204–208, 211, 244, 248–250, 252–253, 257, 263, 267n5, 272–273, 287, 290–293, 293n2, 295n24, 300–320, 323, 411, 420, 497–498, 504, 509–510, 513, 514n1
Modernity 7, 12, 90, 130–131, 163–176, 200, 207, 248–249, 251–252, 256, 277, 278, 359, 401–402, 404, 497, 508, 514n1
Mohanti, C. T. 330
Moi, T. 293, 294n16, 295n22
Moisy, S. von 283, 285
Monk, R. 196
Monrad, M. J. 284–285
Montrose, L. A. 128

Morreall, J. 95
Morris, W. 431
Morrison, T. 334, 498
Most, G. 461n1, 462n9
Mulhall, S. 480
Mulroy, D. 66n10
Murdoch, I. 174, 177n4, 183
Murray, P. 42n23
Music 21, 23–28, 30, 32–34, 45, 50, 51, 52, 62, 108, 121–123, 127, 266, 398, 410, 411, 476, 488
Musil, R. 319n1
Myth 46, 59, 114, 120, 375, 383–384, 396, 407, 412

Nabokov, V. 493–494, 494n4, 515n15
Nagy, G. 21, 23, 24, 34, 35, 37, 38, 40n3, 41n6, 41n7, 41n9, 41n10, 41n14, 41n18, 41n19, 42n24, 42n26, 42n30, 42n31, 42n32
Nancy, J. 201–203, 207, 209, 210, 247, 263–264
Narrative 20, 46, 74, 119, 122, 134, 164, 165, 171, 173, 176, 184–194, 197, 207, 209, 214, 299–307, 318, 323, 324, 342, 349, 360, 365, 369, 371, 373, 376–379, 387, 389, 390n1, 394, 395, 407, 414, 478, 482, 497
Neer, R. 437n2
New, C. 472
Newlands, C. 125
Newton, I. 302–304, 315, 358
Niehues-Probsting, H.S. 158n19, 159n32, 159n33, 159n35
Nietzsche, F. 14, 64, 102, 109, 144, 149, 152–156, 158n27, 159n33, 159n35, 244, 259, 267n7, 291, 293n2, 309, 354, 400, 407, 414, 415
    Beyond Good and Evil 154–155, 286–287
    The Birth of Tragedy 96, 99–101, 111
    Ecce Homo 156, 180, 403
    The Gay Science 152–154, 159n34, 250–251, 258, 514n7
    The Genealogy of Morals 406, 408
    Twilight of the Idols 155, 157n11, 315
Nightingale, A. 47, 66n6
Nisbet, H. B. 416n7
Nobel, A. 287
Novalis 266, 274, 503
Novel, the 12, 95, 162–178, 224, 266, 268n15, 359, 366, 397, 403, 405, 410, 515n15, 515n17
Novitz, D. 360, 362, 470
Nussbaum, M. 73, 76, 165, 171, 177n4, 178n13, 218n8, 243, 373, 377, 385, 390n4, 390n5, 390n9, 417n16, 461n3, 470
Nuttall, A. D. 225, 243

O'Neill, E. 459, 460
Ohmann, R. 424, 425, 438n9
Olsen, S. H. 225–226, 229–230, 242–243, 468, 471, 477
Ortega y Gasset, J. 411
Orwell, G. 158n23
Ovid 338

Paddison, M. 514n11
Pappas, N. 115n1
Parkes, M. 51
Pascal, B. 139, 140, 144
Patterson, A. 124, 136n5
Pavel, T. 474
Payne, M. 118, 421
Paz, O. 133, 134
Peirce, C. S. 414, 415
Perec, G. 497–498
Perloff, M. 68n21, 217
Pessoa, F. 133–134
Petersen, C. 277
Petrarch 39, 54–56
Philip, M. N. 335–339, 341–343, 344n7
Pillow, K. 357, 364
Pindar 450
Pippin, R. B. 165–166, 178n12
Pisco, P. 427
Plato 6, 21–37, 40, 55, 56, 59, 64, 73, 76, 77, 78,
    90–91, 96, 140, 141–146, 149, 157n6, 157n8, 174,
    225, 227, 266, 274–275, 372–373, 407, 415, 445,
    450, 470, 473, 486, 487, 498, 513
  Apology 157n9, 142–4, 145, 512
  Gorgias 22, 47
  Ion 4, 22–32, 34, 41n11, 41n13, 41n17, 41n19, 47
  Laws 22, 452
  Phaedo 390n3, 390n5
  Phaedrus 47, 158n18
  Philebus 141–2, 157n4, 157n10
  Republic 21, 34, 37, 42n23, 46–47, 53, 71–72, 119,
    134, 452
  Symposium 26, 48, 101–103, 105
  Theaetetus 37
Plaatje, S. 323
Plot 6, 74–76, 77, 209, 398, 404, 416n5, 455
Plutarch 451, 454
Poe, E. A. 378
Poiesis 21–22, 29–30, 32–34, 58
Poovey, M. 281–282
Pope, A. 432, 437
Postmodernism 6, 250, 293, 305, 318, 394, 411, 415,
    438n3, 468, 497–498
Pound, E. 63, 136n13, 342, 513
Preminger, A. 45
Propp, V. 376, 378,
Proust, M. 164, 207, 244, 299, 306–307, 311–315,
    317, 318n1, 320n9, 342, 497
Purdie, S. 157n3, 158n18
Pynchon, T. 497

Quine, W. V. O. 231

Ramsay, F. 492
Rand, A. 417n18, 487, 491
Rao, R. 323
Réage, P. 487

Realism 272–273, 280–282, 285, 287, 291, 293n2,
    294n8, 301, 302–306, 310, 315, 318, 319n5,
    320n7, 399–400, 409–410, 411, 510
Relihan, J. C. 159n29
Rengakos, A. 39
Ricoeur, P. 382–385, 391n11, 417n15
Riede, D. G. 136n11
Riefenstahl, L. 494, 495n7, 496
Rilke, R. M. 256, 260–261, 298–299
Rivkin, J. 416n3
Robbe-Grillet, A. 292, 410
Robinson, J. 421, 439n10
Rocco, C. 91n5
Romanticism 59, 62, 114, 201–205, 209–210, 213,
    216, 249–268, 271–272, 277, 290, 358–359,
    402–403, 503, 513
Ronen, R. 134
Rorty, A. O. 76, 77
Rorty, R. 247, 248, 253, 257, 267n2, 414, 415,
    417n20, 417n21
Rosen, C. 266
Rosen, S. 66n6
Ross, A. 267n1
Rothstein, A. 41n4
Rousseau, J.-J. 62, 66n18, 180, 405, 417n10
Rush, F. 502
Rushdie, S. 323, 326, 442–448, 449, 454–455, 460
Russell, B. 231
Russell, D. A. 47
Ryan, M. 416n3
Ryle, G. 468

Said, E. 324, 326–327, 330
Sand, G. 273, 280–281, 283, 291, 294n8, 295n21
Santayana, G. 53, 59
Saro-Wiwa, K. 325
Sarraute, N. 410
Sartre, J.-P. 13, 190–191, 193–196, 275, 306,
    308, 318, 325, 351–352, 355, 356, 362–363,
    365, 380, 414
Satire 56, 96, 163
Saussure, F. de 42n25
Sayles, J. 113–115
Schapiro, M. 421, 422
Schelling, F. 357
Schiller, F. 60–61, 136n5, 271, 274, 276–281, 283,
    286, 289–290, 291, 294n5, 295n22, 401–402,
    404, 405, 511
Schlegel, A. W. 62, 201–202, 511
Schlegel, F. 204, 217n2, 217n3, 217n4, 253, 265–266,
    274, 276, 503
Schleiermacher, F. 217n2
Schoenberg, A. 248, 252, 266, 267n5
Schopenhauer, A. 164, 165
Schor, N. 273–274, 281
Schott, R. M. 294n6
Searle, J. 474
Segal, C. 79–80, 92n6

Shakespeare, W. 82–86, 92n11, 97, 99, 100, 103, 104,
    136n7, 228–229, 278, 394, 402, 412–413, 471,
    476, 496, 505
  All's Well That Ends Well 106–109
  Hamlet 83–86
  King Lear 83
  Measure for Measure, 238–241
Shaw, G. B. 286, 291
Shay, J. 461n6
Shelley, P. B. 60, 287
Sherman, N. 91n4
Shklovski, V. 376
Shoat, E. 325–326
Shusterman, R. 481
Sibelius, J. 248–250, 252
Sidney, P. 55–56, 61, 236, 240
Sifsakis, G. M. 462n10
Simon, C. 410
Singer, A. 381
Sittenfeld, C. 488
Skepticism 110, 171, 215, 253, 257–258, 283
Slatkin, L. 19, 21
Smith, S. 333
Snell, B. 49–50, 400
Socrates 22–23, 25, 27–35, 47–48, 102, 117, 140,
    141–146, 148–151, 157n9, 158n13, 158n18, 182,
    390n3, 390n5, 512
Sommer, D. 327, 344n8
Sonnet, the 54–55
Sophocles 78–82, 91n5, 104, 371, 375, 379, 386, 400,
    457–458
Sorabji, R. 461n2
Soyinka, W. 325
Spanforth, A. 398–399
Spenser, E. 124–129
Spinoza, B. B. de 58–59
Spitzer, L. 421
Spivak, G. C. 327, 331–332, 334
Staten, H. 92n12
Statius 449–450
Stein, G. 63, 96, 199, 204–209, 210, 213, 215, 217n5,
    218n10
Stendhal 170–171
Stern, R. 494n4
Sterne, L. 3, 410, 488, 497
Stevens, W. 63, 67–68n21, 434–437
Stewart, S. 66n11
Stolnitz, J. 468
Stowe, H. B. 487, 492
Strier, R. 136n7
Strindberg, A. 275
Sturma, D. 267n3
Style 6, 10, 12, 35, 100, 165, 170, 171, 223, 224, 242,
    266, 281, 329, 420–440, 493
Suetonius 452–453
Suleri, S. 330
Summers, D. 421, 438n5
Sutherland, K. 394
Swift, J. 140, 157n12

Szafraniec, A. 5
Szondi, P. 92n8

Tagore, R. 323
Tanner, M. 156
Taylor, C. 248, 262, 263, 267n8, 267n12, 417n19
Theocritus 118–125
Thilo, G. 123
Thiong, 'o, N. wa 323
Titian 427
Todorov, T. 376, 377
Tolstoy, L. 63, 288
Toulmin, S. 166
Tragedy 36–39, 71–93, 95, 97–98, 103–104, 115,
    117, 144, 164, 285, 369–370, 373–374, 375, 379,
    386, 390, 391n14, 398–400, 402, 404, 457, 459,
    462n10, 488
Trauma 88–91, 313–314, 315, 374, 427
Trotsky, L. 276
Tupper, M. 240
Tututola, A. 323
Twain, M. 477, 496

Unger, R. M. 167

Valéry, P. 67n21
Van Es, B. 136n9
Van Sickle, J. 120, 122
Velleman, J. D. 388–390
Vera, Y. 334
Vernant, J. 78, 135n2
Vico, G. 57–58, 59, 62, 64
Vidal-Naquet, P. 78
Virgil 39–40, 42n34, 121–125
Viswanathan, G. 323

Wagner, R. 266, 496, 515n16
Walcott, D. 338–339
Walker, S. F. 132
Walton, K. 360, 470, 474
Wang, O. 258
Warnock, M. 349, 356
Watson, J. 333
Watt, I. 163, 438n8
Weber, M. 413
Weinberg, B. 281, 294n7, 294n8
Weinbrodt, H. 177n1
Weinstein, P. 319n1
Weinstock, S. 66n5
Weston, M. 473
Whale, J. 365
White, H. 468
Whitman, W. 223
Wilde, O. 290–291, 293n2, 294n19, 295n20,
    295n21, 394

Williams, B. 254
Williams, R. 87
Williams, W. C. 207
Wimsatt, W. K. 96, 99
Winterbottom, M. 47
Wirsén, C. D. 288–290, 294n13, 294n18
Wittgenstein, L. 7, 14, 63, 139, 140, 156, 182, 195,
    199, 211–214, 216–217, 218n7, 218n8, 218n9,
    230, 234, 239, 256, 262, 351–356, 359, 362, 367,
    414, 415, 420, 426, 428, 439n14, 440n15
Wölfflin, H. 422
Wollheim, R. 420, 421, 425, 426–429, 438n6,
    438n7, 439n11, 439n13
Woolf, V. 63, 207, 244, 289, 293n2, 305, 319n1, 334,
    488, 497
Words, 231–236, 239, 242, 262, 396–397, 493–494
Wordsworth, W. 9, 60, 261, 264, 342, 344n4,
    357–358, 410

Preface to Lyrical Ballads 62, 129, 254–56, 262
The Prelude 248–250, 259, 328–329, 342
"Resolution and Independence" 129–31
Working through 9, 10, 12–13, 74, 84,
    447, 477
Wright, R. 487

Xenophanes 47

Yeats, W. B. 433–434, 437
Young, R. J. C. 331
Yourcenar, M. 462n8

Zink, M. 55
Zola, E. 224, 283, 287, 288, 291, 293n2, 294n12

96385379R00319